CW01369756

THE ENGLISH BENEDICTINE
CATHEDRAL PRIORIES

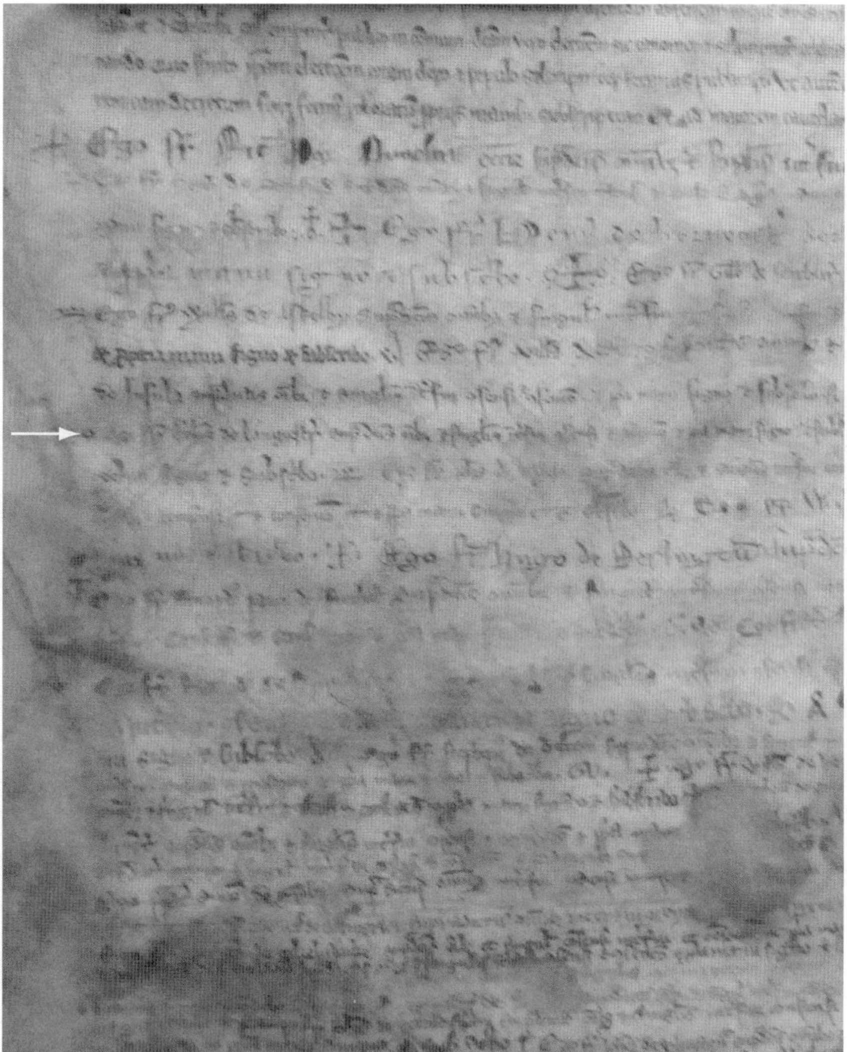

I suggested the document reproduced here, when asked for advice on a possible frontispiece, and I offered to provide some account of it. With characteristic graciousness Joan readily accepted, and so gave me the opportunity to say how delighted I am to see her book published, after many years work on the Durham cathedral muniments. In the process she gave to those who have had them in their care the benefit of comparisons and questions arising from her findings elsewhere, and that with a diffidence that was not entirely appropriate, but nonetheless all the more effective. By such contributions those responsible for major collections are greatly helped to identify what is commonplace and what is truly remarkable. Among the dossier of parchment documents arising from the election of Anthony Bek as bishop of Durham in 1283 this one (DCM, Misc.Ch. 5709a) was evidently not regarded as needing protection from the ravages of rain and rodents, but it confirms the choice made by individual monks of Durham, who appended to it, each in his own hand, a subscription and signs manual, e.g. at →

⋏ *Ego* brother Robert of Lanchester to the above stated, all and each, have been present, consented and do consent and with my own hand do sign and subscribe ⋏ + *Ego*… +

Three important things are revealed. First, the handwriting habits of each monk, making it possible to identify their work in other contexts, notably Thomas of Westoe's list of books acquired in Oxford c.1300, and also the marginal annotations by him and his fellows in texts that they used in the course of their studies; Dr Meryl Foster has shown how much can be gained from these in her doctoral thesis. Second, that each monk evidently had his own supply of ink. Third, that each monk used a personal sign; this could have been used to identify items regarded as personal, such as ink-pots, platters, clothing and bedding, thereby ensuring that the results of one monk's misuse would not be visited on his more careful colleagues. Acrimony would otherwise have arisen, if one man's tendency to rest his elbow on the table caused a hole in his habit, and another was expected to bear the consequences. Much later, with the advent of printing, monks rapidly came to count particular books among their personal belongings, and the fore-edge of paper leaves lent itself to adding not only ink titles but signs such as those seen here, witness DCL Inc. 48.

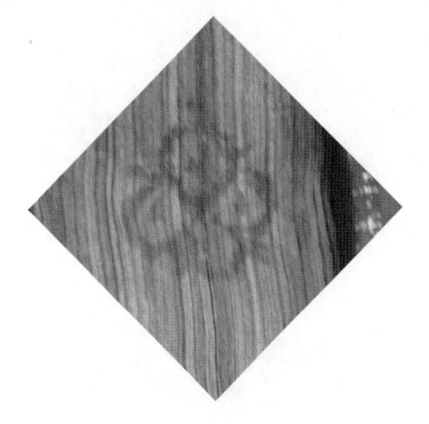

Alan J. Piper, Durham

The English Benedictine Cathedral Priories: Rule and Practice, *c.* 1270–*c.* 1420

JOAN GREATREX

OXFORD
UNIVERSITY PRESS

OXFORD
UNIVERSITY PRESS

Great Clarendon Street, Oxford OX2 6DP

Oxford University Press is a department of the University of Oxford.
It furthers the University's objective of excellence in research, scholarship,
and education by publishing worldwide in

Oxford New York

Auckland Cape Town Dar es Salaam Hong Kong Karachi
Kuala Lumpur Madrid Melbourne Mexico City Nairobi
New Delhi Shanghai Taipei Toronto

With offices in

Argentina Austria Brazil Chile Czech Republic France Greece
Guatemala Hungary Italy Japan Poland Portugal Singapore
South Korea Switzerland Thailand Turkey Ukraine Vietnam

Oxford is a registered trade mark of Oxford University Press
in the UK and in certain other countries

Published in the United States
by Oxford University Press Inc., New York

© Joan Greatrex 2011

The moral rights of the author have been asserted
Database right Oxford University Press (maker)

First published 2011

All rights reserved. No part of this publication may be reproduced,
stored in a retrieval system, or transmitted, in any form or by any means,
without the prior permission in writing of Oxford University Press,
or as expressly permitted by law, or under terms agreed with the appropriate
reprographics rights organization. Enquiries concerning reproduction
outside the scope of the above should be sent to the Rights Department,
Oxford University Press, at the address above

You must not circulate this book in any other binding or cover
and you must impose the same condition on any acquirer

British Library Cataloguing in Publication Data

Data available

Library of Congress Cataloging in Publication Data
Library of Congress Control Number: 2010943361

Typeset by SPI Publisher Services, Pondicherry, India
Printed in Great Britain
on acid-free paper by the
MPG Books Group, Bodmin and King's Lynn

ISBN 978–0–19–925073–8

3 5 7 9 10 8 6 4 2

Ad memoriam coniunctis dilectissimi

Foreword

I would like to begin by pointing out that this comparative study of the English Benedictine cathedral priories is selective in its approach in two respects. To be precise these are, first, the relatively short time frame of about a century and a half that is encompassed and, secondly, the limited range of topics that are treated. It will be helpful to offer a brief explanation of the background from which this work developed. More than forty years ago I first encountered the wealth of information stored on the obedientiary and manorial accounts of Winchester cathedral priory while studying the economic aspects of the monks' administration. Having been alerted to the impressive amount of detail that could be gleaned from these sources I realized that they could provide us with an insight into the lives of monks within their community; and, when used in conjunction with other contemporary records, it would be possible to piece together a biographical framework for most of the monks whose names appear in the documents. It soon became clear that such a study would benefit by focusing on the cathedral monasteries as a group, thereby ensuring that where one of them might be devoid of evidence on a given subject or at a given period of time another, or others, would have extant records to fill the gaps. Further research thus expanded the field of study to include all the southern cathedral priories and resulted in the publication of the *Biographical Register of the English Cathedral Priories of the Province of Canterbury, c. 1066–1540* (Oxford, 1997). This present work is best described as a supplement or sequel to the *Register* in its attempt to answer at least a few of the many remaining questions about these men who chose to become Benedictines. Who were they; where did they come from; what formed the pattern of their daily life and routine through the successive stages of their monastic life; what and where did they study; how did they spend their declining years? In writing this second book I have benefited from further extensive use of the primary source material that was gathered for the *Register* but not included there because it was not directly connected to any named individual monk.

To this study I have added Durham cathedral priory, the only Benedictine chapter among the northern cathedrals. It was omitted from the *Register* because the careers of the Durham monks had been delineated by Alan Piper; the results of his masterful work were finally published in 2007 in the third volume of the *Durham Liber Vitae* project. To avoid any possible confusion I would draw attention to a slight but noteworthy difference between the method followed in naming the Durham monks and its equivalent in the other eight cathedral priories. In the former case the spelling of place-names has been modernized since most of the towns and villages where the monks' families originated were local or regional and readily identifiable. In the latter case the catchment area was much wider and several of the cathedral priories were located relatively near to one another; thus identification of the monks' origins was rendered difficult if not impossible by the variations in spelling which, in turn, are aggravated by the frequent duplication of place-names in different parts of the country. For this reason in my *Register* I left the names as they appear in the records. In addition, I included the common prefix 'de' before a toponym whenever it occurred in the primary sources; Alan Piper preferred 'of'. To deal with these differences of style I have adopted a simple compromise by adhering to his spelling of toponyms but substituting, 'de' for 'of' so that all the monks referred to in this work will have a uniform designation. By the early fifteenth century the 'de' was beginning to be omitted; this explains the apparent inconsistency that appears around and after that date.

In summary, my prime concern has been to follow as closely as possible the Benedictine postulant from the day of his admission to the monastery to the day of his death, to observe the internal affairs in which he participated and played his assigned role of responsibility. Finally, I am fully aware that in the course of completing this task I have deliberately retained a number of repetitive passages in the text because some topics reappear in different contexts; I have judged it expedient not to distract and discourage readers by making it necessary for them to stop and search for other relevant passages, which the subject indexes seem often reluctant to divulge. Moreover, I envisage a number of readers who will wish to consult only certain specific details and will have neither time nor inclination to read the entire volume from cover to cover.

Cambridge
Translation of St Benedict 2009

Acknowledgements

This, the long delayed sequel to my *Biographical Register of the English Cathedral Priories*, was, like its predecessor, generously supported by the British Academy. My gratitude to the Academy and to several other foundations that provided funds for my first years of research also extends to a multitude of friends, colleagues, associates, scholars, and students among whom are numbered librarians, archivists, and archaeologists; many of them have been acknowledged by name in the *Register*. On this occasion I hope to be forgiven for not repeating them all; instead, I will mention here those whose continuing advice and help, and critical appraisal accompanied by encouragement have sustained me in this enterprise. Without the unfailing kindness of Alan Piper I would have lacked both the courage and the knowledge to include the Durham monks in this study. He generously shared with me his then unprinted register of the monks, responded to all my requests for information, frequently providing me with more than I had asked. However, if I have misjudged or misinterpreted any of the Durham manuscripts and muniments the error is mine not his. I am also indebted to Barrie Dobson, who has contributed a number of significant studies on Durham and Canterbury cathedral priories; our friendship was brought about through David Knowles over forty years ago when we met at the entrance to the British Museum. The portions of this study that are devoted to an examination of the manuscripts acquired by the monks for their libraries would not have been possible without the recent publications by Richard Sharpe and Rodney Thomson whose catalogues have been listed in the bibliography. Both of them have come to my rescue with a speedy response to my appeals for enlightenment. Three archaeologists have brought clarity to my reconstructions of the layout of monastic cathedral cloisters: Anne Holton-Krayenbuhl at Ely, John Crook at Winchester, and Chris Guy at Worcester. Roy Haines has kindly continued to keep me up to date with regard to his work on the monk bishops whose careers are of mutual concern. I am also grateful to have had access to two unpublished doctoral theses, Meryl Foster on Durham priory and Claire Noble on Norwich priory, both of which provided me with constructive commentary and fresh insights. Finally, I would like to thank Denise and Philip Bilton for their perseverance through every stage of my manuscript and for preparing the final draft for the press with their accustomed expert precision. The patience and cooperation of the Oxford University Press editors past and present during the lengthy period of gestation of this book also merits grateful acknowledgement.

Contents

List of Plans	xv
I Introduction	1
1. The general historical context	2
2. Cathedrals in a monastic precinct	19
3. Cathedral monks: numbers, names, and family backgrounds	32
II The early years of monastic life	50
1. Admission and clothing	50
2. Probation, claustral studies, and profession	64
III The community of professed novices and junior monks	89
1. Monastic routine and study during and after ordination	89
2. Continuing studies outside and intellectual pursuits inside the cloister	125
IV The years of maturity and responsibility: the duties of obedientiaries and senior monks	160
V Feria, fast, and feast: the rhythm of the liturgical year	236
VI The closing years: illness, age, infirmity, and death	289
VII Conclusion	322
Appendices: Books for study and leisure	333
I. Grammar	335
II. History	348
Bibliography	365
A Manuscript sources	365
B Works in print with abbreviations	370
Index of Manuscripts	393
General Index	398

List of Plans

1. The Medieval Priory of Christ Church. (From Margaret Sparks, *Canterbury Cathedral Precincts, A Historical Survey*. Permission: Margaret Sparks).
2. Durham Cathedral Priory. (Permission: The Surtees Society).
3. St Mary's Priory, Worcester Cathedral. (Permission: Jill Atherton).
4. Norwich Cathedral Priory. (From A.B. Whittingham's plan of Norwich Cathedral and precinct. Permission: Norfolk Record Office, NRO, MC 186/61).
5. St Andrew's Cathedral Priory, Rochester. (Permission: Jill Atherton).
6. Ely Cathedral and Priory. (From A History of the Courty of Cambridge and the Isle of Ely: Volume 4 (OUP, 1953). Permission: the Executive Editor).

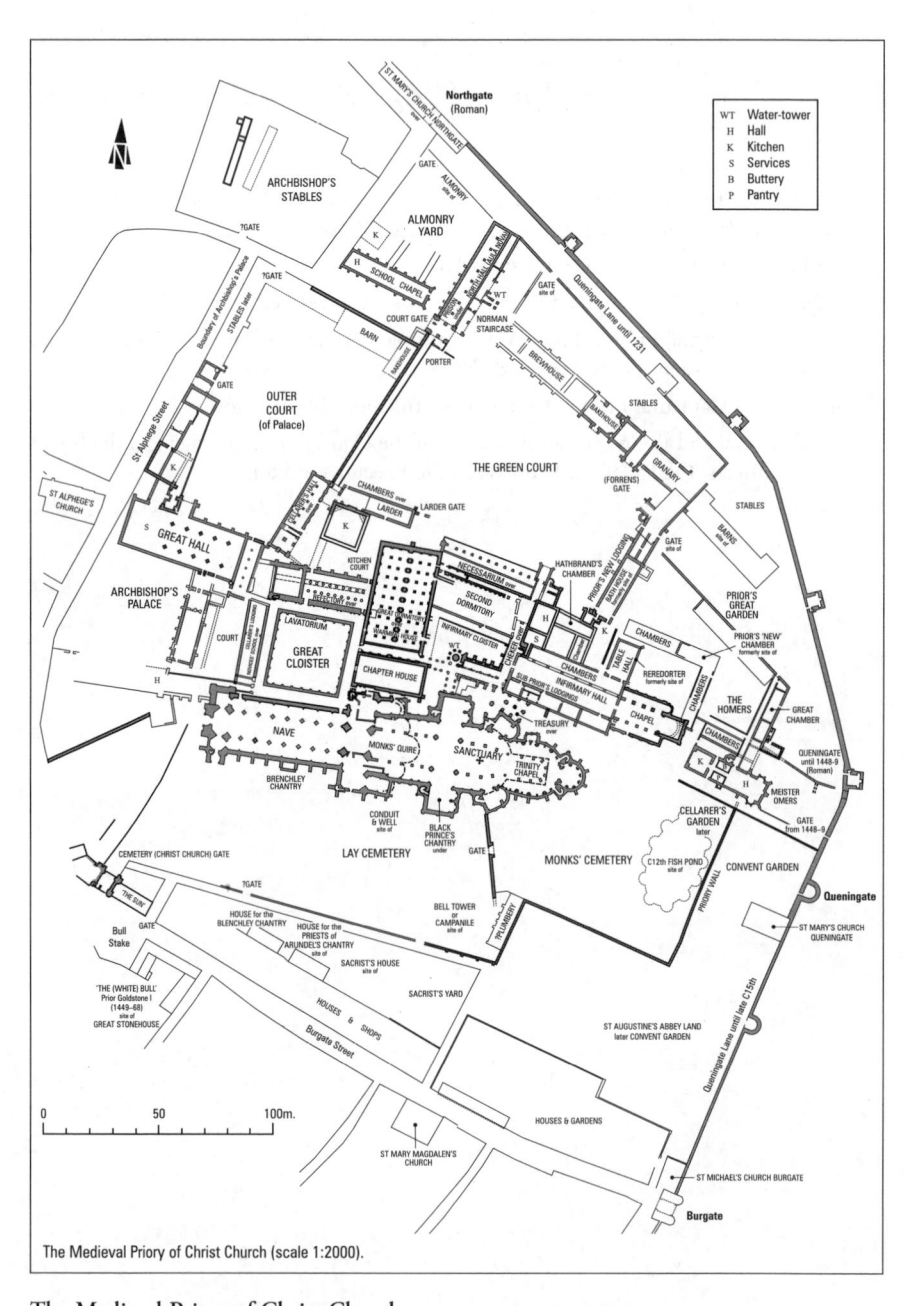

The Medieval Priory of Christ Church

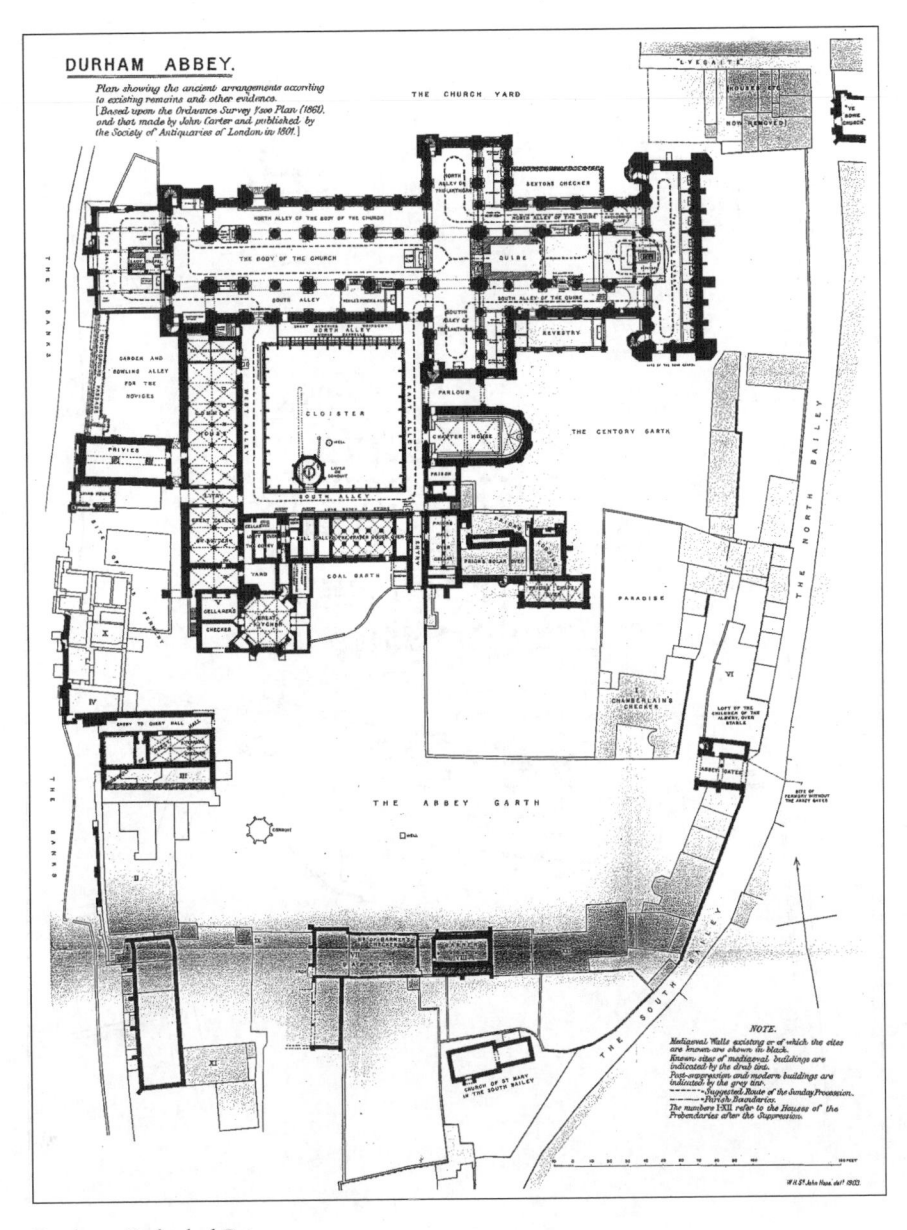

Durham Cathedral Priory

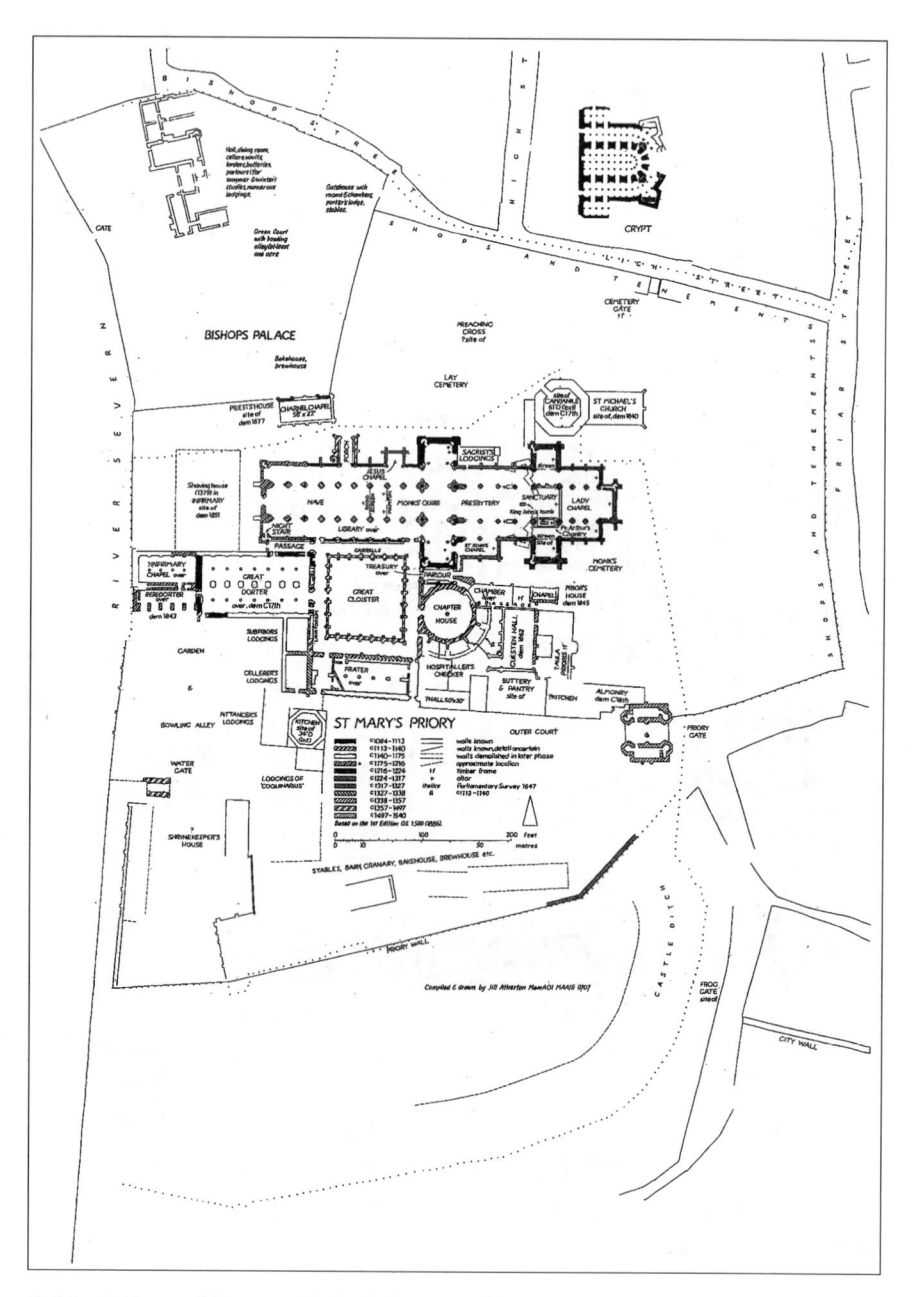

St Mary's Priory, Worcester Cathedral

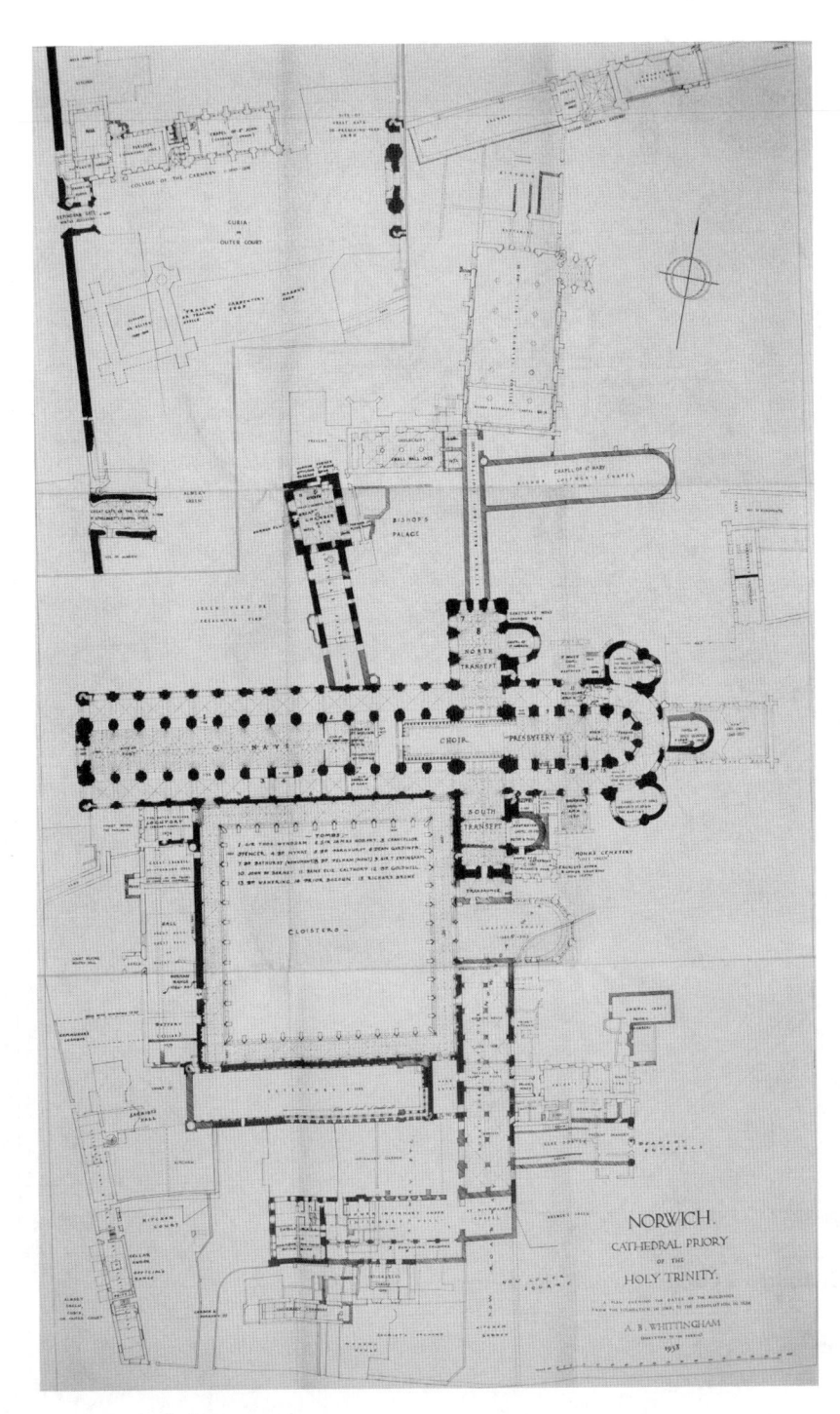

Norwich Cathedral Priory

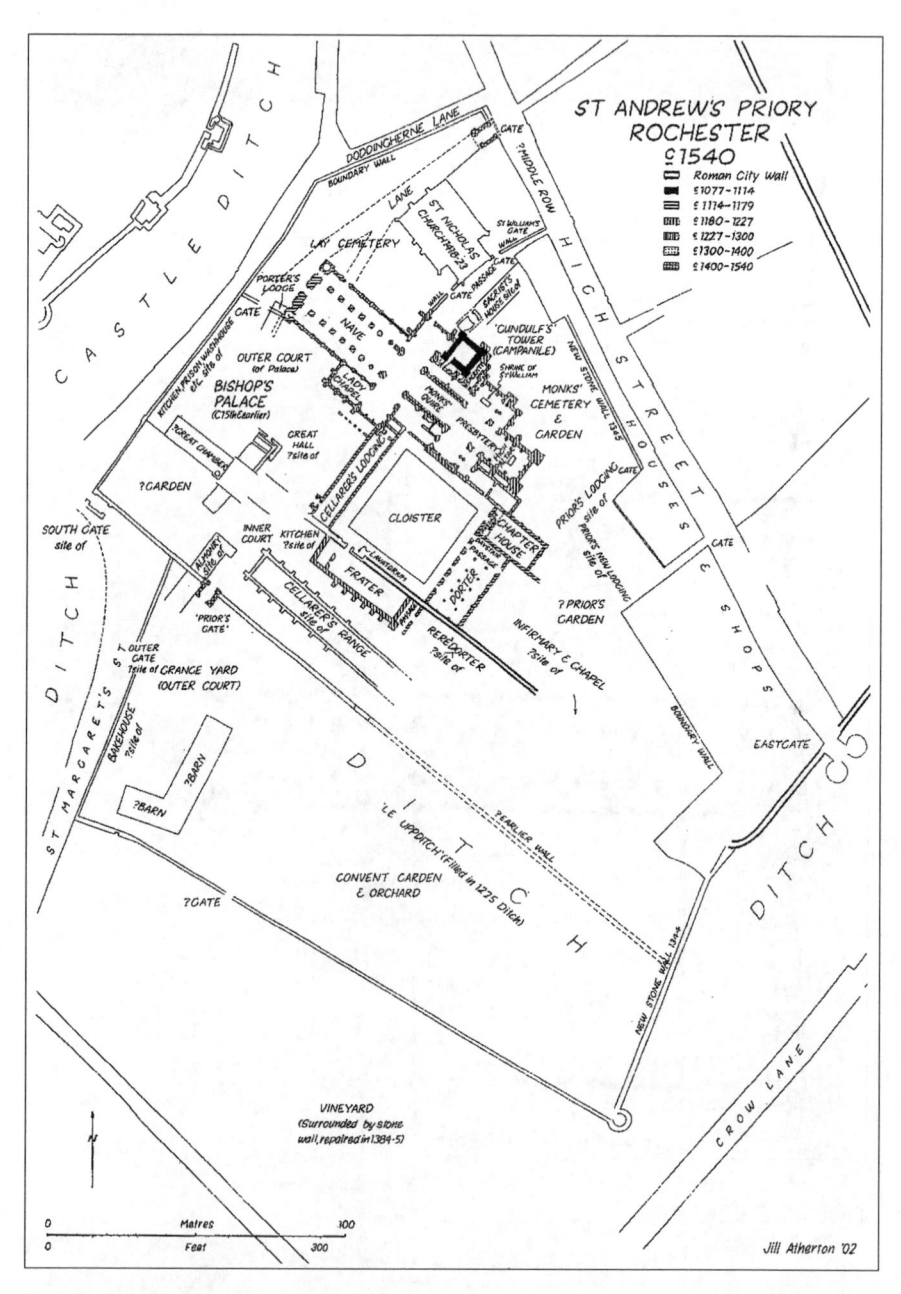

St Andrew's Cathedral Priory, Rochester

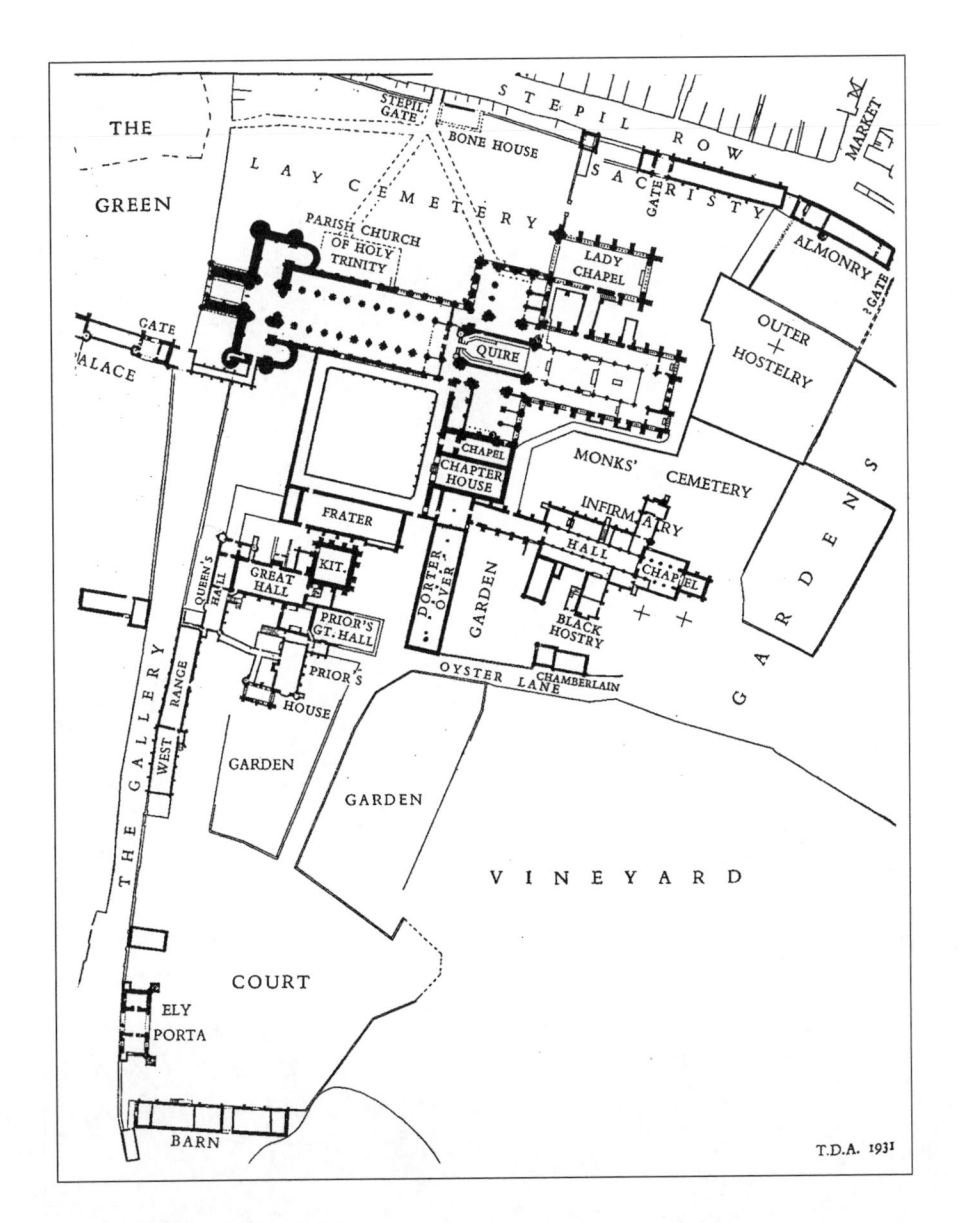

Ely Cathedral and Priory

I

Introduction

Ecce quam bonum et quam jucundum habitare fratres in unum.

Ps. 133:1[1]

The purpose and profile of this work

We may perhaps benefit from the occasional reminder that there are as many approaches to the study of English monasticism as there are historians who sit down to write it. The resulting narratives and their interpretation will, in every case, be *sui generis*, although all or most of them will have been largely dependent on the same facts and records. The reason for this is more obvious today than it was in 1902 when J. B. Bury bravely asserted that 'history is a science, no less and no more'.[1] Today we accept that all historians come to their work equipped with their own intellectual understanding, mental outlook, and personal experience, all of which inevitably leave an imprint on the text.

There are, broadly speaking, three ways in which the English medieval Benedictine communities may be treated: by means of a general survey of all monasteries, both great and small, which were home to the Black Monks prior to the sixteenth-century dissolution; by means of a study devoted to the history of a single house; or by means of a comparative study of a group of houses within a limited time span. I have chosen the third option in the belief that by focusing on the nine cathedral priories through an extended fourteenth century (*c.* 1270–1420) I will avoid the limitations both of the general overview, which can do little more than skim the surface, and of the detailed investigation concentrated on one particular monastery, which leaves scant room for an appraisal of its place in the contemporary religious scene.[2] The *termini ante* and *post quem* are, to some degree, arbitrary but have not been chosen without due consideration. A significant proportion of the evidence on which this book is based comes from original sources which, with a few exceptions, are in short supply before the later thirteenth century; the earlier material, mainly chronicles, charters, and royal and papal documents, can prove informative but it rarely provides more than fragmentary detail

---

[1] J. B. Bury, 'The Science of History' in F. Kern (ed.), *The Varieties of History*, (Meridian Books, Cleveland/New York, 1956), 210.
[2] The nine Benedictine cathedral priories were Bath, Canterbury, Coventry, Durham, Ely, Norwich, Rochester, Winchester, and Worcester.

that is often unreliable, unverifiable, and of uncertain date. The choice of a convenient halting place for this study at the beginning of the second decade of the fifteenth century serves to draw attention to the momentous gathering of 1421 at Westminster convoked by King Henry V to bring about a reform of the Black Monk houses. All Benedictine prelates were summoned to attend; sixty were present, together with over 300 monks and others.[3] This was an extraordinary assembly, almost without precedent, when royal intervention in monastic affairs necessitated self-scrutiny in public by what proved to be a reluctant body of religious dignitaries.

This introductory chapter will set the cathedral priories in their historical background, and will be followed by a description of their geographical setting and of the layout of their monastic buildings within the precinct. A series of succeeding chapters will then take the aspiring monks through the admission procedures, their clothing in the monastic habit, year of probation and study, further study leading to ordination, and their appointments to office within the monastery. In other words we will attempt to follow the monks as closely as possible throughout their monastic careers from the day of their arrival until their death or, in a few cases, departure.

1. THE GENERAL HISTORICAL CONTEXT

During the course of the thirteenth century the Black Monks gradually lost their hitherto pre-eminent position and influence in contemporary society, an influence which had already been challenged in the eleventh and early twelfth century by the Cluniac and Cistercian reformers' return to a stricter interpretation of the Rule of St Benedict.[4] A second blow was probably more damaging: the growing predominance of the regular black canons or Augustinians in the same period, in combination with the rise and rapid expansion of the mendicant movement in the thirteenth century. Before the end of that century the monastic cloisters as the chief centres of learning had been superseded by the nascent universities at Oxford and Cambridge; the monastic response to this transition was to found halls on both sites and send selected monks for university training.

The late tenth, the eleventh, and the early twelfth centuries in western Europe have been rightly singled out by medieval historians as worthy of high praise for some remarkable artistic and intellectual achievements, most of them produced within the precincts of church and cloister. There was an outpouring of creative energy for the most part by monastic artists and craftsmen working in their respective media and, at the same time, by monastic writers and scholars extending the frontiers of knowledge in many areas of learning and producing texts to communicate the fruits of their thought and preserve them for future generations. It was, in short, a time of exploration and expansion of man's mental and spiritual universe.

---

[3] Pantin, *Black Monk Chapters*, ii, 98–9.
[4] I use three modern editions of the Rule; see the Bibliography under the abbreviation *RB*.

There is an abundance of evidence that the English monks experienced and participated in this stimulating environment; we have only to consider what remains of the monastic churches and cloisters constructed or renovated in this period and of the surviving manuscript collections from the former monastic libraries. However, as with all forms of human endeavour, the creative powers and originality that had inspired this productivity were destined to lose their impetus and to decline. Although there is little to suggest that succeeding generations of Black Monks wasted much time in lamenting the lost glories of their order, many historians, who have confined their studies to the period before 1300, have perhaps inadvertently implied that the succeeding age was by comparison of less interest and significance. In so doing they have failed to pay attention to the more modest activities that occupied fourteenth-century monks as they strove to respond to changing needs and concerns both inside and outside the cloister. English Benedictines in that century have yet to be judged on their own merits and in the light of their Rule rather than against the background of the exceptional achievements of earlier centuries. Pronouncements concerning rise and decline, success and failure, I should like to suggest, are largely based on the still prevailing view that the fourteenth-century cloister produced few Benedictine scholars, teachers, writers, or preachers whose fame enhanced their house and order and that, on the contrary, it saw the beginning of an era of laxity and worldliness to which episcopal injunctions frequently drew attention.

The survival of episcopal registers in large numbers has furnished historians with a wealth of material concerning the internal organization and discipline of monasteries, usually emphasizing the bishop's authority and point of view. The unfortunate loss of all but a few of the chapter ordinances from monastic registers rules out the possibility of knowing the chapters' processes of decision-making in introducing new regulations and implementing change and reform either on their own initiative or as the result of papal and episcopal mandates. This is but one example of the type of problem facing the historian who, when attempting to interpret the contents of extant records, encounters the lacunae in the evidence and strains for clues that could help to narrow the gaps. Another problem comes to the fore when we begin to reflect on the way medieval monks represented themselves, how they thought and felt, their texts and works of art being our sole informants. Our task is to study the monastic *mentalité* while bearing in mind that our ability to understand and interpret is significantly affected by our own *mentalités*.[5] In selecting these nine cathedral monasteries, whose economic, social, and cultural settings are in many ways so alien to our own, I am therefore aware that even the codicological and archaeological remnants do not reveal past realities when divorced from the background out of which they emerged.[6] The eschatological outlook of the monks offers one example of this divide between then and now with its longing for the final goal, the heavenly Jerusalem of which the monastic community was in

---

[5] J. Le Goff, *Medieval Civilization* (Paris, 1964, trans. Blackwell, Oxford, 1988), viii.
[6] G. Spiegel, *The Past as Text: The Theory and Practice of Medieval Historiography* (Johns Hopkins, Baltimore, 1997), 53.

itself meant to be a foretaste, and which was made visible daily in the liturgy and the public and private readings.[7]

Since the unifying theme in the history of monks and monasticism is the Benedictine Rule, we would do well to allow it to serve as both guide and judge for the present study. To proceed by means of this model has several advantages, the first being that it ensures a constant reminder of the pre-eminence of the Rule in the monks' daily life whether at their prayers, their domestic and administrative tasks, their intellectual labours, or their recreation. Secondly, from the point of view of *mentalités*, the Rule formed the monks' outlook and attitude to the world of their day; and thirdly, the Rule has survived the test of time through a millennium and a half and is familiar to us today because it remains in use. The monastic ideal of perfection is of historical significance because it is the cornerstone on which the whole monastic edifice rests, without which the monastic life cannot be understood.[8] The practical guide for those attracted by this ideal is to be found in the Rule which every monk was expected to learn by heart during his novitiate. There were daily readings from the Rule at the morning chapter; the threefold promise of *obedientia*, *stabilitas*, and *conversatio morum* made at the time of profession stressed the daily commitment to persevere; and the implications of profession were expounded by the senior monks and in the many commentaries and treatises for regular instruction on the Rule and on monastic life.[9] This is not to say that in the monastery heavenly ideal and earthly reality were often found in close embrace, but rather that the goal was never entirely lost to view, as some historians have concluded on the basis of episcopal censure following visitation. Moreover, if we may generalize on the basis of figures drawn from the records of the cathedral priories, the monastic ideal continued to appeal to young men after, as well as before, the Black Death and also right up to the eve of the dissolution, although numbers never regained their former strength when the Black Monks had been alone on the scene before the arrival of other orders challenging their monopoly.

The French historian of *mentalités*, Jacques Le Goff, has remarked that 'medieval men were dominated by a sense of insecurity which determined the basis of their attitudes' and he described this insecurity as both material and moral.[10] He would probably argue that the fears which haunted them to their dying moments drove many into the monasteries. To be convincing he would need to explain why there are no signs of any substantial exodus among those who became disaffected by the relentless striving to measure up to the daily obligations prescribed by the Rule. Assuredly the aspiring monk would have been aware of, and perhaps even influenced by, the material security enjoyed within the cloister; but it must have been a real sense of vocation that motivated his desire for the perseverance necessary to follow the way of perfection that would lead him unerringly to

---

[7] *RB*, C.4, 46: 'Vitam aeternam omni concupiscentia spiritali desiderare'.

[8] *Si vis perfectus esse*, Christ's words to the rich young man, Matt. 19, 21. See the remarks of Knowles in similar vein in *MO*, 692–3.

[9] This still applies, as do the daily readings from the Rule; the words of profession also remain unaltered.

[10] Le Goff, *Medieval Civilization*, 325.

salvation.[11] Of course, this is not to deny that for many monks perseverance entailed a daily slog, and obedience to the Rule was at times more lukewarm than fervent, closer to the letter than to the spirit.

Despite the changing political and economic circumstances the monastic culture of the fourteenth century was continuous with the traditions of the previous century. There were certainly fluctuations between peak moments of observance and scholarly achievement followed by decline and renewal. But underneath there was always 'a general level of virtue amongst the average monks... [and] the existence of obscure but zealous religious of whom the chronicles have nothing to say but who, like invisible columns supported the whole edifice'.[12]

In this study of the cathedral priories there is also a second theme to be taken into account. It has its origin in the problems caused by their anomalous position as monastic chapters in a cathedral setting subject to direct episcopal oversight. The persistent efforts to limit and, where possible, eliminate the bishop's controlling influence as titular abbot in the monks' domestic and external affairs was a source of frequent tension and from time to time provoked bitter disputes. The relations between the bishop and his monastic chapter had no parallel in the major abbeys and the secular cathedrals. The former were generally free from episcopal oversight except at times of visitation, and some houses like Glastonbury and Bury St Edmunds were exempt from all episcopal jurisdiction. It is true that the secular cathedral chapters from time to time experienced difficulties with their bishops especially during the fourteenth century. However, deans and canons at each secular cathedral were governed by their own particular customs and statutes which varied considerably from one cathedral to another; they did not operate as a community except to perform the daily services in choir and attend chapter business meetings, and in both instances only the residentiary canons were involved.[13]

Origin and early history of the cathedral priories

Most of the nine English Benedictine cathedral priories came into existence soon after the Norman conquest.[14] However, in the case of Canterbury, Winchester, and Worcester cathedrals there is evidence of a monastic presence, reflecting the influence of the tenth-century reform movement, and at Winchester even earlier in the seventh century.[15] Bath, Coventry, and Ely were abbeys of Anglo-Saxon foundation promoted to cathedral status in the first decade of the twelfth century.

---

[11] The past tense is employed because it applies to my study, but the present tense is equally applicable to most of the general statements above. See Knowles, *MO*, 692–3.

[12] Leclercq, *Love of Learning*, 251. In employing the term 'culture' here I follow Dom Leclercq's definition: 'from a very general point of view, culture includes an overall conception of the world and of life, and the means for expressing it, that is to say, language and the arts', ibid., 44.

[13] See Edwards, *Secular Cathedrals*, especially C.1 and C.2.

[14] Carlisle cathedral was also served by regular clergy after *c.* 1122x1133, in this case by canons of the Augustinian order.

[15] For brief summaries see Knowles and Hadcock, *Medieval Religious Houses*, and for the tenth-century reform movement see the introduction in T. Symons (ed.), *Regularis Concordia: The Monastic Agreement* (NMT, Edinburgh, 1953).

Durham and Norwich were instituted as both cathedrals and monasteries in 1083 and 1096 respectively, and at Rochester, where a cathedral had been in existence since 604, the changeover came with the arrival of monks in the early 1080s.

When Lanfranc, prior of the Norman abbey of Bec and abbot of Caen, arrived to take up his appointment as William the Conqueror's archbishop of Canterbury he therefore found himself greeted by a monastic chapter. As head of this community he assumed the role of abbot and composed a set of monastic constitutions to regulate the practical details of daily life and observance.[16] Copies of these were soon passed on to other cathedral monasteries like Durham and probably Worcester.[17] In the historical memories of their chapters the names of several of the more notable monk bishops have remained fresh to the present day: William de St Calais or Carilef, for example, the first Norman bishop of Durham (1080–96) who brought in the monastic community, made it responsible for the cult of St Cuthbert and planned the present cathedral;[18] Herbert de Losinga, the first Norman bishop of Norwich (c. 1094–1119) who laid the foundation stone of his cathedral in 1096 and introduced the monastic chapter;[19] Henry de Blois, a monk of Cluny and brother of King Stephen, who occupied the see of Winchester (concurrently with the abbacy of Glastonbury) from 1129 to 1171, a patron of art and architecture who brought the twelfth-century renaissance to his cathedral and city;[20] and Wulstan of Worcester (1062–95), the only Anglo-Saxon bishop who survived the Conquest for any length of time, and who had previously been prior of the cathedral monastery.[21]

Wulstan was one of the small group of cathedral monks who advanced from the rule of his cathedral community to the rule of the diocese of which that cathedral was the mother church. In his own lifetime he, like Lanfranc, was able to continue to reside among his monks as their titular abbot—the title that soon came to be assumed by all bishops of monastic cathedrals—although his diocesan and other public responsibilities, including attendance at the royal court, often called him away. With the demise of the first few monastic bishops however, this harmonious relationship had already begun to break down as both sides became aware of growing tensions arising out of overlapping and conflicting interests and claims. The ideal community envisaged by Lanfranc and put into practice at Canterbury, Durham, Norwich, and Rochester could not be adapted to function in new

---

[16] Printed in Lanfranc, *Monastic Constitutions*.

[17] Ibid., xxii.

[18] See 'William of St Calais, First Norman Bishop of Durham' in H. S. Offler, *North of the Tees: Studies in Medieval British History* (Variorum, Aldershot, ed. by A. J. Piper and A. I. Doyle, 1996), V, 258–79; and A. J. Piper, 'The First Generations of Durham Monks and the Cult of St Cuthbert' in G. Bonner, D. Rollason, C. Stancliffe (eds), *St Cuthbert, his Cult and his Community to AD1200* (Boydell Press, Woodbridge, 1989), 437–46.

[19] See D. Wollaston, 'Herbert de Losinga' in Atherton, *Norwich Cathedral*, 22–35 and B. Dodwell, 'Herbert de Losinga and the Foundation', ibid., 36–43.

[20] See Y. Kusaba, 'Henry of Blois, Winchester, and the 12th-Century Renaissance' in Crook, *Winchester Cathedral*, 69–79.

[21] Wulstan's life has recently been examined in a detailed and meticulous study by Emma Mason, *St Wulfstan*.

circumstances with their accompanying pressures affecting both bishops and monks.[22] For our purposes it will be sufficient to provide an outline of the main developments that impinged on the relations between bishops and their monastic chapters during the twelfth and thirteenth centuries.

For their part the bishops had become too involved in diocesan business and matters of church and state to watch over the day-to-day concerns of their monastic chapter and its members, while the latter could not repress a desire for independence in managing their own affairs. Thus one major source of disagreement concerned the degree to which the bishop could be allowed to continue to interfere in strictly monastic affairs and included the right of the chapter to enjoy free election of the bishop *qua* abbot although the abbot in this case was also the ordinary. In a number of important spheres, however, they remained bound together; and the separation of rights and responsibilities including the division of property and possessions, posed thorny problems that were often not easily or amicably solved.

The need to arrive at a fair division of the cathedral church's patrimony, hitherto geared to the needs of a single household, arose because it was now required to support two separate establishments both of considerable size. According to the monastic historian, Symeon of Durham, Bishop William of St Calais made this division between himself and his chapter in 1083, shortly after the monks' arrival. While the settlement was probably less precisely stated than Symeon suggests, in practice it appears to have worked as there is no evidence of any later major disagreement.[23] At Winchester, on the other hand, difficulties appeared almost at once under Bishop Walkelin (1070–98), the Conqueror's chaplain, and his successor William Giffard (1100–29), who had served William Rufus as chancellor. Although Walkelin divided the cathedral revenues into two equal shares he soon took back some of it for the construction of his cathedral; Giffard acted similarly by appropriating some of the income from the monks' churches for his expenses, but he later relented.[24] For the monks of St Swithun's, however, a permanent settlement over the division of income from lands and churches was not achieved until 1284.[25] Other monastic chapters experienced similar difficulties; at Canterbury the division of lands is clearly stated in the late eleventh-century Domesday *Monachorum* although this did not prevent Archbishop Baldwin from usurping a number of monastic estates for some length of time.[26] The creation of the see of Ely in 1109 necessitated a division of the lands of the former abbey to accommodate the new bishop; this probably took some time although reliable evidence is lacking. What is

---

[22] Knowles, *MO*, 623–4; probably Archbishop Thomas Becket (d. 1170) was the last to try to live with his monks whenever possible, Smith, *Canterbury Cathedral Priory*, 4. See also Gervase, *Opera Historica*, i, 48.

[23] See Alan Piper, 'The Cathedral and its Monastic Community' in D. Pocock (ed.), *St. Cuthbert and Durham Cathedral, a Celebration* (City of Durham Trust, Durham, 1995), 97.

[24] The stormy relations followed by touching reconciliations are recorded in *Annales Winton.*, 39, 48–9.

[25] The charters are to be found in *Reg. Pontissara*, 419–24.

[26] See Smith, *Canterbury Cathedral Priory*, 5.

certain is that the Ely monks soon benefited from bequests and donations made specifically to them without reference to bishop or cathedral church.[27]

In every case, however, the stresses and strains of the often fragile relations between the monastic chapters and their bishops/abbots occupied a prominent space in the early post-Conquest annals and chronicles. Elections were at the centre of controversy because the cathedral monks *qua* cathedral chapter continued to assert their right to choose their own bishop and the same monks *qua* monastic community claimed free election of their own superior (i.e. abbot). The early, somewhat informal procedure in the election of a diocesan by means of a gathering of clergy and people had been superseded in the twelfth century by a more formal structure limited to an electoral body; in 1184, for example, a dispute arose between the monks of Canterbury and the bishops of the province when both claimed their rights in the election of an archbishop.[28] Although the fourth Lateran council, in 1215, gave cathedral chapters the sole right to elect the bishop, the problem was not laid to rest. There were other parties whose interests were also at stake. In England it was of vital concern to the king to exercise his influence over episcopal elections in order to ensure the promotion of candidates in, or available for, the royal service in church and state on whose support and fidelity he could rely. Since a royal licence was required before a chapter could proceed to an election, the king no doubt often declared his preference when interviewing the monks who presented their prior and convent's petition to elect. Some early elections were carried out in his presence when the delegation of monks was sufficient in number to act as an electoral body.[29] The pope's not infrequent interventions in elections by monastic chapters were often the result of appeals directed to him by thwarted monks, a frustrated king or archbishop, or all three. The monks of Durham enjoyed two free elections in the middle of the twelfth century, although the second required an appeal to the pope to overcome the archbishop of York's refusal to confirm their choice.[30] The episcopal election in 1215 at Norwich of Pandulf Masca, papal subdeacon, was in the shadow of the baronial ultimatum to King John when the latter urgently needed papal support; the Worcester annalist remarks that the Norwich community had voted according to the pope's direction.[31] The situation at Winchester during the six-year vacancy in the see between 1238 and 1244 reveals the strain on the monks, who were also

---

[27] Miller, *The Abbey and Bishopric of Ely*, 74–5. Studies of the monastic economy and financial organization such as this have not been lacking because of the abundance of surviving financial records which have proved a rich source for historians.

[28] Baldwin, bishop of Worcester, was the final choice agreed by both parties after six months of negotiations, *Fasti*, ii, 5; see also Knowles, *RO*, i, 257.

[29] E.g. in 1184 the Rochester prior was summoned to Westminster with twelve of his monks in order to elect a bishop, Flight, *Bishops and Monks of Rochester*, 290 no. 536 (with manuscript references). There is also similar evidence at Winchester in 1238 when four monks went to Reading to request a licence to elect a bishop; there can be little doubt that this delegation had been appointed by the prior and chapter as the electoral body who were prepared to perform their task in the royal presence, *CPR (1232–47)*, iii, 226.

[30] The bishops were William de Sancta Barbara (1142–52) and Hugh du Puiset (1152–95); see *Fasti*, ii, 30.

[31] *Annales Wigorn.*, 404–5.

without a prior during most of this period. They went through the formalities of election for both offices several times in each case, repeatedly thwarted by the king and constantly appealing to the pope. The outcome was eventually satisfactory, but only after they had been so worn down that the seven members of the chapter appointed as electors in the fourth round failed to agree and it was the pope who cast the deciding vote.[32]

Although monks frequently tried to put a member of their own community, usually the prior, into the episcopal office during the twelfth and thirteenth centuries they were only sporadically successful. There were two early monastic bishops of Bath,[33] both previously abbots of Glastonbury; the only one of Coventry, Walter Durdent, had been prior of Canterbury until elected to the see in 1149.[34] The first monastic bishop at Durham after St Calais was the Durham monk Robert de Stichill, elected in 1260, who was followed by Robert de Insula in 1274; both had been priors of the dependent cell at Finchale. There were two other monk bishops at Durham before the dissolution: Richard de Kellawe in the early fourteenth century and William Sever at the beginning of the sixteenth century.[35] During the entire thirteenth century there was only one monk bishop, Roger de Skerning, at Norwich, in contrast to Ely where the abbots of Fountains and of Bury St Edmunds, together with a subprior of Ely, occupied the see for sixty-two years of the century.[36] At Winchester and Worcester monastic bishops were few and far between before 1270. Almost a century after Henry de Blois' death in 1171 the St Swithun's chapter was once again divided, and on this occasion both candidates were monks; however, the pope quashed the election and provided John of Exeter, chancellor of York.[37] During the same period there were three monastic occupants of the see of Worcester but the total number of years involved was only eight, and only one of the three, Silvester de Evesham (1216–18), was a monk and prior of that cathedral priory.[38] The case of one of the two monastic bishops of Rochester after Ascelin (d. 1148) serves to demonstrate that monks did not always benefit from choosing one of their own number. When in 1278 the chapter were successful in promoting their precentor, John de Bradefeld, to the episcopate there was much

---

[32] The episcopal candidates were Ralph de Neville, bishop of Chichester, and William de Ralegh, bishop of Norwich; the latter was finally appointed through the pope's intervention. The priors in question were Andrew, appointed by the king claiming his right *sede vacante* and John de Cauz similarly appointed. See *Fasti*, ii, 86, 89 for a résumé and further references.

[33] Both assumed the title of bishop of Bath and Glastonbury: Savaric Fitzgeldewin (1191–1205) and Jocelin of Wells (1206–42); see *HRH*, i, 52 for references.

[34] *BRECP*, 142; Saltman, *Theobald*, 115–16.

[35] Kellawe was only in office for five years and Sever for three years; M. Robert de Graystanes was elected by the monks in 1333, consecrated by the archbishop of York and enthroned before having to give way to the king's choice, Richard de Bury, *Fasti*, vi, 107, 109. For the Durham monks see also *LVD*, iii, C.752 (Kellawe), C.801 (Graystanes). Sever had not been a monk of Durham; see *HRH*, iii, 91, under Senhouse.

[36] For Norwich see the references in *Fasti*, ii, 57–8 and for *Ely*, ibid., ii, 46–7. Norwich also had one monk bishop in the mid-twelfth century, William de Turba (1146/7–74), ibid., ii, 56; Ely had none.

[37] A summary is to be found in *Fasti*, ii, 86–7 under the names Andrew de London and William de Taunton; see also *BRECP*, 710, 739, under the same names.

[38] The others were Baldwin, the Cistercian abbot of Forde and future archbishop of Canterbury (1180–4) and Henry de Soilli, abbot of Glastonbury (1193–5).

rejoicing because he was a product of their own monastery school and beloved for his peaceful nature and humility; they thought they had found another Gundulf. They were soon bitterly disillusioned for, once elected, as the chronicler tersely commented, *mutatus in virum alium*; however, they were not deterred from electing their prior, Thomas de Wouldham, in 1291.[39]

When the monks in the cathedral communities compared notes with their brethren in some of the major Benedictine abbeys such as Peterborough, Gloucester, Reading, and Tewkesbury they might well have concluded that, for the most part, their day-to-day relations with their bishops/titular abbots, both monastic and secular, had certain advantages. While it is true that the abbot followed the episcopal practice of having separate lodgings, and thus lived apart from the other monks, yet he retained his establishment within the precinct; therefore the community must have constantly felt his presence and authority even when he was physically absent from choir, chapter, and refectory. The bishop, on the other hand, was in general a distant figure who, with certain important exceptions that will be discussed below, did not interfere in the domestic affairs or internal organization of the cathedral monastery. The persistent attempts in the thirteenth century to get rid of these exceptions and free the chapter entirely from episcopal control were continued with moderate success in the fourteenth.[40] It must always be borne in mind, however, that on certain occasions during the year, such as the Ember day ordinations and the Easter and Pentecost solemnities, the monastic church was taken over by the bishop for the performance of his functions, as diocesan, and the general populace thronged the nave. This dual role of the monastic cathedral church was one anomaly from which there was no escape; but there is no sign that the monks had any objection to it.[41]

One of the major sources of irritation was the bishop's right, and in an episcopal vacancy the king's right, to nominate the prior. In every case but one an episcopal rather than a royal licence was required for the election of a prior followed by episcopal confirmation of the elect; the exception was Coventry, the prior of which, as a tenant-in-chief of the crown, was obliged to seek a royal licence.[42]

The earliest of the agreements worked out was that between the bishop and monks of Worcester in 1224; it was in the form of a compromise that continued to work smoothly until the eve of the dissolution but, perhaps not surprisingly, remained a unique arrangement since it worked in the bishop's favour: the convent chose seven candidates to present to the bishop who then made the final selection of one of them.[43] It remains uncertain how early the monks of Bath and Coventry began to assert control over their own elections; Bishop William de Bitton I granted free election to the monks of Bath in 1261, and at Coventry two late twelfth-century priors, Moses and Joybert, were probably chosen by the monks. We can be

---

[39] *BRECP*, 593; Ascelin had formerly been prior of Dover. See also *ODNB* under Bradfield and Wouldham.
[40] See pp. 53–57.
[41] Apart from ordination ceremonies in the cathedral, Durham appears to have been an exception to this episcopal/diocesan 'takeover'.
[42] *BRECP*, 338. This was not realized by Susan Wood in *English Monasteries*, 50.
[43] *Fasti*, ii, 102; the document is printed in *Acta Stephani Langton*, 160–3.

fairly sure that before the end of the thirteenth century what may have been custom in these two cases had been established by right.[44] At Durham the first evidence of a free election of a prior was that of Thomas I (1158x1162); he was chosen *communi consilio fratrum*, but soon afterwards deposed by Bishop Puiset, regretting his initial favours to the convent when they continued to show their strength in opposition.[45] An episcopal charter on his deathbed in 1195 restored the free election of the prior, and the monks took the precaution of obtaining royal confirmation from King John in 1204. However, episcopal confirmation of their right was not forthcoming until it was written into the agreement, *le Convenit*, between bishop and convent in 1229.[46] Winchester was the only other cathedral priory to achieve this complete independence from episcopal intrusion in prioral elections, but only in 1284 after a series of disputes.[47] Elections at St Swithun's were further complicated by the fact that the two archdeacons, of Winchester and Surrey, were accustomed to participate. Since their appointment pertained to the bishop, theirs was an alien presence in the chapter for it is unlikely that they remained immune to outside pressures. In 1243, for example, they sided with the deposed Prior Andrew who had been nominated by the king against the monks' wishes.[48] They were removed from the chapter in prioral elections in 1311 but continued to be summoned for episcopal elections into the fifteenth century.[49]

As neither dates nor documents have been found for Norwich and Ely priories we must fall back on the earliest reliable record of a free election of the prior by the chapter. This occurred in 1257 at Norwich when an inquiry, set up to settle the claims on each side, after examining witnesses concluded that the bishop's rights were limited to the issuing of a licence to elect and the confirmation and admission of the prior elect.[50] By 1271 the Ely monks seem to have been free of episcopal intervention, although some years earlier a mandate from Gregory IX (1227–41) had laid down that no outsider was to be imposed on them as prior and that they were free to conduct their own elections according to the Rule of St Benedict.[51]

---

[44] *Bath Priory Reg.* no. 251. See *HRH*, 41 for Moses and Joybert; see *BRECP*, 10, 48, 361 for priors Walter de Anno and Thomas de Winton (Bath) and Henry de Leycester I (Coventry).

[45] *HRH*, i, 43. Prior Bertram was also freely elected in 1189, Scammell, *Puiset*, 133–5, 139; the charter is in ibid., 261–2.

[46] Scammell, *Puiset*, 261. The terms of *le Convenit* are transcribed in *Feodarium*, 212–17 and, more recently, in vol. 25 of *English Episcopal Acta, Durham, 1196–1239* (Oxford University Press/British Academy, London, 2002), 277–83.

[47] *Reg. Pontissara*, 428. As Susan Wood points out, this was equivalent to the monks admitting that the bishop was their patron in return for surrendering his abbatial rights, *English Monasteries*, 52.

[48] One of the archdeacons and six of the monks were nominated by the chapter to act on their behalf in the election of a bishop in 1243, *CPL*, i (1198–1304), 199–200. Note that a papal grant of free election of the bishop in 1204 had included the phrase 'with the counsel of the archdeacons', Goodman, *Winchester Chartulary*, no. 45.

[49] In 1311 Bishop Woodlock arbitrated in the suit of the archdeacon of Surrey against the prior and chapter, deciding that the archdeacons had no right to take part in elections of a prior, Winchester College Muniment no. 1013. Greatrex, *Common Seal Register*, no. 316 records their presence at Bishop Waynflete's election in 1447.

[50] *Close Rolls*, x (1256–9), 66, 137–8; see also Wood, *English Monasteries*, 51 where she points out that here, too, the decision reduced the bishop's status to that of patron rather than titular abbot.

[51] CUL, EDR G/3/28 (*Liber M*), 20A.

Gregory IX also issued a directive to the Christ Church monks to settle their election procedures: in their case the archbishop was called in to act as *scrutator* of each individual monk's vote and to announce the name of the successful candidate to the chapter. The papal pronouncement came in the wake of an impasse after Archbishop Edmund of Abingdon had forced Prior John de Chatham to resign and the monks, in the archbishop's absence, had proceeded with the election of a new prior, for which defiant act they had been excommunicated.[52] This Canterbury arrangement was also in use at Rochester after 1239; and there it should be noted that, almost a century later, the archbishop upheld the bishop's claim that in his scrutiny of the votes his conscience alone was empowered to discern which was the choice of the *sanior pars* of the chapter.[53] By this method episcopal supervision of elections to the priorate at Canterbury and Rochester was maintained until the dissolution.

There were two other sources of contention between bishop and chapter which endured over a long span of time without being settled definitively; these concerned the admission and profession of monks and the appointment and dismissal of obedientiaries. In the period before 1270 the arrangements in these matters must have been gradually worked out, and only later would custom have been regulated and procedures written down. Since the results point to considerable variety in practice, we may infer that these differences originated and developed under the influence of particular personalities and circumstances, the details of which are largely unknown.

With regard to admission and profession the monks of St Cuthbert and St Swithun were successful in gaining complete independence from episcopal control. In *le Convenit* of 1229 the bishop of Durham conceded profession to the prior in chapter but retained his prerogative to hear the professions repeated in his presence at the profession mass at which he pronounced the solemn blessing. In the mid-thirteenth century the bishop's role in the ceremony lapsed and this precedent, once established, was never dislodged. The decision to accept or reject candidates seems to have always been the prior's.[54] In the *ordinacio* or composition of 1284 Bishop Pontissara gave up all claims to have any say in admissions to St Swithun's priory; the prior was to enjoy *liberam administracionem*, which must be taken to include profession since there is no evidence to the contrary.[55] In contrast, the episcopal registers at Worcester and the priory register, known as the *Liber Albus*, contain a mass of correspondence relating to both the admission and profession of monks. This consists mainly of petitions of the prior to the bishop to perform one

---

[52] *Fasti*, ii, 11 with references. The method of election, *via scrutini*, was one of three alternatives used, the other two being *via compromissi* (by nomination of a small number of monks to be the electors) and *via Sancti Spiritus* (by inspiration).

[53] This is no doubt what frequently occurred in practice both at Canterbury and Rochester, BRECP, 579–80; Wood, *English Monasteries*, 50–1.

[54] See *le Convenit* for profession, *Feodarium*, 213 and the remarks of Foster on Bishop Stichill's failure to restore episcopal rights in 1272, 'Durham Priory', 56. Dr Foster's remarks on admissions are in ibid., 52–3.

[55] *Reg. Pontissara*, 426–8; for their part the prior and convent gave up a number of manors to the bishop. In the fourteenth century the prior and chapter did not hesitate to refuse to comply with requests for admission of persons recommended by the bishop, the king, and possibly even the pope.

or other of the rites and of commissions of the bishop to his official or to the prior to act in his stead.[56]

The regulations for the admission and profession of monks to Christ Church were similar to Worcester. Although the prior obtained a bull from Gregory IX (1227–41) authorizing him to receive the profession of novices *sede vacante*, the archbishops persisted in holding on to their right to issue the required licence *sede plena* despite repeated efforts on the part of the monks.[57] The relevant correspondence occupies many pages in both the archiepiscopal and priory registers as at Worcester, but at Canterbury the undercurrents of tension on both sides and the shadow of resentment on the part of the monks are more pronounced in some of the letters and petitions.[58] The bishops of Bath, Coventry, Norwich, Ely, and Rochester also continued to claim what they regarded as their 'abbatial' rights over admission and profession in the fourteenth century, without reference to the terms of any previously agreed settlement; at Norwich, however, a dispute with Bishop Despenser required arbitration in the 1390s.[59] An entry dated 1236 in the *Magnum Registrum Album* of Lichfield refers to the bishop's right to profess novices at Coventry, and another entry of 1249 in the same register is a copy of the prior's petition to the bishop asking him to receive the profession of seventeen novices; there are no later entries in the episcopal registers, and we may therefore assume that this large number of professions was not due to a sudden increase in vocations but to a delay caused by the necessity of coming to an agreement with the bishop on procedures to be followed.[60] The absence of later entries in any of the Coventry/Lichfield registers forbids any certainty as to the continuation of this practice.

St Benedict himself provided for some differentiation of functions within his monasteries when he prescribed the duties assigned to the cellarer, the kitcheners on the weekly rota, the monk in charge of the infirmary, and the guestmaster.[61] Lanfranc's *Monastic Constitutions* outline the duties of a cantor (or precentor), sacrist, chamberlain, cellarer, guestmaster (or hostiller), almoner, and infirmarer; and this division of responsibilities was extended during the course of the twelfth century to include a growing number of administrative offices or obediences in the hands of monks called obedientiaries.[62] The majority of these offices, of which

---

[56] The reference to profession in the composition is in *Acta Stephani Langton*, 162; examples are given in *Annales Wigorn.*, 496–7 (1289), 534 (1297).
[57] Smith, *Canterbury Cathedral Priory*, 7, and CCA DCc Reg. A, fo 391.
[58] Many of these letters have been extracted from the priory registers and edited by Sheppard, in *Lit. Cant.*
[59] See, for example, *Reg. Drokensford*, fo 270 (Bath). For Norwich see NRO DCN 40/9 (Priory Reg. IX), fo 26, which is an admission *c.* 1319/20, and under Robert de Chattegrove in *BRECP*, 494; see also Tolhurst, *Norwich Customary*, 224. The only Norwich reference concerning profession before the final composition of 1411 is in a petition to the pope in 1398 and demonstrates the prior's persistence in claiming the right to profess novices, in this case because of the bishop's negligence, NRO DCN 42/17. For an Ely profession see Reg. Lisle, fo 16, 2nd foliation. The earliest profession I have found at Rochester is in 1324, *Reg. Hethe*, 132.
[60] *Magnum Reg. Album*, 153 (fo 280 in MS 28 in Lichfield Cathedral Library); ibid., 135 and fo 196.
[61] *RB*, C.31, C.35, C.36, C.53.
[62] Lanfranc, *Monastic Constitutions*, 118–34.

there came to be between fifteen and twenty in every cathedral priory, were provided with an endowment in the form of manorial estates, churches, rents, and pensions to ensure an adequate income to cover their expenditures. These obedientiaries and the heads of the dependent cells were required to produce accounts for annual inspection by the prior and senior monks.[63] The appointment and dismissal of obedientiaries in English Benedictine monasteries pertained to the abbot or prior, generally after consultation with the senior monks; it was a strictly domestic matter carried out in accordance with procedures previously determined by the chapter. Since these arrangements were unacceptable to bishops *qua* abbots of cathedral priories, who insisted on their rights in this regard, the cathedral monks had to appeal to higher authorities. In each case the issue was eventually resolved after a lengthy process similar in its successive stages to the election controversies and their final outcome in compromise. It will suffice to provide a summary of the results for each of the cathedral priories.

William Hunt was probably correct in suggesting that when Bishop John de Villula transferred his see from Wells to Bath in 1090 he assumed his right as abbot to appoint monastic office-holders, namely the sacrist, cellarer, and probably the precentor.[64] The earliest extant episcopal register, that of Bishop Drokensford (1309–29), contains examples of such appointments, usually at pleasure, and also of his appointment of a prior for the dependent cell at Dunster.[65] The later registers have similar entries through the next two centuries without providing any evidence of previous consultation with the prior and chapter although we may presume that this would have taken place informally. On one occasion, which may be regarded as exceptional, the prior petitioned the bishop in 1326 to collate John de Eston to the office of precentor; before granting the request the bishop procured a notarial statement safeguarding his right of appointment.[66] For lack of evidence to the contrary we may infer that the bishops of Coventry/Lichfield at an unknown, early date lost or failed to exercise their right to appoint obedientiaries in Coventry cathedral priory. In the fairly complete series of episcopal registers there are no entries concerning such appointments, but one interesting reference to the institution of an obedientiary office occurs in a papal letter to Prior Roger Coton in 1399. The pope was responding to the prior's request by confirming the prior's ratification of a deed of his predecessor, Prior William Brythwalton (1249–80). The latter during his priorate had been responsible for instituting the office of pittancer with the stipulation that the income from the endowment was for the benefit of the subprior and chapter. A later document further clarifies the arrangements by

---

[63] There were other obedientiaries who probably did not present accounts since none have survived, but customs varied from one cathedral priory to another: the subprior, librarian, and refectorer at Durham, for example, and the hostiller or guestmaster at Winchester were among this non-accounting group.

[64] *Bath Priory Reg.* xliii–xliv. De Villula was another bishop who began by confiscating monastic estates, but later restored them, ibid., xliv.

[65] BRECP under Matthew (precentor, 1311), 34; Robert de Sutton (cellarer and sacrist temporarily, 1310), 42 and R II [?Richard] (prior of Dunster, 1301), 37. The earliest known prior of Dunster is Hugh II in 1186, ibid., 29.

[66] BRECP, 23–4.

declaring that appointments and dismissals of this obedientiary were in the hands of the subprior and chapter.[67] Since no comparable information has emerged from the records of the other cathedral priories this may have been a unique form of settlement.

The disagreements about obedientiary appointments at Durham and Winchester were also resolved by the compositions between bishop and chapter that settled the disputes about prioral elections. In *le Convenit* of 1229 Bishop Poore conceded the right of the prior of Durham, *cum consilio capituli*, to appoint and remove monk officials *sicut expedire viderit*, a grant that Bishop Puiset had specified in his deathbed concessions.[68] The Pontissara *ordinatio* of 1284 granted similar powers to the priors of St Swithun's, *prout viderint expedire*.[69] Over a century earlier, in 1172, Bishop Henry de Blois had issued a charter granting similar rights which his successors had largely ignored, and in vacancies such as that of 1239 the king had ordered the keepers of the bishopric to appoint his nominees.[70] The date of the settlement of obedientiary appointments at St Mary's Worcester remains uncertain, although it is clear that during the thirteenth century the monks, with one significant exception, must have freed themselves from episcopal control. The exception was the sacrist's office which in 1278 was at the centre of a dispute between Bishop Godfrey Giffard and Prior Richard de Feckenham. The background can be only partially reconstructed although the implication is that the sacrist's obedience was at stake: the bishop was not only appointing the sacrist to his office in the priory but also employing him in the episcopal administration. This problem was never resolved and remained a continuing source of friction through the next two and a half centuries.[71] The Worcester composition of 1224 mentioned only one minor obedientiary appointment, which suggests that such appointments were at the time not a problem although there is no clue to the rights on either side in this matter. The agreement dealt with the appointment of two feretrars or *tumbarii* at the tomb and shrine of St Wulstan; one of these was henceforth to be appointed by the chapter and one by the bishop, thus ensuring that the proceeds from offerings would be divided equally between them. It was specified that in both cases these officials could be either monks or *clerici*.[72]

The four remaining cathedral priories—Ely, Canterbury, Rochester, and Norwich—were obliged to submit to the bishop's nomination to four or five of the obedientiary offices which, in each case, included those of the subprior, cellarer, sacrist, and chamberlain and at all but Ely, the precentor. At an inquisition in Ely in 1302 it was established that it was the custom for the bishop to collate to four

---

[67] *CPL*, v (1396–1404), 192 and ibid., ix (1431–47), 424. Coton and Brythwalton are in *BRECP*, 351, 348.
[68] *Le Convenit* in *Feodarium*, 213; for the reference to Puiset's charter see note 45 above.
[69] *Reg. Pontissara*, 428.
[70] The charter is in *Reg. Pontissara*, 625 and Goodman, *Winchester Chartulary*, no. 3; the royal nominations are in *Close Rolls*, iv (1237–42), 158.
[71] The letter is in *Reg. Giffard*, 96; for a full account of the sacrist's impasse see my *Monastic or Episcopal Obedience: The Problem of the Sacrists of Worcester*, Worcestershire Historical Society, Occasional Publications no. 3 (Evesham, 1980). For Richard de Feckenham see *BRECP*, 805.
[72] *Acta Stephani Langton*, 162.

obedientiary offices *in pleno capitulo*.[73] What this involved in practice is still unclear although F. R. Chapman some ninety years ago shed light on the procedure followed in the appointment of one of these, namely the sacrist. Basing his conclusions mainly on the correct definition of the terms employed in the relevant deeds, he advanced the view that in most cases the bishop followed the recommendation of the prior and chapter and confined the exercise of his prerogative to the *prefectio* of the monks presented to him. Chapman rightly draws attention to a ruling of Innocent III to this effect, namely that the 'consensus Episcopi et Conventus in eorum constitucione requiritur, ita in eorum amocione requiratur'.[74] This fails to clarify how the *consensus* of both parties was obtained at Ely; but at Christ Church, where archiepiscopal appointments were customary in the late twelfth century, the process is well documented from the late thirteenth century onwards.[75] Both the priory registers and those of the archbishops record frequent correspondence on this subject, many of the prior's letters containing lists of three names proposed for the office in question and the archbishop's replies naming the monk of his choice and often authorizing the prior to perform the *prefectio*.[76] This method of appointment prevailed until the dissolution, despite the evidence of frequent frustrations on both sides caused by the monks' persistent attempts to bypass the regulations and the archbishops' equally persistent insistence on maintaining the rights of their predecessors. There is no record of the Rochester monks sending their bishop any lists of names from which to choose his preferred candidate for office, but the observance of the monastic customs of Christ Church no doubt explains the Rochester bishops' practice of appointing the same five monastic officials. Entries in the episcopal registers and a late fourteenth/early fifteenth-century priory register show the bishop removing (*amocio*), absolving (*absolucio*) and appointing (*prefectio*) in accordance with the prior's nomination.[77]
In addition to the five obedientiary offices over which the bishops of Norwich exercised their right of appointment, there were the offices of the prior of five of the six dependent cells. The origin and early development of these dispositions are obscure for want of evidence. The single mid-fourteenth-century record of the respective roles of the prior and bishop in these appointments comes from a priory register: in his letter the prior requested the removal from office of the prior of the cell of Hoxne and enclosed three names from which the bishop was to choose a

---

[73] Dugdale, *Monasticon*, i, 487; *Cal. Inq. Misc.*, i, item 1877.

[74] Chapman, *Sacrist Rolls*, i, 175; this ruling was given following the report of a commission examining the relationship between bishops and cathedral monasteries. See also ibid., i, 172–3. When Bishop Arundel replaced the chamberlain in 1377 he remarked 'cuius officii collacio, amocio et perfectio [*sic*] ad dominum dinoscitur notorie pertinere', CUL EDR G/1/2, fo 23v; what precisely did he mean?

[75] Smith, *Canterbury Cathedral Priory*, 33, referring to a bull of Urban III in 1187 confirming the archiepiscopal right to appoint the prior, subprior, precentor, sacrist, and chamberlain. Another papal decree to the same effect was obtained in 1219, CCA DCc Reg. I, fo 40.

[76] E.g. in CCA DCc Reg. I, fo 175, which is a copy of Archbishop Winchelsey's letter to the prior and convent (dated 1295) requesting the names of monks to be sent to him; in *Reg. Winchelsey*, 1305–6, there are also several examples of the archbishop choosing one of the three names presented.

[77] E.g. BL MS Cotton Faustina C.v, fos 13v, 14 (1384, 1385); see also *Reg. Hethe*, 380–1 (1326).

successor.[78] In the ordination of Archbishop Arundel in 1411 the offices over which the Norwich bishop claimed rights were to be filled by his appointment of the single nominee presented to him by the prior and senior members of the chapter *absque contradictione*.[79]

An introduction to the monastic chapters of Bath and Coventry must include a brief explanation of their special status. They were the two cathedral priories that had to learn to cooperate or contend not only with a bishop but also with a cathedral chapter of canons. This is because each see had two focal centres, i.e. two cathedrals, presided over by one bishop. At every episcopal election monk delegates from Bath cathedral priory had to meet with the delegates of the canons of Wells cathedral to participate jointly in electing a bishop agreeable to both parties; a similar procedure took place with Coventry monks and Lichfield canons participating on equal terms. These terms applied only after the two sees had been united, that is from 1238 in the case of Coventry and from 1245 in the case of Bath.[80] Coventry was unique in one other respect, already mentioned, that of military service due to the crown, an obligation that continued in force after the abbey had been transformed into a cathedral priory in 1102. Holding their monastic estates as a barony the chapter were required to notify the king on the death of the prior, seek a royal licence to elect a successor and request the royal assent to the elect.[81] At Durham the bishop's extensive temporal jurisdiction included the confirmation of the election of a prior by virtue of his royal prerogative as lord of the palatinate.[82]

So far I have been concerned with drawing attention to some of the most significant features that distinguished the cathedral priories from other major Benedictine houses. Other differences that accentuated their anomalous status are scattered *passim* through surviving records, for example, the hard won rights of several of the cathedral priors to have custody of the spiritualities of the see during a vacancy.[83] There were also the perennial headaches, often leading to altercation, brought on by the attempts to agree on procedures for the ceremonial occasions when bishop and prior had to share their dignity as mitred prelates. Controversies also arose over the existence and extent of the rights of some bishops to appoint a number of lay officials and servants to posts in the priory. Reference to these and other problems will be made in the appropriate place in the chapters that follow.

---

[78] NRO DCN 40/10 (Reg. X), fo 38, with the date assigned in *BRECP*, 535, under William de Lenn I.

[79] NRO DCN 40/1 (Reg. I), fos 267–70; the offices named are those of subprior, sacrist, cellarer, precentor, chamberlain, master of St Paul's hospital, and all the priors of the dependent cells except for St Leonard's.

[80] There are brief summaries in *BRECP*, 336–7 (Coventry) and ibid., 1–2 (Bath).

[81] *BRECP*, 338. The bishop of Rochester was alone among the bishops in his feudal subjection to the archbishop of Canterbury rather than to the crown, a post-Conquest development described by Brett in 'The Church at Rochester', 21–2.

[82] *HDST*, clxix, concerning Bishop Skirlaw's confirmation of John de Hemingbrough as prior in 1391; the phrase was *racionae nostrae prerogativae regiae*. For Hemingbrough see *LVD*, iii, C.932.

[83] The priors of Canterbury, Norwich, and Worcester were successful; see Churchill, *Cant. Administration*, I, 551–61, 194–207, 184–93.

Having noted the frequency of the dissension and conflict that prevailed in monastic cathedral cloisters we must conclude that they reveal a depressingly human situation, with ideal and reality some distance apart. It would be wise, however, to refrain from judgement until we have proceeded further in our effort to understand what motivated the monks to behave as they did: how did they reconcile their monastic priorities with the situations where they engaged, seemingly with a minimum of hesitation, in disputes and litigation? At times the Rule by which they professed to live appears to have been overlaid by the pressing concerns of the moment, with consequent lapses of charity and disruptions of peace. When Prior Henry Eastry (1286–1331) of Christ Church reminded Edward III of his personal monastic commitment to poverty he used the following explanation: 'veullez savez, tres cher Seignur, qe jeo ne ay terres, ne rentes, ne altres biens, ne chateaux, de temporalte ne de espiritualte, partenantz a moy en severalte'.[84] These words should not be too lightly dismissed as little more than equivocation, a clever ploy to wriggle out of an awkward situation. While it is true that large monasteries such as Christ Church were well above the poverty line there was, nevertheless, a constant concern on the part of those responsible to procure adequate supplies to feed and clothe a large community which included not only monks but many employees and a constant stream of guests. The individual monk had renounced personal possessions; everything in the monastery was held in common and distributed according to need, as Prior Eastry made clear to the king.[85] Sincerity of motive and behaviour, however, does not guarantee harmony in human relations even between monks, and what a monk preaches to his brethren may contradict his subsequent actions. When Baldwin, abbot of Forde, came to Canterbury as archbishop his commitment to the same Rule as the monks did not prevent misunderstanding and conflict nor, unhappily, did it effect reconciliation.[86] If there is need for further persuasion to accept that the cathedral monks, with whom we are concerned, generally acted in good faith or at least tried to do so, it should be noted that in some ecclesiastical and even monastic circles comparable situations occur today, although statements and actions may be more subdued and subtle.

It should now be clear that my principal aim is to view the cathedral monasteries in their fourteenth-century surroundings and in their dual role as Benedictine communities and custodians of cathedral churches. This entails an examination of the details of the daily routine, in other words the practical side of monastic life. It also includes the attempt to understand how the monks saw themselves as they fulfilled their obligations and carried out their assigned duties through the successive stages of their monastic career. Inner thoughts and reflections seldom occur in the written sources, but occasional remarks from the pens of a few monks may be

---

[84] Sheppard, *Lit. Cant.*, i, no. 277.
[85] *RB*, C.33. It must be admitted that by the fourteenth century the monks were receiving cash allowances to purchase some of their necessities; see below *passim*.
[86] Reconciliation, unity, and mutual love are the underlying themes of Baldwin's sermons; e.g., sermons 11 and 15 in *Balduini de Forda Opera, Sermones, De Commendatione Fidei*, ed. D. N. Bell, *CCCM*, xcix (1991), 173–9, 229–52.

taken as speaking for many and will, from time to time, shed light on our undertaking.[87]

2. CATHEDRALS IN A MONASTIC PRECINCT

Monasterium autem, si possit fieri, ita debet constituit omnia necessaria, id est aqua, molendinum, hortum vel artes diversas intra monasterium exerceantur.

RB, C.66, 6

St Benedict could not have foreseen or even imagined the future existence of cathedral monasteries nor their urban setting. Although he does not recommend any particular location where his monks should settle, there is no doubt that he assumed they would seek a remote site beyond the reach of outside interference and the distractions and temptations of the world and its noise. Monastic cathedral chapters, however, were especially afflicted by both of these: as resident chapters of the mother church of the diocese and subject to episcopal surveillance, and as monastic enclaves in an urban setting.[88]

A monastic cathedral church combined features common to both secular cathedrals and abbey churches. Tombs, effigies and chantry chapels of former diocesan bishops, for example, occupied prominent positions in the nave and choir of all cathedrals while similar memorials in an abbey church were largely confined to honouring the monastic community's own abbots. Both monastic cathedral and abbey church generally had two screens at the eastern end of the nave, one being the rood screen of wood or stone; the other, the *pulpitum*, a bay further east, would have formed the western boundary of the monastic choir.[89] In addition, for the bishop's use, monastic and secular cathedrals were furnished with an official seat or throne in a conspicuous location near the high altar.[90]

Although monastic in their origin, by the later middle ages a cloister and adjoining chapter house were features to be found in both the monastic precinct and the secular cathedral close. By contrast, the layout of other buildings within precinct and close reflected the customs and requirements of the residents: in the case of the cathedral priory a community of some forty to seventy monks had to be accommodated, but the number of canons in residence in the secular cathedral

---

[87] See J. Leclercq, 'The Monastic Tradition of Culture and Studies', *American Benedictine Review*, 11 (1960), 102–3.

[88] Monastic cathedral chapters, however, do not seem to have regarded themselves as, *vis-à-vis* Benedictines, occupying an anomalous position.

[89] At Winchester and Ely the *pulpitum* was situated at the eastern end of the nave in the second bay, Crook, 'East Arm and Crypt of Winchester', 21.

[90] The archbishop of Canterbury had three official seats in the cathedral: one behind the high altar for his enthronement, one at the east end of the choir for use when pontificating, and one at the west end of the choir when he was acting as titular abbot, C. S. Phillips, 'The Archbishop's Three Seats in Canterbury Cathedral', *Antiquaries Journal*, 29 (1949), 26–36. The impressive throne constructed by Bishop Hatfield at Durham in the second half of the fourteenth century is situated on the south side of the choir; the spiritual and secular sides of his lordship are powerfully displayed by its height, size, and decoration.

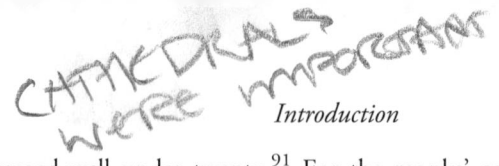

close averaged well under twenty.[91] For the monks' communal life a refectory, kitchen, dormitory and infirmary were necessary; each of the canons, on the other hand, ran his own private household.

Although the political and cultural predominance of the Benedictine abbeys was in decline by the end of the twelfth century, cathedral establishments became increasingly influential in their urban setting.[92] That Benedictine cathedrals retained a position of prestige in the fourteenth and early fifteenth centuries was due, however, not only to their location on important communication routes for king and magnates—Winchester and Canterbury for example—but also to the presence of high-powered bishops like Thomas Langley at Durham (1406–37), John Hotham at Ely (1316–37), William Bateman at Norwich (1343–55) and William Wykeham and Henry Beaufort at Winchester (1366–1404; 1404–47). Of the nine monastic cathedrals all but two, though secularized as the cathedrals of the new foundation under Henry VIII, have continued to function to the present day. One of the two, namely Bath, lost its cathedral status which, before the dissolution of the monasteries, it had shared with Wells; the other, Coventry, was totally demolished soon after the monks were removed.[93]

While the layout of the buildings in a monastic enclosure was based on a general plan to which the cathedral priories on the whole adhered, there were in several cases significant variations; these can usually be explained by the nature of the site and its surroundings. All nine Benedictine cathedral priories, being located in important urban centres, were able to obtain many of their basic commodities close at hand, and benefited from ready access to a potential labour force to serve the multifarious needs of a large monastic household. On the other hand, the urban monastery was often hard pressed to find adequate space for its requirements since expansion was curtailed by the close proximity of an already congested urban area. The provision of fresh water within the precinct for drinking, washing, and other domestic uses was a prerequisite as was an adequate system of drainage to remove waste and sewage. A river or stream close at hand was desirable for the conveyance of heavy goods by barge and boat and for swifter and more comfortable travel for officials and messengers when road travel was hazardous. Water power was also required to drive the mill that was considered essential to the well being of the monastery in supplying flour for the monastic bakehouse.[94]

The monastic cathedrals were all in close proximity to the rivers that wound their way through or around the towns in which they were situated. Sublime masterpieces of the skill of medieval architects, masons, and sculptors they were centres of

---

[91] See Edwards, *Secular Cathedrals*, 70–8.
[92] Morris, *Cathedrals and Abbeys*, 204–5.
[93] Although the bishop to this day retains the title 'Bath and Wells' his former cathedral at Bath is now usually known as Bath Abbey. Coventry was also retained in the episcopal title 'Coventry and Lichfield' until 1918 when its own bishopric, that had enjoyed only a brief existence between 1121 and 1238, was restored and a separate diocese created.
[94] St Benedict himself had specified the need for water, a mill, and a garden within the monastery precinct so that the monks would be self-sufficient, *RB*, C.66, 6 (see the quotation at the beginning of the chapter); eight centuries on, the needs were the same but the context of self-sufficiency had been eroded.

attraction and of pilgrimage, overshadowing the adjacent clusters of humble dwellings and shops. Thus, the river Avon lay to the east of Bath cathedral priory, with only an expanse of meadow and orchard between the precinct wall and the river bank; there were two fish ponds in this area to supply the kitchens, and a mill was situated on the river east of the precinct.[95] The cathedral priory in Coventry lay on high ground close to the river Sherbourne on its northern boundary;[96] Durham cathedral priory and castle were set on a peninsula high above the river Wear which encircled them on all but the northern approach, where the town dwellings and market sheltered below the castle walls; Ely cathedral and monastery had been perspicaciously sited on a slight elevation above and about half a mile to the west of the Great Ouse; the Stour lapped the city walls of Canterbury a similar distance north of the cathedral; and the broad sweep of the Medway was in close proximity to both Rochester castle and cathedral which were situated above its western bank.[97] The Wensum was the eastern boundary of the precinct of Norwich cathedral priory and the Severn lay only a few yards below the western limits of Worcester cathedral and monastic buildings; both of these priories were provided with water gates used by bishops and monks, the remains of which have survived to the present day. At Winchester the Itchen ran close to the walls of Wolvesey palace, the bishop's residence, situated just beyond the eastern boundary of the cathedral precincts; there was also a mill stream flowing inside and close to the eastern wall of the close with a mill called Le Flodes.[98]

Urban monasteries found it far more difficult than those in rural areas to obtain access to an unpolluted source of drinking water; the existence of wells in the cloister garth, as at Canterbury and Durham for example, or elsewhere within the precinct, would not have ensured a sufficient supply for all the needs of a large monastic community. At Canterbury, therefore, springs were sought outside the town, and their water was conveyed to the priory precinct by means of an intricate network of pipes and conduits. The twelfth-century source was a large spring-fed pond in the Old Park at North Holmes three-quarters of a mile to the north of the city. Superimposed on a mid-twelfth-century plan of the monastic precinct is a bird's-eye view of the course followed by the incoming water as it flowed through the cloister and surrounding monastic buildings, and of its outgoing passage via the drains to the city ditch. The plan delineates a complex system of

---

[95] Manco, 'Bath Priory', 93–5; it was known as Monk's Mill. Another mill, the Isabel Mill, was located just outside Ham gate, the southern entrance to the precinct, on a stream running down to join the Avon, ibid., 95.

[96] Brian Hobley has pointed out that the northern boundary of the priory extended beyond the river where the priory fish ponds were located and along the banks of which were two mills, 'Excavations at the Cathedral and Benedictine Priory of St. Mary, Coventry' Birmingham and Warwickshire Archaeological Society, Transactions 84 (Birmingham, 1971), 87.

[97] At an unknown date, probably in the twelfth century, a sailor by the name of Reiner may have sailed up the Medway and moored below the castle before knocking at the priory gate to seek admission as a monk. He offered to the community his boat which was sold for 40s., *BRECP*, 628.

[98] Crook, 'Monastic Buildings of St Swithun's', 5–6, where the author also describes the monastic drainage system known as the Lockburn. See also J. Crook, 'Winchester's Cleansing Streams', *Winchester Cathedral Record*, nos 53 and 54 (1984, 1985), especially no. 54, 15–24.

pipes, pressure tanks, and drainage channels and includes explanatory notes to facilitate the repairs and adjustments that would have been required from time to time in the plumbing and sanitary arrangements, which were still in use at the dissolution.[99] In this way clean water was supplied to the *lavatoria*, the kitchen, infirmary, guest hall, laundry, baths, and brewhouse and throughout the monastic complex wherever it was needed. It is safe to assume that a system bearing similarities to the one that existed at Canterbury would have been found in the other cathedral monastic precincts. Fresh water piped from Beechen Cliff on the far side of the river Avon supplied the monks of Bath who also reaped the benefit of thermal springs within the precinct; the healing waters, however, were also a burden inasmuch as they attracted large numbers of visitors including royalty, many of whom, with their company of retainers, had to be accommodated.[100] Worcester priory made use of springs rising in the prior's park at Battenhall on the northern outskirts of the city; when these proved insufficient the monks found a spring in St John's on the far side of the Severn. They ultimately settled for the spring on Henwick Hill just beyond St John's, the pipes being conveyed across the river on the city bridge north of the cathedral.[101] During the fourteenth century, whenever the Worcester system broke down through faulty pipes the monk cellarer was obliged to pay for water to be brought to the priory from other sources.[102] Unfortunately, Canterbury is the only cathedral priory where details of the waterworks have been preserved in documentary form. Elsewhere, archaeologists have been and are engaged in reconstructing plans of the medieval arrangements with the help of information that can be gleaned from surviving records; the relevant expenses itemized on the accounts of monastic officials, and charters and leases dealing with property rights and transfers are major sources used in conjunction with on site excavation. The result of such reconstruction has recently been exemplified at St Swithun's Winchester where the drainage system through the precinct has been traced.

The daily liturgical rites of mass and office were performed in the choir of the cathedral church by the monastic community for whom the vast and splendid interior must at times have failed to inspire the chant when cold and damp

---

[99] It is to be noted that the cathedral priory was itself in the north-east quarter of the city. The waterworks plan is found in what is known as the Eadwine Psalter, a Canterbury manuscript, now Cambridge, Trinity College MS 987. It has been reproduced and described most recently in F. Woodman, 'The Waterworks Drawings of the Eadwine Psalter' in M. Gibson, T. A. Heslop, and R. W. Pfaff (eds), *The Eadwine Psalter, Text, Image and Monastic Culture in Twelfth Century Canterbury*, Publications of the Modern Humanities Association, 14 (London, 1992), 168–77.

[100] Manco, 'Bath Priory', 83, where the royal lodgings within the precinct are described.

[101] Noake, *Worcester Cathedral*, 113; see also charter no. 133, *Carta aqueductus ab Henewyk usque Prioratum* in the *Liber Pensionum*, 42; this is dated in the eighth year of Henry [IV].

[102] In 1354/5 and 1376/7, for example, WCM C.62, 69; the latter account provides the explanation 'in aqua petenda ob defectu pipe per vices, xij s. viij d.', and is printed in Hamilton, *Compotus Rolls*, 19. The *cursus communis* is referred to in a grant of a corrody within the Worcester precinct in 1334, WCM Reg. A.5, fo 156v, but as yet no excavation has uncovered it. There are similar expenses recorded at Durham, where women were employed to carry water up from the Wear, Fowler, *Account Rolls*, ii, 526, 529, etc., in the 1330s; in 1311/12 the explanation was *pro defectu conducti*, ibid., i, 9.

The English Benedictine Cathedral Priories: Rule and Practice

penetrated through every layer of clothing.[103] At an overall length of 555 feet Winchester was the longest of the nine cathedrals, while Bath cathedral at its greatest medieval extent was only 390 feet. Canterbury, Durham, and Ely were all over 500 feet long; Norwich was close at 481 feet, Coventry and Worcester were both 425 feet; Rochester was by far the smallest at a mere 324 feet. Indeed, the dimensions of Rochester cathedral make it the most modestly proportioned, the height of the nave being only 55 feet, whereas the naves of Ely, Canterbury, and Norwich measure over 80 feet. The other cathedral naves were between 68 feet (Worcester) and 78 feet (Winchester) in height.[104] The monks' responsibilities with regard to their church did not cease when the daily round of services had been duly celebrated, for the day to day maintenance and repair of the cathedral fabric was also in their charge. In practice building operations, in the form of reconstruction, extension, and new work, as we shall see, were a constant presence around the cathedral and monastic buildings in the fourteenth century, and the problem of the division of responsibility between bishop and chapter for the expenses incurred sometimes produced friction rather than cooperation.

With the exception of Canterbury and Coventry, where urban development came close to the south side of the cathedral, the cloister was usually on the south side of the church, its north walk stretching along the outer wall of the nave with access between them by means of a doorway at either end.[105] The main domestic buildings, in which much of the daily work was centred, opened off the other three sides of the cloister thus affording shelter from the elements in stormy weather. More than a covered passage between the monastic quarters and the church, the cloister was at the heart of community life, a place where monks were accustomed to spend many of the daylight hours in reading and studying in the carrells fitted into the window arcades overlooking the garth.[106] With recesses for book cupboards in the wall and the windows opposite glazed, as had become increasingly common by the early fourteenth century, the monks were able to pore over the scriptures and patristic commentaries in relatively light and warm surroundings which gave some degree of comfort.

---

[103] Surviving records from the thirteenth century reveal that the monks of at least five of the cathedral priories received papal dispensations to wear suitable caps (*pilea/pillea*) in choir during the winter months: Canterbury (Sheppard, *HMC VIIIth Report*, 317, from Reg. A), Coventry (*CPL*, i, 269), Ely (CUL EDR, *Liber M*, 41), Winchester (Goodman, *Winchester Chartulary*, no. 155), Worcester (*Liber Pensionum*, no. 147).

[104] These measurements are, with the exception of Coventry, provided by John Harvey in *Cathedrals of England and Wales* (Batsford, London, 1974), 218–43; the length given for Norwich includes the eastern extension of the Lady chapel (before its destruction in the mid-sixteenth century), and for Winchester the western extension of the porch (before *c*. 1350). The length of Coventry cathedral has been established by recent excavations, M. Rylatt, 'Revisiting the Archaeological Evidence for the Priory' in Demidowicz, *Coventry's First Cathedral*, 68.

[105] Keith Lilley explains the choice of the site on the northern side of Coventry cathedral 'by the need to provide a water supply from, and drainage to, the river Sherbourne and possibly because it kept the monastic offices more secluded, away from the town to the south', 'Coventry's Topographical Development: the Impact of the Priory', in Demidowicz, *Coventry's First Cathedral*, 81.

[106] At Winchester there are no remaining indications on the two surviving outer walks that it was ever stone vaulted as were Norwich and Worcester, Crook, 'Monastic Buildings of St Swithun's', 17. The study desks or carrells were usually on the north side of the cloister to obtain maximum exposure to the light from the south-facing windows.

The east cloister walk normally ran southward from the eastern entrance to the church along and beyond the west wall of the south transept, giving access to the chapter house, the building immediately south of this transept.[107] It was generally rectangular in shape with, at Durham, Norwich, and probably Coventry, an apsidal east end; Worcester was unique among cathedral priories in being at first circular and later, after rebuilding in the fourteenth century, polygonal.[108] The refectory or frater was usually located in the south cloister range (but the north range at Canterbury and Coventry), near the entrance to which stood the *lavatorium* where piped water provided the monks with washing facilities before meals. The position of the convent kitchen was naturally close to the frater, either to the south or north, but at Worcester, where uncertainty remains, it may have been to the west.[109] The monks' dormitory or dorter was on an upper floor, the entrance and stairway being in the west range at Durham and Worcester; however, it was in the east range south of the chapter house at Winchester, Rochester, Ely, and Norwich, and at Canterbury and Coventry in a similar eastern position to the north. In all cases the reredorter was attached in such a position that the waste could be carried away through water channels beneath. At Canterbury, Coventry, and Rochester some of the cellarer's offices and stores occupied part of the west range of cloister buildings, but his hall at Canterbury was close to the main kitchen, in the south-west corner of the Green Court; it was on an upper floor over the pentice leading to the North Hall or Aula Nova. The west range at Norwich, and possibly at Winchester, was the site of the guest hall or *hostillaria/hostilarium*; elsewhere, for example at Ely, there was more than one hall with chambers in the precinct set aside for guests: the inner hostelry close to the prior's dwelling and the outer hostelry, for the less distinguished visitors, adjoining the almonry and near the almonry gate. The great hall for guests at Worcester occupied a site near the prior's lodging to the east of the chapter house. At Canterbury there was also a distinction of rank made when housing the visitors, and accommodation was provided in several buildings within the precinct. At Durham some of the guests were lodged in a hall that was located in the western part of the outer precinct, south of the monastic kitchen and

---

[107] At Rochester, however, the cloister was moved eastward in the early twelfth century, perhaps because the bishop's palace and outer court occupied much of the site on the south side of the nave. The north cloister walk thus ran eastward from the south transept for most of the length of the south choir aisle and the western entrance opened directly into the choir, T. Tatton-Brown, 'Three Great Benedictine Houses in Kent: Their Buildings and Topography', *Archaeologia Cantiana*, 100 (1984), 171–88. Bath may have been another exception as there is some evidence to suggest that before the dissolution the north walk was not attached to the nave or choir but only to the south transept, Manco, 'Bath Priory', plan, 90.

[108] See N. Stratford, 'Notes on the Norman Chapterhouse at Worcester' in *Medieval Art and Architecture at Worcester Cathedral* (British Archaeological Society, Transactions, London, 1978), 51–70 especially 56–7.

[109] Two references I have noted suggest the westerly position: (1) a reference to the *camera superior* between the dormitory and the kitchen, WCM Reg. A.5, fo 383v (in 1395); (2) a reference to the kitchener's door next to the *plumbum dormitorii*, printed in Hamilton, *Compotus Rolls*, 19 (in 1376/7). At Winchester the site of the frater remains uncertain but it probably stood 'in the south-west corner of the cloister', Crook, 'Monastic Buildings of St Swithun's', 36.

the infirmary.[110] The almonry offices were most frequently found close to the gate where food and clothing could be conveniently dispensed to the poor and needy; Canterbury, Ely, Norwich, and Worcester adhered to this plan, and probably the other cathedral priories did also.

The infirmary complex was virtually a self-contained monastery within the precinct, a small-scale replica of the monastic buildings by which it was surrounded: it had its own cloister, chapel, kitchen, and hall as well as a few private chambers. Here there was more variation in location: at Canterbury, Coventry, and Ely the infirmary was sited east of the dorter and therefore to the east of the cloister; at Bath and Worcester the complex was to the west of the west front of the cathedral church; the Norwich position was directly south of the south cloister range; the Durham site lay to the west of the south cloister range; at Winchester it is now believed to have been situated along the south side of the great cloister and attached to the frater which, according to current thinking, was the north walk of the infirmary's little cloister, its chapel, hall, and chambers being on the other three sides.[111]

The prior's lodgings included a hall, kitchen, chapel, and private chambers. In three of the priory precincts these were placed to the east of the refectory where the latter was in the south cloister range. At Winchester this meant south of the dorter and adjoining the east walk of the infirmary cloister; at Durham and Norwich, however, this meant south of the chapter house; and at Norwich the entrance was via a ground-floor passage under the dorter to the prior's hall and chambers which were on its eastern side. The prior's dwelling at Worcester was in the area south of the south-east transept of the cathedral; at Ely it was south of the monastery kitchen which, as we have seen, was south of the cloister; at Bath it is believed to have been in the west range of the cloister.[112] In the late thirteenth century at Christ Church, Prior Eastry extended his apartments on the north side of the infirmary by adding new chambers; later priors following his example provided further accommodation

---

[110] The Aula Nova, the guest hall at Canterbury near the north or Court gate, pertained to the office of cellarer who at Christ Church performed most of the duties that pertained to the guestmaster elsewhere; see Sparks, *Canterbury Precincts*, 64–5. The prior and other obedientiaries, however, also played their part in accommodating visitors. At Winchester guests may have been lodged on the upper floor of the west cloister range above the office of hordarian (who was equivalent to the cellarer). A more recent conclusion is that St Swithun's guest hall may have been in the eastern part of the precinct beyond the prior's hall, in other words, the three northern bays of the so-called Pilgrim's Hall, of which the three southern bays were the guestmaster's lodging, personal communication from John Crook.

[111] To be more precise, the Canterbury infirmary cloister was east of the great dorter but south of the second dorter; its hall and chapel extended eastward close to the presbytery and corona of the cathedral church; see Sparks, *Canterbury Precincts*, 39–41. There is some uncertainty as to the Bath location and at Worcester the unresolved question centres around the position of the buildings *vis-à-vis* the dorter and reredorter, i.e. either due west of the west front of the church or south of the reredorter. The existence of a second entrance to the dorter on the side near the parlour of the infirmary inclines me to the latter option; the reference is in WCM C.76. Willis's plan favouring the first option may be found in his *Architectural History*, ii, 316. For Winchester see Crook, 'Monastic Buildings of St Swithun's', 43.

[112] For Bath see Manco, 'Bath Priory', 88–9; For Winchester see Crook, 'Monastic Buildings of St Swithun's', 31.

for their own use and for that of their guests in other locations to the north and east of Eastry's hall.

By the late thirteenth century it was not only the prior and infirmarer who ran their own households and separate establishments. Although the 'offices' of some of the major obedientiaries like that of the cellarer were usually adjoining or in the vicinity of the cloister, others, for example those of the almoner, sacrist, and chamberlain, were often in the outer courts of the precinct. The sacrist's range at Norwich was to the north-east of the cathedral near the Bishopgate entrance into the precinct; this was the centre of his operations for work on the church fabric and monastic buildings. An inventory dated 1436 shows that his quarters were substantial and in more than one location: the rooms listed include the sacrist's exchequer, two upper chambers, two study rooms described as above the cloister, a [dining] hall, kitchen, larder, slaughterhouse, wax house, lead house, and carpenter's and glazier's quarters.[113] Both the almonry and the sacristy at Ely occupied a position along the northern extremity of the monastery wall that bordered Stepil Row; at Worcester the sacrist's house was attached to the north wall of the cathedral between the west and east transepts, but the location of his workshops for the maintenance of the cathedral fabric is unknown. At Canterbury the almonry yard and buildings were partly outside the court gate while the sacrist's lodging was close to one of the small gates in the southern wall that opened into Burgate Street. The site of the chamberlain's office at Worcester, comprising his personal quarters, a chapel, and several other rooms, is uncertain, but it was probably not far from the tailor's premises which were near the west front of the cathedral, and the latter included a private chamber which at different times was occupied by a retired monk, a doctor, and others.[114]

The inner core of the monastic precinct, consisting of the church and domestic buildings around the cloister, was also encircled by groups of other service buildings that, together, comprised the outer core. Among these were a bakehouse, brewhouse, smithy, mason's yard, shops for the tailor, carpenter, and other craftsmen, and storehouses for grain and other commodities. In addition there were areas set aside for gardens, vegetable plots, orchards, at Ely a vineyard, and the monks' and lay cemeteries. Finally, and still within the precinct, there were several stables and enclosures for domestic animals such as dogs, pigs, poultry, and cattle. The site of the bakery and brewery at Canterbury was in a range, in the north-eastern sector of the Green Court, that included stables and a granary. Both the brewhouse and fishponds at Winchester were probably in Mirabel Close, a garden in the south-east corner of the precinct and, close to the brewhouse, the pig-sty.[115] The frequent

---

[113] NRO DCN 1/4/75. For a more detailed description of the contents of the inventory see Noble, *Norwich Gardener's Rolls*, 3–4.

[114] The sacrist's office and the almonry are described in Sparks, *Canterbury Precincts*, 79, 69–72. Since the piece of land on which the Worcester tailor's quarters (*sartrinum*) were situated was returned to the monks (in 1226) by the bishop, one may probably infer that it bordered his property on the north side of the cathedral, *Annales Wigorn.*, 419.

[115] WCL Receiver's Account for 1334/5 ... *porcaria infra clausum Bracini*, printed in Kitchin, *Obedientiary Rolls*, 231.

references to the baker and bakehouse and to the brewery on the Worcester cellarer's accounts give no hint as to their location, but record, for example, the expenses for repairs to an upper room in the brewery suggesting that it may also have served as living quarters, perhaps for the brewster himself.[116]

It is clear that accommodation of priory personnel, permanent staff, other residents, and transient employees, was available in many of the buildings within the precinct. Rooms above the Edgar gate at Worcester were occupied by Henry Bruyn, one of the prior's councillors, and M. John Derl[?yn]ton, *clericus* in the 1390s. While the former obtained his lodging in return for his continuing *bono gestu et consilio*, the latter paid £50 for the privilege of obtaining room and board within the priory as a corrodian or pensioner with all his needs and those of his horse catered for during his lifetime.[117] In this same decade Richard Winchcombe, recently appointed archdeacon of Gloucester, solved his housing problem by paying £80 to the Worcester cellarer and receiving in return life occupancy of comfortable quarters known as St Oswald's chamber. This was described in the grant as an upper room lying between the dormitory and the convent kitchen.[118] As an episcopal appointee who played a leading role in diocesan administration his presence in their midst would have enabled the monks to benefit from his counsel, especially in their relations with the bishop. In 1348 the archdeacon of Surrey, M. Richard Vaughan, acting as legal adviser to the prior and chapter of Canterbury, was given the use of a newly-built solar opposite the new hall of the infirmary; and John Buckingham, bishop of Lincoln, retired to Canterbury in 1398 and took up residence for the final year of his life in Meister Omers. This dwelling provided accommodation for distinguished visitors and was located immediately to the east of the infirmary chapel close to the prior's lodging.[119]

Corrodies in monastic houses were frequently commandeered by the king and queen in their concern to provide for royal officials and retainers whose years of useful service were past. An impressive amount of correspondence on this subject survives in cathedral priory archives; it includes demands for pensions, subsistence, and in some cases accommodation within the precinct. While there can be little doubt that medieval kings were usually short of funds, the monastic communities, understandably, did not welcome these intruders and tried to refuse them as often as they dared since they were a costly burden on the house which had its own retired personnel to care for. In 1334 the Coventry monks were supporting three royal corrodians, at least one of whom was given lodging, probably within the precinct.[120] On learning of the death of a former employee in the royal household whom he had imposed upon the Ely prior and chapter, Edward II lost no time in

---

[116] WCM C.71.
[117] WCM Liber Albus, fos 375 and 363v. Corrodians and corrodies will also be commented on pp. 195–6, 316–17.
[118] WCM Liber Albus, fo 383v and WCM C.76.
[119] Vaughan was professed as a monk a few years later, *BRECP*, 309–10. Buckingham did not enter the community but became a member of the Christ Church confraternity and bequeathed his pastoral staff and vestments to the prior and chapter, Woodruff and Danks, *Memorials of Christ Church*, 181–2.
[120] *CPR (1334–8)*, 38.

sending a successor. The monks reluctantly agreed to accommodate him in their hostelry, the prior compensating the hostiller by an extra 20s. per annum.[121] Among the many other categories of persons who were given lodging within the confines of the priory were doctors, chaplains, and construction workers like smiths and masons, who were often under long-term contracts to the prior and chapter. John de Bathonia, physician, for example, was appointed to care for the sick monks in Bath priory in 1329 and was assigned a room in the gate house, while M. John de Bosco in the same year had a room in the infirmary at Worcester and his horse was assigned stabling.[122] During much of the fourteenth century the almoner at Canterbury gave bed and board to five secular chaplains in his household in addition to his *familia*, clerks, and guests.[123] Two secular chaplains in 1386 were provided with lodgings at Durham, one in a chamber which boasted a fireplace and a latrine and the other in a room adjacent to the office of the terrar, the obedientiary who served as the monks' land agent.[124] Also at Durham in 1321, Thomas de Qwermington, a smith, was put up in a small chamber on the east side of the church.[125]

From the scattered references to gardens on the obedientiary accounts it would appear that there were many open spaces between buildings, some of which were under cultivation and others laid out for recreation and enjoyment. Two cathedral priories, Winchester and Norwich, included monk gardeners among the lesser obedientiaries, and some of the latter's accounts have survived. These name some of the vegetables and herbs that were grown to supply the convent kitchen as well as the apples, pears, and nuts harvested for the refectory table; there was enough room on his allotment to keep poultry, cows, and bees.[126] The gardener at St Swithun's also produced apples, keeping them in a storeroom to serve to the community during Advent and Lent.[127] At Winchester space within the precinct must have been at a premium even before 1335, for the monks also had gardens outside; in that year the prior and convent obtained licence from the king to rebuild an arch or screened passage from Mirabel Close in the south-eastern corner of the precinct over the monastery and city walls and also over the ditch and high road, all this to enable the monks to have a private means of access between the two gardens.[128] An important feature of the infirmary gardens was the herbarium, which was both decorative and of practical use in medical treatment. The prior and major obedientiaries who had their own establishments also had their own gardens where they could walk and take the air. Some contained fruit trees which on occasion yielded bumper crops: the Ely chamberlain, for example, sold apples and pears from his garden in 1350.[129] At Winchester the almoner's garden, located next to the

---

[121] BL Add. MS 41612, fos 62, 63.
[122] *Bath Priory Reg.* item 630 p. 121; WCM Liber Albus, fo 135.
[123] CCA DCc almoner accounts 25–59 *passim*.
[124] DCM Priory Reg. II, fo 214v.
[125] Ibid., fo 76; this room may have been within the sacristy.
[126] Noble, *Norwich Gardener's Rolls*, 31, 32, 33, 36, 37, 41, and *passim*.
[127] Kitchin, *Consuetudinary*, 29.
[128] Goodman, *Winchester Chartulary* no. 275 and *Cal. Inq. A. Q. D.*, Pt i, 341.
[129] CUL Add. MS 2957, fo 26.

The English Benedictine Cathedral Priories: Rule and Practice 29

Southgardyn belonging to the gardener, had within it a cider press suggesting that he preferred to sell surplus cider.[130] He also sold sizeable amounts of grass and, therefore, one section of this garden must have been meadow subject to periodic mowing.[131] Privacy was ensured in this and, presumably, in the other gardens in the St Swithun's precinct by means of walls and locked gates.[132] Both the precentor and chamberlain at Ely had ponds in their garden and the cellarer at Durham had a dovecote.[133]

In most of the cathedral priories cemeteries for both monks and laity were also to be found within the confines of the monastery. At Ely, Norwich, Rochester, Winchester, and Worcester the lay cemetery was on the north side of the cathedral with access from the street through a gate in the precinct wall; at Rochester, Worcester, and Ely there was a parish church in this area and at Worcester also a carnary chapel.[134] An open space on the north side of Norwich and Winchester cathedrals was set apart for lay burial. At Norwich it was in the Green Yard between the bishop's palace and the Erpingham gate; here there was also a carnary chapel and, in the fifteenth century if not before, an outdoor pulpit.[135] The former site of New Minster, Winchester (which moved to Hyde in 1110), conveniently on the town side of the precinct, was the only lay cemetery for all the city parishes; between it and the north side of the cathedral was the sacrist's garden known as Paradise. The lay cemetery at Canterbury was situated on the south side of the cathedral, being the town side and accessible through Christchurch gate; this location, like the other lay burial grounds, was remote from the monastic enclosure. At Durham, however, the centory or cemetery garth for the monks' final resting place occupied an area bounded on the west by the eastern end of the chapter house and on the north by the south-eastern section of the cathedral. In the twelfth century there was a lay cemetery at Bath west of the west front of the cathedral which was also the site of St Mary of Stalls church.[136] The monks' cemetery at Rochester and at Bath occupied land to the north-east of the cathedral church. Monastic burials at other cathedral priories, including Canterbury, took place in the area south of the church; for Ely, Norwich, Winchester, and Worcester it was the area east and south of the south transept.[137] Thus, only at Canterbury and Rochester were both monastic and lay cemeteries, although of course separated, on

---

[130] Kitchin, *Obedientiary Rolls*, 402, 403, 407.
[131] It is possible that the meadow was a field lying outside the precinct because the phrase often used, from 1386/7 onward, is receipts either *de exitu gardini et herbagii*, ibid., 412, or *de exitu gardini et prati*, ibid., 423.
[132] Ibid., 423.
[133] CUL Add. MS 2957, fo 43, and Add. MS 6391, 59 (Ely); Fowler, *Account Rolls*, i, 48 (Durham).
[134] For Ely see 204; the Rochester church was that of St Nicholas, built in the early fifteenth century and at Worcester that of St Michael. The church of St Mary in the Marsh at Norwich was in the outer precinct to the east of the infirmary, in an area known as Brewer's Green.
[135] See B. Dodwell, 'The Monastic Community', in Atherton, *Norwich Cathedral*, 247.
[136] Manco, 'Bath Priory', 80. At Bath the picture is complicated by the presence within the twelfth-century precinct of St James' church and a chapel dedicated to St Nicholas, ibid., 79 (plan), 80–1.
[137] At Canterbury and Worcester this means east and south of the south-east transept.

the same side of the cathedral: Canterbury on the south and Rochester on the north.

There was one more group of buildings that existed just beyond the outer monastic precinct. These comprised the official residence, or palace, of the bishop. Because of diocesan responsibilities combined with duties in the royal service, bishops were frequently absent for long periods. Some of them preferred to make their principal residence elsewhere, the Worcester bishops at Hartlebury castle, for example, and by the late thirteenth century the Durham bishops preferred Bishop Auckland to their castle in close proximity to the cathedral.[138] The Bath and Coventry bishops chose to reside in the close of their secular chapters at Wells and Lichfield respectively. At Bath the bishop's house was in the south-west part of the monastic precinct. Rarely occupied, it was leased by the bishop to the prior and convent in 1336 to provide them with additional accommodation for staff and others; but he reserved his right to stay there when visiting Bath.[139] The bishop's palace at Coventry was in the south-eastern corner of the precinct;[140] Wolvesey palace, the Winchester bishop's residence, was also situated in a south-easterly position outside the monastery wall. There was, however, a convenient footbridge over the wall and the millstream (a tributary of the Itchen) that flowed parallel to the wall inside the precinct. This provided a private passageway for the bishop from Wolvesey to the bishop's door into the cathedral's south presbytery aisle. At Durham, Norwich, and Worcester the episcopal residence was on the north side of the cathedral. As lord of the palatinate the bishop of Durham exercised both spiritual and temporal jurisdiction, and his headquarters were in the castle situated between the cathedral and the town. Norwich bishops were in closer proximity to their cathedral church; the southern end of Losinga's palace was, in fact, attached to the north wall of the nave with a connecting door in the fourth bay from the east. Bishop Salmon and his successors removed the palace a few yards further north and east, and in the early fifteenth century Bishop Wakering arranged for a covered walkway between the north transept and the southern entrance to the palace. The Worcester palace, like the nearby monastic buildings in the west cloister range, was close to the bank of the river Severn and less than a hundred yards from the cathedral. Situated west of the west range of the Canterbury cloister most of the archbishop's palace buildings extended not only to the west, but also to the north of the nave of the cathedral; the Rochester bishops occupied a similar situation but on the south side of the cathedral nave because of the southern layout of the monastic buildings. At Rochester also, because of the more easterly position of the west cloister range, the bishop's outer court adjoined the south wall of the nave and cloister. The westerly site was also found at Ely, the bishop's gateway lying to the south-west of the western entrance to the cathedral with the Gallery lane running north and south between the episcopal and monastic precincts.

---

[138] It is to be noted that Bishop Auckland was the site of a collegiate church.
[139] Manco, 'Bath Priory', 92–3.
[140] K. Lilley, 'Coventry's Topographical Development: the Impact of the Priory' in Demidowicz, *Coventry's First Cathedral*, 82.

This description, aided by the accompanying plans, makes it clear that, apart from the presence of a cathedral church and an episcopal palace, the layout of cathedral priories hardly differed from that of major Benedictine abbeys.[141]

The dependent priories

Five of the cathedral priories were responsible for small dependencies or cells, some near at hand and others more distant. Coventry, Winchester, and Worcester did not enjoy the benefits and thereby suffer from the additional burden of obligations involved in this relationship, one which required constant oversight. Durham, for example, had eight cells and Norwich five or possibly six. These were small replicas of the cathedral priories manned by a small number of Durham and Norwich monks. Most of them trace their origin to the twelfth and early thirteenth centuries. The Durham cells most remote from the mother house were Coldingham, north of Berwick in the diocese of St Andrews, Lytham, on the Lancashire coast, and Stamford in Lincolnshire, all several days' journey from Durham. Farne and Holy Island were both islands off the Northumbrian coast, while Jarrow and Wearmouth were within closer range near the mouths of the rivers Tyne and Wear respectively. Closest of all was Finchale, also on the river Wear, only a six-mile walk downstream from Durham and frequented by the monks for refreshment and recreation. The Norwich dependencies of Aldeby, [King's] Lynn, and [Great] Yarmouth were all in Norfolk, the latter two in coastal towns, the parish church in both cases being attached to the priory. Hoxne in Suffolk was close to the Norfolk border, and the remaining two priories were within or close to Norwich itself.[142] One of these was the hospital of St Paul or Normanspital, an almshouse, for both men and women, in the north-eastern part of the city of which one of the monks was master. The monk appointed to the mastership of St Paul's was numbered among the obedientiaries at Norwich, and provided services similar to those of the almoner at the almonry gates.[143] The other was St Leonard's priory in Thorpe wood on the hill across the river Wensum, about one mile east of the cathedral. Bath cathedral priory had a cell attached to the parish church at Dunster in south-west Somerset and several properties in southern Ireland, the care of which was usually undertaken by a monk.[144] Felixstowe, on the south Suffolk coast near Walton, the only dependency of Rochester cathedral priory, was several days' journey for monks and

---

[141] The plans are on xvi–xxi the prior's lodging within the cathedral precinct would have been similar to that of the abbot.

[142] Aldeby was in south Norfolk not far distant from Yarmouth priory.

[143] The master of Kepier, a hospital just outside Durham, was on at least one occasion a monk, e.g. in 1311, when Hugh de Monte Alto was permitted to accept this position to which he had been nominated by the bishop, DCM Priory Reg. II, fo 55v; see also *LVD*, iii, C.747. At Warkworth, Northumberland, in the mid-thirteenth century, two Durham monks were resident beside the chapel of St Mary Magdelene; see the details and references in Knowles and Hadcock, *Medieval Religious Houses*, 79.

[144] These were located at Waterford and Cork and were described in 1345 as 'the Priory of St John the Evangelist of Waterford, with the house of St John of Cork' and the prior was named as the 'prior of Waterford and Cork', *Bath Priory Reg.* items 888, 885, pp. 177, 176.

messengers travelling back and forth. Christ Church Canterbury claimed Dover priory in the 1130s, but the latter continued to assert a large degree of independence, admitting and professing its own monks, for example, the only dependency among the cathedral priories where there were two distinct and separate communities in this quasi-independent relationship.[145] Because Ely did not acquire any cells prior to the mid-fifteenth century they do not come within the scope of this study.[146]

There were also three Benedictine halls or hostels for monk students in Oxford and one in Cambridge. Two of these, both in Oxford, were considered as dependencies of their founding priories, Canterbury and Durham; they were established in the early fourteenth and late thirteenth century respectively to ensure the continuity of the monastic regimen in the university setting. The Canterbury monks at first stayed in a hall near the church of St Peter-in-the-East, but in the mid-fourteenth century they moved to larger premises which, after the dissolution, became part of the college of Christ Church. Land that was later to be purchased for the foundation of Trinity College was the site of the Durham monks' hall until 1540.

This brief survey of the smaller dependent cells or priories permits us to visualize the cathedral monasteries with their satellites in their medieval setting. It will need to be kept in mind as we turn to the study of the members of the monastic community, who lived within the cathedral precincts and the cells, and of the clerical and lay personnel who served them.

3. CATHEDRAL MONKS: NUMBERS, NAMES, AND FAMILY BACKGROUNDS

Ecce pietate sua demonstret nobis Dominus viam vitae.

RB, Prol., 20[147]

Background of the Rule

In the prologue to his Rule St Benedict addressed candidates seeking admission to the cloister as follows: 'quod dulcius ab hac voce Domini invitantis nos, fratres carissimi? ... Ergo praeparanda sunt corda nostra et corpora sanctae praeceptorum obedientiae militanda'.[148] It was for those who responded to the divine call that Benedict had founded his *dominici scola servitii*, a community engaged in learning to know and serve Christ. Although monastic formation begins in the novitiate, it is

---

[145] Binham and Wymondham, cells of St Alban's Abbey, also exercised some independence. Canterbury's Irish possessions were relinquished in 1255, being made over to the convent of Tintern (or de Voto) which paid an annual pension to Christ Church in return, CCA DCc, CCL Cart. Antiq. I, 237, 245 and also Sheppard, *Lit. Cant.*, ii, nos 907, 908.

[146] The two cells that became subject to Ely in the 1440s were Spinney (Cambs) and Molicourt or Mullicourt (Norfolk); the latter was probably only a grange; see *VCH Cambridgeshire*, ii, 252, 208.

[147] See Kardong, *RB*, 14.

[148] *RB*, Prol., 19, 40.

in fact a lifelong process of transformation because its aim is to inculcate a new set of values and bring about a complete reorientation of mind, heart, and will. Benedict does not hesitate to warn the aspirants of the hardships, humiliations, and even sufferings that they would endure; but these are outweighed by 'the unspeakable sweetness of love' that they would begin to experience.[149]

Admission to an English Benedictine house in the later middle ages was dependent on character and qualifications, as well as on a serious intention to persevere in the monastic life. After having been accepted and received by the monastery to which they had applied, the fourteenth-century monks, with whom we are here concerned, were subjected to a course of training and instruction similar to that given to their predecessors, and to their successors up to the present day. In this the Rule held a prominent place: it was read to them three times at intervals during the year of probation, to ensure that they understood the terms of their commitment before making their profession.[150]

For the historian to examine the medieval novice in the light of the latter's understanding of the Rule is hardly possible without the aid of autobiographical records or personal memoirs which are few and fragmentary for English monastic houses. What is possible and, indeed, essential for the historian is to constantly bear in mind the impact made by the Rule on the daily routine, on fraternal relations, on human weakness in the face of trial, and on the inner struggle which accompanies spiritual growth. The fact that these latter also remain for the most part hidden does not preclude our reading and interpreting such evidence as is at our disposal in the light of a sustained effort to view the Rule as the touchstone. By frequent reference to the Rule and its implications this approach should serve to differentiate the present study from other similar studies, many of which have failed to appreciate sufficiently the inner motivation underlying monastic life, especially when the outward manifestation is markedly devoid of any distinguishing features to identify its *raison d'être*. Monastic studies in the past have tended to concentrate almost exclusively on the Rule itself or on selected details of Benedictine history; it is time to weave these two strands together for they belong to a single theme.

Irrespective of temperament and temptations the medieval monk must have frequently experienced within himself the tension between the ideal towards which the Rule was urging him and the concrete reality of his puny endeavours and recurrent failures. At times the ideal appears to have been submerged by the cares and anxieties of the administrative and other duties assigned under obedience; but the periodic call for a return to stricter adherence to the Rule on the part of the monks themselves reveals an awareness of the problems and of the unease experienced in the presence of increasing laxity and worldliness.

The major portion of the Rule consists of practical arrangements for the day-to-day organization of community life. In several chapters, however, the ideal and the goal shine through Benedict's teaching. In two verses of Chapter 4, for example, he sums up the whole aim of the monastic life in four words: *nihil amori Christi*

---

[149] *RB*, C.58, 8; *RB*, Prol., 50, 49.
[150] *RB*, C.58, 9, 12, 13.

praeponere, and the final goal almost as briefly: 'vitam aeternam omni concupiscentia spirituali desiderare'.[151] Chapter 72 describes the 'good zeal' that monks need to acquire, and in so doing Benedict sums up the aim, the goal, and the means to attain the goal in one word: love.

Unlike the orders of canons and friars, the three orders adhering to the Rule of St Benedict were not founded for the purpose of performing a specific function on behalf of the Church.[152] The distinctive feature of the monastic way of life as Benedict portrayed it is the source both of its strength and of what has often proved to be its weakness. For the father of western monasticism the sole end in view was the *disponibilité* of the individual monk and the community for God.[153] This *disponibilité* explains how it is that Benedictine history records the activities of monks who were missionaries, scholars, teachers, preachers, writers, and artists as well as those who were contemplatives, mystics, and solitaries. All of these occupations at different times and under different circumstances have been perceived as the response to the divine will in the light of contemporary needs, as the means at that particular moment to the single end which is always the glory of God. When any of the means ceases to be subordinate and becomes the end, there is urgent need of reform. The Benedictine way of life is essentially the Christian life lived within a clearly defined framework that binds its members to celibacy, obedience under the abbot or prior, and stability. It should be noted that this last does not oblige the monk to remain at all times within the monastic enclosure. Even extended periods of absence may be permitted if sanctioned by the superior, but absence was always meant to be the exception, never the norm.

Estimating numbers

There was a wide range of choice open to a young man considering the religious life in late thirteenth-century England. Being by this time no longer the unique form of monasticism because of the presence of more recent orders founded since the Conquest, the Benedictines were experiencing competition especially from the friars, whose apostolic work in an urban setting proved attractive to energetic young men drawn by the missionary fervour of the mendicants as they moved from town to town preaching.[154] The Benedictines, for their part, remained aloof from seeking publicity and did not go to the market place to seek recruits; they seem to have depended largely on word passed on through the medium of relatives, friends, benefactors, and other contacts made in the course of outside ecclesiastical

---

[151] Vv. 21 and 46 respectively. C.36 (care of the sick), 1, and C.53 (hospitality), 15 are also to be noted.

[152] Both the Cluniacs and Cistercians, which had their origins in monastic reform movements of the tenth century and eleventh century respectively, continued to adhere to the Rule of St Benedict; see Knowles, *MO*, 145–50, 199–200.

[153] There is no exact English equivalent of this word used by Manning in his edition of *RB*; see his notes to C.72, pp 192–3. Available and free from all [other] occupations go some way to express what is implied by *disponibilité*.

[154] It is worth recalling that the cathedral priories were all located in the centre of towns.

affairs or business dealings. Nevertheless, despite the all too few surviving records of monastic population and the unreliability of most of them, it seems probable that numbers in many of the larger monastic establishments were fairly stable from the late thirteenth century to the Black Death in the middle of the fourteenth century. Furthermore, by and even before 1400 some of these houses had recouped all or most of their losses during the plague. For example, Durham was the largest house in England with 110 members in the community in 1300 of whom between thirty and forty would have been stationed in the cells.[155] According to the Durham *Liber Vitae* the total number of monks in Durham and the cells was eighty-eight in 1343; six years later a note in the kalendar of a Durham breviary informs us that the plague carried away fifty-two monks. By 1374, however, there had been a substantial recovery with at least eighty monks recorded at the time of Prior Fosser's death.[156] The lasting effects of the fourteenth-century crises on the monastic population can be seen in all of the cathedral priories in the fifteenth century; for example, in the case of Durham, the total numbers averaged about seventy of whom about thirty were assigned to dependent cells.[157] Christ Church Canterbury, next in size, had in the region of seventy-seven monks in 1309/10. An unknown number perished in the plague, although it is clear that the drop in numbers was much less than that at Durham, there being sixty-six brethren in 1356/7. Numbers declined slightly in the 1360s and 1370s but had risen to eighty-six in 1404/5.[158] Ely numbered about fifty in the 1320s and 1330s, was reduced to twenty-eight by the plague and had risen to forty-seven by 1367/8.[159] At Winchester sixty-four monks were present at an election in 1325, but there were only about forty-two professed monks in 1404.[160] Worcester like Ely suffered heavy losses in the mid-century epidemic; numbers were just under fifty in 1348/9 before the plague struck, and were slow to recover; by 1397/8, however, there were forty-eight monks.[161] These numbers can only be approximate even when the records abound because of the contradictory figures that occur frequently and of the impossibility of ascertaining whether or not all members of the community have been included. On the particular occasion when names or numbers are reported, for example, at least a few monks are likely to have been absent for various reasons. Calculations in any given year can be even more hazardous for the cathedral priories of Durham

---

[155] I owe the estimates of the number of Durham monks to Alan Piper, and it is worth noting that the much lower numbers actually present even on an important occasion such as the election of a bishop reveal the perennial difficulties in recalling a dispersed community to the mother house; only about 68, for example, were present at the election of Richard de Kellawe as bishop in 1311, DCM Locellus VI, 9a.

[156] The breviary is BL MS Harley 4664, fo 130v.

[157] Dobson, *Durham Priory*, 54; these are the calculations of Barrie Dobson in ibid., 54–5, before the Harley reference came to light, note 156 above.

[158] CCA DCc chamberlain's accounts 3, 42, and 57. In the fifteenth century there were several occasions when up to 90 monks are reported, e.g., in 1454/5 (or 1456/7) CCA DCc prior's account 15; in 1429/30 the chamberlain accounted for 88, ibid., chamberlain's account 59.

[159] CUL Add MS 2957, 20–2 (chamberlain's account); ibid., 26; CUL EDC 5/3/16 (chamberlain's account).

[160] *Reg. Pontissara*, 556–7; Greatrex, *Reg. Common Seal*, no. 68, p. 24 (election of Prior Nevyle).

[161] WCM C.352 (precentor's account); C.23 (chamberlain's account).

and Norwich where monks were moving back and forth between the mother house and the dependent cells; the latter were often, but not always, excluded from the count.

The reduction in monastic income in the second half of the fourteenth century necessitated a policy of restraint with regard to admissions to the cathedral priories, as to major abbeys and minor monasteries alike, in the wake of the Black Death. The calamitous death toll among the general population caused a widespread and prolonged economic crisis affecting both rural and urban communities by the shortage of labour and rise in prices; like their secular neighbours the monks experienced the consequent decline in farm produce on their manors as well as in rents from their tenants. Apart from some fluctuations in numbers during the fifteenth century, to be explained in part by periodic recurrences of contagious diseases, the monastic population of the cathedral priories appears to have been relatively stable as far as can be estimated. Barrie Dobson remarks on the 'numerical stability' at Durham through the fifteenth century to the dissolution and on the success of the Christ Church community in maintaining its complement of monks.[162] Ely and Winchester show slight fluctuations in numbers during the same period followed by what might have been the start of an increase just before the dissolution, while Worcester and Norwich suffered from a gradual, slight, but not consistent decline.[163] The two cathedral priories that were paired with secular cathedrals and shared the same bishop were, with Rochester, the smallest of the monastic chapters having cathedral status. Prior to the Black Death there were about thirty-four monks at Bath, thirty-three at Rochester, and thirty-six at Coventry.[164] It appears that both Bath and Rochester were slow to recover after the Black Death as there were only seventeen members of the Bath community in 1377 and only twenty-four named at Rochester in 1385/6.[165] Early fifteenth-century numbers at the three priories ranged from nineteen at Bath, twenty-two at Rochester to twenty-six at Coventry.[166] However, the few surviving figures show a noticeable rise at Bath in mid-century to twenty-six monks followed by a levelling off to twenty-two which seems to have continued until the 1520s; Coventry suffered a slight decline over the same period while Rochester remained probably more or less stable with just over twenty monks.[167]

---

[162] Dobson, *Durham Priory*, 53; Dobson, 'Monks of Canterbury', 119.
[163] J. Greatrex, 'Some Statistics of Religious Motivation', *Studies in Church History*, 15 (1978), 179–86 at 182–3 (Ely); Kitchin, *Obedientiary Rolls*, 291, 294, 301 (Winchester).
[164] For Bath, *Bath Priory Reg.* no. 344, dated 1344; several monks are known to have been absent in Ireland and Dunster. For Rochester, *Reg. Hethe*, fo 157 (533–4); for Coventry, *Annales Burton*, 379, where there had been 36 in 1214, CUL MS Ee.5.31, fo 240–240v.
[165] For Bath, TNA E179/4/2; for Rochester, CKS DRc F.13 (chamberlain's account). See also *BRECP*, 237 for Coventry.
[166] *Reg. Bubwith*, no. 1271 (Bath, dated 1412); Reg. Prior Shepey, fo 121v (Rochester, dated 1409); Reg. Burghill, fo 207 (Coventry, also dated 1409). In 1447 numbers at Bath were up to 26; see *BRECP*, 3.
[167] At Bath there were 22 in 1525, *Reg. Clerk*, no. 477; at Coventry 22 in 1524, *Blyth Visit.*, 116–17, and at Rochester there were 23 in 1532, Reg. Fisher, fo 156. See also *BRECP*, 3, 337, 583. Note: later fifteenth-century and early sixteenth-century statistics of the monastic population of the cathedral priories have been included in order to rectify the still widely held view that monastic recruitment was already in decline during the century before the dissolution, a view which in fact

The English Benedictine Cathedral Priories: Rule and Practice 37

In the larger cathedral priories there is a discernible general policy that governed the number of applicants accepted at any one time for the year of probation. It was mainly determined by the aim of filling the vacant places caused by death or departure, bearing in mind the need to assure an adequate supply of food and other basic necessities for the well being of every professed monk.[168] The entries at Christ Church Canterbury between 1285 and 1420 can be studied because of the fortunate survival of a list of monks from the early thirteenth century to 1534 which groups the names according to the date of profession. This record in what is often described as the Causton (or Cawston) manuscript reveals that admissions to the priory occurred most frequently at intervals of two to three years, although there were also one- and five-year intervals reflecting, no doubt, the availability of suitable candidates. The lists also show that from two to twelve entered together, with six to eight occurring often.[169] There are similar but less informative lists at Durham in the *Liber Vitae* covering the years from *c.* 1083 to *c.* 1482, with several gaps. These also indicate that groups of six to eight were often admitted together and that three-year intervals were common.[170] The average yearly intake at Canterbury and the average yearly mortality rate between 1286 and 1361 can be estimated from the Cawston manuscript as 2.8 and 2.7 monks respectively, thus demonstrating the aim to maintain a numerical equilibrium.[171] A similar pattern appears at Durham where the average annual number of candidates admitted was two between 1390 and 1446; the yearly death rate was also two.[172] Similar figures for the other cathedral priories are more sporadic and less reliable.

However, when it comes to assessing the number of junior and senior novices in some of the cathedral priories other classes of evidence may be substituted in partial compensation. The provision of clothing and bedding by the chamberlain, the record of professions in episcopal and priory registers, the distribution of pittances and cash allowances, and ordination lists may all be usefully exploited in ways that their original compilers could not have envisaged.[173] Extracting the statistics from

---

continues to affect some of the judgements on the entire post-plague era, i.e., from the mid-fourteenth century onwards.

[168] Optimum totals had been set in earlier times at between 60 and 70 for the major houses, numbers being based on the income in cash and kind derived from their properties. As late as 1393, for example, Bishop Wykeham exhorted the Winchester monks to raise their numbers from 46 to 60 in accordance with custom *ab antiquo*, BL MS Harley 328, fo 18. At the beginning of the fourteenth century Bishop Walpole had ordered the Ely monks to restore their full complement of 70, Evans, *Ely Chapter Ordinances*, 14.

[169] These have been printed from CCL Lit MS D.12 (the Cawston MS) and Cambridge, Corpus Christi College MS 298 by Searle, *Lists of Christ Church*, 155–96. It should be noted that not all the dates are those of profession; I have found some to be admission dates which are therefore a year earlier.

[170] *LVD*, iii, 129–436 provides a chronological list.

[171] Obit lists in the manuscript are complete for the period 1286 to 1361.

[172] Dobson, *Durham Priory*, 51. This compares well with the average annual entry rate that has been calculated as 2.7 monks between 1321 and 1340, Foster, 'Durham Priory', 42. These averages, however, conceal important details of fluctuations which on examination, as Alan Piper has shown at Durham, reveal changes in policy determined by financial stringency; after Prior Walworth's accession in 1314, for example, no monks were admitted for a period of seven years. See Piper, 'Size and Shape of Durham', *passim*.

[173] Pittances may be described as 'treats'; see below 214–15.

such records reveals the inherent difficulty of interpreting evidence that is at once sparse in quantity and often ambiguous in wording. For example, the novices' issue of clothing and bedding as entered on the Worcester chamberlain's accounts probably provides a reliable count, if the distinction between the terms *novicii*, *juniores*, and *juvenes* can be clarified and if we may assume consistency on the part of the accountant. While Canterbury and Durham monks continued to be classed as novices until ordination to the priesthood, and as senior novices once they had been professed, at the other cathedral priories the terms in use are not easily defined. At Worcester the monks to be presented to the bishop or his deputy at the time of profession were always named as novices.[174] The terms *juniores* and *juvenes* here were probably interchangeable: in 1395/6 four young men were clothed in the habit, which was provided by the chamberlain, thus becoming *novicii*, and the following year he provided bedding for eight *juniores*; probably the four novices were now professed and included among the *juniores*.[175] The numbers of the *juniores* when recorded are consistently higher than those of the *novicii*: novices entering in groups of two to four every two to four years, moving on to the next stage after only a year to join the other *juniores* in preparing for priestly ordination is the likely explanation.[176] At this stage they often spent four to five years in the company of those who had recently made their profession, pursuing their studies in a community which numbered nine *juniores* in 1351/2, eight in 1396/7, fifteen in 1411/12, and eight in 1421/2.[177]

Monks of St Swithun's Winchester were admitted and professed by the prior without recourse to the bishop and, unfortunately, the priory register in which their names would have been entered has not survived.[178] However, episcopal registers record ordinations to the minor order of acolyte which for the monks usually took place within their first or second year, often shortly after profession. On the strength of this assumption it is possible to surmise that these groups of acolytes had been, or still were, novices together: eight in 1326, four in 1347, seven in 1350, five in 1377, three in 1400, and four in 1403.[179] However, the intervals are too long and irregular in the fourteenth century to allow any pattern of frequency to emerge.

---

[174] E.g., on 30 April 1360, WCM Liber Albus, fo 226v; on 4 January 1393, ibid., fo 363v. In their petitions to the bishop the priors usually stated that the novices in question had worn the novice's habit for a year, *Liber Albus* no. 536 (Nov. 1311), WCM Liber Albus, fo 363v (Jan. 1393).

[175] I have so far turned up only two fourteenth-century references to *juvenes* at Worcester, on the pittancer's account for 1349/50 and on the chamberlain's account for 1351/2; the former is ambiguous in its statement that three *juvenes* were professed, WCM C.292. Were they *juvenes* before and after profession? No clarification is provided by the chamberlain's statement on his account in 1457/8 when he referred to seven *juvenes* at the time of their profession and seven 'confratres juvenes in prima tonsura eorum', ibid., C.44; was he referring in both cases to the same seven?

[176] These estimates are based on the frequent petitions, many in the priory register the *Liber Albus*, from the prior to the bishop requesting his presence for the profession ceremony; see note 174. However, between 1370 and 1373 it can be shown by comparing two lists of monks that eleven were professed, a higher number than usual, probably because the recovery of numbers after the Black Death had been slow, WRO, Reg. Lynn, 89, *Reg. Sed. Vac.*, 290.

[177] WCM C.11, 22, 30, 33; these are all from the chamberlain's accounts.

[178] Only Canterbury and Durham have surviving manuscripts that contain a record of names.

[179] HRO Reg. Stratford, fo 143; *Reg. Edington*, ii, nos 757, 817; *Reg. Wykeham*, i, 285, 351, 356.

During the first twelve years of Henry Beaufort's episcopate (1404–47) sixteen acolytes were ordained in twos and threes.[180]

No reference to the term '*novicii*' has been found at Winchester. Instead, *juvenes* was used or, more frequently, *juvenes in scola*; that these latter were young monks is made clear in two statements: at Bishop Waynflete's election in 1447 the three most recently professed monks present were classed as *juvenes*; in 1495/6 the hordarian lists the hierarchical order in the community ranging from the prior and senior obedientiaries through the *fratres extra scolam* to the *juvenes in scola*.[181] Because of the impoverished state of the sources the *juvenes* first come to light only in the late fourteenth century. From then on they make frequent appearances on the accounts of a number of obedientiaries who provide money for them to purchase knives, an essential multipurpose instrument, which they obtained at the annual September fair of St Giles. The anniversarian gave four *juvenes in scola* a total of 3s.8d. in 1384/5 and also in 1385/6 for this purpose, increasing the sum the following year to 5s.10d. because there were seven *juvenes*.[182] There were six in 1391/2, five in 1400/1, four in 1405/6, only two in 1408/9 but five in 1409/10; the numbers are too few and far between to estimate the rate of progression or detect any pattern with regard to admission.[183]

One of Bishop Bateman's injunctions following his visitation of Norwich cathedral priory in 1346/7 mentions the novices.[184] The item in question makes it clear that they were accustomed to purchase their drinking vessels and spoons from the obedientiaries probably soon after their admission.[185] Only two recorded instances, one of admission and the other of profession, survive from the period under study: in 1414 Bishop Courtenay commissioned the prior to receive the profession of six novices; and the following year four named monks were accepted for the year of probation.[186] The fact that these four were not professed until three years later, presumably on account of their being below the minimum age, raises the irresolvable question of the frequency of this practice at Norwich. The other references relating to the newcomers in the cathedral priory concern their purchase of drinking cups from the refectorer who entered the names and sums received on his accounts, many of which fortunately survive. Thus in 1307/8 Nicholas de

---

[180] I.e., 1404–16; HRO, Reg. Beaufort, fos A, Cv, E, Fv, Mv, O; the second volume of Beaufort's register has long been lost.

[181] Greatrex, *Reg. Common Seal*, no. 316, Kitchin, *Obedientiary Rolls*, 301.

[182] These accounts were recently found to be among the Worcester Cathedral muniments: WCM C.534 (1384/5), 533 (1385/6), 534a (1386/7). It should be noted that on these and other accounts there are annual gifts of a few pence on the feast of the Holy Innocents to other *juvenes* who were the boy bishop and his companions, too young to have been monks; they were almost certainly attending the almonry school; see below 250–1.

[183] LPL ED69 (a hordarian's account, 1391/2); Kitchin, *Obedientiary Rolls*, 284 (hordarian, 1400/1); ibid., 287 (hordarian, 1405/6); ibid., 213 (*custos operum*, 1408/9); ibid., 291 (hordarian, 1409/10).

[184] The injunctions have been printed with commentary by Cheney, 'Norwich Cathedral Priory', 93–120.

[185] Ibid., 115.

[186] NRO Reg. Courtenay, fo 202v; *BRECP*, 510–11 (John de Fornsete), 517 (Robert Hardwyk), 553 (Geoffrey Sall), 568 (William de Walpole).

Kirkeby paid 8s., in 1376/7 Simon Harpele paid 6s.8d., and Bartholomew de Scrowtby his fellow novice, 13s.4d.; Clement Thornage also spent 13s.4d. for his in 1409/10.[187] Usually for one or, at most, two drinking cups these purchases, entered as receipts on the refectorer's annual account, afford little insight into the total number in the Norwich novitiate at any one time. On a few occasions, at least, other obedientiaries came to the aid of a novice short of money by generous contributions.[188]

Nomenclature at Ely illustrates another variation in terminology. The words *novicii, juniores*, and *juvenes* were all in use in the context of the monastic study programme where they appear to be synonymous.[189] However, with regard to the distribution, in kind or in cash, of bedding and clothing the brethren were frequently divided into the three categories of *fratres* (or sometimes *capellani* or *sacerdotes*), *diaconi*, and *subdiaconi*. Thus in 1288/9 the chamberlain provided bedding to the monks under these three headings; five of them were in deacon's orders and seven in subdeacon's. The presence of novices in the community in this year is confirmed by the mention on the same account of a *convocatio noviciorum et aliorum sociorum*.[190] Are they included among the subdeacons? In a similar distribution in 1336/7 fifty-one monks received summer tunics; it seems clear that this amounted to all members of the community since bedclothes were provided for the same number, of whom seven were deacons and nine subdeacons.[191] There is even less information on the account rolls and elsewhere in later years and only a few recorded professions, where names are given, in the episcopal registers, the earliest of which dates from 1337. Three made their profession in 1389, another three in 1392, two in 1394 and six in 1404; ordination as acolyte followed profession either on the same day or within a few months in every case except for one who withdrew or died.[192] To these figures we may, with some degree of confidence attach a few others, of earlier or later dates, based on the names of monks whose first appearance at Ely is on ordination lists under the heading 'acolytes'. Seven novices received this order between 1341 and 1347, one a group of three and two other groups of two; again, ten were ordained between 1376 and 1384, two groups of three and two of two.[193] In 1412 five acolytes occur together and in 1419 six.[194] While it is not possible with the few statistics available to see any pattern or policy regarding the numbers of novices admitted and professed, what is both reasonably clear and also

---

[187] *BRECP*, 531 (Nicholas de Kirkeby II), 517 (Harpele), 555 (Scrowtby), 564 (Thornage).
[188] See below 61.
[189] E.g., CUL Add MS 2957, 28 (1367/8, *novicii*); ibid., 36 (1389/90, *juniores*); CUL Add MS 2956, 157 (1368/9, *juvenes*).
[190] CUL Add MS 2957, 15 (1288/9).
[191] Ibid., 22.
[192] CUL EDR Reg. Fordham, fo 5v (1389); ibid., fo 179 (1392); ibid., fo 181v (1392); ibid., fo 198v (1404).
[193] CUL EDR, Reg. Montacute, fo 106v (1341); ibid., fo 116v (1345); CUL EDR, Reg. de Lisle, fo 85v (2nd foliation)(1347). CUL EDR, Reg. Arundel, fo 117 (1376); ibid., fo 125 (1379); ibid., fo 129v (1382); ibid., fo 132v (1384).
[194] CUL EDR, Reg. Fordham, fo 261 (1412); ibid., fo 272 (1419).

significant is that there seems to have been no failure of candidates presenting themselves at Ely during the fourteenth and early fifteenth centuries.[195]

Most of the known professions at Rochester cathedral priory occur in the late fourteenth and early fifteenth centuries in the surviving register of Prior John de Shepey.[196] They took place in groups of two and three and include the unusual occurrence in 1396 of two profession ceremonies during the year.[197] The ordinations of acolytes usually followed within a year and suggest a similar trend of mainly two or three grouped together, but also from time to time a single novice; there appear to have been five of the latter during the episcopate of Hamo de Hethe.[198] Because the community was a comparatively small one and candidates for admission few in number, they were probably received with a minimum of delay as long as they met the requirements. The profession of twelve monks at Bath cathedral priory in the presence of Bishop Drokensford in 1326 is puzzling as this must have represented over a third of the community.[199] It is doubtful that there was such a large influx at one time but there is no intimation of the cause of what may have been an unusually long waiting period for some of them; on the other hand, there may have been at the time an exceptionally high mortality among the monks or an injunction from the bishop to increase their numbers, or possibly both. Surviving accounts of four other profession ceremonies record that two were of a single novice, one of two novices, and one of four; and all are in the early fifteenth century.[200] Acolyte references are also few and far between and one of these presents an unusual set of circumstances. In 1292/3 when the sees of Bath and Canterbury were simultaneously vacant the prior of Christ Church became responsible for arranging for the ordination of thirteen monks of whom four were denoted as acolytes and two exorcists; presumably these six were recent arrivals, but no further details are known.[201] Acolyte ordinations are too rarely recorded at Bath to be informative. There is only one recorded instance of a profession at Coventry and

---

[195] It is also worth noting that in 1534 10 of the 34 monks present at an episcopal visitation were not given the title *dom'* and were therefore not yet priests; this is a significant number of novices and/or juniors and is not to be dismissed lightly as a scribal slip, CUL EDR, Reg. Goodrich, fo 90v.

[196] He is the second prior by this name; see *BRECP*, 635. His register, now BL MS Cotton Faustina C.v, also contains one special licence to the prior from the archbishop (the see of Rochester being vacant) to admit and clothe two new arrivals and to receive the profession of one novice who had been a secular priest, fo 42v.

[197] William Tonebregg II and Henry Stoke were professed in May, *BRECP*, 643, 640, and William de Mawfeld I in September, ibid., 620. Four were admitted and professed in 1443, CKS DRb, Reg. William Wells, fos 67, 71v. The profession of seven monks in 1522 and eight in 1527 (CKS DRb, Reg. John Fisher, fos 91, 121v) was probably exceptional, but could have marked the beginning of an increase in monastic vocations similar to that at Ely; see note 195 above.

[198] *BRECP*, under Peter de Hethe, 611; John de London II, 617; William de Hadlo, 608; William de Farindone, 602; William de Strode I, 641.

[199] *Reg. Drokensford*, 276.

[200] John Appleby and Henry Bradelegh, both alone but both in 1413, *BRECP*, 11, 16 respectively; William Shirborn and Robert Chiew together in 1414, ibid., 41, 18; William Bonar, Richard Dunster, William Pensford, John Wydecombe in 1423, ibid., 15, 22, 36, 49.

[201] *Bath Priory Reg.* no. 415 where all the names are given. The order of exorcist is the minor order preceding that of acolyte; the remaining six monks were in deacon's and subdeacon's orders and all of them were to be promoted to the next order as yet unreceived.

it took place in 1249 when the prior and chapter petitioned the bishop on behalf of sixteen unnamed monks. In this case a disagreement between the prior and chapter and the bishop over rights and procedures had been the cause of the increased number of novices waiting to make their profession.[202] The five recorded acolyte ordinations are all confined to the 1470s and 1480s; three of these were of a single novice, one was of two, and one of three.[203] The presence and number of novices in the priory are noted in 1479 when the pittancer gave to eight novices a small sum for treats on the feast of Holy Innocents, and in 1518 when six professed novices were present at an episcopal visitation.[204] The fact that four of the six remained in the novitiate for six years suggests that they would have entered in their mid- to late teens.[205]

Family backgrounds and connections

Candidates for admission to the cathedral priories were no doubt prompted by hopes of entering long-established and prestigious communities within whose precincts there existed a wide range of occupations that gave scope for many talents and temperaments. Unfortunately, only a few casual references shed light on the families whose sons were numbered among the members of the cathedral chapters between 1270 and 1420. Nevertheless, we may postulate a geographic location for parents and relatives in the majority of cases where the monks were known by their places of origin (toponyms), the baptismal name usually being followed by the preposition 'de' and the name of the town, village, or hamlet.[206] Some, probably most, also had family names (patronyms), but these are only occasionally found in the records. Among them are, for example, Philip Aubyn, or de Worcester, who became prior of Worcester in 1272 and who was probably related to James Aubyn his contemporary, a citizen of Worcester.[207] Others are the Rochester monk John Horold, otherwise de Roffa or Rochester, and William Uppehulle or de Corston, monk of Bath.[208] Even before the mid-fourteenth century, however, the toponym cannot be accepted as an unexceptionably reliable indicator of family origins because of the increasing mobility of both the urban and rural populations. John le Devenish or de Devonia, monk of St Swithun's, came from a prominent Winchester family two of whom were mayors of the city during his lifetime.[209] The case of Adam de Cirencestre, monk of Worcester, also illustrates a family move from one location to another because his father was known as Robert de Dymok of

---

[202] Lichfield Cathedral Library, *Magnum Reg. Album*, fos 196, 280.
[203] LRO, Reg. Hales, fos 213v, 222, 273, 284v, 209.
[204] Birmingham City Archives 168237 (DV 2); *Blythe Visit.*, 17. Only three obedientiary accounts, all of the late fifteenth century and early sixteenth century, survive for Coventry.
[205] *Blythe Visit.*, 86, 117.
[206] A few monks are known to have been given a new Christian name.
[207] *BRECP*, 772–3.
[208] Ibid., 631, John de Roffa I; ibid., 20, William de Corston.
[209] Ibid., 685.

The English Benedictine Cathedral Priories: Rule and Practice 43

Cirencester.[210] In addition to the migration of families from one region to another there is the inescapable problem posed by the frequent duplication of place names within a comparatively small area. With two Stratfords, three Astons, three Uptons and three Whittingtons occurring within the diocese of Worcester no certainty is possible as to the former abode of Worcester monks bearing these toponyms.[211] Despite these and other uncertainties, some general conclusions can be cautiously presented on the basis of a study of over 5,000 monks.[212] One of these is that the majority of monks in the cathedral priories came from within the neighbouring region and, not surprisingly, the cathedral town itself and its encircling villages were well represented.

In the century and a half under study eleven Ely monks came from Ely while fourteen had lived within approximately a twelve-mile radius that included Downham [Market], Stretham, Soham, Stuntney, Isleham, and Lakenheath.[213] Most of the remaining monks were also fairly local but, because of the small area of Ely diocese, a good number were drawn from the bordering dioceses of Norwich and Lincoln, Walsingham, for example, contributing six and Spalding five. About fifteen monks of Norwich are known to have had family connections in the city itself or in the encircling suburban villages of Catton, Lakenham, Sprowston, Thorpe, Plumstead, and Witton. The family of one, usually known as William Worstede (prior, d. 1436) but also as de Norwich, had probably originated in the wool town of that name in the north-eastern part of the diocese, the home of the famed woollen cloth.[214] The families of two other monks, Guy and Hugh, with the toponym de St Edmund were very likely members of the city parish of St Edmund in Fishergate, and the family of another, Nicholas Burgate, probably lived in the vicinity of the city gate at the southern end of Ber Street. Another twelve monks can be linked by their toponyms to [King's] Lynn, Yarmouth, and Hoxne, all sites of dependent cells of the cathedral priory.[215] As for the remainder of the monks, their toponyms with few exceptions point to a markedly insular community where even the three from Ely and another three from Cambridge stand apart from the large

---

[210] Dymock is a village about 15 miles north-west of Gloucester; Cirencester is over 20 miles south-west of Gloucester.

[211] One cathedral priory whose monks' toponyms have been analysed and plotted on a map is Worcester; see Greatrex, 'The Local Origins of the Monks of Worcester'. See also Greatrex, 'Who were the Monks of Rochester?'

[212] Among the other uncertainties are the variations in the spelling of toponyms which render identification of some at best problematic. The Durham monks are not included in the 5,000, but a similar conclusion has been suggested by Alan Piper for the local or regional origins of the majority.

[213] Those known by name in the cathedral priories between 1270 and 1420 numbered 140 at Coventry, 170 at Bath, 206 at Rochester, 285 at Ely, 290 at Worcester, 316 at Winchester, 320 at Norwich, 560 at Canterbury, and c. 500 at Durham. The figures are based on BRECP for all but Durham where the information has been obtained from LVD, iii, 184–345.

[214] For William Worstede/Worsted see BRECP, 573–4; the spelling is now Worstead.

[215] Another cell, that of St Leonard's, was at Thorpe or Thorpe Wood on the eastern outskirts of the city of Norwich as already mentioned; there were two monks named Thorp. There are several other Thorpes in the county of Norfolk, as there is also another Plumstead; but in both cases the locations next to Norwich have connections with the cathedral priory—the church at Plumstead provided income for the precentor—thus strongly indicating that they are probably the right choices.

majority of local brethren.[216] A different picture emerges from a study of the Bath and Coventry priory toponyms. Seven monks were named Bath, none with known aliases, and, although an unknown number appear to be local from places like Bathampton, Corston, [Newton] St Loe, and the uncertain Combe, there are others from more distant towns including two from Wells, one from Bristol, one from Dover, one from Exeter, and another from Winchester. There were also five with the toponym Dunster where the dependent cell of Bath priory was located. Coventry's position in the centre of midland England made it a crossroads for the traffic of goods and the home of prosperous wool merchants and drapers. Two monks were from families resident in the borough and a third, with the toponym St Nicholas, probably from the parish of St Nicholas on the northern outskirts beyond Bishop Gate. There were a few with local village names such as Corley and Stoke and others slightly further off, such as Maxstoke and Packington; but this smallest of the cathedral priories seems remarkable in drawing a sizeable number of recruits from other urban centres, some of them from other counties and dioceses. There were four or five from Leicester and one from each of Derby, Dunstable, Nottingham, Northampton, Daventry, and London; the families or forebears of these monks may of course have migrated from these towns to Coventry.

The toponym Winchester or Winton was given to eight monks of that cathedral priory between 1270 and 1420, and to three others the toponym Hyde, the site of the Benedictine abbey on the northern edge of the city.[217] Surrounding villages such as Micheldever, Sparsholt, Winnall, and Tichborne account for seven more; and the village of Marwell a short distance south of Winchester for six, one of whom was the prior and bishop, Henry Woodlock de Merewell.[218] Surrey and Wiltshire towns and villages are also included: three from Guildford, two from Farnham, three from Marlborough, four from Salisbury, three from Enford, and one from the Vale of the White Horse, Berkshire. Further afield, there were four monks from Oxford, four from London, one from Glastonbury, one from Canterbury, one from Worcester and another from Pershore. As the Norman capital of England, whose bishop ranked second in the episcopal hierarchy after the archbishop of Canterbury, Winchester retained its privileged status throughout the later middle ages and the cathedral priory continued to have a wide catchment area. However, it is well to bear in mind that in the later fourteenth and fifteenth centuries some of the toponyms, like that of John le Devenish, almost certainly refer to the former locations from which families had emigrated one or more generations earlier.[219] An analysis of the origins of Worcester monks must take

---

[216] It must always be borne in mind that this study covers only the century and a half between 1270 and 1420. In the 'final' century before the dissolution the picture probably changed; among Norwich monks, for example, toponyms, if they are still true toponyms at this late date, include Canterbury, London, nine Norwich (some with aliases), and Shrewsbury.
[217] The city of Canterbury also boasted two Benedictine monasteries in close proximity, St Augustine's being only a few yards from the Christ Church eastern precincts.
[218] For Woodlock's career see *BRECP*, 749–50.
[219] The recently compiled gazetteer of the streets and tenements with the names of the residents amply confirms this point; see D. Keene, *Survey of Medieval Winchester*, Winchester Studies, 2 ii

into account the presence of six other Benedictine monasteries of distinction within the diocese: Evesham, Gloucester, [Great] Malvern, Pershore, Tewkesbury, and Winchcombe. A total of fourteen monks, or their parents or progenitors, came from these towns to Worcester in the period under study.[220] The city of Worcester provided eight monks, including Philip Aubyn and Simon Crompe who retained their patronyms, another who was probably of the parish of St John [Bedwardine], another of St Wulstan which may refer to the cathedral, and two from Sidbury, the area south of the cathedral.[221] The towns and villages of the surrounding region, however, supplied by far the largest number of monks, for example five from Huddington with nearby Crowle, five from Droitwich, and two from Inkberrow. In addition, the cathedral priory attracted young men from Hereford diocese: Ledbury, Leominster, Tenbury, and Hereford city accounting for seven during the period under study, and many other places like [Much] Wenlock, Kingsland, Presteigne, and Hay on Wye each supplying one.[222] This sizeable contingent from the Hereford area can no doubt be partly explained by the dearth of independent Benedictine monasteries in that diocese, the priories of Leominster and St Guthlac in the city of Hereford being attached to Reading and Gloucester abbeys respectively. In addition, Worcester like Coventry drew on west midland and Shropshire towns, in this case Shrewsbury and Ludlow, which provided five monks between them. Beyond this radius there were few, for example, only two with the toponym Winchester and one, London; in this respect Worcester priory bears some resemblance to Norwich in its insularity.

There are many duplicates among the Kentish toponyms of Canterbury and Rochester monks because of their proximity to each other within the same diocese. Thus Dover, Maidstone, Sittingbourne, [Isle of] Sheppey, and Strood supplied both priories, a total of seventeen in each case. In contrast, while monks with family connections in Eastry, Thanet, and Winchelsea added up to twenty-eight at Christ Church, there were none with these names at St Andrew's Rochester; however, seventeen with the toponyms of Leeds, Meopham, Rainham, and Southfleet joined the Rochester community while none went to Canterbury. There were five monks at Rochester whose family homes were inside the town, including one with the name Suthgate, and three more from adjacent Chatham. Christ Church monks included six with the toponym Canterbury, as well as seven known as Westgate, one as Redyngate [Riding Gate] and ten others from the parishes of Sts Elphege, Margaret, Mildred, Paul, and Peter and the environs of St Augustine's abbey.[223] Indications of monks with more distant origins present at both priories were the toponyms Colchester, Glastonbury, Cornwall, Leicester, Gloucester, Oxford, and

(Oxford University Press, Oxford, 1985), the biographical register of property holders being on 1135–1398.

[220] Between 1200 and the dissolution this total rises to 25.

[221] There were no churches in Worcester dedicated to St Wulstan, nor in the region. The medieval spelling of Sidbury was usually Sudbury.

[222] See the reference in note 211 above.

[223] Three other toponyms may also refer to city parishes or chapels as yet unidentified, namely St Laurence, St Nicholas (?possibly at Wade), and St Walerico; see also the reference in note 211 above.

London; eight Christ Church monks and five Rochester monks went by the name London. Christ Church also had two monks named Ledbury, two named Ludlow, and one each with the toponym Coventry and Norwich; this last, Walter de Norwyco, appears to have had contemporary connections in that city or diocese.[224]

Durham's remote situation in the north-east is reflected in its cathedral monastery whose membership by the later thirteenth century was almost exclusively confined to the region. The monks' toponyms take in County Durham and the three bordering counties of North Yorkshire, Cumbria, and Northumberland; a radius of fifty miles would encompass all but a few of the towns and villages represented, while a thirty-mile radius would cover the majority. As at Bath and Norwich the location of some of the Durham cells was the recruiting ground for a few monks, Holy Island (Lindisfarne) providing five in the period under study, Wearmouth two, Lytham one, and Stamford possibly two or three.[225] Eighteen monks using the toponym Durham were to be found in the priory together with three from the adjacent communities of Elvet and Sherburn. Towns and villages within close range, Hartlepool, Kelloe, Lanchester, Lumley, and Newcastle for example, and the more distant centres of Carlisle, Northallerton, Masham, Hexham, Ripon, and Barnard Castle together accounted for some fifty monks; the former group was well within the thirty-mile radius and the latter within or very close to the fifty-mile radius. Further afield York, Beverley, and Lincoln provided six monks between them while nine came from Rothbury and Bamburgh in Northumberland.[226] Southern England is represented by the toponyms of two monks only, one from Abingdon and one from Canterbury. Among the few family names recorded with the place name of origin are Nicholas Russel of Durham, Henry Wild of Stanhope, and Roger Postle of Greatham; in addition there were some monks with patronyms only, Vavasour, Launcells, Luttrell, and Marmion for example, whose backgrounds remain unknown.[227] A survey of the origins of Durham monks between 1270 and 1420 suggests, therefore, that they were a more geographically localized community than most of their southern cathedral priory brethren with the possible exception of Norwich, but all nine cathedrals were alike in drawing their main support from the families of the surrounding region.[228]

The social status of these families is of interest and significance. Remarks on this subject are often limited to the general statement that most of the monks in the

---

[224] He had some dealings with the master of the cellar at Norwich cathedral priory in 1320/1 and was proctor for the Canterbury chapter with regard to the appropriation of a church in Norwich diocese; his appointment in these matters is not likely to have been mere coincidence. See *BRECP*, 245.

[225] Stamford Bridge near York is much closer to Durham than the cell at Stamford near Peterborough.

[226] Five from Bamburgh and another five from Lindisfarne, the former probably influenced by its proximity to the latter.

[227] These monks' biographies are to be found in *LVD*, iii, C.742 (Russsel), C.761 (Wild), C.771 (Postle), C.913 (Vavasour), C.945 (Launcells), C.798 (Luttrell), C.874 (Marmion). Was William Barry of Welsh origin (C.1026)?

[228] It is to be noted that there was one thirteenth-century monk of Ely, William de Dunelm, whose family may have had connections with Durham. For further details of the origins of Durham monks to 1333 see Foster, 'Durham Priory', 45–50.

cathedral priories and major abbeys at this time could be counted among the middle ranks of urban and rural society, the families of merchants, artisans, landholders, free tenants, and the like.[229] This generalization may be regarded as broadly true, but it requires qualification based on further research into the history of local families, a study which is still in its early stages. Social status like geographic location is subject to change over the course of time as a few of the examples that have already come to light make clear. Monastic cathedral communities were not homogeneous in terms of the composition of their membership. The social standing of the monks in Winchester, for example, ranged from the son of an unfree manorial reeve to the relative of a countess. The former is represented by Ralph Mascal whose father, John Mascal, one time farmer of the St Swithun's manor of Stockton in Wiltshire, was manumitted in 1417 some six years after Ralph entered the priory.[230] The countess was Elizabeth of Juliers, the wife of John, earl of Kent, to whom the monk William Gilers/Julers was related as his name makes clear and, through her, to the ruling families of Juliers and Hainault.[231] Few Durham monks were recruited from the ranks of the lower classes, as far as we know, but illegitimacy proved no hindrance to Robert de Stichill, who, while serving as prior of Finchale, in 1260 was elected bishop of Durham.[232] Again, the family of Robert Lawerne, monk of Worcester in the early fifteenth century, probably had at some time been keepers of the mill at [Temple] Laughern since his brother's name was Richard Mulleward.[233] Another Worcester monk, Ranulph de Calthrop, a century earlier, was probably of even humbler origin because his admission to the priory was preceded by an official inquiry to investigate the circumstances surrounding his birth. The findings entered in the episcopal register concluded that his status was both free and legitimate, a necessary qualification for all candidates seeking admission to a monastic community; but, since records such as this one are rare, one can assume that in most cases the sworn statement of the applicant himself or his parish priest would have been deemed sufficient.[234] Contemporary with Calthrop at Worcester was John de Harley, the son of Henry, lord of the manor of Harley near Pershore; and contemporary with Lawerne was John de Dudley, whose studies at Oxford in the early 1390s benefited from two letters of recommendation from no less than Thomas of Woodstock, duke of Gloucester, and a similar supporting letter from the duchess.[235] Dudley's family background is unknown but the Gloucester connection is impressive. Thus, a form of what could be

---

[229] Dobson, *Durham Priory*, 58 sums up this view in much the same words. Before 1333, however, Meryl Foster found relatively few monks who were members of merchant families, Foster, 'Durham Priory', 52. Brief references to a few of the monks' family connections have been found by Alan Piper; see, for example, *LVD*, iii, C.699, C.711, C.903, C.957, C.982, C.1046.

[230] *BRECP*, 715; Ralph was unusual among his contemporary brethren as one of the few who was never known by his toponym.

[231] Ibid., 695; it will be remembered that Edward III married Philippa of Hainault.

[232] Foster, 'Durham Priory', 52.

[233] *BRECP*, 831–2.

[234] Ibid., 784; Ranulph's parents' name was Scot and their home was at Calthorpe, Oxon., which was then in the diocese of Lincoln.

[235] Ibid., 817, 797–9 (John de Dudley I).

described as 'Christian communism' may be glimpsed through these few examples if, in practice, the monks adhered to St Benedict's frequently repeated counsel of mutual respect and service in charity irrespective of age or seniority within the community. To what extent social distinctions lingered or were dissolved cannot be estimated for lack of sufficient evidence; it is probable that both high born and low were assimilated into the ranks of the 'middle-class' majority among the brethren, and in this way social distinctions would have largely disappeared.[236]

A brief study of the patronyms of some Worcester monks was able to link their probable origins to local landed families; however, only an extensive prosopographical survey over a wider area that takes into account all the families who lived in the vicinity of monastic establishments could begin to be conclusive in finding answers to this and other questions.[237]

Among the other questions which require attention is that of the monastic properties as a recruiting ground for future monks. The lands and churches belonging to the cathedral priories would have been a fairly regular meeting place of monks and local residents when the former made their rounds to supervise farming operations, to collect rents and tithes, to hold courts, and to carry out pastoral duties in the churches in their care. At Worcester a rough estimate spanning three centuries yielded an average of about one monastic recruit in ten in this category.[238] When our focus is limited to the years 1270–1420, the period under study, similar calculations produce a figure of just over one in every ten monks at Ely, just under one in ten at Norwich, one in eight at both Canterbury and Rochester, and only one in fourteen at Winchester. The higher proportion at Canterbury may be explained by the survival of an almost complete record of the monks; for Rochester, with a comparatively meagre amount of information available, it would be wise for the present to conclude that what has survived has weighted and probably distorted the results. The vagaries of destruction and survival may also explain the surprisingly low figure for St Swithun's. Probably the ten per cent ratio for the southern cathedral priories, with the exception of Canterbury, may for the present be taken as a tenable approximation of the average number of monks who were recruited from priory lands and parishes.[239]

Finally, the family background of a few cathedral monks is suggested by patronyms that denote occupations. There are, for example, two named Butler at Worcester and one at Bath, one Chamberlain at Winchester, and a Tinctor, the latter also occurring at Worcester in its English form of Dyer. There is a Warner [Warrener] at Durham and a Spicer at Canterbury. When the prefix 'le' is included, as in two of the Butlers and the Spicer, and the preposition 'de' precedes the

---

[236] Episcopal visitation records do uncover failings of monks which could be labelled as snobbishness and other manifestations of pride, but the evidence does not allow us to attribute any of them to social distinctions. One reason for requiring monks to converse in Latin may have been to eliminate the class divide between those whose background was English speaking and those who had been brought up as French speaking.
[237] Greatrex, 'The Local Origins of the Monks of Worcester'.
[238] Ibid., 145.
[239] These calculations are based on *BRECP*.

occupational name as in Capella at Canterbury and Ostillaria at Winchester, it may be that the occupation was still applicable; and it is to be noted that all the above monks but one commenced their monastic lives before 1300.[240] By the early fifteenth century it had become increasingly common to add the monks' family names to their place of origin, William Wells *alias* Martin, or in reverse order, Henry Langham *alias* Ely.[241] With this shift in nomenclature patterns more occupational names come into view, Chandler, Fisher, Gardener, and Goldsmith being among the most frequent, which might well have become attached as family names over three or four generations. If these were common previously we are left in ignorance, apart from a rare exception like that of Robert de Thaneto *alias* Hayward, who was professed at Canterbury in 1306.[242] Even in the fourteenth century it is likely that these names had ceased to be meaningful in terms of denoting family occupation and social standing. There is, however, one clear case at Worcester cathedral priory in the mid-fourteenth century where the name Mason meant precisely what it implies, for John the Conversus *alias* Mason was put in charge of the construction of the new main entrance gate to the priory precinct.[243] Two further examples of occupational backgrounds known through other contemporary evidence are found at Ely: although the patronym Aurifaber or Goldsmith does not seem to have been used, the father of Prior John Salmon (1292–9) was Salomon the goldsmith, and Prior Alan de Walsingham (1341–63) was widely admired as a skilled goldsmith when he was only a junior monk.[244]

---

[240] These names have a variety of medieval spellings given in *BRECP*, where they are found under Boteler and Botiler, 778 (Worcester); Botyler, 16 (Bath); Chamberlayne, 682 and Tynctor, 742 (Winchester); Dyere, 801 (Worcester); Spicer, as Spycer, 290 (Canterbury); Marcellus de Capella, 230 (Canterbury); John III de Ostillaria, 706 (Winchester). There were two Durham monks with the surname Warner in the early fifteenth century, *LVD*, iii, C.1056, C.1097.

[241] These are both Ely monks: Wells, later prior, entered the monastery in 1419, *BRECP*, 459; Langham entered in 1400, ibid., 421.

[242] *BRECP*, 301.

[243] Ibid., 826–7; the ascription '*Conversus*' signifies that he was a lay brother. By the fourteenth century *conversi* were rarely found among Black Monks; in the cathedral priories only two others have been noted: William de Corston and William de Nubbeley, both at Bath in 1325, ibid., 20, 35.

[244] Ibid., 436, 453–4.

II

The Early Years of Monastic Life

1. ADMISSION AND CLOTHING

Noviter veniens quis ad conversationem, non ei facilis tribuatur ingressus.

RB, C.58, 1[1]

Procedures for admission

In September 1298 Archbishop Winchelsey addressed the prior and chapter of Christ Church cautioning them not to accept recruits with undue haste even when there were empty places to fill.[2] St Benedict's recommendation to keep the eager young postulant waiting outside the monastery gate for several days served, no doubt, in his day as a test of character to discourage the faint hearted at the outset.[3] Prerequisites for admission to the cathedral monasteries in the later middle ages included letters of character reference and scholastic attainment. Although bishops, like Ralph Walpole of Ely, were quick to admonish the monks when numbers had fallen, the surviving evidence indicates that all applicants underwent a selection process which was never a mere formality. Walpole himself was concerned on both counts. Following his visitation of the cathedral priory in 1300 he ordered the prior to raise their numbers to the statutory total of seventy by accepting any *scholaris* or *clericus* who, moved by the Holy Spirit, humbly petitioned to be received provided that he was worthy of approval and was *litteratus*. The bishop then went on to order the examination of those who sought admission by a committee consisting of the prior with the assistance of three or four monks elected by the chapter, after which the successful applicants were to be presented to the community.[4] Eighty years later William Wykeham raised the same issue of declining numbers at St Swithun's while insisting that the monks' genuine problems, brought on by rising costs and decreasing revenues, were to be swiftly eliminated by better management of their resources; in the 1380s this was surely an unrealistic hard-line approach.[5] Walpole had been presented with the reverse side of the problem in his day and had been sufficiently astute to relate it to the very different circumstances of the pre-Black

---

[1] See Kardong, *RB*, 462–79.
[2] CCA DCc Cart. Antiq. A.193e.
[3] *RB*, C.58, 1–5.
[4] Evans, *Ely Chapter Ordinances*, 14–15.
[5] *Reg. Wykeham*, ii, 389–90.

Death era. When the approved candidate was presented to the chapter, he had told the monks to let no objections be put forward based on the pretence that there was insufficient income to provide for their maintenance.[6]

Some of the details of what was expected of prospective candidates can be drawn from exchanges of correspondence between priors, bishops, teachers, and patrons. The subject of one of these exchanges was Edmund de Basyng, who applied for admission to Christ Church Canterbury in 1324. A letter of refusal or, rather, postponement was sent from the prior and chapter to his patron [*alumpnus*] stating that they had discussed Edmund's case and were impressed by the favourable report concerning his personality and potential. Nevertheless, for the present they found him insufficiently skilled in the arts of singing and reading and deficient in knowledge of grammatical terms; when his competence in these subjects had improved they would welcome him into the community.[7] A protégé of Edward III was turned down unequivocally by the prior and chapter of Worcester in 1328 after an inquiry into his character and his family background in *les parties ou il nasquit*; on obtaining some disturbing information they decided to reject him on the grounds that *il n'est pas convenable*.[8] The following year the bishop of Worcester, Adam Orleton, fared no better when he urged the prior and chapter to accept his friend, Reginald de Thurtlestane, who was apparently already a clerk. Upon examination he was discovered to be 'in litteratura et aliis ut est moris minus sufficientem'.[9]

From time to time Christ Church had applicants from among the secular clergy, from Benedictines of other houses of the order and from monks and canons of other orders. These were also subjected to an examination before acceptance. In the case of Henry de Selverton, a novice at the Augustinian priory of Kenilworth in 1336, the prior arranged for a trusted deputy to conduct the interview and examination 'super articulis contentis in quadem cedula praesentibus interclusa'.[10] When it was a notable monk graduate desiring to transfer to Christ Church from Abingdon 'on account of his devotion to St Thomas and the other Canterbury saints'—the usual formula—his acceptance was not in doubt. All that seems to have been required of Henry de Wodehull, D.Th., in 1361 was the necessary licence from his abbot. One may presume that he was well known to the Christ Church monks studying at Canterbury College Oxford.[11]

---

[6] Evans, *Ely Chapter Ordinances*, 15.

[7] Sheppard, *Lit. Cant.*, i, no. 131; he did not reapply. W. A. Pantin refers to this case and neatly summarizes the entrance requirements for admission to Christ Church in *Canterbury College Oxford*, iv, 52.

[8] WCM Liber Albus, fo 133; the king's reply, fo 133v, expressed his understanding and acceptance of the decision. The inquiry may have uncovered canonical impediments to admission or deficiencies of character. In a customary of St Augustine's Canterbury, written in the first half of the fourteenth century but containing earlier material, there is a lengthy passage listing the questions that should be put to a candidate in order to ascertain his true character and intentions, Thompson, *Customary of St Augustine*, i, 261.

[9] WCM Liber Albus, fo 134.

[10] Sheppard, *Lit. Cant.*, ii, no. 606; see also *BRECP*, 284.

[11] The fact that Wodehull, a monk of 28 years standing at Abingdon, had come into conflict with his abbot over the manner of his inception at Oxford seems to have proved no barrier to his reception at Canterbury, *BRECP*, 322.

The fourteen *articuli* that were copied into the Christ Church priory Register 'L' deal exclusively with questions of physical fitness, moral rectitude, and freedom from any obligations and from servile status.[12] More precise details of the scholastic requirements are not supplied, but the above examples make it clear that in addition to the references as to character and status a certain level of elementary education was essential which included singing, reading, and [Latin] grammar. By the early fourteenth century, and even before, this learning was available in grammar schools in many urban centres; grammar schools in the cathedral cities of Canterbury, Durham, Ely, Worcester, and Norwich had been founded and were maintained by the bishop.[13] Elsewhere, in the absence of local schools informal teaching was undertaken by chantry priests, chaplains, and parish clerks. In addition, there was Winchester College, established by Bishop Wykeham to prepare boys for further, advanced studies at his recently founded New College in Oxford; in its list of Winchester alumni only one became a monk at St Swithun's. He was Nicholas de Bysshopestone who left the College to enter the monastery in 1402 and was ordained acolyte the following year by Wykeham himself.[14] The monastic cathedral chapters had also been educating young boys in their almonry schools, but the evidence that these provided a training ground for future monks is surprisingly scanty. Only five names have been recorded, four of them together at Christ Church in 1468 and so outside the limits of this study.[15] The fifth was John de Bradefeld, who was elected bishop by his fellow monks at Rochester in 1278 and was reported as having received his early education in the monastery.[16]

There is one other documented example of a monk with an almonry school background whose qualifications have also been recorded, confirming and supplementing the details given above. He was Robert de Weston, a Worcester monk, who spent his early years at the abbey school of Glastonbury near his parental home at Weston, Somerset. Letters of recommendation were furnished by his schoolmaster, Master Edward, and by the abbey precentor, John de Wygornia. Their report explained that his father held lands of the abbey by free tenure, praised his character

---

[12] Sheppard, *Lit. Cant.*, i, no. 314; these may be compared with the list in the *Customary of St Augustine*, note 8 above, but they are expressed in different terms.

[13] See the map in Orme, *English Schools*, 147, and Chapter 5 *passim*. Prospective Durham monks whose parents lived in the environs of Howden and Northallerton in the fourteenth and fifteenth centuries could have attended the schools there; both were peculiars in the jurisdiction of the Durham prior and chapter who appointed the masters; see A. F. Leach, *Early Yorkshire Schools*, 2 vols, Yorkshire Archaeological Society, record series, xxvii, xxxiii (1899–1903), xxxiii, 60–2, 84–7.

[14] *BRECP*, 679–80. Bysshopestone/Bishopstone, now Bushton in Wiltshire was one of the priory manors, J. Greatrex, 'The Reconciliation of Spiritual and Temporal Responsibilities: Some Aspects of the Monks of St Swithun's as Landowners and Estate Managers, *c.* 1380–1450', *Hampshire Studies*, 51 (1996), 77–87 at 78–9.

[15] *Chronicle Stone*, 106. Dobson apparently assumes without providing evidence that 'the great majority of Durham monks entered religious life after education at the convent's almonry school', *Durham Priory*, 61. Two fifteenth-century priors, Wessington and Ebchester, stated that they had received their early education in the convent 'grammar school', presumably the almonry school, DCM Locellus II, 4, Locellus XXI, 23; but no others are known by name.

[16] *BRECP*, 593.

and behaviour, and stressed his potential in singing. There was no hesitation about his acceptance at Worcester and he was admitted in November 1323.[17]

Neither the Christ Church *articuli* nor, as far as we know, any of the letters of reference produced by the applicants for admission to the cathedral priories mention an age qualification. Nevertheless, the minimum age for entry had been laid down by the English Black Monk chapter in 1278 as eighteen.[18] Infractions of this ruling can be found but their frequency remains in doubt because precise data are rarely obtainable. It is clear, however, that this was not considered to be a regulation to which strict adherence was required and cases were decided on their individual merit.[19] When we have the means of determining the length of time between admission and ordination to the priesthood it is possible to make an approximate calculation as to the age of entry because the minimum age for priestly ordination was set by canon law at twenty-four; nevertheless, here too there were exceptions made particularly in time of plague and pestilence and the consequent high mortality among priests as well as laity.[20] On the basis of the admittedly patchy information available for the years between 1300 and 1540 a rough calculation suggests that only a few monks were admitted to Canterbury, Winchester, Worcester, or Durham below the age of eighteen.[21]

There was a frequent exchange of correspondence between bishops and priors not only over the suitability of candidates for admission but also over admission procedures. As stated earlier this problem was one of those relating to their respective rival claims to jurisdiction.[22] The Canterbury archiepiscopal and priory registers reveal the persistent attempts on both sides to safeguard their prerogatives while reiterating the principles on which they believed their respective positions to be based. In practical terms, however, the result in any particular case was often a working compromise acceptable to both 'on this occasion' [*hac vice*].[23] This bargaining policy is especially evident during the time of Archbishop Stratford

---

[17] *BRECP*, 891–2; the precentor, John de Wygornia/Worcester may have been influential in Weston's choice of a distant cathedral monastery in preference to Glastonbury or another abbey nearer his home.

[18] Pantin, *Black Monk Chapters*, i, 99; this repeated the decisions of the first chapters of both the southern and northern provinces of the English Black Monks in 1219 and 1221 respectively, ibid., i, 10, 99, 234. However, there is a slight change in wording: *infra vicesmum annum* in the ones of earlier date and *nisi nonum decimum annum attigerit* in the later one; the minimum age thus appears to have been lowered by a year in 1278.

[19] The 1219 and 1221 statutes, referred to in the previous note, added the qualifying clause 'nisi commendabilis utilitas vel necessitas...' which probably continued to prove useful as guidelines. Stephen de Howden, for example, was about sixteen when he entered Durham cathedral priory in 1281, DCM 3.6.Pont.10; for his monastic career see *LVD*, iii, C.723.

[20] These calculations are based on *BRECP*. See Harvey, *Living and Dying*, 119–20 for a discussion of the comparable situation at Westminster Abbey. See also Greatrex, 'Prosopographical Perspectives', 130–2.

[21] For Durham see also Foster, 'Durham Priory', 53–4 and Dobson, *Durham Priory*, 61. Calculations made by Alan Piper led him to conclude that although the evidence is patchy and frequently uncertain an average age of 20 at the time of entry is a reasonable estimate.

[22] See pp. 12–13.

[23] *Hac vice* or *ista vice* are phrases occurring frequently in letters of the archbishops and of the Canterbury priors.

(1333–48) who had been promoted from the see of Winchester where the bishop had no say in the admission of monks to St Swithun's. In 1337 he ordered Prior Oxenden not to accept anyone into the Christ Church community without first obtaining a licence from him as had been the custom recorded in the registers of his predecessors.[24] This led to a spate of letters in which the prior's personal deference and conciliatory approach were in contrast to the strongly worded declaration by the corporate body of the prior and chapter who stated their rights clearly: to them 'pertinet clericos ydoneos ad habitum et ordinem regularem...admittere quandocumque viderint expedire'. As for the archbishop's rights: to him they said 'pertinet...clericos...admissos antequam habitum recipiant regularem, quando commode fieri poterit, intueri et ipsos, sine difficultate quacumque benignis affectibus acceptare'.[25] During this period of contentious exchange between the chapter and the archbishop, Prior Oxenden was succeeded by Robert Hathbrande, who attempted to improve relations while still pressing the monks' case by notifying the archbishop that he was in the process of admitting new monks to replace the lately deceased; he suggested that Stratford might desire to have them presented to him, *si fieri posset commode* before they received the monastic habit or, if this should prove difficult to arrange, 'on that occasion' [*ista vice*] would he kindly authorize them to go ahead with the clothing ceremony.[26] Several years later, in 1341, after the admission of eight 'worthy persons' the prior and chapter requested the archbishop, *ista vice de gratia speciali*, to dispense with the necessity of introducing them to him before clothing.[27] A second letter followed, in reply to one from the archbishop, insisting on their unequivocal rights which could be traced back 'beyond the memory of man'; the request for the dispensation concerning clothing was repeated and the *ista vice*.[28] Dissension over admission procedures at Christ Church may have reached a dramatic climax in Stratford's day but there were a few lesser repercussions visible both before and after his time. We are, of course as always, dependent on the surviving evidence of which in this case there is little. Intimations of the presence of a strain between the convent and Archbishop Winchelsey are suggested by the guarded wording of his letter to the prior in 1304. In it he conceded *ista vice* that they should go ahead with the clothing of a monk because he was *agentibus in remotis*.[29] Archbishop Islip seems to have sidestepped the issue, probably avoiding confrontation, by authorizing the prior in 1361 to receive twelve monks, *hac vice*, whom he had neither seen nor approved as was his right according to custom, provided that they were *habiles, decentes et honeste [persone]*. He did not refer to the prior's claim to have the right to admit, but

---

[24] Sheppard, *Lit. Cant.*, ii, no. 630.
[25] Ibid., ii, nos 631 and 632.
[26] Ibid., ii, no. 680.
[27] Ibid., ii, no. 711.
[28] Ibid., ii, no. 713.
[29] *Reg. Winchelsey*, 1326. The monk is named as M. Richard de Haselarton, who appears neither in *BRUO* nor *BRECP*; Causton's entry for 1303/4 has one *magister*, Richard Vaughan, whose name was inserted there, although he did not enter the monastery until 1352, thus according to him the appropriate seniority of rank in the community, a rare privilege.

did make it clear that he was granting permission to clothe.[30] In the early 1370s Archbishop Wittlesey issued four commissions to the prior to clothe monks in the habit.[31] When his successor, Simon Sudbury, sent a commission to the prior and chapter in 1376 he gave instructions that five or six worthy clerks were 'to be admitted to the habit' without being presented to him *ista vice*.[32] By resorting to the regular use of commissions of this kind the later archbishops succeeded in holding on to their prerogative in principle while generally ceasing to intervene in practice.[33]

A cursory investigation into the procedures at Worcester cathedral priory gives the impression that in practice the bishop had more control over the admission of monks than we have seen at Canterbury; this, however, is far from certain. In *c.* 1309 we find Prior John de Wyke explaining to Bishop Walter Reynolds the custom of their church on this point: clerks who applied to enter the monastery were admitted by the prior and chapter after which they were presented to the bishop for his *assensum*; they were then clothed in the monastic habit. In this particular instance, the prior continued, he found it necessary to clothe them at rather short notice; and, since the bishop was absent from Worcester, would he kindly appoint his official to take his place.[34] Consistent with this explanation is the heading of an entry in the priory register under the year 1317, which is a copy of the vicar-general's commission to the prior and chapter and which reads 'Commissio pro clericis monach [?aliter] vestiend[is]'.[35] Confusion and doubt arise, however, when this document is compared with another entry, also dated in the same month and relating to the same function, that survives in the episcopal register. The latter is entitled *Commissio pro admissione monachorum Wygorniensium*; it requires one of the bishop's officials to perform his episcopal duties in respect of two clerks *ad ordinem monachalem... admittendis* whom he, in compliance with the customs of the church, is required to examine for their suitability.[36] The prior and chapter are clear as to what is involved, but it is not certain that the bishop's secretarial staff were as clear and concerned about precision with regard to enrolling the details.[37] The careful wording found in the priory records and the ambiguity in those of the

---

[30] LPL Reg. Islip, fo 180 headed *Commissio ad recipiendum xij monachos in ecclesia*...

[31] LPL Reg. Wittlesey, fos 56v, 57v, 62v (2); in each case the heading of the document is *Ad induend'*, with both 'admit' and 'clothe' included in the text of three of them.

[32] LPL Reg. Sudbury, fo 30; the marginal title is *Commissio ad induendum clericas personas in habitu regulari*.

[33] Probably the commissions had been discussed with the prior in advance before final copies were sent in order to try to forestall the possibility of rejection.

[34] WCM Liber Albus, fo 41v. The custom, or customs, mentioned do not survive; there is nothing relevant in the 1224 composition (*Acta Stephani Langton*, 160–3).

[35] WCM Liber Albus, fo 80v.

[36] *Reg. Cobham*, 10–11. The form of the word '*admittendis*' suggests a future action, and the introduction of the word '*examinacio*' seems to add a new dimension to the bishop's right of receiving them. Moreover, there is no reference to clothing in the monastic habit. Note that this entry also appears at the end of Bishop Maidstone's register, 106 (the manuscript is paginated).

[37] The two letters are not identical, the one in the priory register was sent from London on 14 September, and the other was from the bishop himself in Yorkshire on 13 September. There seems to be a duplication of orders, but this does not affect the case.

bishop are continued in later documents. The monks, for example, gave to their enrolled copy of a commission from Cobham in 1323 the title *Commissio pro noviciis examinandis* which suggests that since they were referred to as novices they had already been admitted.[38] Bishop Adam Orleton's two commissions, on the other hand, use the heading '... ad recipiendum et examinandum j clericum ad ordinem monachalem presentatum'.[39] In 1341 Wulstan de Bransford, former prior and now bishop, was careful to state in his register that he had admitted two clerks, presented to him by the prior and chapter, to the monastic habit.[40] The latest episcopal commission concerning admission to appear in the *Liber Albus*, dated 1352, appoints the prior to act on behalf of Bishop Thoresby 'ad admittend[os] monach[os] ad habitum religionis'.[41] Although Bishop Tideman de Winchcombe in 1399 appointed two commissaries to act for him when three *persone* in the priory were waiting to be presented, it seems that in the second half of the fourteenth century most bishops followed Thoresby's example in commissioning the priors to perform the ceremonies attached to admission, thus obviating any further need to spell out the respective rights and responsibilities of the parties involved.[42]

Comparatively little information has survived concerning the admission of monks at the other cathedral priories. Procedures at Durham and Winchester had long been an internal affair arranged by the prior and chapter; and at Bath, Coventry, and Ely there is no evidence of episcopal intervention in priory affairs before the ceremony of profession. The Rochester monks apparently followed the Canterbury custom, with no known periods of strain and possibly aided by the fact that five of the bishops were Benedictines whose combined episcopates covered ninety of the one hundred and fifty years under study. In the only priory register to survive there is a single entry recording a commission to Prior John de Shepey II from Archbishop William Courtenay in 1389 during the vacancy of the see; it authorized the prior to admit, receive, and clothe two *clericii*.[43] In 1392 when an Augustinian canon of St Osyth's priory applied to join the Rochester community—a move which meant a change both of house and of order—only the prior and chapter were involved.[44] The one episcopal register containing commissions to the prior and chapter concerning the admission of monks is that of William Wells, formerly abbot of St Mary's York. Although they are later than the period of this study by some twenty years they probably followed those of his predecessors, which have not survived. In one of them the bishop stated that he had received and examined the two novices in question and ordered the prior and chapter to clothe and instruct them.[45]

---

[38] WCM Liber Albus, fo 113v.
[39] *Reg. Orleton*, items 513 and 776 dated 1328 and 1330 respectively.
[40] *Reg. Bransford*, no. 1024.
[41] WCM Liber Albus, fo 210v and WRO Reg. Thoresby, 24.
[42] WRO Reg. Tideman de Winchcombe, 73. See, for example, Bishop Alcock's commission to the prior to 'admit five persons as monks' c. 1479, WRO Reg. Alcock, 31.
[43] BL MS Cotton Faustina C.v, fo 42v.
[44] Ibid., fo 57.
[45] CKS DRb Reg. Wells, fo 33; the second commission on fo 67 is similar.

There must have been serious dissension at Norwich over the disputed rights of bishop and prior pertaining to the admission of monks. Unfortunately, the mutilation of the episcopal registers after the dissolution and the incomplete state of those surviving from the priory deprive us of the kind of evidence that survives from Canterbury and Worcester. However, the problem comes to light in a sheaf of documents preserved in the cathedral archives of Norwich; they include papal and archiepiscopal instruments and reveal details of the longstanding dispute between Bishop Henry Despenser and the monks which came to a head in the 1390s, was brought to an end by Archbishop Arundel's decree in 1411 but seems to have flared up again in the 1440s.[46] The case between prior and bishop was, in the course of a succession of appeals and counter appeals, taken before the courts of Canterbury and Rome and also before the king's council after it had reached the ears of Richard II.[47] Despenser's death in 1406 before a permanent settlement was in place, was followed by Arundel's decree five years later; this upheld the customary rights of the cathedral priory over the admission of monks concerning which they had petitioned Pope Boniface IX in 1395. According to their account at that time the newly arrived novices were first received by the prior and convent and afterwards presented to the bishop for his blessing and the kiss of peace.[48] Arundel's *articulum de monachandis* stated that the prior and chapter should retain their authority over the examination and admission of monks before presenting them to the bishop prior to clothing.[49]

It is not surprising that all the cathedral priories aimed to have the right to regulate what they considered to be their own community affairs. The bishop's role as titular abbot had, with regard to admission and other matters, developed into a mutually obstructive relationship from which neither side could escape without loss of dignity. It is regrettable but not surprising that controversy and antagonism between the bishop and the prior and convent tended to be recorded in detail and carefully preserved by both sides for future reference. A case in point is the prolonged and bitter dispute between Bishop Reginald Bryan and Prior John de Evesham at Worcester in the 1350s where there is little doubt that personal animosity fuelled both sides and ended only with Bryan's death on the eve of his translation to Ely.[50] Nevertheless, we should not be misled into thinking that rancour dominated the cathedral precinct. The warmth and affection exhibited by Archbishop Stratford and the Christ Church community in their later

---

[46] The collection of documents is in NRO DCN 42/2/16–29; the composition between Bishop Thomas Brouns and the prior and chapter in 1444 is in NRO DCN Reg. I, fo 267 and also in NRO DN Reg. Brouns, fos 110v–11v; on fo 109v of the bishop's register, two monks were received by the bishop *ad osculum et benedictionem* as prescribed in 1411.
[47] CPL, 5 (1396–1404), 318.
[48] CPL, 4 (1362–1404), 526.
[49] NRO DCN Reg. I, fo 267v–68.
[50] Bryan's register and the priory's *Liber Albus* record the successive stages of the conflict through mutually accusatory letters, episcopal inhibitions, and appeals to Canterbury and Rome; the matters in dispute included at least one over the admission of novices (WRO, Reg. Bryan, i, 42) and, among others, over the prior's right to pontificalia and the bishop's visitatorial rights, see Greatrex, 'Prior John de Evesham', 69–71.

correspondence show that they had put their quarrels behind them and had embraced reconciliation and peace in the true spirit of Christian charity.[51]

Dies ingressus: entry into the novitiate

When the monastery gate closed behind the newly admitted monks-to-be they understood that they had left one world to enter another. This transition was soon to be made visible by the exchange of the secular clothes in which they had arrived for the religious habit. For those who had been accepted at Canterbury and Ely we have extant lists of the essentials prescribed, the 'necessaria noviciis noviter ad religionem venientibus providenda', as the heading reads in an Ely manuscript of the fifteenth century:[52]

'In primis debent provideri ij cannas.	cloths
Item j matras.	mattress
Item ij paria blankettys.	blankets
Item ij paria straylys.	bed covers
Item iij coverlytis.	coverlets
Item j furytpane.	
Item j blewbed de Sago.	?blue cloth
Item j cuculla cum froco.	cowl (monastic outer garment) and frock
Item j tunica nigra furrata.	black tunic with fur
Item j tunica nigra simplex.	black tunic
Item ij tunice albe.	white tunics
Item j amica nigra furrata (amicto).	black hood with fur
Item j amica simplex.	hood
Item j zona cum j powch, cultello, tabulis, et pectine, filo et acu in le powch.	belt, pouch, knife, writing tablet, comb, thread and needle or pen
Item j parva zona pro noctibus.	small belt for night wear
Item iij paria staminorum.	woollen shirts
Item iiij paria bracarum cum Brygerdel et poynts.	breeches
Item ij paria caligarum.	footwear
Item iiij paria de le sokks.	socks
Item ij paria botarum pro diebus.	day boots
Item j par botarum pro noctibus.	night boots
Item j pylche.	fur lined cloak

---

[51] See the judicious remarks of R. M. Haines in *Archbishop John Stratford: Political Revolutionary and Champion of the Liberties of the English Church ca. 1275/80–1348*, Pontifical Institute of Mediaeval Studies, Studies and Texts 76 (Toronto, Ont., 1986), 59–63; the restoration of good relations between the archbishop and the prior and convent is evident in letters no. 696 and 762 in Sheppard, *Lit. Cant.*, ii.
[52] LPL MS 448, fo 106v, printed in Stewart, *Architectural History of Ely*, 232–3. This fragment is written in an early fifteenth-century secretary hand and is a fragment only of regulations for novices of an unknown, earlier date. It lacks the section dealing with the clothing ceremony of the novice but describes the daily routine and is followed on the same folio by a memorandum which is dated 1430.

Item iij paria flammeole.	?cloths, bandages
Item iij pulvinaria.	cushions or pillows
Item j pileo albo pro noctibus.	white night cap
Item ij manitergia.	towels
Item j pokett pro vestibus lavandis.	laundry bag
Item j schavyngcloth.	
Item j crater.	basin
Item j ciphus murreus.	cup of maple wood
Item j cochlear argenteum.'	silver spoon

The *necessaria* may be usefully compared with the only other list surviving from the cathedral priories, namely the one in the notebook of William Glastynbury, a Canterbury monk who recorded the items and their cost at the time of his admission in 1415:[53]

'Expense

In primis pro j lecto de Wynchester	xxij s. viij d.	bed
Item in j lecto de say	x s. vj d.	bed of woollen material
Item in ij paribus de strayl'	x s.	bedcovers
Item in j pari blankettis	viij s. iiij d.	blankets
Item in uno materas	iiij s. ij s.	mattress
Item in iij paribus vestium secretarum	vj s.	underclothes
Item in iiij velaminibus	iiij s. ij d.	
Item in j pulvinari	iiij s. iiij d.	cushion
Item in j bolster	iij s.	bolster
Item in j pilio albo	iiij d.	white (night)cap
Item in j pelvi	iij s. xj d.	basin
Item in ij paribus ocrearum	iiij s. viij d.	thigh boots
Item in j pari ocrearum nocturnarum	v s.	leggings for nightwear
Item in viij paribus meteynys	xx s.	
Item in j sona cum bursa et cultello	xviij d.	belt, purse, knife
In iij amisicis (?amictis)	vij s. iij d.	?hoods
In j panno pro rastura	xij d.	shaving cloth
In j panno pedali	viij d.	?foot cloth
In velamine pro pressura	iiij s.	
In iij habitibus	xxviij s.	monastic habits
In ij tunicis albis	v s. vj d.	white tunics
In j tunica nigra	vj s. viij d.	black tunic
In ij tunicis furratis	xxiiij s.	tunics with fur

[53] The notebook is now Oxford, Corpus Christi College MS 256 where the list is on fo 180; it was printed in Pantin, *Canterbury College Oxford*, iv, 118. Like Stewart and Pantin I have deliberately retained the hybrid Latin English text, but have supplied translations where possible.

In j nigro pilio	vj d.	black cap
In j braccali cum punctis	vij d.	breeches with?
In j canamas	ijs.	
In j pari pyncis	vj d.	
In j pari tabellarum cum pectine eburneo		tablets with comb of ivory
In barbitons'	v d.	?shaving
In ij paribus caligarum	xviij d.	footwear
	Summa viij li. ix s. v d.'	

Although a century probably separates these two lists, aptly described by W. A. Pantin as 'the monk's trousseau', they are remarkably similar.[54] Both, for example, require bedding and specify mattress, pillows, sheets, and blankets; both include items of clothing worn by monks like the tunic, amice, footwear, and night caps; both also require a belt with pouch attached containing the essential multifunctional knife. It is noteworthy that Christ Church novices were provided with three habits, costing over nine shillings each, presumably acquired through the chamberlain and made by the tailor under his direction. The term 'habit' was generally taken to include such items as the cowl and *froccus* and perhaps the shirt, all of which are listed as separate items at Ely.[55] Unfortunately there is only one specific reference to novices' clothing on the surviving chamberlain's accounts at Canterbury, that of the purchase of grey cloth in 1336/7 for the purpose of making hose or stockings (*caliga*) for five novices; ordinarily, it seems, he made no distinction between their clothing supplies and those of the rest of the community.[56] There was one occasion, however, in 1373/4, when the Canterbury treasurers' account showed a payment of £11 19s. to *diversis fratribus pro habitibus*, possibly because the chamberlain's account showed a deficit of about £20.[57] Writing equipment in the form of writing tablets occurs on both lists, but only the Ely novice was expected to have towels, a laundry bag and, for his own use in the refectory, a wooden drinking bowl or mazer and a silver spoon. Most, if not all, of the Christ Church monks are also known to have had the use of their own mazers and spoons assigned to them for life; they were often of silver and were used by successive generations of monks. A 1328 indenture, for example, records *cuppe, ciphi, coclearea* and other items of silver being returned to the treasury on the death of several

---

[54] Pantin, *Canterbury College Oxford*, iv, 119. There is a resemblance to the corresponding section of the regulations for novices formulated by the general chapter of the Benedictines of Canterbury province c. 1277/9. These regulations concerning the observance to be followed in the novitiate were inserted at the end of the customary of St Augustine's Canterbury (now BL MS Cotton Faustina C.xii) transcribed by Thompson, *Customary of St Augustine*, 389ff. Pantin regarded this as a 'small customary' that was part of 'a very ambitious attempt at the enforcement of uniformity', *Black Monk Chapters*, i, 109.
[55] Compare Barbara Harvey's lecture describing the clothing worn by the monks at Westminster Abbey in *Monastic Dress*.
[56] CCA DCc chamberlain's account 12.
[57] CCA DCc treasurers' account 5; there were two treasurers in office together at Canterbury.

monks.[58] In this Canterbury probably followed the custom that prevailed at Norwich where the novices purchased their mazers from the refectorer to whom they had been returned for safekeeping and repair after the death of the previous owners.[59] In reminiscences, written down in the late sixteenth century, an elderly ex-monk of Durham recalled that: 'every Monke had his Mazer severally by himself that he did drink in'.[60]

If the would-be Benedictine had been obliged to acquire at his own cost all the items listed he would have faced a considerable burden of expense according to William Glastynbury's evaluation of £8 9s. 5d. which in fact omits mazer and spoon, surely two of the more costly items on the Ely list. The provincial chapter of the English Black Monks was not slow to recognize that the need to find this sum was proving a deterrent to potentially desirable candidates who applied for admission, and that it had the effect of prompting them to turn to other orders which made no such charges. Accordingly, in 1343 the chapter issued a statute to the effect that 100s. should henceforth be provided toward meeting the expenses of a new monk's clothing.[61] It is clear that from the outset this was inadequate in many instances and, not surprisingly, we find that from time to time monk obedientiaries made donations to impecunious novices: in 1375/6 the precentor at Norwich gave 7s. 8d. to a novice *ad ingressum* and in 1377/8, 6s. 8d. to another *ad intrationem de gratia*.[62] Again, in 1391/2 the Worcester almoner contributed 20s. to three novices 'propter eorum paupertatem in primo ingressu'.[63] The extent of the financial assistance offered to newcomers to the cathedral priories remains uncertain; it is likely that at Canterbury the 100s. provision did not apply because the Christ Church monks distanced themselves from the provincial chapters by persisting in their refusal to attend.[64] It may be that the majority of recruits accepted by this prestigious house would have been able to afford the outlay, but not all. In the case of James Hegham, in 1370 the chamberlain spent £8 5s. 7d. 'pro habitu et necessariis ad ingressum' for which sum he petitioned the monk auditors for an allowance on his account, thereby suggesting that this may have been an unusual occurrence.[65]

The Durham chamberlain's annual accounts record substantial purchases of cloth and other supplies for novices, some of which were for the outfitting of the new arrivals. The reference to the *Rastura noviciorum* on the accounts in the 1360s

---

[58] Sheppard, *HMC IXth Report*, 90. In 1466 William Chichele I (*BRECP*, 117) was using four silver spoons which had previously belonged to William Chartham [?]II (*BRECP*, 114); this information is found in an inventory in Canterbury Reg. N, fo 59.
[59] See above, 39–40.
[60] *Rites of Durham*, 81.
[61] Pantin, *Black Monk Chapters*, ii, 50; in 1444 this statute was reissued with no increase in the amount, ibid., ii, 206.
[62] NRO DCN 1/9/14, 1/9/16; the Norwich sacrist also contributed an unknown sum to a novice *pro intratione* in 1396/7, ibid., 1/4/41.
[63] WCM C.181.
[64] See below, ■.
[65] CCA DCc chamberlain's account 53 (1370/1); in this account his expenses exceeded his receipts by £15 6s. 8d., half of which went to his contribution to Hegham, who must have been without any financial support.

and later distinguishes them from the senior novices because the tonsuring ceremony usually took place at the time of clothing; under the heading *Rastura noviciorum* in 1402/3, for example, the chamberlain listed his expenses in providing six novices with bedclothes, boots, knives, belts and, for each, two *capucia* and one *pellicia*.[66] Several of these items have their counterparts on the Ely and Canterbury lists, the *capucium* presumably being an alternative for *cuculla* and the pelisse being rendered by '*pylch*' at Ely. To complete their monastic wardrobe the Durham novices had probably acquired other essentials at their own expense before entry, and the chamberlain himself may have included in his account additional items for their use without supplying the necessary detailed information on which the historian depends.

For details of the procedures followed at the cathedral priories for the clothing ceremony of novices we must rely on the Constitutions of Lanfranc and ordinances found in several Christ Church registers and manuscripts which would have guided those who were about to be clothed as monks in the correct way of presenting their petition to receive the monastic habit.[67] No preliminary instructions are mentioned although undoubtedly there would have been an introductory programme at every monastic house; in the St Augustine customary, for example, the novices were given two or three days of instruction based on the Rule and Hugh of St Victor's *De institutione noviciorum* together with practical details concerning the monastic routine and the novice's deportment.[68] On the appointed day the Christ Church novices were escorted into the chapter house, each accompanied by the *magister* to whom he had been individually assigned.[69] Prostrating themselves before the prior or the presiding official (*presidens*) they made their request to receive the monastic habit: '... requirimus misericordiam dei et vestram totiusque conventus ut habitum monachi nobis concedere velitis'. On rising they listened to an admonition stressing the hardships that awaited them if they embarked on the way of holy obedience according to the Rule. Their response was 'presto sumus et parati ad faciendum quicquid nobis precipietur pro salute animarum nostrarum'.[70] Each novice in turn genuflected before the prior and kissed his feet in humble subjection;

---

[66] DCM chamberlain's accounts for 1362/3, 1365/6, 1366/7, and 1402/3.

[67] Lanfranc, *Monastic Constitutions*, 154–6; CCA DCc Reg. A, fo 391; BL MS Cotton Galba E.iv (Prior Eastry's memorandum book), fo 72–72v; there are also sixteenth-century copies in BL MS Arundel 68, fo 73 and LPL MS 20, fo 1v. These are similar to but less detailed than the comparable section in the St Augustine customary, Thompson, *Customary of St Augustine*, i, 402–6; in this volume the section 389ff was drawn up by the Benedictine general chapter *c*. 1277–9 at which Christ Church was not represented.

[68] Thompson, *Customary of St Augustine*, i, 402; see also the preceding note and note 54 above.

[69] In Lanfranc's *Monastic Constitutions*, the novice was brought in by the guestmaster, 154. The novice master at Christ Church was known as the *magister ordinis*; he was assisted in his responsibilities by a number of senior monks or *magistri* each of whom was charged with instructing a single novice; see Pantin, *Canterbury College Oxford*, iv, 53–4. There was probably a similar custom at Durham as there were seven *magistri noviciorum* in 1344/5, DCM hostiller's account for that year; again, in 1398/9 the feretrar referred to the *noviciis et magistris suis*, ibid., feretrar's account.

[70] This follows fairly closely the wording in Lanfranc, *Monastic Constitutions*, 154, but without the response beginning *presto sumus*, LPL MS 20, fo 1v.

returning to their places the novices prostrated themselves a second time and repeated their petition begging the:

> misericordiam dei et vestram ut oretis pro nobis dominum quatinus concedat nobis ita suscipere habitum monachi quod sit ad honorem dei et ad salutem animarum nostrarum et honorem huius ecclesie et ad utilitatem omnium nostrorum.

The prior replied to this request by commanding the brethren to make fervent prayer on their behalf. The novices then departed with their *magistri* to be clothed and to be tonsured at the same time.[71] A set of instructions for Christ Church novices, which was derived from Lanfranc's Constitutions, has been preserved in a late thirteenth-century copy entitled 'Instructio noviciorum secundum consuetudinem ecclesie Cantuariensis'. This omits the ceremonies of admission and clothing, and begins with the directions for the tonsuring which was to take place immediately after admission in a private and appropriate place; the church before the introit during mass, the infirmary chapel or the abbot's chapel were suitable places recommended by Lanfranc in his Constitutions. The novice was to be shaven and shorn (*tonsus et rasus*) and to shed his old clothing signifying that he had put off the old man and put on the new. No mention of the new clothing occurs, however, until the third chapter which states that on the day following his tonsuring the novice was to be taught by his master how to put on and take off the habit and how it was to be worn with fitting modesty and dignity.[72] The Benedictine general chapter's instructions issued in the 1270s describe in more detail the ceremonies of tonsuring and clothing in the habit. The former was to take place during the singing or chanting of the seven penitential psalms and the litany, while the latter began with the washing of the novices' feet. New drawers, hose, and daytime footwear were then put on followed by the shirt, tunic, and/or pelisse, this last item to be provided by the novices' *magister*. Next the cowl and *froccus* were put on by those who were already *clerici*, and the scapular replaced the *froccus* for those who were still *laici*; finally, the hood and the belt with its attached purse containing knife and comb.[73] Two Worcester monks received the monastic habit in October 1277 and two Winchester monks were given their *prima tonsura* in February 1362, both statements presumably referring to the same ceremony of 'making the monk'; unfortunately, even such meagre details are rarely found for monks of most of the cathedral chapters.[74]

Now duly clothed and tonsured, the novice commenced his year of probation.

---

[71] LPL MS 20, fo 1v. Tonsuring took place immediately before clothing in Lanfranc, *Monastic Constitutions*, 156.

[72] Excerpts from the *Instructio noviciorum* (contained in MS 441 of Cambridge, Corpus Christi College, fos 359–91) have been printed in Lanfranc, *Monastic Constitutions*, 198–220, the chapter concerning tonsure being on 198, and on the habit, 200. The *Instructio* has been dated to *c.* 1250–75; ibid., liii.

[73] Thompson, *Customary of St Augustine*, 405; see also note 54 above for details of the manuscript in which the ceremonies are described.

[74] For the two Worcester monks, see under John de Harleye and John de Wyke in *BRECP*, 817, 897, and for the two at Winchester, see under John de Haselwode and Thomas de Lymyngton, ibid., 699, 712.

2. PROBATION, CLAUSTRAL STUDIES, AND PROFESSION

> Si adhuc stetirit, tunc ducatur in ... cellam noviciorum et ... probetur in omnia patientia; ... certis temporibus occupare debent fratres ... in lectione divina.
>
> RB, C.58, 11; C.48, 1[75]

The monastic background of study

The year of probation was given over to learning in preparation for profession. The new recruits embarked without delay on a programme of study in which there were two principal objectives. Instruction in the monastic way of life was the primary aim, as prescribed in the Rule of St Benedict and interpreted in its later commentaries; and this was accompanied by an introduction to the customs of the house in which the novice had received the habit. The English Benedictine monasteries were independent of one another but, apart from Christ Church Canterbury, were members of a federation which met periodically to discuss matters of mutual concern and, where it was deemed necessary, to reach joint decisions regarding conduct, routine, and policy. Before 1336 there was a general chapter in each of the two provinces of Canterbury and York, and after that date a single provincial chapter for both provinces.[76] The newly agreed directives at these assemblies were intended for incorporation into the customary of each house while remaining subject to alteration over the course of time, both at the discretion of the individual chapters and by consensus of the general, and later the provincial, chapters. By contrast, the Cluniac and Cistercian reform movements of the tenth and eleventh centuries developed, within the Benedictine framework, a centrally organized system in which Cluny and Cîteaux were the mother houses whose authority extended over all subsequent foundations made by their respective orders.[77]

Although all Benedictine monasteries compiled their own individual customaries, the similarities between them were more striking than the differences because all had their source in the Rule. The latter, however, was cast in fairly general terms, apart from the notable exception of the detailed requirements concerning the performance of the daily sevenfold office.[78] The purpose of the customaries, therefore, was to spell out the precise regulations and practical arrangements by which each monastic community was governed and which were essential to its smooth functioning. No particulars were omitted, from the number and kind of dishes to be served to each monk in the refectory and the sleeping arrangements in the dormitory to the appropriate chants for the seasonal antiphons and responses at mass and office and the distribution of clothing and other allowances during the year.

---

[75] As Fry, *RB*, 447 points out, St Benedict 'does not specify ... studies for novices' other than these readings and the Rule itself. See also C.48, *passim*.
[76] See Pantin, *Black Monk Chapters*, i, xi–xii.
[77] For the early history of Cluny see Knowles, *MO*, 145–8, and for Cîteaux, ibid., 208–66.
[78] *RB*, C.8–C.18, and Lanfranc, *Monastic Constitutions*, xx–xxv.

Unfortunately, we cannot look to the customaries of the cathedral priories to furnish us with many details of the day-to-day arrangements for each house because, with the partial exception of Norwich, none survive except in an incomplete or fragmentary state. Nevertheless, we can piece together enough to enable us to visualize the pattern of daily and seasonal activities within the cloister by means of these; and they can be supplemented by other records among the cathedral priories' muniments which contain information of the kind usually supplied by customaries. We can also have recourse to a few other extant Benedictine customaries such as those of Bury St Edmunds, St Augustine's Canterbury, Eynsham, and Westminster.[79]

The section devoted to novices attached to the St Augustine's customary was 'drawn up apparently by the authority of the general chapter, and ... [probably] intended for use in all of the houses of the province of Canterbury'.[80] Whether or not it was universally approved and adopted throughout the southern province is unknown.[81] In the sections concerned with novices *post ingressum* there are several allusions to their educational programme. The intervals between the canonical hours during the day, for example, were to be spent *in cellam seu scolam* under instruction by their master, who was to begin by expounding chapters five, six, seven, and eighteen of the Rule; these deal with obedience, silence, humility, and the order in which the psalms are to be said (in the daily office). The novice master was also to comment on the daily readings of the Rule in order to encourage the novices to strive after perfection in accord with both Rule and Gospel and to remain at all times inwardly attentive to the *doctrina Christi*.[82] It should be noted that these daily readings of the Rule in chapter were followed by a brief exposition in the vernacular or in French by the prior or presiding monk.[83] As for the local

---

[79] The customaries of Bury St Edmunds and of Eynsham were both edited by Antonia Gransden: *The Customary of the Benedictine Abbey of Bury St Edmunds in Suffolk*, Henry Bradshaw Society, 99 (Chichester, 1973) and *The Customary of the Benedictine Abbey of Eynsham in Oxfordshire*, 'Corpus Consuetudinum Monasticarum', 2 (1963). The other two were edited by E. M. Thompson and published together as *Customary of the Benedictine Monasteries of Saint Augustine, Canterbury, and Saint Peter, Westminster*. *The Customary of the Cathedral Priory of Norwich*, edited by J. Tolhurst, Henry Bradshaw Society nos 23 and 28 (London, 1902–4), is largely confined to liturgical rites. Surviving customaries at Winchester and Worcester are concerned with priory estates and tenants; for Winchester there is also *A Consuetudinary of the Fourteenth Century for the Refectory of the House of S. Swithun in Winchester*, ed. G. W. Kitchin, as well as a mixed collection of customs and probably chapter ordinances, mainly twelfth century, in BL Add. MS 29436, fos 72v–80. Also, for Worcester and Ely there are tantalizingly brief references to the precentor's purchase of vellum and paper, in 1388 'pro libro consuetudinar' claustri . . . copiando', WCM C.366 (Worcester) and in 1373/9, CUL Add. MS 2957, 45 (Ely).

[80] Pantin, *Black Monk Chapters*, i, 109 and Thompson, *Customary of St Augustine*, 389–429; on 407 this treatise is referred to as an *opusculum* for the use of novice masters. (The manuscript reference is BL Cotton Faustina C.xii fos 186–99.)

[81] Greater uniformity was certainly the aim, but could never be enforced.

[82] Thompson, *Customary of St Augustine*, 406. In the preface to his injunctions of 1308/09 John Salmon, bishop of Norwich and former prior of Ely, cautioned his monastic chapter that the interpretation of the Rule always had to take into account changing times and circumstances and differences in character and temperament, *Studies in Norwich Cathedral History*, ed. E. H. Carter (Jarrolds, Norwich, 1935), 19, a somewhat unreliable transcription of NRO DCN 92/1.

[83] Thompson, *Customary of St Augustine*, 390; Pantin, *Black Monk Chapters*, i, 95 (1278), the revised version of the statutes of 1277; an addition to the 1278 revision states *in vulgari seu gallico*.

observances which are described as *variae... et multae*, the masters were to carefully select for the novices those which were relevant to their status during their probationary year.[84] It is significant that the *doctrina Hugonis*, that is Hugh of St Victor's *De institutione noviciorum*, was mentioned not only here, *post ingressum*, but also previously, *ante ingressum*, where it was coupled with the Rule. The prospective novice had thus been informed in advance as to the basic texts that he would be required to study.[85] In the same years, 1277–9, the chapter of the southern province also drew up and published a new body of statutes, one chapter of which regulated the novices' study programme by spelling out some of the practical details. It was laid down that every novice was henceforth expected to demonstrate his mastery by heart of the entire psalter, the Rule, hymns, canticles, versicles and responses, antiphons, invitatories, and other prescribed liturgical material before [priestly] ordination.[86]

Monastic routine

We may compare the general chapter proposal with the set of instructions drawn up for novices at Christ Church Canterbury that survives in a mid-thirteenth-century manuscript inscribed with the name of Richard de Wynchepe.[87] The volume is written in one neat but pedestrian gothic book hand throughout and consists of a collection of treatises of which the 'Instructio noviciorum secundum consuetudinem ecclesiae cantuariensis' is only one. The other items, however, would also have been suitable for novices.[88] Knowles summed up the *Instructio* as 'a directory derived from Lanfranc's Constitutions' to the relevant section of which it bears some resemblance; but Lanfranc makes only brief references to the novices and there is virtually no information about what is required of them during the first twelve months.[89] The *Instructio* makes up for this deficiency, at least in some respects, but leaves many questions unanswered. For example, it makes passing references to the obligation to study, but only in naming the times during the day when the novices were required to go with their books to the west side of the cloister; there, seated on their bench [*forma*], they could easily be observed and any questionable behaviour reported.[90]

---

[84] Thompson, *Customary of St Augustine*, 407.

[85] Ibid., 409 and 402.

[86] Pantin, *Black Monk Chapters*, i, 73–4; these requirements were stated in the 1277 statutes, and they were reaffirmed in the statutes of 1343 after the publication of the constitutions of Pope Benedict XII in the bull *Summa Magistri*, ibid., ii, 50. See also Thompson, *Customary of St Augustine*, 420.

[87] Wynchepe is not known to have been a novice master, but he served as chamberlain and sacrist before being sent to Dover as prior in 1268; see *BRECP*, 331.

[88] This manuscript is now Cambridge, Corpus Christi College 441 where the *Instructio* occurs on 360–91 (paginated in red by Archbishop Parker). In the Eastry catalogue (James, *ALCD*) item no. 1420 can be recognized as this manuscript of which the contents remain virtually identical to the list entered by the monk compiler of the catalogue. See footnote 72 above.

[89] Lanfranc, *Monastic Constitutions*, liii. Lanfranc had confined his directions with regard to novices to three paragraphs, ibid., 156–8. See also ibid., 212–20.

[90] Cambridge, Corpus Christi College MS 441, p. 385. The Eastry catalogue records two copies: James, *ALCD*, item nos 1352 and 1420 (pp. 115, 121). There would almost certainly have been a

The Christ Church *Instructio* and the St Augustine's treatise follow a similar arrangement in introducing the newly clothed novices to the daily regimen, first showing them their allotted places in choir, dormitory, and refectory and explaining the correct comportment and gestures that were relevant to each. Both sets of instructions next proceed to go through the horarium for ferial (ordinary) days and for festal days, together with an explanation of the changes that occur to mark the seasons of the liturgical year.[91] Further instruction in these liturgical and other observances would continue during the course of the year while the novices were acquiring familiarity with the complexities of ceremonial variations as they actually occurred. Both the sweetness and the severity of the Rule are made clear as are the necessity of the discipline of outward conformity in gesture, word, and act accompanied by prompt obedience to every command; only in this way would the young monk attain to an inward spirit of humility and mutual love grounded in the monastic zeal of St Benedict.[92] This spirit was nourished by the frequent homilies and daily readings in the chapter house which was described as the 'refectory of the soul', where the 'bread' shared was the '*verbum vitae*' and where 'dominus nobiscum loquitur, instruit, docet, corripit, arguit et castigit et punit'.[93] In order to deepen his understanding of this 'word of life' the novice had much to learn: prayer and meditation to enlarge his spiritual capacity and study to enlighten his intellect.

An extract from what appears to have been an Ely customary with instructions for novices occurs in a collection of miscellaneous tracts possibly bound together by Robert Wells (alias Steward), the last prior of Ely and first dean of the new foundation. The quire in which they occur, in what is now Lambeth Palace Library MS 448, also contains two folios describing monastic sign language and the list of clothing and equipment required by the novice at the time of admission.[94] Comprising seven folios the quire is written in an early to mid-fifteenth-century secretary hand, and may have been copied from a lost Ely customary or from later extracts. The fact that it has features in common with the Christ Church and general chapter directives suggests that all three may have ultimately been derived from a common source. However, the Ely fragment introduces a few homely details that breathe life into the novices' routine. Ely novices were also assigned places for study [*sedilia*] in the western walk of the cloister where, after the conventual mass, they were allowed to converse, but only about matters concerning the Rule and the monastic observances [of the house]. At meal times in the refectory they were to

---

supplement to the *Instructio* outlining a study programme for the use of novice masters at Christ Church but possibly only in notebook form.

[91] Thompson, *Customary of St Augustine*, 409–20; Instructio, caps 12–16, 26–36, 49, and on 386–7 (where the chapter numbering breaks down).

[92] *RB*, the final chapter [72]: 'De bono zelo quod debent monachi habere'.

[93] Instructio, chapter 23: 'De capitulo et de hiis qui ibidem fiunt', 371–4.

[94] LPL MS 448, fos 100–6v of which two folios are numbered 101. These signs have been translated and edited by David Sherlock, *Signs for Silence: The Sign Language of the Monks of Ely in the Middle Ages* (Ely Cathedral Publications, Ely, 1992). A brief account of the profession ceremony is found on fo 103. The Eastry catalogue at Canterbury, *ALCD* no. 1352 (p. 115), includes an *Instructio signorum monasticorum* which has not survived.

make use of table napkins to avoid soiling their habits, and at bedtime before settling down to sleep they were to sit on their beds and say a paternoster and an ave.[95] Juniors are distinguished from the novices in being assigned certain duties such as the distribution of psalters among the group of novices waiting at their *sedilia* for the bell calling the community to vespers.[96] At certain times during the day the novices were occupied with their books at their *sedilia*, and at other times, e.g., before the evening *collatio*, they sat there in contemplation.[97] Towels, which were kept hanging in the dormitory, were brought down to the cloister for the daily washing of feet at the *sedilia*.[98] The Durham novices also pursued their studies in the west walk of the cloister where, by the early fifteenth century and probably earlier, they were allocated wooden 'pewes or carrells' with a desk for their books, in full view of the stall of the novice master who sat opposite them.[99]

In preparing his several volumes on Canterbury College Oxford, Pantin reconstructed in outline the academic programme of study for novices and junior monks in the Christ Church cloister prior to the selection of the most promising among them for higher learning at the university. In so doing he, too, noted that they 'had to go through a double training, [both] religious and scholastic'.[100] After brief comments on the former he proceeded, in line with his purpose, to focus his attention on the latter. In this study, by contrast, the attempt will be made to view the whole monk in whom both the spiritual and the intellectual formation were intended to advance together.

Our aim to preserve this wholeness, however, does not preclude us from making use of the distinction noted by Pantin; indeed, it will be followed here. However, it is important that at the outset we become aware of the intimate connection between the two as demonstrated, for example, in the study of the same texts in two complementary but different ways. Soon after their admission the novices were introduced to the practice of reading and listening to the Scriptures prayerfully;[101] this *lectio divina* was both a public or communal activity and a private occupation. In the lessons heard at Matins (Vigils) and at *Collatio*, which took place between Vespers and Compline, the assembled community listened together while other times during the day were set aside for private reading.[102] The purpose of these

---

[95] LPL MS 448, fo 100v, 101.
[96] Ibid., fo 101v; in 1346/7 the chamberlain contributed 23d. towards the [repair of the] *formulae* of the novices; this probably refers to the *sedilia*, CUL EDC 5/3/7.
[97] LPL MS 448, fo 101 *bis*.
[98] Ibid., this washing was done *honeste*, or modestly, like the removing of clothes in the dormitory at night.
[99] Fowler, *Account Rolls*, i, 225 (almoner, 1416/17), ii, 464 (feretrar, 1423/4); see the description of the carrels in *Rites of Durham*, 83, 84–5. There is also an earlier reference to carrels in Durham MS C.iv.24. The Christ Church novices' school is shown on the west side of the cloister in a plan produced in Collinson, *History of Canterbury Cathedral*, Plan I, xxvi. In Eastry's day there is a reference in CCA DCc Reg. K, fo 220 to a cistern *iuxta schola noviciorum*, which is also shown on the plan. One of Prior Thomas Chillenden's achievements, between 1391–1411, was a *nova schola monachorum*, Sheppard, *Lit. Cant.*, no. 992 (p. 116).
[100] W. A. Pantin, *Canterbury College Oxford*, iv, 53.
[101] *RB*, C.4, 55; C.48 *passim*; the writings of the Fathers would also be included here.
[102] See the remarks in Kardong, *RB*, 384 on *lectio divina* and those in Fry, *RB*, 447. Examples of references in *RB* are C.9, 8 (Matins); C.4, 2 (*Collatio*); C.48, 1 and C.73, 3–5 (private reading).

readings was to nourish the monk's meditation and prayer and enable him to progressively appropriate 'the Word in view of forming his life' by, in and through it.[103] This Word, in order to be taken to heart, must first be imprinted on the mind, that is, memorized. Jean Leclercq has succinctly described the close link between reading, meditation, and memorization, this last being 'what inscribes ... the sacred text in the body and in the soul'.[104]

Devices for training the memory had been in use since classical times in all areas of learning including, for example, the rules of Latin grammar, and the organization of historical data; the technique was also applied to the memorization of the Rule and the psalter, obligatory for novices. Hugh of St Victor maintained that memory was nothing less than the basis of learning; the use of mnemonics, far from our present-day restrictive meaning of rote, furnished its practitioner with an inner storehouse of wisdom, a library of texts, neatly catalogued and indexed, and available for instant use.[105] In the prologue to his *Chronica*, a handbook of historical materials, composed *c.* 1130 for his students embarking on the first stage of scriptural exegesis, Hugh propounded a practical method for acquiring the *ars memorativa*. By way of illustration, he turned to the psalms to show the way to visualize each one by its number and *incipit*.[106] In our eyes the usefulness of this stratagem should have been marked by the widespread circulation of copies, but the evidence to date suggests that this may not have been the case; among the cathedral priories, however, Canterbury, Durham, Rochester, and Worcester are known to have possessed Hugh's *Chronica*.[107] Indeed, his more popular *Didascalicon*, or medieval scholar's guide to the arts,

---

[103] Fry, *RB*, 447.
[104] Quoted in Mary Carruthers, *The Book of Memory: A Study of Memory in Medieval Culture* (Cambridge University Press, Cambridge, 1990), 88 (from Leclercq, *Love of Learning*, 90). It should be noted that the Rule prescribed readings *ex corde recitanda* at the night office and similarly at lauds, *RB*, C.9, 10; C.10, 2 (memoriter); C.12, 4.
[105] Carruthers, ibid., 82, 106–8 and Chap. 3, 80–121 *passim*.
[106] Ibid., 82; the prologue itself, which is entitled *De tribus maximis circumstantiis gestorum*, has been transcribed by Carruthers in Appendix A, *Book of Memory*, 261–6; see note 104 above. In her Appendix C of this book (281–8), she provides a translation of Thomas Bradwardine's *De memoria artificiali* (i.e., on acquiring a trained memory); the only identified copy in Benedictine cloisters was at Durham where it had been copied by Robert Embleton II (*LVD*, iii, C.1096; fl. 1423–48). This manuscript of 'miscellanea' is now Cambridge, Fitzwilliam Museum MS McClean 169. See also Grover Zinn, jr, 'Hugh of St. Victor and the Art of Memory', *Viator* 5 (1974), 211–34. In memorizing the psalms it is almost certain that the novices began by spending some time repeating assigned verses aloud together under supervision, and there can be little doubt that this discipline taught them the correct pronunciation and intonation long before they fully understood the meaning of the words. On this point it is of significance to note that Tibetan monastic teaching today gives memorization a prominent role from the day of admission to the monastery.
[107] The *Reg. Anglie de Libris* lists nine religious houses where it had been located before *c.* 1309; these include Christ Church Canterbury, 247, and it is probably this copy which occurs in item no. 175 of the Eastry catalogue, James, *ALCD*, 36. There was a copy at Durham according to *Cat. Vet. Durham*, in a 1416 list described as *ponitur in claustro*, 109. Twelfth-century Rochester and Worcester copies have recently been identified in British Library MSS Royal 4 B.vii and Cotton Claudius C.ix respectively; see Julian Harrison, 'The English Reception of Hugh of Saint-Victor's *Chronicle*' in *The Electronic British Library Journal* (2002), 1–33 at 2–3.

suggests by inference that mnemonic techniques were widely known and practised.[108]

Academic instruction

In contrast to the strictly monastic and spiritual training, the academic or scholastic instruction given to the novices was in part a continuation of the basic education they had previously received in order to qualify for admission. Nevertheless, these studies were also primarily designed to provide the intellectual skills that would enable them to penetrate more deeply the meaning of the sacred texts: *credo ut intelligam* came first, but it was to be followed by *intelligo ut profundius credam*.[109] Knowledge of the liberal arts was seen as the stepping stone to an understanding of the Scriptures of which grammar formed the foundation. A study of the surviving grammatical manuscripts shows that the medieval definition of grammar extended far beyond the rules governing Latin syntax, the rudiments of which at least had to be mastered prior to admission to the monastery. The purpose of the course in grammar was to teach students 'to write correctly, to pronounce correctly what is written, to understand correctly what is pronounced and to explain or expound what is understood'.[110] In order to achieve this end it therefore included both orthography, concerned with writing and spelling, and prosody, introducing metre and accentuation; the practical aspect of the latter was of particular significance when applied to pronouncing correctly the words and phrases constantly chanted or intoned in the performance of the divine office. Although the 1337 Constitutions of Benedict XII prescribed instruction in grammar, logic, and philosophy for cathedral priories and all Black Monk houses in England, Pantin expressed doubts that Canterbury monks were taught anything more than grammar in the Christ Church cloister; it was surely due to the lack of explicit evidence that he thought logic and philosophy were reserved for the select few who were sent up to Oxford.[111] This conclusion fails to take into account the presence, among the library volumes in the cathedral cloisters, of grammatical texts that speculated on

---

[108] Chap. 11 of Book 3, entitled *De memoria*, urges the student 'in omni doctrina breve aliquid et certum colligere, quod in arcula memoriae recordatur, unde postmodum, cum res exigit, reliqua deriventur', *Hugonis de Sancto Victore Didascalicon De Studio Legendi: A Critical Text*, ed. C. H. Buttimer (Catholic University of America Studies in Medieval and Renaissance Latin no. 10, Washington, 1939), 60–1. See also Carruthers, *Book of Memory*, 92, and Jerome Taylor's English translation: *The Didascalicon of Hugh of St. Victor* (Columbia University Press, London and New York, 1961), 93–4, 120.

[109] St Anselm's phrase is in chapter 1 of his *Proslogion*, vol. 1, p. 100 in *S. Anselmi Archiepiscopi Opera Omnia*, ed. F. S. Schmitt, 6 vols (Edinburgh, 1946–61); the second phrase is my own addition.

[110] 'Recte scribere, recte scripta pronunciare, recte pronunciata intelligere, intellecta exponere', quoted in J. N. Miner, *The Grammar Schools of Medieval England: A. F. Leach in Historiographical Perspective* (McGill-Queen's University Press, Montreal, 1990), 151, from BL MS Harley 5751, fo 246v.

[111] Wilkins, *Concilia*, ii, C.7, 594. Pantin, *Canterbury College Oxford*, iv, 54–5. It must be admitted that although a monastic visitor was expected to inquire whether or not the young monks were being taught grammar, logic, and philosophy we have next to no information as to the answer to the question or if, indeed, it was actually asked; see Pantin, *Black Monk Chapters*, ii, 82, 84 where the date when these visitation articles were drawn up is given as *c*. 1363.

the nature of grammar itself by raising logical and metaphysical questions. During most, or perhaps all, of the first year, the novices' physical and mental energies were expended in acquiring familiarity with the monastic horarium and in applying themselves to the task of learning the prescribed texts.[112] While the whole of Compline, the final office of the day, was normally recited from memory and during the winter months took place after darkness had fallen, at Ely an episcopal ordinance of 1300 commanded the provision of books and candles in choir for the novices so that they could take part before they had become word perfect in the recitation of the psalms and prayers.[113]

Prescribed texts

About half a century later, also at Ely, three novices presented a petition to the prior or, perhaps, the novice master. From his reply we may infer that it probably contained their request to be admitted as full members of the chapter, which usually took place towards the end of the year of probation.[114] The reply, headed *Exortacio facienda Noviciis post petitionem*, cites short passages from a number of authorities, for which accurate references are supplied in the text; these quotations may have been derived from a reading list prescribed for use in the novitiate some of whose contents, by this time, would have been introduced to the novices. These books are the Rule, the Old and New Testaments, St Ambrose's commentary on Luke, Gregory the Great's *Moralia in Job*, Bernard of Clairvaux's *De praecepto et dispensatione*, Hugh of St Victor's *De institutione noviciorum* and probably his *De beatae Mariae virginitate*, and Hugh de Folieto's *De claustro animae*; there are also three references to canon law, two of which quote the *Liber extra de statu monachorum*. The only surviving medieval library catalogue compiled for novices in the cathedral priories comes from Durham and is dated 1395. Comparison with the Ely list of references shows that both included the Rule, Bernard's *De praecepto*, and Hugh of St Victor's *De institutione*.[115]

Taking these few titles at Durham and Ely as required texts for novices we will proceed by checking for copies in the other cathedral monasteries and taking note of any treatises bound with them in the same volume on the grounds that their physical proximity may be indicative of a common purpose. Let us begin with the Rule, the cornerstone of Benedictine monasticism and the day-to-day handbook for the individual monk. For this reason, although no copy of the Rule survives from Bath cathedral priory, there must have been at least several available to supply the needs of the twenty-five or so monks in the community before the Black Death. However, in light of the fact that all but a dozen volumes once belonging to this

---

[112] See above, 64–6.
[113] Evans, *Ely Chapter Ordinances*, 7; the elderly monks who had forgotten the words were also included in this dispensation. A statute was issued by the general chapter of the Black Monks in 1343 ordering the distribution of candles at the night office (matins) to the *indigentibus* so that the chanting *plenius atque melius decantetur*, Pantin, *Black Monk Chapters*, ii, 35.
[114] CUL EDC 1B/6.
[115] *Cat. Vet. Durham*, 81–2.

house have disappeared, the loss of the Rule is hardly surprising.[116] Among the seventy volumes so far identified as having belonged to St Swithun's no copy of the Rule has been found. St Mary's Coventry, however, with a survival rate in books and book catalogues only slightly higher than that of Bath, does include the record of one copy in a mid-thirteenth-century list of thirty-three titles; all of these were copied by John de Bruges, possibly a precentor/librarian, but they have subsequently been lost.[117] Only a single copy is known to have belonged to Norwich priory—the one that still survives—despite the fact that, with its satellite cells, it was the largest community after Durham and Canterbury.[118] The monks of St Etheldreda's possessed a well-worn, late twelfth-century text of the Rule annotated in the margins by a variety of hands, one of which warns the reader that 'obedientia est melior quam virtutes'.[119] This is a composite volume in which eighteen booklets and treatises on diverse subjects were bound together.[120] A single copy of the Rule is recorded in an early twelfth-century catalogue of Rochester books but there are no known copies extant.[121] The earliest surviving text of the Rule in England belonged to the monks of Worcester; written in Latin it dates from the eighth century.[122] A second copy dated some three centuries later is in Anglo-Saxon with a Latin gloss.[123] Most of these copies of the Rule, including the one in the Durham novices' book cupboard and the Ely copy, formed only part of a volume; at some point of time they were united with other treatises and booklets for reasons which will be discussed below.[124]

For Christ Church and St Cuthbert's there is a fortunate conjunction of surviving texts and medieval book catalogues that enable us to form a more complete picture of the contents of these libraries than of those in the other cathedral monasteries. At Canterbury it is clear that multiple copies of the Rule were the norm, and the current depleted figures arising from the vagaries of more substantial loss and destruction elsewhere must not be allowed to influence and distort our judgement. Five copies of the Rule from Canterbury survive, dating from the eleventh to the sixteenth century.[125] Some fifteen copies (one of these in English) are listed in the library catalogue compiled under Prior Eastry in the early

---

[116] The *Reg. Anglie de Libris* lists nineteen titles from Bath (no. xiii, 317–18) and Leland noted only six in the 1530s, Sharpe, *EBL*, at B8.

[117] The list is in Sharpe, *EBL*, at B23, where the Rule is item 9.

[118] Now CUL MS Kk.3.26, fos 135v–146v (coll. 491–536).

[119] Oxford, Bodley Laud misc. 112, fos 92v–103; the added quotation is on fo 94. I am indebted to Michael Gullick for examining this manuscript at my request; he judges that it has probably existed more or less in its present form since the time of Prior Robert de (Longchamp) Ely, *c.* 1194–7.

[120] The name Robert Steward [Wells] is on fo 432v, at the end of the volume and Archbishop Laud's hand is on fo 1v.

[121] Sharpe, *EBL*, at B77.71.

[122] Now Oxford, Bodley MS Hatton 48. The facsimile edition of the Rule based on this manuscript is vol. 15 in the series *Early English Manuscripts in Facsimile*, ed. D. H. Farmer (Rosenkilde & Bagger, Copenhagen, 1968). It has been associated with Worcester since at least the late eleventh century.

[123] Now Cambridge, Corpus Christi College MS 178.

[124] See below 75–6.

[125] These are BL MSS Royal 7 E.vi (fos 574–93), Cotton Tiberius A.iii, Arundel 68; Oxford, Bodley MS Lyell 19; LPL MS 20 (abbreviated version).

fourteenth century; this number would have been sufficient to supply the text of the Rule to each of the five or six novices who were in the process of memorizing it and there would have been another ten copies available for use by the remaining sixty or sixty-five members of the community.[126]

Surviving Durham copies number six, four of which remain *in situ*. Both the Latin and the Anglo-Saxon texts of the Rule are found in Durham Cathedral MS B. IV.24, a late eleventh/early twelfth-century manuscript in which the Latin version is so well-thumbed and marked by notations in the margin that it may have been at one time the copy used for the daily readings in chapter; bound with it were a martyrology and the customs of Canterbury, no doubt those of Lanfranc.[127] According to an inventory of 1391/2 it was then kept in the *communi armariolo* in the Spendement, a small storeroom on the west side of the west cloister walk close to the novices' carrels.[128] Durham Cathedral MS B.III.8 contains a late fourteenth/early fifteenth-century copy of the Rule; MSS B.IV.26 and B.IV.41 of approximately similar date include the text with an alphabetical index. Cambridge, Jesus College MS 61 is the fifth copy and is dated *c.* 1400; in addition Jesus College MS 41 contains an imperfect fifteenth-century copy. In the novices' book cupboard at Durham there was also a *tabula* to the Rule in addition to the Rule itself but in a separate volume; both of these, the *tabula* and the Rule, were bound with other treatises and have subsequently been lost.[129] Among the items under the heading *Cronicae* in a 1416/17 book catalogue occurs a volume of which the description suggests that it was similar to Durham Cathedral MS B.IV.24 in having two texts of the Rule, Latin and Anglo-Saxon, along with other treatises which appear to be the same in both the medieval catalogue and Rud's *Codices . . . Dunelmensis*; in 1416/17 it was in the hands of the prior.[130] The fact that, in comparison with the Canterbury catalogue of Prior Eastry, the Rule is less well represented in the Durham medieval catalogues may seem surprising since the element of post-dissolution loss is not such a significant factor that has to be taken into account here. How copies of the Rule were distributed and shared among Benedictine novices remains ultimately uncertain; memorization may have been facilitated by vocal repetition in concert

---

[126] In James, *ALCD*, the item nos are 291, 292, 294, 540, 542, 720, 1039, 1300, 1514, 1579, 1603, 1606, 1634, 1683; it is of course possible, and even probable, that of these items some survive among the seven named in the previous note, but there is insufficient evidence to identify them. The numbers of monks and novices *c.* 1330 derive from the chamberlain's account, CCA DCc chamberlain, nos 24 and 25.

[127] R. A. B. Mynors, *Durham Cathedral Manuscripts to the End of the Twelfth Century* (Oxford University Press, Oxford, 1939), 44; it was one of the many volumes bequeathed to the cathedral priory by Bishop William de St Carilef (d. 1096).

[128] *Cat. Vet. Durham*, 30; it is listed among the books in the section *Cronicae*.

[129] Ibid., 81, 82; the *tabula* would have been some sort of index, perhaps no more than a list of chapter titles. Two of these manuscripts are missing from the list of Durham manuscripts in the facsimile edition of the Rule (note 122 above), 27–8, which was limited to those of English origin and provenance; MSS B.III.8 and B.IV.41 must have been judged to have been produced abroad.

[130] *Cat. Vet. Durham*, 107A^2; although the initial words on the second folio of each differ, in the later 1416/17 entry these words have been struck out, thus suggesting that they had been written in error. The prior was probably John Wessington, who was elected in November 1416.

as well as by individual study, but some method of sharing must have been in operation.

Some of the treatises that were often found with the Rule were undoubtedly intended for the instruction of novices in their introductory year of monastic life; the text of the Rule assigned to the Durham novices, for example, was bound with Hugh of St Victor's *De institutione noviciorum* and St Bernard's *De praecepto et dispensatione*, both of which we have already noted at Ely. These two popular works were written some time before the middle of the twelfth century, the former for Augustinian novices at St Victor in Paris where Hugh was master of the abbey school and the latter by the Cistercian abbot of Clairvaux (d. 1153) at the request of two Benedictine monks of Chartres.[131] Both treatises came to be highly regarded by novice masters because they were recognized as practical, introductory guides for those who had left the world to set out on the way of perfection, *ad perfectionem conversationis*, by means of which they were led to expect that they would arrive ultimately *ad celsitudinem perfectionis*.[132] In strict accord with the teaching of St Benedict, encapsulated in these two phrases from the final chapter of the Rule, it was made clear to the novices that conversion (*conversatio*) was an ongoing process to be learned through unceasing self-discipline in gesture, speech, and act which, as Hugh explains, produces the fruit of virtue and humility. Bernard stresses stability within the cloister and obedience to the abbot or superior, but at the same time he defines in some detail the limits of obedience and the circumstances under which the monk would cease to be bound by his promise made on the day of his profession.[133]

These were not by any means the only instruction manuals for beginners in monastic life, but the cathedral priories' medieval library catalogues and the volumes that still survive combine to imply that they were the two most often prescribed formative texts.[134] Either with or without the Rule the presence of one or both of them should be noted in manuscripts consisting of an apparently miscellaneous collection of treatises bound together. In some cases, if the binding predates the dissolution, there may be fairly convincing reasons to consider this 'miscellany' as a compilation of reading material deliberately selected for use in the novitiate. One of the volumes in the Durham novices' book cupboard may be taken as a model to demonstrate the possible range of preferred choices found with the

---

[131] Record of the novices' Durham copy is in *Cat. Vet. Durham*, 82K. The text of the *De institutione* has been printed in *PL*, 176, cols 925–52. No less than 27 variations in the title of this work are given in R. Goy, *Die Überlieferung der Werke Hugos von St. Viktor* (Hiersemann, Stuttgart, 1976), 340–1; some of the more common listed are *De instructione novitiorum, De informatione novitiorum, Speculum monasticae disciplinae*. Jean Leclercq and H. M. Rochais have edited vol. 3 of *S. Bernardi Opera* (Rome, 1963) in which the *De praecepto* may be found, 253–94.

[132] *RB*, C.73, 2.

[133] The two treatises also occur with the Rule in James, *ALCD*, the Eastry catalogue, item nos 542 and 1063 (Canterbury).

[134] By way of comparison and in order to stress that our knowledge is dependent on the chance survival of evidence, it should be noted that a fifteenth-century catalogue of selected authors in the library of St Mary's Abbey, York, had six copies of the *De praecepto* and ten of *De institutione*. Of the monastic cathedrals only Canterbury and Durham are known to have had multiple copies and there is no extant record of any copies of either at Bath and Winchester.

Rule. In addition to two indexes (*tabulae*), one to the Rule and another to the *De praecepto*, there were about a dozen items including the following:[135] an exposition on the Lord's prayer; a tract on confession; Uthred de Boldon's *De substantialibus regulae monachalis*;[136] *Abbas vel prior*, which was an exposition and commentary on monastic law and discipline in the light of the papal reforms implemented by the constitutions of the 1330s;[137] several sermons of St Bernard on the compassion of Christ and the compassion of the Virgin Mary; Richard of Wetheringsett's *Summa* of ecclesiastical discipline;[138] and an imperfect text of the Constitutions of Otto.[139]

Recommended reading material

These items may be loosely classified within the following categories: works on prayer and the spiritual life of the cloister, on monastic discipline and profession, on the faith and teaching of the Church, and on papal legislation pertaining to Benedictines along with statutes issued by the English provincial and general chapters of the Black Monks. Either with or without the Rule these texts, one or more of them, frequently appear in volumes which on first sight seem to be merely a miscellaneous collection of treatises bound together for no obvious reason. In at least some cases, however, there are fairly persuasive if not completely convincing reasons to consider them as collections incorporating reading and reference material compiled for the use of novice masters and novices. An examination of several potential candidates for this category among the many composite manuscripts formerly held by the cathedral priories should serve to strengthen this hypothesis.

Since the compilers of both the Eastry and Durham catalogues have kindly itemized the contents of many of the volumes listed it is not difficult to pick out several examples from those that appear to have miscellaneous contents. Eastry item number 1579 is one of these in that it includes the Rule, the *De institutione* of Hugh, meditations of Bernard, an exposition of the Lord's prayer, an anonymous treatise on the sacraments, and another entitled *Questiones de theologia*.[140] Number 1576, which lacks both the *De institutione* and Bernard's *De praecepto*, contains a *Tractatus super regulam beati Benedicti* together with some fundamental teachings essential for newcomers to the monastic life; these comprise explanatory treatises

---

[135] *Cat. Vet. Durham*, 82K.

[136] This treatise goes by a variety of titles; in the list here it is *De professione monachorum* but the inclusion of the incipit 'Novicio inquirenti' resolves any doubt that it might have been John de Beverley's *De professione monachorum*.

[137] This treatise probably comes from the pen of a Durham monk who may well be Uthred himself; see Pantin, *Black Monk Chapters*, ii, xviii and Sharpe, *Latin Writers*, 699.

[138] Other titles used are 'Speculum ecclesiasticorum', Summa theologiae de symbolo de officio sacerdotum'; its incipit by which it is also often known is 'Qui bene presunt [presbyteri]'.

[139] That is, the constitutions of the papal legate, Otto (1238) directed to the reform of the English Black Monks; these were reported in detail by Matthew Paris in *Chronica Majora*, iii, 499–517. One further item bound in this composite volume and entitled *Sinonoma* is almost certainly the work of Isidore of Seville, *Synonyma de lamentatione animae peccatricis*, the description of the spiritual journey from despair to hope through repentance and amendment of life. The printed text is in Isidore Hispaniensis, *Opera Omnia*, ed. F. Arevalo, vol. 6 (Rome, 1802), 472–523.

[140] James, *ALCD*, 131.

on the ten commandments, the creed, the Lord's prayer, the virtues, and several incentives to true repentance in the form of a commentary on the psalm *Miserere mei domine*, Pope Innocent III's *De miseria hominis* [*sic*] and a questionnaire used in preparing for confession.[141] Another, item number 542, has some twenty titles in addition to the Rule, the *De praecepto* and the *De institutione*; these include a *De professione monachorum* possibly by the Dominican William Peraldus, the *Institutio [Instructio] noviciorum secundum consuetudinem Cantuar. Ecclesiae*, meditations attributed to Bernard, the *De cognitione verae vitae* by Honorius Augustodunensis (here attributed to Augustine), sermons of which one was on the passion of Christ, and Richard Praemonstratensis on the canon of the mass.[142] Finally, there can be no doubt that one volume at Christ Church had been compiled for use in the novitiate, namely item number 1300, which had only four items: the Rule, an unattributed *De professione monachorum*, and two sets of rubrics, one 'De usu divini officii in ecclesia Cantuar.', and the other 'De sonitu et consuetudinibus Cantuar. Ecclesiae'.[143] There is one surviving Christ Church manuscript from the second half of the fourteenth century which may also have been among those recommended for use in the novitiate because it, too, was a compilation of instructive texts. Now Cambridge, Corpus Christi College MS 137, the contents include the popular commentary on the Rule by Bernard Aiglerius, abbot of Monte Cassino (d. 1282), expositions of the Lord's prayer, and the Salve Regina, homilies addressed to monks by 'Eusebius Gallicanus' and two treatises of Hugh of St Victor, one being the *De instructione noviciorum*.[144] Also bound in this volume is a well-worn copy of the anonymous *Philosophia monachorum* which portrays the life of charity enjoyed by religious in the cloister in stark contrast to the life of misery and sin persistently afflicting men in the world; it urges the renunciation of ambition to excel in acquiring knowledge of the schools in favour of learning the divine wisdom which indwells the heart.[145]

[141] James, *ALCD*, 130–1. The treatise on the Rule may have been by Aelmer, although this was described as a *Sermo super regulam beati Benedicti* in item no. 253 of the same catalogue; it has not survived. See Sharpe, *Latin Writers*, 27, for the explanation concerning its probably mistaken ascription to Eadmer. The *Miserere mei, Domine* is most likely to be Psalm 50, in which for 'Dominus' read 'Deus'; it is one of the seven penitential psalms. There were also unidentified sermons in this volume and a work attributed to Bernard with the title *De moribus et vita honesta*.

[142] James, *ALCD*, 66. There was also a treatise concerning Thomas Becket and another entitled *De divinis scripturis* attributed to Anselm. The *De professione monachorum* has several other earlier attributions, namely Roger of Caen, Alexander Nequam, and Anselm of Bec and Canterbury; see Sharpe, *Latin Writers*, 584. John de Beverley's treatise by the same or a similar title was composed too late for it to have been in the Eastry catalogue.

[143] James, *ALCD*, 112.

[144] The conjectural identity of 'Eusebius Gallicanus' is discussed in F. L. Cross and E. A. Livingstone (eds), *The Oxford Dictionary of the Christian Church* (3rd edn, Oxford University Press, Oxford, 1997), 574–5. Hugh of St Victor's *De instructione noviciorum* is here given one of its many variations of title: *De disciplina clericorum*.

[145] The theme of human misery and its remedies was dwelt upon at length by many medieval writers, including Pope Innocent III in his widely read *De miseria humanae conditionis*. Jean Leclercq has commented at length on this, the only known copy of the *Philosophia monachorum*, in his 'Études sur le vocabulaire monastique du moyen âge' in *Studia Anselmiana* 48 (Rome, 1968), 145–50; he includes extracts from this Christ Church manuscript, now Cambridge, Corpus Christi College MS

Dover priory's dependence on Christ Church was, in most respects, less than that of the Durham and Norwich cells, and one sphere which enjoyed autonomy was its library. It did not rely on the cathedral to supply its literary needs but operated independently and, by 1389, it had built up an impressive collection of more than 400 volumes. In that year the precentor, John Whytefeld, compiled a catalogue of 'precocious sophistication and astonishing detail'.[146] Its fortunate survival enables us to pinpoint a section in which at least five volumes can be identified as intended for novices; all contained the Rule and one or both of Bernard's *De praecepto* and Hugh of St Victor's *De instructione* along with other items such as Hugh de Folieto's *De claustro animae*, William Peraldus's *De professione monachorum*, *Signa monachorum Dovorre*, *Norma professionis monachorum Dovorre*, and *Decreta concernentia ordinem monachorum*. Another volume in this same section of the catalogue is the *Formula noviciorum* of David of Augsburg, a fourteenth-century Franciscan friar.[147]

It is clear that the Durham novices were not restricted to the study of the few books recorded in the 1395 inventory of their cloister book cupboard. Other books were listed as on loan to them from the Spendement collection: for example, in 1416 to one novice a volume in which Smaragdus's *Diadema monachorum*, Augustine's *De vita et moribus clericorum* and *Collationes abbatum* were bound together; in the same inventory, to another novice, the [*Soliloquium*] *de arta animae* of Hugh of St Victor and a *De fide, spe et caritate* also attributed to Hugh; to a third, Hugh de Folieto's *De claustro animae*.[148] All of these works can be described as in the category of spiritual reading appropriate for beginners in the religious life, and copies are known to have been held by most, probably all, of the cathedral priories. There was also at Durham one composite volume no longer extant whose contents, itemized in the 1395 inventory of the *communi armariolo*, suggest that it would have been very profitable for novice reading. It consisted of Hugh of St Victor's *De informatione* [*sic*] *noviciorum* and Bernard's *De praecepto et dispensatione*, Hugh de Folieto's *De claustro animae*, a treatise *De professione monachorum*, probably the one by the Durham monk John de Beverley (d. 1349), letters [*epistolae*] by Bernard and Jerome, sermons to monks by 'Eusebius Gallicanus', and the *Diadema monachorum* of Smaragdus.[149]

Several of the surviving manuscript compilations would also have provided instruction and spiritual nourishment for the probationary year Durham novices.

---

137. It shows, he says, the continuity of monastic tradition in its frequent citations from patristic writings, with little attempt at originality for which there was felt to be no need.

[146] Stoneman, *Dover Priory*, vi.

[147] Ibid., items 206a–209e, 212, pp. 109–10; Peraldus's treatise is here entitled *Tractatus super regula monachorum*. Item 214 is the *Formula noviciorum* of David of Augsburg. Only a few copies have been found in English Benedictine monasteries, Durham being one of them.

[148] *Cat. Vet. Durham*, 95I, 97C; the spendement or treasury was situated near the north-west corner of the cloister under the dormitory. The *Collationes abbatum* were probably the sayings of the desert fathers, i.e. the *Collationes patrum* recommended by St Benedict in *RB*, C.73, 5. More details of the novices' books and studies are given by Piper, 'The Libraries of the Monks of Durham', 232.

[149] *Cat. Vet. Durham*, 70G where the *De informatione noviciorum* is ascribed to the wrong Hugh and the sermons of 'Eusebius Gallicanus' are ascribed to Caesarius of Arles.

Some of the writings to which they were introduced were in-house products, composed by two members of their own community whose combined careers spanned the greater part of the fourteenth century; these were John de Beverley, who was active in the 1330s and 1340s, and Uthred de Boldon, who died in 1397 after more than fifty years in the monastery. Both men championed the cause of defending and promoting the Benedictine form of monasticism in response to two contemporary problems: the competing attraction of the mendicant orders and the increasing threat of heresy that had been aggravated by John Wyclif's attacks on ecclesiastical and clerical orthodoxy. Both men served as priors of Durham college and both played an influential role in the triennial Black Monk chapters, John de Beverley between 1338 and 1343 and Uthred in the 1360s.[150] One form of response to the challenge from other orders lay in demonstrating 'the antiquity, sanctity, and dignity of Benedictine monasticism and its services to the Church and to learning'.[151] These circumstances also brought home the periodic need for self-examination, that is for the reinterpretation and reassessment of the essentials of monastic life in order to convince the contemporary generation of its intrinsic value and continuing relevance. With such thoughts in mind John de Beverley wrote a commentary on the Rule which, alas, has not survived; nor, surprisingly, has it been recorded in any of the medieval Durham book catalogues.[152] Testimony to John's concern for the novices lies in his tract *De professione monachorum* of which there are two remaining copies in Durham manuscripts.[153] With frequent reference to Bernard's *De praecepto* this short composition makes amply clear the penalties of breaking the profession promises of obedience, stability, and *convers[at]io morum* and spells out the extent and limits of obedience.[154]

Uthred was a prolific writer on a variety of themes several of which were informative for novices; the *De substantialibus regulae monachalis*, for instance, begins with the words *Novicio inquirenti*.[155] It then proceeds to demonstrate at some length the 'origin and lawfulness of the monastic life' by identifying its presence in the prophets of the Old Testament, in Christ and the Apostles in the New Testament, and in the early Church before the time of St Benedict. The *substantialia* of the 'monastic life' as envisaged by Uthred are continence, abdication of material possessions, and obedience, to all of which every man is naturally subject in varying degrees according to circumstance, status, and so on. St Benedict's profession promise introduced a distinctive form of obedience 'according to

---

[150] The careers of both monks are summarized in *BRUO*, i, 183, 212–13, and *LVD*, iii, C.838, C.888.

[151] Pantin, 'Origins of Monasticism', 189.

[152] Its existence is known through several references, e. g., by Uthred in *De substantialibus regulae monachalis* (DCL MS B.IV.34, fo 80). Richard de Wallingford, abbot of St Albans (1327–36), also wrote a commentary on the Rule which has been lost; see Sharpe, *Latin Writers*, 518.

[153] DCL MS B.III.30, fos 42–43v; BL Add MS 6162, fos 42–4.

[154] The title listed in Rud's *Codices...Dunelmensis* was *De declaratione professionis nigrorum monachorum*, 172. There is also in this work a reference to Abbot Richard de Wallingford's prologue to the lost Rule of St Benedict.

[155] It is to be found in DCL MS B.IV.34, fos 80–96v, and is listed in the 1395 inventory of books, *Cat. Vet. Durham*, 71F with his *De perfectione vivendi*.

the Rule of St Benedict' as the basis of his ordering of monastic life directed toward a more perfect observance of the law of Christ. The treatise is cast in a dialectical framework by means of argument, counter-argument and resolution. It is probable that it had only a limited circulation since few copies seem to have survived, and among the other cathedral priories only Norwich is known to have possessed a copy.[156] A second work of Uthred, the *De perfectione vivendi*, was probably designed as a continuation of the *De substantialibus*.[157] Both are considered by Pantin to be 'an attempt to work out a constructive theory of the religious life' firmly founded in biblical history, and Uthred's aim was to demonstrate that monasticism is 'something deeply rooted in man's nature as a rational being'.[158] The complex development of Uthred's themes in these two texts prompts a question regarding the level of intelligence and understanding of the inquiring young novice to whom it was purportedly addressed; it would surely have required some interpretative commentary on the part of a senior monk or novice master.

A second question arises as to the actual method of presentation of these and of other novice texts in general. When first introducing them to his charges the novice master must have taught them by means of a judicious exposition, probably in the vernacular, adapted to suit their abilities. Only after this initial period of instruction would the texts have been put directly into their hands. With this *mise-en-scène* in place it would be a reasonable assumption to view the selection of treatises in some manuscripts as having been made for a dual purpose: to provide essential source material for the masters and study material for the novices. This conjecture draws attention to a perplexing question with regard to more precise details of the curricular programme: which treatises were on the agenda during the probationary year and which were studied later during the second and third years, after profession? On the basis of the response to the Ely novices' petition for admission to profession a partial answer may be inferred; but there is no indication as to how or when, in practical terms, they actually acquired familiarity with the chosen texts.[159]

At Canterbury most of the evidence relating to manuscripts containing collections that bear upon our present inquiry is, as we have seen, dependent on the entries in the thirteenth-century Eastry catalogue. At Durham it is possible to examine surviving manuscripts, which furnish fuller detail than the itemized lists of contents of Christ Church as the latter are often so concise as to be difficult to interpret with any certainty. In several of the Durham manuscripts it is possible to discern a pattern of choice similar to that identified above at Canterbury and Dover. Thus novice masters appear to have been making similar selections but, a wide range of choice being available, there is some variation. For example, the Durham volume now Tanner MS 4 in the Bodleian Library, Oxford, contains a

---

[156] Sharpe, *Latin Writers,* lists attested copies at St Albans and Bury and notes that the Norwich copy, in Cambridge, Emmanuel College MS 142, is incomplete.
[157] In DCL MSS B.IV.34, fos 93–111 and A.IV.33, fos 116–21; the latter is only an extract.
[158] W. A. Pantin, 'Two Treatises of Uthred of Boldon on the Monastic Life', in R. W. Hunt, W. A. Pantin, and R. W. Southern (eds), *Studies in Medieval History Presented to F. M. Powicke* (Oxford University Press, Oxford, 1948), 363–85 at 382 and 383.
[159] See above 71, for the texts quoted by the novice master.

collection of treatises in thirteenth- and early fourteenth-century hands, including the *Formula noviciorum* of David of Augsburg complete in three books and a *Speculum de utilitate religionis regularis*; other treatises were also incorporated into this collection which may reflect the interests of the monk owner[s] more than the specific needs of the novices. Nevertheless, sermons of which some are attributed to Augustine, a *Flores* (i.e. choice extracts) *Augustini* and portions of biblical and psalm commentaries in this volume would have provided informative and stimulating matter for both teacher and taught.[160]

A second example may be found in MS 41 of Jesus College Cambridge. It is one of several Durham compilations that have been described by Pantin as 'a useful collection of tracts on monastic discipline', bringing together items such as the Rule, St Bernard, *Abbas vel prior*, papal constitutions for Benedictines with provincial chapter statutes, and treatises on monastic origins and hagiology.[161] In this instance fourteenth- and fifteenth-century hands have copied the Rule which is accompanied by a *tabula*, an imperfect *Speculum religiosorum*, that is, a treatise on ecclesiastical discipline and doctrine, several more *tabulae*, one on Bernard's *De praecepto* by Uthred and another on *Abbas vel prior*, also perhaps by Uthred, who may have been the original author of this latter work; the volume also contains the Constitutions of Benedict XII as well as provincial chapter statutes of 1343 and Durham chapter ordinances of 1417. In the light of what has been postulated above, this volume, and possibly others, may have been compiled with a specifically instructional role in mind as a reference for the instructors and, at some appropriate stage, for those being instructed. It would also, of course, have served as a readily accessible reference for general consultation.

The presence of manuscripts with similar contents in the libraries of other cathedral priories suggests that, although novice masters were free to make their own choice of texts for novices, their selection also revolved around similar themes if not identical treatises. A Norwich priory volume, for example, whose binding dates from the middle of the fourteenth century, consists of the Rule together with six other treatises. One of these, which immediately follows the Rule, is the *Tractatus de professione monachorum* of William Peraldus which here lacks both title and author;[162] the other works included are two *Flores* attributed to Augustine and Bernard, a brief *Summa theologiae magistralis* and Richard of St Victor's *De contemplatione*. The *De claustro animae* of Hugh de Folieto and the *Speculum religiosorum* of Peraldus were also available to Norwich monks and novices in two

---

[160] From the binding it would seem that the manuscript is the result of a medieval compilation, but the incomplete state of the biblical commentaries remains unexplained unless the portions were deliberately selected. There is another incomplete copy of the *Formula noviciorum* still in Durham in DCL MS B.IV.42; it is included in a volume that otherwise consists mainly of indexes (*tabulae*) to facilitate the process of tracking down references to the most frequently cited sources such as the Dialogues and Homilies of Pope Gregory the Great, the *Diadema monachorum* of Smaragdus, and writings of Augustine.
[161] Pantin, *Black Monk Chapters*, ii, pp. ix–x, xv, xviii. *Abbas vel prior* is described on 75 above.
[162] Now CUL MS Kk.3.26 The Rule is on fos 135v–46v and the *Tractatus* fos 147–62v (modern numbering); the latter is identified by its incipits to the prologue 'Tractatus iste qui est de professione monachorum, tres habet partes', and to the work 'Cum displiceat domino infidelis . . .'

separate volumes; the former is written in a clear late thirteenth/early fourteenth-century hand with many elongated pointing fingers in the margins and profile sketches of stern monks saying 'nota'; the latter in a hand of similar date has been provided with a *tabula* of subjects arranged alphabetically. Both these treatises are the sole contents of their respective volumes with one, probably both, inscribed with the name of Henry de Lakenham, prior (d. 1310). The *Speculum* has few annotations apart from one in the margin of the prologue which reads: 'Nota in isto capitulo quod monachos nolentes erudiri', perhaps a comment from a frustrated novice master![163] Two of the volumes purchased by Simon Bozoun during his priorate (1344–52), which do not survive, have been tentatively identified as commentaries on the Rule by Bernard of Monte Cassino.[164] If so there were three copies of this work at Norwich in the mid-thirteenth century since Robert de Donewich, a contemporary of Bozoun, possessed a volume which contained Bernard on the Rule, along with copies of the treatises of Folieto and Peraldus named above.[165]

No such collections are in evidence at Worcester, but there are two separate volumes which feature the two best known of the surviving works of the ninth-century Abbot Smaragdus. Both date from the twelfth century; both were continuing to be consulted in the sixteenth century and, presumably, during the time between. Brother Thomas Wulstan noted that he *perlegit* the *Diadema monachorum* in 1529 while he was a young priest monk serving as chaplain to the prior, and brother Roger Neckham D.Th., inserted his name in the commentary on the Rule.[166] Additional evidence of the persistent borrowing of the *Diadema* is provided in a Christ Church list of books sent away for repair in 1508; it included a tenth-century copy which still survives.[167] In fact, five other copies are known to have been in the library collection at Canterbury, four in the Eastry catalogue and another surviving early fourteenth-century copy now in Lambeth Palace Library.[168] The borrowers at Worcester and Canterbury cannot be identified as novices, but a brief perusal of the seventy short chapters of the *Diadema* is sufficient to indicate that the contents would have been valued for the

---

[163] CUL MS Ii.4.35 (Folieto), CUL MS Ii.4.15 (Peraldus). The name Henry de Lakenham has been almost obliterated in the latter manuscript because of the shorn margins and the title appears only as the *Tabula erudicionis religiosorum* at the end; the marginal quotation is on fo 5.

[164] I.e., Bernard Aiglerius (d. 1282); the list of Bozoun's books is in Sharpe, *EBL*, at B58 where the two probable copies of Bernard are items 12 and 16.

[165] CUL MS Kk.2.21; for Donewich see *BRECP*, 501–2.

[166] The *Diadema* takes up the whole of BL MS Royal 8 D.xiii and contains the inscription of three other sixteenth-century monks' names in addition to Wulstan; Oxford, Bodley MS Hatton 40 consists entirely of Smaragdus's commentary where Neckham's name appears on fos 62 and 164v. For these two monks see *BRECP*, 896, 855–6.

[167] This early copy is now CUL MS Ff.4.43 and must surely be either item no. 118 or no. 1721 in the Eastry catalogue, James, *ALCD*, 30 or 139 respectively; it was sent for repair by William Ingram, who identified it by the second folio, ibid., no. 268 (p. 162). For the monk Ingram see *BRECP*, 209 (William Ingram I).

[168] The other copies in the Eastry catalogue are item nos 54, 1170, and 1343, ibid., 22, 104, and 114 respectively; the Lambeth copy is LPL MS 180 and could be one of the three listed immediately above.

clear and direct exposition of topics beginning with prayer which, the author stresses, is foremost in importance. In the second chapter, *De disciplina psallendi*, he describes the virtuous monks in choir 'non solum voce, sed corde psallentes'.[169] Succeeding chapters on obedience, penitence, confession, the virtues, love of God and neighbour, and the contemplative life confirm that it was a handbook of spiritual teaching which could survive the test of time and remain applicable at all stages of monastic life, to instruct and inspire the young and to refresh and invigorate the jaded. The presence of copies of the *Diadema* also at Durham, Rochester, and Winchester provide further evidence of the esteem in which Smaragdus's teaching continued to be held, at least within the cathedral priories.[170]

Among the comparatively small number of manuscripts known to have belonged to the Ely monks there is one which survives as an apparently miscellaneous jumble of some twenty-eight items, many of them short and incomplete or fragmentary. The attempt to disentangle why and when the contents were bound together may never be successful but, in light of the evidence presented above from other miscellanies, it takes only a slight stretch of the imagination to see a possible motive in amassing some of the collection especially if a novice master had been responsible. We find in this volume the Rule, amplified by many marginal annotations in a variety of hands; there are also spiritual treatises and meditations by Augustine and Bernard, treatises on penitence, a short exposition on the Lord's prayer and several items for reference purposes including the biblical *Distinctiones* of Peter Cantor (d. 1197) and an elementary grammatical treatise by the English Augustinian Alexander Nequam (d. 1217).[171] The presence of the textbook on grammar introduces a question concerning the amount of time devoted to teaching this subject in addition to the strenuous schedule set before the first-year novices during the course of their monastic and spiritual formation.[172] One may assume that growth in knowledge of Latin vocabulary and in solving the complexities of grammatical construction, together with a certain amount of biblical exposition especially of the psalms, would have been given some place in the timetable. Again, it must not be forgotten that within the study programme musical training played a significant role. Lengthy periods of frequent practice would have been required to ensure that the chants for mass and office were performed not only with due reverence and devotion but also as perfectly as the musical talents within the community could be trained to achieve. The lament of a novice monk that survives in a Norwich manuscript dramatically expresses the difficulties that he, and no

---

[169] *PL*, 102, cols 593–690; the quotation is found in col. 596.

[170] There are two Durham copies, one in a list in *Cat. Vet. Durham*, 70D dated 1395, and the other survives as DCL MS B.II.33 (early thirteenth century). The Winchester *Diadema* is written in a late twelfth-century hand and is in a volume also containing *Vitas patrum*; until recently it was Winchester College MS 18, but is now housed in Winchester Cathedral. There was one copy at Rochester according to the early twelfth-century catalogue, Sharpe, *EBL*, at B77.61.

[171] This manuscript is now Oxford, Bodley MS Laud misc. 112. See note 119 above.

[172] It must not be forgotten that everyday use of the monastic sign language was another skill to be acquired during the formative year. At Ely this consisted of some ninety different gestures; see note 94 above which also provides details of the Christ Church book *Instructio signorum monasticorum*.

doubt others, were experiencing in learning to follow written notation in the mid-fourteenth century.[173]

We also need to make room for the times allocated to the novices for recreation, generally within the monastic enclosure and the gardens inside the precinct during the first year. Periodic bloodletting, or flebotomy, would also have interrupted the regular schedule of studies several times in the year and was always followed by a few days of relaxation of routine and a more appetizing diet. There were community celebrations in the refectory on certain feasts and occasional entertainments by travelling musicians, actors, and jesters, all of which relieved the monotony of the daily timetable. Some of these themes will receive attention in the appropriate section in later chapters.

In this preliminary search among the book collections held by the cathedral priories we have singled out some that appear most likely to have been earmarked for use in the novitiate. Since it is impossible to determine at what point any particular text was introduced, I have selected and described those which were probably the most easily assimilated and digested by a novice in his first year of monastic life. The following chapter will discuss the later stages of the novitiate study programme that continued after the solemn rite of profession had been celebrated.

Profession: procedures and ceremony

Our knowledge of the procedures leading up to profession is derived from two main sources, namely the biographical detail available for individual monks, and the regulations laid down in surviving customaries and chapter ordinances. It is again necessary to tread circumspectly because the records are patchy and any resulting interpretation of events will inevitably bear the marks of this deficiency.

Biographical information in a limited number of cases provides dates for both the admission and profession of monks, and the range of variations exposed may be seen as sufficiently broad to allow us to consider that we have to hand a typical cross-section. For Thomas Talbot and John de Teukesbury at Worcester, for example, there was a ten-month interval in 1352 in the wake of the plague when numbers had been greatly reduced; there was an even shorter interval for Peter de Oxney and John Bertram at Canterbury who waited only a brief four months and six months respectively before their profession in March, 1373.[174] The four Norwich monks who entered the cathedral priory in June 1415 but were not professed until April 1418 were probably kept waiting because they had been admitted under age, at about fifteen or sixteen years.[175] An unusual case occurred at Canterbury in 1336 after a group of seven had been received into the novitiate.

---

[173] In the context of a poem in old English; BL MS Arundel 292, fo 70v.
[174] *BRECP*, 882 (Talbot), 883 (John de Teukesbury I). Bertram was clothed in September 1372, ibid., 88 and Oxney/Stone in November of the same year, ibid. 251; both were professed in March 1373.
[175] For minimum age requirements for admission see above 53.

Five of them were so eager for profession that Prior Richard de Oxenden was persuaded to request the necessary permission from Archbishop Stratford for fear, as he reported, that if disappointed they might leave the monastery. The archbishop was adamant in his refusal.[176] In the event all five remained and were professed at the appropriate time, like the great majority for whom the relevant dates are known. The required year of probation was a healthy safeguard for both the monastic community and the novices in that it offered an adequate testing time for both parties.[177]

For all but two of the cathedral priories preparations for the solemnization of profession required adroit handling similar to those preceding admission.[178] When the time came for the prior to inform the bishop and request his presence at the ceremony there was an exchange of correspondence, some of which survives in episcopal and priory registers, providing details of the dates involved and of the candidates' names. As noted above the bishops remained in principle opposed to any diminution of their rights of jurisdiction over their monastic chapters, but in practice they frequently commissioned the priors to deputize for them. The day and hour set by the prior were often inconvenient for prelates whose many other responsibilities necessitated continual journeying within the diocese and beyond.[179] It is to be noted that the treatise drawn up by the c. 1277–9 general chapter and copied into the St Augustine Customary includes regulations concerning episcopal participation in the profession ceremony 'in cathedrals and other churches' where the bishop's presence was normative. It specified a three-month advance warning of the date proposed by the abbot or prior and compliance on the part of the bishop or his commissary within the month after the date. There is no firm evidence that these prescriptions were strictly adhered to in the cathedral priories.[180] Durham and Winchester, however, had earlier gained their independence from episcopal control in matters of the admission and profession of novices; it is for this reason that, in these two cathedral priories, there exists little or no information regarding names and precise dates. The majority of the monks of St Swithun's and St Cuthbert's do not make an appearance in the records until their first ordination, and it is fortunate that the Winchester episcopal registers survive, with their ordination quires more or less complete for all but eighteen years of the century and a half of this present study. At Durham, by contrast, the registers for

---

[176] *BRECP* under Robert de Duffelde (141), John de Exeter (155–6), Thomas Gyllyngham (185), Henry de Selverton (284), James Whyte I (319). Sheppard, *Lit. Cant.*, ii, no. 621 (p. 155). Selverton had previously been a novice at the Augustinian priory at Kenilworth and had arrived at Christ Church only a few weeks before the request was made to the archbishop.

[177] The probationary year had been laid down in canon law and was incorporated in the 1278 statutes of the general chapter of the Black Monks of Canterbury province, Pantin, *Black Monk Chapters*, i, 99.

[178] The two exceptions were Durham and Winchester.

[179] On occasion the bishop sent an official of his household to take his place. One wonders if the priors ever connived to arrange dates when they were fairly sure that the bishop would be absent.

[180] Thompson, *Customary of St Augustine*, 422. Canterbury priory Register L (CCA DCc Reg. L) includes many samples of the exchange of correspondence between archbishops and priors regarding both the admission and profession of monks in the fourteenth century (c. 1318–67) and the archbishops' registers are equally well supplied.

more than half of these years are missing; however, the lists of monks in the Durham *Liber Vitae*, which are grouped by date, go some way towards providing a chronological framework although there are several gaps in this record.[181]

Having obtained the requisite licences from all the parties concerned, a professed monk occasionally moved from one monastery to another. This transfer (*migratio*) necessitated a second profession because the original promises of stability in his previous monastery and obedience to its superior ceased to be valid.[182] Henry de Wodehull, a monk of Abingdon of twenty-eight years' standing, obtained permission in 1361 to transfer to Christ Church because of his devotion to St Thomas [Becket] and the other Canterbury saints, together with his desire to lead a stricter life. This was the usual formula employed which at times concealed more practical motives; in this case it was probably a dispute between Wodehull and his abbot at the time of his inception at Oxford. No doubt, as a doctor of theology he was highly acceptable to the Canterbury monks, who assigned him a place among them in the order of seniority to accord with the date of his former profession at Abingdon in 1333.[183] Despite their quasi-subservient relationship to Christ Church, Dover monks were also subject to this second profession when they transferred to Canterbury because their original profession had been to the prior there; the single known instance of this is John Marchall I, who, transferring from Dover, was professed with six other Christ Church monks in 1401.[184]

By the close of the probationary year the Rule in its entirety had been read to the novices three times: after two, eight, and twelve months respectively.[185] If, after the final reading, they had convinced the novice master that they remained steadfast in their intent they were then given a final and solemn warning that they should now be ready to commit themselves for life, fully aware that in so doing they would no longer be free to depart.[186]

According to the early fourteenth-century manuscript which contains a copy of the customary of St Augustine's Canterbury the novices were to assemble three days before the profession rites were scheduled to take place in order to receive instructions for writing out their own professions.[187] The general chapter treatise is similar but less precise. Both follow almost identical wording:

---

[181] The *Liber Vitae* commemorates by name not only the monks of Durham but also many benefactors, and religious and laity associated in confraternity with them. It has received exhaustive scrutiny by recent scholars in the three-volume *LVD* in which the biographical register of Durham monks compiled by Alan Piper has supplied most of the missing names, *LVD*, iii, 129–436.

[182] For a résumé of transfers by cathedral priory monks see Greatrex 'Prosopographical Perspectives', 133–5.

[183] BRECP, 322. The practice of clothing and professing secular priests without delay applied in cases of mature and eminent men in mid-career, and their order of seniority was based on their ordination; see John Kynton and Richard Vaughan, ibid., 216, 309–10.

[184] Ibid., 230.

[185] RB, C.58, 9–13; one hopes that they were well on the way to memorizing it.

[186] Ibid., C.58, 14–15. There are significant points on the juridical aspects of monastic profession to be gleaned from Richard Yeo's 'The Structure and Content of Monastic Profession' in *Studia Anselmiana*, 83 (Rome, 1982), especially Chap. 6, 167–97.

[187] Thompson, *Customary of St Augustine*, 13; the manuscript is now BL Cotton Faustina C.xii.

Ego, frater N., ... promitto stabilitatem meam et conversionem morum meorum et obedientiam secundum regulam sancti Benedicti, in hoc monasterio, quod est constructum in honore N. sancti vel sanctorum, coram Deo et sanctis ejus, et in presencia domini archiepiscopi, episcopi ... vel prioris vel procuratoris N.[188]

An early thirteenth-century profession slip which survives at Durham has been reproduced in Plate No. 31 in Rollason, *Symeon of Durham* where the saints named are the Virgin and St Cuthbert, the Prior Thomas [Melsonby], and the monk concerned, William, priest.[189] Seven fifteenth-century fragmentary slips of Durham monks, which are also extant, have been dated by Alan Piper as *c.* 1420.[190] Unfortunately, profession slips record only the baptismal names of the monks and, therefore, identification is rarely possible. The problem is highlighted at Bath in 1326 when Bishop Drokensford was present in the cathedral for the profession of twelve monks, five of whom were named John![191] The only known exception is the occasion of Henry Fouke's profession at Worcester which took place on 4 February 1303 in the Lady chapel of the cathedral priory. His profession slip was copied into the *sede vacante* register kept by the Worcester priors and was followed by a statement giving his full name and those of the three others professed with him. Brother Henry, acolyte, made his promises in the presence of John de Wyke, prior 'auctoritate curie Cantuariensis gerentis curam officium et administracionem spiritualium in civitate et diocesis Wygornie sede vacante anno elapso post mortem domini Godefridi episcopi'.[192] This clause appended to the profession makes clear the unique status of the priors of Worcester who, in 1268, had acquired the right, during vacancies of the see, to exercise episcopal jurisdiction in spiritualities within the city and diocese. *Sede plena*, the bishop's approval and presence had to be requested, with dramatic timing in September 1310, when two Worcester novices made their profession on the day of Walter Reynolds' installation as bishop; they did so before the reading of the gospel at the high mass immediately following the installation.[193]

Most professions were less spectacular but, for the novice, no less solemn occasions. The candidates were carefully rehearsed by their novice masters in the

---

[188] Thompson, *Customary of St Augustine*, 13 and 424; see also *RB*, C.58, 17–18.
[189] The reference for the original document is DCM Misc. Charter 6067a. Another profession slip of similar date is Misc. Charter 1a.
[190] These slips are listed as DCM Misc. Charter 7221. I owe many of the details given here and elsewhere to the unfailing kindness of Alan Piper. An inventory of the feretrar's office dated 1418 states that the profession slips were kept 'in armariolo qui subest proximo pavimento ex parte boriali', Fowler, *Account Rolls*, ii, 461.
[191] Somerset Record Office, D/D/B. Reg. I (Drokensford/Droxford), fo 270. It seems surprising that at a date when there were probably not more than thirty-five to forty monks in the priory such a large number of novices would have been accepted together. It is to be noted that, on this occasion, the form of profession has been copied into the bishop's register.
[192] WCM, Reg. A.1 (Sede Vacante), fo 15 where there is a profile of a monk drawn in the margin; and the full names of all four monks are supplied below the profession: Henry Fouke, David de Presthemede, Simon de Solers, Roger de Stevintone; see *BRECP*, 807–8, 864, 874, 877. The profession has been omitted from the printed edition of the Register.
[193] WCM Liber Albus (A.5), fo 45v. The two monks were Wulstan de Bransford and Simon Crompe (de Wygorn'); see *BRECP*, 779–80, 792–3.

order of proceedings according to the details approved by the 1277/9 general chapter of English Benedictines. Later copies of the form in use at Christ Church differ only slightly from the one earlier agreed for all monasteries, a strong indication that, at Canterbury and probably elsewhere, there was little change in the later middle ages right up to the dissolution.[194] What follows is a reconstruction based on all four sources.

On the morning of profession the novices were led by their master into the chapter [house], where the community was already assembled and, prostrating themselves before the president (the archbishop, bishop, or prior), made their petition to receive the habit of profession and the blessing of the president. They were warned once again of the harshness of monastic life and replied *Presto sumus et parati*... as on the day of admission the year before. After they had begged for the forgiveness of God and of all the brethren whom they had offended, the president also begged the monks to pardon the novices' offences; in addition, he urged the entire assembled community to be reconciled one with another *ex intime cordis totaliter*. The chapter ended, everyone processed out, the novices bringing up the rear and following their master to their quarters. If the profession slip had not been written out previously it was now to be prepared by each novice in readiness for the mass that was about to follow. Immediately after the gospel had been read and the creed chanted the cantor began to intone the *Miserere mei, Deus* (Psalm 50/51) followed by the convent, while the novices processed in order to the steps in front of the altar where carpets had been put down and their profession habits, consisting of *cucullae* and *frocci*, laid out in readiness. During the chanting of this psalm they lay prostrate in front of the altar, but rising at once after the closing *Gloria Patri*, each in turn read out in a clear voice his profession, marking it with the sign of the cross in his own hand in place of a seal; then, after genuflecting, he placed the slip on the altar symbolizing that, with this document, he was offering himself. Returning to their former [prostrate] position, the novices repeated together the words of Psalm 118/119: 'Suscipe me Domine secundum eloquium tuum et vivam; et non confundas me ab expectacione mea', the convent responding with the same words; this was done thrice in succession, each time in a higher tone. A series of prayers followed and the Holy Spirit invoked in the hymn *Veni Creator*. After being sprinkled with holy water, the novices arose and their profession habits were blessed. One by one in order they genuflected before the officiant and with hands raised had the *cucullae* and *frocci* they were wearing removed, the officiant addressing each novice personally 'Exuat te Dominus veterem hominem cum actibus suis.' Next, clothing them in the garments just blessed he said to each in turn 'Induat te Dominus novum hominem qui secundum Deum creatus est [in justicia et sanctitate veritatis]'. The whole assembled community commencing with

---

[194] For the reference to the 1277/9 customary issued by the general chapter see above 66; the relevant pages in Thompson, *Customary of St Augustine* are 423–6. The three surviving manuscripts containing the Christ Church rite of profession are (1) priory Register A (CCA DCc Reg. A) in a brief section also containing early fourteenth-century chapter ordinances, fo 391–391v; (2) BL MS Arundel 68, fo 73–73v (15th century); (3) LPL MS 20, fos 2v–3 (early 16th century).

the officiant then embraced each of the newly professed. The mass then continued and the novices all received communion. For three days following they remained in seclusion, head and face covered by the hood of the *cuculla*.

It is unclear whether or not the profession habit of *froccus* and *cuculla* differed in any respect from the two garments which had been removed during the ceremony. The *cuculla*, or cowl, was a workaday garment, ankle-length and with little or no sleeve; the *froccus*, *froggus*, or frock was a more formal garment, full-length with ample sleeves. They were the two outer garments and at the profession rite both were worn together, the *froccus* possibly on top of the *cuculla* although the wording is ambiguous.[195] Since no distinction between these two sets of garments is mentioned it seems likely that for profession the novices were provided with fresh, clean, if not new, *cucullae* and *frocci* to symbolize their putting on the 'new man'.

Now fully-fledged monks, with profession behind them, the novices were eligible to participate actively in the daily chapter meetings, sharing with their brethren the *secreta capituli* from which they had hitherto been excluded.[196] For the next few years their studies would continue in preparation for priestly ordination which by the late thirteenth century had become the norm for all monks.

---

[195] The 1277/9 regulations are ambiguous. Barbara Harvey supposed that the two were never worn together, *Monastic Dress*, 14; perhaps this occasion was an exception? It would appear that the professed monk's *cuculla* and *froccus* differed from those of the novice.

[196] They continued to be known as novices, or sometimes juniors (*juniores*) at least until they had received priest's orders.

III

The Community of Professed Novices and Junior Monks

1. MONASTIC ROUTINE AND STUDY DURING AND AFTER ORDINATION

> ... ab ipsius [via mandatorum Dei] numquam magisterio discedentes, in eius doctrinam usque ad mortem in monasterio perseverantes ...
>
> RB, Prol. 50[1]

The unknown author of the *Rites of Durham*, recalling the former life in the cloister, stated that the novice members of the community pursued their studies for seven years.[2] His remarks are vindicated by the fact that William de Kelloe and John de Aycliffe, who were admitted or professed *c.* 1360/1 and ordained priests in 1364, were described as senior novices as late as 1366.[3] At Worcester, three years after their priesting in 1389/90, Thomas de Barndesley II and William de Hydeshale were still novices, and Thomas de Broghton professed in 1391 was deemed a novice after his priesting the following year.[4] The term *juniores*, most frequently found at Winchester, probably refers to this senior group.[5] Although Durham is the only cathedral priory from which comes a specific reference to the length of time spent in the novitiate, it should be noted that young monks in the other cathedral priories very rarely played a noticeably active role within their community until several years after ordination to the priesthood. While studies directed by the novice master and other senior monks would have continued in preparation for this major event, the three or four years immediately following would have provided scope, at least for the more studious, to develop their own particular fields of interest with a modicum of guidance or supervision and, at the same time, to test their ability to discharge minor responsibilities within the enclosure. Benedict's sole purpose in setting before his monks a lifelong

---

[1] Fry, *RB*, 166–7.
[2] *Rites of Durham*, 96.
[3] The profession dates have been assigned by Alan Piper in *LVD*, iii, C.959, C.960; the ordination date is in DCM Reg. Hatfield, fo 106.
[4] *BRECP*, 774 (Barndesley), 825 (Hydeshale), 781 (Broghton).
[5] No mention of *novicii* has been found in the Winchester muniments, but it is clear that *juvenes*, who are frequently referred to, were monks; see Greatrex, *Common Seal Register*, no. 316, p. 101. At Canterbury in 1296 Ralph de Apuldor, who had been professed seven years earlier, was named as a *junior*, *BRECP*, 76.

commitment to learning was, as we have seen, to ensure a constant growth in understanding which, primarily through the study of the scriptures, would stimulate both mind and heart in the search for God.[6]

For the great majority of monks these formative years were spent entirely within the cloister, with the exception of a select few who had demonstrated an intellectual prowess that would benefit from higher studies at the university. Numbered among those who were sent up were some who had not completed the full sequence of ordinations; John de Holyngbourne of Rochester cathedral priory, for example, was licensed by Prior John de Shepey II to study at Oxford in October 1382 two months before his ordination to the subdiaconate; again, Nicholas Morton of Worcester had been professed for only about three years when he was sent to Oxford in 1354, and he did not receive priest's orders for another three years; and Thomas Browne of Christ Church was a student at Canterbury College Oxford in 1414, four years after profession and four years before being ordained priest.[7] Early departures for Oxford, however, were the exception and, behind the decision in each individual case, factors based on age, maturity, and monastic commitment as well as intellectual competence must have played determining roles.[8] Monk scholars from the cathedral priories who were given the opportunity to pursue university studies will be treated in the next chapter.

From profession to ordination

It would be misleading to attempt to impose a pattern on this period in the medieval novice's life. To begin with, the length of time involved shows what appear at first sight to be surprisingly extensive variations, the two extremes for which evidence is forthcoming being under one year and seven or more years.[9] Even the abundance of documentary material that survives from Canterbury and Durham provides us with only scanty information regarding precise dates of profession and priestly ordination for more than a relatively small proportion of the monks of these two cathedral priories. Of the total number of monks admitted between 1270 and 1420 a rough estimate indicates that only twenty per cent of those at Canterbury and twenty-five per cent of those at Durham can be included in this group. Moreover, even the attempt to arrive at any figures such as these is

---

[6] See Fry, *RB*, Appendix 6, 'The Role and Interpretation of Scripture in the Rule of Benedict', 467–77. With regard to Durham see Piper, 'The Monks of Durham and the Study of Scripture'.
[7] *BRECP*, 612 (Holyngbourne), 851 (Morton), 102 (Browne).
[8] It should be borne in mind that a considerable financial outlay was involved in each case which was often a heavy burden on the monastic community.
[9] See *BRECP*, 835 for John de Legh II of Worcester cathedral priory who was already in subdeacon's orders when he was professed in January 1393; ordained deacon in March and priest in May of the same year, he must have previously completed a course of training in preparation and he should have been at least 24 years of age. In the few other identifiable cases of seemingly rapid promotion circumstances may have been similar. At the other end of the spectrum the Winchester monk, Thomas de London, waited for seven years after his ordination as acolyte in 1373 before receiving priest's orders (*BRECP*, 711), and five of the nine Canterbury monks professed in 1309 were not priested until seven and a half years later. See p. 94.

itself fraught with pitfalls. For example, there can be confusion and uncertainty regarding the actual dates of admission (or entry) and of profession; fortunately, however, the interval between the two did not exceed a year and was sometimes less. In this present study, in the absence of clear evidence that distinguishes one from the other, I refer to profession on the presumption that this was a date of major significance in monastic life: it was both the solemn moment of personal commitment on the part of those who read aloud and signed their threefold profession promise; and it was also, at the same time, the public record on the part of the community of their acceptance and recognition as full members, with all the pertaining rights and responsibilities.[10] It would most likely have been on that occasion, not when they were admitted and clothed, that their names were inserted into the *liber vitae* of their monastery. The names of the monks found in the Durham book of that name are now found, with their approximate profession dates, in the *Liber Vitae* recently published.[11] At Canterbury there remain two late fifteenth/early sixteenth-century copies of what may be described as profession lists dating from the monks' return to Canterbury from exile in 1207 and an obituary list from 1286, both incomplete. The manuscript preserved in Canterbury is associated with Thomas Causton (d. 1504), who held many offices in the cathedral priory including that of *magister ordinis*, in charge of the novices.[12] The other copy, which is similar to the Causton manuscript, has come to rest in the Parker Library at Corpus Christi College Cambridge.[13] No *libri vitae* survive from the other cathedral priories, but the necessity for episcopal participation in the ceremonies of admission and profession and in the rites of ordination assured the entry of an official record in the bishops' registers and, where these survive, they furnish valuable information.[14] Dating problems have to be faced and resolved as far as possible in order to ensure a reliable degree of accuracy in the effort to render visible prevailing trends and to clarify and substantiate at least some of the observations arising from a close examination of the sources relevant to this study.

It will be helpful to begin with some of these observations. At Durham the average length of the interval between admission/profession and priestly ordination was slightly under three years; at Canterbury it ranged between three and five years.[15] With fewer figures available for the other cathedral priories it becomes less meaningful to try to make similar estimates; at Worcester, for instance, only about forty monks' records within the confines of this study retain both dates,

---

[10] However, I do admit that sometimes it is clearly stated that a particular date refers to clothing or admission; see, for example, *BRECP*, 259, under the Canterbury monk John Pyrye.

[11] *LVD*, iii, 129–436.

[12] *BRECP*, 110.

[13] It is MS 298, fos 1–22 (pp 143–86).

[14] As noted above both Winchester and Durham were free of episcopal intervention with regard to the admission and profession of monks but ordinations to major orders were the universal prerogative of bishops.

[15] These are only estimates and, as such, should be quoted with caution; averages are not a sound basis for judgement since they cloak the extent of the wide variations and cannot take into account the lacunae in the primary sources. The Durham average has been provided by Alan Piper.

and of this number slightly over half were ordained to the priesthood between two and four years.[16] One issue at stake here is the extent to which the cathedral priories adhered to the Black Monk chapter statutes concerning both the minimum ages for admission and profession and those laid down in the Clementine Constitutions for the successive stages of ordination.[17] Having attained his nineteenth year a young aspirant could be received as a novice and professed a year later. He was at that point already eligible for ordination to the subdiaconate and diaconate; but he had then to wait until his twenty-fifth year before receiving priest's orders. Thus, for such an aspirant, the interval between profession and priestly ordination should never have been less than five years. The fact that it often was less suggests either that most of the young men who sought to enter monastic life were aged twenty or more, or that many were admitted and/or ordained under age. Basing their arguments on the relatively few known exceptions, some scholars have concluded that at least some of the strictures regarding age were often disregarded. Surviving evidence points to a few papal dispensations for specified individuals or groups under age usually in times of crisis when priests were in short supply, and to the occasional *post facto* papal absolution for the reception of priest's orders under age.[18] These facts, however, actually go some way toward suggesting that the regulations were taken seriously. Moreover, additional substantive evidence has recently come to light in the form of a licence granted by Pope Eugenius IV to Prior William Molassh of Christ Church during the 1430s; it gave to him and to his successors permission to allow Canterbury monks to receive minor orders in their seventeenth year, subdeacon's and deacon's orders in their nineteenth year, and priest's orders in their twenty-second year. An accompanying proviso stipulated that the newly ordained monk-priests were not to celebrate mass outside the monastic precincts until they had attained the regular canonical age. A few years earlier, in 1414 a similar dispensation, requested by Prior John de Hemingbrough at Durham, had been granted by Pope John XXIII without any strictures attached; this also was to apply not only to

---

[16] Where admission and profession dates are lacking and the first entry is that of ordination as acolyte, I have assumed that this commonly took place within the year of profession and have therefore increased the time span by one year; see also note 15 above.

[17] The admission and profession age requirements are stated in the Black Monk chapter statutes of 1277/8 (Pantin, *Black Monk Chapters*, i, 99); those laid down for ordination are to be found in the *Liber Clementinarum* I.6.iii (early 14th century). Note that 'having attained the nineteenth year' is usually taken to mean 'eighteen years of age'; but there is a slight ambiguity in this phrase with regard to all the ages specified.

[18] In 1364 and the following year William de Greneburgh, prior of Coventry, was granted permission to dispense six and ten monks respectively in their twenty-second year to be priested because so many members of the community had died in outbreaks of the pestilence, *CPL*, iv (1362–1404), 39 and 47. Again, in 1390, the Rochester prior was given an indult by Boniface IX for the early ordination of six monks for similar reasons, ibid., iv, 366. No crisis was specified, however, when John Wycliffe, monk of Durham was ordained priest by Bishop Langley on 2 April 1412 in his twenty-second year; he had been chosen as one of the nine clerks who benefited from a dispensation granted to the bishop in a bull of Alexander V, *Reg. Langley*, i, 170, ii, 7. Thomas Nesbitt was similarly dispensed and ordained the same year, ibid., i, 171.

Hemingbrough but to his successors in office as well.[19] The first among the cathedral priors, however, who obtained this privilege for himself and his successors was Alexander de Totyngton of Norwich in 1401/2 when he received a faculty from the pope allowing members of his community to be ordained priest in their twentieth year.[20]

Adherence to the Canterbury dispensation can fortunately be tested at one point of time, on the eve of the dissolution, when there has been a tendency to conclude that lax and irregular practices were on the increase. A surviving list of some fifty-eight monks, which may have been drawn up for Thomas Cromwell in c. 1538/9, gives the age after each name as well as a brief character reference;[21] when these are combined with the available profession and ordination dates the results demonstrate that in all but a very few cases these men were not receiving priest's orders before they were twenty-one or twenty-two; and they had been professed at about nineteen or twenty years of age, or even slightly later in a significant number of cases. Although many of the last few generations of Christ Church monks were ordained priests only a short time after their profession, it is almost certain that this was done in conformity with the regulations concerning age as stated in the dispensation and proviso granted to Prior Molassh.

Transferred to the earlier period that is the focus of this present study, the above observations can prove helpful when applied to the individual differences in the novices' progression from profession through the several stages of ordination. For example, when four Canterbury novices were professed together in October 1361 two of them received priest's orders two years later in December 1363, the third in March 1365 and the fourth in September 1367.[22] Similarly, at Rochester Robert Shorne and two others made their profession in June 1391 and, although Shorne was priested two years later, one of his brother novices was made to wait until February 1396 and the other until September 1397 before being permitted to follow suit.[23] The most plausible explanation is that, aside from the few cases in which priestly ordination was delayed because of ill health, failure to complete learning requirements, or uncertainty on the part of the novice master (and perhaps of the novices themselves) as to their suitability, these differences in the dates of advancement were determined by age requirements. The ages of a few of the Durham monks, which have been preserved in the chapter muniments, lend

---

[19] BL MS Arundel 68, fo 71v (Canterbury); DCM Priory Reg. II Parva, fo 65v (Durham). The latter has been printed in *HDST*, ccxxv–ccxxvi. At Bury St Edmunds the abbot and his successors received a dispensation to the same effect in 1418, *CPL*, viii, 391. The abbot of Westminster also acquired a similar privilege in 1477, Harvey, *Living and Dying*, 119–21. However, as Barbara Harvey remarked, these were all probably restricted to celebrations of mass within the cloister, ibid.

[20] *CPL*, v (1396–1404), 357; this does seem surprising, but Barbara Harvey's comment in note 19 above must surely have applied.

[21] London, TNA State Papers Henry VIII, no. 116, fos 44–6 and printed by Pantin in *Canterbury College Oxford*, iii, 151–4.

[22] The four were, in chronological order, John Sandwich I (*BRECP*, 278), Laurence Tent (ibid., 299), John Gloucestre I (ibid., 169–70), William de Dover III (ibid., 140); there were, in fact, nine professed together in 1361, but information concerning the other five is incomplete.

[23] For Robert Shorne see *BRECP*, 637; the other two were Simon Gillyngham (ibid., 606) and Thomas de Ealding (ibid., 601) respectively.

94 The Community of Professed Novices and Junior Monks

further support to the significant role played by age both in the admission and profession of novices and in their progress through the stages of ordination. With the evidence at his disposal Alan Piper has calculated that in the period between the late thirteenth and early fifteenth century the average age of entry was 'just short of 23' with the range between about 17 and 30.[24] John de Hemingbrough, for example, was about 25 or 26 when he was admitted/professed *c*. 1352, and John Wessington, who succeeded Hemingbrough as prior in 1416 was about 20 when he entered monastic life *c*. 1390; when the latter celebrated his first mass four to five years later he would have been well within the minimum age for receiving priest's orders.[25] Piper sees no closely fixed age for admission at Durham and supports the view that variations in the length of time before priesting are a direct reflection of this flexibility. A similar approach to admission was probably taken in other cathedral priories and is strongly suggested by the differing ordination dates of the Canterbury and Rochester novices named above. Even more persuasive at Christ Church is what must have been the outcome of Prior Eastry's decision in October 1309 to profess a group of nine novices, whom he must have previously admitted at an age younger than was usual, because seven of them waited for seven and a half years before being ordained priests in May 1317.[26]

Progression through ordinations

It is reasonable to assume that those novices whose progress through the four stages of ordination was unusually swift had entered the monastery in their early twenties having already completed sufficient formal schooling to prepare them for speedy advancement. If they had received instruction from a priest or chaplain, as suggested above, they would have acquired a practical knowledge of liturgical procedures in addition to the rudiments of Latin grammar and chant; the fact that many novices were ordained as acolytes within a year after profession lends plausibility to this supposition.[27] Apart from these conjectures the type and extent of their pre-

---

[24] For the dates of admission/profession of Durham monks I have relied on Alan Piper's computations.

[25] The account of Prior Hemingbrough's death recording his 'almost sixty-six' years of monastic life is in DCM Locellus I, 7; Wessington's death notice occurs on a surviving obituary roll printed in *The Obituary Roll of William Ebchester and John Burnby, Priors of Durham*, ed. James Raine, Surtees Society 31 (1856), 72. More biographical details for Hemingbrough are given in *LVD*, iii, C.932 and for Wessington, ibid., C.1028.

[26] One of the nine died and the priestly ordination date of another is unrecorded. The rest are in *BRECP*: Robert de Aldon, 70; John de Lenham, 222; William de Mallyng, 230; Denys de St Margaret, 272; Thomas de Sandwyco, 280; William de Thrulegh, 306; John de Valoyns, 309. Alan Piper noted a probably similar younger group of seven at Durham in 1428 who waited over four years before receiving priest's orders. See also Harvey, *Living and Dying*, 119–21 where the evidence available for Westminster indicates a similar policy in operation.

[27] Acolyte is the senior of the minor orders and the first of those requiring episcopal ordination. However, there is one known exception to this general rule: in July 1456 the prior of Durham received papal permission for himself and his successors to confer minor orders, *CPL*, xi (1455–64), 109. In a few cases ordination as acolyte preceded profession, e.g. by six days for William Regeweye in 1401 at Canterbury, and by four days for William de Mawfeld I in 1396 at Rochester (*BRECP*, 262 and 620 respectively). For Henry Stoke, also of Rochester, the order of acolyte was conferred in 1396, four months after his profession (ibid., 640).

monastic education remains hidden from view. In the novitiate they must have had to undergo at least a basic course in theological and doctrinal matters pertaining to the duties of a priest such as are found in the *Oculus sacerdotis* written by the parish priest William de Pagula in the first half of the fourteenth century; as a practical guide ready to hand for consultation it found a home on many monastic shelves, and copies have survived from Ely, Worcester, Canterbury, and Norwich.[28] Another useful text, from the mid-thirteenth century, and acknowledged by Pagula as an influential source for his writings, was the *Summa de doctrina sacerdotali* or, more often, *Summa qui praesunt presbyteri* of Richard de Wetheringsett which has already been suggested above as one of the possible choices during the first year; it was found in at least four of the cathedral priories: Canterbury, Durham, Norwich, and Worcester and probably also Rochester.[29] Texts such as these covered a wide range of topics drawing on canonical as well as theological authorities, and taking in their stride creeds, sacraments, the ten commandments, virtues and vices, and the gifts of the Spirit.

Among the works frequently occurring in the cathedral priories' medieval libraries many are known only by the titles recorded in medieval book lists and cannot be precisely identified but, considered as a group, they comprise a substantial body of reference material on sacramental doctrine and liturgy. There were, for example, close to fifty titles in the early fourteenth-century Christ Church book catalogue which can be identified as belonging to these categories, many of them anonymous or supplied with dubious attributions. Moreover, the presence of other seemingly similar treatises and *libelli* among the miscellaneous contents of some of the extant Canterbury manuscripts adds weight to their former multiplicity. Also, it is surely significant that twelve copies of Pope Innocent III's *De sacro altaris mysterio* were recorded at Christ Church in Prior Eastry's catalogue, a strong indication that it was recommended there; by comparison, in the late fourteenth century as many as twelve copies were available for the use of monks at Peterborough Abbey, although their community was little more than half the size of Canterbury.[30] Both Durham and Norwich had copies, the latter still surviving in an abridged form.[31] The *De*

---

[28] For a summary of William de Pagula's career and writings, see *BRUO*, iii, 1436–7 (under 'Paul') and W. A. Pantin, *The English Church in the Fourteenth Century* (Notre Dame University Press, Indiana, 1962), 195–202. Pagula's *Oculus sacerdotis* and other works are listed among a number of books named in an Ely MS, now LPL 448, on fo 119v; the context suggests that they formed part of the priory book collection but none of this group have survived. Two fourteenth-century Worcester copies have come to rest in the Bodleian Library: Bodley MS 828 and Hatton MS 11 (first part). A late thirteenth/early fourteenth-century Canterbury *Oculus* survives in Canterbury Cathedral, Lit. MSS D.8 and D.9 (53 and 54), and one of the fourteenth century formerly belonging to Norwich is now located in Cambridge University Library, MS Ii.2.7.

[29] The references are Eastry catalogue item nos 719, 746, 1515, James, *ALCD*, 78, 80, 127, and a surviving copy still at Canterbury, Lit. MS D.9 (54); Oxford, Bodley MS Rawlinson C.4, and in 1395 a copy was in the novices' book cupboard, *Cat. Vet. Durham*, 82K (Durham); CUL MS Ii.4.12 (Norwich); WCM MSS F.71, Q.22 and Q.27 (Worcester); BL MS Royal 10 B.ii (Rochester).

[30] The Canterbury copies are discussed in Greatrex, 'Innocent III's Writings', 188–9, and those of Peterborough are listed in *Peterborough Abbey*, Karsten Friis-Jensen and James M. W. Willoughby, eds, Corpus of British Medieval Library Catalogues, 8 (British Library/British Academy, London, 2001), 207 under the title 'De missarum mysteriis'.

[31] A Durham copy, recorded in *Cat. Vet. Durham*, 26A³ in a list dated 1391 is probably not to be identified with the copy in the surviving Durham MS, BL Harley 5234 although some of the contents are identical; the *Cat. Vet. Durham* title is *De canone misse*. The Norwich abridgement, *Super officio misse*, is now CUL MS Ii.1.22.

sacramentis Christianae fidei or De sacramentis ecclesiae of Hugh of St Victor was a lengthy treatise of which part two is devoted specifically to the sacraments of the church; a twelfth-century copy of this section of the treatise which belonged to Durham is now Cambridge, King's College Library MS 22. Other extant copies include three formerly at Christ Church and now located in Oxford and Cambridge libraries, and probably two at Rochester.[32]

There was, in fact, no shortage of texts from which novice masters could make selections to pass on to those who had been marked out for early ordination. It will be sufficient, however, to cite a few further examples from among the many available to the cathedral priory novices, those on the fast track, and probably some of the others as well; the choice in every case would have been made at the discretion of the novice masters and would more than likely have consisted of selections rather than the whole text. The twelfth-century Paris master, John Beleth, wrote one which circulated widely, most commonly under the title *Summa de ecclesiasticis officiis*; in one hundred and sixty-five short chapters clearly signalled by captions it dealt with the monastic office, the mass, and the distinguishing features of each of the liturgical seasons throughout the year.[33] About a century later a Norwich monk, Simon de Elmham, bought a copy; was he perhaps a novice master?[34] Canterbury possessed two copies in the early fourteenth century one of which is extant; Durham had at least one which has survived but was noted as incomplete by the monastic librarian, Thomas Swalwell, in the early sixteenth century.[35] Beleth made extensive use of a number of earlier writers like Ambrose, Gregory the Great, Bede, Amalarius of Metz, Rupert of Deutz, and especially Honorius Augustodunensis's *Gemma animae*. This last, also a liturgical treatise, borrowed freely from, among others, Amalarius, whose own treatise, *Liber officialis*, was found at Canterbury, Ely, and Rochester.[36] Honorius had spent some time in England in the early twelfth century where he developed close connections with Canterbury, Rochester, and Worcester.[37] It is therefore not surprising to find

---

[32] Possibly two copies were formerly in the Durham monastic library, *Cat. Vet. Durham*, 21B², E², N, 67A², B², D. Extant Christ Church copies are found in Oxford, Bodley MS 379, Cambridge, St John's College MS 130, and Cambridge, Trinity College MS 346, all three the full-length version. Two late twelfth-century Rochester manuscripts, now BL Royal 2 D.vi and 8 D.v*, also contained part or all of Hugh's treatise.

[33] It has recently been edited by Herbert Douteil in *CCCM*, 41 and 41A (Turnhout, 1976); Pierre-Marie Gy OP dates its third recension to 1160–4, André Vauchez, Barrie Dobson, Michael Lapidge (eds), *Encyclopedia of the Middle Ages*, 2 vols (James Clarke, Cambridge, 2000), i, 772–3.

[34] This is now CUL MS Ff.5.28. There are two monks named Simon de Elmham, one of them prior 1235–57, whose inventory of books purchased does not include Beleth, Sharpe, *EBL*, at B58. The second Simon de Elmham was a member of the Norwich community in the 1290s, *BRECP*, 505–6.

[35] The Eastry catalogue, James, *ALCD*, item nos 1201 and 1258 and Oxford, Bodley MS 196 (Canterbury); BL MS Harley 4725 (Durham) where Swalwell's annotation is on the list of contents on the front flyleaf.

[36] There may have been three copies of Amalarius, a ninth-century liturgical scholar, at Canterbury, listed in the Eastry catalogue, James, *ALCD*, as item nos 73–5 (p. 24), two of them described as incomplete; the twelfth-century Ely copy is now Cambridge, Corpus Christi College MS 416 and the Rochester copy first appears in the early twelfth-century catalogue, Sharpe, *EBL*, at B77.63.

[37] See V. I. J. Flint, *Honorius Augustodunensis*, in *Authors of the Middle Ages* (Variorum, 1995), vol. 2, no. 6, 100–7.

copies of the *Gemma animae* at Canterbury and Rochester and two surviving copies of another of his writings, the *Sigillum sanctae Mariae*, still at Worcester, which would probably have had the *Gemma* as well.[38]

The bulky *Rationale divinorum officiorum* of William Durandus has recently been judged 'the liturgical synthesis *par excellence* of the middle ages'.[39] After its appearance in the late thirteenth century it may have gradually superseded earlier authors, many of whom Durandus, like his predecessors, had drawn on for source material.[40] In 1443 Canterbury College Oxford kept a copy chained in the chapel *pro divino officio celebrando* but no other Canterbury copy has been traced.[41] At both Durham and Worcester there were two copies, three of which and a *tabula* to the fourth have survived.[42]

The examples selected and described above were only a small fraction of the titles available in the cathedral priories. Moreover, among the numerous *libelli* and treatises of unnamed authorship that are recorded in medieval catalogues and included in extant manuscripts it is highly probable that some were home productions by individual members of the monastic community, in many cases with novices in mind. Ownership does not necessarily imply authorship; nevertheless a thirteenth-century *Tractatus super canonem misse* with the name attached of Thomas de Stureye, a Canterbury monk, could have been his own compilation especially if he had been responsible for instructing those soon to be ordained to the priesthood.[43]

Any post-profession study programme had to make allowances for the fact that the novices would be receiving major orders during these years, and time would have been set aside to make the necessary preparations for each of these significant

---

[38] The Canterbury *Gemma* is in Oxford, Bodley MS 196 along with John Beleth's *Summa*, note 33 above; that of Rochester is BL MS Royal 6 A.xi; the two Sigillum texts at Worcester are MSS F.71 and Q.66 (incomplete) and there is a third copy from Worcester in CUL MS Kk.4.6, all three twelfth to thirteenth century. An anonymous *Gemma animae* is listed in *Cat. Vet. Durham*, 26C².

[39] Cyrille Vogel, *Medieval Liturgy, an introduction to the sources*, revised and translated by William G. Storey and Neils Krogh Rasmussen (The Pastoral Press, Washington, 1986), 15. The text has recently been edited by A. Davril and T. M. Thibodeau in *CCCM*, 140, 140A, 140B (Turnhout, 1995–2000).

[40] These included extracts from Ambrose, Augustine, and Gregory among the Fathers and more recent writings such as the *Gemma animae* of Honorius, the *Summa* of John Beleth, and the *De mysteriis* of Innocent III.

[41] Pantin, *Canterbury College Oxford*, i, 4; Dover had one copy by 1395, Stoneman, *Dover Priory*, BM 1.87.

[42] The Durham copies are Aberdeen University Library MS 2740 (Forbes of Boyndlie) which may be the one listed in the 1395 inventory in *Cat. Vet. Durham*, 76A², and the *tabula* to the text is in Durham cathedral MS B.III,29, fos 76–79v; the Worcester copies remain *in situ* as Worcester cathedral MSS F.124 and F.129. The fact that the last prior of Worcester, William More, bought a printed copy of the *Rationale* in 1528 may have no significance apart from illustrating a contemporary interest in obtaining the printed editions of manuscripts already owned; More's book purchases are listed in Fegan, *Journal of William More*, 412.

[43] The *Tractatus* is the first item in this manuscript of miscellanea which is now Oxford, Bodley MS Digby 4. There were, in fact, two late thirteenth-century Christ Church monks named Thomas de Stureye. Only a few biographical details of these contemporaries, known as 'senior' and 'junior', have been found; both had small collections of books which became subsumed into the monastic library after their deaths; see *BRECP*, 295–6.

occasions in monastic life. Ordinations were held on the four Saturdays in Embertide, one of the three days of fasting that were prescribed for each of the four seasons of the church's year. They were generally conducted by the diocesan bishop in the cathedral church, but exceptions were not uncommon depending on his own personal convenience. Monk novices were accompanied and presented by a senior monk, often the precentor, as in 1337 when a group of *juvenes* of St Swithun's were supervised by Nicholas de Enford on their journey *versus ordines*; they stayed at the priory manor of Whitchurch en route [? to Salisbury] at a cost of three shillings.[44] Ralph de Derham of Ely travelled to three locations for his ordinations: to St Mary's church outside Trumpington Gate in Cambridge for acolyte's orders in 1376; the next two orders, those of subdeacon and deacon, were on home ground in the Ely Lady chapel; his priestly ordination took place in the chapel of the episcopal manor at [Fen] Ditton.[45] Although few ordination lists survive for Norwich monks, scraps of information can be gleaned from the accounts of obedientiaries such as the communar who regularly contributed to the travelling expenses of the ordinands and their supervisor. Seven monks were ordained in Ware and two in Ipswich in 1348/9 and an unstated number were taken to Thetford and to Holt in 1362.[46] On the occasion of the new priest's first celebration of mass, with family and friends in attendance, the religious ceremony was followed by a repast of bread and wine or beer to which many of the obedientiaries contributed in cash or kind. The amount given varied, perhaps reflecting the financial status of the obedientiary office at the time. Each of two unnamed Durham novices received 6s. 8d. for this refection from the hostiller in 1388/9 and 1392/3 respectively.[47] Thomas Broghton at Worcester was given *exennia* by three obedientiaries in 1391/2; the hostiller contributed 21d. and the almoner and chamberlain 3s. 8d. each.[48]

The fact that the order of acolyte was often conferred on novices either a few months before or shortly after their profession enabled them to assist the monks in major orders at the altar during mass. Promotion to the subdiaconate and diaconate in turn extended their liturgical functions; the deacon, for example, was assigned to read or sing the gospel at mass on major feasts, but only those who possessed a *solempnem vocem* were chosen at Christ Church Canterbury.[49] Priestly ordination brought about an increase in dignity and status; in practical terms it was a ministry for which the novices would have been well prepared, some gradually, others more speedily. However, the priest novices, in company with the other novices, would have remained within the precinct to continue their studies; the only requirement

---

[44] WCL, Whitchurch manor account, L38/0/107.
[45] *BRECP*, 404. For the minor order of acolyte see note 27 above; the three major orders were those of subdeacon, deacon, and priest.
[46] NRO DCN 1/12/27 and 1/12/30.
[47] DCM hostiller's accounts 1388/9, 1392/3. See also Harvey, *Living and Dying*, 118 for a similar practice.
[48] WCM C.215, 181, 19. While the Worcester cellarer reports on his 1376/7 account (WCM C.69) a gift of wine for eight monks who celebrated their first mass during that year only two names have been preserved. (This account has been transcribed by Hamilton in *Compotus Rolls*, 10–23; the reference is on 16.)
[49] CCA, DCc Reg. K, fo 214.

which separated them from their fellow novices was that their names were on the mass rota as they were expected to say mass at least every four days.[50] It was their task to celebrate using one of the many chapels, chantry chapels, and altars; an example of this practice occurs in a memorandum written in a fifteenth-century hand in a copy of Book Two of the *Liber Eliensis*; it states that two junior monks in priest's orders were to celebrate the anniversaries of two named lay benefactors.[51] Only at Ely is there a specific reference to a novices' chapel but it seems likely that a chapel set aside for the use of novices would have been the norm rather than the exception.[52] Monastic communities unlike those of the preaching orders were in no haste to give responsibilities, either within the monastery or outside it, to their junior monks, and the up to seven-year induction period allowed ample time for acquiring knowledge and skills for undertaking the pastoral duties of preaching and hearing confessions.

Claustral lectors and lectures

The larger cathedral priories such as Canterbury and Durham would have been accustomed to having at any one time a group of novices some, or perhaps all, of whom might have exhibited differences in the standard achieved in their previous schooling and in the resulting speed of their advancement in study in the novitiate. Individual timetables or programmes for two or three were probably common and may explain the presence of several novice masters at Durham, as well as non-monastic *magistri* and monk lectors at Canterbury. In 1344/5 the Durham hostiller's account states that on St Cuthbert's feast he gave knives to seven novice masters as well as to ten novices, and in the 1380s and 1390s similar items were recorded by the feretrar without specifying the precise number in either case.[53] At Canterbury, in addition to the novice master, or *magister ordinis*, each novice was assigned to a senior monk known as the *magister regule* who was responsible for the monastic formation of his charge, which included supervising the memorization programme begun in the probationary year and seeing it through to a successful completion on the day of examination (*redditus*) before a board of seniors. The scant evidence available shows four monks who took between two and seven years after profession to pass this test; these might have been either before or after priestly ordination even though a Black Monk chapter in 1277 had decreed that the *redditus* should precede it.[54]

---

[50] Pantin, *Black Monk Chapters*, i, 70–1, an ordinance of the general chapter of Canterbury province 1277/9; it was also included among the injunctions issued by Bishop Kellawe to the Durham monks in 1314, DCM Priory Reg. II, fo 50v.

[51] This manuscript is now Cambridge, Trinity College MS 1145; the reference is on fo iiib.

[52] The chapel is mentioned in the Ely sacrist's account of 1402/3, a partial transcript of which survives in CUL Add. MS 2956, 165.

[53] DCM hostiller's account, 1344/5; feretrars' accounts, 1383/4A, 1387, 1398/9B.

[54] Pantin, *Black Monk Chapters* (southern province), i, 73–4; the list of texts for memorization is given above, 66. Alexander Staple I's *redditus* took place in 1440 a mere two and a half years after profession and therefore probably before he became a priest; Richard Godmersham II, on the other hand, was professed in January 1450 but not examined until August 1457 (unless he had failed an earlier test) when he was almost surely a priest although still described as novice, *BRECP*, 290–1, 171. Archbishop

There are frequent passing references to the masters and lectors appointed to instruct the novices but these furnish only brief and scanty details as to what was actually being taught. At Durham, where there were up to seven *magistri noviciorum*, the classes may have been divided into several groups according to ability, each with its own master; but it is also possible that there was a rota of masters who, while fulfilling their teaching assignments, may have been temporarily released from other obligations.[55] Both of these alternatives are given weight by the fact that in 1364/5 the hostiller distributed a small sum among *diversis fratribus pro informatione juvenorum*.[56] It may have been a valid complaint at the time, made by a Durham monk *c.* 1357/8, that there was no qualified teacher [*magister artium*] for the monks; but another source, a tantalizing fragment of a letter which may not be far removed in date, speaks of a *confrater* giving lessons in logic in the convent.[57] Periodic internal visitations among the Benedictines organized by the meetings of the general and provincial chapters were often perfunctory and seldom brought to light any serious breaches of discipline or neglect of the regulations within the cloister. This would seem to highlight the significance of the report of the monk visitors who came to Durham from St Mary's Abbey York, *c.* 1384–93; their *comperta* drew attention to the lack of an 'instructor claustralis, sive magister... ad instruendum monachis in primitivis scienciis, videlicet gramatica, logica et philosophia, secundum... statuta Benedictina'.[58]

At Christ Church between the mid-1270s and 1314 a succession of Franciscan lectors instructed the monks in theology; one may presume that novices attended some of these claustral lectures at the discretion of their master.[59] The friars may

---

Winchelsey's injunctions to Christ Church in December 1298 included the stricter requirement for the novice to be examined before profession by two senior monks who were solemnly to swear to the chapter that he had fulfilled the probationary year learning requirements *de servicio sic sufficienter reddito*, Graham, *Reg. Winchelsey*, 821; the operative word must have been *sufficienter*!

[55] DCM hostiller's account 1344/5. Alan Piper is inclined to agree with these suggestions, and postulates that the subprior, as the monk responsible for the internal regime within the cloister, may have had overall charge of the novices.

[56] Ibid., 1364/5 account. The only master known by name is William de Kibblesworth, who received small sums from several obedientiaries in 1415/16 *pro informacione noviciorum*, DCM accounts of the almoner, feretrar, and hostiller for this year. Among these *diversi fratres* who instructed the young monks, the monk in charge of the library would surely have been included; Henry of Kirkstede, librarian at Bury St Edmunds in the mid-fourteenth century, was also a novice master during this period, R. H. and M. A. Rouse, *Henry of Kirkstede*, Corpus of British Medieval Library Catalogues (British Library/British Academy, London, 2004), xxxii–li.

[57] DCM 1.9.Pont.1b (no *magister artium*); DCM Misc. Charter 6063, which may have been a letter from Prior William de Cowton to the subprior, may mean only that lectures in logic were desirable but not as yet a regular part of the curriculum. For Cowton see *LVD*, iii, C.768.

[58] Pantin, *Black Monk Chapters*, iii, 83 (from DCM Misc. Charter 5634) with reference to the Constitutions of Benedict XII, dated 1336, published by the English provincial chapter in 1343; see Pantin, ibid., ii, 231, Ca^m 6^m [*De studiis*].

[59] See Pantin, *Canterbury College Oxford*, iv, 3, and also the extracts from Christ Church monastic accounts which record payments, two of them to named lectors, viz., ibid., 167, 174, 176 Robert [Fulham]. Commenting disparagingly on the Canterbury chapter's decision to appoint Franciscan lectors, one of the continuators of Gervase's Christ Church chronicle remarked that such an unprecedented decision augured ill for the future, *Opera Historica*, ii, 281. Friar Robert de Wodeheye, for example, who died in 1306/7 *legebat theologiam in claustro* for twenty-four years or more, LPL MS 20, fo 116 and Pantin, *Canterbury College Oxford*, iv, 174.

have held the position of master lector but they probably never had a monopoly on lecturing within the cloister since Martin de Clyve, a monk of Christ Church and often given the title *magister*, was a lector in 1295 who gave instruction in dialectic and theology according to Archbishop Winchelsey's directive on his behalf.[60] However, the first named member of the cathedral community to be appointed lector, or master lector, in the place of the Franciscans was Stephen de Feversham II soon after his return from several years of study at the university of Paris; he remained in this office until his death in 1326.[61] All of his successors were Oxford graduates with doctorates in theology, some of whom were involved in teaching within the monastery possibly even before and probably during their university studies as well as after their inception.[62] Franciscan lectors may have been appointed elsewhere as Decima Douie believed to be the case at Worcester cathedral priory in 1285. Although her statement was based on uncertain evidence her reasoning, that a theological grounding in the late thirteenth century was best provided by the Franciscans, was sound.[63] Because of the similarity in date and with the application of similar reasoning, the reference at Norwich in 1290/1 to a lector, *frater* John, may also refer to a Franciscan; Norwich, like Worcester, was home to a Franciscan convent and *studium*, the friary being next door to the cathedral.[64] For the next century and a half the records of the Norwich chapter are silent on the subject of claustral instructors until, in 1429/30, a *magister theologie* is mentioned in connection with repairs to his chamber.[65] Had this post been filled throughout the intervening period as laid down for cathedral churches and greater monasteries in decrees issued by the third and fourth Lateran Councils of 1179 and 1215, requiring them to support a university graduate as lecturer? Or are these few surviving references intimations of a developing Benedictine concern to promote learning in the cloister long before Benedict XII's reforming constitutions for the order? Probably both were influential factors, and should be associated with the general chapter's decision to open a hall for monk students at Oxford.[66]

At Worcester there is more evidence to suggest that the Lateran decrees had been faithfully obeyed. In *c.* 1305, for example, the abbot president of the Black Monk chapter wrote two letters to the prior of Worcester urging him to resume the

---

[60] *Reg. Winchelsey*, 1309.
[61] *BRECP*, 160.
[62] Such a monk instructor was Hugh de Sancto Ivone, ibid., 271–2.
[63] Decima Douie, *Archbishop Pecham* (Clarendon Press, Oxford, 1952), 165–6. The underlying problem about Robert de Crull, the lector in question at Worcester in 1285, is that while there is little doubt that he was not a monk, there is little certainty that he was a Franciscan; and his appointment to the 'convent of Worcester' is ambiguous because although the word 'convent' was sometimes applied to the cathedral priory it could also refer to the Franciscan friary, *Reg. Giffard*, 263.
[64] NRO DCN 1/4/10, sacrist's account. Excavations on the Franciscan site south of the cathedral have recently taken place.
[65] NRO DCN 1/10/17, infirmarer's account.
[66] The Lateran decrees may be found in N. P. Tanner (ed.), *Decrees of the Ecumenical Councils*, 2 vols (London: Sheed and Ward; Washington, D.C: Georgetown University Press, 1990), vol. 1, 211–25, 230–71; the Constitutions of Benedict XII are in Wilkins, *Concilia*, ii, c.7, 594. Lateran III addresses cathedrals and monasteries in its concern that free access to learning be made available to poor scholars, but Lateran IV with similar concerns refers only to metropolitan churches.

lectures on the Scriptures which had lapsed for the previous two years. However, should there be no one at that time qualified within the community, he was not to fill this post by recalling one of his monk students from Oxford before he had completed his studies.[67] The monk whom Prior John de Wyke had in mind was probably Richard de Bromwych, who obtained his first degree in 1305. By 1317/18 he was lecturing to the Worcester monks and probably some years earlier as he incepted in theology at an unknown date between 1305 and 1312.[68] Ranulf de Calthrop and John de Saint Germans, two of Bromwych's contemporaries at Worcester and, like him, doctors of theology were in demand to lecture in other Benedictine houses, Calthrop at Ramsey abbey for an unknown period before 1318 and Saint Germans at St Augustine's Canterbury in 1308–10 and possibly later; both these appointments were as lectors in theology.[69]

There is an underlying uncertainty surrounding the specific functions performed by lectors and masters who taught in cathedral priories. Did their duties usually include the instruction of novices as well as more senior brethren, and how frequently did the appointment include the requirement to give public lectures for the benefit of secular clergy? Because these three classes of audience can rarely be distinguished I have chosen to include here all of the patchy information that remains concerning education in the cathedral priory cloister in the surmise that professed novices would probably have benefited directly or indirectly from much of it. Only Worcester has left evidence of occasions when a series of public lectures was held in the chapter house, one in the 1340s and another about a century later. The monks, John de Preston II and John Lawerne I, were appointed to perform this function; both were Oxford trained and both lectured on the Sentences of Peter Lombard.[70] For young monks who were showing promise as potential candidates for university study such lectures would have been a challenging introduction to the higher spheres of learning.

Two monk instructors appear at Ely in the 1360s: Roger de Norwich I and Robert de Sutton II. Norwich received a small sum *pro informacione juniorum monachorum* twenty years before his inception at Cambridge in 1384/5 and perhaps before he went up to university; in the late 1380s he was again being remunerated *pro instructione monachorum*. The long duration of his university studies suggests that he may have continued to teach in the community intermittently, as the short distance between Ely and Cambridge would have rendered this feasible. Nothing is known about Sutton's university credentials if he had them, probably because of the lamentable gaps in the Ely muniments; he was *instructor juvenum* between 1367 and 1369 and perhaps longer. Also, he was very likely the

---

[67] These two letters have been printed by Leach in his *Documents... Education*, 29–33. The word *theologia* does not appear; in its place the phrases *sacram scripturam* and *sacre pagine* are used to describe the subject of the lectures to be given.

[68] *BRECP*, 782–3. He returned from a short stint as prior of Abergavenny in 1325 at the urgent request of the prior as he was once again required as lecturer.

[69] Ibid., 784 (Calthrop); 869–70 (St Germans); for Calthrop see also Pantin, *Black Monk Chapters*, i, 181–5.

[70] *BRECP*, 865 (John de Preston II); 830–1 (John Lawerne I).

priory's most gifted preacher for he was chosen to give the opening sermon in 1373 at a metropolitan visitation.[71]

While novices appear to have shared with their senior brethren in some of the lectures given within the cloister, there is another combination for teaching purposes that comes into view at both Winchester and Worcester in the sixteenth century and half a century earlier at Ely. Here, junior monks are found sharing one of their masters with the young pupils in the almonry and song schools. John Potynger was appointed by the prior and chapter of St Swithun's in 1538 to teach grammar to *confratres nostros juniores*, to the *pueros capelle nostre* and to the boys who were being educated *ex elemosina*.[72] The Worcester priory schoolmaster in 1501 was employed to teach 'fratres nostros et scholasticos domus nostre elemosinarie [in] grammatice vel arte dialectice'.[73] For the best part of two decades in the mid-fifteenth century a secular priest, John Dounham junior, is known to have been engaged in giving daily lessons in grammar to the junior monks and almonry boys at Ely.[74] These appointments illustrate some of the combinations put into practice by the priors and their advisers for the mutual convenience of teachers and taught, as well as for the well-being of the entire monastic community and the smooth running of their daily regimen; they were probably not an innovation in the mid-fifteenth century but earlier confirmation is lacking.

The cathedral priory novices have been observed bending over their books in the cloister, and it has been noted that any specific curriculum of studies, especially for the years immediately following profession, continues to elude even the most diligent researches. This may well be because the arrangements were flexible, possibly even verging on the *ad hoc*, as would seem to have been the policy with regard to the shortened course for those preparing for early ordination as priests.[75] Because of the autonomous status enjoyed by the majority of Benedictine houses it is not surprising that regulations for post-profession study programmes are not to be found among the statutes issued by the triennial Black Monk chapters. However, the fact that only bare fragments occur of most of the surviving customs and ordinances issued by any of the individual cathedral priories is disappointing.[76]

Like the 'bare ruined choirs' and other surviving monastic remains, manuscript books are witnesses to the past; in addition, the book has the advantage of being articulate. It speaks through its text to us as it has spoken to others, although our understanding and interpretation of its contents will differ from those of earlier readers because none of us can escape from the confines of our own particular age,

---

[71] Ibid., 427 (Roger de Norwich I); 446 (Robert de Sutton II).
[72] WCL, Priory Reg. III, fo 83v; see also *BRUO (1501–40)*, 459 whose biographical account refers to Potynger's education at Winchester College and New College, Oxford. For the Ely boy choristers see Evans, 'Ely Almonry Boys', 155–69.
[73] Printed in Leach, *Documents . . . Education*, 93 from WCM Reg. A.VI (2), fo 17.
[74] Greatrex, 'Benedictine Observance at Ely', 77–93 at 80.
[75] See above 93–4.
[76] One such fragment is a note on the Ely precentor's account for 1373/4 that he paid for 'j Consuetudinar' & j Gradal illuminand' hoc anno 22s 9d', CUL Add MS 2957, 45 (Bentham transcripts). A Worcester reference occurs on the precentor's account for 1388, WCM C.366; he bought vellum *pro libro consuetudinar' claustri*.

circumstances, and environment. Nevertheless, to a limited, though by no means insignificant, extent manuscripts put us in close if not direct touch with those who commissioned, ordered, purchased, and read them in successive generations. Even when it is only seldom that we discover which monks were actually reading them, we know that at a certain point of time they were selected by monks as essential or, at least, desirable and useful reading material for members of the community. For this reason it cannot be considered a digression to examine the contents of the cathedral priory libraries in some detail. In 1960 Jean Leclercq pleaded for more research into the inner life and thought of ordinary monks, in other words to focus less on what they did and more on what they were. By looking carefully at what they read and wrote, I suggest, we should begin to glimpse the motivation of mind and heart.[77] Although monastic studies were focused on the Bible there were many volumes in monastic libraries on other subjects such as grammar, history, and science. Scripture and theological studies will be discussed here.[78]

Scripture studies: the use of patristic biblical commentaries

Dominican novices at an early stage received daily lectures on the Bible, and the Benedictines could hardly have provided less for their novices.[79] Indeed, apart from the Bible itself, of which a good number of copies have survived, the existence of a multitude of glossed Bibles, biblical commentaries, concordances, dictionaries, *tabulae*, and other reference aids in the cathedral priory book cupboards and on their library shelves underlines the life-long commitment of the monk to the study of the sacred texts.[80]

Novice masters and lectors in the cathedral priories had to hand a variety of biblical commentaries ranging from those of the Fathers to more recent and even contemporary writers. Of the earlier commentators, for example, Ambrose and Bede were, and seemingly remained, among the most popular. Ambrose's Super Lucam is found in the earliest extant inventories of books at Rochester and at Durham where a copy was also said to be *in libraria* in 1395.[81] The Bath entry in the mid-fourteenth-century *Registrum Anglie de Libris*, consisting of a mere nineteen titles, also names this Lucan commentary as does the Eastry catalogue at

---

[77] Jean Leclercq, 'The Monastic Tradition of Culture and Studies', *American Benedictine Review*, 11 (1960), 99–131.

[78] Grammar and history will be discussed in the two appendices.

[79] M. M. Mulchahey, 'First the Bow is Bent in Study...', *Dominican Education before 1350*, Pontifical Institute of Medieval Studies, Studies and Texts, 132 (Toronto, 1998), 133. It is also worthy of note that after profession, the young friars (*juvenes*) continued to study for another two years and remained free of most other tasks, ibid., 106–7.

[80] How many monks had Bibles of their own? The Eastry catalogues name some twenty-eight Christ Church monks whose Bibles or portions thereof had been placed in the library, presumably after their death; and a good number of other monks had had in their possession copies of one or more books of the Old and New Testaments, James, *ALCD*, 28–148 *passim*. Many monks' names are also attached to glossed books of the Old and New Testaments.

[81] Sharpe, *EBL*, at B77.41 (1122/3 Rochester catalogue); *Cat. Vet. Durham*, 3, 57D^1. *Libraria* must here refer to cloister as the new library was not constructed before 1414–18.

Canterbury of slightly earlier date.[82] In the response to the Ely novices' petition for profession there is a passing reference to Ambrose's Luke which has already been noted.[83] Among Bede's biblical expositions, those on Mark, Luke, and the Acts of the Apostles were available at Canterbury; Durham had all four gospels *de manu Bedae*; those on Mark and Acts are listed in the early twelfth-century catalogue at Rochester.[84] Bede's commentary on Mark was also at Worcester at an uncertain date, and a copy of his *Quaestiones super Genesim* was reportedly seen by Leland on his visit to Ely (*c.* 1536–40).[85] Augustine's commentary *De Genesi ad litteram* was familiar at Bath, Canterbury, Durham, Norwich, and Worcester, and also at Rochester where the precentor, Elias II, was probably responsible for procuring this volume before 1202.[86] Two other patristic commentators whose works, assuredly, found a place in all the cathedral priories were Jerome, a contemporary of Augustine, and Gregory the Great, who was pope from 590 to 604. It is Jerome's Vulgate version of the Bible, translated by him from Greek and Hebrew texts, that was gradually accepted by the Church for use in its liturgical services;[87] and it was Gregory, himself a monk and founder of monasteries, who also provided the followers of St Benedict with a life of their founder, copies of which must have belonged to every monastic community that adhered to the Rule. Among the cathedral priories, at Rochester, Canterbury, Durham, Ely, and Worcester several manuscripts containing Gregory's *Dialogi* with the *Vita* have survived.[88] His commentary on the book of Job, *Moralia in Job*, as it was frequently named, also seems to have retained its popularity among Benedictines, certainly in the cathedral priories where medieval book catalogues and surviving manuscripts combine to provide abundant evidence of its presence, with two or

---

[82] Rouse, *Reg. Anglie de Libris*, 317 (Bath): this register was a Franciscan project to compile an early 'union list' of patristic and a few later select writings owned by English religious houses; unfortunately, it remains far from complete. The Eastry catalogue in James, *ALCD* lists one copy of Ambrose on Luke: item no. 49.

[83] See above, 71.

[84] James, *ALCD*, Oxford, Bodley MS 217 (Mark), Eastry catalogue: item no. 87 and Cambridge, Trinity College MS 46 (Luke), item no. 88 (Acts), and item no. 89 (Mark); Rouse, *Reg. Anglie de Libris*, 248 (Canterbury); Rouse, *Reg. Anglie de Libris*, 164 (Mark, Luke, Acts), *Cat. Vet. Durham*, 16D² now DCL MS A.II.16 (Durham); Sharpe, *EBL*, at B77.70, B77.35c (Rochester).

[85] The Worcester commentary, now BL MS Royal 4 B.xiii, was written in the twelfth century but its presence in the library there was not noted until the early 1600s and so it may have been a late arrival. For Ely see Sharpe, *EBL*, at B28.2.

[86] Rouse, *Reg. Anglie de Libris*, 317 (Bath); James, *ALCD*, Eastry catalogue, item nos 1, 2, 110 (Canterbury); *Cat. Vet. Durham*, 2, 17G, 63AC (now DCL MS B.II.27) (Durham); Sharpe, *EBL*, at B62.20a, bound with Augustine's commentary on John and at St Leonard's cell in 1424 (Norwich); BL MS Royal 5 C.i (Rochester); for Elias see *BRECP*, 601.

[87] For a brief account of the various early editions and translations of the Bible see Christopher de Hamel's *The Book, a History of the Bible* (Phaidon, London, 2001), 13–38.

[88] One Rochester copy of the *Dialogi*, of which Book II contains the *Vita*, is now BL MS Royal 6 B.ii, and another copy may have been in MS Royal 5 E.ii; see Sharpe, *EBL*, at B77.46. Rouse, *Reg. Anglie de Libris* records a copy at Christ Church, 248, and the Eastry catalogue lists several copies, James, *ALCD*, item nos 151, 156 (?), 157, 1169, one of which may now be Cambridge, Trinity College MS 79. Durham manuscripts included DCL A.III.11; an Ely manuscript of the tenth/eleventh century is now in LPL, MS 204; a Worcester manuscript of similar date is in Cambridge, Clare College MS 30.

more copies at Canterbury, Durham, Rochester, and Worcester and single copies at Norwich and Winchester.[89]

Lists recording repairs, including the binding and chaining of Christ Church books in 1508, together with those of volumes in the library of Canterbury College Oxford between 1443 and 1524, and of similar lists of Durham College Oxford in the late fifteenth century, suggest that many of the above commentaries continued to be consulted—and were consequently the victims from wear and tear—throughout the period covered by this study and probably until the dissolution.[90] William Ingram's list of 1508, for example, includes Ambrose on Luke and Bede on Mark and Luke, several of Jerome's Old Testament commentaries and Gregory's *Moralia*.[91] Augustine's *Super Genesim ad litteram* had appeared at Canterbury College Oxford more than half a century earlier where it was listed in 1443 among the warden's books kept in his study.[92] As early as 1315 Durham monks at Oxford had been equipped with Augustine and Bede on Genesis and the second part of Gregory's *Moralia*; these commentaries were still on hand for the monk students in c. 1390–1400 when the *Moralia* was listed as complete in two volumes.[93] Bede's Mark, now BL MS Royal 4 B.xiii, written in a twelfth-century hand, belonged to the Worcester monks; nevertheless, purchases made by the Prior William More between 1518 and 1533 perhaps lend some further weight to the continuing reliance on these patristic writers as well as to the pleasures of print. Volumes containing the works of Ambrose, Augustine, Jerome, Gregory, and Bede ordered from London were quite likely to have been complete editions although only in the case of Augustine is this stated explicitly.[94]

---

[89] In the Eastry catalogue there are two items, nos 537 (an abbreviated copy) and 738 (extracts); Cambridge, Trinity College MS 123, written at Christ Church in the twelfth century, contains the second part of the *Moralia* (Canterbury). Two manuscripts remain *in situ* at Durham, DCL B.II.32 (*in libraria* in 1395, *Cat. Vet. Durham*, 63A[6]) and B.III.10 (a copy of the first part only) was at Oxford in 1416, *Cat. Vet. Durham*, 96A[2], and other copies are recorded in *Cat. Vet. Durham*, 63. Three Rochester manuscripts in the BL Royal Collection, MSS 3 C.iv, 6 C.vi (both twelfth century) and 6 D.vii contain the *Moralia*, the last mentioned being a fourteenth-century copy to which the precentor, Thomas de Horsted (*BRECP*, 613) added a *tabula*, and in which in the 1460s or 1470s Thomas Wybarn inserted his couplet warning readers to treat the volume with care (ibid., 649–50). A concordance and a *tabula* to the *Moralia* are found in Worcester cathedral MSS, Q.24 and Q.25, both of which were probably made at Worcester, but the *Moralia* for which they were intended has/ have been lost. Two Norwich copies are recorded at St Leonard's in 1424, and another copy was at Yarmouth in the fifteenth century, both cells of Norwich, Sharpe, *EBL*, at B62.17, B62.18 (abbreviated), B62.19 (*tabula* to the *Moralia*), B64.17. There is also one surviving Norwich MS, possibly one of the foregoing, now CUL MS Ii.2.22. The library of Balliol College Oxford (MS 15) houses the second volume of what was formerly a thirteenth-century Winchester copy of the *Moralia*.

[90] The 1508 list of Christ Church books repaired and the Canterbury College Oxford inventory of 1524 where these may be found are in James, *ALCD*, 152–64 and 165–72 respectively. Durham College inventories of books have been edited by W. A. Pantin, 'Durham College Catalogue', 240–5; H. E. D. Blakiston, 'Some Durham College Rolls', 1–76 at 35–41.

[91] James, *ALCD*, Ingram item nos 134 (Ambrose on Luke, 157), nos 120–1 (Bede on Mark and Luke, 156), nos 100–4 (Jerome, 156), nos 131–2 (Gregory, 157).

[92] Pantin, *Canterbury College Oxford*, i, 4 (item no. 32).

[93] Blakiston, 'Durham College Rolls', 36, 37, 36; Pantin, 'Durham College Catalogue', 241.

[94] The list was recorded in Prior More's journal and has been included in Sharpe, *EBL*, 662–73: B117.16 (Ambrose), B117.11 (Augustine), B117.14 (Jerome), B117.15 (Gregory), B117.52 (Bede; this last is probably not complete).

The appropriation of recent and up-to-date exegetical writings

An enduring adherence to the teaching of the Fathers did not preclude an openness to more recent developments in scriptural exegesis. Long before there was a monastic presence at Oxford, English Benedictines in general and some of the cathedral monasteries in particular were keeping abreast of the new trends across the English Channel. Hugh of St Victor, master of the abbey school of that name in Paris from 1133, manifests this awareness of changing times by his teaching in which he is seen attempting to retain a balance between the traditional monastic approach to biblical study and the new 'scholastic' approach that was in the process of emerging in the secular cathedral schools of France, especially Paris. Practised within the cloisters, the monastic discipline of reading reflectively and of inwardly digesting the biblical and patristic texts was giving way in the schools to an intellectual, 'scientific' examination of both the Bible and patristic commentaries.[95] Traditional authorities were being compared, differences in interpretation discussed and debated, and the literal meaning of passages of scripture re-examined in the light of renewed study of original Hebrew and Greek texts on which the Latin Vulgate had been based. The Bible continued to be the primary source for both approaches to learning but this did not prevent the tension between the two from developing into contrasting, even contradictory views that later came to affect both monks and schoolmen. Hugh's all-encompassing definition that the study of sacred scripture *is* theology became more narrowly defined in its university setting as the principles and methods followed in the teaching of other disciplines were now being applied to theology. Composed in the late 1120s, Hugh's *Didascalicon de studio legendi* guided students through an orderly programme of study in which the various branches of knowledge provided the building blocks whose cornerstone was finally revealed in the exposition of the sacred scriptures. His was a high standard of scholarship which was combined with fidelity to the monastic practice of liturgical devotion and contemplation; but the balance was soon to be tipped in favour of the new theology being taught in the secular schools. The *Didascalicon*, a handbook written for the Victorine novices, does not seem to have attracted the attention of many English Benedictines; among the cathedral priories only Canterbury and Durham record its presence. There are three copies in the Eastry catalogue and a fourth containing extracts, and two copies listed in 1390 at Durham in an inventory of the Spendement.[96] There may also have been a copy at Norwich

---

[95] The transition is vividly described in Smalley, *Study of the Bible*, Chapters III and IV. See also R. W. Southern, *Scholastic Humanism*, especially vol. ii, *The Heroic Age*, 7–147 for a more general survey of developments in the twelfth-century Paris schools. To the naming and description of the 'modern' texts I have deemed it expedient to add a few brief remarks about their authors and to outline the contemporary background in which they were produced.

[96] James, *ALCD*, Eastry catalogue item nos 170, 171, 1607 and 38 (excerpts); *Cat. Vet. Durham*, 21C^3, D^2 and 97C^3, D^2 where the same two copies are mentioned. The *Didascalicon* was often paired with the same author's *De institutione noviciorum* to form 'deux volets d'un unique programme d'éducation intellectuelle et morale', H. B. Feiss, P. Sicard et al., *L'Oeuvre de Hugues de Saint-Victor*, Sous la règle de Saint Augustin (Brepols, Turnhout, 1997), i, 11.

c. 1291 when a scribe was paid 7s. 4d. by the master of the cellar *pro libris Magistri Hugonis*.[97]

From Hugh's day onwards there is a noticeable increase in the number of biblical commentators, most of whom were both masters in the schools and nascent universities and members of the mendicant orders.[98] The wider range of choice is reflected in the diversity of authors whose writings began to be acquired by the cathedral monks even before the Benedictine general chapter in the 1270s decided to set up a house of studies in Oxford. Surviving evidence suggests that Durham may have been alone among the cathedral priories to have procured the complete set of postills of the books of the Old and New Testaments by Hugh of St Cher, a French Dominican who was lector of the order's *studium* at the convent of St Jacques, Paris; at least two of these were the gift of Prior Bertram de Middleton in 1258, that is within Hugh's lifetime. It is improbable that the Christ Church library holdings would have lacked this important text, but the only, admittedly slender, clue to its possible presence there is the fact that an unnamed work of Hugh was sent for repair in 1508.[99] The theological writings of Thomas Aquinas, a Dominican contemporary of Hugh of St Cher, were more widely known than his biblical expositions, but several of the latter were available at Canterbury, Durham, Norwich, and probably Worcester. Early fourteenth-century copies of his postills on the four gospels are listed in two volumes in the Eastry catalogue under the name of the Christ Church monk William de Ledebery, who may have acquired or had a long-term loan of them from the monastic library; they are probably to be identified with MSS 132 and 133 now in Trinity College Cambridge.[100] Durham cathedral library retains Thomas's commentary on Matthew and Mark,[101] and an undated mid-fifteenth-century Yarmouth inventory of books includes Matthew. The latter volume displayed a Norwich class-mark indicating that it had probably been temporarily transferred from the cathedral; to it was added, in 1444/5, Thomas's Mark which a scribe had been hired to copy, perhaps for the use of John Folsham, who had recently obtained a first degree at Oxford and was prior of Yarmouth in the 1440s.[102] A letter written by Prior John de Wyke of Worcester in 1306 to the abbot of nearby Evesham makes it clear that the abbot had lent the

---

[97] Sharpe, *EBL*, at B57.3. Hugh's exegetical writings were limited to several Old Testament commentaries, one of which on the Lamentations of Jeremiah survives *in situ* at Worcester (MS Q.48), and a Canterbury volume that includes Ecclesiastes and Lamentations is in Oxford, Bodley MS 345 (cf. James, *ALCD*, Eastry catalogue item nos 807, 808).

[98] See Smalley, *Study of the Bible, passim*.

[99] These are DCL MSS A.I.8, A.I.12–16; for Prior Bertram see *LVD*, iii, C.410. The Canterbury reference is in James, *ALCD*, item no. 20 (p. 153). For a summary of Hugh's contribution in the field of biblical commentaries or postills see Lesley Smith, *Masters of the Sacred Page*, 69–72; see also Smalley, *Study of the Bible*, 269–74 and *passim*.

[100] James, *ALCD*, item nos 1777, 1778 (p. 140) and repaired in 1508 (item nos 15, 16 (p. 153). An alternative title frequently found for one or more of Thomas's gospel commentaries was *Catena aurea Matthei* etc. or *Catena aurea in quatuor evangelia*. For William de Ledebery see *BRECP*, 220 where the Trinity College manuscripts, however, are not mentioned.

[101] DCL MS A.I.11, which was in the library by, and probably before, 1390 (*Cat. Vet. Durham*, 73Q).

[102] See Sharpe, *EBL*, at B64.3 and the preceding paragraph in Sharpe's text; for Folsham see *BRECP*, 509–10. Was Yarmouth like Stamford a haven for studious monks?

prior a manuscript of Aquinas on Luke for the purpose of having it copied; since only the single gospel commentary was named it is likely that the other three were already, or soon to be, at Worcester.[103] Another Dominican who taught at St Jacques in the late thirteenth century was Nicholas Gorran, several of whose postills on books of both Testaments were obtained by the cloister libraries at Canterbury, Durham, Rochester, and Worcester. His postills on the Pentateuch have been inscribed with the name of the Christ Church monk Thomas de Stureye I, who was serving as subprior in 1270 and must have acquired this volume soon after it was written.[104] Durham possessed Gorran's postills on the Pentateuch and on Luke, and Rochester a volume containing his commentary on the Psalms.[105] At Worcester Gorran's postill on Matthew has marginal annotations probably in the hand of Richard de Bromwych, who was sent up from Worcester to Oxford in the first decade of the fourteenth century.[106]

One of the most learned and influential exegetes of the later middle ages was the French Franciscan friar Nicholas de Lyra, who was a master of theology at Paris in the early years of the fourteenth century and whose *Postilla litteralis in vetus et novum testamentum* (composed between 1322/3 and 1331) became the standard commentary for the following three centuries.[107] It was Nicholas's primary concern to produce an improved and up-to-date guide to the Hebrew biblical text and to include an historical explanation of Jewish tradition; he represents, in the words of Beryl Smalley, 'the culmination of a movement for the study of Hebrew and rabbinics'.[108] Surviving evidence shows that his writings found a place in five of the cathedral priories. Both Old and New Testament postills were at Canterbury, but there are no records that can be dated before *c.* 1415 when the first part of the Old Testament arrived as a deferred bequest; a presumably complete set of four volumes, and a further volume on the Old Testament were in the college library at Oxford in 1501 and a two-volume set was repaired at Christ Church in 1508, a strong indication that several copies were circulating among Canterbury monks, and it may surely be assumed that these were not all recent acquisitions.[109] The

---

[103] The Worcester letter is in WCM Reg. Sede Vacante, fo 21; the printed *Register*, 59, omits the author's name.

[104] This manuscript survives as Oxford, Bodley MS Laud misc. 161; it is item no. 921 in James, *ALCD* (Eastry catalogue) in the list of books that had belonged to Stureye, whose biographical details are in *BRECP*, 295. Gorran's canonical epistles were at Canterbury College in 1443, Pantin, *Canterbury College Oxford*, i, 5, item no. 40.

[105] Durham, DCL MSS A.I.6 and A.III.31 respectively, although it must be said that the former was procured only in 1446; however, it may have been a replacement volume. The Rochester volume is now BL MS Royal 2 C.v.

[106] WCM MS F.67; the hand of Richard de Bromwych has been tentatively identified by R. M. Thomson in annotations to this manuscript; Thomson has also noted that, although there is evidence that the library was being put to good use in the later twelfth century there is little indication that Worcester monks were in direct touch with the output of the Paris Schools until their monk students began to acquire them at Paris and Oxford, *Medieval Manuscripts in Worcester Cathedral*, 42, xxiii–xxiv.

[107] See Christopher Ocker, *Biblical Poetics before Humanism and Reformation* (Cambridge University Press, Cambridge, 2002), 179–83.

[108] Smalley, *Study of the Bible*, 355; see also her remarks, ibid., 274.

[109] The *c.* 1415 reference to what is now Oxford, Bodley MS 251 may be found in *BRUO*, under Richard Courtenay, i, 502; the 1501 set of volumes occurs under the theological works in an Oxford

Durham copies of Lyra include his postills on the Old Testament from Genesis to Job, the Psalms, the Pauline and canonical epistles, and the Apocalypse. The subprior, Robert de Blacklaw, commissioned the scribe William de Stiphol to copy the postills of which the first half of the Old Testament was completed in 1386.[110] Lyra's postills, like the commentary of Aquinas on Matthew, were at Yarmouth priory in the fifteenth century, on loan from the cathedral library at Norwich.[111] The Rochester monk John de Whytefeld was instrumental in obtaining a copy of Lyra on the Pentateuch, Psalms, and Job which he probably acquired shortly after they were completed since he disappears from view some time after 1342.[112] At Worcester, on the other hand, there survive four late fourteenth-century volumes comprising the complete set of Lyra's postills on both Testaments, all probably with the *ex dono* of John Grene, volume three retaining the detail that he procured it *ad communem utilitatem claustralium* in 1386.[113]

It must constantly be borne in mind that, quite apart from the tragic and heavy losses sustained by all monastic libraries at the dissolution, there remain numerous listings of anonymous glosses, commentaries, and postills of which the authors cannot be identified; as a result, none of our investigations will ever succeed in yielding more than a small proportion of these much sought-after details concerning the contents of medieval libraries. However, even the little that remains of cathedral priory cloister holdings furnishes evidence for an arguable case in support of a continuing devotion to scriptural studies on the part of the monks of these communities as well as a persistent effort to keep in touch with the scholarly output of their contemporaries. Additional evidence that the university contingent of monks played an important role in the acquisition of new texts for their libraries will be given in part two of this chapter.

The significance and use of the Psalter

One Old Testament book has until now received no more than a passing mention for the reason that it requires separate treatment. Because the book of Psalms formed an integral part of the monastic office its words and phrases were constantly on the lips and in the mind of every Benedictine as soon as he had begun to commit them to memory early in his novitiate. Indeed, it was the most used of all the books of the Old Testament, and commentaries on the psalms became more numerous

---

inventory of that date, Pantin, *Canterbury College Oxford*, i, 39, item nos 1–3, and the first two items on the 1508 repair list are in James, *ALCD*, 152.

[110] These remain at Durham as DCL MSS A.I.3–5; MS A.I.4 is listed in *Cat. Vet. Durham*, 51M², and A.I.3 ibid., 51K². For Blacklaw see *LVD*, iii, C.966.

[111] Sharpe, *EBL*, at B64.18; it also has the Norwich class-mark. One of the two sixteenth-century monks of Norwich named Robert Catton had a copy of Lyra on the Apocalypse which is now CUL MS Ii.1.23; see also for Catton, *BRECP*, 492–3 where this volume has been omitted.

[112] Now BL MS Royal 4 A.xv which has been heavily annotated by a variety of hands; the section on the psalms is dated 1326, i.e. the year in which Lyra completed them. For Whytefeld see *BRECP*, 647.

[113] WCM MSS F.25–8; the flyleaves for F.25, F.26, and F.27 have been lost. For Grene, later prior, see John Grene I in *BRECP*, 812–3.

than those on any of the other biblical books. In almost every generation between Augustine and Nicholas de Lyra there appeared new contributions to the interpretation of these one hundred and fifty religious prose poems that had sprung from the hearts of the Hebrew people to express their joys and bewail their sufferings. The psalms were, of course, intended to be understood and interpreted within a Christian perspective, the underlying theme that was constantly borne in mind by all Old Testament commentators, who never failed to draw attention to the fulfilment of the divine promise in the person of Christ. Some of the authorities from whom passages were selected to provide explanations accompanying the psalms in the early glossed Bibles were named; others have been subsequently identified. The result indicates that most of the extracts are from the Fathers including Jerome, Augustine, and Bede; but among the later commentators there were three twelfth-century Paris masters who were notably in demand: Anselm of Laon (d. 1117), Gilbert of Poitiers (d. 1154), and Peter Lombard (d. 1160). All three produced postills on the psalms which were incorporated into the standard gloss of the Bible as well as existing as separate manuscripts that were widely copied and consulted.[114] We find, for example, that while the Christ Church monks were supplied with copies of Augustine's *Enarrationes in psalmos* and Jerome's commentary, long before Eastry's day they had also acquired five copies of the commentary by Anselm of Laon, three of which were denoted as having been in the possession of named monks. Two of the latter were Azo and Walter Durdent, both mid-twelfth-century members of the Christ Church community.[115] The Coventry monks also possessed Anselm's psalm commentary thanks to the industrious monk scribe who copied it *c.* 1240 along with thirty-two other volumes.[116] There are three copies of Gilbert of Poitier's commentary at Canterbury listed in the Eastry catalogue one of which was identified as having belonged to Alured the hermit.[117] As to Peter Lombard's psalm commentary, no less than fifteen copies occur in the Eastry catalogue and, of these, seven or eight have names of previous monk owners attached.[118] Since five of these monks were members of the Christ Church chapter in the second half of the twelfth century and one, Prior Wibert, died in 1167, the

---

[114] For a general introduction to the careers and contributions of these three exegetes see Southern, *Scholastic Humanism*, ii, *passim*.

[115] James, *ALCD*, Eastry catalogue, item nos 324–6 (Augustine); no. 199 (Jerome); nos 787, 996 which had belonged to an unidentified monk Gregory; no. 997 (Durdent); nos 1005, 1015 (Azo) (Anselm of Laon). See *BRECP*, 81 (Azo), 142 (Durdent), and 181 (Gregory I, II, III).

[116] Sharpe, *EBL*, at B23.24c; the volumes which comprise Bruges' handiwork are listed, ibid., 110–13.

[117] James, *ALCD*, item no. 1003; the other copies are nos 1006 and 1007.

[118] Ibid., item nos 737; 788 (this and a copy of Anselm of Laon's psalm commentary, no. 787, may have been given by Archbishop Thomas Becket); 854 and 855 (two volumes given by Herbert de Bosham, pupil of Lombard and secretary to Archbishop Becket); 897 and 898 (two volumes); 981 (Prior Wibert's copy); 985 (William Brito's copy); 1016 (Azo's copy); 1019 (Absalom's copy, possibly a monk but as yet unidentified); 1023 (Felix III's copy); 1044 (M. Humphrey's copy); 1058; 1075; 1206 (M. Warin's copy); 1299 (Thomas de St Valerico's copy); 1337. For these monks see *BRECP*, 319 (Wibert I); 100–1 (Brito); 81 (Azo); 159 (Felix); 206 (M. Humphrey); 314 (M. Warin); 274 (St Valerico).

arrival of Lombard's commentary can probably be dated to within the author's own lifetime and certainly to within a few years of its completion.[119]

Although the Durham cloister book shelves do not display multiple copies of any of the psalm commentaries by Anselm, Gilbert, or Peter Lombard, insufficient evidence may be the cause rather than lack of zeal or interest on the part of the monks. We may never know if the thirty or so glossed psalters in the 1391 inventory, distinguished only by incipits of their second folios, may conceal further copies of these and other psalm commentators.[120] However, we know that Laurence, who held the office of prior c. 1149–54, had not been slow in acquiring Anselm's postills on the psalms and also those of Ivo of Chartres, who was better known for his writings on canon law than on the scriptures. Gilbert's postills in two volumes were also in the Durham book collection according to the same twelfth-century catalogue in which Prior Laurence's books are listed; DCL MS A.III.10 which has survived *in situ* is Gilbert's exposition of psalms eighty to one hundred and fifty.[121] Three copies of Peter Lombard's postills on the psalms are listed in Durham catalogues; all have been successfully identified and found to be extant in the cathedral library.[122] The Durham monks were also able to consult Nicholas Gorran on the psalms, probably well before 1395 when it first appears in a book inventory; it, too, still survives at Durham and the hand is late thirteenth century.[123] The presence of Hugh of St Cher's five volumes of postills covering all the books of the Bible has been already noted at Durham; his psalm commentary is found in the second volume which was reported to be *in libraria* in 1395.[124] Glossed psalters which were not identified by an author may have been a compilation of several commentators, in other words like the book of Psalms as it appeared in the *glossa ordinaria* of the complete Bible but existing for convenience as a separate volume. In listing a number of these psalters, all with second folios, the monk librarian in 1395 added further details of interest in naming, for example, Thomas Rome, student and bursar at Durham College Oxford in the 1390s, as responsible for obtaining an *Expositio super psalterium* which had been placed *in libraria* in 1395.[125] Again, five monks' names are attached to psalters in the 1416 inventory, among them Rome, now currently consulting a different gloss.[126]

---

[119] Lombard completed his biblical gloss early in the 1140s. Biographical details of the five Canterbury monks are in *BRECP*, Azo (who had copies of the psalm commentaries of both Anselm and Peter Lombard), William Brito, M. Humphrey, M. Warin, Wibert. Felix III occurs around 1200, ibid., and Thomas de St Valerico in the 1220s. For all of these the references are in note 118 above.

[120] *Cat. Vet. Durham*, 13–14, and in the 1416 inventory, 88–9; several of these survive still *in situ*, e.g. DCL MSS A.II.11–13 (all in French), A.III.9, A.IV.2. There are also other unattributed *notabilia* and *sermones* on the psalms in the 1391 inventory, e.g. ibid., 26, 27, 28, etc.

[121] *Cat. Vet. Durham*, 8 (Anselm); 3 (Gilbert); for Prior Laurence see *LVD*, iii, C.96.

[122] *Cat. Vet. Durham*, 51H, and now DCL MS A.II.9 inscribed with the name Thomas Swalwell, *LVD*, iii, C.1221; *Cat. Vet. Durham*, 88a⁴ and now DCL MS A.II.10 inscribed William Pocklington, C.1004; *Cat. Vet. Durham*, 51K and now DCL MS A.III.7, inscribed Robert de Brackenbury, C.894.

[123] *Cat. Vet. Durham*, 68A and DCL MS A.III.13.

[124] DCL MS A.I.13.

[125] *Cat. Vet. Durham*, 51L² where Rome is already described as *sacrae paginae professor*, for Rome see *BRUO*, iii, 1587–8, and *LVD*, iii, C.1008.

[126] *Cat. Vet. Durham*, 88S.

William Pocklington, prior of Finchale, Henry Ferriby, who returned from Finchale to be master of the Galilee [chapel] in 1416, William Durham, and John Ryton had also borrowed glossed psalters.[127] The significance of these examples of a few monk borrowers is admittedly limited to demonstrating their continuing interest and good intentions—familiar sentiments not unknown today—and the visible functioning of the library at this particular time.[128]

There is no sign of Peter Lombard's commentary on the psalter at Norwich before 1495 when a twelfth-century copy was given to the cathedral priory by the rector of St Mary in the Marsh, the parish church within the precincts close to the south side of the monastic infirmary.[129] It is most unlikely, however, that the monks were still relying only on the glosses of Jerome and Augustine which survive together in a single fourteenth-century manuscript.[130] Surviving evidence from Rochester shows that the monks there were well equipped and at an early date. Nicholas Gorran, Anselm of Laon, and Gilbert of Poitiers on the psalms are all represented: Gorran's postills, which survive as BL MS Royal 2 C.v, were acquired for the cathedral priory by Robert de Gelham, who became a monk only a few years before Gorran's death in *c.* 1295; Anselm's gloss is listed in the 1202 catalogue as is that of Gilbert.[131] In addition, although Lombard's exposition on the psalms does not appear, Peter Comestor's gloss on Lombard's gloss does.[132] Evidence of the former contents of St Swithun's library, as noted above, is woefully lacking; all that can be traced is a twelfth-century copy of Cassiodorus's commentary on the psalms which is also recorded at Canterbury and Durham.[133] The better survival rate at Worcester reveals a copy of the postills on the psalter by Gilbert of Poitiers which was probably made at Worcester in the late twelfth century.[134] Unfortunately, the only complete copy of Lombard's commentary now in the cathedral library is of uncertain provenance and may be a post-dissolution acquisition; there is also, however, a twelfth-century fragment in a pastedown which may indicate the presence of an earlier copy.[135] An illuminated twelfth-century glossed psalter, that may have been donated to the Worcester monks by Bishop John de Pagham (d. 1157), consists of the text accompanied by the *glossa ordinaria* which

---

[127] *Cat. Vet. Durham*, 88A[4], 88F, 88N, 89Y; see *LVD*, iii, C.1004, C.1044, C.1035, 1021. Neither Ferriby nor Ryton were sent to Oxford. Ferriby may have been one of the rare breed of monk scribes/illuminators at this date as he was recompensed for his work in illuminating a gradual in 1413/14 in the almoner's and feretrar's accounts for that year (although the feretrar named him 'Richard'), Fowler, *Account Rolls*, i, 224; ii, 459. Apart from this reference Ryton, who seems to have been sent to Stamford in 1409/10, is not heard of after that date.

[128] I say 'continuing' because the youngest of these five monks had been a priest for ten years in 1416, and so all of them were senior monks.

[129] This manuscript is now CUL MS Ii.3.24.

[130] Now CUL MS Kk.2.19.

[131] For Gelham see *BRECP*, 605. The commentaries of Anselm and Gilbert are listed in Sharpe, *EBL*, at B79.139, B79.66; Gilbert's postills were a gift from Bishop Ascelin in the 1140s.

[132] Sharpe, *EBL*, at B79.64.

[133] WCL MS 4. There are several copies of Cassiodorus on the psalms in the Eastry catalogue at Canterbury, e.g. item nos 328–30 (in three parts); DCL MS B.II.30 (Durham).

[134] WCM MS F.163.

[135] WCM MSS F.47 and F.71 respectively.

includes passages from, among others, Anselm of Laon.[136] Its survival has permitted identification of one source of the gloss and serves as an example of the type of contents of other glossed psalters that no longer exist.

The acquisition of the new research and study tools

The spread of institutions of learning in the twelfth century spurred on the development of scripture studies in new directions; encouraged and guided by their masters students questioned, discussed, and compared passages of the Bible in renewed efforts to draw out their meaning. These activities were accompanied by the development of new and more sophisticated organizational techniques to facilitate this enterprise in the form of research tools and finding devices; verbal concordances and subject indexes (*tabulae*) were compiled in response to the new demands imposed on biblical and patristic texts. 'The most important tools of biblical scholarship devised in the Middle Ages' were, in the words of Richard and Mary Rouse, 'the *glossa ordinaria* and the verbal concordance.'[137] English Benedictines soon availed themselves of these reference aids if we may judge by surviving evidence from the cathedral priories. We may take the prevalence of biblical concordances, for example, the most complete and successful version of which owes its origin to the Dominicans at St Jacques, initially under Hugh of St Cher. A surviving copy of one of the St Jacques Concordances dating to the late thirteenth or early fourteenth century was assigned to the study of the prior of Christ Church according to a note on the first folio.[138] The idea that lay behind the Concordance was the need to provide speedy access to Scripture by assembling in alphabetical order all the words in the Bible and providing in each case all the references to the passages in which they occurred. There would no doubt have been another copy for the general use of the community, but those listed in the Eastry catalogue are identified only by a general title such as *Concordantie biblie*.[139] The Durham monks were assiduous collectors of St Jacques productions as has already been observed; a copy of the Concordance was obtained for them through Robert de Graystanes early in the fourteenth century and the origin of two others has not been identified.[140] As early as 1290/91 the master of the cellar at Norwich paid five shillings to have two *Concordaunces* bound; most probably these were still

---

[136] Now Oxford, Bodley MS 862.
[137] Rouse, *Authentic Witnesses*, 191. The *glossa ordinaria* would only have been suitable for use by monks who had previously undergone at least several years of preliminary study of the fundamental texts.
[138] Cambridge, St John's College MS 51; this is the third edition of the Concordance produced at St Jacques and was in existence by the mid-1280s.
[139] James, *ALCD*, item nos 1176 (p. 105), 1180 (p. 105), 1229 (p. 108), 1567 (p. 130).
[140] This is DCL MS A.I.2; Pantin, *Canterbury College Oxford*, i, 4, item no. 18. Graystanes (or Greystones) was a member of the Durham community between c. 1304 and 1333/4. Two other concordances, DCL MSS A.III.12 and B.III.22 which are probably identical, should be described as biblical subject indexes, see Rouse, *Authentic Witnesses*, 203. *Cat. Vet. Durham*, 53, has a section headed *Libri Concordanciarum*, three of which were *ex dono* of monks: Gilbert de Elwick, Thomas Lund, and Robert de Graystanes according to the 1395 inventory. All had been active in the first half of the fourteenth century; see *LVD*, iii, C.786, C.816, C.801.

circulating in the fifteenth century and may have been the two listed in inventories at the cells of St Leonard's and Yarmouth.[141] The Norwich monks may have been well acquainted with the achievements of Cardinal Hugh as it was presumably one of their number who annotated their copy of Martin Polonus's *Chronica pontificum et imperatorum* in a fourteenth-century hand; in the margin opposite the Dominican author's laudatory remarks about his fellow Dominican Hugh, a [monk] reader and annotator has summarized the passage in the text which states that the cardinal 'totam bibliam postulavit et primus auctor concordanciarum [erat]'.[142] A few frustratingly brief biographical notices of authors were inserted in a section of an Ely manuscript miscellany covering the fourteenth and fifteenth centuries, among which occurs William de Montibus and his *concord[anc]ias litteras super bibliam*; the attribution to William is probably mistaken, but this is noteworthy as being the sole surviving evidence of the possible presence of this genre of texts that can be connected with the cathedral priory.[143] Thomas de Horsted, one of whose additions to the Rochester cathedral library has been mentioned above, obtained the St Jacques third Concordance for his community probably in the 1340s or 1350s while he was precentor; some years later, in 1390, this volume, described as 'concordancias pulchras in magno volumine fratris Thome de Horstede' was one of a group of manuscripts given on loan jointly to Bishop William de Bottlesham and a local rector.[144] If the monks were content to part, even temporarily, with this indispensable reference tool we are surely not straining the evidence to suggest that they possessed a second working copy.[145] The fact that there is no clear indication of the presence of the third and final version of the St Jacques Concordance at Worcester is, at first sight, surprising because of the fortunate survival of a relatively large number of that cathedral priory's medieval holdings; the lack of surviving inventories of books, however, unlike those of Canterbury and Durham, renders it impossible to fill in some of the missing titles, of which this would no doubt have been one. There is a single reference to the purchase of one volume of Hugh the cardinal by Prior William More in 1531 but it is

[141] Sharpe, *EBL*, at B62.23 (St Leonard's) and B64.7 (Yarmouth); Richard Sharpe has tentatively identified the latter, which has a cathedral-library class-mark, as the third concordance compiled at St Jacques.
[142] CUL MS Ii.3.7, fo 75; the manuscript is heavily annotated on almost every folio in the same hand. Friars from the Dominican convent in Norwich, situated only a short walk from the cathedral, seem to have co-operated with the Benedictines and the other houses of friars in a joint teaching programme in the fourteenth century; but details of any mutual sharing of books and lecturers are sparse, see William J. Courtenay, *Schools and Scholars in Fourteenth-Century England* (Princeton University Press, Princeton, 1987), 106–11.
[143] LPL MS 448, fo 119v.
[144] The Concordance is now BL MS Royal 4 E.v; the loan is in Sharpe, *EBL*, at B83.2. For Horsted see *BRECP*, 613 and above 106, n.89.
[145] In 'The Verbal Concordance to the Scriptures' by R. H. and M. A. Rouse, *Archivum Fratrum Praedicatorum*, 44 (1974), 5–30 the authors comment on the expense involved in producing the St Jacques Concordance, but they also observe that by the 1340s it was assumed that every priest whose duties included preaching would have had access to a copy, ibid., 22, 24 (quoting Thomas Waleys OP, for whose writings see Sharpe, *Latin Writers*, 685–7).

unidentifiable beyond the fact that it was not the *Biblia cum postilla*.[146] All that remains is an early *Pars concordantium* identified by Rodney Thomson as a fragment of the second or English version which was an unsatisfactory replacement of the first edition, did not circulate widely, and was soon superseded by the third Concordance.[147]

There had been less ambitious precedents for this genre of information providers. One group consisted of alphabetically-arranged distinction collections whose purpose was to compile and distinguish, or explain, the various senses in which words were used in the Scriptures, often accompanied by short passages illustrating their meanings. Distinctions first appeared in the final decade of the twelfth century although St Jerome's *Liber interpretationis hebraicorum nominum*, which occupied a place in most monastic libraries, could be seen as an early precursor.[148] Peter Cantor's *Distinctiones Abel* or *Summa Abel*, and Maurice the Englishman's *Distinctiones* were two biblical distinctions of this type which were to be found in some of the cathedral priories before the end of the thirteenth century. The Ely monks were using Peter Cantor, which had been bound with other treatises that included the Rule and an anonymous *Definitiones quaedam breves rerum variarum* also in alphabetical order (*absolutio* to *zelus*).[149] The Rochester copy of Cantor survives in the British Library as MS Royal 10 A.xvi, written in the thirteenth century; Worcester acquired an early fourteenth-century copy but it may not have been a library volume there until some time later.[150] However, the joint purchase of Maurice's *Distinctiones* by eleven monks of Worcester affords an insight into one of the ways in which some of them chose to make use of small sums they received, in gifts or pocket money, in order to augment the cloister book collection. One of these monks was John de Wyke, prior from 1301 to 1317; and only one of them, the controversial John de Dumbleton, studied at Oxford where, probably before the turn of the century, he might have procured the manuscript.[151] Christ Church

---

[146] Sharpe, *EBL*, at B117.53. Prior More purchased a number of printed texts of authors whose writings in manuscript form were already in the cathedral library.

[147] Rouse, 'Verbal Concordance', 16–17, 26–7 and Thomson, *Medieval Manuscripts in Worcester Cathedral*, under MS F.175.

[148] The Eastry catalogue lists at least seven copies of this reference work of Jerome, James, *ALCD*, item nos 209, 910, 940, 1090, 1305, 1415, 1573. There were also copies at Durham and Rochester: *Cat. Vet. Durham*, 1, a twelfth-century catalogue, and again in the 1395 inventory, 58E (Durham); and Rochester in 1122/3, Sharpe, *EBL*, at B77.29d. At the end of the twelfth century it acquired a new lease of life when it was revised and re-arranged alphabetically; it was then often found bound with the Bible, e.g. at Norwich in Oxford, Bodley MS Auct. D.4.8 (13th century).

[149] Oxford, Bodley MS Laud misc. 112; Cantor's alphabet ran from Abel to *zelus*. The *Definitiones* is also of the *distinctiones* genre.

[150] The Worcester press-mark is MS F.130; unfortunately there is no evidence of its presence in the cathedral priory before the mid-fifteenth century; see Thomson, *Medieval Manuscripts in Worcester Cathedral*, 92.

[151] Maurice, whose dates are uncertain beyond the middle and second half of the thirteenth century, was also known as Maurice of Provins and Maurice Hibernicus. The Worcester copy is WCM MS Q.42. The eleven monks are in *BRECP*: Laurence de Badminton (773), Nicholas de Coulsdon (792), Gilbert de Dodynham (797), John de Dumbleton (800), John de Harleye (817), Hugh de Inceberg (826), Robert de Wich (893), Thomas de Wych I (897), John de Wyke (897–8), Simon de Wyre (900), Henry de Wyrmintone (900). Maurice's *Distinctiones* run from *abiectio* to *zona*.

also acquired a copy at a similarly early date; it was in the hands of John de Wy, who died in 1302. Another copy was one of the seven volumes in the possession of Robert Poucyn before his death in 1310.[152] At Durham there was at least one copy of Maurice by 1395, and Yarmouth priory had on loan from the mother house at Norwich a copy for an unknown length of time in the fifteenth century.[153] One set of theological distinctions was compiled by a Benedictine, Ranulph Higden of St Werburgh's Chester (d. 1364); it circulated in two versions, one of the second half of the fourteenth century and the other early fifteenth, both of which were at Worcester. John de Fordham's name is in the earlier version which he gave to the library; he was at Oxford, although probably not continuously, from the 1390s until his election as prior in 1409.[154] If Canterbury had a copy of Higden's *Distinctiones* it was listed in the catalogues by title only, but a Durham copy, in a volume containing a miscellany of manuscripts, has on the front inside cover above the list of contents *utiles valde*. This phrase is rendered all the more meaningful by the addition of indexes or *tabulae* to several of the treatises including Higden's *Distinctiones*.[155]

While only a small number of English Benedictines wrote biblical or theological works for circulation, many were involved with the indexing of manuscripts already in their possession, a self-effacing task of service to their community that should not be underestimated. These indexes proliferated in the fourteenth and fifteenth centuries, many of them being anonymous as well as homemade, and others ordered from professional scribes. It is to be noted that Simon Bozoun of Norwich purchased several during his priorate (1344–52).[156] Christ Church, like Norwich, had a *tabula* to the *Speculum historiale* which in 1508 was to be found in close proximity to the *Speculum* for speedy reference.[157] Entire volumes devoted to *tabulae* were among the finding aids with which the Durham library was equipped. One of these, procured by William Appleby, possibly while he was librarian in the 1390s, consisted of seventeen *tabulae*; another had ten and a third, which was obtained by Thomas Lund, was a *Tabulae alphabeticae* to Augustine's *Civitas Dei* and Gregory's *Moralia*; he may have obtained it, along with several other volumes, during his years of study in Oxford in the 1320s.[158] A volume entitled *Tabulae alphabeticae in varios auctores*, which William Seton was responsible for providing, was completed in 1438 with indexes to no fewer than thirty-six titles.[159] Henry Fouke, who was given a number

---

[152] James, *ALCD*, Eastry catalogue item nos 1614 and 1734 respectively. See *BRECP*, 327 (John de Wy I) and 257–8 (Poucyn).

[153] The Durham *Distinctiones* is listed in *Cat. Vet. Durham*, 53G, and that of Yarmouth in Sharpe, *EBL*, at B64.6.

[154] The earlier version is WCM MS F.128 and the later MS F.80. For Fordham see *BRECP*, 805–7.

[155] This is now LPL MS 23.

[156] Sharpe, *EBL*, at B58.5 (*Tabula originalium*); B58.18 (*Tabula* to Gregory's Moralia in Job); B58.19 (Tabula to Vincent of Beauvais' *Speculum historiale*); B58.20 (Tabula to Gratian's *Decretum*). For Bozoun see *BRECP*, 486.

[157] Canterbury Cathedral MS 100; in 1508 this volume was probably no. 141 in Ingram's list, James, *ALCD*, 157, while the *Speculum* itself was no. 151, (p.) 158.

[158] DCL MSS B.III.31, B.III.28, B.III.27; other volumes of *tabulae* are MSS A.III.35 (*super Bibliam*), B.III.27, B.IV.42, B.IV.43, C.III.13, C.IV.21. William Appleby's career is summarized in *LVD*, iii, C.1001 and Thomas Lund, ibid., C.816.

[159] DCL MS B.III.29; this may have been an in-house production; Seton's biographical details are in *LVD*, iii, C.1116.

of responsible positions at Worcester between the 1320s and 1340s, was at the same time much involved with the chapter library, both in acquiring and annotating manuscripts and in personally compiling a number of indexes in order to facilitate their use by himself and his brethren. A treatise on canon law by William de Pagula, two volumes of sermons and a Franciscan *Speculum beatae Mariae virginae* are among his contributions as an indexer.[160] In the second half of the fourteenth century, William de Thornham of Rochester cathedral priory undertook the task of providing a subject index for the library copy of the *Super unum ex quatuor* or *De concordia evangelistarum* of Zacharias Chrysopolitanus, a French Premonstratensian canon who completed this 'cross-referenced merging of the Gospel accounts' in the middle of the twelfth century.[161] The manuscript was procured for the monastery by Prior Alexander de Glanvill a century later, and was presumably continuing to fill the need that had originally prompted its compilation so that, in Thornham's day, an accompanying *tabula* was warranted.[162]

Further developments and acquisitions

The production of a continuous and comprehensive biblical commentary written in the form of a chronological narrative and amplified by the incorporation of historical material from Jewish, pagan, and other Christian sources—this was the achievement of Peter Comestor. On relinquishing his teaching post at Notre Dame, Paris, he retired to the abbey of St Victor where, in the late 1160s or early 1170s he completed his *Historia scholastica*.[163] Although he made use of the *Unum ex quatuor* of Zacharias, Peter chose to go beyond the limitations of a concordance by providing readers of Scripture with a single sequence of historical events from creation in Genesis to the resurrection and ascension of Christ at the end of the Gospels; to this he added information to assist in the identification of persons and places referred to, and in the resolution of textual problems. Less than a century later the *Historia scholastica* had become so universally popular that there were complaints that everyone was reading Comestor in place of the Bible.[164] The impressive number of copies in the cathedral libraries would seem to vouch for the accuracy of this statement: for example, by the 1320s there are records of at least thirteen at Christ Church, and in 1389 no fewer than twelve copies are listed in the

---

[160] WCM MSS F.131 (Pagula); F.157, Q.64 (sermons); Q.65 (*Speculum*). Fouke was clearly a studious monk but, as far as we know, was not sent to Oxford; see *BRECP*, 807–8 and Thomson, *Medieval Manuscripts in Worcester Cathedral*, xxvi–xxviii.

[161] This manuscript survives as BL Royal 3 C.vii; the quotation is from Rouse, *Authentic Witnesses*, 48.

[162] For these Rochester monks see *BRECP*, 643 (Thornham), 606 (Glanvill). One surviving volume of this *Unum ex quatuor* or *Concordia evangelistarum*, now at Winchester (WCL MS 8), may have been written there but it lacks any medieval ownership identification; another volume belonged to Worcester (now BL MS Royal 4 D.xii). The former dates from the second half of the twelfth century and the latter, which came to Worcester in the fourteenth century, from the first half of the thirteenth.

[163] For a recent appraisal of Peter's career and writings see D. E. Luscombe, 'Peter Comestor' in Katherine Walsh and Diana Wood (eds), *The Bible in the Medieval World, Essays in Memory of Beryl Smalley*, Studies in Church History, Subsidia 4 (Blackwell, Oxford, 1985), 109–29.

[164] The Franciscan friar Roger Bacon (d. *c.* 1294) is reputed to be the source.

catalogue of its cell at Dover.[165] If the estimated date of the completion of the *Historia* is accurate it seems remarkable that three named Canterbury monks who died or left in the 1180s had copies in their possession; since two of them were known as *magistri*, could they have studied in the Paris schools and have remained in touch after their return?[166]

Four copies of the *Historia* remain at Durham to the present day and an uncertain number are recorded in the late fourteenth-century inventories.[167] In *c.* 1377 John de Aycliffe, then head of the Durham establishment at Oxford, lent a volume for three years to John de Bolton, almoner; one of the three items in this manuscript was a copy of the *Historia scholastica*.[168] Henry Helay, who was appointed prior of Stamford in 1422, had nine books belonging to him sent there for his use and one of these was his copy of the *Historia*.[169]

Rochester and Worcester were also well supplied with Comestor's biblical history. The 1202 Rochester catalogue records one copy; Bishop Hamo de Hethe, who died in 1346, gave his monks another which was part of a bequest of ten volumes that were to be available for the use of [secular] clergy in general and penitentiaries in particular.[170] In 1390, when the prior and convent loaned a copy to the rector of Southfleet, there must have been enough copies in the cathedral priory book cupboards to satisfy the needs of the community, and the two surviving copies in the British Library may have been among these. One of them, BL MS Royal 2 C.i, in a thirteenth-century hand, had been acquired at an unknown date by Ralph de Stoke, whose presence in the community is otherwise unrecorded.[171] Unfortunately there is some uncertainty about when one of the Worcester manuscripts, now in the cathedral library, first arrived to join the book collection there;

---

[165] Some of the copies were incomplete. The Canterbury copies in the Eastry catalogue (James, *ALCD*) are as follows: item nos 637, 722, 975, 1047, 1060, 1084, 1171, 1181, 1208, 1219, 1340, 1619, 1651; no. 1084, which belonged to Nigel Wireker, may probably be identified with Cambridge, Trinity College MS 342. For Wireker see *BRECP*, 320–1; for the Dover copies, see Stoneman, *Dover Priory*, 299.

[166] The three were M. Warin, who died in 1180 as prior of Dover (Eastry catalogue item no. 1208); M. Humphrey, who died in Rome in 1188 (no. 1047); and Robert de Hastings, who left to become abbot of Chester in 1186 (no. 975). Biographical details are in *BRECP*, 314, 206 and 266 respectively. Another copy that had belonged to Geoffrey de Romenal (d. 1301) was at Oxford in 1443, and kept among the chained books in the chapel, Pantin, *Canterbury College Oxford*, i, 3 (item no. 2).

[167] The four are DCL MSS B.I.33, B.I.34, B.II.36, B.III.20. *Cat. Vet. Durham*, 18 lists four in 1391, three of which are incomplete: B^2, C^2, T, S; and four are listed in 1395 *Cat. Vet. Durham*, 53A^3, B^3, C^2, and 54D^1, two of which have been identified by their second folios as MSS B.I.33 and B.I.34 (late twelfth century). MS B.III.20 (mid-thirteenth century) was still in use in the second half of the fifteenth century when Thomas Pickering (*LVD*, iii, C.1168) and John Manby (ibid., C.1181) inscribed their names.

[168] DCM Misc. Charter 2477.

[169] *Cat. Vet. Durham*, 116.

[170] These are in Sharpe, *EBL*, at B79.105 and B82.6; some of the monks were also appointed as penitentiaries.

[171] The rector of Southfleet's loan is in ibid., B83.3a; the second surviving manuscript is now BL MS Harley 23. Recently, another probably earlier manuscript of the *Historia*, formerly at Rochester, appeared at a sale at Christie's, London; see their catalogue, *Valuable Illuminated Manuscripts, Printed Books and Autograph Letters* (28 November, 2001), Lot 10; it was probably written at Rochester *c.* 1190s and may be B79.105 in Sharpe, *EBL*.

but five others can be identified as present in the monastic library in the early to late twelfth and late thirteenth century.[172] One of the five (MS F.37) found its home at Worcester during the 1290s thanks to the combined efforts of two monks, Thomas de Segesbarowe and John de Wyke. The former died in 1299 while in Rome on a proctorial mission, and a fellow Worcester monk, Henry de Newynton, was sent to Rome to retrieve his books and possessions; the latter, John de Wyke, became prior in 1301.[173] MS Q.44 is inscribed with the name of John de Bromesgrove, whose known years as a monk of Worcester are 1298/9 to 1306. There is no evidence that any of these four monks had studied at Oxford, although some of their brethren were sent up as students during these years.[174] One of the three other manuscripts (F.1) is a well-worn volume showing signs of constant use subsequent to its early arrival at Worcester around the middle of the thirteenth century.[175]

Three of the remaining cathedral priories owned at least one copy of Comestor's history: John de Bruges, the mid-thirteenth-century monk-scribe at Coventry copied it for his brethren *c.* 1240; the Ely monks loaned a copy in 1277 to the rector of Suburn (?Sudbourne, Suffolk) for life, a fair indication that they had other copies for their own use; a Norwich *Historia* was recorded at the nearby cell of St Leonard's in 1424, which implies that the cathedral priory had reserved at least one copy for the fifty or so monks at the mother house.[176]

Theological studies

The lectures given by the Worcester monk John de Preston II in the chapter house of the cathedral priory around the middle of the fourteenth century were, as noted above, based on the *Sententiarum libri IV* of Peter Lombard written two centuries earlier.[177] Although by Preston's day it had been long established as the university text in theology, the influence and importance of the Sentences was not limited to the lecture halls of academic institutions as the Worcester evidence clearly demonstrates. The attraction and usefulness of Lombard's accomplishment lay not in any innovation, for it consisted largely of extracts from the Fathers on various topics that brought together the differing and sometimes contradictory opinions—the so-called *sic et non* approach—to which a reasonable, harmonious solution was usually added by Peter; this eliminated the need to look for further references. With the exception of Bath and Coventry evidence survives to confirm that all the cathedral priories had copies. The Canterbury inventory in Prior Eastry's day lists some twenty of them, together with an additional copy in Eastry's own possession; there

---

[172] The doubtful manuscript is WCM F.133, whose presence can be traced no further back than the 1520s.
[173] For Segesbarowe, Wyke, and Newynton see *BRECP*, 871, 897–8, and 858 respectively.
[174] For Bromesgrove see ibid., 781–2 where MS Q.44 has inadvertently been omitted.
[175] The remaining two Worcester copies of the *Historia* are MSS F.71, in an early thirteenth-century bookhand which came to the cathedral library during the course of that century and Q.51 of about the same date but containing only a small portion of the text.
[176] Sharpe, *EBL*, at B23.24 (Coventry); ibid., 128 (Ely); ibid., B62.16 (Norwich).
[177] For Preston see above 102. Peter Lombard died in *c.* 1160.

were also many commentaries, treatises, *quaestiones*, and *notulae* on the Sentences by authors known and unknown.[178] Thirteen copies of the Sentences are listed among the books of individual monks of whom two died in the 1180s and two others were active in the first three decades of the thirteenth century.[179] Close links between the Christ Church monks and their Benedictine brethren across the Channel form the most likely explanation for the early and continuing acquisitions by Canterbury. Moreover, these were the very years in which Prior Honorius led a delegation of his monks to Rome in the course of the chapter's dispute with Archbishop Baldwin; and this journey was followed shortly afterwards by the monks' seven-year exile in northern France during the controversy between King John and Pope Innocent III over the choice of candidate to the primatial see of Canterbury.[180] One of the monks who accompanied Prior Honorius on his travels was M. Humphrey, and of those who returned from exile M. John de Sittingborne heads the list. It is likely that their copies of the Sentences were procured during their years abroad when their travels would have brought them into contact with many of their continental brethren with whom they sojourned en route.[181] Furthermore, when Pope Innocent III issued the summons to the fourth Lateran Council in 1215 Prior Walter of Christ Church was among the monastic superiors called to Rome where he and his entourage would have had opportunities for the purchase of manuscripts to add to their book collection.[182]

These opportunities would also have been afforded to the priors of Coventry, Durham, and Worcester who, with Walter of Canterbury, were among those in attendance at the Council; but it must be admitted that there is no concrete evidence to allow us to substantiate these speculations. However, the inclusion of

---

[178] See James, *ALCD*, item nos 348, 601, 638, 724, 806, 912, 1046, 1062, 1085, 1172, 1207, 1220, 1247, 1554 (now CUL MS Ff.3.19), 1570, 1617, 1618, 1774, 1804; Eastry's own copy is item no. 5, p. 143. John le Spycer (d. 1336) had had his own copy which had also belonged to William de Ledebery (d. *c*. 1328) but it was reported lost in 1338, James, *ALCD*, item no. 1774 (p. 140), item no. 22 (p. 148). Bonaventure's commentary on Book IV, for example, is item no. 602, an anonymous *notule*, no. 639, a *tractatus*, no. 1451 and a *quaestiones*, no. 1596.

[179] For M. Warin (d. 1180) and M. Humphrey (d. 1188) see *BRECP*, 206 and 314; for Nigel Wireker (*fl* 1189–1215/16) and M. John de Sittingborne (d. *c*. 1238), ibid., 320–1 and 289. The other ten monks died between *c*. 1240 and *c*. 1328; and John le Spycer, who had borrowed the copy that had belonged to William de Ledebery, failed to return it to the library before his death in 1336. See *BRECP*, 290 (Spycer), 220 (Ledebery), and James, *ALCD*, item no. 22 (p. 148) and item no. 1774 (p. 140). A copy that had belonged to Robert Poucyn (d. 1310) with an accompanying *tabula* that may have been compiled by him had been sent to Canterbury College by 1443, Pantin, *Canterbury College Oxford*, i, 4 (item 8); for Poucyn see *BRECP*, 257–8.

[180] Prior Honorius's biographical details are given under Honorius III in *BRECP*, 203–4. When the monks were expelled from Christ Church they were welcomed and given hospitality by their Benedictine brethren at St-Omer and neighbouring monasteries.

[181] See note 180 above for M. Humphrey and M. John de Sittingborne, but note that since Humphrey died of plague in Rome his books would have been returned to Canterbury by one of his fellow monks. It should also be noted that there were rival parties of Christ Church monks who journeyed to Rome to press for papal approval in a disputed election to the primatial see in 1205/6; this involved the presence at the Curia of some thirty members of the cathedral priory before it was settled. The fact that these two monks were designated *Magistri*, suggests the possibility that they had attended one of the cathedral schools in Paris or perhaps Chartres.

[182] See Greatrex, 'Innocent III's Writings', 193–4.

one copy of the Sentences in the late twelfth-century Durham catalogue is proof of its early arrival there.[183] An uncertain number of copies, along with many of the Sentence commentaries, are listed in the late fourteenth- and early fifteenth-century catalogues and there are five surviving volumes, two of which were in the hands of known monks: Thomas de [Novo] Newcastle, whose monastic career spans the years *c.* 1269 to 1313/14, and Thomas Lund, who was at Oxford in the 1320s.[184] Eleven copies of Lombard's Sentences acquired by Worcester monks are extant and still *in situ* today. Four or five of these, however, may not have entered the library until long after the closing date of this study. Of the remainder, MS F.8 contains notes by both Henry Fouke (occ. 1303x1340/41) and John de St Germans, who may have taken it to Paris where he studied *c.* 1310–15. The name of William de Grymeley (occ. 1283x1308) appears in MS F.98, and the hand of John de Preston II has been tentatively identified in MS F.134 which he may have used in preparing his Worcester chapter house lectures.[185] Another copy of the fourth book only, now at Peterhouse Cambridge, has a *memoriale* inscription with the name Robert de Diclesdone (occ. 1300x1317).[186] Among the books that formerly belonged to Ely cathedral priory the only known copy of the Lombard's Sentences is a single fourteenth-century manuscript now in Cambridge University Library.[187] In 1272/3 the major Norwich obedientiary known as the *custos cellarii*, or master of the cellar, paid the sum of twenty shillings *pro j libro Sentenciarum* which he procured from a member of the Jewish community in the city.[188] Books II, III, and IV survive in a fourteenth-century Norwich manuscript now in Cambridge; and the 1424 book list of St Leonard's dependent cell in the Norwich outskirts includes a copy, from which one may again presume that the library of the mother house had an adequate number of copies to suit the needs of the much larger community there.[189] The Rochester monks had acquired a copy before 1202, perhaps even as early as Christ Church; it was in two volumes, each of which was given by a named individual, both of whom, it has been conjectured, were teachers in local schools.[190] Two other copies were obtained by priors: Prior John whose manuscript purportedly dates from the late

---

[183] *Cat. Vet. Durham*, 3.

[184] For the texts (and commentaries) listed in ibid., see 22–3, 54A¹, B¹, C¹, D², 98–9. The five manuscripts are Durham MSS DCL B.I.1, B.I.2, B.I.3, B.I.4 and Cambridge, Jesus College MS 15 (which is probably to be identified with *Cat. Vet. Durham*, 99P); MSS B.I.1 and B.I.2 were procured by Thomas de Newcastle and Thomas Lund respectively and were late thirteenth-century productions. For Newcastle (professed *c.* 1269) see *LVD*, iii, C.702 and for Lund (professed *c.* 1309) ibid., C.816.

[185] For these lectures, see above 102. WCM MSS F.8, F.46, F.134, Q.32 (book IV only) and Q.47 are written in thirteenth-century bookhands and came to Worcester early, while MSS F.53, F.64, F.88, and F.176 may not have arrived before the sixteenth century. For Fouke, St Germans, Grymeley, and Preston, see *BRECP*, 807–8, 869–70, 814, and 865 respectively; Fouke's handwriting is referred to in Thomson, *Medieval Manuscripts in Worcester Cathedral*, 9, and Preston's in ibid., 95. Marginal annotations in MS F.8 may also be in Preston's hand, ibid., 9.

[186] Peterhouse MS 71. For Diclesdone, see *BRECP*, 797.

[187] CUL MS Ii.2.15; the last eleven folios contain a subject index of the scriptural passages and their biblical sources.

[188] The phrase is *acquietat[o] in judaismo*, presumably in Norwich; Sharpe, *EBL*, at B57.1.

[189] The Cambridge manuscript is CUL Ii.4.38 and the one recorded at St Leonard's is in Sharpe, *EBL*, at B62.26.

[190] Sharpe, ibid., at B79.63.

thirteenth century and Prior John de Westerham, who procured one before his death in 1321; it is written in an early fourteenth-century hand and still survives.[191]

A century after Peter Lombard had completed his Sentences a theological masterpiece was penned by the Dominican friar Thomas Aquinas (d. 1274). The latter, like a number of other scholars and teachers in the later twelfth and the thirteenth centuries, had himself previously written a commentary on the Sentences which was also acquired by some of the cathedral monasteries.[192] Thomas's *Summa theologica*, however, was an exhaustive study commencing with the nature of God and going on to consider God's relationship with humanity, followed by a detailed treatment of Christ and the sacraments of the Church. Monastic communities like Canterbury recognized it as an indispensable source book and were eager to obtain it.[193] The one surviving copy at Christ Church, which consists of the first part of the *Summa* only, has been identified with one in the Eastry and Ingram lists.[194] The earliest possible dates for its presence at Canterbury are dependent on two of the first known possessors: Andrew de Hardys (d. 1305) and Robert Poucyn (d. 1310). The former had been sent as a student to Paris in 1303/4 with Stephen de Feversham II but the latter had no known university connections.[195] The Durham monks may have obtained a copy at about the same time because Thomas de Westoe, who was a member of the community between *c.* 1272 and 1321, bought *tota Summa* in four volumes as well as Lombard's Sentences in three; in all he purchased in Oxford about twenty books *c.* 1300 and annotated several including the fourth book of the Sentences (DCL MS B.I.6) and the third part of the *Summa* (DCL MS B.I.17).[196] Of surviving copies of the *Summa* there remain at Durham four of the *pars prima*, one *pars prima secundae*, three *pars secunda secundae* and two *pars tertia*, all thirteenth- and fourteenth-century productions.[197]

An early arrival of the *Summa* is also recorded at Norwich by the master of the cellar in 1313/14; he paid the impressive sum of twenty-seven shillings for one volume, the *secunda secundae*. Three of its four parts were among the forty-eight books listed in the 1424 inventory at St Leonard's among which, as has been noted earlier in this chapter, were included a number of basic texts and reference works

---

[191] The identity of Prior John is uncertain, but see *BRECP*, John I, 614, and for Westerham, ibid., 647; the earlier volume is now among the dean and chapter Rochester muniments, CKS DRc/Z20, and the later is BL MS Royal 11 C.i.

[192] At Christ Church, for example, the Eastry catalogue records several copies of Thomas's commentary, most of them listed in separate manuscripts for each book of the Sentences: James, *ALCD*, item nos 913–15 (three of the four books), 1669–71 (four books in three), 1781–2 (two of four).

[193] The Eastry catalogue in James, *ALCD*, lists the following copies with their owners: nos 1621 (Andrew de Hardys), 1666–7, 1673–4, 1733 (Robert Poucyn), 1779–80, 1784–5 (William de Ledebery), 1805–7 (Walter de Norwico). These monks are in *BRECP*, 189, 257–8, 220, 245–6 in the above order.

[194] James, *ALCD*. The first part (Eastry item no. 1666) (Ingram, item no. 12), is now Cambridge, Trinity College MS 384.

[195] See *BRECP*, 257–8 (Poucyn) and 189 (Hardys).

[196] See Foster, 'Durham Priory', 395–402 and also A. J. Piper and M. R. Foster, 'Evidence of the Paris Booktrade, about 1300', in *Viator*, 20 (1989), 155–60. For Westoe see *LVD*, iii, C.707.

[197] These are DCL MSS B.I.8–17, most of which have been found in *Cat. Vet. Durham*; several also were sent to Durham College, *Cat. Vet. Durham*, see, for example, 40A², D³.

that were presumably being consulted from time to time, possibly for practical purposes such as preaching.[198] The three or four monks residing at St Leonard's were in charge of the nearby chapel of St Michael where their ministrations would have been pastoral and have required the preparation of homilies. Although between 1348 and 1450 only two of the cell's priors received university training, Simon Bozoun, who retired as prior of the cathedral priory in 1352 and for a few months was in charge of St Leonard's, may have brought some of his books with him.[199] Because our knowledge of the collection of books formerly belonging to the Rochester monks is largely dependent on twelfth- and early thirteenth-century catalogues, scarcity of evidence for the acquisition of later works is not surprising. However, a fourteenth-century copy of the commentary of Aquinas on the fourth book of the Lombard's Sentences has fortunately survived and was in the possession of Thomas Broun or Bruyn, a member of the Rochester community c. 1384x1412; this in itself suggests the presence of the Sentences and the *Summa* which like countless other manuscripts were subsequently destroyed or lost.[200] Three of the four books of the commentary on the Sentences by Aquinas survive at Worcester as does a Sentence commentary by one of the monks, Richard de Bromwych, who was a student at Oxford and lector at Worcester in the early years of the fourteenth century.[201] Bromwych also had a copy of the *Pars prima secundae* of the *Summa* which he annotated and this, along with two copies of the *Secunda secundae*, also remains in the cathedral library, as does the *Pars tertia* which is bound with a second copy of the *Prima secundae*; this last, however, may be a late arrival at Worcester. One of the *Secunda secundae* was acquired before 1299 by Thomas de Segesbarowe and may have been one of his books retrieved by Henry de Newynton in Rome after Segesbarowe's death in that year.[202]

It is hardly necessary to point out that the choice of texts available for the use of senior novices, as they continued to pursue their studies in Scripture and theology, was not limited to the books selected and described above. What is assuredly certain, however, is that these were among the most highly regarded and eagerly sought titles between the late twelfth and early fifteenth centuries. Moreover, the means by which books were acquired demonstrates the active role played by the cathedral monks in keeping abreast of the most recent writings of European scholars. In its turn this activity reflects the persistent efforts of precentors,

---

[198] Sharpe, *EBL*, at B62.28–30.
[199] The list of priors of St Leonard's is virtually complete between 1348 and 1535, and the two who had been monk students were Walter de Stokton in the 1340s and John de Dereham in the 1390s; see *BRECP*, 559 and 499–500 respectively. For Bozoun's career see ibid., 486 and for details of his books, Sharpe, *EBL*, at B58.
[200] For Broun/Bruyn see *BRECP*, 594 where two monks of this name are listed; I have arbitrarily assigned the manuscript now BL MS Royal 9 C.iv (not Cotton, as is mistakenly stated there) to the later of the two.
[201] WCM MSS F.107–9 are the three volumes of Aquinas's commentary; F.139 was Bromwych's copy. For Bromwych see also *BRECP*, 782–3, and note that he passed it on to Henry Fouke for 20s., ibid., 807–8.
[202] Bromwych's annotations are in WCM MS F.101; the two copies of the *Secunda secundae* are MSS F.102 and F.103; the *Pars tertia* is F.104. For Segesbarowe see *BRECP*, 871, and ibid., 858 for Newynton.

librarians, and other members of the monastic cathedral chapters to ensure that their shelves were furnished with up-to-date works. Here, then, we have solid evidence of the continuing presence of a core of intellectually-minded mature monks seriously intent on advancing their own learning facilities and also on encouraging and stimulating at least some of the younger monks, the group which included the senior novices, to follow suit. This intellectual core would probably never have numbered more than a few, but it was sufficient to maintain the Benedictine tradition of study in succeeding generations. Lacking the details of how such studies were ordered and directed, we have tried to gain access to the monk readers by means of a consideration of what was provided for their reading. The sparse evidence concerning the frequency of recourse to certain volumes has been partially compensated by examples of continuity of use throughout the period of this study and beyond; moreover, occasional glimpses of lectors and public lectures in the cloister have supplied additional insights into the novices' educational surroundings. For the cathedral priories of Bath, Coventry, Ely, and more especially for the larger and more prominent Winchester, the disappointingly few manuscripts that survive should not distort our judgement; rather, we should now be allowed to propose the reasonable conclusion that at least some of the books described above were at one time on the shelves of their libraries, and were being read and consulted. For the cathedral priories in general actual proof that a given monk had in fact read a given book may be almost non-existent, but the continuing acquisitions to the book collections are themselves evidence of the presence and support of a readership that must have numbered at least a studious minority among successive generations of monks.

2. CONTINUING STUDIES OUTSIDE AND INTELLECTUAL PURSUITS INSIDE THE CLOISTER

> Ante omnia sane deputentur unus aut duo seniores qui circumeant monasterium horis quibus vacant fratres lectioni.
>
> *RB*, C.48, 17[203]

While only a select few were sent to university the majority of young monks, who remained at home, were gradually inducted into the diverse affairs of a complex organization that was dependent for its smooth running on the mutual co-operation of all departments. In this final period before they were called on to assume responsible positions they would gain experience through a variety of assignments while, during this same period, several of their fellow classmates in the novitiate were furthering their studies at Oxford or Cambridge. The brethren left behind to continue their training and their studies in the cloister were given

---

[203] Although this particular verse may be concerned specifically with Lenten readings, Chapter 48 of the Rule deals with both the intellectual and the manual work in which the monk will be engaged throughout the year. Reference is made to five different times during the day when, in between the hours set aside for the liturgical offices, the monks *lectioni vacent*.

the opportunity to continue their reading and learning in these last few years of relative freedom from administrative responsibility; it was a period in which they had time to develop their own intellectual interests, aided and encouraged by the like-minded among those senior brethren who frequented the quiet places set aside for study.[204]

Monks of the cathedral priories at university

The late thirteenth-century joint resolve on the part of English Benedictines to take advantage of the benefits of attendance at the newly established institutions of higher learning was a move of great consequence.[205] It brought the chosen monks into direct contact with a secular world where intellect was dominant, theology on the way to becoming professionalized, and scholasticism and the art of disputation were coming into vogue. It is true that the monks were to some extent shielded in being set apart from other students. At Oxford they resided in a monastic hall which was administered under the direction of the Black Monk chapter of Canterbury province until 1336, and after that date by the provincial chapter comprising both Canterbury and York provinces.[206] Gloucester Hall or College, which depended on regular contributions from all participating monasteries, was up and running in the 1290s under a *prior studentium* appointed by the southern chapter to ensure that the obligations of the Benedictine Rule were faithfully observed.[207] Among the early residents of the Hall during the first decade of its existence were Hervey de Swafham from Norwich and John de St Germans and John de Dumbleton from Worcester.[208]

Neither Canterbury nor Durham cathedral priories were participants in this corporate venture, the former because it persisted in refusing membership in the Black Monk chapter on the pretext of its self-proclaimed pre-eminence within the English Benedictine hierarchy, and the latter because it had made independent arrangements for its own monks to study at Oxford before the Benedictines of the northern province of York were united with those of Canterbury in a single chapter. Thus Canterbury and Durham Colleges had their separate beginnings as cells of their respective mother houses, distinguished by their presence and purpose in an academic setting. Although a few Durham monks were lodging in Oxford as early as the 1280s, the actual foundation of a regular college was delayed for a century

---

[204] E.g., the carrels in the cloister, probably close to the book cupboards which are still to be seen in the north walk of the Ely and the east walk of the Worcester cloisters. Durham carrels were in the north walk and those at Canterbury in the south walk.

[205] Pantin, *Black Monk Chapters*, i, 75, *De studio*; also ibid., 100–1, no. 31, and 129–33, no. 43. See also J. Catto, 'University and Monastic Texts', in Morgan and Thomson, *The Book in Britain*, 219–29.

[206] The papal constitution *Summi Magistri* was responsible for uniting the two English provinces into one, Pantin, *Black Monk Chapters*, ii, v; it also laid down the requirement that one monk in every twenty should be sent to university; ibid., ii, 55–7.

[207] Or prior *domus sancti Benedicti Oxonie*, as the monk in charge was described in a letter to the abbot of Thorney c. 1290/1291, Pantin, *Black Monk Chapters*, i, 133.

[208] BRECP, 561, 800, 869 (Swafham, Dumbleton, and Saint Germans respectively). Among the few *priores studentium* known by name two, John de Fordham and Thomas Ledbury subsequently became priors of Worcester; Fordham was *prior studentium* c. 1401x1407; ibid., 806 and Ledbury c. 1417x1423, ibid., 833.

until, in 1381, Bishop Hatfield's endowment secured its future viability.[209] At Canterbury it had been Prior Eastry's policy to send his monks to study at the university of Paris: Richard de Clyve was there in 1288, and Andrew de Hardys and Stephen de Feversham in 1303/5.[210] The earliest evidence of Christ Church monks at Oxford occurs *c.* 1331 when a private hall was hired for three students, and the rudiments of a college came into existence thirty years later. However, it was only after a series of prolonged and frequently critical negotiations between the prior and convent and a succession of archbishops that agreement was reached; and a final revision of the college statutes enabled the monks to pursue their studies in peace.[211] Nevertheless, the financial condition of both the Canterbury and Durham establishments in Oxford remained uncertain until adequate funding had been assigned, for which the major source was derived from the income of appropriated churches.

A hostel for Benedictines was initially set up in Cambridge under the aegis of John de Crauden, prior of Ely (1321–41), only to be taken over by Bishop William Bateman to provide for the needs of the clergy of his diocese of Norwich. Over the next century several other hostels or halls were used by the Black Monks; but the details of their location, their students, and wardens are sparse, and a common house of study for Benedictines did not come into existence until the 1420s. Ely was the only cathedral priory that consistently sent its monks to study at Cambridge, no doubt because of the close proximity, a line of reasoning that does not seem to have impressed the Norwich chapter which required its monks to make the longer journey to Oxford until the mid- to late fifteenth century.[212]

In recent years the monastic connections with the university of Oxford and the history of Canterbury, Durham, and Gloucester Colleges have been receiving the long deserved attention of historians resulting in an impressive output of publications.[213] Since my intention in this study is to focus on the activities and careers of monks

---

[209] The early history of Durham College is described by R. B. Dobson in *Durham Priory*, 343–50. For a more recent and more detailed account prior to 1381 see Meryl R Foster, 'Durham Monks at Oxford: A House of Studies and its Inmates', *Oxoniensia*, lv (1990), 99–114.

[210] *BRECP*, 125–6 (Clyve), 189 (Hardys), 160 (Stephen de Feversham II). Hardys and Feversham may have encountered another English student monk at Paris, John de St Germans of Worcester, ibid., 869–70.

[211] The first three students were Hugh de St Ives, James de Oxney, and Roger de Godmersham, ibid., 271 (St Ives), 251 (James de Oxney I), 171–2 (Godmersham), W. A. Pantin's four-volume study, *Canterbury College, Oxford* provides details of the foundation and early history in vol. iv, 1–50. For a brief but informative comparative study of Canterbury and Durham Colleges see also R. B. Dobson, 'The Black Monks of Durham and Canterbury Colleges: Comparisons and Contrasts', in Wansbrough, *Benedictines in Oxford*.

[212] A brief account of the early history of the Benedictines in Cambridge is given by P. Cunich in P. Cunich et al. (eds), *A History of Magdalene College Cambridge, 1428–1988* (Magdalene College Publications, Cambridge 1994), 1–8. For details and for a register of Ely monks who studied at Cambridge see Greatrex, 'Rabbits and Eels', 312–28. For Norwich *eadem*, 'Monk Students from Norwich', 555–83.

[213] For example, J. Catto and R. Evans (eds), *The History of the University of Oxford*, i, *The Early Oxford Schools* (Clarendon Press, Oxford, 1984), in which M. W. Sheehan has written a section on 'The Religious Orders 1220–1370', 193–223. The second volume, entitled *Late Medieval Oxford*, continues with 'The Religious Orders 1370–1540', by R. B. Dobson, 539–79. See also the reference to *Benedictines in Oxford* in note 211 above.

residing in the cathedral cloisters and their dependencies (apart from Oxford) I have judged it unnecessary to include what can readily be found elsewhere. This section, therefore, will be limited to providing some general comparisons with regard to the cathedral priories, e.g., the numbers of monks sent for university study, the lengths of their stay, and the degrees obtained. These will be followed by a brief description of some of the responsibilities assumed by the priors and obedientiaries on behalf of their absent charges in meeting their expenses, supplying their needs, and supervising their progress: in other words, the monk students as perceived, directed and supported by their superiors and brethren in the cloister.

Numbers, courses, degrees

A reasonably accurate numerical estimate of the university attendance of monks can be obtained from the surviving records of six of the nine cathedral priories. All of these were well above the requirement imposed on the major monasteries to send one monk in twenty for further study in the halls of higher learning.[214] The Norwich prior and chapter averaged one in seven and Worcester one in nine from the late thirteenth century onwards, while Winchester sent approximately one in thirteen beginning in *c*. 1306 when the first known St Swithun's monk arrived in Oxford.[215] One in ten among the Ely monks occurs at Cambridge from *c*. 1340, while Canterbury and Durham supported one in five or six after their respective colleges were established on a reasonably sound footing in the 1380s, both colleges accommodating about seven or eight monk students and secular scholars at any one time.[216] However, much less than half of this privileged group of monks was given the opportunity to stay long enough to return with a degree; most of them were obliged to be content with two to five years' absence from their brethren in the cloister. In fact, from their first arrival in Oxford to their departure at the dissolution only 29 out of 81 Norwich monk students returned with a degree, only 17 of 37 Ely monks (at Cambridge), 14 of the 34 from Winchester and 20 of the 48 from Worcester. For Canterbury and Durham the figures are about half and half: 55 of the 112 monks at Canterbury College and 44 of the 90 at Durham College.[217]

---

[214] See note 206 above.
[215] With the exception of Durham priory, for which I benefited from the computations of Alan Piper, these figures derive from my own research; see also Greatrex, 'English Cathedral Priories and . . . Learning', 396–411. The earliest known Winchester monk student was Philip de Lusteshall, *BRECP*, 711. It is worth noting that on two occasions, in 1343 and 1408, the prior of St Swithun's was fined by the provincial chapter because of his failure to send monks to Oxford, Pantin, *Black Monk Chapters*, ii, 22 and iii, 149. On the other hand, two unnamed monks were at Oxford in the period 1398–1402, Kitchin, *Obedientiary Rolls*, 421 (almoner), 284 (hordarian), HRO W53/14/2 (chamberlain); on the strength of these references it behoves us not to overlook the probability that there were monk students at other times of whose names there is no record.
[216] The estimates in my earlier articles of cathedral monks' university attendance have been revised here and, therefore, these may be found to differ from some of the figures previously stated which did not make adequate allowances for the differences in the dates of college and hostel foundations. In fact, with regard to Durham College, its financial security was not finally achieved until 1405, Dobson, *Durham Priory*, 349.
[217] These are also my own calculations based on my *BRECP* and Alan Piper's register of Durham monks, *LVD*, iii, 201–345. Figures for the cathedrals of Bath, Coventry, and Rochester are too sparse to be informative although a small number of monks from these three priories are recorded at Oxford; those known by name occur in my *BRECP*, *passim*.

The English Benedictine Cathedral Priories: Rule and Practice   129

The course of study and the length of time allowed for it were individually determined by monastic superiors. After their grounding in arts subjects in the cloister cathedral monks for the most part were sent to read theology, although a small number were directed to follow the course in canon law. In fact, no Durham or Worcester monks proceeded to take a law degree; Canterbury produced only seven canonists as did Ely, while Norwich produced six and Winchester two. There may have been additional monk students of canon law but, unless they graduated, their field of study was rarely stated; and it is generally assumed that those who were recalled before completing the degree requirements were likely to have been theologians.

A number of reasons combine to explain why many students had to be content with only two to five years in the centres of higher learning. In the first place it was not deemed important or even desirable to study for any longer than was necessary to learn to preach and teach the articles of faith and doctrine.[218] In the second place it was very costly as will soon become clear. Moreover, monks could be recalled at any time, as was Adam Easton *c.* 1357 by the prior of Norwich, who required his presence for the purpose of preaching at a critical moment when the friars in the city were alleged to be spreading false opinions and thwarting the Benedictines in the cathedral.[219] Easton's travelling expenses between Norwich and Oxford in one year amounted to £7 14s. 8d., an exorbitant sum, a large proportion of which was no doubt explained by the fact that he was wont to carry with him a quantity of heavy tomes.[220] Monk students could also be required to return to their monastery from time to time, probably to demonstrate their preaching skills in the cathedral on important holy days and festivals. Thomas Brinton, one of Easton's brethren at Norwich and his contemporary at Oxford, was sent for in order to give the homily on Good Friday in 1356; his round trip cost a mere 5s. 4d.[221] John Wodeward was recalled to Worcester for this purpose twice in 1405/6 and his fellow monk Richard Barndesley twice in 1419/20; the former preached on Christmas Eve and again on Good Friday and the latter on an unspecified occasion and on the feast of the Assumption.[222] These return visits provided an opportunity for the prior and his advisory council to assess the progress of their monk students and to decide when they had acquired the knowledge and skills for which they had been sent. Barndesley and Wodeward, for example, were recalled after only four or five years at Oxford, while William Hertilbury their fellow monk, who had probably gone up to Oxford from Worcester with Barndesley, was permitted to stay on for a further six or more years to complete a first degree in theology.[223]

---

[218] Pantin, *Black Monk Chapters*, ii, 75. See also Greatrex, 'Benedictine Monk Scholars', 213–25.

[219] This was stated in a letter from the prior of Norwich to the *prior studentium* at Gloucester College, *BRECP*, 502 under Easton, with additional references. Easton's exceptional intellectual gifts, however, were recognized and he was allowed to continue his studies several years later; he incepted in theology *c.* 1365 and was himself appointed *prior studentium*, ibid.

[220] The obedientiary known as the communar was responsible for these expenses, e.g., NRO DCN 1/12/30 (1363/4).

[221] *BRECP*, 487 under Brinton and NRO DCN 1/12/29 (communar's account).

[222] *BRECP*, 894 (Wodeward), 773 (Barndesley); their expenses were paid by the precentor, ibid.

[223] Ibid., 821; Hertilbury is recorded as returning twice, once to preach and the second time for no specified reason. By, and probably sometime before, 1433 he was *in theologia bacallarius*, ibid.

During the same period, i.e. between 1405/6 and 1423/4, a third Worcester monk was pursuing his theological studies at Oxford; this was Thomas Ledbury, who incepted D.Th. in 1423/4 after some seventeen or eighteen years of study.[224] The sacrist, John de Cleve, travelled from Worcester to Oxford for the ceremony and feast and brought with him 40s. as a gift to the new doctor.[225] The accounts of some obedientiaries record contributions to mark this occasion not only by a personal gift but also by a payment toward defraying the heavy expenses incurred at the time of inception; the latter included university fees and obligatory gifts in addition to the cost of the feast at which the regents and other university dignitaries were suitably entertained. In 1384/5 when the Ely monk Roger de Norwich incepted in theology at Cambridge the cellarer contributed 20s. to the costs and at the same time sent a gift of 10s. by way of congratulation.[226] The prior of Canterbury had to foot the bill for the inception of two monks in 1410/11. His accounts for that year record the massive outlay of £118 3s. for John Langdon and Richard Godmersham. These expenses were only the culmination of a lengthy period of continuing financial support which, for Godmersham, covered sixteen or seventeen years; in addition to his studies, however, he could be said to have earned his keep by administrative duties as warden of Canterbury College during the last ten years of his stay.[227] Painfully aware of the financial strain of inception costs the provincial chapter of the Black Monks had set up a common fund in the mid-fourteenth century to provide grants to ease this burden. William Worstede, monk of Norwich and soon to be elected by his brethren as prior, was one of those who are known to have benefited; he received £25 in 1423 as noted on the account of the two presidents of the chapter.[228] Unfortunately a Durham monk at Oxford *c.* 1341 had no recourse for extra funding when his prior told him that money would not be forthcoming to pay inception costs on account of the recent Scottish depredations of their lands and of the *impositio nonarum*.[229]

It is therefore unsurprising that an anxious Worcester monk, John de Dudley, was reluctant to burden his brethren with the expenses of his inception on top of those he had already incurred over a thirteen-year stay in Oxford from 1379 to 1392. Four letters have survived to reveal his hesitation and search for advice and, doubtless, for practical assistance as well. Two of these letters are from Thomas of Woodstock, duke of Gloucester, and a third from the duchess his wife, all three

---

[224] For Ledbury's career see ibid., 833–4; it is probable that, for at least part of this lengthy period, he was made to divide his time between Oxford and Worcester.

[225] Ibid., 787 (Cleve) and 833 (Ledbury).

[226] Ibid., 427 (Roger de Norwich I). The Durham monk William Ebchester was given small sums by at least four obedientiaries in commendation of his successful completion of a B.Th., DCM accounts of the feretrar, hostiller, sacrist, and terrar for the year 1420/1, *LVD*, iii, C.1053.

[227] Pantin, *Canterbury College Oxford*, iii, 63–7 and iv, 191. John Langdon I's career is in *BRECP*, 217 and that of Richard Godmersham I ibid., 170–1; the former was a theologian, the latter a canonist.

[228] Pantin, *Black Monk Chapters*, iii, 90; for Worstede, *BRECP*, 573–4.

[229] H. E. Salter, W. A. Pantin, H. G. Richardson (eds), *Formularies Which Bear on the History of Oxford, c. 1204–1420*, 2 vols, Oxford Historical Society, new series, vols vi, v (Oxford, 1942), iv, 225. The *impositio nonarum* refers to the parliamentary grant of March 1340 as an aid to alleviate Edward III's increasing burden of debt in the opening years of the Hundred Years War; see M. McKisack, *The Fourteenth Century (1307–1399)* (Readers Union, Oxford University Press, London, 1964), 162–3.

addressed to the prior urging him to find the money to allow the unfortunate monk to proceed to his doctorate. Presumably Dudley had previously approached the duke and duchess, who had listened sympathetically to his problem; but there is no evidence that their practical help extended beyond sending letters to the prior, whose reply was somewhat vague but generally favourable. In the event Dudley did incept and received 20s. from the prior, presumably as a gift. The provincial chapter also came to the rescue by allocating an unspecified amount, although this sum was reported as still unpaid some six years later and therefore some person or body remained out of pocket.[230]

Student funding

In addition to the income derived from appropriated churches that was assigned to the support of monk students, contributions in cash and kind were required from obedientiaries, the size of whose contributions must have been predetermined by the prior and senior monks. This was a necessity since the appropriated churches not infrequently failed to yield the amount at which they had originally been valued, and the shortfall had to be met by the individual (cathedral) monastic chapter. It would appear that students were at times obliged to do without or go into debt. Thomas Hosyntre, a Worcester monk student who died in 1444/5 at Gloucester College where he had been resident, left the Worcester cellarer to settle his outstanding bills: 23s. 4d. to the college butler, and 18s. 8d. to named people in Oxford; the final total, which also included sums owed by two of Hosyntre's fellow monk students, exceeded £20.[231] Books placed in Oxford loan chests also suggest needy monks who had disregarded papal regulations concerning volumes entrusted to their safe-keeping while they were at the university. Benedict XII's Constitutions had laid down that records were to be kept of the books removed from monastic libraries for the use of monk students, with the individual monk's name attached in each case.[232] However, the wardens of Gloucester College would have experienced difficulty in keeping track of their students' actions concerning the collections of books brought by the monks from their monasteries. Nicholas Hambury of Worcester, for one, probably did not hesitate for long before pledging an early twelfth-century copy of Augustine's *Enchiridion* in the Seton chest in the 1460s.[233]

Due to the loss of vast numbers of the annual accounts of monk obedientiaries and also to the abbreviated, shorthand form in which the surviving rolls were written it is impossible for the most part to work out, with any degree of precision, the actual amount paid for a given monk student's upkeep and other expenses to

---

[230] *BRECP*, 797–9 (John de Dudley I). Some eighty years earlier Ranulf de Calthrop, one of the first Worcester monks to incept, found himself in debt and sought contributions from the obedientiaries, one of whom, the cellarer, sent £4, ibid., 784 (under Calthrop).
[231] Ibid., 825 (Hosyntre).
[232] Pantin, *Canterbury College Oxford*, iv, 155.
[233] *BRECP*, 815 (Hambury); the volume is now BL MS Harley 3066. See also Thomson, *Medieval Manuscripts in Worcester Cathedral*, 92, under MS F.130 which Hambury also owned.

cover an academic year at university.[234] The sums despatched from the home cathedral priory, as entered on the accounts, often fluctuated for reasons rarely recorded, with the result that we are left with only a partial picture based on the fragments that survive. Nevertheless, when the extant materials are brought together they render visible the general conditions under which the cathedral monks fared at Oxford and Cambridge.

Thanks to a fairly continuous run of a good number of the Worcester obedientiary accounts it is possible to discern signs of a pattern in the annual distribution of payments on which the usual complement of two students were dependent. Before the appropriation of Overbury church and its attendant chapels was completed the bishop, Wulstan de Bransford, who had previously been prior, sent John de Lemenstre, a fellow monk, to Oxford in the mid-1340s and supported him out of his own episcopal revenues.[235] In 1346/7 the Worcester cellarer reported that he had allocated from his funds the sum of £7 11s. 5d. per annum for two monk students; not until 1382/3 was this amount increased to £12 for two.[236] In addition the chamberlain contributed an average of £3 for clothing and bedding; the sacrist paid 4s. for wax candles for lighting, and the kitchener supplied 8d. per monk per week to cover the cost of meals.[237] In addition the almoner and other obedientiaries often recorded small sums usually classed as gifts; and the pittancer doled out the annual pittances, or pocket money, to all the monks present and absent, the usual amount being about 16s. each.[238] As noted above, the precentor was charged with meeting the students' travelling expenses as well as those of any messengers riding back and forth between Worcester and Oxford with letters and summonses to return home when need arose.[239] There are also occasional references on the accounts to a few of the conveniently situated Worcester priory manors to the effect that students stopped en route for meals and accommodation; these expenses were charged to the manor and entered on the manorial account. Thus the bailiff of Cropthorne in 1411/12 and his counterpart at Blackwell the following year included the cost of entertaining the journeying monk students.[240] A century earlier the reeve of Grimley had been ordered by Prior John de Wyke to provide

---

[234] For example, a number of diverse items were frequently listed together in a single entry on the account roll and only the total cost stated.

[235] This episcopal generosity may have been unparalleled; no other example has yet turned up. *Reg. Bransford*, no. 828 and *BRECP*, 779–80 (Bransford), 836 (John Lemenstre I).

[236] WCM C.61, C.70. The papal bull authorizing the appropriation is dated 2 October 1347 (fifth year of Clement VI); it has been printed in *Liber Pensionum*, no. 68, pp 18–19. One of its stipulations was that some of the income from Overbury should be used to support two monks at the university; see also *CPP*, i, 121. The delay in reaping any financial benefit was no doubt partly due to the expenses involved including £110 to the proctor acting on the chapter's behalf, WCM Liber Albus, fo 205.

[237] E.g. WCM C.12 (1379), C.16 (1389) chamberlain's accounts under the heading *coopertur*'; C.425 (1423/4) sacrist; C.124 (1393/4), C.142 (1422/3) kitchener. These expenses were also, no doubt, borne by the above obedientiaries on behalf of their brethren at home, but the cost would have been less.

[238] The pittancer's annual distribution is regularly recorded on his surviving accounts; see, for example, WCM C.309 (1372/3).

[239] In 1383/4 the precentor paid 11s. 2d. for two returning students and their horses, WCM C.363; and in 1419/20 he spent 18s. 9d., C.375.

[240] WCM C.565 (Cropthorne), C.538 (Blackwell, near Tredington).

two large cheeses for two Worcester monk scholars at Oxford.[241] Calculations from surviving evidence strongly suggest that a Worcester monk student seldom, if ever, was in receipt of the full £15 per annum prescribed by the provincial chapter c. 1363.[242]

Winchester records suggest a similar pattern, although informative details are fewer than those at Worcester because of the frequent lacunae. For example, all but a few fragments of the accounts of the receiver or treasurer are missing on which the major payments to monk students would have been entered. From the hordarian's income, next in size to that of the receiver, no more than 10s. per annum per student seems to have been the average contribution *in exhibitione*.[243] The Winchester chamberlain regularly sent each student a *curialitas* of 2s. to purchase a knife at the local fair along with 20d. as his share *in exhibitione*; the *custos operum* gave 5s., the almoner 6s. 8d. *in curialitate* and the anniversarian 2s. 6d.[244] A few of the extant manorial accounts of St Swithun's provide additional details in recording the stopovers of monks travelling back and forth between Winchester and Oxford. Whitchurch (Hants) was one of the manors conveniently located for their journeys and probably a frequent resting place for saddle-weary monks. Thomas Nevyle and Thomas Shirebourne stopped there in 1389/90, on which occasion their horses ate four bushels of oats while the monks dined on chicken.[245] Hurstbourne also catered for monk students, accommodating Thomas de Chilbolton four times during the year 1393.[246] In the 1340s the manor of Woolstone was ordered to send cheese to Oxford for the St Swithun's monks and in 1364 ten capons were delivered; in 1374/5 Ralph de Basyng's inception feast was supplied with twelve capons from the same manor.[247]

Like the prior and convent of Worcester the Norwich community had been committed to the Oxford foundation from the beginning and made frequent contributions toward the construction of the college buildings.[248] Before the appropriation of the church of Sprowston in the 1360s the Norwich obedientiaries were making regular contributions to support their brethren at Oxford. Following its acquisition, in accordance with one of the terms imposed by Hugh de Sprowston on relinquishing the advowson, it became the student monks' duty to celebrate

---

[241] Ibid., C.582.
[242] Pantin, *Black Monk Chapters*, ii, 78.
[243] Kitchin, *Obedientiary Rolls*, 281, 284. In 1381/2 there were three students receiving 10s. each from the hordarian, ibid., 280.
[244] Ibid., 365, 366, 370, 371 (chamberlain); 214 (*custos operum*); 413, 416, 421 etc. (almoner); 203, 206, and in Worcester Cathedral Muniments C.534, C.535 (anniversarian). These and other anniversarian accounts have not been returned to Winchester. The number of students in receipt of these sums of money is not always specified.
[245] WCL L38/0/123 (Whitchurch Hundred compotus roll); for biographical details of Nevyle and Shirebourne see *BRECP*, 721–2, 734–5.
[246] WCL L37/8/12 (Hurstbourne account); Thomas de Chilbolton I's career is summarized in *BRECP*, 682.
[247] TNA SC6/756/10 (1342), SC6/756/19 (1364), SC6/757/2 (1374/5). For Ralph de Basyng, whose doctorate was in canon law, see *BRECP*, 670.
[248] In 1291/2 and 1292/3 the master of the cellar contributed 15s. 3d. *ad studium Oxon' erigendum*, NRO DCN 1/1/10 and 11; in 1304/5 66s. 8d. ibid., 1/1/17; in 1320/1 69s. 9d. ibid., 1/1/28.

mass daily at Gloucester College for him and his family.[249] However, little if any benefit accrued for a number of years on account of a continuing deficit in the payments due from Sprowston as the prior of St Leonard's explained on his account when, on two occasions in the 1380s, he gave an additional sum to the monk students *ex defectu rectorie de Sprowston*.[250] The full £10 at which the advowson had originally been valued does not appear to have been paid to the monk students except during five years in the first two decades of the fifteenth century.[251] This particular payment was made by the master of the cellar, the equivalent of the receiver, treasurer, or bursar in the other cathedral priories. He also itemized on his accounts a number of payments to students under a variety of categories such as *pro communibus* and *in donis* or simply *pro scolaribus*. Fortunately for us he took the trouble to name some of the recipients and to record inception dates when he allocated extra funds under *expense forinsece* 20s. to John de Hoo, for example, who incepted in 1377/8.[252] Most of the other obedientiaries made fluctuating contributions, occasionally specifying the particular item for which the money was intended, the chamberlain, for example, adding two to three shillings for spices to his usual 'pension'.[253] On several fourteenth-century Norwich accounts the precentor, communar, and master of the cellar paid some of their contributions to the subprior who may have been, for a time at least, responsible for collecting them and passing them on to the students.[254]

In 1313/14 the infirmarer at Norwich entered two payments on his account: 10s. 8d. for the students and 4s. 6d. for their clerk; this is a pertinent reminder that student monks were usually accompanied to the university by one or more tonsured attendants who provided for their domestic and probably other needs.[255] The chamberlain, who chose to label his payments to students as *pro communibus* and *ex gratia*, added further details in 1339/40 when he sent 6s. 8d. to John de Stukle and Odo for their *pellicia*; Odo was most probably a clerk *socius* rather than a monk.[256] Before 1383/4 it seems likely that the students' clothing and

---

[249] *CPR* xii (1361–4), 20. As Benjamin Thompson has observed, this was in essence a chantry which, in this case, favoured both the student monks and their benefactors; see his introduction to the volume which he edited: *Monasteries and Society in Medieval Britain*, Harlaxton Medieval Studies, vi (Paul Watkins, Stamford, 1999), 12–13.

[250] NRO DCN 2/3/14 (1386/7), ibid., 2/3/15 (1388/9).

[251] Ibid., 1/1/68 (1400/1), 1/1/69 (1402/3), 1/1/70 (1411/12), 1/1/73 (1416/17), 1/1/75 (1420/1). Of course, we need to bear in mind that the full £10 may have been paid in the years for which the records have not survived.

[252] NRO DCN 1/1/55; the master of the cellar's regular contribution this year amounted to 15s. 10d., and a further 15s. 10d. which failed to be paid until the following year, ibid., 1/1/56.

[253] Ibid., 1/5/3 (12945); many accounts fail to record an entry *pro speciebus*, but it appears again in 1425/6, ibid., 1/5/53, and one may be fairly certain that the chamberlain made contributions to the monk students in the intervening years.

[254] The master of the cellar gave the subprior 20s. in 1309/10 and 1310/11 *pro communibus* for Alexander de Sprowston, NRO DCN 1/1/19, 21; the precentor paid the subprior 4s. in 1353/4, 1/9/7 and the communar 41s. 4d. for Adam Easton in the summer of 1364, the year of his inception, 1/12/30. This responsibility of the subprior probably ceased after 1364 since there are no later references. For Easton and Sprowston see also *BRECP*, 502–3, 557.

[255] NRO DCN 1/10/1.

[256] NRO DCN 1/5/11.

bedding requirements were supplied from the chamberlain's office because after this date his accounts show a considerable increase in the amount paid; thus he must have begun to pass on to the Oxford monks themselves the responsibility for purchasing some of their own supplies on the spot.[257] At Norwich it was the communar who provided for the monks' travelling expenses and for the transport of their books and other baggage; in 1345/6 these items amounted to 26s. 8d. for John de Betele, 6s. 8d. for John de Stukle and 26s. 8d. for two others.[258] The refectorer regularly contributed between 3s. and 6s., with an additional payment on the occasion of an inception; he also provided silver spoons for the Oxford students and noted in his 1392/3 inventory that six spoons were currently in their care.[259] Even the monk gardener, an obedientiary whose annual income averaged no more than £15, gave his few pence to the student support fund.[260] These payments, though numerous, when added together were insufficient; the total, even with the amount received from Sprowston, would hardly have been an adequate provision for more than one monk; and we know that the usual number of Norwich monk students was not less than two.[261] However, our inability to explain this apparent deficiency on the part of prior and chapter should not, *ipso facto*, lead to an adverse judgement but, rather, to the realization that there must have been other sources of funding which remain unknown, either because they were unrecorded or because the relevant records have been lost.

Between 1416 and 1418 three monk students from Ely obtained degrees at Cambridge, one a bachelor's and two doctors'. The exact length of time these studies involved is unknown although one of them, John de Yaxham B.Cn.L, had probably begun his student career in 1396/7 in which year the Ely treasurer had paid £4 2s. for his maintenance.[262] In the 1340s, and perhaps earlier, the monastic chapter appears to have agreed on a sliding scale of payments by means of which eight or more of the obedientiaries calculated the amount to be set aside by their office to support the monk students at Cambridge during the year of the account being rendered. Thus, the treasurer, almoner, cellarer, hostiller, and granator paid a halfpenny in the pound while the sacrist, chamberlain, and precentor paid a full penny in the pound. How were these rates assessed? Apparently not on the relative size of the income of each of the offices concerned since the receipt totals of most of the obedientiaries showed wide variations from year to year.[263] These computations may explain how the treasurer arrived at a sum close to £4 per annum per student, which is the amount on several occasions recorded in the 1380s and 1390s

---

[257] Before 1383/4 the amount paid was usually 13s. 4d. per student and after that date twice this amount or more, NRO DCN 1/5/18 and succeeding accounts.
[258] Ibid., 1/12/25, 26. For Betele see *BRECP*, 483, and for Stukle ibid., 560.
[259] John de Hoo received 13s. 4d. when he incepted in 1377/8, *BRECP*, 525 and NRO DCN 1/8/46; the inventory that includes the spoons is ibid., 1/8/48.
[260] Noble, *Norwich Gardener's Rolls*, 34, 37, 40, 43, 45 etc.
[261] See Greatrex, 'Monk Students from Norwich', 555–83.
[262] CUL EDC 1/F/13/16 and Add. MS 2957, 72; and see *BRECP*, 465 (Yaxham).
[263] It is, of course, possible that for these computations the individual obedientiary's contribution had been reckoned at a percentage of a fixed amount that is not recorded. The references to these payments occur *passim* on the obedientiary accounts; see *BRECP*, 384–5.

and again in the 1420s and 1430s.[264] In 1337/8 John de Bekkles and Walter de Walsoken were sharing 60s. *pro vesture*; ten years later the chamberlain was providing 46s. for the clothing and bedding needs of John de Sautre and Thomas de Lincoln and, in addition, 2s. 3½d. calculated on the basis of his quota of 1d. in the £. In the 1350s and 1360s in the wake of the plague, however, the only recorded sum paid by the chamberlain to the monk students was 2s. 3d. for two; the explanation may be that financial stringency had caused him to revert to an earlier arrangement by which replacements of clothing and bedding were furnished direct from the chamberlain's stores.[265] The cellarer at Ely took care of the monk students' expenses for meals by means of an allowance which amounted to 3½d. per week for John de Bekkles in 1341/2 and to which he added his annual payment of 8½d. based on the levy of ½d. in the £. By 1384/5 the weekly food allowance had risen to just under 6d. for each Ely monk student at Cambridge, while John de Dudley of Worcester and other fellow monks at Oxford in the 1380s and 1390s were each allowed 8d. per week.[266] The contrast may not be a valid one, however, from which to draw conclusions because of the proximity of Ely priory to Cambridge; this would have facilitated deliveries of foodstuffs from the monastic larder and kitchens to the university Black Monk hostel, and the student monks themselves could travel back and forth the same day by water or road. The Ely sacrist's share in the students' support fund in the late 1350s was 5s. 10¾d. for one and in 1368/9 double that amount because there were two, as there were in 1414/15 when the same amount was paid.[267] The granator's contribution averaged 4d., if we may judge by the surviving account rolls; the hostiller 2s. 6d.; and the *custos* of the Lady chapel 8d., all three of them also for two students.[268] For the inception feast of Simon de Banham in 1366, after twelve or more years of theological studies at Cambridge, the granator made an additional contribution in the form of twelve quarters four bushels of wheat and nine quarters four bushels of malt, no doubt ingredients for an adequate supply of bread and ale; the chamberlain made a cash payment of 2s. 3d. and other obedientiaries would also have made similar offerings.[269] Other contributions in kind were sent to Cambridge for inception celebrations: 260 rabbits from the manor of Lakenheath, for example, by order of the cellarer for Roger de Norwich in 1384/5; he also made payments of 20s. and an

---

[264] For example in 1389/90 (CUL EDC 1/F/13/13); 1396/7 (1/F/13/16); 1423/4 (1/F/13/18); 1428/9 (TNA SC6/1257/4); 1434/5 (SC6/1257/5).

[265] *BRECP*, 390 (Bekkles), 455 (Walsoken), 437 (Sautre), 422 (Lincoln). The amount, described as 'pension', was 2s. 3d. in 1360/1 and 1367/8, CUL EDC 1/F/3/14 and 1/F/3/16, but later accounts do not specify the amount as a separate item.

[266] CUL EDC 1/F/2/9 (cellarer). In this same year the sacrist made contributions to Bekkles and Walsoken *ex curialitate* of 11s. 11d. and 6s. 8d. respectively, Chapman, *Sacrist Rolls*, ii, 107; some of this money may have gone toward the food allowance. The cellarer's account for 1384/5 is CUL EDC 1/F/2/25. For Dudley's living allowance see WCM C.121, 123.

[267] In 1357/8 and 1359/60 for example, Chapman, *Sacrist Rolls*, ii, 178, 190; 1368/9 CUL EDC 1/F/10/16; 1414/15 CUL Add. MS 2956, 167.

[268] For the granator e.g., CUL EDC 1/F/4/14b (1375/6), 1/F/4/15 (1377/8), 1/F/4/17 (1383/4); for the hostiller CUL EDC 1/F/5/4 (1381/2), 1/F/5/5/ (1387/8); for the *custos* of the Lady chapel CUL Add. MS 2957, 54 (1359/60), ibid., 56 (1367/8).

[269] For Banham's inception, see *BRECP*, 390 and CUL 1/F/4/14, 1/F/3/15.

additional 10s. *in exhennia* to the new doctor. In 1396/7 the menu for Edmund de Totyngton's inception feast was enhanced by the gift of two eels courtesy of the precentor.[270]

Some of the Ely monk students were probably required to interrupt their studies to take on temporary responsibilities in the cathedral priory and at least one monk, the Roger de Norwich named above, seems to have been both teaching the junior monks in the cloister in the 1380s and at the same time continuing his Cambridge theological studies.[271] Although there is no mention of monk students returning to Ely to preach in the cathedral, four of them were licensed in May 1415 to preach in any church [? in Cambridge] appropriated to the monks; their homiletic skills could have easily been assessed, however, since they were able to return to their home monastery more frequently than Norwich and Worcester monk students to theirs.[272]

The financial arrangements in place for the monk students of Canterbury and Durham Colleges were, in some respects, similar to those in operation for their brethren from the other cathedral priories who were in residence at Gloucester Hall. There was one principal difference, however, in that these two colleges were administered as cells of their mother houses while Gloucester Hall, as we have seen, was subject to the provincial chapter of the English Benedictines. The wardens of these two colleges were treated as senior obedientiaries and, as such, the Canterbury College warden was chosen from a list of three names presented to the archbishop by the prior and chapter; the Durham College warden was appointed by the prior after consultation with senior monks.[273] Five warden's accounts dating from the 1380s and 1390s survive for Canterbury College and nine from the 1390s for Durham College; there are also some later accounts of both, most of which fall outside the period of this study.[274] The largest item among the receipts recorded by the Canterbury warden, William de Dover, in 1382/3 was the sum of £86 which,

---

[270] Roger de Norwich also received money from the chamberlain whose account provides interesting details of his contribution: 13s. 4d., and a further 3s. 4d. in procurations laid down by the provincial chapter based on ½d in the £ for the current year and the two years following, *BRECP*, 427 (Roger de Norwich I). For Totyngton ibid., 451.

[271] Ibid., 427; this is almost certainly the correct explanation for the fact that Norwich continued to receive his university maintenance allowance from the treasurer while he was also teaching in the cloister; at first he received payment *pro informatione juniorum monachorum* and in later years *pro instructione monachorum*. The difference between the two phrases may indicate a different group within the monastery to whom he was assigned.

[272] Ibid., 424, where the other three names are listed under Henry Madyngle. If the licence was intended to apply only within the town limits of Cambridge the church of St Andrew the Great in the market place would alone have fitted the description; however, there were other parish churches in close proximity, i.e., Impington, Swaffham Prior, and possibly Newton, which were also appropriated to Ely. There may have been an unusual situation here because it was Archbishop Chichele and not Bishop John Fordham who issued the licence; Fordham was possibly abroad.

[273] For Canterbury College appointments see Pantin, *Canterbury College Oxford*, iii, nos 43, 44, 49, 56, 57 etc.; in other words the appointments followed the same procedure as those to a number of the other obedientiary offices, see above 15–16. For Durham College see Dobson, *Durham Priory*, 347.

[274] Pantin has transcribed the Canterbury College accounts in *Canterbury College Oxford*, ii, 124–47. The Durham College account of 1392/3, followed by several mid-fifteenth- and sixteenth-century rolls, have been transcribed by Blakiston in 'Some Durham College Rolls', 56–60, 61–71; these and other college accounts are among the muniments in Durham.

although the source was not stated, was presumably derived from the appropriated church of Pagham in Sussex.[275] There were, of course, other sources of income, notably sums paid by the priory treasurer for the expenses of monk students and secular scholars, and for the maintenance and repair of college buildings; but the surviving college accounts reveal that the warden's receipts amounted to only about £90 per annum.[276] The earliest surviving series of Durham College accounts runs from 1389, with gaps, to 1433. The 1392/3 account lists substantial sums received from appropriated churches as well as pensions and oblations from the chamberlain and his fellow obedientiaries including, as at Norwich, the master and wardens of the cells; the total receipts for this year amounted to £263 20d.[277] By the opening years of the fifteenth century both colleges were on a sufficiently secure financial footing that they were able to embark on a substantial building programme of which there are visible remains to this day.[278]

Although the Canterbury and Durham obedientiaries, like their counterparts in the other cathedral priories, were equally committed to the well-being of their brethren at university, a guaranteed, albeit fluctuating, income in the fifteenth century meant that both colleges were, on the whole, well able to provide for their students. Obedientiary contributions were, therefore, not as crucial to the monk students' welfare as they appear to have been in the case of the other cathedral priories. The 1392/3 account of Robert de Blacklaw, Durham College warden, records, along with the receipts from the appropriated churches, the *oblationes* from two obedientiaries in the Durham cloister and also £4 16s. from the Durham chamberlain *pro oblationibus et pannis lineis*.[279] A further entry on the receipt side

---

[275] Pantin, *Canterbury College Oxford*, ii, 129. The account of 1371/2 recorded the receipt of £86 13s. 4d. from Pagham but only £50 the following year, ibid., iv, 184, 185. For William de Dover III see *BRECP*, 140–1.

[276] See Pantin, *Canterbury College Oxford*, iv, 108–12 where the Canterbury and Durham college account-keeping methods are compared and contrasted. There seems to be a noticeable disparity between the Canterbury and Durham accounts in terms of the total receipts, an explanation for which remains hidden by the complexity of the accounting systems and the loss of many accounts.

[277] Blakiston, 'Some Durham College Rolls', 57. There were four appropriated churches, namely, Bossall, Ruddington, Fishlake, and Frampton, three of which occur on the 1392/3 account.

[278] Canterbury College was built on a site north of St Frideswide's Priory (now Christ Church), and Durham College on the site of Trinity College. Gloucester Hall has been enveloped by the buildings that now make up Worcester College. See CCA DCc MS Scrap Books B68 for details concerning the construction of Canterbury College under Prior Thomas Chillenden (1391–1411). For the equivalent at Durham see Dobson, *Durham Priory*, 349–50, where there are additional references. The origins and location of Gloucester College are described by James Campbell in 'Gloucester College', in Wansbrough, *Benedictines in Oxford*, 37–47.

[279] Blakiston, 'Some Durham College Rolls', 56 and *LVD*, iii, C.966 for Blacklaw. The sums of £5 from the communar and of £2 from the feretrar were the monk students' share in the yearly distributions paid to every member of the community by these two obedientiaries. The chamberlain may have distributed clothing as required to the monk students whenever they were in Durham or, more likely, he gave them the amount of money to which they were entitled each year under his *in rebus ordinatis*; the total in this category amounted to over £50 in 1378/9, DCM chamberlain's account. Since the student body regularly received 20s. from the chamberlain in the 1370s and later, it is unlikely that this was intended for clothing and bedding the amounts for which would surely have varied according to the number and needs of those who resided in the college. The 20s. was therefore probably a general contribution (*oblatio*) which on the 1392/3 account (note 274 above) we see included with the clothing.

of this same college account was £13 3s. 4d. which was explained as *de pensione* from the obedientiaries and the cells, with the exception of far-distant Coldingham.[280] The Durham bursar's accounts in the 1370s and 1380s also record similar amounts sent to the college; they may possibly be linked with the fairly frequent contributions of 20s. from the almoner, chamberlain, and feretrar and unspecified sums from the hostiller, sacrist, and others which may have been turned in to the bursar for delivery to the college.[281] The debit side of the 1392/3 college accounts specifies a payment of £38 4s. 10d. *in communis* to the monks and their boys and to the servants for their stipends; the sum of £30 8s. was also allocated to the prior and his *socii*, that is the warden, bursar, and a third senior monk who were named as the accountants at the head of the roll.[282] Durham monk students about to set out on the long journey south to Oxford were, on occasion, the recipients of donations from one of the obedientiaries: Uthred de Boldon received 6s. 8d. in 1367/8 from the sacrist, Robert de Masham the same amount from the chamberlain in 1395/6, and Robert Hornby 3s. 4d. from the terrar in 1416/17.[283]

The extant Christ Church treasurer's accounts scrutinized in conjunction with those of the Canterbury College warden elucidate some interesting features of the financial arrangements in place for the latter. The monk students, or fellows as they were called, like their student counterparts at Durham College, received an allowance known as 'commons', in this case a weekly payment for their board which, although subject to some fluctuation, averaged about 20d. per person; this was two and a half times the sum allocated by the Worcester monk kitchener.[284] Under the heading *pensiones et liberationes* on the 1382/3 Canterbury College accounts the warden and his six brethren also received £17 10s. to cover their personal expenses for the first quarter, a salary in all but name as Pantin describes it, and probably comparable to the sum specified for the prior, *socii*, and monks at Durham College.[285] The payments to the monk students of both colleges, although couched in slightly different terms, suggest that both had developed similar arrangements which allowed a greater degree of economic independence than was feasible for a group of monasteries cooperating to provide communal living arrangements for

---

[280] Blakiston, 'Some Durham College Rolls', 56.
[281] In 1378/9, for example, John de Aycliffe (*LVD*, iii, C.960) and his student brethren (*socii*) received £13 6s. 8d. and again in 1380/1 and 1383/4, DCM bursar's accounts for the years in question. These sums may have been delivered by the subprior; in 1379/80, for example, the subprior received £8 for repairs at Oxford from the prior's *dona et exennia* according to the bursar's account for that year. For the almoner's contributions see his account for 1397/8A and 1411/12A under pensions; for the feretrar, his account for 1376/7 and later accounts; for the hostiller and other obedientiaries *passim* on their accounts of similar dates, where individual items are usually lumped together and only the totals are given. The chamberlain's contributions have been discussed in note 279 above.
[282] Blakiston, 'Some Durham College Rolls', 56–8.
[283] DCM accounts of the sacrist, chamberlain, and terrar for the years stated; none of these journeys relate to the first year at Oxford; for Masham see *LVD*, iii, C.1016 and Hornby ibid., C.1047.
[284] The 1393/4 and 1394/5 college accounts list them as *co[mmun]es* week by week often recording the number of monks who received them, Pantin, *Canterbury College Oxford*, ii, 132, 134, 137–9; concerning Worcester see above 132.
[285] Pantin, *Canterbury College Oxford*, ii, 129. See also ibid., iv, 112–15 where Pantin provides further details and historical explanation. At Durham the number of monks involved is not known.

their monk scholars. The corporate organization that underpinned Gloucester College—where monks of the six other cathedral priories formed only a minority among the Benedictines sent up to Oxford from all parts of the country—would have become immeasurably difficult to run had there been any decision to bring under central control all the College's financial affairs; thus, the monk students remained directly dependent on their mother house and the arrangements seem to have verged at times on the *ad hoc* when payments were delayed.[286]

The Christ Church treasurer's accounts appear to be unique in furnishing information about the monk student's academic habit, or *cappa scolastica*, which was made of brown cloth [*burnetus*] and was prescribed by the Benedictine statutes to be worn not only at university but also elsewhere on formal occasions.[287] The treasurer paid 20s. to Thomas Dover in 1381/2 so that he could purchase his *cappa* on first going up to Oxford.[288] The same sum was given to John Aleyn the following year when he had just incepted and been named warden of Canterbury College; presumably this was a replacement for the one he had worn for the previous eight to ten years during his theological studies at the university.[289] Payments for the *cappa* were often combined with the travelling expenses from Canterbury to Oxford, as in 1380/1 when Henry Henfeld was given 50s. to cover the cost of both.[290]

Watchful oversight of monk students

Adam Easton was by no means unusual in having his university studies interrupted by an order to return to his monastery to undertake certain duties.[291] Other monks with a similar experience can be found both at Canterbury and at Durham. William Gyllyngham, for example, probably first went up to Canterbury College in 1375/6 and completed the requirements for a bachelor's degree in theology *c.* 1381/2. He was then recalled to Christ Church, where he served as master lector in the cloister for the next eight years, but was probably permitted to continue his Oxford studies on a part-time basis because he was finally able to qualify for inception in 1395. William de Hethe and Thomas Everard were also called upon to interrupt their studies, the former to be claustral lector in Canterbury in the 1340s and the latter to serve as one of the two treasurers in 1388/9.[292] Robert de Blacklaw's university

---

[286] Unfortunately, no Gloucester College accounts survive; if some were to come to light this statement might require qualification or correction. Ely monk students at Cambridge were probably subject to similar arrangements in the Benedictine hostels there.

[287] Pantin, *Black Monk Chapters*, ii, 177, for the decree of the provincial chapter, 1426. However, it must have been considered appropriate, if not essential, at an earlier date; see also Pantin, *Canterbury College Oxford*, iv, 119.

[288] *BRECP*, 139.

[289] Ibid., 71–2 (John Aleyn I).

[290] Pantin, *Canterbury College Oxford*, iv, 188; *BRECP*, 195, which, however, omitted to mention that the travel costs were included in the 50s.

[291] See above 129.

[292] Gyllyngham was master lector from 1382 to 1390, but his precise whereabouts between 1390 and 1395 are uncertain, *BRECP*, 185–6 (William Gyllyngham I). William de Hethe served as lector while working on his doctorate in theology, ibid., 200 (William de Hethe I). Thomas Everard, who

career followed a similar pattern during his time at Durham College. He was at Oxford some time prior to 1376, was then recalled and, in 1379, appears as *socius* of the feretrar; by 1379/80 he was back in Oxford.[293]

Among some of the monks whose university studies have been described above as broken by spells back at home in the cloister there may be a few others, like Robert de Blacklaw, who appear to have been simultaneously absorbing their texts and holding down an obedientiary office. However, this may indicate no more than the fact that the two occupations for a short time overlapped while the monk made the transition from the one to the other; the dates at our disposal are insufficiently precise to establish certainty. Thomas Nevyle, for example, later to become prior of Winchester, was seemingly an Oxford student and also the St Swithun's almoner in 1389/90; it is, of course, conceivable and probable that a deputy or subalmoner was responsible during Nevyle's absence.[294] John Lawerne of Worcester was appointed almoner in 1448/9, the year in which he incepted and delivered a series of lectures at Oxford.[295] The Durham monk William Appleby is found accounting simultaneously for the offices of almoner at Durham and college warden at Oxford between August 1404 and February 1409; although here again a deputy could have performed the responsibilities attached to the Durham office. With no evidence of a shortage of manpower why was Appleby's name found occupying both positions?[296]

In addition to their studies, external duties were imposed on some of the university monks, who were commissioned as proctors or proxies to represent their prior and convent at the triennial chapters of the Black Monks. The gatherings were usually held at the Cluniac priory in Northampton which was relatively close to Oxford and to Cambridge. This arrangement proved to be particularly advantageous for the priors of Durham and Rochester who would have been obliged to travel long distances in order to attend in person. Among the wardens of Durham College who performed this function were Robert de Blacklaw in 1402, William Appleby in 1405, and Thomas Rome in 1411.[297] At least two Rochester monk students attended a number of chapters on behalf of their superior: John de Holyngbourne in 1384, 1387, and 1390 and John de Ealding in 1393 and 1402.[298] Had more priory registers survived we would undoubtedly

---

was at Canterbury College between 1379 and 1395, might have spent the year 1388/9 in dividing his time between studying theology and balancing the priory account books, but he must have had an assistant in the treasurer's department, ibid., 155.

[293] DCM bursar's accounts 1376/7; feretrar's pyx receipts 1379/80; in September 1381 he was appointed warden of Durham College, BL MS Cotton Faustina A. vi, fo 81. For Blacklaw's biographical details see *LVD*, iii, C.966.

[294] *BRECP*, 721; on the other hand, he may have been at Oxford for only part of the year.

[295] Ibid., 830–1 (John Lawerne I).

[296] DCM accounts of the almoner and college warden for the years in question and *LVD*, iii, C.1001 for Appleby. The uncertain lengths of term and vacation may also enter into the seeming overlapping of positions.

[297] Pantin, *Black Monk Chapters*, iii, 212. For Rome see *LVD*, iii, C.1008.

[298] *BRECP*, 612 (Holyngbourne), 600–1 (Ealding); the prior was John de Shepey (1380–1419), ibid., 635 (John de Shepey III).

have further names to add to these few examples. As pointed out above, preaching duties in Cambridge were assigned to four Ely monk students while they were engaged in study there in 1415.[299]

Monk students were always summoned to return to the monastery for episcopal and Black Monk chapter visitations, and for elections of both bishop and cathedral prior since these involved the participation of the full chapter.[300] However, surviving lists of absentees and records of the appointment of deputies to vote on their behalf make it clear that not infrequently there were a few who, for one reason or another, were not present on these important occasions. Thomas Nevyle, for example, was absent at Gloucester College in 1390 when two Rochester monks visited St Swithun's as commissaries of the Black Monk chapter, which made appointments to conduct monastic visitations at each of its triennial chapters and received the visitors' completed report at the following chapter. Three Winchester monks, also students at Oxford, were unavailable to sign a composition with the bishop, William Wykeham, in 1393 in the wake of his visitation which had resulted in a contentious set of episcopal injunctions.[301] By way of contrast two Worcester monks were recalled from Oxford in 1409 in order to attend the funeral of Prior John de Malverne; both of them then stayed on to take part in the nominations for the new prior and in his installation. John de Fordham, who was chosen to succeed Malverne, was at the time also at Oxford and had been, perhaps still was, *prior studentium* at Gloucester College.[302] Although John Langdon and several other monk fellows at Canterbury College travelled back to Christ Church for the election of an archbishop in March 1414 on the death of Thomas Arundel, they were not obliged to make a second return journey only nine months later in order to be present at the first official visitation of Arundel's successor, Henry Chichele. In reply to the archiepiscopal summons the Christ Church chapter requested that Langdon and his brethren be excused because they had been 'ad studium generale Oxon[iense causa studii transmissis, et in eodem actualiter studentibus'.[303] Durham College monk students, who faced an even longer journey to their monastery, probably also returned more often for elections than for visitations but the surviving records lack sufficient detail to provide certainty. Robert de Picton (Pigdon), Robert de Blacklaw, and Robert Ripon returned to Durham for the election of John Fordham as bishop in May 1381; but William Appleby, John Bywell, Walter de Teesdale, and Thomas Hamsterley were absent

---

[299] See above note 272.
[300] In the case of elections, only professed monks were eligible to vote.
[301] For Nevyle, soon to be prior, see *BRECP*, 721–2; he was probably still at Oxford, but was present to sign the composition. The three who were absent were Thomas de Chilbolton, Thomas Rudborne, and Thomas Shirebourne, ibid., 682, 731, 734–5 respectively. The controversy with Wykeham has been dealt with in my 'Injunction Book', 242–6.
[302] The two monks, in addition to Fordham, were Richard Clifton and Thomas Ledbury, *BRECP*, 789 and 833–4; for Fordham, ibid., 805–7.
[303] *BRECP*, 217 (John Langdon I); for Chichele's first visitation see CCA DCc Reg. S, fo 71 which has been summarized in Pantin, *Canterbury College Oxford*, iii, 73.

The English Benedictine Cathedral Priories: Rule and Practice 143

presumably because they remained at Oxford.[304] In July 1408 at the episcopal visitation of the recently elected Thomas Langley as bishop of Durham, William Appleby, warden of Durham College, along with Robert Hornby, William de Kibblesworth, and John Fishburn junior were absent from the list of those who participated, again because they were probably at Oxford.[305]

Constant oversight of monk students on the part of their prior is attested in a brief, undated correspondence between two Norwich monks and Prior Robert de Langele (1310–26). One of the letters is addressed to John de Mari, who is known to have been at Oxford from about 1317/18, another to both de Mari and Martin de Middleton and a third to Middleton.[306] All three are responses to letters from the monk students which have subsequently been lost, and it is clear that they contained requests for advice and direction. In one letter the prior gives them both permission to stay on at Oxford after the end of term in mid-August if they should feel so inclined. Middleton, who was following the course in canon law, received the prior's approval to make arrangements for continuing his studies and, in the same letter, the prior went on to express surprise that de Mari had not yet requested permission to take his bachelor's degree in theology. His hesitation, in the prior's view, was to be attributed to the fact of de Mari's diminutive stature and self-effacing temperament. The message must have been passed on by Middleton because the third letter from the prior acknowledges receipt of de Mari's request to proceed to the degree and to begin his lectures on the Sentences of Peter Lombard.[307]

College libraries

Few details have survived concerning the books borrowed by individual monks from their cloister libraries to take with them to university. There is one list of Worcester volumes which can be dated approximately to the 1430s and which is connected with John Lawerne's first year or two at Oxford; the books were probably also shared with his fellow monk students, Isaac Ledbury and John

---

[304] DCM Priory Reg. II, fos 198–200v. Blacklaw, Pigdon (Picton) and Ripon were in Oxford on 10 May but had returned to Durham before 30 May when they were chosen as *compromissarii*, or electors, for the election. Pigdon, a senior monk, appears to have been in Oxford in the years 1380x1383 but his presence was probably for administrative or financial purposes rather than for study; for references see note 305 below.

[305] DCM College Warden accounts for 1407/8, 1408/9. In the record of those present at the visitation the masters/wardens of the dependent cells were all included except for the two most remote from Durham: Coldingham and Oxford, Storey, *Reg. Langley*, i, 68. The careers of the named monks are in *LVD*, iii as follows C.956 (Picton), C.966 (Blacklaw), C.985 (Ripon), C.1001 (Appleby), C.990 (Bywell), C.992 (Teesdale), C.1000 (Hamsterley), C.1047 (Hornby), C.1018 (Kibblesworth), C.1038 (Fishburn junior).

[306] V. H. Galbraith transcribed the letters, from NRO DCN Priory Reg. IX, fos 30, 57, in 'Gloucester College' in Salter, *Snappe's Formulary*, 377–8.

[307] Pantin tentatively dates the third letter to *c.* 1321, *Black Monk Chapters*, iii, 321. In addition to these three letters from the prior there is a fourth, also in Priory Reg. IX (fo 61v), which is addressed to de Mari and Roger [de Eston] recalling them to Norwich in July 1325 because of the death of Bishop John Salmon. Eston's biographical details are in *BRECP*, 507.

Broghton. The thirty titles have been identified as in Lawerne's hand and appear to represent a record of what had been allocated to the three during their time at Gloucester College. It must be admitted that the selection, which consisted of a few biblical commentaries, Innocent V on the Lombard's Sentences, several grammatical and classical works, two volumes of sermons and little else of significance, fails to suggest a rigorous programme of study.[308] As to the library at Gloucester College, we know that it was under construction in the 1420s and that John Wethamstede, abbot of St Albans, provided the money according to the abbey's monk chronicler, John Amundesham.[309] In general, we find monks being given allowances for the purchase of books, most of which would either have been passed on to their student brethren or would have become available for community use when they ultimately found their home in the cathedral library. John de Aston of Worcester was given 20s., a goodly sum, by the cellarer in 1294/5 which was specifically *ad libros*.[310] Richard de Bromwych and Ranulf de Calthrop, fellow monks and close contemporaries of Aston at Oxford, almost certainly benefited from similar donations from one or more of the Worcester obedientiaries; indeed, some of their acquisitions may be among the volumes that survive in the cathedral manuscript collection: MS F.79, for example, Henry of Ghent's *Quodlibetae*, which contains both Bromwych's name and an *ex libris* of the priory in a later hand, and part of MS F.124, theological *Quaestiones*, which on fo 60 states 'Liber sancte Marie Wygornie...ex dono Ran[ulfo de Catthorp'.[311]

With regard to the contents of the Canterbury and Durham College libraries the surviving evidence is more rewarding. From the mid-fifteenth century onwards there are a number of inventories of Canterbury College marking the retirement of one warden and the appointment of his successor. One hundred and two books were listed in 1443, and to this number had been added another thirty volumes by 1459.[312] That the nucleus of the college collections came on loan from the mother house is attested by the presence of books formerly belonging to deceased monks who had had no known university connections, for example, a *Hugucius cum Britone* with the name of Thomas de Stureye junior (d. 1298) inscribed in it and

---

[308] The list, together with additional details and commentary, can be found in Sharpe, *EBL*, 659–60. It may well be no more than a random collection of books chosen by the three monk students with no direct bearing on their courses of study, but possibly filling in some of the gaps among the books available in the Gloucester College library about whose contents nothing is known. Details of the three monks are in *BRECP*, 830–1 (John Lawerne I), 832–3 (Ledbury), 780–1 (Broghton).

[309] *Annales Monasterii S. Albani, a Johanne Amundesham monacho...A.D. 1421–40*, ed. H. T. Riley, Rolls Series, 2 vols (1870–1), ii, 200. In the record of the abbot's achievements the chronicle includes the 'factura unius Librarie pro Ordine et in fabricatione cujusdam Capellulae' which, together with a *clausura circa gardinum*, cost £108.

[310] Two of Aston's books survive in Worcester Cathedral Library, MSS Q.13 and Q.33, both of which contain notes and *questiones* composed by him and presumably written in his own hand. His grant is recorded on the cellarer's account for 1294/5 which has been printed in Wilson and Gordon, *Early Compotus Rolls*, 30; the payment was made *per preceptum prioris*.

[311] Bromwych and Calthrop are in *BRECP*, 782–3, 784. See also Thomson's remarks on their surviving manuscripts in his *Medieval Manuscripts in Worcester Cathedral*, 50–1 (MS F.79) and 85–6 (MS F.124).

[312] Some of these lists have been printed by Pantin in *Canterbury College Oxford*, i, 3–6 (1443), 11–16 (1459).

a copy of Peter Lombard's Sentences which had been used by Robert Poucyn (d. 1310). Books from the Christ Church cloister library were also 'signed out' to individual monk students to take with them to Oxford, the titles of which were to be recorded and a copy sent to the college warden by the monastery succentor.[313] The earliest Durham College inventory of books to have been preserved is included in the college *status* for 1315. It contains some thirty-five volumes among which were found some of the essential writings of Gregory, Bede, Anselm, Peter Comestor, and William Brito which had already been introduced in the novitiate; there was also a volume of Thomas Aquinas which had been obtained by Robert de Graystanes, who may well have been at Oxford when the *status* was compiled.[314] He was but one of a number of Durham monks and monk students who were instrumental in acquiring books both for the college and for the cathedral library from the early days of the Durham foundation in Oxford. Among these Thomas de Westoe is especially noteworthy in that, despite no known connection with the Durham house of studies, he was responsible for the purchase of some twenty-five books *c.* 1300, of which five survive at Durham to this day.[315] The transfer of books from Durham to Oxford during John Wessington's term of office as chancellor, or librarian, of the cathedral priory in the first decade of the fifteenth century is demonstrated by two surviving lists. Their contents, mainly biblical texts and commentaries, suggest that they may have been sent to replace college copies probably worn out through constant use.[316]

Return and responsibility

Monks returning from the university, with or without a degree, rejoined their community to assume the same place in the order of seniority that had been entered in the official record on the day of their profession. No special privileges were conferred on them and no particular office was reserved for them; not surprisingly, however, they were often appointed to be librarians and claustral lectors as already noted.[317] It may seem remarkable that there is little sign of a division within the

---

[313] Ibid., i, 3, item nos 5 and 4, item 8; biographical details of Stureye and Poucyn are in *BRECP*, 296 (Thomas de Stureye II), 257–8 (Poucyn). By 1524 the college library had grown to almost 300 books, James, *ALCD*, 163–70. The succentor was the precentor's deputy and the precentor commonly acted as librarian. Christopher de Hamel suggests that the increasing number of students and books being sent up to Canterbury College from Christ Church had the detrimental effect of depriving the monks in the cathedral priory of their reading and reference materials, C. de Hamel, 'The Dispersal of the Library of Christ Church, Canterbury, from the Fourteenth to the Sixteenth Century', in James Carley and Colin Tite (eds), *Books and Collectors: Essays Presented to Andrew Watson* (British Library, London, 1997), 263–79, at 266.
[314] Blakiston, 'Durham College Rolls', 35–8. The Aquinas volume, *Prima pars summae*, now DCL MS B.I.10, is only one of many procured by Graystanes and coming to rest in the cathedral priory library collection; see *BRUO*, ii, 814, for his career and *LVD*, iii, C.801.
[315] The list of Westoe's acquisitions is in Cambridge, Jesus College MS 57 (Q. G. 9), fo 168v; it has been transcribed and analysed by Meryl Foster in her thesis, 'Durham Priory', 331–6, 395–402, where the extant volumes, all of which are by Aquinas, are described in some detail. For Westoe's career see also *LVD*, iii, C.707.
[316] *Cat. Vet. Durham*, 39–41 and for Wessington's biographical details *LVD*, iii, C.1028.
[317] See above 102 and below 179.

cathedral priory communities between the university-trained monks and the monks whose studies had been confined to the cloister. Among the many complaints that came to the fore during episcopal visitations a mere one to this effect has been found, and it was only eight years before the dissolution. In 1532 the Norwich precentor, John Sall, roundly condemned two monk scholars, Richard Norwich and Thomas Morton, who for the previous five or six years had been absent at Oxford. Sall reported that since their return they had been putting on airs and sowing discord among the brethren.[318] A more profound problem that caused disquiet in the consciences of many Benedictines was an increase of doubt about the appropriateness of their presence in the university halls of learning. It must have been one of the topics of discussion from time to time among monk students and their brethren in the cloister. A single instance of its occurrence as the subject of a disputation has come to light in a student notebook of the Worcester monk John Lawerne, who was at Oxford between c. 1432/3 and 1448/9.[319] Two authorities, Jerome and Gregory the Great, are quoted to the effect that the monastic rule binds the monk to remain within the cloister and to pray; but a third position, based on an unspecified ruling *ex decretis* is interpreted to allow a religious to aspire to the academic status of doctor.[320]

In the opening years of the sixteenth century one monastic superior is known to have openly expressed dissatisfaction with the growing spirit of individualism and independence displayed by monk students. The reaction of Abbot Kidderminster of Winchcombe to this situation was to propose an end to university study for his monks and to make arrangements for further studies in a 'university' within the monastic enclosure.[321] Despite the failings of the likes of Richard Norwich and Thomas Morton the cathedral monasteries appear to have remained at least overtly unimpressed by such a radical measure of reform—which may have been seen by some as a misguided return to the past—after some two centuries of the university connection; and they continued to send their quotas of monks to Oxford and Cambridge until the dissolution.

The continuity of studies within the cloister

It may seem pointless to discuss the reading interest of the recently professed and ordained novices and junior monks in the cloister because concrete evidence is slight, and any attempt to build on it could be dismissed as sheer speculation. However, if we extend the terminal date of this study into the second half of the

---

[318] *BRECP*, 543 (Morton), 545–6 (Richard Norwich II), 553–4 (John Sall II). See also Jessop, *Visitations of Norwich*, for the transcription of this visitation, especially 264, 266. Norwich, appointed to preach the Latin homily at the opening mass, was, perhaps, unwise in choosing as his text 'Be ye therefore perfect as your heavenly Father is perfect' (Matthew, 5:48); and there may have been an overdose of self-assurance in his delivery.

[319] The notebook is now in the Bodleian Library, MS Bodley 692; for Lawerne, see *BRECP*, 830–1.

[320] MS Bodley 692, fo 6. James Clark kindly drew my attention to this passage which I had failed to notice.

[321] See Greatrex, 'Cathedral Monasteries', 133.

fifteenth century and refrain from insisting on the need to know the precise moment when particular books were acquired and read, we are free to make a few constructive observations on the basis of the facts available. It will be necessary to look at those books which can be attached to named monks, with dates and other details where possible. This is an admittedly limited objective, confined to the study of a few hundred Benedictine monks of the nine cathedral priories in fourteenth- and fifteenth-century England. To fill out the picture it would be necessary to place these monastic communities within the broader background of contemporary trends and developments in the fields of higher learning. Attention would need to be given to monastic book-production although its heyday had passed before 1200, to the impact and influence of the schools of Paris in the later twelfth century followed by Oxford and the arrival there of Benedictines a century later, and to the building up of the cathedral priory book collections and their organization and management. Reference will be made to these developments as they affected, or were affected by, the individual monks who have made and will make an appearance in the relevant section of this chapter and later chapters below. It must be remembered that the amount of time and attention available for precentors to devote to the production, care, and acquisition of books was limited by their overriding responsibilities in instructing and conducting their brethren in the daily performance of the musical components of the liturgy. Moreover, they, like their fellow obedientiaries, were often subject to frequent transfers from one office to another. These facts serve to explain the absence of any sign of a sustained policy with regard to the development of the library collections during the period of this study. As has already become clear many, if not most, volumes were added through the initiative of enterprising monks of whom the majority were those who had the benefit of university training.

We have seen that monks who remained in the cloister continued to keep in touch with their more scholarly brethren in whose company they had previously prayed, worked, and studied in the novitiate. It appears that John Wodnesburgh, a Canterbury monk at Oxford in the 1420s and 1430s, continued to have need of Jerome's *De interpretatione hebraicorum nominum* and, believing that his brother in religion at Canterbury, William Glastynbury, had a copy in his keeping asked for it to be sent to him.[322] This means that, in theory at least, both monks found this reference work of practical use in their continuing biblical studies. The survival of Glastynbury's personal notebook provides us with further references to two of the texts he consulted, namely, Augustine's sermons and his commentary on St Paul's letter to the Romans.[323]

The choice of reading material on the part of a few cloistered Canterbury monks many years earlier was recorded by the librarian whose 1338 inventory of missing books has fortunately been preserved. From it we learn of the delinquency of Philip

---

[322] Pantin, *Canterbury College*, iii, 88, item 98; Pantin has tentatively dated this letter to 1432. For Wodnesburgh *BRECP*, 323.
[323] These are identified and described in Greatrex, 'Culture at Canterbury', 172; the notebook is now Oxford, Corpus Christi College MS 256.

de Wykham and William de Cantorbury, who had been monks for less than five years; the former had failed to return a copy of the *Sententia super librum physicorum* and the latter a *Vita sancti Thomae martyris* which he had borrowed from the communal book collection (*de communi*).[324] Another junior monk, Richard de Merstham, in his tenth year of profession, had misplaced two or more volumes: the *libri Cassiodori senatoris* and Everard de Béthune's grammatical work *Grecismus*.[325] Older monks like Thomas Undyrdown senior, for example, had borrowed and, subsequently, lost five books bound in one volume of unspecified works by Archbishop Anselm; it had formerly belonged to Simon de St Paul, an elderly monk whose name is associated with this and five other books in the Eastry catalogue.[326] Undyrdown was also in default over John de Bocton's copy of Brito, *Super prologos Biblie*, one of eight volumes that were placed in the library after Bocton's death in 1307.[327] If the monk or clerk who compiled or copied the final section of the Eastry catalogue has done his work accurately Walter de Norwyco (d. 1328) left a personal library comprising some nineteen volumes or items. This was a monk who served as cellarer, warden of manors, and subprior during the quarter century before his death, but he was not too overburdened by these major responsibilities to be prevented from accumulating important theological works of Thomas Aquinas and Peter Lombard, several canon law texts, philosophical treatises, and sermons.[328] These, along with several other examples from the early decades of the fourteenth century, indicate that books were being acquired by and circulating among non-university monks within the community at Christ Church.[329]

In the last two centuries before the monasteries were dissolved there are disappointingly few signs to indicate that library volumes were circulating within the monastic community. The extensive loss suffered by the cathedral library at Canterbury when its magnificent collection was dispersed at the dissolution and the fact that relatively few of the surviving books have any indication of individual

---

[324] James, *ALCD*, 147 which contains a full transcription of this list, 146–9, from Canterbury CCA DCc Reg. L, fo 104; further reference to Wykham may be found in *BRECP*, 328 and to William de Cantorbury I, ibid., 108–9.

[325] James, *ALCD*, 147.

[326] For Simon de St Paul's collection of books see item nos 1715–20 in James, ibid., 138, and for biographical details *BRECP*, 273–4; for Undyrdown, ibid., 309. Since it has been assumed that the Eastry catalogue had been completed by the time of Prior Eastry's death in 1331, and since all the other monks named in the catalogue were dead by that date it is surprising to find Simon's books placed in the library at least seven years before his death in 1338; possibly he had to give up reading due to failing eyesight after more than half a century of monastic life.

[327] John de Bocton's monastic career is in *BRECP*, 92 and his books are listed in James, *ALCD*, 72 item nos 635–42 or 643; 642 is the volume of Brito.

[328] The range of de Norwyco's intellectual interests suggests a university connection, and it is conceivable that during the twelve years between his profession and his first obedientiary appointment he may have been sent to Paris or Oxford. However, there is no evidence that he was ever a student as there is for several of his contemporaries at Christ Church; see, for example Stephen de Feversham II in *BRECP*, 160, and de Norwyco, ibid., 245–6 where the reference to the list of books is supplied. Attention should be drawn to Prior Eastry's impressive collection of books deposited in the library after his death in 1331; they numbered 26 theological and biblical texts and 44 volumes of canon and civil law, James, *ALCD*, 143–5.

[329] For further examples see James, *ALCD*, 146–8; and note that Eastry is not numbered among the university monks.

ownership preclude all possibility of either comparison or contrast with the preceding period.[330] However, a few of the exceptions to this otherwise bleak picture will confirm that the practice continued, at least among some who can be named thanks to surviving records.

One of these was William Chartham, who was a contemporary of William Glastynbury. Sometime before his death in 1448 he put together his own book, a *Speculum parvulorum*, which was expressly intended 'ad multorum parvulorum delectationem et utilitatem'. Prompted by his own experience as a child he wanted others to enjoy and benefit from the moralizing narratives found in the lives of the saints, the *Gesta Romanorum* and exempla collections that he had enjoyed.[331] In 1520 John Salisbury added his name and the date to the flyleaf.[332] Also passed on to Salisbury was a *Vitae sanctorum Cantuariensium* much of which was the work of Richard Stone in copying from earlier accounts of the life and miracles of Dunstan, Anselm, and others.[333] Stone's collection of books has been preserved in an undated inventory of the contents of his *cubiculum*, presumably compiled at the time of his death in 1508. The location of his *cubiculum*, or cell, is not stated; but it was likely to have been within the Christ Church cloister since there is not a single shred of evidence of his presence at Oxford. Apart from service books his personal library consisted of some thirty volumes nearly half of which are described as printed, historical writings, grammatical texts, and lives of saints and church fathers being prominent.[334] Two other monks, contemporaries of Stone, displayed an interest in books and literary pursuits. These were Laurence Wade, who in 1497 completed an English verse translation of the life of Thomas Becket, and William Ingram, who compiled a list of 306 books which were sent for repair in 1508. Ingram held the office of *custos martyrii* that year, but took on the additional task of recording the titles of the volumes together with their second folio incipits and their location in the library above the prior's chapel.[335]

Despite the several informative library catalogues of the late fourteenth and early fifteenth centuries which have survived from the monastic library at Durham, and despite the impressive collection of surviving books, there are relatively few to

---

[330] Richard Sharpe has kindly pointed out to me that many of the books acquired after *c.* 1170 would have been of little interest to most post-dissolution collectors, who were keen to possess the earlier texts, with the result that many of the former have disappeared; this may explain the disappointingly low survival rate of Christ Church manuscripts with ownership inscriptions and other data.

[331] The book is now MS 78 in Lambeth Palace Library and the quotation is on fo 1; other details of William Chartham II are found in *BRECP*, 114.

[332] John Salisbury III is in *BRECP*, 276.

[333] See M. R. James, *A Descriptive Catalogue of the Manuscripts in the Library of Lambeth Palace* (Cambridge University Press, Cambridge, 1930), 250–4.

[334] The inventory was printed by Pantin in *Canterbury College*, i, 88–90, and Stone's monastic career is in *BRECP*, 293.

[335] Wade's text is in Cambridge, Corpus Christi College MS 298, fos 1–56v; his sources were two of the early Latin lives of Becket, one by Herbert of Bosham and the other by John Grandisson, bishop of Exeter (d. 1369). Ingram's list was printed by James in *ALCD*, 152–64; both monks are in *BRECP*, 209 (Ingram I), 311 (Wade). By 1390 the Durham librarian was including second folio incipits in his inventory, *Cat. Vet. Durham*, 10 et seq.

which individual monks' names can be attached. Acquisitions in these years, and earlier as well as later, came mainly through the initiative of Oxford monks; but some of the volumes that were brought, or sent, back to Durham would undoubtedly have been consulted by monks who had remained behind in the cloister. The dearth of evidence, as Meryl Foster noted, makes it virtually impossible to ascertain when and how most of the books were obtained and to what extent they were used, since ownership inscriptions and identifiable marginal notes are rare. There are indications of some potential enthusiasm for study in an early fourteenth-century letter written by an unnamed prior of Durham to the prior of the cell of Finchale asking for the return of certain books which were needed for the brethren in the Durham cloister who, without them, were in danger of becoming *ociosi*.[336]

Among the small numbers of non-academic Durham monks who left their mark on extant volumes is William de Guisborough senior. Elected prior in 1321, when he was in his mid-fifties, he resigned almost immediately remarking that he preferred the quiet of the cloister; his contribution to the library was a book of dictaminal treatises.[337] An older contemporary, Thomas de Wolviston, spent some of his free time in copying the texts that make up the major portion of what is now BL MS Harley 5234, a largely didactic and devotional collection of writings including the *Elucidarium* of Honorius Augustodunensis, an anonymous *florilegium* with the title *Flos florum*, Innocent III's *De miseria* and *De missae mysteriis* and meditations of St Bernard.[338] This volume, probably augmented by a few other similar works, was continuing to circulate in the mid-fifteenth century when both John Mody and Thomas Caly had it in their possession.[339] During Robert de Brackenbury's uneventful monastic life (*c.* 1342–91) he amassed a miscellaneous collection of books suggesting a wide variety of interests and an inquiring mind, unless his motivation was limited to that of a bibliophile. His personal library included theology (Peter Lombard and Thomas Aquinas), medicine (Constantinus Africanus), history (William Gemeticensis and Martin Polonus), canon law (Gregory IX's *Decretales*), Isidore of Seville's one-volume encyclopaedia and sermons (Peter Chrysologus).[340] Four other Durham monks of the later fourteenth century

---

[336] Foster, 'Durham Priory', 268, 270–1; the letter quoted is found in a Durham priory register (*Registrum Parvum*) now BL MS Cotton Faustina A.VI, fos 15v–16.

[337] His name was spelled Gisburne in this volume which remains at Durham as DCL MS C.IV.24; his career is summarized in *LVD*, iii, C.726.

[338] The section written by Wolviston and later incorporated into the library—ex *dono et labore* as he inscribed it—occupies fos 19 to 197, the inscription having been inserted at the top of fo 2v; see also *LVD*, iii, C.694.

[339] These monks were contemporaries in the 1440s and both were university monks; see *BRUO*, ii, 1287 (Mody) and ibid., i, 342 (Caly). Prior William Ebchester had passed on the volume to Caly; the *ex dono* is on fo 4v of the manuscript. For all three monks see also *LVD*, iii, C.1071 (Mody), C.1131 (Caly), C.1053 (Ebchester).

[340] Most of these books survive at Durham: DCL MSS A.III.7 (Lombard), B.I.9 (Aquinas), C.I.19 and C.IV.12 (Constantinus), BL MS Harley 491(Gemeticensis), and Oxford, Bodley MS Laud misc. 603 (Polonus), DCL MSS C.II.3 (Decretales), B.IV.15 (Etymologies), Bodley MS Laud misc. 641 (Chrysologus). The Lombard volume was given him by Emery de Lumley, a Durham monk who died about two years after Brackenbury entered the monastery; had he been sufficiently prepared in order to benefit from the Sentences while still a very junior novice? He served in the relatively minor offices of refectorer, granator, and infirmarer for brief terms only, during almost half a century in the cloister,

may be selected because of their association with books which they acquired, lent, or borrowed. Robert Constable was the owner of grammatical works by Alexander de Villa Dei, while William de Killerby procured (*ex procuracione*) a copy of the *Sermones super Evangelia dominicalia* of James de Voragine (Januensis) bound with Robert de Basevorn's treatise *De arte predicandi*.[341] Killerby held a succession of offices in the 1370s and 1380s and was chaplain to the prior before his death in 1392/3. He ensured his perpetual remembrance on fo 9 of his volume by commissioning a portrait of himself kneeling before St Cuthbert, who holds the crowned head of St Oswald in the crook of his left arm, within the frame of the initial 'H'; a scroll between them is inscribed with the words 'Confessor vere Kyllerby, gaudia quere'.[342]

With regard to the lending of books, John de Bolton, who had a quarter of a century of monastic life and experience behind him, was careful to record the contents of a book that he lent to a fellow monk *c.* 1377 and to specify the length of the borrowing period. John de Aycliffe, a student and possibly warden of Durham College, was allowed three years in which to read and study the three texts contained in the volume: the *Historia scholastica* of Peter Comestor, the *Liber exceptionum* of Richard of St Victor, and *De fide orthodoxa* by John of Damascus.[343] Richard de Stockton had been a member of the Durham community for some twenty-eight years in 1391 and was hostiller at the time when an inventory of the books in the Spendement noted that he had a copy of books two, three, and four of the Sentences of Peter Lombard. Possibly he had been given permission for a long-term loan; what remains unexplained is why monks' names appear as borrowers in the surviving inventories.[344] On the strength of one list of books and their borrowers at Canterbury and an insignificant number of monks, at both Canterbury and Durham, it would be foolhardy even to conjecture how exceptional these monks were among their fellow non-university brethren. Continuing our search for

---

DCM bursar's account 1349B (refectorer), ibid., 1357/8 (granator) 1363, Loc. X:28 (infirmarer). For Lumley's career see *LVD*, iii, C.789 and for Brackenbury's ibid., C.894.

[341] Constable's manuscript remains at Durham, DCL MS C.IV.26, and Killerby's is MS Mm.3.14 in Cambridge University Library. Constable is C.967 in *LVD*, iii, and Killerby ibid., C.974.

[342] The armorial bearings depicted at the foot of fo 9 were associated with the Brakynbery [*sic*] family of Denton, Durham, in the early sixteenth century, T. Woodcock, Janet Grant, Ian Graham (eds), *Dictionary of British Arms Medieval Ordinary*, vol. 2 (Society of Antiquaries, London, 1996), 400. Is it any more than a coincidence that Robert de Brackenbury and William de Killerby were contemporaries in the Durham cloister? In 1395 this copy of the sermons of Januensis had found its place in the *commune armariolum*, *Cat. Vet. Durham*, 75G. This phrase, according to Alan Piper, referred to the 'general stock of the community's books' not to one particular location; see his 'The Libraries of the Monks of Durham', 213–49 at 218.

[343] These details are found in DCM Misc. Charter 2477; the volume has not been traced. Comestor's text has been described above 118. The *Liber exceptionum* was an encyclopaedic work of which one section, the *Allegoriae*, provided a useful reference work on the spiritual senses of Scripture as a counterpart to Comestor's literal exegesis; see Smith, *Masters of the Sacred Page*, 57–60. A volume with similar, but not identical, contents appears in the 1391 inventory of the Spendement, *Cat. Vet. Durham*, 18B². For Bolton and Aycliffe see *LVD*, iii, C.937 and C.960 respectively.

[344] *Cat. Vet. Durham*, 22Q, *Stokton habet*. This book had been returned to the library by or before 1416 according to the inventory of that year, ibid., 99Q; it was probably back in its place soon after his death in 1408/9 if not earlier. Stockton's career is found in *LVD*, iii, C.970.

intellectually inclined monks in the cloisters of the other cathedral monasteries should furnish some additional evidence to broaden our field of view if not to resolve some uncertainties.

Bath, Ely, and Coventry are unrewarding in this endeavour with the almost single exception of John de Grenborough, infirmarer at Coventry for some thirty years in the second half of the fourteenth century. His medical training probably took place in the cloister under the tutelage of one of his predecessors in charge of the infirmary. He himself tells us that his concern for the sick in his care prompted him to purchase a book containing the *Compendium medicinae* of Gilbertus Anglicus together with other related treatises; he also added his own notes based on other medical authorities to whose writings he must have had access. He mentions that he has consulted English, Irish, Jewish, and Arabic texts and texts from the medical schools of Lombardy and Salerno, some of which, in his judgement, were by ignorant doctors who wrote *multa verba et vacua*.[345]

Between the late thirteenth and mid-fifteenth centuries a handful of Norwich non-academic monks have left their names in surviving books; two of them, both priors, are distinguished by the sizeable collections which they amassed and which found a place in the community library following their death. Henry de Lakenham, who ruled over the cathedral monastery from 1289 to 1310, is often described as *magister*, but the reason he merited this title remains a mystery beyond the fact that his learning must have impressed his contemporaries; and his personal library of at least seventeen volumes may have been the basis of the attribution.[346] Four of these are preserved among the manuscripts in the Cambridge University Library: a *Flores Bernardi*, a collection of the sermons of Bonaventure which two centuries later had passed on to Henry Langrake, the *Liber eruditionis religiosorum* of William Peraldus, and *De claustro animae* by Hugh de Folieto.[347] By using as her guide the library letter-marks which were assigned to them Barbara Dodwell has deduced that there probably were an additional thirteen books of Lakenham that have not survived.[348] In the surviving four there are indications that we have in Lakenham a monk who, in the midst of an active and demanding life as sacrist and prior, was concerned to maintain the contemplative dimension of his Benedictine vocation. Thirty-one books purchased by Prior Simon Bozoun (1326–52) are known from a list which records their titles and the prices paid for each. Only four of these have been

---

[345] This volume is now BL MS Royal 12 G.iv, and Grenborough's remarks are on fo 187v. Some of the contents were added after Grenborough's death; but it is probable that the notes dealing with the illnesses and treatment of two monks, William Haloughton (fo 202) and Richard Luff (fo 215), were either by him or his successor. These three are in *BRECP*, 356 (Grenborough), 357 (Haloughton), 363 (Luff), but the medical diagnoses and treatment were omitted. The *Catalogue of Western Manuscripts in the Old Royal and King's Collections* by Sir George F. Warner and Julius P. Gilson, 4 vols (London, 1921), ii, 69–71 provides a detailed description of all the articles.

[346] Lakenham's monastic career is in *BRECP*, 531–2, where, his involvement in the foundation of Gloucester College is noted.

[347] The four CUL manuscripts are now Ii.1.32 (Bernard), Ii.4.2 (Bonaventure), Ii.4.15 (Peraldus), Ii.4.25 (Folieto); Langrake, a university monk, is found in *BRECP*, 533–4.

[348] Dodwell, 'History and Norwich Monks', 41. See also Ker, 'Manuscripts from Norwich', for his interpretation of the letter-marks.

identified: historical works by Bede and Roger Wendover, geographical itineraries, the *Polychronicon* of Ranulph Higden together with extracts from other historical writings, and a *Flores historiarum*.[349] Bozoun's remaining book purchases combine to form a diverse assortment of subjects, assuredly revealing the presence of at least a few curious and inquiring minds as well as the need, from time to time, for additional or replacement copies of popular or essential reading material. There were, for example, two more collections of historical writings, five volumes of canon law, several theological works of reference with indexes or *tabulae* to some of them and to other texts available in the library, the preaching manual by the Dominican John of Bromyard, a copy of the Koran in Latin translation, and an exposition of the Rule, probably the popular one by the Cassinese Bernard.[350]

Two other Norwich monks, both contemporaries of Prior Bozoun, had copies of this same commentary on the Rule. One of them, Robert de Donewich, was a competent master of the cellar in the 1330s, working strenuously and successfully to reduce the convent debt; but we may assume that he periodically, if not regularly, made time for reflective reading. His book also contained spiritual treatises by William Peraldus and Hugh de Folieto. John de Reynham's copy was similarly provided: in his case with the *De stimulo amoris* by James of Milan and a lament of the Virgin on the passion of her Son. Inscribed on a flyleaf at the end of the volume are the words 'liber Johannis de Reynham monachi Norwici quem ipse in parte scripsit et in parte scribi fecit'.[351] Another monk who was the owner of a collection of texts bound together in one volume was Richard Walsham. He was active as master of the cellar in the 1430s and as prior of the cell of St Leonard in the 1450s before his retirement in order to live a solitary life within St Leonard's precincts.[352] The book, which may well have accompanied him into solitude, contained five items to satisfy a variety of moods and interests: for theological reflection the *Quadripartitus apologeticus* (or *Speculum sapientiae*) of the fifth-century theologian St Cyril of Alexandria, and the *De essentia divinitatis* of ps. Jerome; for spiritual refreshment a very recent work by Adrian the Carthusian, *De remediis utriusque fortunae*, which was written at about the time when Walsham was a novice; for reflective reading extracts from classical authors, the church fathers, and others; and for recreation and mental stimulus a treatise on chess.[353]

---

[349] Simon Bozoun's career is in *BRECP*, 486; the surviving books are now Cambridge, Corpus Christi College MS 264 (Bede etc.), ibid., MS 407 (itineraries), BL MS Royal 14 C.xiii (Higden), Oxford, Bodley MS Fairfax 20 (Flores).

[350] The list of books, found in BL MS Royal 14 C.xiii, fo 13v, is printed in Sharpe, *EBL*, at B58; Bozoun's list also included a *Speculum monachorum*, probably by the same Bernard, B58.16. I am assuming that the books were intended for the use of the community, although possibly not in general circulation until after Bozoun's death.

[351] For Robert de Donewich see *BRECP*, 501–2 and for Reynham ibid., 550; the manuscripts in question are CUL Kk.2.21 (Donewich) and Cambridge, Corpus Christi College 252 (Reynham). Nothing is known about Reynham apart from the fact that he was ill in 1347/8.

[352] See the biographical details in *BRECP*, 568–9, and note that the diagnosis of leprosy may be inaccurate as the doctors consulted pronounced him free of that disease, NRO DCN 35/7.

[353] CUL MS Ll.5.21; the treatise on chess is listed in the contents on a front flyleaf but at some unknown date was removed. What remains is in one hand of the early fifteenth century.

Among the surviving twelfth- to fourteenth-century books from Rochester there are only a few in which non-university monks' names are inscribed and these are most in evidence during the first half of the fourteenth century. The activities of Thomas de Horsted as precentor and librarian suggest that he was assiduous in procuring texts if we may judge by six that survive and trust the inscription *per fratrem Thomam de Horsted* in five of them.[354] The manuscripts include a biblical Concordance, a *Flores Bernardi* containing a request to the reader for prayers for Horsted's soul, Gregory's *Moralia* with a *tabula* compiled by Horsted, part of the *Pantheologus* of Peter of Cornwall, and the *Summa predicantium* by John of Bromyard.[355] In addition, the copy of Augustine's *Civitas Dei* which, along with the Concordance above, were among the books lent to a secular priest in 1390 was described as 'Fratris Thome de Horstede'.[356] The name Robert de Gelham, a contemporary of Horsted, is found in three Royal manuscripts in two of which it is preceded by the problematic *per*. The *Postillae super psalterium* by Nicholas de Gorran has been previously referred to and could have come to the library via Gelham since the text is in a hand of the late thirteenth or early fourteenth century. The collection of treatises by Ambrose of Milan, however, had been in the library since before 1122/3 and therefore *per* may refer to temporary possession by way of a loan. The third volume, which contains biblical commentaries of Isidore and Jerome and is also listed in the 1122/3 catalogue, has a marginal note on fo 84 to the effect that 'Robertus de Gelham est bonus puer'; is this an indication of its use for elementary bible study when Gelham was a novice?[357]

Three monks whose years in the Rochester cloister overlapped with those of Gelham were also in possession of surviving manuscripts. Henry de Mepeham had a twelfth-century copy of Jerome's version of the Pauline Epistles and also a thirteenth-century volume of theological treatises by William Peraldus, neither of which appear in the early Rochester library catalogues.[358] William de Reyersh,

---

[354] The little that is known of Horsted is in *BRECP*, 613. The precise meaning of the preposition *per* followed by a name has been queried by Neil Ker and Richard Sharpe, notably when a monk's known dates are either too early or too late for him to have had any direct involvement in procuring a particular manuscript, Sharpe, *EBL*, 466–7, where the reference to Ker is stated. This scepticism may be relevant to one manuscript; see note 355 below.

[355] The Concordance has been described above, 114; the *Flores Bernardi*, now bound with other texts that are of later date, is BL MS Royal 5 A.x and the request for prayers on fo 1; the *Moralia* and *tabula* are BL MS Royal 6 D.vii, also referred to above, 106, n.89; the *Pantheologus* is BL MS Royal 7 F.iv. Bromyard's preaching manual must have been completed no later than 1348 according to Leonard Boyle, who goes on to point out that Prior Bozoun of Norwich purchased a copy before he resigned in 1352, L. Boyle, 'The Date of the *Summa Praedicantium*', *Speculum* 48 (1973), 533–7 at 537. Thus it is not surprising to find that Horsted had also obtained it for Rochester at a similarly early date. Ker's dating of this manuscript, in Ker, *MLGB*, 163, is somewhat late. These calculations lead to the conclusion that Horsted was precentor in the late 1340s and/or early 1350s, which should be added to *BRECP*, 613.

[356] Sharpe, *EBL*, at B83.5 and B83.2.

[357] Gelham's three Royal manuscripts in the British Library are 2 C.v (Gorran), 6 C.iv (Ambrose), 3 B.i (Isidore etc.); possibly Gelham attended the almonry school. On the vexed question of the meaning of *per* with reference to Gelham see Sharpe, *EBL*, 466, and for the entries in the 1122/3 catalogue ibid., at B77.42 (Ambrose), B77.23 (Isidore). I am confident that it is the same Robert de Gelham whose name is in the three manuscripts, *BRECP*, 605.

[358] These are now BL MSS Royal 4 B.ii (Jerome) and 10 B.ii (Peraldus); the few known details of Mepeham's life are in *BRECP*, 621.

chamberlain and sacrist in the 1320s and 1330s, was responsible for obtaining the third book of Alexander of Hales's commentary on the Sentences of Peter Lombard while, through John de Westerham, the text of the Sentences had previously been acquired.[359] The second half of the fourteenth century produced two monks by the name of Thomas Bruyn (Broun), one of whom obtained a fourteenth-century copy of Thomas Aquinas's commentary on book four of the Sentences.[360] Printed books are also in evidence at Rochester in the case of two which have the inscription 'Johannes Noble monachus Roffensis pertinet'. Noble is not known to have been a student at Oxford but was precentor *c.* 1510. His chosen texts were by Augustine and Ludolf of Saxony the Carthusian; the Augustine volume consisted of a sermon, an exposition on the creed, and a tract on drunkenness which was printed in Cologne *c.* 1474, and the work by Ludolf is his *In Psalterium Expositio* printed in Paris in 1506.[361] Thomas de Horsted may have been a worthy successor to Alexander, precentor of Rochester during the first decade of the thirteenth century, who *vel scripsit vel acquisivit* nineteen books, the list of which was copied into the only one of them to have survived.[362] It may be that Thomas de Horsted was the last to follow the tradition of seeking out and, possibly, commissioning copies; but what has since been lost might have told a different story.

The literary interests of Winchester monks, both those who were sent to Oxford and those who were not, is almost a blank. The meagre total of extant books from a royal foundation which was both monastery and cathedral leaves the historian bereft of evidence. The handful of volumes, whose one-time owners are specified and which remains for our consideration and scrutiny, presents such a diversity of subject matter that it could hardly be an exaggeration to expect the contents of the late medieval library to have been at least as varied in providing for the community's interests. The books include: a volume of extracts from the classical writers Macrobius, Vegetius, and Vitruvius with the *contulit* of H. de Merleburg, a monk of whom nothing else is known;[363] James de Voragine's lives of saints, or *Legenda aurea*, containing a *memoriale* of John de Drayton (*c.* 1283–1307), who was presumably the donor;[364] verse fragments which Prior Nicholas de Tarente *dedit* (d. 1309);[365] the juxtaposition in one volume of the treatise on chess by James

---

[359] Reyersh is found in *BRECP*, 628–9 and the book is now BL MS Royal 9 E.xi; for Westerham's acquisition see above 122–3.

[360] Both of the monks Broun and Bruyn are in *BRECP*, 594; the manuscript survives as BL MS Royal 9 C.iv.

[361] For Noble see *BRECP*, 624; the Augustine work is now BL IA.3420 and that of Ludolf was in the hands of Messrs Maggs in 1964, subsequently sold and since then untraced. Although the title of the latter is unstated, the date and place of publication make it almost certainly this work rather than Ludolf's popular *Vita Christi*; see H. M. Adams, *Catalogue of Books Printed on the Continent of Europe, 1501–1600 in Cambridge Libraries*, 2 vols (Cambridge University Press, Cambridge, 1967), i, no. 1673, p. 675.

[362] Alexander II is in *BRECP*, 589 and his list of additions to the library in BL MS Royal 10 A.xii, printed in Sharpe, *EBL*, at B80.

[363] The name is in a manuscript now Leyden University Library, Voss lat. F.93, and has been dated as early thirteenth century; Merleburg may be an alternative spelling of Marleburgh, *BRECP*, 719.

[364] Now MS CUL Gg.2.18; Drayton's details are in *BRECP*, 686–7.

[365] Now BL MS Harley 315, fos 46 and 47 only; the rest of the manuscript is missing. For Tarente see also *BRECP*, 739.

de Cessolis and the *De regimine sanitatis* of Bartholomew [of Salerno] owned by William Manwode, hordarian in the 1490s;[366] John de Burgo's *Pupilla oculi omnibus presbyteris*, which is to a large extent a revision of the *Ocula sacerdotis* of William de Pagula, a printed book published in Paris in 1501 and acquired *ex provisione* of John Morton in 1518 when he may have been precentor.[367]

In contrast, the fortuitous survival of a substantial collection of books from Worcester cathedral library is sufficiently impressive to incline us to believe that a healthy nucleus of mature non-university monks there were serious about keeping up their studies. Over half of the fifty-four monks whose names appear in surviving books had no university training.[368] Ten of the eleven monks who pooled their pittance money to buy the *Distinctiones Mauricii* somewhere between 1277 and 1301 were in this latter group, and the remainder are scattered unevenly between those dates and the dissolution.[369] Among them monk precentors are often represented. Philip Aubyn or Philip de Worcester, for example, who, before he became prior in 1287 commissioned the copying of Bonaventure's commentary on the fourth book of the Lombard's Sentences.[370] Another, John de Wyke, must have impressed his brethren from his earliest years in the monastery for within ten years of his clothing in the monastic habit he was elected one of the seven nominees for the priorate; not until 1301, however, when he was for the third time one of the nominees, was his appointment approved by the bishop. He was one of the eleven purchasers of the *Distinctiones*; as noted above, he and Thomas de Segesbarowe were jointly responsible for the acquisition of a copy of Peter Comester's *Historia scholastica*, and Segesbarowe himself for part of the *Summa*.[371] Two more monks who served under Prior Wyke have also received mention as providers of books: John de Bromesgrove of Comestor and Robert de Diclesdone of the Lombard's Sentences.[372] In the first half of the fourteenth century Henry Fouke was much in evidence as an avid collector of manuscripts, and his knowledge and skill are demonstrated by his labours in compiling finding-aids to facilitate their use.[373] He foliated and indexed several volumes, annotated and wrote parts of some, purchased others, and commissioned the copying of at least one. There is no record of his attendance at the university although he was frequently in touch with those of his brethren who were, on occasion buying books from them and sharing with

---

[366] The history and rules of the game of chess by this fourteenth-century Dominican in company with the treatise by Bartholomew, owned by Manwode is now Oxford, Bodley MS Digby 31; the treatise on chess also occurs in Bodley MS 58 which belonged to St Swithun's in the fifteenth century. Manwode's career is in *BRECP*, 712–13.

[367] This volume is now Cambridge, St John's College S.5.24; John Morton II may be found in *BRECP*, 720.

[368] The preservation of some 370 volumes, of which two-thirds remain *in situ*, partially compensates for the absence of any comprehensive medieval catalogues.

[369] With reference to the Distinctiones see above 116, and for the dating, Thomson, *Medieval Manuscripts in Worcester Cathedral*, MS Q.42, 143.

[370] Now WCM MS F.167 *quem... scribi fecit*; for Aubyn see *BRECP*, 772–3.

[371] See above 120, 124.

[372] See above 120, 122.

[373] The known details of Fouke's monastic career are in *BRECP*, 807–8; he is not known to have served as precentor.

them in the work of annotation. The unusual extent of our knowledge with regard to Fouke's activities is due to the skilful identification of the handwriting in some thirteen books in addition to the eight in which his name occurs.[374] All of the manuscripts concerned have been dated as emanating from the late thirteenth or early fourteenth centuries and therefore may be considered fairly new in relation to Fouke's own monastic life span, from his profession in 1303 to 1340 when he was still fulfilling responsibilities on behalf of the chapter. The manuscripts may be grouped in the three major categories of theology, preaching, and canon law. Theology is represented, amongst other works, by Peter Lombard's Sentences and commentaries on them, one of the latter being the Oxford lectures of his fellow monk, Richard de Bromwych, which Fouke bought from Bromwych for 20s.[375] There are ten volumes containing sermons and sermon material mainly by friars such as Guy d'Evreux, Nicholas de Gorran, James de Voragine, and Gilbert of Tournai; this last manuscript was obtained by Fouke from Robert de Morton, a fellow monk, in exchange for *quodam iocali eburneo*.[376] One of the works of canon law was the *Summa summarum* of William de Pagula for which Fouke paid 50s., another was Innocent IV on the decretals, and a third John of Freiburg's *Summa confessorum* bought from Richard de Bromwych for 20s.[377] This monk may be compared with Thomas de Wolviston at Durham, both noteworthy bibliophiles whether or not they had the benefit of university training.[378]

In the early fifteenth century another volume was added to the Worcester collection of legal texts, the *Summa* of canon and of civil law by Ranfredus of Benevento; it was 'handed over' by one monk, Richard de Grafton, to another, Thomas de Broghton, who is known to have been precentor in 1411/12.[379] John de Cleve, also precentor several years earlier, may have taken upon himself the copying of the anonymous *Regimen animarum*, a compilation of useful information for the guidance of parish priests; his name is in the opening initial 'O' and the year 1404 is the earliest date in the Easter tables that are included in the manuscript.[380]

---

[374] The distinctive hand of Fouke was recognized by Professor R. M. Thomson while he was working on the catalogue of manuscripts in Worcester cathedral; my reference to manuscripts in BRECP, 808 has been rendered incomplete as a result of Thomson's more recent work.

[375] The commentary by Bromwych is WCM MS F.139. WCM MS F.8 is the Lombard's Sentences and F.2 contains the commentary probably the work of Romanus de Roma, o.p.; both of these volumes have annotations probably in the hands of Fouke. His name also occurs in F.124 which contains theological *quaestiones*, and his hand appears in Q.24 a sermon concordance.

[376] WCM MSS Q.12 (Evreux), Q.53 (Gorran), Q.64 (Voragine), F.77 (Tournai) where the inscription is on fo v verso; for Robert de Morton see BRECP, 851. Other sermon manuscripts connected with Fouke are F.16, F.157, Q.18, Q.46, Q.85.

[377] WCM MSS F.131 (Pagula), F.170 (Innocent IV), F.62 (Freiburg); Fouke also probably owned F.141 (*Apparatus super sextum*), and his name is inscribed in Oxford, Bodley, MS Rawlinson C.428 (*Liber sextus decretalium*).

[378] For Wolviston see above 150.

[379] The manuscript is WCM F.125, written in Italian bookhands of the early fourteenth century; on fo 1 the inscription reads 'Tradatur domino Thome Broctone precentori' at the top, and 'Liberatus per Ricardum Grafftun quondam ob/ligat(us) pro eodem' at the foot. Grafton is in BRECP, 812, and Broghton ibid., 781.

[380] Extracts from the *Summa confessorum* of Raymond [?Pennafort] and the *Oculi sacerdotis* of William de Pagula are included in this volume, now Oxford, Bodley MS Hatton 11, the first part of

Sometime in the last quarter of the fifteenth century Thomas Scheldesley's *constat* appeared in a copy of Peter Comestor's *Sermone... ad monachos et canonicos regulares* bound with Lanfranc's *De officio monachorum*. In 1480 Thomas Streynsham, who was then chamberlain, exchanged his early twelfth-century copy of the chronicle of Florence of Worcester for the *Historia destructionis Troiae* by the Franciscan Guido de Columpnis (d. 1408) which was offered to him by a monk of Great Malvern priory.[381] Between the 1490s and the 1530s four more volumes of sermons have names attached: Thomas Mildenham, precentor in 1491/2 and prior 1495 to 1507, obtained and owned [*constat*] a fifteenth-century mixed collection of some 160 sermons; Thomas Grene (fl. 1504–23/4) obtained a volume of sermons on the Sunday epistles; and the names of William Fordham (fl. 1504–36) and his contemporary John Musard are found in a volume of mainly patristic homilies.[382]

It is true that individual acquisition and ownership of books, and of book borrowing and actual reading among the monks of the cathedral communities remain, for the most part, matters surrounded by uncertainty. Nevertheless, unqualified scepticism should not be allowed the final word. Even pen-trial evidence requires an explanation for the insertion of 'this' particular name in 'this' particular book. In the final analysis, aside from the unequivocal statement of Thomas Wulstan of Worcester, who in 1528 *perlegit* the *Diadema monachorum* of Smaragdus, we cannot be sure that any monk did read the books he had acquired or borrowed and indeed, in some cases, if he personally had acquired or borrowed them.[383] However, we need to recognize that good intentions are a fundamental component of human nature and therefore as applicable to medieval monks in their day as to us in ours. There is enough evidence to allow us to discern signs of a continuing, although from time to time flagging, interest in the pursuit of learning that should be interpreted, in the monastic setting, as primarily motivated by the desire for God. The search for and recognition of original thought or scholarly and intellectual achievement within the monastic cathedral precinct are not the aim of

which was completed in 1343 (fo 105), and William de Pagula's treatise may have been a later addition. If Cleve did not take part in the copying he may have been responsible for commissioning it. These remarks qualify and correct my earlier statement in *BRECP*, 788.

[381] The Comestor manuscript is now CUL Mm.1.19 of which the Lanfranc text is the *Decreta Lanfranci*, printed as *Monastic Constitutions*, under Lanfranc in the bibliography. For Scheldesley and Streynsham see *BRECP*, 871 and 880 respectively.

[382] WCM MS F.10 (Mildenham), Q.17 (Grene), F.93 (Fordham and Musard). The following should be noted: 1) Mildenham regarded F.10 as his personal possession that would be available in the library only after his death (fo 339); 2) the names Thomas Grene, William Fordham, and John Musard may be no more than pen-trials according to R. M. Thomson; and F.93, a text belonging to the first half of the twelfth century, is thought to have originated at Worcester and was therefore presumably in the library; Fordham and Musard, however, could have been borrowers. 3) The comments and suggestions made here have greatly benefited from the judicious remarks of R. M. Thomson in his Worcester manuscripts catalogue *passim*.

[383] Alan Piper has pointed out that modern scholars should not apply their own attitudes to books to medieval monks for whom books were far too costly and difficult to obtain to be content to possess them without the intent of reading them (unpublished personal communication). With regard to Durham his research has revealed the presence of impressive intellectual standards in the community in the later middle ages, Piper, 'The Libraries of the Monks of Durham', 249.

this present study; it focuses, rather, on the ordinary monks who, under obedience, performed their ordinary duties of prayer and service and made time, with varying degrees of success and zeal, to progress in their understanding of what they professed to believe by resorting to the books available.

Note: two appendices will be found below at the end of the final chapter. They are intended to illustrate the potential fruitfulness of a comparative study of the writings available for use by the monks of the cathedral priories. I hope that my survey of the titles in the fields of grammar and history, which reveals the books and authors most commonly featured in the cathedral priory libraries, will encourage further investigations.

IV

The Years of Maturity and Responsibility: The Duties of Obedientiaries and Senior Monks

> Substantia monasterii in ferramentis vel vestibus seu quibuslibet rebus praevideat abbas fratres de quorum vita et moribus securus sit et eis singula... consignet custodienda.
>
> RB, C.32, 1

In the cathedral priories, as in other religious houses, the monk officials were known as obedientiaries because they were appointed by the superior, that is by the abbot or prior, to whom they owed obedience in fulfilling their responsibilities. It has been usual to distinguish several categories within the obedientiary offices by grouping them according to their respective spheres of responsibility—for example, those involved in financial and economic administration, those in charge of the provision of hospitality for friends and strangers, and those responsible for the daily performance of the liturgy in the monastic church and chapels and for the care and maintenance of these sacred places. Alternatively, some have preferred to make a division between those obediences which were required to present an annual account of the income at their disposal and those which do not appear to have been subject to this prescription. In contrast, I have avoided these attempts to impose tidy distinctions which, while intended to facilitate our understanding by clarifying a complex picture, unavoidably oversimplify the day-to-day organization and operation of a monastic community, which was built on a constantly changing set of human relationships and external circumstances. I prefer to stress the unifying element in monastic life, its fundamental motivation stemming from the individual monk's initial decision to follow Christ in obedience to the Rule of St Benedict. The often harsh and bitter reality of the existential situation within the community did not negate the original ideal even when it was clouded by frequently recurring incidences of uncharitable behaviour, serious lapses in discipline, bitter disagreements, and grave offences. In order to preserve a balanced perspective in our study of monastic and ecclesiastical records we should bear in mind that men who became monks continued to be human beings, frail, vulnerable, and subject to the whole range of disorders that are common to all mankind. We also need to be reminded that through the times of laxity, strain, and crisis the quintessential daily round of monastic prayer and praise continued whether by many or few, with diligence and fervour or without. This was in itself a remarkable achievement, rendered possible by the continuous underlying presence of the monastic ideal; often obscure, it remained unquestionably the *raison d'être* of the whole monastic edifice.

The method of treatment of the obedientiary offices has been selective and is therefore uneven in the extent of detail that follows here. Thus, I have chosen to pause only briefly over the chief financial departments, that is with those responsible for the oversight and administration of lands and the custody of parish churches; some of these have been the focus of critical analyses by historians on medieval rural and urban economy.[1] Rather, I have concentrated my attention on the group of obedientiaries whose duty it was to take charge of the more strictly monastic affairs such as the daily performance of the divine office, the maintenance and repair of the cathedral church, the provision of clothing for the monks, the care available for the sick brethren, and the discharge of the charitable obligation with regard to monastic almsgiving and hospitality.

Many, but by no means all, monks in the cathedral communities were appointed to administrative posts during their lifetime. However, when numbers were few some monks were pressed into taking charge of two and, at times, three or more offices simultaneously despite an occasional episcopal admonition to the contrary.[2] It is hardly surprising to find plurality of office in small religious communities where the number of professed monks was little more than equivalent to the number of obedientiary posts occupied. At Bath, for example, between the late thirteenth and early fifteenth centuries there were some eighteen obediences in operation if we include the priors of the two dependent cells at Dunster and Waterford, Ireland. During these years the monastic population at Bath fluctuated

---

[1] For example, to mention only a few, R. H. Snape, *English Monastic Finances in the Later Middle Ages* (Cambridge University Press, Cambridge, 1926); R. Virgoe, 'The Estates of Norwich Cathedral Priory, 1101–1538', in Atherton, *Norwich Cathedral*, 339–60; B. Harvey, *Westminster Abbey and its Estates in the Middle Ages* (Clarendon Press, Oxford, 1977); M. Threlfall-Holmes, *Monks and Markets, Durham Cathedral Priory 1460–1520* (Oxford University Press, Oxford, 2005); R. A. L. Smith, 'The Central Financial System of Christ Church, Canterbury, 1186–1512', *English Historical Review*, July 1940 and reprinted in his *Collected Papers*, London, 1947, 23–41; M. Mate, 'Property Investments by Canterbury Cathedral Priory 1250–1400', *Journal of British Studies*, 23, 1984, 1–21. See also note 163 below.

[2] E.g., Richard Warrewyk, who was both sacrist and treasurer at Coventry cathedral priory in 1402 until Bishop John Burghill issued an injunction ordering his removal from the office of sacrist. *BRECP*, 373. Bishop Richard de Kellawe, himself a monk, told the Durham monks in 1314 that none of them were to hold more than one office at a time, Reg. II, fo 50v.

Vicarii in choro or *in ecclesia*, who substituted or deputized for some of the major obedientiaries in choir for the office, were probably either *claustrales* holding no office or having a position with minor responsibilities. They are mentioned on a number of obedientiary accounts; for example, by the Durham almoner who gave his vicar 6s. 8d. in 1393/4 (DCM almoner's account). Dobson suggests that they were 'secular deputies' without supporting evidence, *Durham Priory*, 69. At Worcester, Reginald Dyere was the *vicarius* or *socius in choro* for the cellarer in 1392/3 (WCM C.76); and at Ely the sacrist's *vicarius* in 1341/2 was William Burdeleys (Chapman, *Sacrist Rolls*, 119). Dyere is in *BRECP*, 801 and Burdeleys, ibid., 394.

and, at the same time, clearly showed a gradual downward trend, from slightly over thirty to the mid-twenties.[3] Similar in size, the monastic community at Coventry has preserved, among its lamentably few surviving records, the names of several pluralist office holders in the fifteenth century.[4] Due to depleting numbers also at Coventry in the last decades before the dissolution this practice became more common.[5]

In the larger cathedral priories there are fewer examples of the simultaneous occupation of more than one obedientiary office; but the explanation in at least one case at Winchester lies in the existence of a grave financial crisis in the 1330s during the priorate of Alexander de Heriard. The chapter drew up a petition urging the prior to take over responsibility for the offices of hordarian, chamberlain, and almoner to reduce and eliminate the debt.[6] Where there were more members in a community to draw from there is abundant evidence that many obedientiaries were provided with assistants or deputies; at both Durham and Ely these were known as *socii*, and at Ely their name was often included on the heading of the annual accounts after that of the obedientiary.[7] Several obedientiary offices were regularly, or from time to time, occupied by two monks jointly; there were usually, for example, two anniversarians at Christ Church Canterbury and sometimes two feretrars are named at Durham, while three treasurers are often found working in tandem at Canterbury.[8] Other deputies such as the succentor, subcellarer, subalmoner, subsacrist, and subchamberlain were second in command in the departments named; and a few of them, like the subcellarer at Worcester, are known to have rendered their own subsidiary accounts.[9] The subprior, who ranked next to

---

[3] Figures are few and far between for Bath cathedral priory, and there are no records as to the numbers in the novitiate; see *BRECP*, 3–4. In 1447 when 26 professed monks assembled to elect a prior one of them, William Salford I, was named as holding the offices of sacrist, cellarer, *custos* of the Lady chapel, and hostiller, and John Lacok was infirmarer, pittancer, and refectorer, ibid., 40, 33.

[4] Richard Drowte was subprior and pittancer in 1486 and John Shepey had combined the same two offices during the previous year, *BRECP*, 354, 369,. Earlier in the century William Haloughton may have been serving as cellarer and pittancer in 1410/11; see ibid., 357.

[5] See, for instance, Thomas Knyghton and John Pope, *BRECP*, 360, 367. In these final years, however, Bath does not appear to have suffered the same decline in numbers; see ibid., 7.

[6] *BRECP*, 700–1; my statement here corrects and clarifies this entry. It should be noted that the office of hordarian was being accounted for by John de Merlawe, who was at the same time receiver (treasurer), ibid., 718 (Merlawe I). There is also a single known case for one year only at Worcester when Thomas Blackwell compiled the 1434/5 accounts for the offices of both the pittancer and the chamberlain, ibid., 776–7 (Blackwell I)—a temporary emergency perhaps?

[7] E.g., in 1321/2 the pittancer was John de Orewell and his *socius*, R. de Yakesham, *BRECP*, 428, 465.

[8] None of these accounts are available in printed form, but see the typed lists in the Christ Church archives for the anniversarians' DCc Accounts 3–9 and for the treasurers' ibid., 1–10. For Durham, an early fourteenth-century chapter ordinance required all masters of obediences to have a *consocius*, DCM Locellus XXVII, 16d.; see the feretrars' accounts for 1381/2 and 1398/9, DCM accounts of the feretrar.

[9] There are over twenty account rolls of the subcellarer extant, between *c*. 1325 and 1493/4, WCM C.431–C.452. At Canterbury in the 1330s the prior had both a chaplain and a subchaplain, see *BRECP* under John Coleshull, 127.

the prior and was vicegerent of the community during the absence of the prior, was often assisted by a third and even a fourth prior to whom he could delegate specific responsibilities when circumstances required.[10]

Income from manorial properties, rents, pensions, and other regular sources of revenue such as benefactions and offerings provided the necessary funds to support the fifteen to twenty major obedientiary offices and those of the dependent cells. In addition, there were a not inconsiderable number of other positions to which monks were assigned, some of them involving small financial transactions; but these have left no records to indicate if they were examined at the annual chapter audit.

If a sacrist of Winchester ever had the opportunity to meet and converse with his counterpart at Ely—possibly at one of the triennial provincial chapters of the Black Monks at Northampton—both of them might well have been surprised by the marked differences between their respective spheres of authority. St Swithun's, for example, was one of only several of the cathedral priories to have a *magister* or *custos operum* among its obedientiaries, who was responsible for the maintenance, repair, and renovation of the cathedral fabric and other buildings within the monastic precinct.[11] At Ely and Canterbury these duties came within the jurisdiction of the sacrist; at Norwich the responsibilities pertained mainly but not exclusively to the sacrist; at Worcester, where there was also a monk *custos operum*, he was entirely subservient to the cellarer.[12] John de Tickhill, chamberlain of Durham in 1354, reported to Bishop Thomas de Hatfield during his visitation that the sacrist was to blame for failure to make the urgent repairs required both in the cathedral church and bell tower; and the remedy, he suggested, was to establish the office of *magister operum*. The bishop does not seem to have followed this recommendation as no such stipulation appears in his injunctions; however, five years later Prior Fosser and his advisers appointed Tickhill to the sacrist's office, perhaps on the grounds that his denunciation implied self-confidence in his ability to be more competent.[13] The presence of monk gardeners follows a

---

[10] Thus, John V was third prior at Bath in 1206 and Nicholas de Bath I fourth prior there in 1364, *BRECP*, 30, 12; Richard de Hegham at Canterbury was third prior in 1359/60 and Nicholas Galeye fourth prior in the 1380s, ibid., 195, 164; Reginald de Barnby was third prior at Durham in 1311, *LVD*, iii, C.684; Philip de Dallyng was third prior at Ely in 1341, *BRECP*, 402–3, and William de Maydenstone occurs in the same office at Rochester in 1333, ibid., 620 (William de Maydenstone I). At Winchester in the 1350s William de Camel occupied the position of third prior; and a fourth prior, John Basyng III, occurs in 1476/7, ibid., 680, 669 (John Basyng). At Worcester there were both third and fourth priors in 1401, John de Upton and John de Legh, ibid., 886, 835 (John de Legh II).

[11] Two surviving accounts have been transcribed by Dean Kitchin in his *Obedientiary Rolls*, 209–23; John III was *custos operum* of Bath cathedral priory in 1206, *BRECP*, 30, and one later reference, dated 1308 suggests that this obedientiary office was also in possession of its own income, BL MS Egerton 3316, fo. 67v; see *BRECP* under William de Hampton I, 27.

[12] See Chapman, *Sacrist Rolls*, *passim*; Smith, *Canterbury Cathedral Priory*, 37–8, where it is stated that the 'heavier building expenses were usually met by public subscription'; for Norwich, see also the role played by the communar and pittancer in the major construction works covering the years 1282/3 to 1329/30, Fernie and Whittingham. *Communar Rolls*, *passim*. In the mid-fourteenth century John Conversus was *magister operum* at Worcester, *BRECP*, 826–7; the cellarer's account for 1376–7, transcribed by Hamilton, *Compotus Rolls*, 20–1, includes the expenses of the construction of the new dormitory.

[13] Tickhill's statement appears in the episcopal *comperta* [report] in DCM 1.9.Pont.1b, his appointment as sacrist in *LVD*, iii, C.883.

similar pattern. The only extant accounts are those pertaining to Norwich cathedral priory, but there are references to holders of this office at Coventry, Ely, and Winchester.[14] At Worcester the gardener's O antiphon celebration was regularly paid by the kitchener, and one may therefore conjecture that the two offices had been combined; the fact that both receipts and expenses from 'the garden' appear on the kitchener's annual accounts supports this combination.[15] Gardeners mentioned on Durham account rolls and elsewhere were usually hired labourers.[16]

Exceptions aside, most of the major obedientiary offices were to be found in all the cathedral priories, although they were not always given the same title. The chief financial officer at Winchester, for example, was known as the receiver; his counterpart at Norwich was the master of the cellar, while Canterbury, Ely, Bath, and Coventry had a treasurer and Durham a bursar.[17] At Worcester early existing accounts reveal a bursar's office combined with that of cellarer, but by 1351/2 the heading on the roll names the cellarer alone.[18] The Christ Church and St Swithun's monks had an anniversarian charged with keeping track of the dates on which benefactors and others were annually commemorated and pittances distributed to the community in the form of small sums as pocket money or tasty treats of food or drink. At Durham the subprior and the communar, and later the bursar and communar dealt with these distributions; the Norwich communar and pittancer are inextricably linked and their respective roles are unclear, but both were concerned with dispensing small gifts to their brethren.[19]

For some unknown reason the monks of St Swithun's developed their own terminology to designate three of their offices within the obedientiary framework, namely those of the hordarian, curtarian, and *depositarius*. The first of these, in terms of the size of his income, appears to have been next in importance to the receiver and was the sole provider of funding for the kitchener's office. The cellarer's role must have been a relatively minor one, but there are no accounts extant apart from two of the late fifteenth century on which his office was combined with that of the curtarian.[20]

---

[14] The Norwich gardener's accounts have been translated and edited by Claire Noble in *Norwich Gardener's Rolls*. The single known reference at Coventry is to John de Merstone in 1287, *BRECP*, 363; similarly, at Ely there is only one on record, Alan de Soham, in the late thirteenth century, ibid., 439. A monk *custos gardini* occurs at Winchester on at least three occasions in the fourteenth century; see Robert de Basyng, Richard de Claverlye, William Lane, ibid., 670, 683, 708.

[15] It was usual, but not universal, for the monk gardener to be chosen to sing the Advent antiphon that began with the appropriate wording O radix Jesse'; see below 243. It is, of course, possible that there had never been a monk gardener at Worcester.

[16] A gardener's stipend occurs from time to time on the Durham bursar's account and in a list of servants attached to the kitchen in 1316, DCM Locellus XXVII, 16b.

[17] For Bath, Coventry, and Rochester there are few references to this office; see *BRECP*, 3, 337–8, 578; the single reference at Rochester suggests that the office, at least temporarily, was linked to that of cellarer, or prior, ibid., 578 nn. 8 and 9; see also R. A. Smith, 'Rochester Cathedral Priory', 47–53. At Winchester treasurer and receiver seem to have been interchangeable terms.

[18] Some of the early bursar/cellarer rolls have been transcribed and edited by Wilson and Gordon in *Early Compotus Rolls*, including the 1351/2 account, 8–53.

[19] See Foster, 'Durham Priory', 167 and Fernie and Whittingham, *Communar Rolls*, 9–13. In the sixteenth century at Worcester a *magister communis cene* appears.

[20] The two rolls have been transcribed in Kitchin, *Obedientiary Rolls*, 380–9; three more rolls, of the early fifteenth century, of the curtarian alone have turned up since Kitchin's day and are numbered W53/14/9–11 in Winchester cathedral library.

According to the fourteenth-century customary of the refectory the curtarian was concerned with the distribution of bread at meal times, but he was also responsible for some of the prior's domestic needs such as his supply of wood, coal, and candles for his separate hospice.[21] To judge by the duties of the *depositarius* it is clear that he—or they, as there were often two—were the equivalent of the pittancer at Bath, Coventry, Ely, and Norwich. Winchester was also unique in its monk *speciarius* whose special concern is, no doubt, suggested by his name which is related to the Latin word for spice.[22]

Financial and administrative officials

The supervision of the manorial estates pertaining to the cathedral priories lay in the hands of one or more monastic officials. Theirs was a heavy responsibility based on the essential need to provide the community with an adequate income to support its members along with a plentiful supply of farm produce to feed them. The Durham bursar was in charge of the major portion of the estates and income of the cathedral priory and shared in other responsibilities within the monastery; he also accounted for the prior's needs and expenditures. The cellarer and granator were financially dependent on the bursar with whom the terrar worked closely in the sphere of estate management.[23] At Bath a granator appears in 1206 and at Coventry a *senescallus terrarum*, or land steward is named in 1409, but the records are otherwise missing or silent.[24] A lengthy series of account rolls has survived from the office of granator at Ely where there was also a *senescallus terrarum* whose name follows that of the treasurer on the heading of the latter's accounts. The granator's duties were limited to the sale and purchase of grain from the manors and other related operations, leaving the manorial administration to the *senescallus*.[25] Archbishop Winchelsey refers to the Rochester *custodes maneriorum* in 1299 in a sternly worded injunction to the effect that their supervisory duties must not extend beyond a two-day absence from the cloister.[26] A few years earlier Archbishop

---

[21] Perhaps the curtarian acted as steward of the prior's hospice, an obedientiary by this name, found only at Ely; see the three early fifteenth-century accounts referred to above in note 20, and the *Consuetudinary* edited by Kitchin, 33–4, item xxi. My previous conjecture that the two offices of cellarer and curtarian were probably held by one and the same monk was based on the two late fifteenth-century accounts which I now consider to have been an exceptional case. It seems more likely that the responsibilities of the curtarian cannot be clearly defined as he appears to have been active in several areas, another of which was riding around the priory manors with the lay land steward to hold the courts and arrange for deliveries of foodstuffs to St Swithun's; see the early manorial court and account rolls *passim* among the muniments in Winchester cathedral library.

[22] See, for example, John Thurston and Nicholas Salisbury I, *BRECP*, 740, 732. There is no evidence that John le Spycer, monk of Christ Church, ever occupied a similar office, ibid., 290; the name is very likely his patronym.

[23] The doctoral thesis of R. A. Lomas, 'Durham Cathedral Priory as a Landowner and a Landlord, 1290–1540' (Durham, 1973), 8–9, provides brief accounts of the role of these obedientiaries as does R. B. Dobson in *Durham Priory, passim*.

[24] See Robert II for Bath, *BRECP*, 39 and Nicholas Caldecote for Coventry, ibid., 349.

[25] The granator's accounts are CUL EDC 1/F/4/1–, and those of the treasurer/*senescallus* ibid., EDC 1/F/13/1–.

[26] *Reg. Winchelsey*, 838–42. There is evidence, at a much earlier date, of monk custodians of single manors on which they were presumably part-time residents; see Robert de Hecham at Southfleet,

Pecham had been even more severe in his denunciation of the Canterbury monks serving as custodians of manors who, so he told them, were not monks but demoniacs: 'sicut enim piscis sine aqua, sic sine monasterio monachus existere afirmatur'; and, therefore, the custodians should be secular officials.[27] On recognizing the unhealthy state of the priory finances, however, he retracted his order and restored the traditional arrangement of monk wardens, one for each of the four custodies into which the widely scattered Christ Church properties were divided.[28] As one of the largest Benedictine establishments in medieval England, Canterbury had found it expedient to include both bartoners and granators as well as monk wardens among its obedientiaries; the bartoner was in charge of the home farm that was located a few miles north of Canterbury and the granator ensured that the convent granary was kept replenished.[29] At Winchester these offices came within the hordarian's mandate with some responsibilities shared with the curtarian.[30] The *senescalli terrarum* there were lay officials who were given a seat on the prior's council and, as prominent landowners in the vicinity and often holders of public office, their advice was highly valued.[31] The Norwich master of the cellar must have chosen laymen of similar standing as his land stewards in the fourteenth century since he paid them a substantial annual pension of £6 13s. 4d.[32] It was the Worcester cellarer himself, who, as the chief financial administrator, dealt directly with the manorial officials, while the subcellarer accounted for the amounts of grain obtained from each of the manors. The presence of a *senescallus domini* appears on many of the cellarer's rolls, but his role and status at Worcester must have been fairly insignificant because he was paid only 40s. a year. Although no accounts survive, Alan is named as the monk *senescallus terrarum* at Ely in 1301/4, and in 1465/6 the name Nicholas Derby, one of his successors in the office, appears jointly with that of John Ely the treasurer at the head of the latter's account.[33]

BRECP, 609, and John de Marchia, ibid., 620 at Haddenham, Oxford, Bodleian Rolls, MS Rolls Bucks, Box 1, No. 4. I owe the latter reference to the Rev'd Dr William Strange.

[27] *Epist. Peckham*, i, 89, no. lxxiii, dated 1280.
[28] A lucid survey of the manorial system is provided by R. A. L. Smith in *Canterbury Cathedral Priory*, ch. 7, 100–12.
[29] There are surviving accounts in the Canterbury archives (CCA) for all three of these obedientiaries: DCc/monk warden (from 1462), bartoner (from 1299), granator (from 1288). Additional accounts are found under miscellaneous accounts (MA) in the priory Registers O and P.
[30] There are two early references to bartoners in the 1230s; see BRECP, 669, 721, under John de Basyng I and Adam de Neubir'. A third reference a century later on the receiver's account links the bartoner with the curtarian, Kitchin, *Obedientiary Rolls*, 232.
[31] Robert atte More, for example, was high sheriff for Hampshire in the 1390s during his tenure of the office of steward and was summoned to parliament as a knight of the shire, TNA Lists and Indexes No. 9, *List of Sheriffs for England and Wales* (1898), 55; *Parliaments of England, Return of Members to Parliament*, Part I (1878); Edward Coudray, who succeeded More, also held both public offices, ibid.
[32] Names are not given on the account, but see the brief description of the Norwich steward in Saunders, *Obedientiary Rolls*, 42–3.
[33] The Ely monks are in BRECP, 387 (Alan II), 404 (Derby), 407 (John Ely VII).

The hostiller and the reception of guests

St Benedict devotes chapter fifty-three of his Rule to the regulations that were to govern the practice of monastic hospitality; these he summed up in the prescription that every guest was to be received as Christ himself. While guests were customarily accommodated and cared for by the guestmaster, or hostiller, two of the cathedral priories, Ely and Worcester, made use of a second obedientiary, the steward of the prior's hospice. There, in separate and more lavish quarters, important visitors were given the equivalent of 'four star' attention. Needless to say, such care was not lacking at the other cathedral priories but it was provided by obedientiaries already in place. However, at Canterbury it was the cellarer who was in charge of the *domus hospitum*, supplying guests and pilgrims with food and accommodation while Master Omer's former lodging, which was situated close to the east end of the infirmary chapel, was set aside for distinguished visitors.[34]

With the exception of Canterbury ordinary guests, including relatives and friends of the cathedral monks and other visitors, were accommodated in the guesthouse or hall (*hostillaria* or *aula hospitum*) presided over by the hostiller. A Durham inventory of the furnishings of the hall in 1348/9 lists and describes an impressive display of colourful bed coverings, some embroidered with roses, birds, and butterflies and some of the beds provided with hanging tapestries.[35] The office enjoyed a large endowment which, nevertheless, proved inadequate to cover expenses for a large part of the later fourteenth century. Lengthy stays, e.g., long-term residents, as well as a succession of short visits had to be catered for, and this usually included stabling and provender for horses. In addition, the hostiller's responsibilities entailed the supervision of the manor of Elvethall and the parish of St Oswald, both within the environs of the city. A large staff of officials, clerks, and servants was necessary to enable him to carry out all his duties. Several Durham hostillers in the late fourteenth and early fifteenth century also acted as terrar, an obedientiary who, originally operating as the prior's land agent, had become dependent on the bursar from whom he received funds for making the rounds of the manors.[36]

The Norwich hostiller's activities can be followed from 1319/20 to the 1420s in an impressive run of some sixty-five account rolls, but they are less informative. Although he was concerned with the accommodation of both travellers and resident workers, his expenses make no reference to the purchase or provision of food which must have been supplied by the master of the cellar and probably the cellarer.[37] In

---

[34] Master, or Meister, Omer had served as clerk to the prior in the middle of the thirteenth century and was given the building subsequently named after him as his official residence. The Christ Church monks were constantly inundated by visitors, large numbers of whom came as pilgrims to Becket's shrine, and their accommodation was a persistent problem. The result was that additional rooms and locations had to be found for them; see Dobson 'Monks of Canterbury', 139–40, for references to these alternative lodgings.

[35] DCM hostiller's account 1348/9; and for 1371 where there is a similar list under *camera* see Fowler, *Account Rolls*, i, 130–1.

[36] Durham hostiller's accounts survive from the 1330s, but the earliest terrar's account is for the year 1401/2; extracts are printed in Fowler, *Account Rolls*, i, 113–40, and ii, 299–303.

[37] There is, however, no clear indication on the accounts of these two obedientiaries that this was the case.

1398/9 he recorded the repair of beds *contra adventum regis* the cost of which was 2s. 8d.; but even in that year his total expenses and receipts amounted to less than £8; his was a very slim budget financed by rents from several city parishes.[38] The five Ely hostiller account rolls that survive from the period of this present study reveal that both food and lodging for guests were in his charge, and his income, derived largely from two churches, was correspondingly larger than that of his Norwich counterpart—it was over £50 in 1387/8.[39] Names of visiting relatives of the monks are occasionally inserted on the roll, and resident corrodians occur from time to time.[40] The hostiller's responsibilities at Worcester must have been reduced because of the presence of a second obedientiary, who took charge of the prior's guests in the separate hospice named above. More important, however, was the substantial contribution made by the cellarer towards the guests' meals.[41] The names of only two hostillers have come to light at Rochester and absence of any accounts for this office leaves the historian bereft of information.[42] A similar situation prevails with regard to both Bath and Coventry where there are no hostillers named before the middle of the fifteenth century.[43] Although Winchester also lacks accounts for the office of hostiller, the gift of the church and manor of Littleton by Bishop Henry de Blois in 1172 toward 'the reception of guests' was carefully preserved among the monastery's charters.[44] Two centuries later this endowment proved to be inadequate to enable the hostiller to provide a priest to minister the sacraments to the parishioners and, as a result, the hostiller himself was furnished with an episcopal licence to take on the task. Since Littleton was only about two and a half miles to the north of Winchester this was probably not too burdensome an addition to his other responsibilities.[45]

Although St Benedict had prescribed that the office of guestmaster was to be placed in the hands of a monk imbued with a reverential fear of God, the little evidence that remains suggests that there were considerable variations in age and seniority among those appointed. John Luttrell at Durham, for example, had been a

---

[38] E.g., NRO DCN 1/7/48.

[39] CUL EDC 1/F/5/1–5.

[40] In 1387/8 the father of Thomas de Ramesey (*BRECP*, 433 under Ramesey I) and the mother of William de Thorp (ibid., 450–1) were guests; a corrodian, William de Eltisle, a royal nominee, was accommodated in the hostelry in 1324, BL Add. MS 41612, fo 63. For further references to corrodians see the General Index under 'corrodies'.

[41] However, although the Ely hostiller like his counterpart at Worcester divided his responsibilities with the prior's guestmaster, his income was much larger. It may be that the prior of Ely chose to entertain more guests in his lodgings than did the prior of Worcester in his. The Worcester cellarer's accounts include a regular heading *Expense hospitum* which amounted to over £11 in 1354/5; and the total was over £13 in 1385/6 under *Expense ob defectu coquina*, which included some of the food and wine purchased for both guest halls, WCM C.62, 71.

[42] The two names are John de Leycestria, *magister hospicii* in 1333, and Walter de Rawe, who was described as *quondam hostiar*' in 1317, *BRECP*, 616 and 628 respectively.

[43] The earliest hostiller known at Bath is William Salford I in 1447 and at Coventry John Eccleshall in 1518, ibid., 40, 354.

[44] Goodman, *Winchester Chartulary*, no. 3.

[45] Three hostillers were given licences between 1373 and 1400: John de Hyde for the year in 1373 and again in 1375, *BRECP*, 704–5; Thomas de Stoke in 1378, 1379, 1387 (ibid., 738); John Mideltone in 1400 and 1402 (ibid., 719).

monk for barely more than eleven years when he was made hostiller in 1311; and it was his first appointment after a brief period as the prior's chaplain. In the 1330s Walter de Scarisbrick, a monk of twenty years' standing, served as both bursar and hostiller. Robert de Claxton was also responsible for these two offices in the 1390s after forty years in the monastery, while Henry Helay was in charge of the combined offices of hostiller and terrar from the mid-1420s for about a decade. Roger de Evesham had been professed at Worcester for almost half a century in 1420, at which date he was in the office of hostiller; in contrast, Walter de Kirkeby's appointment to the same office came after just under twenty years of profession. No further comparisons are possible with regard to the cathedral priory hostillers because of the dearth of evidence.[46]

Custodians of the chapels

Lady altars and Lady chapels of the monastic cathedrals were usually in the care of an obedientiary known as the *custos* or *magister*.[47] At Bath, a *custos capelle* first comes to light in the mid-fifteenth century but must surely have been present earlier since a Lady chapel east of the high altar was rebuilt in the thirteenth century; a similar late appearance is found at Coventry in the early fifteenth century.[48] It is surprising that the first known holder of this office at Rochester occurs on the eve of the dissolution, but the continuing uncertainty surrounding the precise identification and location of the Lady chapel may offer a clue to the possibly late appearance of the *custos capelle* here.[49] A widespread increase in devotion to the Virgin Mary in the thirteenth century found practical expression in the construction of Lady chapels often in the form of an eastern extension to cathedral and abbey churches. Norwich, Winchester, and Worcester like Bath adopted this new fashion; and Ely followed suit in the fourteenth century, with an impressive free-standing structure on the north side of the choir of the cathedral church. At Norwich, however, there is no record of a monk custodian of the Lady chapel; instead, the *magister altaris beate Marie* appears to have been a secular chaplain or clerk who received small sums annually and robes from the sacrist.[50]

---

[46] *RB*, C.53, 21 is the source of St Benedict's admonition. The Durham monks' careers are in *LVD*, iii, C.798 (Luttrell), C.812 (Scarisbrick), C.942 (Claxton), C.1046 (Helay). Evesham and Kirkeby are in *BRECP*, 804–5 and 827–8 respectively.

[47] Liturgical performance in the Lady chapel together with its musical accompaniment will be discussed below in the next chapter.

[48] See William Salford I, *BRECP*, 40 (Bath) and Richard Stoke, ibid., 370. For Bath see also R. Davenport, 'The Cathedral Priory Church at Bath', 25 in Tatton-Brown, *Archaeology of Cathedrals*, 19–30, and Manco, 'Bath Priory', 86; the latter article distinguishes between the Lady chapel in the easternmost arm of the cathedral and a second [Lady] chapel in the nave provided for the laity.

[49] See J. P. McAleer, *Rochester Cathedral*, 161–2, 'The So-called Lady Chapel'.

[50] The *magister summe altaris* was another clerk/chaplain who received 20s. per annum from the sacrist while his counterpart at the Lady altar had a mere 2s. according to many of the sacrist's accounts, e.g., NRO DCN 1/4/25, 32, 37 etc. This would suggest that the latter probably fulfilled another function within the cathedral church or precinct to provide him with sufficient funds to survive—as a chantry chaplain perhaps?

Winchester and Worcester, by contrast, had obedientiaries, the former from as early as 1223 when Adam de Wyg' was *custos* of the Lady altar, while the latter has preserved *in situ* nearly fifty account rolls of the *magister* or *custos capelle* dating from 1356/7.[51] The *custos altaris beate Marie* at Ely was renamed the *custos capelle beate Marie* upon completion of the new chapel in the mid-fourteenth century; and the surviving accounts of this obedientiary, although relatively few in number, begin as early as 1318/19.[52]

By 1311 there was a master of the Galilee [chapel] at Durham where a late twelfth-century western extension of the cathedral church was dedicated to the Virgin Mary. The precise extent of the duties of this obedientiary remain uncertain because references are few and far between and mostly uninformative; he may have been associated with the sacrist's office as the latter was responsible for any repairs or alterations in the Galilee.[53] There was a Lady chapel at Canterbury in the twelfth century situated in the two easternmost bays of the north aisle of the cathedral nave which, in the mid- and late fourteenth century, was in the care of secular clerks who were paid by the sacrist. From Prior Ernulf's time, however, there had also been a chapel of St Mary in the crypt where a monk *custos* was in charge by, and probably before, 1287.[54] In the wake of Archbishop Thomas Becket's murder, in 1170, followed by his speedy canonization, the Christ Church monks found themselves confronted by an unprecedented situation which soon necessitated the appointment of three additional obedientiaries: the *custos corone*, the *custos martyrii* and the *custos tumbe*. The first of these became responsible for the *corona* or eastern extension of the Trinity chapel where fragments of Becket's skull were preserved; the second was in charge of the site of the martyrdom in the north-west transept; the third looked after the tomb in the eastern crypt which was the original burial place. These monk custodians were probably in place long before the names of the earliest holders of the three offices appear in the records in the 1280s.[55] In addition a *custos magni altaris* occurs from time to time in the fourteenth century

---

[51] For Adam de Wyg' at Winchester see *BRECP*, 751; the Worcester accounts are WCM C.248–C.291, C.838, 839.

[52] More precisely, they are about twenty-four in number, some of which are in the form of extracts copied by Bentham, CUL EDC 1/F/7/1–8 and CUL Add. MS 2957, 50–7. The earlier location of an altar dedicated to Our Lady was in the south presbytery aisle of the cathedral (now Bishop West's chapel).

[53] John de Allerton was master in 1311 and 1316, *LVD*, iii, C.749. The Galilee usually refers to the western porch or entrance to a church: see Richard Halsey, 'The Galilee Chapel' in *Medieval Art and Architecture, Durham Cathedral*, Conference Transactions for the Year 1977 (British Archaeological Association, 1980), 60–2.

[54] The sacrist's accounts (CCA DCc sacrist) *passim* record these payments from 1341 onward; there are a few surviving fragmentary sixteenth-century accounts only of the *custos beate Marie in cryptis* in ibid., Miscellaneous Accounts, vol. 36. In 1287/8 John de Thaneto II was *custos*, *BRECP*, 300.

[55] The Trinity chapel was located to the east of the presbytery and high altar. Peter de Ikham was *magister corone* in 1287/8, *BRECP*, 207; Robert de Elham was probably *custos martyrii* in 1285/6 and was followed by Marcellus de Lese in 1287/8, ibid., 150, 222; John de Begbroke was *custos tumbe* in 1287/8, ibid., 84. Fragments of a few sixteenth-century accounts of the *custos martyrii* are in DCc Literary MS C.11. *Cathedral Shrines* by Ben Nilson provides a lucid comparative study in which Canterbury features in some detail; see the index references there under Thomas Becket.

and more rarely in the fifteenth century, who performed his duties in conjunction with the four subsacrists.[56]

The infirmarer and infirmary cloister

The infirmarer, infirmarian, or *magister infirmarie*, like the sacrist, cellarer, and chamberlain, was one of the obedientiary offices essential for the provision of the basic needs of the brethren and, as such, was present in all the cathedral priories from the earliest times. St Benedict devoted chapter thirty-six to the care of the sick, and Archbishop Islip's injunction to the Christ Church monks in 1356 voiced similar concern when he ordered that the brothers in the infirmary were to be treated with compassion *in visceribus... Christi*. Strong words on the same subject were addressed to the Durham monks by Bishop Kellawe in 1314; the sick were to receive adequate meat and drink and a competent doctor was to be provided.[57] Resident medical practitioners were not always in attendance although payment for their services is a regular entry on the accounts of infirmarers and other obedientiaries; an ordinance issued by the monks in chapter at Norwich in 1379 placed responsibility on the infirmarer to find and employ a 'medicum in arte medicine peritum pro conventu sicud solebat facere'.[58] With their own cloister, chapel, and kitchen the occupants of the infirmary were removed from the hustle and bustle prevalent elsewhere within the monastic precinct and thus from undue interference during their convalescence. At Bath cathedral priory, where no obedientiary accounts remain, the earliest known infirmarer, Ralph, appears in 1206; at Coventry, where there is a similar absence of account rolls, the first recorded infirmarer is John de Grenborough, who held the office from *c.* 1353 to *c.* 1380.[59] There is a single surviving fifteenth-century infirmarer's account for each of Ely, Rochester, and Winchester, but for all three cathedral priories early thirteenth-century occupants of the office are known by name.[60] Geoffrey de Totyngton's name heads the earliest of the Norwich infirmarer's accounts which run intermittently from 1312/13 to the sixteenth century, while Henry de Annochia comes on the scene as infirmarer at Worcester in 1302 where a mere ten rolls survive between 1378/9 and 1412. At Norwich the names of sick brethren and their expenses while resident in the infirmary were carefully recorded on the account rolls; and the infirmarer's income, which averaged between £35 and £40 per annum, was sometimes augmented by contributions from other obedientiaries, who charged their own accounts for their

---

[56] Walter de Eastry, John de Copton, and John Coleshull were three of the monks to hold this position during the 1330s, *BRECP*, 147, 129, 127, and John Molond I in 1410/11, ibid., 237. The close connection with the subsacrists is made clear in CCA DCc Reg. B, fo 439 and elsewhere; in *c.* 1404/5, for example, John Shepay I, one of the subsacrists, was also *custos* of the high altar, *BRECP*, 285.

[57] LPL Reg. Islip, fo 123v; DCM Priory Reg. II, fo 50v.

[58] Corpus Christi College MS 465, fo 161v, transcribed in Cheney, 'Norwich Cathedral Priory', 119.

[59] Ralph I is in *BRECP*, 38, as is John de Grenborough, 356, of whom more will be said below, see 295.

[60] For Ely see Walter de Walpole, *BRECP*, 452; for Rochester, Richard de Eastgate, ibid., 601; and for Winchester, Thomas de Henton, ibid., 700.

personal expenses incurred during illness.[61] The Christ Church infirmarers' activities in the period covered by this study are revealed only indirectly because of the loss of all the account rolls; however, we find a monk named Andrew given charge of the infirmary in the first decade of the thirteenth century.[62] Thirty accounts of the Durham master of the infirmary survive between the years 1352/3 and 1420/21, and possibly the earliest known monk in the office dates from the beginning of the fourteenth century.[63] The relative brevity of the few existing accounts seems to suggest that, despite the essential and significant services performed by the monastic infirmarers, with their minimal expenditures they remained largely in the background among their brethren; this view finds corroboration in the additional information that can be gleaned principally from references to infirmarers on the account rolls of other obedientiaries with whom they had regular dealings.

The chamberlain and the provision of clothing

Cathedral priory chamberlains in the fourteenth century approached the provision of clothing and bedding for their fellow monks in different ways. The early arrangements were based on the purchase of several kinds of cloth usually at local or regional fairs, followed by the dyeing, cutting, and sewing operations to produce the various items that made up the monk's wardrobe.[64] In time it became more common for some of the items to be bought ready-made and, later, for the allocation of funds to be distributed to the monks for the purchase of specified or all essentials. These developments, not surprisingly, met with a certain amount of resistance on the part of episcopal visitors familiar with the Rule which made the abbot responsible for the distribution of all the clothing as well as other necessities.[65]

Chamberlains are known by name from an early date; Godricus at Worcester in 1092, Ralph at Rochester c. 1100, Ailricus at Canterbury in the mid-twelfth century, Hilarius at Durham probably late twelfth century, Martin at Bath in 1206, Simon at Coventry and Anselm at Winchester between c. 1230 and 1250 and Richer de Baldeswell at Norwich in the 1260s.[66] Accounts for seven of the

---

[61] *BRECP*, 566 (Totyngton), 771(Annochia). Thomas de Depedale was constantly confined in the Norwich infirmary between 1345 and 1348 costing the infirmarer a total of about 10s., *BRECP*, 499, while Thomas Baa de Elsyng, sacrist, who was ill in 1393/4, charged his office 5s. 8d., ibid., 506.

[62] Ibid., 73–4 (?Andrew IV).

[63] These remain *in situ* in the Durham cathedral archives; somewhat inaccurate extracts are to be found in Fowler, *Account Rolls*, i, 259–70. Richard de Herrington was infirmarer before 1308, *LVD*, iii, C.736.

[64] Dyeing the cloth was sometimes a necessary stage in this process.

[65] *RB*, C.55, 18–19. Ely visitation records reflect the continuing episcopal concern; Ralph Walpole in 1301 and Robert de Orford in 1307 both condemned the distribution of a clothes allowance, Evans, *Ely Chapter Ordinances*, 9, 34; Archbishop Arundel found the practice still prevalent in 1403 and agreed to a compromise, ibid., 55. The problem was discussed from time to time at the periodic meetings of the Black Monk chapter where the preference for fine garments was also an issue when human nature came to the fore, Pantin, *Black Monk Chapters*, iii, 83 (an accusation against Durham monks receiving money *pro vestitu eorum c.* 1384–93) and ibid., ii, 67–9 (letter of the chapter president 1363).

[66] *BRECP*, 811 (Godricus), ibid., 628 (Ralph III), ibid., 69 (Ailricus), *LVD*, iii, C.238 (Hilarius), *BRECP*, 34 (Martin II), ibid., 369 (Simon III), ibid., 666 (Anselm), ibid., 480 (Richard de Baldeswell).

cathedral priory chamberlains survive in varying numbers from three at Rochester of the late fourteenth to early fifteenth century to over one hundred and fifty at Norwich from 1291 onwards. The Ely rolls also begin in the late thirteenth century, those of Canterbury and Worcester in 1308 and 1312/13 respectively, Durham in the 1330s and Winchester in 1399/1400.

The three Rochester accounts record that the twenty-one to twenty-three monks were receiving the comparatively generous sum of 20s. per annum *pro camera*.[67] At Canterbury, in contrast, in 1391/2 the chamberlain's purchases included the item 'in lxx pannis nigris pro lxx habit[ibus]', and the same number of pelisses.[68] Unlike the other cathedral priory obedientiaries who held this office, the Christ Church incumbents remained almost entirely dependent on the treasurers; in the 1350s, however, the increasing debt of the office prompted Archbishop Islip to increase its income by the gift of the rectory of Westerham. In the 1360s and 1370s the almoner made contributions of varying amounts and in 1409/10 several other obedientiaries made donations which enabled the chamberlain to balance his account.[69] The 1407/8 account lists expenditures on many bolts of cloth of different materials as well as the purchase of eighty-two pelisses for eighty-two brethren, and the cost of maintaining the staff in the tailor's quarters amounted to £14.[70] These very brief accounts lack sufficient detail to throw light on any signs of a possible transition to cash allowances in place of cloth during the period of this study.

The Norwich chamberlain had a fluctuating income derived from his properties and tithes; and his heavy outlay on cloth for summer and winter habits, mattresses, and bed coverings often resulted in overspending. In the 1340s payments were entered on the account for some of the items of clothing and bedding; by the 1380s a new entry had appeared with the heading 'Liberatio denariorum conventui pro vestibus et aliis necessariis', under which the ordinary monks each received 5s. twice a year while the prior and several obedientiaries were given larger, specified sums.[71] By 1392/3 the individual monk's cash allowance had risen to 8s. 4d. for each of the two terms.[72] In the same decade and possibly earlier, small sums were augmenting the chamberlain's revenues in the form of 'alms' from deceased brethren, the total in 1419/20 amounting to over £5.[73]

Like his Norwich equivalent the Durham chamberlain had frequent headaches when trying to balance his accounts, his income having a similar provenance also

---

[67] CKS DRc/F. 13–15 (1385/6, 1396/7, 1415/16).
[68] CCA DCc chamberlain's account 56. The pelisse was, in the words of Barbara Harvey, 'a special kind of tunic, made of leather' for cold weather; see her *Monastic Dress*, 14–15.
[69] LPL Reg. Islip, fo 123ʳ; CCA DCc chamberlain's accounts 45–55, 58.
[70] CCA DCc chamberlain's account 57. In the 1420s the chamberlain Thomas Herne (*BRECP*, 197–8) compiled a list of instructions for his successors in the office CCA DCc MS Scrap Book C.112.
[71] NRO DCN 1/5/12, 17; the prior usually received twice as much as the average monk, and some of the obedientiaries charged their own accounts for certain items of clothing thereby reducing their allowance from the chamberlain. In the 1340s Bishop Bateman, in keeping with other bishops, condemned money payments for clothing, Cheney, 'Norwich Cathedral Priory', 110.
[72] NRO DCN 1/5/24; the two terms in this case were denoted by the feasts of the Purification of the Virgin Mary (2 February) and of the Nativity of St John the Baptist (24 June).
[73] NRO DCN 1/5/47. the so-called 'alms' may have been the sums received by the sale of the deceased monk's clothing; see below under the Worcester chamberlain.

subject to fluctuation. In the 1340s a programme of reform was agreed in chapter with the aim of reducing expenditure and improving efficiency in all the obedientiary offices.[74] The chamberlain's account for 1348/9 provides a clue to his implementation of the changes introduced when he inserted a memorandum referring to a sum owed to the prior and the community by his office 'pro rebus ordinatis... per quadam cedulam in qua nomina... fratrum intitulantur propter novam ordinacionem domini prioris factam in capitulo'.[75] A few years earlier the phrase 'in rebus ordinatis et pecunia' for the brethren had appeared on the chamberlain's account as an addition to his other distributions to them.[76] By requiring the office to keep a register of names in order to record what each monk received for his clothing and bedding Prior Fosser was aiming to eliminate waste and undue extravagance. Unfortunately, the surviving accounts, in respect of the *in rebus ordinatis*, are a mere summary presumably based on the detailed records kept through the year. The item on the expense account labelled *in rebus ordinatis* is followed only by the amount spent, which averaged between £40 and £50 between the 1370s and the early fifteenth century. One may, presumably, assume that at least some of this amount consisted of money payments. Small expenses for cloth for such items as shirts, drawers, and towels, and sometimes the ready-made products themselves, are also listed, as are the clothing expenses of the novices for whom the chamberlain continued to provide almost all their needs.[77]

As early as 1288/9 the Ely chamberlain's accounts include small cash allowances, for example, seventeen monks received 3s. each towards the repair of their pelisses while, at the same time, the chamberlain bought thirty new pelisses.[78] Some thirty years later, in 1320/1, the account states that twenty-four *socii* received £36 'pro integra vesture prout patet per nomina eorum', no doubt a list similar to that at Durham; at the same time others, some of them named, received payments for specified items such as shirts and bedcovers, and eighteen brethren were given cash 'pro parte vesture ut patet per partic[ulam] de nominibus. By 1353/4 it looks as though all monks were being paid in cash rather than in kind.[79] However, the 1367/8 account provides a list of items, together with the cost of each, under the heading of the total received by each of the forty-seven monks: thus, tunic 5s., bedclothes 5s., cowl 6d. etc. The list adds up to 30s. 6d. per monk; but it might be that this should not be read as a record of cash payments but rather as a detailed breakdown of the annual cost of furnishing the monk's wardrobe.[80] On the other

---

[74] DCM Locellus XXVII, 16.
[75] DCM chamberlain's account, 1348/9 A. The 1522/3 account lists the names of the monks with the payments made *in rebus ordinatis*.
[76] Ibid., chamberlain's account, 1342/3.
[77] Ibid., chamberlain's accounts *passim*.
[78] CUL Add. MS 2957, 15; other payments include nine monks who received 3s. each for their *frocci* and eight 2s. for their *cuculli*. If this is the correct reading what is the meaning of the entry, to eleven monks *in pecunia*? These cash distributions contravene injunctions of bishops Walpole in 1300 and Orford in 1307, Evans, *Ely Chapter Ordinances*, 9, 34.
[79] Ibid., 20; CUL EDC 1/F/3/11.
[80] CUL EDC 1/F/3/16. There is a problem of interpretation here and, if my solution is plausible, the chamberlain may have reverted to purchasing more clothing ready made (or to making more use of

hand, the wording used in 1384/5 seems to make it clear that money payments were being made to forty-eight monks and the prior *pro vestibus*; and the late 1390s and first years of the fifteenth century found the chamberlain struggling with debt and forced to reduce the payments to 13s. 4d. per monk.[81]

In October 1332 the monastic chapter of Winchester met to discuss the grave financial crisis that threatened their future well-being. It was decided that the prior, Alexander Heriard, would take over several of the obedientiary offices for a period of six years, one of them being that of the chamberlain whose creditors were demanding payment. The prior was to assume responsibility for providing every monk with 30s. *per annum* for clothing and an additional 3s. for their shirts and drawers.[82] There is no further information about the state of this office until 1399/40 when the earliest of the surviving accounts furnishes details of the money allowances distributed to each monk, the sum amounting to 4d. more than it had been seventy years earlier. The young monk novices were not included because they, like the Durham novices, continued to depend on the chamberlain for their monastic apparel most of which, presumably, was made in the tailor's workroom.[83] The income of just over £100 this same year came almost entirely from two manors which had been attached to the chamberlain's office since at least the early thirteenth century.

The Worcester chamberlain functioned with an income that ranged between £80 and £100 during the fourteenth century, amounts fairly close to the annual receipts of his Winchester counterpart from his manors and churches—similar incomes for communities of similar size.[84] At Worcester, however, the chamberlain developed a different mode of operation according to the entries in his accounts. Cloth for habits, shirts, and drawers was still being purchased in the 1390s, although a few monks were the recipients of cash of varying amounts *pro habitus*.[85] Not until a new ordinance, which was promulgated in the 1430s, did a partial transition to money payments occur for some items of clothing.[86] With regard to bedding supplies (*coopertura*), as early as the 1340s the monks were given an annual

---

his staff in the tailor's workshop) in response to a recent episcopal injunction of which there remains no record; whichever the case the list may have been a convenient way of appearing to conform to new restrictions; see above notes 65 and 78.

[81] CUL Add. MS 2957, 35; CUL EDC 1/F/3/24, 27. Seiriol Evans has simplified the transition to money payments by concluding that by 1353 the monks were receiving cash for everything but boots; see his 'The Purchase of Mepal', 117–18. In 1403 Archbishop Arundel's injunctions accepted a compromise, Evans, *Ely Chapter Ordinances*, 55.

[82] The other two offices were those of the hordarian and almoner, Goodman, *Winchester Chartulary*, no. 180.

[83] WCL, W53/14/2.

[84] The Worcester chamberlain also frequently records fairly substantial sums received from the sale of grain and stock.

[85] It is to be noted that the staff of three in the tailor's 'shop' continued to receive, between them, the same amount in wages from about 1320/1 to at least the end of the century.

[86] WCM C.39. However, absent monks such as those who were students at Oxford, were often provided with funds for their clothing needs, see John de Fordham, *BRECP*, 805–7, and John de Dudley I, ibid., 797–8.

allowance of 12s. each, with slightly more for the prior and subprior.[87] In the second half of the fourteenth century the chamberlain's annual receipts were often less than his expenses; on at least one occasion among his creditors were included fellow obedientiaries.[88] A small source of revenue, listed under *Recepte forinsece*, came in the form of the sale of the clothing and bedding of deceased monks.[89]

The offices of precentor, librarian, and prior's chaplain

Since no precentor's accounts have survived from six of the cathedral priories we are entirely dependent on other records, such as episcopal and priory registers, for the few informative details that can be gleaned in them.[90] Where bishops bore the responsibility of appointing the precentor, as they did at Bath, Canterbury, Coventry, and Rochester, their extant registers often provide the only means of knowing the names of holders of this office. Although the precentor was not numbered among the eight *maiores capituli* as spelled out at Durham, and probably elsewhere, his was nevertheless a position of almost continuous responsibility centred on the cathedral church's daily round of offices and schedule of masses.[91] In addition, most monastic libraries and scriptoria were assigned to the office of precentor, with the notable exception among the cathedral priories of Durham where, by the later thirteenth century, a *librarius* had made his appearance.[92] A relatively small income was considered to be sufficient for the effective performance of the duties assigned to the precentor and of maintaining his quarters, often referred to at Ely and Worcester as the *precentoria*. At Ely the yearly receipts ranged between £30 and £35, at Norwich slightly less, while at Worcester the average amount recorded was below £20.[93]

The office of precentor was most frequently entrusted to a mature monk, one who had been professed for twenty or more years. It seems that they often remained in office for only two or three years, but reappointment at a later date was not

---

[87] The novices received 4s. each for their footwear (*botis*), and pelisses from 1351/2 onwards under the heading *Coopertura* although these two items also appear under clothing (*Emptio pannorum*) from time to time. Are these and other apparent inconsistencies attributable to carelessness or to a somewhat nonchalant placing of items under headings which, in fact, seem confusingly varied?

[88] In 1395/6 the chamberlain names on his list of creditors John de Dudley, the infirmarer, and Roger de Shrovesbury, third prior, *BRECP*, 797–8 (John de Dudley I), 873 (Shrovesbury).

[89] This hardly appears to be in strict adherence to the Rule which prescribes that all discarded clothing be stored for giving to the poor, *RB*, C.55, 9. The sums obtained from these sales, which first appear in the 1370s, varied considerably; see below 315–16.

[90] The six are Bath, Canterbury, Coventry, Durham, Rochester, and Winchester.

[91] The *maiores* at Durham were listed as the prior, subprior, sacrist, hostiller, bursar, cellarer, terrar, and feretrar in 1302, DCM Misc. Charter 5668. In 1331 the almoner and chamberlain were substituted for the bursar and feretrar, DCM 2.1 Archid. Dunelm. 4; the omission of the bursar is surprising.

[92] See Piper, 'The Libraries of the Monks of Durham', 217 with references.

[93] The precentor's accounts from Ely, Norwich, and Worcester show receipts from one or two manors and churches plus a few rents from small properties acquired through gifts or purchase; unsurprisingly they were sometimes overdrawn. For the Ely accounts see CUL 1/F/9/1– and CUL Add MS 2957, 38–47; for Norwich NRO DCN 1/9/1/–; for Worcester WCM C.351–.

uncommon.[94] However, in a few instances where precise dates are available a different picture suggests itself. For example, the obituary notice of 1420 for John Borne of Christ Church Canterbury praises his musical achievement as third cantor, succentor, and precentor over a period of thirty years because he had 'inter omnes religiosos regni excellentissimam vocem.'[95] Also at Canterbury, John de Thaneto, who had earlier served as treasurer and as warden of manors, was named precentor in 1300 and remained in the post for thirteen years.[96] It was the precentor's prime function to direct and lead the monks in chanting the daily office and the musical parts of the daily mass at the high altar; Bishop Salmon made this very clear in his injunctions to the Norwich monks on the subject of the divine office. He also reminded the precentor that it was his solemn duty to report negligent and absent monks. Even stronger language had been used by Bishop Robert de Orford little more than a year before when he warned the Ely precentor that no other occupation was to prevent him from being in his place in choir both for the day and the night offices.[97] It was more than likely that he or one of his assistants, the succentor or third cantor, was charged with the instruction of the novices in the intricacies of the chant.[98] The Worcester precentor on several occasions purchased caps for *cantoribus*, while cantors at Norwich received small sums from time to time; a more precise entry on the Durham bursar's account of 1363/4 records a gift of 3s. 4d. to a *fratri cantori*. It is probable that the Worcester and Norwich singers were not monks but men with good voices brought in to sing with the monastic community as both later Norwich and Durham accounts suggest.[99] Also it should be noted that the Lady chapel choir at Ely in 1375/6

---

[94] Nicholas IV had been a monk of Coventry for twenty-six years and was seventy years old when he is recorded as precentor in 1285/6; it is possible that it was not his first appointment to this office or that he had been holding it for many years, *BRECP*, 365. Thomas de Dovorr of Rochester, who was professed in 1346/7 and had been previously cellarer and sacrist, was appointed precentor in 1384, dismissed five months later, reappointed the next year and, after a year in office, was replaced by John Pleme. The latter had been professed for about seventeen years and he remained in office for four years, ibid., 599–600, 627. Hugh Warkworth of Durham also seems to conform to this trend: appointed c. 1416 after just over twenty years in the community he was precentor for all or part of the years between 1416 and 1425, *LVD*, iii, C.1033.

[95] *BRECP*, 95. The name of Geoffrey Bonde, also at Canterbury, should be included; previously a monk of St Albans, he was probably lured to Christ Church by the higher standard of musical performance at Canterbury and became precentor in the 1420s, ibid., 94.

[96] Ibid., 300; Thaneto II had been a monk for twenty years before becoming precentor.

[97] NRO, DCN 92/1 (Salmon); Evans, *Ely Chapter Ordinances*, 33 (Orford).

[98] The absence of evidence should not be a cause for surprise as, for example, no expense was involved that required recording in the precentor's accounts. From the 1340s on the Worcester succentor received 13s. 4d. from the precentor *pro officio suo*, WCM C.351, 355 etc; the Norwich succentor had to be content with 6s. 8d., NRO DCN 1/9/17 etc.

[99] For caps bought by the Worcester precentor, WCM C.359a (1365/6), C.371 (1401/2); for Norwich cantors, NRO DCN 1/9/6 (1352/3). However, in 1380/1 the Norwich precentor charged his account 6s. *in minutionibus cum cantoribus* and therefore these cantors must surely have been monks, NRO DCN 1/9/19. The Durham bursar's account in 1363/4 names the 'brother cantor' but the later accounts fail to clarify the issue. For details about singers and singing in the monastic setting see articles by Roger Bowers, e.g. in note 228 below and for Winchester, 'The Lady Chapel and its Musicians'.

consisted of professed monks and others who were given 3s. 4d. by the monk *custos capelle* under whose authority they presumably functioned.[100]

Other activities of monastic cathedral precentors concerned the provision of liturgical texts and of organists to accompany the singing. The Ely precentor periodically charged his account for the purchase, repair, and replacement of books of antiphons, graduals, and tropes as well as missals for the high altar and other altars.[101] It was the succentor at Worcester who, in 1390/1, undertook the binding of the *magnum librum in choro*, probably the one around which stood those appointed to sing the choral parts of the liturgy.[102] Only a small number of liturgical manuscripts have survived, among which the collection of Worcester musical fragments of early English polyphonic music and the Worcester antiphoner are two of the most important.[103] An extant thirteenth-century breviary and missal that includes prefaces with plainsong contains liturgical evidence of its Ely provenance; and a few tantalizing fragments of Marian motets have been discovered in a manuscript copy of the *Liber Eliensis* where they had been used as binding leaves. But none of these provide any direct insight into the way in which precentors carried out their duties.[104] There is more information available about cathedral priory organs and organists because of the frequent expenses incurred by the precentor and itemized on his annual account. New organs were costly and contributions from the community were welcomed, for example at Canterbury in the 1330s when both John de Copton and Prior Richard de Oxenden gave 20s. and 71s. respectively.[105] At least one monk, namely Reginald de Wearmouth of Durham, was deemed capable of constructing an organ and was rewarded by the prior with a gift of 10s. in 1377/8, while the following year the feretrar gave a small sum for organ repairs.[106] It was the master of the cellar at Norwich who donated 20s. toward similar repairs in 1313/14, but the precentor did so in 1367 and again

[100] CUL EDC 1/F/7/5B (*Custos Capelle*).
[101] Ibid., 1/F/9/5 (1374/5), the binding of antiphons and graduals; the illumination of a gradual, CUL Additional MS 2957 (1373/4), 45; the repair of a missal at the high altar, ibid. (1360/1), 44; the repair of missals, ibid. (1371/2), 45. The Durham hostiller magnanimously bought a processional in 1387/8 and an organ book, together costing 10s., DCM hostiller's account. It was also he who paid fellow monks Nicholas de Allerton and John de Goldsborough, the former for *fabricand'* a missal and the latter an antiphonal in the 1340s, hostiller's accounts for 1346/7, 1347/8 and *LVD*, iii, C.819, C.835.
[102] WCM C.367; the succentor in question may have been Reginald Dyere; see *BRECP*, 801.
[103] See the description of the fragments in Thomson, *Medieval Manuscripts in Worcester Cathedral*, xxiv–xxv and notes; the antiphoner, WCM MS F.160, dates from the thirteenth and fourteenth centuries.
[104] The Ely breviary is now CUL MS Ii.4.20 and the fragments are found in Trinity College MS 1005. See Greatrex, 'Benedictine Observance at Ely', 88–9. The magnificent Ormesby psalter, known by the name of its monk donor, Robert de Ormesby, was assigned to a place in the choir of Norwich cathedral in front of the subprior; the reason for this seemingly unusual provision was not given. See *BRECP*, 546–7 for this Norwich monk; the psalter is now Oxford, Bodley MS Douce 366.
[105] *BRECP*, 129, 250; these sums were entered in Prior Oxenden's day book of his expenses and receipts CCA DCc MS DE 3, fos 32, 36, and more expenses on fos 18 and 19.
[106] It was the bursar who paid on the prior's behalf, DCM bursar's account for 1377/8 and the next year the almoner added his gift, ibid., almoner's account 1378/9; the feretrars' assistance with repairs may have applied to one of the several other organs in the cathedral, feretrars' account, 1378/9A. For Wearmouth see *LVD*, iii. C.951.

in 1380; for his part the Ely precentor reckoned the total cost of extensive organ work in 1396/7 at close to £7.[107] As to organists, by no means all were monks; at Worcester Thomas appears in the late thirteenth century, Adam at Norwich in 1332/3 who received robes from the sacrist, and M. Nicholas at Ely in 1374/5.[108] No reference to secular organists has been found at Canterbury where, because of the large number in the community, there must have rarely been a lack of musical talent on which to draw. Two of the monk organists, John Cranbroke and John Maghfeld, were individually praised as *organista eximius* and a third, William Bonyngton, as 'in cantu et ludo organico egregie eruditus'. The musical career of a fourth, John Stanys, was summed up by a younger contemporary member of the community in his Chronicle: 'Omnem cantum organicum in ecclesia disposuit et gubernavit in magnum laudem et ecclesie honorem.'[109] Another expenditure that fell to the precentor was that of providing organ lessons unless he was qualified to do the teaching himself.[110] An Ely precentor, probably William de Thorp, spent 30s. in hiring an unnamed person to teach his clerk to play; a half-century and more later, Robert Colville, the only known Ely monk organist, was receiving lessons paid for by the precentor and the treasurer.[111]

A comparative investigation of cathedral priory precentors in the period under study discloses that Worcester priors and their senior advisers showed a marked preference for placing studious monks in the office, many with some years at Oxford behind them, and a high proportion who owned or made use of manuscripts. This fact distinguishes Worcester from the other cathedral priories including those like Norwich and Canterbury where there was also an impressive number of monks who were university students and possessors of manuscripts. Of about eighteen known Worcester precentors between 1270 and 1420 six had been sent to Oxford and ten are known to have owned manuscripts; moreover, six names occur in both categories.[112] In addition, of the eighteen, eleven were, on one occasion or

---

[107] NRO DCN 1/1/23, ibid., 1/9/9, 1/9/18, this last specifying two organs in the Lady chapel. The Ely precentor recorded details of all the items involved including the meals of the workmen over a period of thirteen weeks; it seems probable that this refers to the building of a new organ, CUL Add. MS 2957, 46.

[108] Thomas is named as organist in the witness list to a deed, WCM B.925; Adam NRO DCN 1/4/27; M. Nicholas, CUL EDC 1/F/10/19.

[109] *BRECP*, 132 (John Cranbroke I), 229 (Maghfeld), 94 (William Bonyngton I), 290 (Stanys). All four entered Christ Church in the closing years of the fourteenth century and the first half of the fifteenth, a period in which details such as these have been preserved in a Canterbury manuscript containing obits; the monk chronicler is John Stone I, *BRECP*, 293.

[110] This may have been the case at Canterbury where, for example, John Stanys, precentor, was described as an *organista precipuus* in 1421, *BRECP*, 290.

[111] This is recorded on the precentor's account for 1406/7, CUL Add. MS 2957, 47. Robert Colville was later elected prior, *BRECP*, 398–9.

[112] There is, admittedly, a certain element of statistical uncertainty here because of the lacunae in our sources of information; nevertheless, the contrast is sufficiently striking to permit these conclusions which, of course, remain tentative. The ten monks associated with manuscripts are all to be found in *BRECP* as indicated, and those names preceded by an asterisk had been at Oxford: Thomas de Broghton, 781; *Richard de Bromwych, 782–3; John de Cleve, 787; Simon Crompe, 792–3; *William de Grymeley, 814; *John de Hatfeld, 818; *John de Lemenstre I, 836; *John de Malverne I, 842–4; *John de Westbury, 891; Thomas de Wych I, 897; Simon de Wyre, 900.

more, selected from among their brethren to be among the seven nominees for the position of prior presented to the bishop; of these, three were appointed to the priorate.[113] It would seem that Worcester precentors were generally admired and respected by their brethren, although we lack evidence to suggest that this was not true elsewhere. Only three (at the most) Norwich precentors, one, possibly two, at Canterbury, and two at Rochester are known to have attended university.[114]

The precentor's dual responsibilities are reflected in many of the regular expenses on his accounts where he recorded items listing materials and money required for purchasing, copying, repairing, and binding books for the library. Less frequently occur entries of payments to scriptors and illuminators and for benches, lecterns, and other furnishings for the scriptorium and *precentoria*.[115] Unique among the cathedral priories the Worcester precentor and his monk assistant provide a glimpse of their quarters in the late fourteenth and early fifteenth centuries. Between 1387 and 1405, and possible longer, Reginald Dyere was occupied in binding and repairing books and had in his custody the instruments required for this specialized work. The surviving account rolls present us with the picture of active scribal and book production departments at Worcester between *c.* 1345 and 1420. The annual supplement to a 'great chronicle' which was hung [on a stand or lectern] in the church is a regular item recorded for which parchment had to be purchased and a scribe paid.[116] White and red leather for binding books cost 5s. 4d. in 1384/5 and two dozen membranes of vellum *pro libro consuetudinar' claustri* 6s. 8d. in 1388; in this latter year a carpenter was hired to make a chair for the scribe and repair the benches or stools used by the brethren.[117] The scribe who was employed in 1390/1 for an annual stipend of 8s. 10d. must have been commissioned to carry out a lengthier task than earlier scribes, none of whom received more than 1s.[118]

Although a scribe is mentioned in 1301/2 on the earlier Ely precentor's roll, working through Lent for 7s., later records are disappointingly uninformative.[119] One monk, Peter de Norwich, was given 7s. in 1373/4 *pro labore suo* probably in the *precentoria*, but other references are to hired scribes such as Nicholas and Roger

---

[113] The three priors are Simon de Wyre, Simon Crompe, John de Malverne, *BRECP*, 900, 792–3, 842–4.

[114] The page references are all to *BRECP*: for Norwich, Robert de Ely, 506; Richard de Hecham II, 518 (uncertain); Robert de Swanton, 562–3 (uncertain); for Canterbury, John de Eastry, II, 146; Geoffrey Poterel, 256–7 (uncertain); for Rochester, John de Ealding, 600–1; Roger de Stapelhurst, 639–40.

[115] These two words, at least at Worcester, are interchangeable; in 1388 improved lighting was provided in the solar in the *precentoria* where the scribe worked, Hamilton, *Compotus Rolls*, 43.

[116] Dyere was succentor in 1401 and probably earlier, *BRECP*, 801. WCM C.351–8, 361a, 363–5, 367, 370; see Greatrex, 'English Cathedral Priories and . . . Learning', 405, note 32. Similar hanging chronicles have been noted at Durham where the feretrar paid for the writing of a chronicle and the repair of some psalters in 1384/5, Fowler, *Account Rolls*, ii, 44.

[117] WCM C.364, 366. The presence of benches for the brethren suggests that some of them were performing scribal tasks.

[118] Ibid., C.367; does this imply that a lengthy work was being copied, perhaps the customary, begun in 1388?

[119] CUL Add. MS 2957, 38. Michael Gullick's *Extracts from the Precentor's Accounts concerning Books and Bookmaking of Ely Cathedral Priory* (Hitchin, 1985) provides a helpful commentary along with all the relevant entries in Bentham's manuscript volume cited here.

in 1373/4 and John Dallyng in 1396/7 who also repaired books.[120] There are a few references to the purchase of books: a book of the Decretals in 1300/1 for 3s. for the library and *Speculum Gregorii* in 1321/2 for 2s.; and a new set of Easter tables was produced and illuminated in the scriptorium in 1302/3.[121] Supplies of parchment, paper, and the ingredients for making ink and candles are mentioned on several accounts.[122] The chapter ordinances of 1314 reminded the precentor not only to ensure the adequate provision of choir books but also to collect in chapter all books on loan once a year on the first Monday in Lent; he was then to check them against his list before they were returned to the library or the loan renewed. The loss of any volume was to be paid for by the withholding of pocket money and items of clothing until the cost had been made up.[123] This is clearly a reference to a precept in the Rule requiring the distribution of books for Lenten reading.[124] Missing books must have been a perennial problem, and the lists compiled in Lent, which had their origin in the practical clause attached to St Benedict's instruction, were intended to encourage greater diligence in reading. An extant list compiled in the second week of Lent, 1338, by the Canterbury precentor indicates the problem, but at the same time makes it clear that some offenders were outsiders who had taken advantage of the community's willingness to lend.[125]

There is a single reference to the calling in and reallocation of books in Lent on the Norwich precentor's accounts. In 1352/3 he paid 9d. to two boys whose help he had enlisted *in ostens[ione librorum in quadrages[imo.*[126] Like his fellow precentors elsewhere he bought supplies of parchment and ink, but one of his more frequent purchases seems to have been chains to attach books in their assigned places in the dormitory chapel, in the library, and at the precentor's desk in choir.[127] Little expenditure is recorded on books apart from small amounts on binding and repair, and the one instance in 1375/6 when the sum of 23s. 8d. was spent on book repairs and on the tools essential for binding.[128] A partial explanation lies in the fact that in the late thirteenth and early fourteenth centuries substantial expenses were incurred by the master of the cellar to pay for parchment, books, and scribes, and

---

[120] CUL Add. MS 2957, 45–6.
[121] Ibid., 40–2.
[122] Ibid., 41–5.
[123] Evans, *Ely Chapter Ordinances*, 40.
[124] *RB*, C.48, 15–16. A rare surviving example of a precentor's list of Lenten books borrowed by monks of Thorney Abbey has recently been critically examined by Richard Sharpe in 'Monastic Reading at Thorney Abbey, 1323–47', *Traditio*, 60 (2005), 243–78.
[125] James, *ALCD*, 146–9.
[126] NRO DCN 1/9/6; in later years this particular entry may have been subsumed under a general heading with other miscellaneous items.
[127] For references to parchment and ink NRO DCN 1/9/1, 3, 14, 23; for chains in the dormitory chapel, between 1376/7 and 1382/3 seventy-eight were bought, ibid., 1/9/15, 17, 20. Library chains are referred to in 1386/7, ibid., 1/9/23 and the precentor's choirbook in ibid., 1/9/20.
[128] The precentor did purchase two books in 1283, one on the Trinity (the dedication of the cathedral) and the other a copy of the Epistles; this entry, and others relating to books, has been printed in Sharpe, *EBL*, 299. Book repairs occur on precentor's accounts NRO DCN 1/9/3, 5, 9, 14 (including tools).

the sacrist also made similar contributions from his income.[129] Although books continued to be added to the library, some no doubt through the acquisitions of individual monks, the only concrete evidence of additions to the library exists in the mid-fourteenth-century catalogue of Prior Simon Bozoun's books which number thirty-one and were valued at about £35.[130] The precentor makes two references to the production of book catalogues in 1313/15, and again in 1384/5 when green wax was bought *pro tabul' de cathologo*.[131]

The Durham librarians known by name within the period under study number seventeen. Of these only five were university trained and they, along with seven others can be associated with manuscripts by means of inscriptions.[132] Like the general run of precentors discussed above they tended to be monks who had been about twenty years in the community; for many, if not most, of them it was their first appointment, but they were often moved on after several years to hold a variety of obedientiary offices. The position of librarian at Durham was sometimes coupled with that of chancellor and used as an alternative title until about the end of the fourteenth century. The last monk to be given the title of librarian was William Appleby in 1392 who in the same year was described as chancellor like his immediate successors.[133] Chancellors were keepers of the monastery muniments and usually of the contemporary priory register. Thus, a third title was in use in 1312/13 when John de Layton was named as both registrar and chancellor. The following year, 1314, saw William de Durham make his first entry in the register as registrar and at the same time be described as librarian.[134] Three of the monks in the office of librarian/chancellor/registrar were also, very probably, serving as chaplains to the prior during part of this time;[135] this combination, that is of the chancellor/registrar and chaplain, is also found in one of the other cathedral priories, namely Worcester, where the precentor held the post of librarian. It may have been a combination in frequent use but hidden from view through the loss of primary sources.

At Worcester, however, the *Liber Albus* provides us with a fairly full record of the prior's chaplains, one of whose responsibilities was to write the entries in this the

---

[129] Sharpe, *EBL*, 293–9; these expenses were often listed on the *camera prioris* section of the master of the cellar's account. For the years 1313/1316 a Roger de Thurston (Thurnetune), almost certainly the monk (*BRECP*, 565), received a *liberatio pro scriptura*, ibid., 298.

[130] Sharpe, *EBL* at B 58.

[131] NRO DCN 1/9/3, 22.

[132] Alan Piper's list of obedientiaries and office-holders has provided names and dates of known librarians, *LVD*, i, 496, and precentors ibid., i, 499. Only one Durham precentor, Hugh Warkworth (*LVD*, iii, C.1033), had been to Oxford and none of the precentors has been associated with manuscripts.

[133] Appleby is C.1001 in *LVD*, iii; he was followed by Thomas Rome (C.1008) and John Wessington (C.1028), who not only served as chancellor and librarian but also, for part of the time at least, as sacrist.

[134] Layton is C.765 (766) in *LVD*, iii and Durham C.783; precise dates are not available and therefore it is possible that Durham's dates as librarian and registrar may not have exactly coincided.

[135] John de Barnard Castle (*LVD*, iii, C.926) was in fact the prior's chaplain for all, or nearly all, the years of his responsibilities as librarian/chancellor, but the relevant dates for Peter de Durham and Robert de Lanchester (*LVD*, iii, C.915, C.948) leave a measure of doubt.

official priory register. Between 1302 and 1420 some seventeen names are noted in headings to indicate the appointment of a new chaplain: *hic frater—incipit registrum* or *tempore fratris—capellani* are among the most frequent.[136] Almost all of these monks were young with no more than four or five years in priest's orders. This was, therefore, a time when they were still, as *claustrales*, engaged in absorbing the full implications of the monastic life and would, or should, have been open to the counsel and guidance of their seniors, in this case their prior. They were a privileged group who were carefully selected to spend one or two years in the prior's household where their duties also included taking charge of his financial arrangements and accompanying him on manorial visits and other journeys. Of the seven known by name who served as chaplains to Prior John de Evesham (1340–70) three went on to study at Oxford and a fourth, as cellarer in the late 1370s, was one of the prime movers behind the extensive building programme within the cloister and precinct.[137] What little is known about the prior's chaplains elsewhere suggests that they were more often mature if not older monks, or in the case of Ely, secular chaplains whose annual stipend of 40s. was paid by the treasurer.[138] Surviving accounts at Christ Church Canterbury include both those of the prior himself and those of his chaplain. The latter, as at Worcester, dealt with all the prior's household expenses. Archbishop Walter Reynolds restricted the length of the chaplain's appointment to one year in his injunctions of 1315 to his monastic chapter, but even during his lifetime this ruling does not seem to have been strictly enforced.[139] These Canterbury chaplains had generally held one or two previous offices or obediences and sometimes they appear to have been in charge of a second assignment at the same time, although in the absence of precise dates this remains uncertain.[140] None of them appear to have borne any responsibility for keeping the priory registers. The earliest known chancellor, John Westgate, was appointed as third chancellor in 1324, an unprecedented appointment, and one which indicates that generally two were required to keep the registers and other records up to date.[141] In 1349/50 the two names are noted in Register H, and in 1394 and 1411 in Register S, but these entries are sporadic and the present state of the priory

---

[136] E.g., WCM Liber Albus (Reg. A.5), fos 228v, 419v.

[137] The three Oxford monk students were John de Hatfeld, John de Malverne I, who later became prior, and Roger de Bosbury, who was sent up to Oxford both before and after his year as chaplain; they are all in *BRECP*, 818, 842–4, and 778 respectively, and Prior Evesham also ibid., 802–4. See also Greatrex, 'Prior John de Evesham', 64–76. William Power was cellarer in the 1370s and 1380s, *BRECP*, 863–4.

[138] CUL EDC 1/F/13/13 (1389/90), 1/F/13/14 (1392/3), 1 F/13/16 (1396/7); the few treasurer's rolls are generally in a very fragile state and only partly legible. A chapter ordinance of 1304, however, had required the prior to choose a monk as his chaplain, Evans, *Ely Chapter Ordinances*, 25.

[139] LPL Reg. Reynolds, fo 69v–70; John de Gore was chaplain to the prior between 1318 and 1321, *BRECP*, 179–80.

[140] It may either be a case of a swift change of appointments or of a slight overlapping while the change took effect. It seems fairly clear, for example, that John Wodnesburgh II was both chaplain and warden of the manors between 1394 and 1401 and again from 1405/6, and that Stephen Byrchyngton followed suit between 1402 and 1405, *BRECP*, 322–3, 107. The manorial warden's duties necessitated frequent absences from the priory in order to supervise the estates; hence the usefulness of a second or subchaplain.

[141] *BRECP*, 317 (John Westgate III).

registers is far from complete; for all of the monks with the exception of one at the time of his second appointment, it was their first placement in office within the community.[142] At Norwich there were often two chaplains who are recorded on the prior's *camera* account by the master of the cellar; it was he who provided them with practical necessities like boots and shoes and itemized certain expenses as charged *per capellanum* or *per capellanos*.[143] Only five are known by name, and the information about their monastic careers is too scanty to allow for any comparative comment.[144] The presence of two monk chaplains at Winchester on at least two occasions is referred to, in 1334/5 and again in 1393, when John de Haywoode is named as senior chaplain.[145] The prior's expenses occur on two of the few surviving receiver's accounts, both in the 1330s, under the heading 'Expensae pro camera, capella, et elemosina domini prioris.' Thus, it can probably be assumed that those monks who are recorded as paying some of the prior's expenses and distributing alms on his behalf were doing so in their role as chaplains.[146] No references to chancellors have been found at Norwich or Winchester; at Ely there is a single instance of two senior monks who, as chancellors of the chapter in 1390, lent some charters concerning the bishopric to Bishop Fordham.[147] Durham chaplains, of whom there may have been two serving together from time to time, were not burdened with the additional responsibilities assigned to their counterparts; their duties were limited to the constantly demanding charge of the prior's household and his itinerary when he travelled on business or pleasure.[148] Few of them had held any previous office in the community, as far as is known, and about half of them had been professed for less than ten years.[149]

Among the monks who served their turn as chaplains there was a small group who were not assigned to the prior but rather to the bishop where they temporarily became members of the episcopal household. They were especially in evidence at Canterbury and Rochester and, at the latter, more frequently when the bishop was himself a monk and former member of the monastic community. During Hamo de

---

[142] John de Northborne and Thomas de Tilmerstone were chancellors in 1349/50, *BRECP* 244–5 (John de Northborne I), 306 (Tilmerstone); Thomas Bungay and William Elmore in 1394, ibid., 104, 151; Thomas Bungay and Alexander London in 1411; ibid., 104, 224. William de Eythorne's name appears in CCA Reg. G in 1333; he was made chancellor only three years after profession, ibid., 156–7.

[143] NRO DCN 1/1/13, 14, 19, etc., and 1/4/32, 35, 39 etc. (small gifts from the sacrist).

[144] The five are in *BRECP*: Guy de St Edmund or Gido, 552 and 515; John de Henghem I, 521; Ralph de Hulme, 527; John de Thurgarton, 565; John de Tilney, 565. the last two of these were both named as chaplains in 1384/5.

[145] Two are recorded on the receiver's roll for this year receiving their Christmas oblations a year late, Kitchin, *Obedientiary Rolls*, 237.

[146] Robert de Popham distributed the prior's alms in 1337 and William Skyllyng was engaged in paying some of the prior's expenses in 1355/6, *BRECP*, 726, 736. Nicholas de Haywode I is also named as chaplain in 1332, ibid., 699–700.

[147] The monks in question were Peter de Norwich II and Robert de Sutton II, ibid., 427, 446.

[148] This information is provided by the Durham bursar's accounts *passim* under headings such as *elemosina prioris, dona prioris, expensae prioris per maneria*, and *expensae prioris*.

[149] These calculations are based on the *LVD* list of *c.* twenty-eight chaplains during the years 1310 to 1420, i, 502. Four attended Durham College Oxford, three before their appointment as chaplains. The average length of service was about three years. These were, therefore, relatively young monks, not sufficiently mature to be seen as the prior's 'personal advisers', cf. Foster, 'Durham Priory', 147.

Hethe's lengthy episcopate, for example, between 1317 and 1352 six or possibly seven of his brethren were called to serve him, several for periods lasting four or five years.[150] His predecessor, Bishop Thomas de Wouldham, previously prior, had one chaplain from the cathedral priory whom he kept for at least seven years, and Bishop Thomas de Brinton, monk of Norwich, selected one, John de Shepey, whom he also appointed to be receiver of the bishopric.[151] There were no monastic archbishops of Canterbury in the fourteenth century with the single exception of Simon Langham, abbot of Westminster, who was promoted to the see of Ely, translated to Canterbury, and resigned after only two years in the primacy.[152] Nevertheless, several archbishops and priors found it advantageous to have a link between their households in the person of a monk chaplain who could act as an intermediary when the situation required it. Relations between the Christ Church community and its 'titular abbot' were not infrequently less than amicable, an unsurprising outcome of the fact that their respective jurisdictions were too closely convergent for comfort. There is a wealth of extant correspondence between Prior Eastry and several archbishops, for example, in which the ups and downs of their fluctuating rapport are well illustrated.[153] The monk chaplain was in a favourable position to put his chapter's case to the archbishop, to explain at length their requests and offer advice tactfully. Thomas de Goodnyston filled this role for Prior Eastry, who sent him to Archbishop Meopham in 1330/1 with an eloquently worded letter of recommendation. He followed this up a few months later by writing to his monk asking him to intercede with the archbishop on behalf of an imprisoned clerk; and a second letter requested him to arrange for the archbishop to provide letters dimissory for the monks who were ready and waiting to be ordained.[154] However, it was a tactless decision on the part of Archbishop Walter Reynolds to delegate his monk chaplain, Geoffrey Poterel, to implement the corrections and reforms resulting from his first visitation of the monastic chapter in 1314. This inevitably damaged relations between the monks and the archbishop for a number of years because in carrying out his commission Poterel acted in a high-handed manner, apparently failing to consult the subprior and allegedly consorting with the archbishop. The resulting friction within the community took time to heal, and the archbishop did not have another chaplain from Christ Church for at least ten years.[155] Archbishop Robert Winchelsey was better served

---

[150] Hethe's monk chaplains are all included in *BRECP*: John de Borden, 592; John de Faversham I, 603; Peter de Hethe, 611; John de Mepeham II, 622; William Peper, 626; William de Reyersh 628–9 (uncertain); Robert de Southflete III, 638.

[151] Wouldham's chaplain was John de Grenestrete, *BRECP*, 607; John de Shepey III was also elected prior, probably while still chaplain, ibid., 635.

[152] See the entry in *ODNB*.

[153] Many of these letters have been printed in Sheppard, *Lit. Cant.* i., e.g. nos 146, 153, 154, 158, 260.

[154] The three letters are in Sheppard, *Lit. Cant.*, i, nos 318, 396, 376. For Thomas de Goodnyston I see *BRECP*, 179. Meopham and Eastry were almost never on good terms; see R. M. Haines, 'An Innocent Abroad: The Career of Simon Mepham, Archbishop of Canterbury, 1328–1333', *EHR*, 112 (1997), 555–96 *passim*.

[155] For Poterel see *BRECP*, 256–7; the subprior, Simon de St Paul, ibid., 273–4, was standing in for the absent prior in 1315 when he wrote the letter to his superior complaining about Poterel's

by his chaplains; in fact, three of them were called upon in 1319 to testify at the *Inquisitio de miraculis* where they affirmed the sanctity of the archbishop.[156]

Few monk chaplains to bishops have been found in the remaining cathedral priories. At Norwich, the master of the cellar provided *capae* for two *confratres existent' cum episcopo* in 1314/15 but, with the exception of John de Clipesby, who was named as chaplain to the monk-bishop John Salmon in 1320/1, the entries on the accounts fail to distinguish between monastic and secular chaplains.[157] The chamberlain of Worcester reported that in 1346/7 Nicholas de Stanlake was *comorant' cum episcopo*, Wulstan de Bransford, formerly prior of the community, while other references in the 1340s mention one or two monks as with the bishop, possibly Stanlake with another.[158]

There were, in addition, a few monks who, while holding the office of sacrist in their priory, were at the same time employed by their bishop as receivers of the bishopric. Such were John de Ely at Ely in 1378/81 for Bishop Arundel, John de St Briavel at Worcester for bishops Reynolds and Maidstone in 1312/14, and Richard Colys also at Worcester for Bishop Thoresby in 1350.[159]

The almoner's works of mercy and the almonry school

The office of almoner receives no direct mention in the Rule, but among the tools of good works St Benedict's disciples were admonished to 'relieve the lot of the poor, clothe the naked, visit the sick, and bury the dead', and also to 'help the troubled and console the sorrowing'.[160] According to Lanfranc's monastic Constitutions these 'social service' activities were incumbent upon the almoner; but in the course of time they were gradually reduced to the distribution of alms to those who came to the monastery to seek them.[161] However, this was far from the full extent of the almoner's purview. There were hospitals and almshouses dependent on the cathedral priories over which the almoners had oversight and a large measure of control, and toward the upkeep of which a portion of their income was directed. Moreover, an almonry school had long been attached to the almoner's quarters within the monastic precinct where young boys and their master were lodged and fed; this was regarded as a work of charity, although some parents are known to

---

behaviour, CUL MS Ee.5.31, fo 161. In 1324 the prior reminded the archbishop of his failure to appoint a monk chaplain, Sheppard, *Lit. Cant.*, i, no. 123.

[156] The three were Gilbert de Bisshoppiston, *BRECP*, 89–90; Bertram de Eastry, ibid., 144; John le Spycer, ibid., 290. Walter Causton and Archbishop William Courtenay must also have enjoyed harmonious relations because the latter left the monk a legacy of 10 marks on his death in 1396, ibid., 110.

[157] NRO DCN 1/1/24, 1/1/27; in 1320/1 Clipesby was spending at least part of the year at Oxford, *BRECP*, 496. Bishop John Salmon is found ibid., 436 as a monk of Ely.

[158] WCM C.10, 59, 300, 301; for Stanlake see *BRECP*, 876.

[159] For John de Ely IV see *BRECP*, 406–7; John de St Briavel, ibid., 867–9; Richard Colys, ibid., 791–2. At Worcester the bishop's right to appoint the sacrist is discussed above, 15.

[160] *RB*, C.4, 14–19, the chapter on 'the instruments of good works'.

[161] Lanfranc, *Monastic Constitutions*, 132.

have paid fees.[162] Almoners' account rolls survive from seven of the cathedral priories, although the single account from Rochester, dated 1430/1, lies outside the confines of this study. Income was largely, if not entirely, derived from manorial properties, churches, and rents which often proved inadequate to meet expenses as was the case of many other obedientiaries.[163]

A significant issue to be addressed concerning the occupations of cathedral almoners is the form and extent of their almsgiving. At Canterbury, for example, the almoner shared with the cellarer some responsibility for guests and pilgrims, but there are few details;[164] and the modest household expenses for his *familia* and guests included the six priests attached to the almonry chapel who sang masses daily for the king and other benefactors.[165] The charitable activities of the Christ Church almoners should have necessitated some regular dealings, direct or indirect, with the sick and destitute, but there is little surviving evidence to suggest that this was the case. The fact that they were chosen from among the mature and experienced monks who had been professed for at least twenty years and had held other responsible offices might indicate that they were expected to cope with the practical problems of dispensing aid to the poor and needy. On the other hand, it could equally well indicate that it was a charge often assigned to monks beyond their prime who were no longer capable of the rigours of prolonged and strenuous activity.[166] The Canterbury accounts record distributions in both cash and kind to various categories of poor persons that included allowances to the monks themselves.[167] In the 1320s and 1330s among the poor receiving donations in cash were a recluse, poor persons on several of the almonry manors, poor scholars, friars, travellers, and the bedridden. These involved relatively small sums which, even with the addition of the distributions of grain and pulses and small amounts of cash among the needy, made up only an insignificant fraction of the almoner's income. Half a century later the details supplied on the accounts had been reduced to donations to sick brethren and others in the cloister and *diversis pauperibus in*

---

[162] Ibid., 6, 32, 48 etc., refer to the presence of boys, but the *schola infantium* in Lanfranc's day does not seem to have been associated with the almoner. For the payment of fees at Norwich see below ■.

[163] It is not part of my brief to provide an analysis of the precarious financial management of obedientiaries, but it is worth noting that there were a number of factors involved that were beyond their control, among which were the yearly variations in crop and livestock yields, the fluctuations in the labour market, and the cost of essential commodities. The introduction to B. Harvey's *The Obedientiaries of Westminster Abbey and their Financial Records, c. 1275 to 1540* (Boydell Press, Woodbridge, 2002), xix–liv, is to be strongly recommended.

[164] These were the ordinary run of visitors; only the privileged few were put up in grander quarters; see above 27.

[165] The new almonry chapel is first mentioned on the almoner's account of 1317/18 (CCA DCc almoner no. 23); it was dedicated to Our Lady and St Thomas. Most of the money for the upkeep of these secular chaplains was supplied by the treasurers.

[166] Out of some twenty-seven known almoners between 1270 and 1420 there were only three who had been professed for slightly less than twenty years; in fact, four had been monks for forty years and one, Guy de Smerdon, for half a century, *BRECP*, 289.

[167] These allowances are often found under headings such as *caritates et oblationes cum donis fratribus* (e.g., CCA DCc almoner's account no. 42, for 1337). Similar distributions to the brethren, in the form of small amounts of spending money or of treats of food and drink on feast days, are found in the accounts of other obedientiaries as will be noted below 247–50.

patria; and in 1381/2 approximately fifty quarters of mixed grain was made into bread for the poor. Distributions at the gate of leftover food must have occurred daily, but references to this work of monastic charity rarely appear except in archiepiscopal injunctions. Winchelsey condemned the practice of giving portions to friends, relatives, and even dogs, and Islip prohibited any future reductions in the amount collected for the poor and ordered the almoners to live up to their monastic obligations in dispensing alms.[168] While there is no doubt that these figures point to a low level of charitable expenditure on the part of the Christ Church almoner a totally negative judgement made on the strength of the documents available is unsafe. They are far from complete, and the extant accounts convey the impression that their production for the annual audit was not a matter of great concern; in fact it is unsafe to interpret them analytically because of the eccentric habit of lumping individual items together with a single total cost for all of them and of the only intermittent appearances of what were probably regular expenditures.[169]

The existence of the Christ Church almonry school is not in doubt but details of its composition and functioning are shadowy. It is commonly said that these schools were the nursery where the seeds of a monastic vocation were sown. Whatever the case in earlier centuries this was no longer true in the cathedral priories in the late thirteenth century and later. The clothing of four former pupils of the Canterbury almonry school in 1468, recorded in a contemporary chronicle, was presumably a cause for special celebration because of its infrequency; in fact, no other monks who had been educated in the monastery have been identified.[170] The presence of poor, that is non-fee paying, scholars was noted by Archbishop Islip, who commanded the monks not to reduce the customary number they admitted nor to withhold any of their needs; he also ordered them to appoint a competent master.[171] In fact, the *magister scolarum* appears in the almoner's accounts only twice, in 1381/2 and 1382/3, on both occasions receiving small sums *ex gratia*.[172]

---

[168] See CCA DCc almoner's accounts nos 38 (1326/7), 40 (1329/30), 45 (1336/7), 46 (1337/8), 19 (1380/1), 59 (1381/2). Winchelsey's injunctions of 1298 are printed in *Reg. Winchelsey*, 817 and Islip's of 1356 are in LPL Reg. Islip, fo 123v.

[169] The fact that these were the final accounts and therefore a summary of the year's accounting records does not explain the situation, but the fact that the auditors were an 'in-group' largely composed of monks means that much would have been clear to them which is far from clear to us. R. A. L. Smith's negative judgement in *Canterbury Cathedral Priory*, 47, fails to allow for these uncertainties and needs a more sensitive evaluation. Furthermore, entries such as the one in Register K, dated 1322, listing the amount of bread and ale to be given out daily and weekly to the mendicant orders and in memory of Archbishop Lanfranc must also be taken into account, CCA DCc Reg. K, fo 217v.

[170] See above 52. It was usual for the monks to have some say in the selection of boys for the school, and one reference to this practice occurs in 1376 in connection with sick monks confined to the infirmary. If any one of them *scolarem habeat in elemosinaria* he was allowed to have that boy attend to his needs, Sheppard, *Lit. Cant.*, iii. no. 944.

[171] LPL Reg. Islip, fo 123v. From 1398 on the Christ Church chapter maintained in the almonry a succession of two poor scholars from the recently founded college in Bredgar parish church on condition that they proved to be competent in reading and antiphonal chant, Sheppard, *Lit. Cant.*, iii. no. 968.

[172] Who were these *magistri* on CCA DCc almoner's accounts, nos 54/59 and 3? Had they been monks there would almost certainly have been clear indications. If one of the almonry chaplains was

The boys themselves also receive scant mention. Their supplies of clothing and other necessities probably came under the expenses of the almoner's *familia* but this was only clearly spelled out in 1291/2 and 1360/1.[173] References to the purchase of tablecloths specifically for the boys occur several times and to meat and fish for them when home supplies ran out.[174]

Durham almoners carried out major works of mercy in supporting three separate establishments: the infirmary or *domus infirmorum* just outside the main priory gate, the Magdalen hospice for the elderly in Gilesgate where some of the monks' relatives and former priory employees were among those cared for, and the leper hospital at Witton Gilbert a few miles north-west of the city. The infirmary held twenty-eight men and women who received an annual clothes allowance of 4s. each as well as money for salt, flour, and fuel; the Magdalen made similar provisions for five residents as did the leper hospital. Along with the distributions in cash and kind to the poor the almoner was spending an average of £10 a year in the 1360s and, although by the 1390s the accounts provide less precise information partly because of a change of format, the total outlay appears to have remained at about the same level.[175] The daily distribution at the gate of food and beer to the poor from the monks' leftovers also included from time to time clothing, both cast-offs and apparel that had belonged to deceased monks.[176] Like their counterparts at Canterbury the majority of the Durham almoners known by name in the period under study had been members of the community for at least twenty years.[177] Their accounts show that receipts from an income dependent on manors, rents, churches, and the sale of grain and stock increased from *c.* £70 in 1339/40 (the earliest surviving account) to *c.* £90 by 1403/4 when the sum of £29 11s. 1d. was spent on alms-related expenses.[178] While the almsgiving practised by the Durham almoner was selective in its distribution policy it could hardly be judged as lacking in generosity.[179]

The almonry school received mention intermittently from the 1350s onward, but at Durham as at Canterbury there is a frustrating lack of connecting details. The *Rites of Durham* recalls that 'certain poor children, called the children of the Almery...were maintained with learning...and...went dayly to school to the Farmary school, without the Abbey gates'.[180] The monks had their turn in

---

expected to take charge of teaching the boys this would explain the absence of the master's stipend on the accounts since regular payments to the chaplains are recorded.

[173] Ibid., almoner's accounts nos 8 and 49/50.

[174] Tablecloths ibid., almoner's accounts nos 31/32 (1325/6), nos 36/41 (1368/9), nos 24/28 (1372/3), no. 3 (1382/3); meat and fish nos 49/50 (1360/1), no. 52 (1362/3).

[175] DCM almoner's accounts for the years described.

[176] See Foster, 'Durham Priory', 181.

[177] To be more precise, about two-thirds, slightly less than Canterbury; see note 166 above.

[178] The 1403/4A account has been printed in full by Fowler, *Account Rolls*, i, 217–22; the relevant section on alms expenditure is headed *Expense necessarie*, 218. Although the expense totals consistently came to slightly less than the receipts, arrears built up gradually as a result of unpaid debts and loans; on this account the latter were wiped out.

[179] The word 'selective' was employed by Meryl Foster, in 'Durham Priory', 182, by which she summed up the period up to 1350. A similar view is expressed in Harvey, *Living and Dying*, ch. 1.

[180] *Rites*, 91–2; the school was located in the *domus infirmorum* mentioned above.

recommending boys, who were often relatives, as a chapter *definitio* of the mid-fifteenth century makes clear with the reasonable hope that they would be *habiliores ad monachatum*.[181] Both Prior John Wessington and his successor in the priorate, William Ebchester, were products of the almonry school, and several other members of the community who were linked by ties of kinship probably started off as boys in the school.[182] However, this is insufficient evidence on which to conclude that many, if not most, monks had received their early education in the shadow of the cathedral priory.[183] There are frequent references to the schoolmaster, *magister puerorum elemosinarie*, to whom the almoner paid a stipend that varied for no apparent reason; in 1372/3 for his salary and robe he received 39s. 3d. with 2s. added for coal; in 1376/7 he was paid only 6s. 8d.; but in 1390/1 the sum rose to 40s., perhaps according to the number of boys he taught.[184] The boys, for their part, were presented with a new tablecloth in 1406/7 and meat was bought for them in Advent of 1418/19; but it seems that usually they were fed 'the meat that the Master of the Novices, and the Novices left'.[185]

There was a continuing problem at Ely about the diminishing amounts of food that were being distributed to the poor at the priory gate. In 1300 Bishop Ralph de Walpole found it necessary to remind the monks that all surplus food was to be given to the poor, and an ordinance to the same effect was decreed by the chapter fourteen years later which specified that the almoner 'magis liberalem se exhibeat, et elemosinas faciat uberiores'. Almost a century later Bishop Thomas Arundel rebuked the monks for using leftover food in lieu of payment to secular employees instead of leaving it for collection by the almoner.[186] Nevertheless, the fragmentary remains of the fourteenth-century accounts, from which it is impossible to glean any precise figures, convey an impression that in one form or another the poor were receiving an indeterminate but far from negligible portion of the almoner's annual receipts. An annual income that averaged roughly £100 from the usual sources—farms, rents, churches, sale of produce—regularly included between £5 and £8 in contributions from other obedientiaries towards the expenses of almsgiving for the commemoration of former priors, bishops, and lay benefactors.[187] These commemorative alms were distributed in the form of cash, bread, wheat, and other kinds of grain. Changes on the accounts in the manner in which items are grouped and described as well as the sparse number of remaining accounts preclude any attempt to separate alms proper from other donations; thus, although £28 15s. 10d. under *Anniversaria cum elemosina* in c. 1335/6 appears impressive in contrast to under £10 in 1377/8—in this latter year mats, footwear, and linen and woollen

---

[181] DCM Locellus XXVII, no. 15, m. 3, quoted in full in Dobson, *Durham Priory*, 60.
[182] Dobson, *Durham Priory*, 59.
[183] I respectfully beg to differ with the generalization in ibid., 60.
[184] DCM almoner's accounts 1372/3A, 1376/7A, 1390/1A; on one occasion his name, William de Cowton, is entered on the account, ibid., 1394/5.
[185] *Rites of Durham*, 92.
[186] Evans, *Ely Chapter Ordinances*, 17, 38 (quotation), 55–6.
[187] In 1328/9 the amount was £5, CUL EDC 1/F/1/5, and in 1344/5 £8, ibid., 1/F/1/6; the Ely almoner was thus performing the duties of the anniversarian at other cathedral priories.

The English Benedictine Cathedral Priories: Rule and Practice 191

cloth for the poor were included under *Elemosina cum gastell 'convent'*; but it must be remembered that neither anniversary distributions of alms nor other distributions have been taken into account.[188]

There were no hospitals or institutions for the sick and elderly poor under the Ely almoner's care, but on occasion he provided corrodies of bread and ale; there is also one known instance of a corrodian resident in the almonry hospice which served as home for the boys of the almonry school.[189] A chapter ordinance in 1314 spelled out the rules to be followed in the selection of boys for admission. These allowed nominations from both monks and the laity for places limited to a term of four years and forbade anyone from proposing a candidate more than once within eight years.[190] Together with their master the boys were to be supplied with sufficient food and drink of 'high quality', the particulars of which are listed on the accounts under *Expense hospicii*. Meat, fish, butter, cheese, milk, eggs, and ale are recorded in 1375/6 adding up to over £7; two years later some of the meat and fowl came from the almonry grange, and the master received a gown trimmed with fur.[191] As to the almoners themselves, biographical details of the twenty-two known by name between *c.* 1270 and 1436 are sparse and prohibit any conclusions from being drawn about their appointments and seniority.

A similar comment can be applied to the Norwich almoners of whom only nineteen names are known in this same period, and the disappearance of important sections of most of the episcopal registers has deprived us of the vital statistics regarding dates of admission to the priory, and of profession and ordination. As early as 1279/80, when the almoner's receipts amounted to over £70, he listed donations to the poor and to prisoners and lepers as well as quantities of grain (probably made into bread) doled out to mark the anniversary of Herbert Losinga, a former monk of Fécamp and the cathedral priory's first bishop; the total cash value of these food distributions was specified as £35.[192] In later accounts it becomes clear that the Norwich almoner shared with the communar the role of anniversarian, responsible for the distributions to the poor for the annual commemorations of former bishops, priors, and other benefactors, and at the same time that for this purpose he received contributions from fellow obedientiaries.[193] In later years,

---

[188] Extracts from the account for *c.* 1335/6 are in CUL Add MS 2957, 9–10; the 1377/8 account is CUL EDC 1/F/1/10; in this latter year 10s. 6d. in rent from poor tenants in Ely was waived.

[189] In 1324 Simon *dictus* Porter and his wife Margaret were given corrodies of bread and ale, BL Add MS 41612, fo 62v; in the 1270s Nicholas de Cayton, described as perpetual chaplain in the priory, was provided with his own private chamber, his clothing and meals in the almonry, ibid., fo 6. Seiriol Evans' article on 'Ely Almonry Boys' is to be recommended.

[190] Evans, *Ely Chapter Ordinances*, 38–9; although this is the earliest reference to an almonry school at Ely, the wording of the ordinance allows no room for its interpretation as a foundation document.

[191] CUL EDC 1/F/1/8 (1375/6), 1/F/1/10 (1377/8). The surprising reference in 1328/9 (ibid., 1/F/1/2) to twenty-three boys and two masters may be an error for thirteen; the next mention of the number of boys is in 1448 when five were expected, CUL EDR G/2/3, fo xxxv.

[192] NRO DCN 1/6/4, £34 18s. 9d. to be precise.

[193] For the communar see above 164 and below 215; the sums contributed by other obedientiaries are recorded in the receipts section of the almoner's account, e.g., NRO DCN 1/6/8 (1287/8), 1/6/9 (1310/11), 1/6/10 (1328/9). The combined communar/pittancer rolls also list contributions from some of the obedientiaries for anniversary distributions among the monks themselves; in 1316/17, for

however, the headings on the accounts change and proliferate as do the listings of individual items with the result that, at Norwich as at Ely, it becomes impossible to distinguish and separate alms in the strict sense from other gifts and donations. In 1328/9, for example, the heading *Custus pauperum* at Norwich consists of 13s. 9d. to the poor and cloth and footwear amounting to 20s., as well as 2s. to 'scholars' and 20s. to the almoner's nephew on his admission to a monastery in Colchester; twenty years later under [*Expense*] *forinsece* alms of 36s. 10d. were given *pro episcopis, prioribus et monachis*. By 1396/7, the heading *Forinseca et dona* records distributions to the poor *per totum annum* for bishops Losinga and Ralegh 36s. 2d., for Bishop Grey 13s. 4d., and for lepers at the city gates and prisoners in the castle 20s.[194] Although not in the almoner's care, the hospital of St Paul was attached to the cathedral priory and treated as one of the dependent cells with its own monk-warden or master. Founded in the early twelfth century for the sick and infirm poor, after the Black Death it became an almshouse for women. The earliest account of 1422/3 specified that the sisters and staff (*familia*) were furnished with bread, meat, fish, pittances, and oil for their lamps, but it seems that money payments had replaced the provision of food by 1433/4 when thirteen sisters were given 8d. per week and eleven 3d. per week.[195]

Details of the almonry school at Norwich are gratifyingly abundant although questions inevitably remain. The earliest surviving reference to boys in the almonry can be placed during the priorate of William de Kirkeby, that is between 1272 and 1289.[196] Although several almoner's accounts survive from these years the first sign of the presence of a school appears in 1298/9 on the account of the master of the cellar who gave 12d. to the *magister elemosinarie* under his *dona*; however, it is not until 1310/11 that the almoner begins to record payments to the *magister puerorum*.[197] From then on there are frequent, although far from consistent, entries detailing expenses related to the boys' maintenance, most of them listed under *Custus puerorum et familie* or simply *Custus familie*. The items specified are mainly food—meat, fish, eggs, bread, and cheese—without any specific mention of the boys apart from mats and cloth for the boys' table in 1339/40, and an entry in 1378/9 stating merely that 3s. 4d. was spent *circa pueros in advento et LXX* (Lent).[198] After his visitation of the cathedral priory in the 1340s Bishop Bateman

---

example, the feast in commemoration of the two former priors Gerard (d. *c*. 1202) and William de Kirkeby (d. 1289) included delicacies such as porpoise, rice, almonds, figs, and wine and cost over £3, Fernie and Wittingham, *Communar Rolls*, 92.

[194] NRO DCN 1/6/10, 1/6/15, 1/6/27; on the 1345/6 account alms to the poor of 21s. 6d. are found under *Custus familie*, ibid., 1/6/13. Many of the later grange accounts are missing but regular distributions of grain would have continued.

[195] NRO DCN 2/5/1, 2/5/2.

[196] Kirkeby's career is in *BRECP*, 531.

[197] NRO DCN 1/1/13, 1/6/9; on the latter account the almoner spent 27s. 3d. on cloth for *pauperes clerici*, i.e., the boys. The monks attributed the foundation of the school to Bishop Losinga, but see Greatrex, 'Norwich Almonry School', 169–70.

[198] NRO DCN 1/6/12, 1/6/18. One reason for the few references to the purchase of food for the boys is that an unknown quantity of what they consumed, possibly most of it, as at Durham, came from the leftover food in the monastic refectory.

The English Benedictine Cathedral Priories: Rule and Practice 193

was concerned that the almonry boys were not receiving their fair share of the leftover food from the monks' tables and ordered that they were not to be short-changed. He also imposed rules for the selection of boys similar to the Ely ordinance of 1314 by which the monks, in rotation according to seniority, could propose names; and he stressed that only the poor among their relatives were to be eligible.[199] In 1378/9 the almoner reported a deficit amounting to almost half of his receipts of £71 and, in this same year, hardly by coincidence, he is found to be charging fees for some of the places in the school.[200] The parents of two boys who boarded for twelve weeks in the almonry paid 10d. a week, while a third parent paid only 9d. for the same length of time; a fourth was also charged at the weekly rate of 10d. for six weeks. The family names are given—Elys, Beverle, Repp, and Charleton—and the accounts record that the following year the Beverle boy was lodged for thirty-two weeks and Elys for forty-two; these two also stayed on for a third year during which three new names were added.[201] The lists of named boys disappear from the accounts after 1380/1 but were resumed twenty years later when four names are recorded, two of whom were paying the higher rate of 12d. per week *pro mensa*.[202] In later years the boys cannot be clearly distinguished from other named persons from whom the almoner received sums of money. Only two of these fee-paying boys can be identified as relatives of the monks; others would have probably belonged in the category of poor relations, who remain unknown because their maintenance would have gone unrecorded.[203]

Only a few Winchester almoners have been identified by name and an even fewer number at Rochester.[204] The seemingly perennial failings of these obedientiaries, however, as of their fellow almoners at other cathedral priories have been preserved for posterity through the complaints of the brethren to the diocesan in the course of visitation. Bishop Nicholas de Ely sent his injunctions to St Swithun's in 1276, one of which ordered that no one was to remove leftover food from the monks' dining tables except the almoner who was to ensure that all of it was distributed to the poor; half a century later Bishop Stratford found that the poor were still or again being defrauded of their alms which were being taken by *personis suspectis in villa*, the culprits probably being priory servants.[205] Archbishop Winchelsey's 1299 visit to Rochester found the monks less than generous in their almsgiving to the poor who came to them for relief in their distress; he sternly

---

[199] Cheney, 'Norwich Cathedral Priory', 112.

[200] NRO DCN 1/6/18; since there is a twenty-six-year gap in the accounts between 1352/3 and 1378/9 it is uncertain when the change in policy occurred.

[201] Ibid., 1/6/19, 1/6/20.

[202] Ibid., 1/6/30.

[203] The two are the nephews of Richard de Helyngton (Elyngton) and of the unnamed prior of Yarmouth, both in the early 1420s; and the prior of Yarmouth himself paid the fees, ibid., 1/6/47, 1/6/48, 1/6/50. For Helyngton see also *BRECP*, 519.

[204] Between *c.* 1270 and *c.* 1420 twelve Winchester and three Rochester almoners' names are known.

[205] Nicholas de Ely's injunctions were copied into the earliest surviving Winchester episcopal register, that of his successor, John de Pontissara; see *Reg. Pontissara*, 641–4; for Stratford, HRO 21M65/A1/5, fo 173.

reminded them that this was a duty they owed to their patrons and benefactors whose grants and bequests had been intended both to provide sustenance for the community and also to alleviate the suffering of the needy.[206] The earliest surviving Winchester almoner's account of 1309/10 was prepared under the direction of Adam de Hyda, who probably stayed in office for the whole of the next ten years, during which time he spent part of three separate years ill in the monastic infirmary. His medicines, charged to his account, amounted to over 37s., a large sum for one who was operating within an income of no more than £40 per annum. In 1316/17 and later years almost half of his receipts was devoted to the support of the Sustern Spital, a hospital just outside the south gate of St Swithun's that accommodated in that year twenty-two needy men and women. He gave them 3½d. per week for food and 3s. each year for clothing; he also paid the stipend of their chaplain and bought wax and incense for the chapel.[207] Numbers fluctuated and, after the Black Death, decreased; in 1404/5 there were fourteen sisters, who did not receive their full allowances because of the disastrous fire that burned down almost the entire manorial buildings at the almoner's manor of Hinton.[208]

The Rochester almonry boys came to Archbishop Winchelsey's attention in 1299 and resulted in his injunction to the effect that the number of poor scholars was not to be reduced, and their portions of food in future were not to be taken by menials and intruders.[209] The sole surviving almoner's account, dated 1430/1, includes among its expenses eight pounds of candles for the boys, meat in Advent and Septuagesima, and two hundred herrings in Lent; their master's annual stipend was recorded as 20s.[210] The almonry school's presence at Winchester is elusive; references are few and late in date. The *juvenes in schola*, who occur frequently in the accounts of the almoner and of other monks from the mid-1380s onward, are *juvenes monachi* as a 1447 election list makes clear.[211] Shortly before his death in 1404 Bishop Wykeham concluded an amicable agreement with the monks concerning the future provisions for his chantry chapel in the cathedral nave. One of the items lays down the arrangements for the boys living in the almonry school to sing a Marian antiphon there every evening and to recite the psalm *De profundis* along with specified prayers; their recompense was to be 6s. 8d. distributed to them once a year.[212]

Although several late thirteenth-century Worcester almoners have been identified by name, the earliest account is for the year 1341/2; and for only twenty of the

---

[206] *Reg. Winchelsey*, 841.
[207] Kitchin, *Obedientiary Rolls*, 400–1; both men and women are specified until 1390, but in 1395/6 and after only women.
[208] Ibid., 426; Hinton, now known as Hinton Ampner (i.e., of the almoner), was the source of nearly all of the almoner's income.
[209] *Reg. Winchelsey*, 841; only two of the monks are known to have attended the almonry school which the archbishop described as in existence *antiquitus*.
[210] CKS DRc/F11.
[211] *Reg. Common Seal*, no. 316; the names of all the monks present are listed, of whom the three last are descried as *juvenes*.
[212] Ibid., no. 63; the distinction between the almonry boys and the boys who sang will be discussed below 265–70.

next eighty years are there surviving rolls.[213] This scanty collection of rolls has much in common with the accounts of other cathedral priory almoners in the seemingly nonchalant approach to the recording of entries which makes it impossible to interpret them with any degree of accuracy. However, we are provided with glimpses of several functions incumbent upon the Worcester almoner, details of which have not been apparent elsewhere either because they were absent or, possibly, hidden from view. Moreover, the recurrent financial difficulties commonly experienced by many obedientiaries do not seem to have plagued the Worcester almoners in the fourteenth century; in fact they were able to build up a sizeable surplus, by means of the usual sources of income from rents, pensions, and the sale of grain and stock, despite the fact that their annual receipts were modest.[214] It follows that the expenditures on these accounts were relatively small. There is no sign of a dependent hospice for the poor and infirm and only occasional reference to visitors staying in the almonry; for example, the expenses of *diversorum hospitum supervenientium* in 1399/1400 amounted to 8s.[215] A few of the priory corrodians received food and sometimes lodging in the almonry but most of them had initially paid a lump sum for the privilege. Several of these are described as chaplains, and may have been identical to the almonry chaplains who received a stipend on several accounts.[216] One of the chaplains, who was given a corrody in 1321, paid 30 marks down in return for his daily allocation of food and a gallon of good ale for the rest of his life from the almoner, with the stipulation that he was to celebrate mass every day in the cathedral as directed. In 1396 William Weston, another chaplain, also paid 20 marks and was required to carry out similar duties; however, he was to receive from the almoner a yearly stipend of 33s. 4d. and woollen cloth for a robe of the quality provided for armigers, while in old age he was to be guaranteed room, board, and gown.[217] To this form of corrody must be added the so-called monastic corrodies which appear in the receipts section of the Worcester almoner's accounts. The sale of these corrodies was an abuse of the common monastic practice of commemorating deceased brethren by distributing to the poor what would have been their daily portions of food and drink during a set period after

---

[213] These are WCM C.170–90; there is one lengthy gap between 1355 and 1374.

[214] In 1355/6 the receipts were *c*. £64; by 1399/1400 the total had increased to £144 of which almost £55 was surplus, and some of which the almoner turned over to the cellarer to alleviate his debt, WCM C.172, 185.

[215] Ibid., C.185. In the 1340s there are two references to the cost *pro hospicio* of the mother of the monk John de Ankerdom, *BRECP*, 771, but it is not stated where she was lodged, ibid., C.170, C.171.

[216] In 1341/2 the almonry chaplain was paid 20s., in 1387/8 53s. 4d. *preter mensam*, ibid., C.170, C.179.

[217] Copies of these (and other) corrodies were entered in the priory register known as the Liber Albus, WCM Reg. A.5, fos 104v, 384. Corrodies were a useful but risky means of providing ready money for the grantor but offered a lifetime guarantee to receive the basic necessities of food and drink for the grantee; at Worcester the cellarer was the obedientiary who was most burdened with corrodians. The numerous royal demands for corrodies in monasteries to pension off royal servants at the expense of the monks will not be included in this study; it will be sufficient to draw attention to the lengthy correspondence on the subject between Edward II and the prior of Worcester which was edited by James M. Wilson and Ethel C. Jones, *Corrodies at Worcester in the Fourteenth Century* (Worcester Historical Society, London, 1917).

their death.[218] At Worcester this period lasted for a year or thereabouts and its cash value was reckoned at 9d. per week.[219] In the case of John Grene, prior, who died in 1395, the almoner, Thomas Dene, records the receipt of 52s. for his corrody, that is at the rate of 1s. per week for a full year. A noteworthy entry on this 1395/6 account reveals that, in addition to paying the salary of a chaplain for half the year, Dene paid the stipend of William the chaplain employed to celebrate masses for the souls of Prior Grene and a fellow monk also recently deceased.[220] On several occasions, however, the almoner's account makes it clear that the corrodies were not sold; in 1380/1, for example, they were distributed to the poor for the souls of the two monks who had died that year.[221] It is to be noted that among the obedientiaries and other monks a few gave alms both in cash and in kind; Robert de Hambury 5s. per annum *pro elemosina sua* in 1404/5 and for the remaining five years of his life, and the precentor turned over to the almoner four bushels of pulses in 1377/8.[222]

Donations of the almoner in the form of money, food, and grain are scattered here and there on all the surviving accounts, some occurring through the year and others on specified anniversaries. His cash gifts amounted to £4 in 1377/8 and 1380/1 but in the 1390s about 13s. less. Some years earlier, in 1341/2 he was obliged to buy the mixed grain he customarily had made into bread for the poor and also beans and pulses which cost him over £8; and more details of the times and quantities of these distributions appear on the dorse of the account.[223] The anniversaries commemorated at the almoner's expense receive frequent mention on his accounts, but a clear picture of the complex internal arrangements that lie behind them is not easily recoverable and may at times have perplexed even those involved. The almoner's responsibilities, for example, with regard to the

---

[218] In her *Living and Dying*, Barbara Harvey refers to this practice in the context of monastic charity, 13–14, and devotes a lengthy chapter to a judicious study of monastic corrodies, their origin and development, their benefits, and their problems, 178–209.
[219] WCM C.170.
[220] *BRECP*, 812 (John Grene I), 819 (Thomas Hay); the latter's corrody was sold for 38s. at the rate of 1s. per week. As to the chaplains in the almonry to whom reference has been made above, there is often insufficient evidence to allow us to distinguish the several categories into which they appear to fall.
[221] See *BRECP*, 810–11 under John de Gloucestre III and 826 under John de Kyderminstre I. In 1374/5 one half of John de Newport's corrody was assigned to the clerks of the chapel and the other half to the friars minor and friars preachers *BRECP*, 857. These two mendicant orders were regular recipients of small donations in cash and kind for which they responded by praying for deceased monks like John de Stanleye in 1398/9, *BRECP*, 876.
[222] WCM C.187, 188, 189 and see also *BRECP*, 816. The precentor's gift of pulses is on the dorse of the account, WCM C.174, and there are similar small amounts of the same on the dorse of the account for 1380/1 (C.176) given by five other obedientiaries. These donations were for the poor and not oblations for the almoner himself as may have been the case at Durham where the explanatory phrase was *in recompensatione elemosine*; see for example DCM almoner's accounts for 1394/5, 1397/8 A and B.
[223] WCM C.174, 176, 181, 182 record cash donations; ibid., C.170 for the distributions in kind, which are also entered on subsequent accounts. It is worth noting that archiepiscopal and episcopal reprimands of the almoners' negligence in the collection and distribution of alms survive from the early fourteenth century but not later; for Winchelsey's injunction see *Reg. Montacute*, 275 and for Gainsborough, ibid., 266, 267.

anniversary of St Wulstan, former monk and bishop, took the form of distributions of *blada* or bread for the poor and of what was described as the corrody of St Wulstan. A portion of the latter, which seems to have been valued at *c.* £4 a year, on only two occasions appears to have been given to the poor; on other occasions it was sold or assigned to a relative of the prior.[224] William de Molendis (Moleyns), who had bequeathed lands and rents to the almoner's office, was commemorated by money pittances for the monks and bread or money for the poor. Thomas Carter was commemorated in a similar way with the additional expense of 18d. per week which the almoner paid throughout the year to a monk to celebrate masses for Carter.[225]

The almonry school at Worcester is first mentioned on the almoner's accounts in 1380/1 when a resident chaplain was engaged to teach the boys in the almonry; in 1398 their teacher was John Ekynton for whom the almoner purchased cloth for a tunic.[226] Two years earlier, in 1396, one boy who was probably numbered among those in the school, was in the employ of a resident chaplain assigned to celebrate daily masses in accordance with the almoner's requirements.[227] There is, in addition, an undated but probably late thirteenth-century reference to poor *clerici* and their master who from the context may have been part of the almonry school.[228]

It would be wise to refrain from passing judgement on the almsgiving of almoners since the figures on which any estimate of the amounts involved is of necessity based are patchy and ambiguous and the records are far from complete in the details provided.

The sacrist and his domain

Attention has already been drawn to some of the differences between cathedral priory sacrists with respect to their spheres of authority.[229] The office was considered to be one of the senior obedientiary posts to which only an experienced and

---

[224] Ibid., C.170, *blada* or mixed grain, and bread; C.182, the almoner received (?from the cellarer whose accounts C.75, C.76 suggest this) £4 for the corrody *cum coquina*. C.178, C.179, alms; C.172 sold; C.174, C.176, C.177, C.179, assigned to a kinsman of Prior Walter de Legh.

[225] For William de Molendinis see *Annales Wigorn.*, 509; Thomas Carter's connection with the priory is unknown. The probable transfer of some of these commemorative obligations is suggested by the fact that it was the cellarer who gave pittances to the brethren on Carter's anniversary in 1376/7 and in 1385/6 was paying for the masses, WCM C.69, 71; Carter's anniversary first appears on an extant almoner's account in 1387/8 and the payments for masses that same year, C.179.

[226] WCM C.176, 184.

[227] The chaplain was William Weston, whose *carta* containing the terms of his employment is in WCM Liber Albus, fo 384–384v; the boy in question was to serve the chaplain and to be given food and drink and schooling like the other boys.

[228] *Reg. Prioratus*, 130b; this volume provides the Latin text of WCM Reg. A.2. The relevant passage states that the *magister scholarum* was allowed to choose three *clerici* to be numbered among the thirteen poor men for the maundy ceremonies in Lent; it also suggests that the master was teaching not only the *clerici* but also relatives of the monks and others *de elemosina* [?*elemosinaria*] *nutritorum*. Attention should here be drawn to the masterly encapsulation of the latest research on English monastic almonry schools by Roger Bowers in 'Almonry Schools', 177–222.

[229] See above 163.

mature monk could expect to be appointed; and, in fact, only a few of those to whom dates can be safely assigned had behind them less than twenty years of monastic life.[230] Unless there was a *custos operum*, as at Winchester and Worcester, the sacrist's duties combined the maintenance of the cathedral fabric and the provision of the materials necessary for the performance of all the liturgical rites and ceremonies throughout the course of the ecclesiastical year.[231] At Bath, Canterbury, Ely, Rochester, and Worcester the appointment and dismissal of the sacrist lay with the bishop, who from time to time asserted his right against the wishes and advice of the monastic community.[232] John de Powik of Worcester, for example, was already a doubtful character in the eyes of his brethren when, in 1363, Bishop Reginald Bryan named him sacrist.[233] Details of the two-year-long affair were recorded in the priory register before the final resolution of which Powik had disappeared.[234]

Two surviving episcopal registers of the diocese of Bath and Wells cover most of the first half of the fourteenth century, although there are sections missing from both of them. However, neither from before 1350 nor from the subsequent years before 1420 has there emerged more than a handful of sacrists' names, all devoid of any informative detail even though they were appointed by the bishop. A similar situation pertains at Coventry where the registers provide an almost continuous record, and they are virtually complete for the same period; but the bishop's confirmation of the appointment of this obedientiary rarely appears. Two references in the register of Bishop Roger de Northburgh momentarily lift the veil of silence with the information that in the 1320s the sacrist, Richard de Lodbrok, was in need of funds for the cathedral fabric.[235] Like Bath and Coventry, Winchester has no surviving sacrists' accounts with the exception of one dated 1536/7 on which the total receipts were less than £50 and the expenses amounted to a mere 9s. less.[236] However, the two surviving accounts of the *custos operum* must be included in our consideration of St Swithun's because of the division of labour between these two offices. The 1532/3 roll of the *custos operum*, which is conveniently close to that of the sacrist, shows that on the eve of the dissolution it was the former who had the more costly burden of responsibility since he dealt with the maintenance, repair, and construction pertaining to the cathedral church and monastic buildings; the sacrist's duties were limited to the interior furnishings of the church and to

---

[230] When exceptions are in evidence they tend to be at a time when there was a problem of manpower as in the aftermath of the mid-fourteenth-century plague.

[231] Lanfranc's *Monastic Constitutions*, 122–6, provide detailed instructions for this office, but without reference to the maintenance and repair of church fabric.

[232] Norwich should probably be added to this list; see above 15.

[233] BRECP, 864; the office of sacrist at Worcester was the sole obedientiary appointment over which the bishop had any control, see above 15.

[234] WCM, Liber Albus, fos 236–245v; Prior John de Evesham and the monks were finally vindicated and the bishop ordered the absent sacrist to be deprived of his office.

[235] BRECP, 362 and LRO B/A/1/3, Reg. Northburgh, fo 20v; at ibid., fo 24v the bishop made his contribution to the fabric fund by donating to the sacrist the custody of his houses in Coventry together with their appurtenances for a period of three years but without emoluments.

[236] WCL W53/13/16; this roll was transcribed and edited in Kitchin and Madge, *Documents of Winchester*, 19–31. Only five sacrists are known by name between 1321 and 1415.

procuring the materials necessary for conducting the daily services.[237] Rochester cathedral priory sacrists are named from time to time in the episcopal registers in the entries authorizing their appointment and dismissal; the sole surviving account of 1511/12 is too brief to be informative.[238]

The remaining cathedral priory sacrists—those of Canterbury, Durham, Ely, Norwich, and Worcester—are better known to posterity because of the preservation of more numerous records. The Norwich account rolls, for example, begin in the 1270s and survive for fifty of the years between then and 1420. Their existence provides us with the names of some eighteen sacrists, but not more because some of them appear to have continued in office for a number of years; Henry de Lakenham, for one, had a fourteen-year run as sacrist before he was elected prior in 1289, and Richard de Hecham probably thirteen continuous years from 1323 to 1335/6.[239] Both the incomings and outgoings of the Norwich sacrist fluctuated from year to year mainly due to the rise and fall in the amounts received from churches, tithes, manors, rents, and offerings collected in the cathedral and to the amounts required to pay for repairs and construction. The totals were usually well over £100 and sometimes closer to £200, and the sacrist was not infrequently overdrawn. During the first decade of the fourteenth century a free-standing campanile was built, the cost of which was in the region of £250. Additional expenses were incurred, during building operations, to feed and sometimes house the masons and other workers employed.[240] In the 1320s the sacrist experienced another lesser but still major outlay for a new clock to replace the old one; master clockmakers from London came to oversee the construction on the outside wall of the south transept, and the total cost was close to £60.[241] An expenditure of a different kind looms large in 1329/30 because of a lawsuit concerning the rights of the prior and convent in *sede vacante* jurisdiction. The account for that year details the expenses for the sacrist's journey to the papal curia at Avignon and the eleven-week stay while the case was being heard.[242] During the 1330s work was begun on the reconstruction

---

[237] The two *custos operum* rolls are printed in Kitchin, *Obedientiary Rolls*, 209–23, the earlier one dated 1408/9; there are also several fragments of uncertain date, WCL W53/15/2–4. The 1408/9 account shows expenses of £64 10s. while that of 1532/3 was £82.

[238] The account is now CKS DRc/M7.

[239] For Lakenham and Richard de Hecham II see *BRECP*, 531–2, 518; there is a misprint in the latter reference because Hecham was made sacrist in March 1325. A similar lengthy tenure of office occurs in the 1420s and 1430s when Richard de Midelton was in office, ibid., 541. The only surviving reference to the exercise of episcopal authority over the sacrist's appointment is in the register of John Wakeryng, dated 1419, and concerns William de Silton, ibid., 555.

[240] The campanile or belfry was sited on the north side of the west end of the cathedral, just south of the Erpingham gate. Details of the construction actually begin to appear on the sacrist's account in 1297/8 and continue for the next ten years, NRO DCN 1/4/10–17. The mason, John de Ramesey I, was involved during these years as well as in the later construction of the carnary chapel and cloisters; see Harvey, *English Mediaeval Architects*, 240–1. It seems surprising that the total expended on the campanile is found on the dorse of the 1297/8 account ibid., 1/4/12.

[241] NRO DCN 1/4/21–3; see also Gilchrist, *Norwich Cathedral Close*, 255. As Professor Gilchrist notes this may well have been prompted by one of Bishop Salmon's injunctions to provide a reliable clock in order to ensure punctuality for the liturgical services, ibid.

[242] NRO DCN 1/4/24; the total spent according to this account amounted to £168 and required some borrowing from other funds. For Richard de Hecham, the sacrist, and Roger de Eston see

of the cloister, which was largely the joint responsibility of the communar and pittancer who record contributions and legacies from bishops and laity, and not least from monks. Before this was completed the spire was brought down by a hurricane in January 1362 and the presbytery was badly damaged. The following year the sacrist accounts for the additional cost of feeding the men who were working on the reconstruction of the eastern arm of the cathedral, and in 1368/9 he contributed £33 from his office.[243] At Norwich building works figure prominently on the fourteenth-century accounts of the master of the cellar, communar/pittancer and the sacrist, and donations from other members of the community occur on these rolls from time to time, thus making clear that these were projects in which the whole community participated.[244] The particular wealth of detail at Norwich serves as a reminder of our total dependence on the surviving evidence and of the imbalance resulting from the haphazard nature of what remains. It follows that a comparative study such as this can attempt to fill in some of the blank spaces, tentatively and with circumspection, in order to present a more rounded, although admittedly composite, picture without minimizing the characteristic differences.[245]

The Norwich sacrist's responsibility included not only the care of shrines and altars but the collection and disposal of the offerings made by the faithful at the altars and images in the nave and chapels of the cathedral. The absence of an obedientiary, elsewhere known as feretrar or shrine-keeper, may have resulted from the lack of a significant saint, the cult of St William never becoming more than local; offerings at his shrine, when they were for the first time listed separately in 1313/14, were barely more than £1, but between the mid-1380s and 1390s they fluctuated between £8 and £20, only to fall again dramatically to 14s. in 1420/1.[246] The highest sums found in the dozen or so collection boxes in the cathedral were consistently those deposited at the high altar which, despite fluctuations, never fell below £20 a year, were often over £40, and in the 1390s were about £60.[247] The donations of the faithful made up a significant part of the sacrist's annual income, in fact between a third and a half, the remainder being mainly derived from his manors, churches, and rents. The fortunate preservation of one detailed inventory on the reverse of the 1436 account, which registered a change of incumbents in the office, provides an insight into the material extent of the sacrist's sphere of authority. The itemized list describes over twenty separate rooms or quarters in different parts of the precinct; they include his hall,

---

BRECP, 518 (Richard de Hecham II), 507. There are copies of some of the correspondence and a partial account of the proceedings in London and Avignon in NRO DCN Reg. X, fos 1, 4v, 5, 8–33v.

[243] For details of the reconstruction see Fernie, *Architectural History... Norwich*, 183–6; the sacrist's accounts referred to are NRO DCN 1/4/35, 1/4/36.

[244] See, for example, *BRECP*, 524, under Nicholas de Hindolveston; Henry de Lakenham, prior, 531; Richard de Lakenham, 532.

[245] See above 1–2.

[246] NRO DCN 1/4/5, 37–41, 56; see also Nilson, *Cathedral Shrines*, 156–8, 218–21. A probable explanation of the brief but dramatic increase in offerings may be the fact that the Norwich pelterers' guild took St William as their patron, see J. R. Shinners Jr., 'The Veneration of Saints at Norwich Cathedral in the Fourteenth Century', *Norfolk Archaeology*, 40 (1988), 133–43.

[247] For ease of comparison see Nilson's tables in *Cathedral Shrines*, 218–19; in the first two decades of the fifteenth century the amounts received ranged between £57 and £98.

kitchen, and larder together with a granary and bakehouse, two *camerae* over St Catherine's chapel in the south transept, two *studia* over the cloister, a glasshouse, waxhouse, and a lead house, probably situated close to the east end of the cathedral, and of course the vestry or sacristy where the vestments and altar linen were kept.[248] At the same time he would have been responsible for the workmen employed in each of these departments as well as for preparing the schedule of duties for the monks who served as *magistri* of the high and the Lady altar.[249]

Two stages were involved in the appointment of a sacrist at Christ Church Canterbury. The names of three senior monks deemed to be suitable candidates were forwarded to the archbishop, who selected one of them and informed the prior and chapter of his choice. The term of office was generally not more than five years but, among the thirty-six sacrists known by name, there were a few notable exceptions such as Robert de Dover, who probably remained in office from 1303 to 1313.[250] Although only twenty accounts survive between 1341/2 and 1420, names along with some other details can be gathered from a variety of sources. Like his counterpart at Norwich, the Canterbury sacrist was in charge of the maintenance and repair of the cathedral church. In this he was assisted by regular contributions from the treasurers which sometimes amounted to about half of his total receipts. In 1341/2, for example, he received £29 from church pensions and over £44 from the treasury; in 1374/5 his total receipts were almost £124 of which the treasurer's portion was £62.[251] One of the major annual expenses of sacrists was the purchase of wax and candles on which at Canterbury the amount spent was over £43 in 1374/5. Other regular payments included those for bell ringing and organ blowing (*pro organis trahendis*), while the whitewashing of the choir vault in 1391/3 cost £19.[252] Major building work undertaken during the priorates of Henry Eastry and of Thomas Chillenden a century later necessitated a recourse to loans and depended in part on public donations; but the financial acumen and expertise of these two remarkable priors played a major role in their achievements, details of which were carefully recorded and have survived to the present day.[253] Small sums

[248] NRO DCN 1/4/75; the subsacrist was, of course, his assistant.

[249] The two *magistri* regularly received payments from the sacrist, but it remains uncertain whether or not they were always monks; see William de Martham, who was *magister magni altaris* in 1314, *BRECP*, 539.

[250] *BRECP*, 139; first appointed by Archbishop Winchelsey he was also reappointed twice by succeeding archbishops between 1319 and 1324 and 1335 and 1337, ibid. See also John de Guston, whose term of office probably extended from 1373 to 1385, ibid., 184. Appointments were similarly carried out at the other cathedral priories (apart from Winchester and Worcester), but surviving records do not furnish the details provided by Canterbury where they were not infrequently the source of contention between prior and chapter and archbishop.

[251] Canterbury sacrist's accounts CCA DCc 2, 6; when, in the 1390s, Prior Thomas Chillenden, formerly one of the treasurers, gave himself a more central role in the financial administration the sacrist recorded payments from him, ibid., DCc 10.

[252] Ibid., DCc 6 (wax and candles); ibid., 3, 6, 10 (bell ringing and organ blowing); 10, 11 (choir vault); several obedientiaries and monks contributed small sums to the work on the choir.

[253] Eastry's achievements are summarized chronologically in CCA DCc Reg. K under 'Nova Opera in Ecclesia et in Curia tempore Henrici prioris', fo 220–220v. For Chillenden, the so-called 'Anonymous Chronicle', CCA DCc Lit. MS C.14, fos 35v, 34, 34v, 31, 31v provides a chronological record which Eveleigh Woodruff has transcribed, translated, and edited in

were collected by the sacrist and his assistant sacrists from the offertory chests and pyxes placed at the various altars in the cathedral church to receive the donations of pilgrims and the faithful. The total annual receipts from these collections ranged between £4 and £6, the altar of our Lady in the nave attracting the most generous offerings seconded by the altar dedicated to St Peter.[254]

Durham and Canterbury sacrists had much in common, as well as notable differences. Their extant accounts date from 1338 and 1341 respectively, although those at Durham are almost three times more numerous in the eighty years before 1420. Like his opposite number at Christ Church the sacrist of St Cuthbert was responsible for the maintenance of the cathedral fabric and the provision of all the items required for use in all the liturgical rites and ceremonies that were celebrated in the cathedral church. The names of about forty Durham sacrists have been extracted from the records between c. 1270 and c. 1420, most of them senior monks of twenty or more years in monastic life with experience gained in previous obedientiary offices.[255] As far as accurate dates of tenure of the sacrist's office can be determined, few monks held the post for more than three or four years, with the noteworthy exception of John Abel and Thomas D'Autre who remained in office from 1375 to 1384 and 1384 to 1398 respectively.[256] The Durham sacrist accounted for the offerings deposited in the pyxes of St Cross and St Bede in the Galilee chapel and the money boxes at the entrance to the church and near the high altar.[257] These were only small sums in comparison with the amounts collected at the shrine of the revered monk and bishop St Cuthbert (d. 681), responsibility for which belonged to the two feretrars. The sacrist's annual receipts and his expenses were in the region of £100, but he carried over from year to year an increasing burden of unpaid debts.[258]

There is regrettably less detail about building operations on the Durham sacrist and other obedientiary accounts than on those of Norwich. Nevertheless, the sacrist records heavier than average expenditures between 1338 and 1345, for example, when stone masons were engaged in erecting a new buttress *ad gabellum* of the Galilee chapel, and the campanile and north aisle of the cathedral were under repair, and again in 1355/6 when a new window at the west end of the cathedral was inserted. In addition to masons there are frequent references to the stipends

---

Archaeologia Cantiana, 29 (1911), 47–8, at 60–77. R. Willis transcribed a list of Eastry's building works from CCA DCc Reg. I, fo 212 in the same Journal, 7 (1882), 185–7.

[254] CCA DCc sacrist's accounts 2, 6.

[255] Richard de Brompton and Roger de Stanhope, sacrists in the first decade of the fourteenth century, had been monks for forty years! For the period during and immediately after the plague epidemic in the mid-fourteenth century more junior monks were appointed as sacrists; a list of sacrists may be found in *LVD*, i, 500, and for Brompton, ibid., iii, C.663 and Stanhope C.664.

[256] For Abel see *LVD*, iii, C.920 and for D'Autre C.981 (under Audrey).

[257] These receipts totalled between £7 and £10 a year, DCM sacrist's accounts 1355/6, 1362/3, 1381/2A. With the appearance of a monk master of the Galilee in 1311 it may have been his duty to collect the offerings there and turn them over to the sacrist.

[258] His accounts are complicated by this fact of an accumulation of arrears or debts: in 1360/1 this amounted to c. £61; in 1380/1 it had risen to £117 which was finally *exonerat'* or cancelled, DCM sacrist's accounts for these years, the accounts in both cases being labelled 'A'.

paid to carpenters, plumbers, glaziers, and wax and candle makers, and in 1385/6 to repairs to the leadhouse, wrighthouse, and waxhouse.[259] Fleeting references on some accounts serve as a reminder of the sacrist's constant need to ensure an adequate supply of clean vestments in good repair.[260]

Among cathedral priory sacrists the holder of this office at Ely was vested with singularly wide-ranging authority. Evidence for the prominent role he played within his community is provided by the thirty surviving account rolls between 1291/2 and 1420/1.[261] Of the eighteen sacrists in this period whose names have come to light, four were elected to the priorate by their fellow monks.[262] Among the Ely obedientiaries, with the sole exception of the treasurers, the sacrist had considerable estates under his management from which he derived a sizeable income and which was applied 'circa fabricam ecclesie et ea que ad officum suum spectant'.[263] In his own quarters he had charge of a hospice that provided bed and board for a more or less permanent, albeit frequently changing, workforce and at the same time he ruled over a substantial body of regular officials and servants responsible for the day-to-day functioning of the cathedral.[264] Other responsibilities included the supervision of the hospital of St John in Ely, and archidiaconal jurisdiction in parts of the Isle of Ely from which he received a small amount in profits from probate and corrections.[265] At least one sacrist, namely John de Ely, was appointed receiver of the bishopric between c. 1378 and 1381 while continuing to hold his office in the cathedral priory; the only other recorded instance of this dual role, with its inherent potential for a conflict of obedience, occurs at Worcester.[266] The substantial income at his disposal enabled the sacrist to make generous contributions each year to his brethren under the headings of pittances, on the occasion of anniversaries and feasts, and *pro graciis*. The latter, according to the episcopal statutes of 1300, were small sums of money which could be used to purchase unspecified necessities *de licencia et ordinacione prioris*—in other words

---

[259] DCM sacrist's accounts for the years specified, and some of the details may be found in Fowler, *Account Rolls*, ii. 377–85. Large supplies of wax were purchased, on average about 500 lbs, but in the 1370s and 1380s Juliana Gray was employed to make wax, ibid., accounts for 1376/7A, 1385/6.

[260] Ibid., 1362/3, 1377/8, 1371/2 etc.

[261] CUL EDC 1/F/10/1–30 and the collection of Bentham transcripts CUL Add. MS 2956, 160–5; the first fifteen accounts have been transcribed and edited by Chapman in *Sacrist Rolls*.

[262] Their careers are summarized in *BRECP*: Alan de Walsingham (1341–63/4), 453–4; William de Walpole I (1396/7–1401), 452; William Powcher (William de Ely I) (1401–18), 431 and 410; Edmund Walsingham (1418–24), 454.

[263] Most of the other obedientiaries were to some extent financially dependent on the treasurer. The quotation is from the statutes issued in 1300 by Bishop Walpole regarding the responsibilities of the obedientiaries, Evans, *Ely Chapter Ordinances*, 20.

[264] In 1368/9 the sacrist's officials and staff also included three [secular] chaplains and M. Robert Foxton, his commissary, *custodiens iurisdictionem*, CUL EDC 1/F/10/16.

[265] For the origins and later limits of the sacrist's archidiaconal authority see C. E. Feltoe and E. H. Minns, *Vetus Liber Archidiaconi Eliensis* (Cambridge Antiquarian Society, Cambridge, 1917), xxii; in 1371/2 he received 14s. *de iurisdictione*, CUL EDC 1/F/10/18.

[266] John de Ely IV may be found in *BRECP*, 406–7; the Worcester sacrist/receiver is discussed above 186.

'pocket money'. In 1368/9, for example, he gave to his brethren just over £5 for pittances and £7 13s. *ex graciis*.[267]

The Ely sacrist's high profile in the fourteenth century is in great part due to his responsibility of superintending the *novum opus*, as he named it on his accounts, from 1322/3 onwards. The collapse of the central tower in February 1322, which destroyed the western bays of the Norman choir, occurred only months after the foundation stone of the new free-standing Lady chapel had been laid. The progress and completion of these two ambitious projects, only one of which was essential, were to occupy the recently appointed sacrist, Alan de Walsingham, for the next forty years.[268] The coincidence in timing of the start of the Lady chapel building campaign with the fall of the tower necessitated a lengthy and concerted effort on the part of the monks to finance their construction and reconstruction. Although small sums related to the work on the Lady chapel are occasionally recorded on the sacrist's accounts, his concerns centred on the rebuilding of the choir and construction of the octagon and lantern over the crossing.[269] Funding for these, and other building operations was raised from a number of sources. These included gifts and bequests from two of Ely's contemporary bishops, John de Hotham and Simon de Montacute, public subscription in the diocese and contributions from the prior, obedientiaries, and monks who gave up treats and pocket money to assist in reducing the overdraft.[270] Two other building works came within the sacrist's purview, namely the construction of a new up-to-date sacristy, comprising his office and workshops, which was underway immediately after Walsingham's appointment as sacrist, and the new parish church on the north side of the cathedral towards the cost of which the sacrist, Robert de Sutton, contributed over £28 in 1359/60.[271] In the 1380s the sacrist's attention was directed to the construction of a reredos for the high altar, and the details appear on a separate account compiled by William de Ely; the total cost was just under £167 which was only a few shillings short of the total receipts; among the most generous donors were

---

[267] The statute in question is in Evans, *Ely Chapter Ordinances*, 9, and the sacrist's account for 1368/9 is CUL EDC 1/F/10/16. As there appears to have been no anniversarian at Ely it was the pittancer who provided treats for certain feast days, notably those of St Etheldreda and the Assumption as the sacrist frequently specified, e.g. Chapman, *Sacrist Rolls*, ii, 163, 175, 187.

[268] Walsingham's career is summarized in *BRECP*, 453–4; from 1341 to 1363/4 he was prior. The heading *custos novi operis* on the accounts continued until at least 1373/4 (CUL EDC 1/F/10/19); and in 1386/9 (CUL Add. MS 2956, 162) it was replaced by *de novo opere circa magno altare* for which M. Robert de Wodehirst, described as *magister operum*, received a pension of £4, ibid., and see Harvey, *English Mediaeval Architects*, 342–3. See also Greatrex, 'Marian Studies', 157–67.

[269] Lady chapel expenses occur in CUL EDC 1/F/10/3. For the dramatic account of the untiring efforts of the monk John de Wisbech to bring the Lady chapel to completion see *Anglia Sacra*, i, 651–2 and further details about this monk in *BRECP*, 462.

[270] The exact amount of the bishops' contributions remains uncertain; similarly, the sums collected in the diocese and from named persons are rarely supplied by the sacrist with a few exceptions in the 1320s, Chapman, *Sacrist Rolls*, ii, 36, 51, 63. As to the prior and monks themselves, their contributions are listed in ibid., 26, 36, 50, also in the 1320s, and in 1359/60 when the subprior and others donated £6 3s. 4d., ibid., 185.

[271] Work on the new sacrist's quarters is referred to in 1323/4, Chapman, *Sacrist Rolls*, i. 24–5, ii, 41–3 (1323/4), 54–5 (1325/6) etc. The costs of building materials for the new parish church are itemized in ibid., ii, 193–4; it was dedicated to St Cross or St Peter, ibid., i, 104. For Sutton see *BRECP*, 445–6 (Robert de Sutton I).

Richard II and Bishop Thomas Arundel.[272] Difficulties in the attempt to reconstruct the complex fourteenth-century building programme at Ely have resulted in differences of opinion among architectural and other historians of the cathedral priory.[273] It is abundantly clear, however, despite the poor condition of many of the surviving rolls and the many lacunae, that the sacrist played a major role.

Between the years 1270 and 1420 some twenty Worcester sacrists are known by name, three of whom subsequently became priors. Five other sacrists were also nominated by their brethren for inclusion in the list of approved candidates for the prioral office which was presented to the bishop.[274] Thus it may be inferred that, for the most part, the episcopal appointments to the sacrist's office found favour with the monastic community.[275] The fortunate survival of both episcopal and priory registers, in addition to over five hundred obedientiary account rolls, partially compensates for the disappearance of sacrists' accounts before 1423/4, but the latter is the only account for the entire fifteenth century. Like his fellow sacrists at the other cathedral priories he was responsible for the upkeep of the cathedral, that is its fabric and furnishings. In the 1280s. when the reconstruction of the central tower was an urgent necessity, the sacrist Nicholas de Norton was the grateful recipient of a legacy of 60 marks from the executors of Nicholas de Ely, who had been Worcester's bishop from 1266 to 1268.[276] The deteriorating condition of the cathedral some thirty years later aroused the concern and generosity of the then diocesan, Walter Reynolds, who ordered John de St Briavel to remove the tombs and other objects in the cemetery which were impeding repairs to the exterior; in the following year, 1311, the bishop gave the sacrist £33 6s. 8d. as his contribution to the fabric fund.[277] At about the same time the prior, John de Wyke, authorized St Briavel to contract a loan of £100 *in utilitatem et commodum ecclesie*.[278] Bishop Thomas de

---

[272] CUL Add MS 2956, 162–3; William de Ely I is probably William Powcher, who became prior in 1401, *BRECP*, 410, 431.

[273] The reader is advised to consult Phillip Lindley, 'Architectural Programme at Ely', and the same author's Cambridge University Ph.D. thesis, 'The Monastic Cathedral at Ely, c. 1320 to c. 1350' (1985). Recent monographs on the subject include Nicola Coldstream, 'Ely Cathedral: the Fourteenth-Century Work', in *Medieval Art and Architecture at Ely Cathedral* (British Archaeological Association Conference Transactions, 1979), 28–46 and John Maddison, *Ely Cathedral, Design and Meaning* (Ely Cathedral Publications, Ely, 2000), ch. 5, 61–82.

[274] The sacrists who became priors are William de Cirencester I, Simon Crompe, and John de Malverne, *BRECP*, 785–6, 792–3, 842–4 (John de Malverne I). The five who were nominated but not promoted are Robert de Cliftone II, John de Harleye (nominated on two occasions), John de Lyndeseye (nominated twice), Robert de Weston, Stephen de Wytton, ibid., 789–90, 817, 841, 891–2, 900–1. From the relatively few surviving admission dates for this group they appear to have been senior monks.

[275] John de Powik was a notable exception; see above 198. Another was Nicholas de Norton, sacrist on and off between the late 1270s and 1301; the problem in this second instance seems to have centred mainly on Bishop Godfrey Giffard's irritation at the *sede plene* visitation of Worcester by Archbishop Robert Winchelsey and the latter's imperious overruling of the bishop's authority, *BRECP*, 858–9.

[276] *Annales Wigorn.*, 480; the bishop was transferred to Winchester where he died in 1281. For Norton, see note 275 above.

[277] *Reg. Reynolds*, 17; for St Briavel see *BRECP*, 867–9.

[278] WCM Liber Albus, fo 36v. St Briavel served as receiver of the bishopric, *receptor denariorum* for both Bishop Reynolds and his successor, Walter Maidstone, WRO Reg. Reynolds, fo 37, Reg. Maidstone, fo 41.

Cobham also supported the monks in their building operations and was gratefully remembered as being responsible for the reconstruction of the vaulting of the north aisle of the nave.[279] In 1319 he loaned to the sacrist his share of the offerings at St Wulstan's shrine and left £20 to the fabric in his will.[280]

While later bishops, like Henry de Wakefield, are known to have made contributions towards work on the cathedral it is the sacrist's personal involvement that is of primary concern here.[281] Fortunately, the paucity of evidence in the surviving cathedral priory records is partially compensated, during the episcopates of William de Lynn and Wakefield, by a document entitled *Chronologia Edificiarum*; it was copied into a priory register of *miscellanea*, mainly of the sixteenth century with some earlier material such as this item, which names John de Lyndeseye, sacrist, in the left margin.[282] He supervised an extensive building programme for which responsibility was shared with the cellarer.[283] The *Chronologia* attributes to Lyndeseye the completion of the new central bell tower in 1374 together with *unum orologium, clocke vulgariter nuncupatum*. The following year he *fecit* (?completed) a new vault and window in the chapel of St Mary Magdalene, and work on the new choir stalls was begun. The next undertaking was the vault over the choir under the bell tower and a new vault and windows for St Thomas's chapel. This was followed by new vaulting over the nave in 1377 and, in 1379 by the installation of the choir stalls and the new decorative paving in the two chapels named above. Finally, in 1380/1 Lyndeseye saw to the construction of an enclosure/screen between the choir and the presbytery, a new west window in the nave and work over against the enclosure/screen around the Lady chapel situated next to the red door.[284] There is an additional note to the effect that on the night of the feast of St Thomas the Apostle (21 December), 1381, with the new lectern in place in the [upper] choir, the lessons that had been read in the lower choir for twenty-five years were for the first time read in the new location. The summary in this register is the unique record of the culmination of an extensive and prolonged building programme, but details of the financial outlay are lacking.

Feretrars and shrine keepers

The obedientiary office of shrine keeper, or feretrar, where it existed within the cathedral priories, developed in the way best suited to meet the needs of the

---

[279] Willis, *Architectural History*, ii, 108 quoting Leland.

[280] *Reg. Cobham*, 21, 49.

[281] Wakefield was bishop from 1375 to 1395; his contributions are discussed in Willis, *Architectural History*, ii, 113–14. Engel, *Worcester Cathedral*, 182, summarizes funding details.

[282] WCM, Reg. A.12, fo 77v; this document has been copied by antiquarians and extracts have been printed, as, for example, Willis, *Architectural History*, ii, 109 and Appendix, 315–16.

[283] The Worcester cellarer was the equivalent of the bursar or the treasurer at other cathedral priories; however, the cellarer's accounts only provide information about the work being carried out in the monastic buildings excluding the cathedral church.

[284] WCM Reg. A.12, fo 77v; *clausura* here probably means screen. The Lady chapel next to the red door was the nave altar on the west side of the screen; see *Liber Pensionum*, no. 153 and Atkins, *Office of Organist*, 4–7.

particular community. It appears to have been absent at Bath, Coventry, Norwich, and Rochester, whose misfortune it was to lack sufficiently noteworthy saints to attract a significant number of worshippers and pilgrims. The boy martyr William, reputed to have been murdered at the hands of the Jews in 1144 at Norwich, and the baker William from Perth, murdered near Rochester in 1201 while en route to the Holy Land, became the focus of local cults that drew a mere handful of devotees. Their shrines were cared for by the sacrists; the one early sixteenth-century account that survives at Rochester records the receipts of offerings amounting to 36s. 5d. at the tomb of St William and in the chest of *beate Marie*.[285] The shrine of William of Norwich never became more than a minor centre of attraction; with the exception of a brief and unexplained surge in offerings between *c*. 1385/6 and 1414/15, whenever the sacrist provides precise figures for oblations received at each of the collection points in the cathedral the amounts for St William were generally less than £1, in contrast to the £25 to £60 receipts at the high altar.[286] The shrine of St Swithun, bishop of Winchester before his death in 862, was never a mere locally popular cult.[287] Miraculous cures were associated with his relics from an early period and his fame is reputed to have reached Norway in the twelfth century.[288] However, there is no evidence of a feretrar and there are no sacrist's accounts until 1536/7 in which a single entry records that 'de oblationibus ad scrinium S. Swithini hoc anno nihil'.[289]

The earliest known feretrars at Canterbury were Roger de Wrotham, who shared the office with Robert Poucyn in 1287/8, but the first and only account that has been preserved is dated over a century later. In 1397/8 the two feretrars recorded that the total receipts from the offerings at Becket's shrine were just short of £250, some of which was distributed to their brethren in the form of spices, wine, pittances, and oblations on various feasts during the year, notably those associated with St Thomas.[290] Like the *custodes* of the other three locations in the cathedral dedicated to the saint, they turned in their receipts to the treasurers, among whose assignments was the allocation of funds to several of the obedientiaries who were dependent on these distributions to alleviate their financial problems.[291] In the 1390s the changes effected by Thomas Chillenden as prior led to a reduction in the power exercised by the treasurers, with the result that these distributions were meted out by the prior himself. However, in 1397/8 the feretrars seem to be making payments directly to the same group of obedientiaries without recourse to

---

[285] CKS DRc/M7; two seventh-century Rochester bishops, Sts Paulinus of York and Ithamar may have been lost to sight.
[286] See the table in Nilson, *Cathedral Shrines*, 218–19.
[287] The architectural history of the shrine from the late tenth century until its destruction in 1539 is reconstructed by John Crook 'St. Swithun of Winchester', 57–68, in Crook, *Winchester Cathedral*.
[288] See *BRECP*, 729 under Reinald, the Winchester monk who is supposed to have carried a relic of the saint to Stavanger.
[289] This sacrist's account is transcribed in Kitchin and Madge, *Documents of Winchester*, 21.
[290] CCA DCc feretrars' account 1.
[291] Ibid., and treasurers' accounts 1, 2, 3, 5; the obedientiaries receiving 'handouts' were generally the cellarer, chamberlain, sacrist, and the prior's chaplain.

the prior or treasurers.[292] A customary of St Thomas Becket was compiled in 1428 by the sacrist John Viel and the *custos martyrii*, Edmund Kyngston, who were presumably responding to the need for clear and precise regulations to be observed. All the obedientiaries and monks who were charged with responsibilities concerning the sites within the cathedral church where the saint was revered by pilgrims and other members of the public were involved; and the regulations included round-the-clock assignments of monks to watch beside the holy places.[293] The cults of three other archbishops recognized as saints, Dunstan, Elphege, and Anselm, were all but eclipsed by Becket.[294]

As at Christ Church Canterbury there were two feretrars at Durham, one of them being described as *socius*. Names of monks serving in this office have been identified from 1300 onwards, but the earliest known *socius* dates from 1375, four years before the earliest extant account. There is no evidence to suggest that the relationship between the feretrar and his *socius* took the form of obedientiary and deputy or assistant, although the relatively few instances when both names are known would suggest that the *socius* was usually slightly younger, and only two of them went on to be appointed feretrar.[295] Except in the plague years and their immediate aftermath both were senior monks, usually with twenty or more years of monastic life behind them. Their responsibilities were centred almost exclusively on the care of the shrine and relics of St Cuthbert, the seventh-century monk and bishop of Lindisfarne; after three centuries of being conveyed from place to place his body found a permanent home in Durham where it was installed in its prepared shrine in 1104 in the new Norman cathedral. The saint's cult flourished, providing a variable but satisfactory income which was the feretrars' sole source of revenue before 1385; rents from a few tenements gave a small increase after that date.[296] Donations placed in the pyx at the shrine were collected at irregular but frequent intervals and the receipts, recorded by the *socius*, averaged between £28 and £35 per annum between 1376/7 and 1419/20.[297] Two-thirds or more of this amount was distributed among the brethren on five feasts during the year.[298] Only the monks who were resident at Durham at the time a distribution was made were recipients, as the record of the individual names together with the sums received makes clear; it

---

[292] See the sacrist's account rolls in the 1390s, e.g. CCA DCc 10, 11, 9 etc., and the account of the chamberlain, ibid., 56. The direct transfer of money from the feretrars was in operation by and probably long before 1428 when the customary records it.

[293] For Viel and Kyngeston see *BRECP*, 310, 214–15. The customary is in BL Add MS 59616, fos 1–11; see also Turner in *Canterbury Cathedral Chronicle*, no. 70, 16–22.

[294] Archbishop Elphege was also a martyr, having been murdered by the Danes in 1012.

[295] The two were John de Allerton and John Durham senior, *LVD*, iii, C.954 and C.1009; these facts and figures apply only to the period under study. The list of feretrars known by name is in ibid., i, 497–8.

[296] Fowler, *Account Rolls*, ii, 441, under receipts.

[297] The pyx collection dates for 1375/6 are given in Fowler, ibid., ii, 420, where they numbered nineteen; different dates are given on two other surviving lists on the feretrars' accounts for 1379/80 and 1381/2A. Annual shrine receipts are provided by Nilson in *Cathedral Shrines*, 226–7, where two exceptionally large sums are noted: over £63 in 1385/6 and £56 in 1400/1.

[298] The feasts, named on the 1376/7 account, were St Peter *ad vincula*, St Cuthbert in September, All Saints, the Purification, the *inventio sancte crucis*; see Fowler, *Account Rolls*, 421.

is also clear that the variation in the amounts paid—between 4s. and 1s.—were dependent on the order of seniority.[299] Although the expenditures necessary for the maintenance of the shrine were on the whole relatively minor, several accounts reveal that the feretrars were sometimes slightly in the red, and they appear to have had recourse to borrowing small sums from some of their fellow monks and to repaying these debts within a year or two. There were eighteen named 'lenders' in 1381/2, but the details on the following year's account suggests that these debts may have been the acknowledgement of sums that had not been paid at the time of one or more of the distribution dates.[300]

Named Ely feretrars are few and far between. The earliest so far identified is Robert de Rykelyng in 1322/3 and, between his appearance and that of John de Yaxham a century later on the earliest extant account, only seven feretrars have come to light.[301] The presence of a feretrar in 1314 is confirmed by one of the chapter ordinances issued that year. It concerned the sacrist, feretrar, and *custos altaris beate Marie* who were together to account for offerings received at the shrines in the church and, after deducting his expenses, the feretrar was to turn over the remainder to the sacrist.[302] The payments from the offerings made at the shrine of St Etheldreda are recorded on several occasions by the sacrist, for example, in 1349/50 and 1352/3 through John de Croxton and twice in the 1370s through Simon de Banham.[303] These entries on the sacrist's account rolls continued until at least 1406/7 which suggests that the feretrar was not an accounting obedientiary before that date; the transition, therefore, may have taken place around that year or sometime between then and 1421.[304]

The shrine keepers at Worcester were known as tomb keepers, about twenty of whom have been identified between *c.* 1290 and *c.* 1420. In the 1290s the money collected *de feretris et tumbis* is an item in the receipts section on the account of the bursar/cellarer.[305] This entry disappears and, at an unknown date, a division of responsibility was introduced, with the shrine offerings, that is those in the pyx before the image of St Mary going to the sacrist and those at the tombs of Sts Oswald and Wulstan to the *tumbarius*. The guardianship of the shrine and tomb of St Wulstan had been one of several matters in dispute between the bishop, William

---

[299] An account of *c.* 1410, containing five lists of names for the five distributions shows the prior's share as 20s., that of the subprior 6s. 8d. and of novices 1s., and varying amounts in between for the other monks. The names and amounts paid at the feast of St Peter are printed by Fowler, ibid., ii, 457. The feretrars' account of 1407/8 also has lists of names.

[300] DCM feretrars' accounts for 1381/2A, 1382/3.

[301] Both monks are in *BRECP*: Rykelyng, 435 and Yaxham, 465.

[302] Evans, *Ely Chapter Ordinances*, 39.

[303] CUL EDC 1/F/10/11, 12 and Chapman, *Sacrist Rolls*, ii, 147, 149; CUL EDC 1/F/10/18 (1371/2), 1/F/10/19 (1374/5). See *BRECP*, 402 (Croxton), 389–90 (Banham).

[304] The earliest surviving feretrar's account is dated 1421, CUL EDC 1/F/11/1. In 1406/7 Edmund de Thomeston was feretrar, CUL EDC 1/F/10/26; see also *BRECP*, 450.

[305] WCM C.52, dated 1294/5 and transcribed in Wilson, *Early Compotus Rolls*, the reference being on p. 27; on the two previous accounts of 1291/2 (C.51) and 1293/4 (C.51a) *de feretris* alone is used but presumably includes both, ibid., 11, 17. In all three instances the money was delivered *per* a named monk whom I have taken to be a *tumbarius*; see *BRECP*, 773, 839 under Laurence de Badminton and William de London.

de Blois, and the prior and chapter. The settlement in 1224 decreed that the offerings were to be divided equally between the two parties who were each to appoint a reliable monk or clerk to look after their interest.[306] How this division of responsibility evolved in practice, however, is far from clear. Examples of the process by which later episcopal appointments were made show the bishops asserting their right, and they seem to have consistently chosen monks. In the case of John de Hethe, who was dismissed in September 1313, Bishop Reynolds required him to hand over the shrine accounts for the period in which he held office, and the bishop's official and the prior were to act jointly to remove him and appoint a suitable replacement.[307] Only a few months later Bishop Maidstone ordered the removal of John de Briera, who had presumably been Hethe's successor, and the appointment of Roger de Stevintone.[308] In January 1318 Bishop Cobham, being in London, commissioned the prior to appoint on his behalf one of the monks *ad custodiendum feretrum*; writing from Cambridge in December he commissioned his official to make Nicholas de Bradefeld *tumbarius* and order the obedience of the prior and monks. A marginal addition in the episcopal register notes that on this occasion the bishop had acted 'preter et contra voluntatem prioris et conventus'.[309] The specific cause of friction remains unknown. Adam Orleton, Cobham's successor, directed his vicar-general on two occasions to appoint a *custos* of the shrines of the two saints, as did Wulstan de Bransford during his episcopate in the 1340s and John Thoresby in 1351.[310] The appointment of John Thwarton[er] by Bishop Henry Wakefield in 1388 as his choice for one of the two custodians of the shrines fortunately coincides with the third of the surviving obedientiary accounts of the *tumbarius*.[311] John de Teukesbury, who was presumably the monk's choice, appears on the head of the account rolls from 1388 to 1391. He had been a monk for more than thirty years; John Thwarton[er], however, is almost an unknown member of the monastic community, making an appearance only once on the chamberlain's account in 1389/90 because new boots were being made for him. It is to be assumed that these two monks, like their predecessors who had shared the office, would have had some need to co-operate. The accounts are regrettably unhelpful in this respect and, indeed, in virtually all matters pertaining to the shrines. In 1388/9, for example, rents and pensions together made up the total receipts of just over £8; about half of this sum was spent in the provision of wax and production of candles and there were also small expenditures for the maintenance and repair of the shrines.[312] The last extant account of the *tumbarius*, dated 1521/2,

[306] *Acta Stephani Langton*, Appendix iii, 160–3.
[307] *Reg. Reynolds*, 72, 77; for Hethe see *BRECP*, 822.
[308] WRO Reg. Maidstone, fo 5. For Briera and Stevintone see *BRECP*, 780, 877.
[309] *Reg. Cobham*, 5, 13–14; for Bradefeld see *BRECP*, 779. Who would have inserted this critical comment?
[310] *Reg. Orleton*, item 549 (1328), and item 943 in *Reg. Montacute* (1333) where it must have been copied, but is not found in Orleton's register; *Reg. Bransford*, items 599 (1344) and 1001 (1349); WRO Reg. Thoresby, fo 58.
[311] *Reg. Wakefield*, item 795 where the name is spelt Thwartoneys; see also *BRECP*, 884.
[312] WCM C.455. Teukesbury seems to have kept bees for several years to augment the supply of wax, ibid., and C.457, 458.

records the receipt of 7s. in oblations 'ad tumba sanctorum Oswaldi et Wulstani', a sharp contrast to the oblations reported by the sacrist from St Mary's pyx.[313]

Cellarers, kitcheners, and refectorers: the domestic scene

As the monk responsible for the monastery's sustenance the cellarer was a key functionary from the earliest times. The qualities required for the holder of this office and the duties involved were spelled out in detail by St Benedict himself in chapter 31 of the Rule. The material welfare of the brethren had to take into account both the young and the old, the strong and healthy, and the weak and frail with a constant concern to provide for their individual needs with consideration and solicitude. These prescriptions would appear to restrict this position to senior monks of mature and equable temperament; indeed, as far as surviving records show, the majority of the cathedral priory cellarers in the fourteenth and fifteenth centuries were experienced monks whose appointments were commonly for no more than two to four years at a time.[314] Surviving accounts of these cellarers reveal only the general outlines of their responsibilities and activities which are brought to light at Ely, and Norwich from the 1280s, and at Durham from 1307/8.[315] It has been explained above that the office of cellarer at Winchester was tied to that of curtarian and that the Worcester cellarer was equivalent to the bursar or treasurer elsewhere.[316] The earliest remaining cellarer's account at Christ Church Canterbury is dated 1391, the year in which Thomas Chillenden was elected prior and began implementing a reform of the priory's financial system by assuming the role of a prior cum treasurer.[317] This arrangement had the effect of greatly increasing the cellarer's financial dependence on the prior, a situation similar to that already present at Durham, Ely, and Rochester, all of whom were already receiving the major portion of their funding from their bursar or treasurer.[318] The Norwich cellarer derived his income from the manors, churches, and rents attached to his office. There was a sizeable staff employed by the cellarers including cooks, workers in the pantry, larder, bakery, and brewery as well as gardeners and carters and boatmen delivering supplies.[319] Some of the Durham, Ely, and Norwich accounts

---

[313] Wilson, *Accounts...for Henry VIII*, 25, 36; the pyx receipts were over £11, ibid., 37.

[314] This frequent turnover may well imply that the cellarers found themselves shouldering an exceptionally heavy burden of responsibility. However, the Ely monk Alexander de Bury and the Norwich monk John de Carleton remained in office for most of the 1380s; see *BRECP*, 395 (Bury) and 491 (Carleton).

[315] William IV was cellarer at Rochester around 1100, *BRECP*, 648. Cellarers at Bath and Coventry are known from the early and late thirteenth century respectively; see Urban II, *BRECP*, 45 and Henry de Stratton, ibid., 370–1.

[316] See above 164–6.

[317] By 1396 the cellarer was in receipt of £658 from the prior out of his total receipts of £700, CCA DCc cellarer's accounts 1 and 2. It is to be noted that the Canterbury cellarer replaced the hostiller elsewhere.

[318] There is only one extant cellarer's roll from Rochester, dated 1383/4.

[319] For example, at Norwich in the 1380s the cellarer paid over £15 in stipends, NRO DCN 1/2/26, 1/2/27, 1/2/28.

include a so-called diet or kitchen account itemizing weekly and monthly expenditures on food along with other interesting details that will be treated below.[320]

Surviving account rolls of a kitchener and a refectorer at Worcester cathedral priory provide insights into the functioning of the main kitchen in the monastery, and into the role of the refectorer who concerned himself with matters pertaining to the dining hall (*frater*) or refectory. The kitchener's yearly income, from manors, rents, and fishing weirs, fluctuated around the £200 mark in the fourteenth century, and several accounts provide details of the weekly expenditures that were required to feed the brethren. In 1386/7, for example, the amounts varied from 53s. 6d. for an ordinary week to over £4 when the bishop or other important guests were being entertained.[321] Two cooks were on his payroll as well as a boatman *ad portam Sabrine*, a swineherd, a part-time dairymaid and women to clean the larder. His purchases ranged from livestock to pepper and other spices, and included frequent replacements of kitchen utensils.[322] Many of the twenty-four kitcheners known by name between the late thirteenth and early fifteenth centuries also served their turn in the offices of cellarer or subcellarer or both. Since these obedientiaries were together responsible for procuring and supplying the monastic community at Worcester with the food necessary for the physical well-being of all its members, the experience gained in any one of the three offices would have proved profitable in the other two.[323] The Worcester refectorers remain largely hidden from view; only three have been identified by name and only two fourteenth-century accounts survive, both dated in the 1390s and both very brief. In 1393/4 rents, pensions, and tithes and the sale of two drinking cups netted Thomas atte More £4 which he spent on repairs to the refectory windows, table linen, new drinking vessels, and the repair of damaged ones, and wax and candles.[324]

Several of the other cathedral priories mention monk kitcheners who do not appear to have been accounting officials in their own right. At Christ Church Canterbury, for example, Thomas de Holyngborne was appointed in 1330, but the kitchen account for the priory constituted a section on the cellarer's account; the kitchener must, therefore, have been subservient to the cellarer and possibly

---

[320] See below 242–3 where the surviving late fifteenth-century Winchester diet roll will also receive attention.

[321] WCM C.121; this account has been transcribed in Hamilton, *Compotus Rolls*, 24–6, with the dating given incorrectly as 1387/8. The weeks are distinguished by means of the opening words of the Sunday introit. The season of Lent was also a period of higher expenditure WCM C.111, 120, 121, 123. About thirty accounts survive between 1326/7 and 1420/1; but the earliest known kitchener is John de Gloucestre II in 1298, *BRECP*, 810.

[322] WCM C.109a, 114, 116, 120 etc. Some of the animals destined for the larder were housed within the monastic precinct; see my article 'The Layout of Worcester'.

[323] Although the Worcester cellarer was the equivalent of the bursar or treasurer elsewhere his accounts show that he was also concerned with some of the domestic requirements of the community such as expenses of entertaining guests and visiting officials and regular payments to the kitchener and to the prior to augment their income. Some of his responsibilities will receive further attention in the next chapter.

[324] WCM C.416, 417; the three refectorers are Thomas atte More I, Roger de Evesham, and John de Legh II, all in *BRECP*, 847, 805, 835 respectively. The next account is dated 1431/2.

equivalent to subcellarers elsewhere.[325] A similar situation prevailed at Durham where the cellarer's accounts give weekly and monthly kitchen accounts of expenditures.[326] Durham refectorers were dependent on the bursar for a small pension to meet their few obligations. Since their office was unendowed they were exempt from producing an annual account. Many of their needs in the refectory such as candles, and the expenses involved in the washing of tablecloths and napkins, were borne by other obedientiaries.[327] At Ely a single named kitchener occurs in 1319; and an unidentified kitchener is referred to on the kitchen section of the cellarer's 1334 account because he was responsible for purchasing large quantities of eggs, a task that could well have been performed by a lay servant called by the same name.[328] The names of three Ely refectorers appear in the treasurers' accounts and other records between the 1320s and 1420s. The properties by which the office was financed are recorded in a fourteenth century priory cartulary and, although a chapter ordinance of 1314 required the refectorer to submit an inventory of the plate in his care at the annual audit, no accounts have been found.[329] Monk kitcheners occur at Winchester during the fourteenth century, as regular entries on the hordarian's account *in solutis coquinariis* (or *coquinario*); these involve large sums amounting to nearly £250 in the 1330s but decreasing to £182 by 1382.[330] From this latter date onward the payments continue, but to the *coquina* in place of the *coquinarius* and, apart from the identification of Thomas Newton as kitchener in 1393, it seems likely that the hordarian's *coquinarius* was not always a monk.[331] There are also two refectorers in the fourteenth century whose names have come to light, but the presence of this obedientiary is well attested in a surviving undated fourteenth-century customary for the refectory.[332]

---

[325] For Holyngborne see *BRECP*, 203 and much earlier a Hugh de Geround in 1224/5, ibid., 167; no subcellarers have been found at Christ Church. As for refectorers only three early thirteenth-century names have been found and two accounts of the same period.

[326] Fowler, *Account Rolls*, i, 1–55, provides some inaccurately dated extracts from the cellarer's accounts. For the refectorer see DCM bursar's accounts for 1351/2A, 1360/1A, 1374/5A etc.

[327] Between 1300 and 1416 fourteen refectorers' names have come to light, the earliest being William de Dalton, *LVD*, i, 500; the bursar paid 3s. 4d. twice a year to the refectorer from at least 1300/1 onwards, DCM bursar's accounts. The cellarer bought wax and candles for the refectory in 1329/30, 1348/9, and 1377/8 and other years, and the hostiller bought twelve pewter vessels in 1357/8 and 1392/3 DCM accounts for these years. A notice in *Cat. Vet. Durham*, 107O¹, states that a manuscript containing the life of St Ebbe was in the monk's refectory in 1416.

[328] The kitchener is Richard de Spalding, q.v. in *BRECP*, 441, and the cellarer's account for 1334, CUL EDC 1/F/2/2.

[329] See under John de Ramesey II, Ralph de Stisted, John de Bukton II in *BRECP*, 432, 442, 394; the cartulary is EDR G/3/28, Liber M p. 407 et seq., and the ordinance will be found in Evans, *Ely Chapter Ordinances*, 40–1, where it is also stated that, as at Norwich, the mazers and spoons were in his care.

[330] Kitchin, *Obedientiary Rolls*, 262, 265, 268, 271, 274, 279; the name of an earlier kitchener is recorded in *BRECP*, Robert de Godeshulle (*c.* 1311/12), 695. There are also two incomplete rolls of diet accounts dated 1492/3 and *c.* 1514/15, ibid., 307–62.

[331] For Newton see *BRECP*, 722.

[332] Kitchin, *Consuetudinary*, 15–47 *passim*; his needs were at least partially provided for by the chamberlain and curtarian and therefore he, too, may have been exempt from the annual audit, WCL W53/14/2, 9, 10. In the *Consuetudinary* there is mention of a kitchener, who sat at the high table and was, therefore, at the time of its composition, presumably a monk, ibid., 18. The presence of the two refectorers, in 1393 and 1450, is noted in *BRECP*, 752, 728 under Henry de Wynchestre and John Redyng II.

Kitchen expenses and weekly diet accounts are included on the Norwich cellarer's accounts with no reference to a kitchener, but the refectorer's presence is well attested by a collection of some seventy account rolls between 1289 and 1420. The sphere of authority of the twenty-six refectorers who have been identified was largely confined to the monastic dining hall. Receipts from tithes, rents, and sales of grain, hay, and drinking cups provided a small but adequate income that varied between under £5 and over £20 per annum and allowed them to make small payments to the infirmarer on a number of occasions.[333] Their expenditures included the purchase of cups, plates, knives, silver spoons, tablecloths, and towels, and a supply of almonds to mitigate the annual Lenten fast. In 1336/7 Thomas de Brok was moved to write, or to have written, at the head of his account 'Adiutorium nostrum in nomine domini qui fecit celum et terram'.[334] Regulations for the rota of weekly readers during meals in the refectory were laid down by St Benedict in chapter thirty-eight of the Rule. He does not specify who was to be responsible for preparing the list of readers and choosing the texts to be read, but he does refer to the use of sign language at table when necessary in order to ensure that strict silence was kept. Several extant Norwich manuscripts contain directions that point to their having been among the books selected for use in the refectory. A volume of patristic homilies, for example, states the day and time for some of the readings (*lectiones*), the lengthy sermons being divided into sections and later marginal annotations such as *in cena domini ad prandium* provided. Another similar volume also contains sermons by the founding monk Bishop Herbert de Losinga. These two homiliaries were survivors of the 1272 fire, but a third book also contains evidence of use for reading aloud, probably in the refectory; it is a fifteenth-century *Vitas Patrum* which displays red stress marks to indicate correct accentuation.[335] Of the remaining three cathedral priories Rochester, with the exception of William de Bradebourne, is bereft of any evidence of the existence of either a monk kitchener or refectorer. Coventry appears to lack a monk kitchener, but had John Volney as refectorer in 1409. Bath designated a monk named Walter as refectorer in 1206 and another Walter as *quisinarius* in 1242, and a third monk was named *coquinarius* in 1412.[336] No further evidence has yet been found.

The obedientiary offices of anniversarian, pittancer, and communar

These three obedientiaries, of whom one or two occur in most of the cathedral priories, were largely but not exclusively concerned with periodic distributions in cash and kind to their brethren. The pittances and treats were given out in

---

[333] E.g., NRO DCN 1/8/31 (1333/4), 1/8/33 (1334/5), 1/8/36 (1345/6), 1/8/43 (1369/70), 1/8/47 (1386/7). It is possible that these were not donations but payments for some unspecified cause; however, the amounts vary and, though frequent, are irregular.

[334] NRO DCN 1/8/35; it is the final verse of Psalm 123/124; for Brok see *BRECP*, 488.

[335] The two sermon volumes are now CUL MSS Kk.4.13 and Ii.2.19; the *Vitas Patrum* is Cambridge, Corpus Christi College MS 36. All three are briefly described by Ker in 'Manuscripts from Norwich', 255–6, 263. See also Tolhurst, *Norwich Customary*, 198.

[336] Volney is in *BRECP*, 372; Walter V, ibid., 46; Walter VII, ibid., John Norton II, ibid., 35.

celebration of certain feasts, anniversaries, and commemorations; and, therefore, the particular responsibilities involved on the part of each of the three will be more fully treated in the next chapter which follows the order of the liturgical seasons.

Anniversarians are found at Canterbury and Winchester; at Christ Church there were generally two monks named on the head of the account rolls, while at Winchester the rolls have confusingly given him the title of *custos* of the manor of Bushton (Wilts) which was the chief source of his income.[337] Pittancers are known at Bath, Ely, Norwich, Worcester, and Coventry; and at Coventry the institution of the office was attributed to prior William de Brythwalton (1249–80) although the first pittancer known by name does not appear until 1390.[338] There are no pittancer's accounts at Bath and the earliest name that occurs is John Lacok in 1447; of the two surviving Coventry accounts the earlier is dated 1478/9.[339] The fourteenth century Ely accounts reveal that the pittancer frequently had a *socius* whose name was also recorded on the head of the roll, but the office itself was in place as early as 1233.[340] Nicholas de Bradefeld, the first known pittancer at Worcester, appears in 1314/15, some twenty-five years before the earliest surviving account of which there are thirty before 1420.[341] Thomas de Rillington held the office of communar at Durham in 1303 and some twenty of his successors have been identified before the earliest of the few surviving accounts in 1416.[342] The Norwich pittancer and communar are best described as linked in an anomalous partnership. As Fernie and Whittingham observed, the communar had 'an extremely varied round of duties' which often appeared to overlap with those of fellow obedientiaries when, for instance, he footed the bill for some of the monks' travel expenses and made payments to monk students at Oxford. There was only one account, although it was often divided into two separate sections. The names of two monks head the joint accounts in the 1290s, but the later accounts record only one. Those of the Norwich communar reveal that he was the obedientiary most heavily involved in the building works undertaken in the precinct in the late thirteenth century and through much of the fourteenth century.[343]

---

[337] The earliest surviving account roll of the Canterbury anniversarian is dated 1348/9 but only three others survive between that date and 1420/1. Winchester accounts are more numerous—from 1369/70 to 1427 a total of ten remain, most of them to be found among the Worcester cathedral muniments. There were mid-thirteenth-century holders of this office at both priories, for example, John de London I and Henry Stordy at Canterbury and Philip Trenchefoil at Winchester, *BRECP*, 224, 294, 740.

[338] See *BRECP*, 348 for Brythwalton and ibid., 347 for the earliest named pittancer, John de Bromlegh in 1390; the reference to the institution of the office is not in *BRECP* but in LRO Reg. Burghill, fo 123.

[339] For John Lacok, *BRECP*, 32–3; in 1478/9 he is listed as holding three offices: those of the refectorer and infirmarer as well as pittancer.

[340] Ely pittancer's accounts number ten between 1309/10 and 1420; the earliest known pittancer is named simply N., in a cartulary, *BRECP*, 426.

[341] Bradefeld is in *BRECP*, 778–9.

[342] For Rillington see *LVD*, iii, C.759 and for the list of communars ibid., i, 496.

[343] Fernie and Wittingham, *Communar Rolls*, contains a transcription of the account rolls from 1282/3 to 1329/30 with a lengthy introduction that convincingly resolves many of the apparent contradictions and also describes the later building programme as recorded in the later fourteenth- and early fifteenth-century communar accounts; the quotation is on p. 11. The two monks named in the 1290s are Elyas de Hoxne and Roger de Dorobina; see *BRECP*, 526, 502.

Priors and obedientiaries of the dependent cells

Among the cathedral priories there were three kinds of dependent priories, or cells, distinguished by their relationship with their 'mother' house. The most straightforward was that in which the cathedral and chapter exercised unlimited overall authority over their cells as was the case with regard to Durham, Norwich, Bath, and Rochester; the second was a more discrete or detached relationship which was expressed in the degree of independence allowed or asserted, as seen in the connection between Christ Church Canterbury and Dover; the third is best described as little more than a monastic presence in properties and establishments in southern Ireland where both Bath and Canterbury had acquired possessions.[344] Coventry, Ely, Winchester, and Worcester had no dependencies in the period under study although there has been some confusion about the status of Little Malvern priory *vis-à-vis* Worcester whose relationship is at best uncertain.[345] The Ely connection with Spinney and Mullicourt as dependent cells does not predate the mid-fifteenth century. The aim of this section is to examine briefly the way in which these relationships worked out in practice.[346]

Durham

In addition to Durham College Oxford there were eight priories or cells dependent on Durham cathedral priory. When they were founded or refounded in the eleventh and twelfth centuries it was an era of generous individual benefactions and of general goodwill and mutual co-operation between monks and their secular neighbours. From the late thirteenth century onwards, however, the small monastic outposts, though operating as cells, were primarily concerned with the supervision of the local estates pertaining to the mother house. These remote properties tended to become more of a liability than an asset and most of the cells experienced difficulties in striving to maintain the financial independence from the mother house that was expected of them.[347] There was little if anything else, however, in which the cells were allowed to exercise any independence of judgement or action.[348] Nevertheless, in practical terms

---

[344] The Oxford colleges established for the monks of Canterbury and Durham were also dependencies but have been discussed above, 126–30.

[345] The fact that two Worcester monks, John de Dumbleton in 1299 and Richard de Wenlok in 1379, were appointed or licensed by the bishop to go to Little Malvern as prior does not imply dependent status; see *BRECP*, 800, 890.

[346] For a comparative study covering all the English dependent priories see Heale, *Dependent Priories*.

[347] In addition, a chapter ordinance of 1308 required most of the cells to pay an annual *auxilium* to the mother house, Foster, 'Durham Priory', 93. Barrie Dobson's lucid chapter on the Durham cells in his *Durham Priory*, 297–320 is to be highly recommended, and I gratefully acknowledge my reliance on some of his conclusions. He makes the important point that the 'Durham monks, with their obsessive interest in the traditional liberties and possessions of Saint Cuthbert's church, were naturally devoted to the preservation . . . of their cells', ibid., 297.

[348] By the terms of *Le Convenit* of 1229 the prior of Durham had the right to appoint and remove all obedientiaries including the priors of cells situated within the diocese of Durham; for *Le Convenit* see above 11.

the more distant cells could adapt some of the prescribed *dicta* to suit their own perceived best interests. With an average community of less than half a dozen monks the full implementation of all the *minutiae* to be observed for the correct performance of the divine office as well as the responsibility of the administration of the cell and its estates could prove a formidable challenge.

At least two-thirds of the monks who were professed at Durham between 1270 and 1420 were sent by the prior to spend a year or more away from the mother house in one of the cells.[349] This frequent to-ing and fro-ing between Durham and the cells was no doubt beneficial to the community resident in Durham, which suffered less from inner tensions than monasteries without dependent priories. There is abundant evidence of these journeys of monks to and from the cells in obedience to the prior because their travelling costs appear on the bursar's accounts. Younger monks may not have always enjoyed being posted far from the mother house, but some older monks were content to retire in one of them as did Richard de Whitworth at Coldingham in 1325 and Robert de Walworth at Finchale in 1391 and at Jarrow three years later.[350] Despite the long journeys involved the priors of cells took an active part in the affairs of the mother house. They were expected to attend the annual chapter at Durham and render their accounts, and they were summoned to episcopal and prioral elections. The priors of Coldingham and Finchale were chosen to be *compromissori* in the 1313 election of Prior Geoffrey de Burdon and six of the priors voted in the 1381 episcopal election.[351] Episcopal visitations of Durham priory were considered of less consequence and were often, in fact, endured with a bare semblance of good will. In response to the bishop's citation to the effect that all monks, no matter where they were located, were to appear before him, the Durham prior's polite but firm rejoinder was invariably to the effect that it was necessary for a few monks to remain in the cells 'ad deserviendum deo et beato Cuthberto' and 'ad custodiendam cellam . . . et celebranda divina officia'.[352] There is some slight evidence of visitation of the cells by the prior of Durham as, for example, in Prior William de Cowton's notice of his proposed visit to Coldingham in 1330.[353] References to problems within the cells are noted from time to time: a chapter ordinance of 1316 admonished the priors and master of cells to treat their fellow monks *curialiter et humane* and the latter to be obedient *humiliter*; and an episcopal visitation of the cathedral priory in Prior Cowton's day exposed the neglect and lack of care given to sick monks in the cells.[354]

---

[349] The known priors, obedientiaries, and monks of the cells are listed by name in *LVD*, i, 503–16.
[350] DCM Priory Reg. II, fos 88v, 313–313v; Whitworth and Walworth are in *LVD*, iii at C.796 and C.903 respectively.
[351] DCM Priory Reg. II, fos 16v, 198v; for Burdon see *LVD*, iii, C.731.
[352] DCM Priory Reg. II, fos 105, 262; nevertheless, in 1381 at the election of John Fordham as bishop seven priors were present, ibid., fo 204.
[353] Ibid., fo 100v, DCM Misc. Charter 2645; Cowton's career is in *LVD*, iii, C.768.
[354] Durham Locellus XXVII, 16c., Misc. Charter 2645. Accusations of maladministration also occur and were dealt with, e.g. DCM Reg. Hatfield, fo 23v. In 1354, William de Goldsborough was sent to Coldingham to oversee corrections after visitation, DCM 2.8.Pont.9; for Goldsborough see *LVD*, iii, C.843.

The most remote was the priory of Coldingham situated in the Scottish borders north of Berwick and therefore subject to the jurisdiction of the bishop of St Andrews to authorize the admission of the prior and obedientiaries appointed by the prior of Durham.[355] Priors known by name are plentiful from the 1270s on and also some sacrists as well as a few almoners; the latter two offices were sometimes in the hands of one monk because there were rarely more than three monks in the cell in addition to the prior.[356] The choice of priors was confined to senior monks who had usually demonstrated their competence in previous appointments at Durham and occasionally in other cells; and their average stay at Coldingham was from about seven to ten years. Longer appointments, such as that of John de Aycliffe between 1396 and 1416, were probably broken by periods of absence.[357] There were two brief but dramatic sojourns as prior, those of Robert de Graystanes, for whom 1333 was the culmination and conclusion of his career, and of John Fosser, who was elected prior of Durham in 1341 only a year after his arrival in Coldingham.[358] Situated in alien territory and exposed to bands of raiders and troops on the march the cell managed to survive until 1478 when it was abandoned to the Scots.

In contrast to the remoteness of Coldingham the priory of St Godric at Finchale was only a short ride or easy walk from Durham along the river Wear. As such it was a popular resort for monks, a place for recreation and rest, where they were sent *causa spaciandi*, in the phrase frequently used. Although there was almost always a transient group of visiting monks enjoying a change of air, the prior, subprior, and cellarer were permanent members of the community, and with them resided another seven or eight monks, some of whom were sick or elderly and retired from active service. One of the ongoing complaints heard at visitations was that in a small community, which was top-heavy with infirm and decrepit monks, there were too few left to perform the divine office fittingly.[359] The numerous account rolls that survive from 1303 are brief and relatively uninformative.[360] However, the fact that the names of the three regular office holders are, on the whole, well recorded makes it possible to discern a few details about the monks appointed to the highly desirable position of prior of Finchale. Of all the cells it was the most favoured location by the majority of monks, next to Durham itself, whether as obedientiaries or as simple resident members. Possibly by a deliberate and astute

---

[355] Examples of letters requesting the admissions are transcribed from priory Register II in Raine, *Coldingham*, 13, 34, 43–4. Application to the king of Scotland was also necessary for the restoration of the temporalities.

[356] In 1330/1 Alan Piper has found five, but this was probably unusual and the stay of several of them may have been brief, *LVD*, i, 504.

[357] Aycliffe is C.960 in *LVD*, iii; another example is Robert de Claxton, ibid., C.942, prior of Coldingham for many of the years between 1374 and 1391, but known to have been hostiller at Durham in 1387/8.

[358] Graystanes obtained his D.Th. from Oxford in 1333, was sent to Coldingham, and elected bishop by his brethren. The archbishop of York confirmed the election and consecrated Graystanes, who was enthroned at Durham on 18 November; but the monks' choice was overridden by the king's choice of Richard de Bury, and within a few months Graystanes died. Graystanes is C.801 and Fosser C.817 in *LVD*, iii.

[359] For example, DCM Misc. Charter 2645, *c.* 1329 in date.

[360] Extracts have been transcribed and edited by James Raine in *Finchale*.

decision of a succession of Durham priors the turnover of Finchale priors, who were invariably senior monks, was fairly frequent, averaging no more than four to five years with only a few notable exceptions. Detachment and mobility were important factors in monastic life in maintaining discipline and order and in enabling the Durham prior to keep in touch with the state of affairs in the individual cells in between the annual Ascensiontide chapters. Of the Finchale priors whose term of office was extended, the widely esteemed monk scholar Uthred de Boldon stands out by the fact that between 1367 and 1396, the year of his death, he was appointed prior no less than four times, being recalled from time to time to fill other offices and carry out various commissions. During the last five years of his final appointment as prior he was given a monk assistant, designated as warden, to take over the essential administrative duties because he had become *sene et debilite confractus*.[361] At the same time Uthred was also provided with a chaplain who, in 1394, was Richard Haswell, a young monk only recently ordained priest. His responsibilities were more personal: to say the canonical hours with the infirm prior and to care for his round-the-clock needs by sharing his chamber at night.[362]

Other less commendable facets of community life at Finchale come to light in a sharply reproving letter from the Durham prior who had heard that some monks kept hunting dogs, a practice strictly forbidden. Another letter reveals some diligent monks complaining that their studies were being severely hampered due to the disappearance of canon law texts from the Finchale library; the Durham prior ordered their immediate return.[363] During the arbitrary and disruptive rule of the two controversial Durham priors Richard de Hoton (1290–1300) and Geoffrey de Burdon (1313–21), the monks of Durham and those in the cells became deeply divided over the conflicting issues involved. Finchale was close enough to Durham to make its collective presence felt, and for a time it functioned as a dissident group in opposition to the official position at Durham.[364]

It will be sufficient for the purposes of this study to treat the remaining cells of Durham more briefly by drawing attention to their distinguishing characteristics. For Lytham, for example, in its remote and isolated location on the Lancashire coast it was not alien marauders who were a constant threat, as at Coldingham; it was, rather, the neighbours who provoked a running feud against the small community which resulted in frequent litigation. There were never more than two or three monks, who were expected to fulfil their monastic duties and supervise their properties; in the event they found themselves involved in interminable legislation in which the Durham prior advised them to act with *modesta monachali* in order to promote peace and concord.[365] The priors appointed to Lytham were

---

[361] Boldon is C.888 in *LVD*, iii; details of his career are also summarized in *ODNB* and of his university career in *BRUO*. The quotation is from the letter of appointment to Roger de Mainsforth (*LVD*, iii, C.986), in BL MS Cotton Faustina A.vi, fo 85.
[362] BL MS Cotton Faustina A.vi, fo 92; Haswell is C.1027 in *LVD*, iii.
[363] BL MS Cotton Faustina A.vi, fo 9, fos 15v–16; both letters are undated.
[364] The troublesome years of prior Burdon have been thoroughly scrutinized by Jean Scammell in 'The Case of Geoffrey Burdon'; those of Hoton are covered by C. M. Fraser in *Antony Bek*, and her recent entry in *ODNB*.
[365] BL MS Cotton Faustina A.vi, fo 15–15v.

senior monks with experience in administrative office, and a good number of them remained there for six or more years. However, at least four of them requested permission to return to the mother house, one of them, Richard Haswell, after an intermittently fraught nineteen years.[366] The extant Lytham account rolls, of which there is an almost complete run from the early thirteenth century, are brief; but they record the expenses of travel between Lytham and Durham on various occasions, such as the annual chapter which the prior was obliged to attend.[367]

The dependent priory of St Leonard's Stamford shared several features in common with Coldingham and Lytham: its long distance from Durham and its location in another diocese, in this case that of Lincoln.[368] All three cells were engaged in administering their surrounding estates, but Stamford provided an additional service in offering Durham monks travelling to and from the south of the country—Oxford and London being frequent destinations—a welcome stopover on the long journey. About twenty account rolls survive from the period covered in this study but, like the accounts of other cells, their routine contents are relatively uninformative.[369] Of the more than twenty priors recorded in this period the average appointment was of three to five years' duration; there were a few who remained slightly longer and one, Robert de Picton, who ensconced himself in pseudo-independence for twenty-eight years, from 1391 to 1419, the longest period in office in any Durham cell.[370] On several occasions between 1340 and 1387 the Stamford prior fulfilled the role of proctor, representing the Durham prior at the triennial provincial chapter of the English Benedictines which met at nearby Northampton.[371] Relations between St Leonard's and the adjacent town of Stamford and local society, with a few exceptions, were cordial; and the prior was, from time to time called on to play a minor role in the ecclesiastical affairs of Lincoln diocese.[372] The distinctive characteristics of this small community, where there usually were no more than the prior and two or three monks, was that it appears to have been recognized as a place suitable for study as early as the 1260s.[373] In 1314 the bishop, Richard de Kellawe, himself a monk of Durham, numbered among his

---

[366] DCM Priory Reg. III, fo 140; Haswell was allowed to return to Durham in 1431 and was appointed almoner, C.1027 in *LVD*, iii.

[367] Extracts of some of the accounts, the originals of which remain at Durham, have been edited by Henry Fishwick in *The History of the Parish of Lytham in the County of Lancaster*, Chetham Society new series 60 (Manchester, 1907), 73.

[368] Lytham was in the archdeaconry of Richmond within the diocese of York. As at Coldingham it was necessary to go through diocesan channels to validate the appointment of priors; see, for example, Prior Fosser's letter to the bishop of Lincoln concerning the appointment of Robert de Hexham as prior in 1348, DCM Priory Reg. II, fo 132v. Hexham is C.864 in *LVD*, iii.

[369] The accounts and other related materials are in the DCM Stamford archive.

[370] Piper's 'Stamford Priory' recounts the history of the cell; Picton's repeated disobedience is treated in Part ii, 5–6. For Picton see also *LVD*, iii, C.956.

[371] Pantin, *Black Monk Chapters*, iii, 210–11, to which should be added the appointment of John de Hemingbrough in 1387, DCM Priory Reg. II, fo 251; after this date monks from Durham College Oxford took over this responsibility. For Hemingbrough see *LVD*, iii, C.932.

[372] See the summary in Piper, 'Stamford Priory', pt ii, 2–4.

[373] Barlow, *Durham Annals and Documents*, no. 57.

injunctions to his brethren one to the effect that monks *habiles ad studendum* should be sent to Stamford; and a few years later one of the depositions made by a monk at an episcopal visitation urged that more monks be sent there *pro profectu studii*.[374] The results of these recommendations can be seen in the 1330s and later when a significant number of monks were sent from Durham to Stamford within three or four years of their profession. Nicholas de Lusby, Robert de Hallington and Uthred de Boldon were among these. Their first stay preceded their studies at Oxford and all returned for a second time as Oxford graduates, Lusby and Hallington as priors.[375] Evidence from book ownership adds weight to the cell's intellectual emphasis. Among the non-university set of monks who were sent to Stamford early in their monastic life some, such as Peter de Durham and John de Barnard Castle in the 1350s, can be identified as possessors of manuscripts that were later placed in the library at Durham; manuscripts owned by two of the monk graduates named above also found their way to the library shelves.[376] As to the contents of the library at Stamford no evidence has been found beyond a short list of nine volumes that accompanied Henry Helay when he was appointed prior in 1422.[377]

The two neighbouring cells of Holy Island and Farne were both located on islands off the Northumberland coast.[378] Not more than eight miles apart from each other they were, nevertheless, remote and isolated from the rest of the world and yet near enough to the Scottish border to be exposed to occasional raids. Both being associated with Sts Aidan and Cuthbert they were regarded by the Durham monks as hallowed sites over which it was their duty to retain control. The Holy Island community was never free of financial problems that sometimes threatened its survival, and numbers were reduced from five or six to two or three by the early fifteenth century. Farne, where Aidan and Cuthbert in their day had both retreated for periods of solitude, became known as an eremitical refuge in the twelfth century but gradually developed into a fully-fledged but minuscule cell.[379] The succession of known masters, or *custodes* as they were addressed, begins at the end of the thirteenth century while those of Holy Island go back a century earlier. The frequent turnover of both the heads of these cells and of the monks at both cells probably reflects the reluctance on the part of monks, who enjoyed the more comfortable amenities and greater stimulus at Durham, to be posted to smaller

---

[374] DCM Priory Reg. II, fo 50v–51, Misc. Charter 2645.

[375] Piper, 'Stamford Priory', ii, 10–12; Lusby, Hallington, and Boldon are C.857, C.866, and C.888 in *LVD*, iii.

[376] For Durham and Barnard Castle see C.915 and C.926 in *LVD*, iii, and for Lusby and Boldon see note 375 above. The books belonging to these are also listed by Piper, Watson, *MLGB Supplement*, 88 (Durham), 87 (under Castro Bernardi ii), 93 (Lusby), 86 (Boldon). In the later fourteenth century the younger monks were being sent directly to Oxford bypassing Stamford where older monks replaced them.

[377] Helay, C.1046 in *LVD*, iii, had been a student at Durham College; the list of books has been transcribed in *Cat. Vet. Durham*, 116.

[378] Holy Island is often known by its other name of Lindisfarne and Farne is one of the cluster of Farne islands, distinguished as Inner Farne.

[379] Around the middle of the century two Durham monks had retired there as hermits.

houses which lacked them.[380] It is to be noted, however, that several masters of Farne were reappointed, William de Hexham for example, whose first posting was in 1326 for about a year, and who returned three times for short periods of one to two years, going back to Durham in between to serve in the offices of bursar, cellarer, and hostiller.[381] One of the few who remained for longer periods without a break was Richard de Sedgebrook, whose name heads the Farne accounts from 1357/8 to 1362/3 and again from 1368/9 to 1377/8.[382] He is the presumed owner of BL MS Arundel 507 which is a compilation of prayers, devotional treatises, and miscellaneous material, some probably in his hand. Alongside, but separate from, the small community the eremitical tradition on the island was continued in the mid-fourteenth century through the presence of at least one solitary who was presumably a Durham monk.[383] He is known only because of the survival of his meditations which are in Durham Cathedral MS B.IV.34.[384] In 1318 the monks of Farne benefited from the arrival of a doctor who was given a corrody for life, presumably in return for his services.[385] The medical problems may have thus been alleviated, but it seems that the cell was afflicted by serious misconduct which Hexham on his first arrival was ordered by the Durham prior to eliminate by correcting and punishing the *crimina et excessus* of the brothers and by restoring *observancias regulares*.[386]

Holy Island seems to have had prolonged disciplinary problems during the first half of the fourteenth century. The prior and his brethren were sharply reprimanded by their superior, the Durham prior, for failing to carry out their obligations with regard to the round of offices both day and night. This was followed by a second letter from Durham ordering the Holy Island prior to discipline two named monks on account of their misdemeanours.[387] The correspondence continued and, although we do not have any of the replies from the Holy Island prior, some of the contents may be inferred in the next letter from the prior of Durham addressed to his sons in the island community. They were firmly reminded of their duty to respect the senior and elderly monks and to give honour and reverence to their prior, Gilbert.[388] These stern orders were probably sent shortly after Gilbert de Elwick's appointment as prior of the cell in 1328 since at that time Prior Cowton had informed Elwick, newly invested with a doctorate in theology, that the cell was in a bad state and he was counting on Elwick to institute reform.[389] Surviving

---

[380] The lists of monks resident in the cells, compiled by Alan Piper, is less complete than those of the priors and therefore one cannot be certain without further evidence; see *LVD*, i, 503–16.
[381] Hexham is C.800 in *LVD*, iii; his last appointment was in *c*. 1340.
[382] Accounts survive from 1357/8 in the Durham muniments; for Sedgebrook see *LVD*, iii, C.936.
[383] See Pantin, 'The Monk-Solitary of Farne'.
[384] See Farmer, 'Meditations'. The manuscript was later in the hands of Peter de Durham; see above 221.
[385] DCM Priory Reg. II, fo 55.
[386] Ibid., fo 88.
[387] BL MS Cotton Faustina A.vi, fo 8–8v, 8v–9; the prior of Durham, identified only as 'W', was probably William de Cowton, 1321–41, and the monks were referred to as 'R' and 'B'.
[388] Ibid., fos 10–10v.
[389] DCM Priory Reg. II, fo 98v. Elwick was prior from 1328 to *c*. 1346 with several gaps; see C.786 in *LVD*, iii.

statutes for Holy Island which were issued in this period clearly demonstrate the determination to tackle and resolve the unrest and laxity in the cell. They prescribed in detail the daily routine necessary for the regular life to which all Durham monks were committed. The only concession indicating some awareness of the problems arising from the shortage of monastic manpower was the permission to reduce the required daily chapter to two or three times a week.[390] The problems that assailed Holy Island in the first half of the fourteenth century were no doubt matched elsewhere, more especially when monastic life was impaired by the lack of adequate numbers to share the weight of the assigned responsibilities; at such times difficulties were exacerbated by the clash of temperaments and the tendency of human nature to prevail over divine charity.

The twin cells of Jarrow and Wearmouth were in close proximity to each other and both were only a short distance from Durham.[391] Both owed their foundation as independent monasteries to the Northumbrian monk Benedict Biscop in the late seventh century. When a group of monks from these two monasteries were brought to Durham by Bishop William of St Calais in the late eleventh century to form the nucleus of a monastic community attached to the cathedral, Jarrow and Wearmouth became dependent priories. Durham and Jarrow were closely linked by a further bond in the person of Bede, who spent his entire life as a monk, first at Wearmouth and then at Jarrow; and his remains were later buried in the Galilee chapel of the cathedral.[392] Communications between the mother house and the two cells were easy to maintain; visits back and forth were frequent and supervision of discipline readily observed.[393] Despite the convenient location of the two cells the turnover of masters and monks was as frequent as for the more distant dependencies. There were rarely more than two monks in addition to the master; in 1323, for example, at Jarrow when summoned to a visitation the total in residence was two, and in 1362/3 the same number was reported.[394] The pattern of short repeated appointments of senior, experienced monks as masters, similar to those at Farne and Holy Island, is also found at Jarrow where, for example, Emery de Lumley went from Jarrow to be prior of Lytham, returned to Jarrow, was sent to take charge of Finchale and then back to Jarrow.[395] Thomas Legat's tenure of the office of master, however, stretched between 1381 and 1393 with two short gaps when his whereabouts are unknown.[396] At Wearmouth, with the exception of John de Bishopton, who held the mastership from 1369 to 1386, the appointments

---

[390] DCM Locellus XXVII, 4.
[391] Jarrow was situated close to the mouth of the river Tyne, and Wearmouth, or Monkwearmouth, near the mouth of the Wear as its name implies. The former was dedicated to St Paul and the latter to St Peter.
[392] For Bede's writings see above 105 and below 353–4.
[393] The Durham bursar's accounts record the travel payments made *passim* e.g., DCM bursar's account 1278/9.
[394] DCM 2.7.Pont.2b. See also Raine, *Jarrow/Wearmouth*, 45. Accounts of Jarrow survive at Durham from 1313 and those of Wearmouth from 1321.
[395] Lumley is C.789 in *LVD*, iii; these appointments occupied the years 1326 to 1344.
[396] Legat is C.953 in *LVD*, iii; it is, of course, possible that he remained at Jarrow.

varied in length between two and six years.[397] Among monks, as far as is known, the stay was not more than a year at a time, but there is evidence of a few returning later for a second year such as Simon de Darlington at Jarrow in 1354 and again in 1368/9, and Thomas Esh at Wearmouth in 1407/8 and probably again in 1414/15.[398] Alan Piper points out that frequent changes of personnel in the cells served to dilute the objections of the majority of monks who were averse to being deprived of the amenities available at Durham; he also notes that it lessened the possibility that an evolving coterie of indolent monks would have the chance to relax the prescriptions of the Rule.[399]

Fragments of surviving, often undated, correspondence from the prior of Durham to the masters of Jarrow and Wearmouth shed some light on the type of day-to-day issues with which all three had to cope. There was, for instance, the need to provide for the retirement of Prior William de Tanfield in 1313 when he resigned the priorate at Durham. The solution reached was to appoint him master of Jarrow where he was provided with a pension and various perquisites as well as one or two monk companions approved by the prior.[400] A letter from one of the three priors with the name William, very probably William de Cowton, concerned a monk, recovering from an illness at Farne, who was to be sent to Jarrow as soon as a boat could be found to convey him. A change of plan necessitated another letter to inform the master no longer to expect the convalescent because it had been decided that he was to return to Durham.[401] The master of Wearmouth received a tactful letter in the late 1340s from Prior John [Fosser] about a monk J[ohn] de N[orton] currently visiting the cell on a three-week holiday; the monk was to remain at the cell and to be won over to accept this directive *cum bono animo* by *diversis salubribus exhortationibus*.[402] Fosser had himself been master of Wearmouth before his election as prior in 1341, and Norton was appointed master there in 1349; it is thus probable that when writing the letter Fosser already had the appointment in mind and chose this way to prepare his choice of candidate. Twenty years later, during his second short term as master, Norton received a letter from Fosser recalling the monks resident in the cell to a visitation at Durham by Bishop Hatfield; in keeping with the usual practice it included the admonition against leaving the cell without enough monks to ensure the continuity of the divine office and the performance of other essential duties.[403] Prior Fosser may have been

---

[397] Bishopton is numbered C.919 in *LVD*, iii.
[398] Darlington is C.861 and Esh C.1010 in *LVD*, iii; both were senior monks at the time of their first visit.
[399] Piper, *Durham Monks at Jarrow*, 17.
[400] DCM Priory Reg. II, fo 21v; Tanfield died eight months later. In fact, he had been a monk of St Mary's abbey, York, and, at the time of his appointment in the wake of the turbulent priorate of Richard de Hoton, he was prior of Wetheral, a dependent priory of St Mary's; see *LVD*, iii, C.1389.
[401] BL MS Cotton Faustina A.vi, fo 16–16v; Cowton was prior from 1321–40/1, C.768, *LVD*, iii.
[402] The first quotation is from *RB*, C.5, 16 in the chapter on monastic obedience; the second is in BL MS Cotton Faustina A.vi, fo 16v.
[403] DCM Priory Reg. II, fo 262. There is a slight uncertainty about John de Norton, C.853 in *LVD*, iii; I have followed Piper's suggestion that for 'Neuton' we should read 'Norton', but see John de 'Neuton' or 'Newton', C.893.

admonished for posting monks to the cells who challenged some of his decisions in chapter, and there is no doubt that it was often viewed by monks as a punishment.[404] However, there was another challenge constantly facing the prior which the monks probably rarely entertained, and that was to plan and direct the almost continuous movement between the mother house and the cells. Arrangements could easily become complicated, and consideration for those to be transferred required patience and diplomacy. To maintain a balance between these conflicting issues was not always achieved, nor always achievable.

Canterbury

By definition St Martin's priory, Dover, was a dependency of Christ Church Canterbury, but any further similarity to Durham ends here.[405] From the early twelfth century the patronage of the priory was at the centre of an ongoing dispute in which the contenders included the crown, the archbishop of Canterbury and the prior of Christ Church.[406] Most of the early Dover priors were monks of Christ Church chosen and appointed by the archbishop; but between 1289 and 1351 the choice reverted to monks of Dover, who were also archiepiscopal appointments.[407] An agreement was reached in 1350 between Archbishop Islip and the prior and chapter and finalized six years later in a royal charter by which Dover priory was annexed to Christ Church, but the archbishop retained his right of appointment.[408] After this date monks of both Dover and Christ Church are found in the office of prior and, apart from this continuing connection, there was little if anything else in common. A few Canterbury monks like Stephen Tygh and Robert Lynton obtained licences from the archbishop to move to Dover, and a few like John Marchall moved in the opposite direction.[409] It is to be noted that between 1270 and 1420 there were six Christ Church monks with the toponym Dover and before and after these dates eleven, in other words a total of seventeen. Two of the Christ Church monks appointed as priors of Dover returned to Canterbury with pensions and were given preferential treatment, but they were not permitted to resume playing a part in chapter or other community activities. William de Dover paid 10 marks per annum *pro mensa sua et famuli sui* on his return in 1396/7 and Walter Causton for the same fee was given a private chamber for himself and his servant and was allowed to dine with the prior or cellarer.[410] Never more than a

---

[404] See Harbottle, 'Hatfield's Visitation', 95.
[405] This may serve to explain, if not entirely to excuse, my forbearing to refer to Dover in the introduction to the Canterbury section of my *BRECP*.
[406] Details are given in Haines, *Dover Priory*; see also for a brief summary, Stoneman, *Dover Priory*, 3–4.
[407] *HRH*, ii, 96–8.
[408] Sheppard, *Lit. Cant.*, ii, no. 782; *Reg. Langham*, 274–5.
[409] *BRECP* has the details, 308 for Tygh, who went to Dover under a cloud in 1423, and Lynton (II), ibid., 228, who transferred in 1466. John Marchall I, ibid., 230, came to Canterbury in 1401.
[410] Ibid., 140–1 (William de Dover III), 110 (Causton). Precaution was necessary when dealing with the return of Christ Church monks seconded to Dover as the case of the temperamental Richard de Wynchepe demonstrates, ibid., 331. He had tried to get involved in the internal affairs of the chapter both during and after his term at Dover.

small community Dover priory managed to preserve a substantial degree of independence. Novices were admitted and professed *in situ* and, by the late fourteenth century, the monks had accumulated an impressive collection of books which was at their disposal.[411] Surviving correspondence reveals the persistence of friendships forged between Canterbury monks within the Christ Church cloister when distance separated them. The William Glastynbury who kept in touch with some of his contemporaries who were sent to Oxford also remained in contact with another friend, John Coumbe, after he was appointed prior of Dover by Archbishop Chichele in 1435. Glastynbury, with another contemporary, John Waltham, spent a holiday with Coumbe at Dover by the latter's invitation.[412]

Bath

Bath cathedral priory had two dependent cells, at Dunster in south-west Somerset and at Waterford in southern Ireland. Although within the same diocese as its mother house the former was located at the opposite end of the county, and it was acquired by gift in the late twelfth century. The priors, of whom a few names are known, were monks of the cathedral priory chosen by the prior, who had the right of appointment, subject to episcopal confirmation. There were probably rarely more than three monks in residence, although the roll call at the selection of Thomas Lacok as prior of Bath in 1447 names five.[413] Seven monks with the toponym Dunster are numbered among the members of the monastic community at Bath; this may imply that cordial relations existed between the local inhabitants of Dunster and the monks in the priory of St George who lived in their midst. To add possible weight to this suggestion, at least one prior of Dunster on retirement preferred to remain in the cell there rather than to return to Bath; and one monk, Robert Hendeman, obtained a papal licence in 1401 to leave the unhealthy and infectious air in Bath if he became ill and go to Dunster or to Ireland.[414]

There is more information of the movements of monks between Bath and Waterford for the purpose of administering the Irish estates.[415] These had been acquired in the early thirteenth century when the hospital of St John at Waterford together with its scattered properties were affiliated to Bath as a dependent priory or

---

[411] The dependencies of St Alban's abbey also admitted and professed their own recruits. For the Dover library and its catalogue see Stoneman, *Dover Priory*.

[412] For Glastynbury see *BRECP*, 169; for John Coumbe II, *BRECP*, 130 and for John Waltham I, ibid., 313.

[413] *Bath Priory Reg.* lxvii; the original intention according to a charter issued by Prior Robert de Clopcote of Bath in 1330 was that there should be a prior and four brothers, ibid., no. 694.

[414] The monk was Robert de Sutton, *BRECP*, 42–3; he was described as a monk of Dunster in the deed concerning his pension, *Bath Priory Reg.* no. 736. Hendeman is in *BRECP*, 28. See, however, K. L. French, 'Competing for Space: Medieval Religious Conflict in the Monastic-Parochial Church at Dunster', *Journal of Medieval and Early Modern Studies*, 27 (1997), 215–44. In this paper the author claims that there was an ongoing dispute lasting more than two centuries between the monks and the parishioners over the responsibility for and the maintenance of the church building. In my view she rather dramatically overstates her case.

[415] The Canterbury monks also had property in Ireland but chose to exercise their authority from a distance through resident agents.

cell. From that time on there were usually two monks there mainly for administrative purposes and sometimes called attorneys. By observing the activities of some of the ten known monks who were sent as priors, or *custodes*, of the cell we begin to appreciate the difficulties of managing overseas properties even though most of the practical measures employed are hidden from view. By 1306 reports of poverty and mismanagement had become sufficiently alarming that Prior Robert de Clopcote undertook to make a personal visit which resulted in his absence from Bath for the better part of a year.[416] His success in alleviating the problems was probably temporary and limited because two appointments of priors for Waterford in the late 1320s and early 1330s proved to be disastrous. One of these was Hugh de Dover, who was recalled by order of Archbishop Meopham after he had conducted a *sede plena* visitation of the cathedral priory.[417] Thomas de Cyrcestre, one of the monks who had been sent to Ireland to take charge of the priory livestock, may have been the one who made his complaint to Meopham against the ill treatment he had received at Dover's hands; but the Irish problem was not solved by the latter's removal.[418] The next appointee, Thomas de Foxcote, had been precentor at Bath prior to his departure for Ireland in 1332 where he was in charge for an indeterminate period until his final removal in 1346. In retirement, despite the accusation that he had misused hospital/cell funds, Prior John de Iforde permitted him to remain in Waterford and allowed him to occupy a room in the infirmary. He then proceeded to make life difficult for his successor, John de Bloxham, who nevertheless was willing to accept several renewals of his initial appointment as prior.[419] John de Stone, Bloxham's successor, also appears to have avoided any further need for intervention from Bath; his lengthy tenure of the office, from 1362 until the late 1370s, implies that both he and the prior of Bath were at least reasonably satisfied with the *status quo*. But there were always problems lurking below the surface; in this case one of them was the inability to communicate with the natives of Waterford. It came to the fore in 1463 in a complaint against John Lamport, who was accused of failing in his pastoral duties because he did not know the language.[420]

Rochester

To the monks at Rochester their cell at Felixstowe, or Walton St Felix, must have been a mixed blessing. For one thing it was far away on the Suffolk coast, possibly more easily reached by sea than by land in some seasons of the year; either way it involved an arduous journey. The church and manor of Felixstowe had been given to the monks before 1100, and two or three monks were in residence there by and possibly before 1174 when the name of the first known prior, Aufredus, is

---

[416] *BRECP*, 19–20 (Clopcote).
[417] Ibid., 22 (Dover).
[418] Ibid., 21 (Cyrcestre).
[419] Ibid., 24 (Foxcote), 15 (Bloxham).
[420] Ibid., 42 (Stone), 33 (Lamport); presumably most of the monks sent to Waterford would have had problems, at least initially, in the matter of communicating with the local inhabitants.

recorded. The church was used by both the monks and the local inhabitants who were its parishioners, and the cloister was little more than a set of adjoining secular buildings.[421] Robert de Waletone, who was prior shortly afterwards, probably c. 1202, had a collection of six books with him at the cell which were later incorporated into the Rochester library.[422] Only nine other priors of Felixstowe before 1420 have been identified; two of them, John de Hertlepe and Robert de Southflete, were elected to the priorate at Rochester immediately afterwards and a third, John de Ealding, was an Oxford graduate who had served as precentor both before and after his term at Felixstowe.[423] Only one, Henry Raundes, seems to have shown any sign of being a doubtful character. In March of 1382, for reasons unknown, he had been required to renew his promise of obedience to Prior John de Shepey II; in May he was sent to Felixstowe with a letter to the prior there stating that he was to remain at the cell under observation to ensure his obedience to the Rule. At the end of November he was appointed *custos* of the cell in place of John Morel, who must have made a favourable report to Prior Shepey. After a six-year stay at Felixstowe Raundes was released from his charge because 'nequit ibidem diutius commode ministrare'.[424] The decision to give him the office appears to have had no ill results. There is one reference to the ineligibility of monks to take part in prioral elections while serving in the cell. In 1333 at the election of Prior John de Shepey I it was stated that monks at Felixstowe were not entitled to vote and that this was in accordance with ancient custom.[425] The origin of this unusual regulation does not appear and there is no known parallel in any of the other cells of the cathedral priories.

Norwich

The six Norwich cells have much in common with those of Durham. However, there were some notable differences: their relative proximity to the mother house and their location within the diocese of Norwich. Another feature distinguishing them from the Durham cells is the identical origin of four of them—St Leonard's Norwich, St Mary's Aldeby, St Margaret's King's Lynn and St Nicholas' Yarmouth—which came into being through the initiative of Herbert Losinga, who transferred his see to Norwich c. 1005 and established his cathedral with its attached priory. The other two dependencies, St Edmund's Hoxne in Suffolk and St Paul's hospital, an almshouse in Norwich, became subject to the cathedral in the early twelfth century. The visitation of the cathedral priory by Bishop

---

[421] Aufredus is listed in *BRECP*, 590. See R. Gilyard-Beer, 'The Buildings of Walton Priory', *Proceedings of the Suffolk Institute of Archaeology*, 33 (1975), 131–49, at 138–41. The reference on pp 142–3 to the presence of a prior and thirteen monks, from the *Calendar of Inquisitions Post Mortem*, 4, in 1307 is surely incorrect.
[422] *BRECP*, 646 (Waletone); see also the latter's list of books in Sharpe, *EBL*, at B79. 236–41.
[423] *BRECP*, 611 (John de Hertlepe I), 638 (Robert de Southflete II), 600 (Ealding).
[424] Ibid., 628 (Raundes), 635 (Prior John de Shepey II).
[425] BL MS Cotton Faustina C.v, fo 66; *BRECP*, 634–5 (Prior John de Shepey I).

Bateman c. 1346/7 revealed the need to enforce a stricter régime which the bishop proceeded to do in a series of strongly worded injunctions, several of them directly concerned with the cells. He specified that no monks who were *vagi, leves et indomiti* should be sent to the cells; that those in the cells were not to leave the monastic precinct without licence from the prior of the cell and they were always to have a companion, preferably a monk; that those who were *apti* should study scripture and canon law and at other times give themselves *diligenter* to prayer and devotion. The priors of cells were required without fail to present their accounts annually in chapter and each cell was ordered to make a fixed annual payment to the treasury at Norwich.[426]

St Leonard's priory was situated within sight of the cathedral, no more than a short walk across Bishopgate bridge over the Wensum to Thorpe Wood. The proximity had both advantages and disadvantages for the prior and his community of three or four monks. Communications in person or by messenger were both easily and swiftly delivered. Books in the cathedral library could be consulted and borrowed with little effort or delay if they were not to be found among the forty or so volumes housed in the upper chapel of the cell.[427] Moreover, the sociable exchange of news and views between the two communities could be arranged without advance planning apart from the required exeat. However, there were certain obligations placed upon the prior and his brethren at St Leonard's by chapter ordinances imposed in 1351 and 1379. Both required the prior and monks to take their place in the cathedral at the office of second vespers on principal feasts, and the later ordinance extended this ruling to include their mandatory presence at both first and second vespers for the feast of the Trinity, after which the prior and one monk were to return to the cell while the other two stayed on to sing matins with the convent. The prior was also expected to join the monks in the cathedral on several other holy days, and he and his brethren were to attend mass on the feasts of the Epiphany and the Purification.[428] About three dozen account rolls survive from 1349/50 to 1420, all in the name of the prior who was the one and only accounting officer. The first of these was Walter de Stokton, who had spent three or four years at Oxford before being sent to St Leonard's.[429] Simon Bozoun, prior of Norwich from 1344 to 1352, was appointed prior of St Leonard's in his retirement, where he was to be exempt from the observances and the regular discipline incumbent on Benedictine monks except for the essentials required by the Rule such as the promises made at the time of profession.[430] He would probably have enjoyed a quieter life with time to enjoy reading some of the

---

[426] These injunctions were transcribed and edited by Cheney in 'Norwich Cathedral Priory', 93–120 at 106–7, 108, 114. The books available for use at Yarmouth are discussed below 234.

[427] See the list, dated 1424, printed in Sharpe, *EBL*, at B62.

[428] Cheney, 'Norwich Cathedral Priory', 117, 119–20; I have given only a summary of the obligations. Note that in 1379 there were four monks at St Leonard's. See also M. Heale, 'Veneration and Renovation at a Small Norfolk Priory: St. Leonard's, Norwich, in the Later Middle Ages', *Historical Research*, 76 (2003), 431–49.

[429] *BRECP*, 559.

[430] NRO DCN 40/10 (Priory Reg. X), fo 40.

books he had acquired while at Norwich.[431] However, it seems likely that he died within the year since John de Hedirset heads the account as prior for 1353/4.[432] Two of the priors remained in office for lengthy periods: William de Rykinghale for over ten years, from 1358 to 1369, and Richard de Blakeneye for nineteen, from 1386 to 1405; both had held at least one obedientiary office at Norwich previously.[433] The principal source of revenue, in fact almost the entire income of the cell, came from oblations which were placed by the faithful in several pyxes in the priory church, the one beside the image of St Leonard being the most popular.[434] In 1375/6 over £26 was collected and twenty years later close to £17.[435] Among the expenses listed on the brief accounts are the cost of entertaining visiting brethren from the cathedral and other guests, including the succentor and *socii* on 6 November, St Leonard's day.[436] The only monk known to have retired at St Leonard's is Richard de Walsham after forty-six active years of monastic life; he served in several of the major offices including those of master of the cellar and sacrist and, finally, prior of St Leonard's when he was already ill. In 1456 he was allocated a newly constructed dwelling in the garden of the cell where he could live in solitude with a servant in attendance.[437]

St Paul's hospital, Norwich, was unique among the cells in that instead of housing a small monastic community it offered accommodation for a number of poor men and women—twenty according to the early thirteenth-century constitutions.[438] The master or *custos*, a monk of the cathedral priory who may not have been resident, was assisted by a procurator who received the newly admitted and worked under the master's direction. The earliest masters known are John de Plumstede and Richard de Skerninge in the late thirteenth century about whom little else is known.[439] The six fourteenth-century masters whose names have been found in the records are also shadowy figures about whom few details survive apart from brief notices of their appointments to other obedientiary offices. All the accounts before 1422/3 have perished and after that date a mere six are extant. The earliest roll shows that the income was derived from rents and tithes and it conforms to the usual format found in the other obedientiary accounts, recording contributions to anniversaries, pensions, and other communal expenses such as chapter negotiations. Under the heading *aula sororum* £13 14s. were spent in

---

[431] For his biographical details see *BRECP*, 486; for the list of his books, Sharpe, *EBL*, at B58 and above 152–3. A *studium* with desks is mentioned in 1388/9 when a new window was inserted, NRO DCN 2/3/9.
[432] NRO DCN 2/3/2; there is no account for the year 1352/3. For Hedirset *BRECP*, 518–19.
[433] *BRECP*, 552 (Rykinghale); 484 (Blakeneye).
[434] The statue is described in an inventory of the cell, dated 1424, which was transcribed and translated by Bensley in 'St Leonard's Priory', 198–201.
[435] NRO DCN 2/3/8 (1375/6), 2/3/17 (1396/7).
[436] E.g., ibid., 2/3/9 (1386/7), 2/3/9 (1388/9), 2/3/12 (1394/5), 2/3/17 (1396/7).
[437] *BRECP*, 568–9; and see above 153 for his reading material.
[438] NRO DCN 2/5/8; the hospital is sometimes referred to as Normanspital reputedly after its first master, *BRECP*, 544.
[439] *BRECP*, 548 (Plumstede); 556 (Skerninge).

providing for the inmates' food and lighting, but in later accounts money payments were substituted.[440]

The cell of Hoxne was at least a two-day journey from the cathedral priory, almost due south and close to the border between Norfolk and Suffolk. In his *History of Norfolk*, the eighteenth-century antiquary Francis Blomefield cites a cartulary long since vanished, to the effect that seven or eight monks were resident in the community to which a school for the local children was attached; he also notes that two of the pupils were supported by the monks and may have received room and board.[441] It is frustrating that no further evidence has come to light to corroborate or amplify these details attributed to Hoxne. Intimations of some intellectual activity are possibly to be read into the existence of a fragment of a book list recently discovered on the dorse of the account roll of 1395/6. Much of it is illegible but enough is clear to show that it included four volumes of history, one volume of sermons, the Rule of St Benedict, and works by Hugh of St Victor and William de Pagula.[442] The earliest account is uncertainly dated but probably before 1336, and it is the second year of Robert de Ormesby's priorate; since he paid off the debt of Peter de Donewich it may be presumed that the latter had been Ormesby's predecessor at Hoxne.[443] The earliest prior known was Hervey according to Blomefield but his dates, and those of several of his successors which derive from the same cartulary, are unknown. Even for many of the fourteenth-century priors, like Donewich and Ormesby, only tentative dates and indefinite lengths of tenure of office can be assigned. Short appointments appear to have been the norm, with the exception of Geoffrey de Norwich, who was probably prior continuously between 1407 and 1418.[444] The 1394/5 account names two monks on the dorse of the roll, one being John de Jernmuth the prior and the other Nicholas Geyton, presumably his deputy; this is the only occasion when more than one monk at the cell is known by name.[445] There were evidently only two monks there according to an undated letter probably written by Robert de Langele, prior of Norwich from 1310 to 1326, to the prior of Hoxne; he was ordered to appear in chapter for the bishop's visitation while his *consocius* was to remain behind in charge of the cell.[446]

The nearest, but by no means neighbouring, cell to Hoxne was St Mary's Aldeby in south-eastern Norfolk which, in turn, lay to the south-west of the cell of Yarmouth. One of its distinctive features was that the prior was also, as it were, the parish priest and the priory church served as the parish church.[447] Bishop Salmon's injunctions of 1309 referred to the presence of five monks at Aldeby at that date and only three at Yarmouth; to make numbers even he ordered that one

---

[440] NRO DCN 2/5/1–7; see also Saunders, *Obedientiary Rolls*, 147–8.
[441] Blomefield, *Norfolk*, vol. iii, 607–10.
[442] NRO DCN 2/6/2; the list was brought to our attention by Martin Heale.
[443] *BRECP*, 546–7 where Ormesby's gift of an illuminated psalter to the cathedral priory is described; Donewich held a succession of obedientiary offices after Hoxne, ibid., 501.
[444] Ibid., 545.
[445] Ibid., 528 (Jernmuth); 515 (Geyton).
[446] NRO DCN 40/9, Priory Reg. IX, fo 39v.
[447] NRO DN Reg. 1/2, Reg. Ayermine, fo 79v.

monk from Aldeby was to be despatched to Yarmouth.[448] Numbers had been reduced, at least temporarily about ten years later, when Robert de Langele, the Norwich prior, summoned the Aldeby prior and his two brethren.[449] Only one prior has been identified before their names are stated on the account rolls, the series of which begins in 1380/1; unfortunately, all are brief, relatively uninformative, and before 1422/3 consist only of a series of undifferentiated items. A three- or four- year posting, or less, seems to have been common for Aldeby priors as far as can be ascertained. John de Bedingfeld, the earliest known prior, only makes one appearance when he was commissioned by the vicar general to hear the nuns' confessions at Bungay, and an approximate date can be attributed only because the bishop had appointed the Norwich prior, Laurence de Leck (1352–7), to act on his behalf.[450] John de Thurgarton was sent to Aldeby as prior in 1403 after service in several other obedientiary offices at Norwich; his name is at the head of the cell accounts for that year and the following seven, before he returned to the cathedral priory to become sacrist.[451] A secular priest is regularly named on the accounts, often included among the *famuli*; he was, no doubt, assisting the prior with the cure of souls in the parish and he probably lived in the priory.[452] Offerings from the collection boxes in the church and at a cross or crucifix amounted to £5 or £6, and other items on the accounts were similar to those on the accounts of other cells.[453] Two fourteenth-century monks and one fifteenth-century monk have the toponym Aldeby, a fact which may have little significance; on the other hand it may be construed to suggest that the monastic community was favourably regarded by the parishioners and other locals. While there is no evidence to indicate what books in addition to service books were to be found in the cell, one of the three monks, Adam de Aldeby, was the owner of a late thirteenth-century *Liber glossarum*, a volume containing biblical and other reference material.[454]

Losinga's dependent priories of St Margaret at [King's] Lynn and St Nicholas at [Great] Yarmouth were unique among the Norwich cells for several reasons. In the late middle ages both found themselves in urban centres which owed a large part of their prosperity to the fact that they were flourishing ports, Lynn on the Wash at the mouth of the river Ouse and Yarmouth on the North Sea at the mouth of the Yare. The former, west and slightly north of Norwich was over forty miles from the

---

[448] NRO DCN 92/1; there is also a transcription and translation, not altogether reliable, in E. H. Carter, *Studies in Norwich Cathedral History* (Jarrold, Norwich, 1935), 19–24.

[449] NRO DCN Priory Reg. 40/9, fo 5v; the others were Adam de B[edingham] or B[elagh] and J. de D. who were to remain in the cell. For Langele see *BRECP*, 533 and for Bedingham and Belagh ibid., 481–2.

[450] *BRECP*, 481 (Bedingfeld); the commission of Leck as vicar general is in the episcopal register, NRO DN Reg. 2/4, fo 145v, but Leck's commission to Bedingfeld is in NRO DCN Priory Reg. 40/9, fo 20. For Leck, *BRECP*, 534.

[451] *BRECP*, 565.

[452] NRO DCN 2/2/1, 2/2/4 etc.

[453] The phrase is *de ecclesia cum cruce*, e.g., NRO DCN 2/2/1 (1380/1); 2/2/2 (1397/8); 2/2/4 (1400/1); the cell was seriously in the red in these years.

[454] The volume has a Norwich cathedral press-mark; see Ker, 'Manuscripts from Norwich', 257; when I last saw the volume, *c.* 2002, it was in the Bridewell Museum, Norwich; Aldeby is in *BRECP*, 478.

mother house while the latter, almost due east, was about half that distance. In both towns, as at Aldeby, the priory church was also the parish church, and the prior was addressed as the prior of the cell of the parish church.[455] The priors were assisted in their pastoral role by their brethren and several secular chaplains whose stipends are referred to on the account rolls.[456] The priors were regularly licensed by the bishop to hear the parishioners' confessions; but they and/or other monks were apparently involved in other pastoral duties in 1362 when they were exposed for celebrating mass in oratories and private places in houses belonging to parishioners. The latter were warned by the bishop that they would be excommunicated for this offence unless a licence had been sought and obtained.[457] It does not require more than a slight stretch of the evidence to suppose that these masses were probably for the benefit of housebound souls, some perhaps critically ill, and that the monks had been delated to the bishop by resentful members of the parish.

Both priories operated on much larger budgets than the other cells, expenses of over £200 at Lynn are recorded by the prior on the earliest surviving account of 1370/1 and a similar amount at Yarmouth in 1355/6, the first account there.[458] The offerings of the faithful at both priory/parish churches were substantial: at Lynn about £100 in 1370/1 and at Yarmouth a similar figure in 1386/7.[459] Payments to the mother house during the course of the year under variable headings such as pensions, contributions, and donations amounted to *c.* £30 at Lynn in 1393/4 and close to £40 at Yarmouth in 1386/7.[460] It may seem surprising to find these relatively large sums being managed by a handful of monks but, with regard to the community at Lynn, there is some evidence to suggest that there were fluctuations in numbers depending on the presence of monks for short-term residence. One of the regular items of expenditure is that of the cost of monks travelling back and forth between Norwich and Lynn, many of which are described as 'in cariag[io monachorum cum bonis eorundem'; in 1373/4 and 1399/1400 this amounted to over £4; it seems likely that, despite the distance from Norwich, Lynn was regarded as a favourable location for monks to rest or recover from illness.[461] Ralph de Martham was prior of Lynn from 1372/3, probably continuously, until

---

[455] E.g. by Bishop Alnwick *c.* 1430, NRO DN Reg. 5/9, fo 102.

[456] E.g. at Yarmouth in 1355/6, NRO DCN 2/4/1; in most years they are lumped together with other stipends. For Lynn they were put with various other items, ibid., 2/1/6 (1381/2), 2/1/20 (1393/4).

[457] Licences to hear confessions are found in Bishop Ayermine's register where, in the 1320s he issued them to the three priors of Aldeby, Lynn, and Yarmouth, NRO DN Reg. 1/2, fo 79–79v. The warning letter from Bishop Percy is NRO DCN 43/74; by contrast, in 1412 Bishop Burghill gave permission to the Coventry monks to celebrate mass in oratories on their manors or other oratories wherever they happened to be staying, Reg. Burghill, fo 203v.

[458] NRO DCN 2/1/1, ibid., 2/4/1; twenty-three accounts of Lynn are extant between 1370 and 1420 but a mere five from Yarmouth.

[459] NRO DCN 2/1/1, 2/4/2.

[460] Ibid., 2/1/20, 2/4/2; it is difficult to interpret correctly and to extract accurate figures because of the ambiguous and idiosyncratic way in which the accounts were compiled, and also because of their brevity.

[461] Ibid., 2/1/2, 2/1/3, 2/1/5, 2/1/11, 2/1/21. This is a puzzling phrase; it assuredly does not mean that the monks were literally being transported; is it likely that the word *cariagio* is intended as a general term to include the expenses of horses and the conveyance of baggage?

his death there in 1393; the total cost of conveying his body and his books back to Norwich, together with the expenses of his brethren at the cell who travelled to the cathedral priory for *le enterment* and back, came to over £6.[462] Later the same year the new prior, John de Carleton, arrived; the charge of 73s. 6d. on the account is explained in interesting detail: 'in cariag' monachorum et donis datis et expensis factis in adventu nostri prioris ad Lenn'.[463] Other known priors at Lynn from Adam de Schipdam c. 1285 to Thomas de Hevyngham, who in 1421/2 also died at Lynn, bring the total to fourteen, several of whom spent five or more years there.[464] A similar pattern emerges at Yarmouth, at least with regard to the six priors who have been identified. One of them was William de Claxton, who, as far as is known, was in office for only a few months in 1326 before his election as prior of Norwich.[465] Claxton had studied at Oxford, as had Laurence de Tunstale and John de Hoo and, among priors of Lynn, John de Mari and Richard de Folsham were both graduates.[466] Books would surely have been important to these priors, and to other priors and monks stationed at Lynn and Yarmouth; Hevyngham's books, like those belonging to Martham, were returned to Norwich and reallocated to other monks including John de Dereham and William Worstede.[467] In their role as librarian two precentors of Norwich visited the cells, William de Penteney to Lynn in c. 1386/7 *pro libris videndis*, and Thomas Cawmbridge in c. 1415/16 to Yarmouth several times during the year.[468] There is an undated fifteenth-century inventory of the book collection at Yarmouth consisting of about twenty-two volumes as well as fifteen service books, all of them bearing a Norwich pressmark.[469] There is no record of the library at Lynn, except for a single reference on the 1392/3 account to the purchase of a book of sermons for Sundays by James de Voragine and a second similar volume.[470]

Two priors of Lynn came into contact with the tiresome and irritating Margery Kempe and both seem to have treated her with kind forbearance. One of them, Thomas de Hevyngham, had apparently been allowing her to receive communion in the monks' own (private) chapel within the cloister until a brother, just recently posted to Lynn, announced that he would boycott the chapel if she were present. Hevyngham told her and her priest confessor that they would have to be content to

---

[462] For Martham, see *BRECP*, 539.
[463] For Carleton, ibid., 491; the account referred to is NRO DCN 2/1/20.
[464] *BRECP*, 554–5 (Schipdam), 523 (Hevyngham).
[465] Ibid., 495.
[466] *BRECP*, 495 (Claxton), 567 (Tunstale, prior in 1361), 525 (Hoo, D.Th. and prior between 1386/7 and 1406); 538–9 (Mari, D.Th., prior 1348), 510 (Folsham prior 1398/1407, B.Th. according to NRO DCN 38/2).
[467] *BRECP*, 499–500 (Dereham), 573–574 (Worstede).
[468] NRO DCN 1/9/23, 1/9/31(5); see also *BRECP*, 548 (Penteney) and 493 (Thomas Cawmbridge I) where their visits to these cells are not mentioned.
[469] The list is printed in Sharpe, *EBL*, at B64; the Norwich pressmark suggests that the books were borrowed and returned and that Yarmouth, unlike St Leonard's, did not possess a permanent collection of its own.
[470] NRO DCN 2/1/21; the second volume was by 'uno doctore vocato gem?a fr' evangel' dominical' '.

use the parish church.[471] Shortly after obtaining a doctorate, *c*. 1421, John de Dereham was sent to Lynn as prior where he probably remained continuously until 1446. During this time he found himself embroiled in a lengthy dispute with two rival factions among the parishioners of St Margaret's. According to Margery's dramatic and strongly approving account Dereham took a firm stand in support of the rights and dignity of the church and against the proposed changes that would have threatened them; in the end his patience and perseverance were rewarded.[472]

Finally, an interesting statistic regarding the names of monks admitted and professed at Norwich between *c*. 1270 and 1480 is worth noting. A total of fourteen monks, seven from each cell, bore the toponym Lynn or Yarmouth.[473] No reliable comment can be imposed on this slender evidence beyond the fact that there were probably some family connexions in the two towns for some of them and that the monks on the whole were likely to have had good relations with their parishioners.

---

[471] *The Book of Margery Kempe*, translated by B. A. Windeatt (Penguin Books, London, 1985), ch. 57, 178; in the church she cried so loudly that those inside and even outside were disturbed.
[472] *The Book of Margery Kempe*, ch. 25, 94–6; for Dereham see *BRECP*, 499–500.
[473] *BRECP*, 534–6 (Lenn), 528–9 (Jernmuth).

V

Feria, Fast, and Feast: The Rhythm of the Liturgical Year

Licet omni tempore vita monachi quadragesimae debet observationem habere'
In sanctorum vero festivitatibus vel omnibus sollemnitatibus, sicut diximus Dominico die agendum ita agatur.[1]

The chronological order, which has been conspicuous until now, will be interrupted in order to describe and fit into place some of the salient features that marked the course of the liturgical year. Many of these regular seasonal occurrences, like the celebration of some of the anniversaries, have already been mentioned but others, like the periodic *minutiones* or blood-letting, have until now been omitted. The topics to be treated in this chapter are selective and, once again, heavily dependent on evidence provided by the wealth of information that can be extracted from obedientiary account rolls, together with significant additions from other manuscript sources.

Liturgical manuscripts for mass and office

Monastic observance of Advent and Christmas, Lent and Easter, and other solemnities at the cathedral priories was centred on the prescribed liturgical rites, the diligent preparation and correct performance of which demanded priority of time and attention on the part of the entire community. To attempt a detailed reconstruction of all of these liturgies and rites as they would have been celebrated is outside the scope of this study and, indeed, is scarcely possible given the paucity of the essential evidence.[2] Among the relevant surviving manuscripts are a few choir psalters, one of which would probably have been reserved for each monk in the place assigned to him in the monastic choir. These liturgical psalters contained the one hundred and fifty psalms of the Old Testament book of that name together with additional material intended to accompany the daily recitation of the office. Frequently included were private prayers to be said before and after the office, canticles, collects, antiphons, hymns, the Athanasian creed, a litany or two and,

---

[1] *RB*, C.49, 1; C.14, 1; these are two contrasting but not incompatible precepts which together constitute the rhythm of monastic life and serve as aids in dispelling monotony and accidie.

[2] It is also beyond the competence of this author. See, however, *The Liturgy in Medieval England*, the impressive study recently completed by Richard Pfaff in Chapter 6 of which he examines customaries and office books of several of the cathedral priories.

sometimes, a kalendar on the opening folios. The psalms were not numbered, but the main liturgical divisions were denoted by the size of the opening initial. There were slight variations in the distribution of psalms among the offices but, in general, the prescriptions of St Benedict as specified in the Rule remained in force.[3] Several psalters survive from Christ Church Canterbury with the current users' names inscribed; one, dating from the early eleventh century, was in active use almost five centuries later when William Ingram wrote on folio iv 'si quis invenerit hunc librum restituat dompno - -'. Two earlier possessors of this same psalter were William Hadlegh, subprior in the 1470s, and John Waltham to whom Hadlegh had passed it on.[4] A later thirteenth/fourteenth-century psalter belonged to one of the two John Holyngbornes who were members of the Canterbury community between the mid-fifteenth and the early sixteenth centuries.[5] At Durham in 1417 the chancellor, John Fishburn, checked the books kept in the chancery/spendement and compiled a list which has fortunately been preserved.[6] One section of the list bears the heading *psalteria non glosata* which, from the description of the additional contents of many of the twenty or so psalters, can be identified as choir psalters. Several had the names of monks inscribed: Roger de Mainsforth, William Durham, Henry Ferriby, and John Oll, who were members of the community of St Cuthbert between the mid-fourteenth and the mid-fifteenth centuries. Four of the psalters were stated to have been allocated for the use of novices and one was noted as having been at the cell of Lytham.[7] In addition, a surviving psalter, dating from the twelfth to the fifteenth century contains not only a kalendar, collects, canticles, the office of the dead and so on, but also sermons and Easter tables.[8]

---

[3] *RB*, C.9–C.19; the seven daytime offices were lauds or matins, prime, terce, sext, none, vespers, and compline and the night office was vigils or nocturns. For a detailed description of the choir psalter, its structure and use, see Andrew Hughes, *Medieval Manuscripts for Mass and Office* (University of Toronto Press, Toronto, 2004), 50–2, 226–31.

[4] The psalter, now BL MS Arundel 155, contained a kalendar and most of the other items listed above, and some of the prayers at the end have Anglo-Saxon interlineation. The three monks are in *BRECP*, William Ingram I, 209; William Hadlegh I, 187; John Waltham II, 313–14. The list of missing service books dated 1338, in James, *ALCD*, 148, includes a psalter that in the early twelfth or thirteenth century had been in the possession of a monk named Silvester (*BRECP*, 288, which has omitted this reference). Prior Eastry's personal psalters are listed among his *Libri de officiis ecclesiasticis* bequeathed to the community, James, *ALCD*, 145.

[5] This is now LPL MS 558 and it includes a kalendar, a section of hymns, and the office of the dead with musical notation. The two monks are in *BRECP*, 201–3, where I have followed M. R. James' catalogue description in assigning the psalter to the later Holyngborne; however, he did not know of the existence of an earlier namesake. In addition there are two thirteenth-century psalters now in the Bibliothèque national, Paris, MS Lat. 770 and MS nouv. acq. lat. 1670, neither of which I have seen. Canterbury Cathedral MS 62, listed as *Preces*, may also be considered as a choir psalter, of fourteenth/fifteenth-century date.

[6] John Fishburn senior is C.1031 in *LVD*, iii; details of the location of book collections are in Piper, 'The Libraries of the Monks of Durham'.

[7] Mainsforth (*c.* 1369–1409/10) is C.986 in *LVD*, iii; Durham (*c.* 1395–1438/9), C.1035; Ferriby (*c.* 1400–53/4), C.1044; and Oll, C.1074, was in deacon's orders in 1416 and named as donor of one of these psalters as a replacement for one that had been stolen. The list is printed in *Cat. Vet. Durham*, 114–16.

[8] Now Cambridge, Jesus College MS 23.

None of the choir psalters that are survivals from the other cathedral priories can be identified as having belonged to a particular monk with the single exception of the Ormesby psalter at Norwich. Embellished with superb illuminations it was the gift of the monk Robert de Ormesby, probably in the late 1330s, with the understanding that it was to be permanently placed in front of the subprior's stall in choir.[9] There are also three fourteenth-century Norwich choir psalters and two of the thirteenth century, all containing additional material as described above.[10] The list of service and other books copied by the industrious Coventry monk John de Bruges in the mid-thirteenth century draws attention to the periodic necessity to replace the essential 'tools of the trade'; these included a psalter for Prior Roger de Walton and a psalter and diurnal (for the day hours of the office) for the infirmary.[11] Of the two Ely liturgical psalters, both of thirteenth-century origin, one included the four gospels as well as the common additions and the other had musical notation in the margins which has been partially removed by shaving.[12] A single extant Winchester psalter of the twelfth century is remarkable for its abundance of brightly coloured, albeit somewhat crude, illuminations; it is also distinguished by the presence of both the Latin and the French texts of the psalms in parallel columns on each page, and the usual additions are included.[13] A surviving late twelfth-century psalter of Worcester provenance has the name 'dan John Stanley' and the date 1395 on a back flyleaf; however, although there was indeed a monk of that name and date, it may be doubted whether he had more than a passing personal connection with the book, the pristine condition of which reveals little sign of use.[14] These few examples of choir psalters suffice to show some of the variations in their contents which were regarded as expedient adjuncts to the books in daily use for the recitation of the office.

The sparsity of medieval liturgical manuscripts that remain from the cathedral priories and, indeed, from English monasteries in general can be attributed to their constant, if not daily, use with the resulting wear and tear and also, especially with regard to sacramental liturgical rites such as the mass, to post-dissolution destruction. Only two surviving cathedral priory missals are known, of which one from Durham is of fourteenth-century date. It was assigned for use at the altar of St John the Baptist and St Margaret, one of the nine altars at the eastern extremity of the

---

[9] See S. C. Cockerell and M. R. James, *Two East Anglian Psalters* (Oxford, 1926); the Ormesby psalter is now Oxford, Bodley MS Douce 366. For Ormesby see *BRECP*, 546–7.

[10] The fourteenth-century psalters are now BL MS Harley 3950; Oxford, Bodley MS Lat. liturg. f. 19; Oxford, Wadham College MS A13.7; those of the thirteenth century are Durham, Ushaw MS 7 (which I have not seen) and LPL MS 368 to which has been added the office of the Blessed Virgin Mary.

[11] Sharpe, *EBL*, at B23.11, 23; for Bruges and Walton see *BRECP*, 348, 372.

[12] BL MS Harley 547 contains the gospels, and Oxford, Bodley MS Laud lat. 95 the musical notation.

[13] F. Wormald's *The Winchester Psalter* (Miller and Medcalf, London, 1973), is one of several commentaries on this manuscript, now BL MS Cotton Nero C.iv.

[14] Now Oxford, Magdalen College MS lat. 100, the kalendar of which may be compared with that found in the Worcester antiphoner (Worcester MS F.160) according to R. M. Thomson, *Medieval Manuscripts in Worcester Cathedral*, 109. For John de Stanleye see *BRECP*, 876, where there is no reference to this manuscript.

cathedral church; the consecration folios are darkened from use and strips of green cloth are attached as markers extending below the foot.[15] A fifteenth-century missal which may have belonged to the Norwich monks also remains, if the inclusion of the propers for the feast of the dedication of the cathedral can be regarded as substantial evidence.[16]

Numbered among other manuscripts for mass and office was the antiphoner, represented by the Worcester antiphoner which dates from the early thirteenth century with later additions. A choir book containing the chants for the office, it is a unique survival and has recently been critically examined in detail to show that it is, in fact, a compilation of several books all concerned with the correct observance of the daily services.[17] Another essential volume, commonly referred to as the *temporale*, provided a kalendar together with the propers, that is those portions of the liturgy appropriate to the observance of the succession of seasons of the church year; a second volume, or *sanctorale* fulfilled a similar role by providing the propers for the celebration of saints' days. These, like the antiphoner, were for use by the choir. A single volume made in the early thirteenth century for the Worcester community combined both the *temporale* and *sanctorale* and continued in use at least into the fifteenth century, as the many additions and alterations in a variety of hands make clear.[18] The medieval monastic breviary was akin to, and often indistinguishable from, the choir psalter but was generally understood to incorporate the complete text of the office. Several of these have survived among cathedral priory manuscripts. One, described as the 'burnt breviary' of Canterbury origin consists of only a few late fourteenth-century fragments.[19] Another, of thirteenth/fourteenth-century date at Durham was in use in 1521 when it was given by the last prior, Hugh Whitehead, to Richard Crosby, who had been professed about eight years before. Marginal additions in different hands provide evidence that it had been in constant, or at least intermittent, use by individual monks of previous generations; the antiphons for feasts have been supplied with musical notation, and the text has

---

[15] The kalendar in this missal, which is now BL MS Harley 5289, has been included in Wormald's *English Benedictine Kalendars after AD 1000*, i, 163. A thirteenth/fourteenth-century *graduale* also probably from Durham and containing the choral chants for the propers of the mass survives as Cambridge, Jesus College MS 22.

[16] The cathedral was dedicated to the Trinity; the missal, now Downside MS 26524, was examined by Dom Aelred Watkin in the *Downside Review* (1940), 444–6.

[17] See Thomson, *Medieval Manuscripts in Worcester Cathedral*, under MS F.160, 108–9. Thomson has also examined and commented on the fragments of late thirteenth-century polyphonic music from Worcester which have been removed from manuscript bindings after being discarded as out of date, and subsequently used for rebinding in the fifteenth and sixteenth centuries, ibid., xxiv–xxv, xlvi. The two eleventh/twelfth-century Winchester tropers that are now Oxford, Bodley MS 775 and Cambridge, Corpus Christi College MS 473 should be mentioned, see W. H. Frere, *The Winchester Troper*, Henry Bradshaw Society, viii (London, 1894), and most recently the facsimile edition by Susan Rankin (British Academy/Stainer & Bell, London, 2007).

[18] Now Worcester manuscript Q.26, and see Thomson, *Medieval Manuscripts in Worcester Cathedral.*, 134.

[19] It remains at Canterbury as MS Add. 6; see the astute commentary by Pfaff in *The Liturgy in Medieval England*, 242.

been embellished with many highly decorated and illuminated initials.[20] An Ely breviary of c. 1300 is a small volume of originally over three hundred folios which combines the texts of both office and mass, the latter being furnished with some musical notation. Many folios are darkened and worn from age and use. It may have been a *vade mecum* taken by monk priests on journeys outside the monastery, and evidence for such private and personal use is provided by the insertion of additional prayers in blank spaces, for example the words of absolution said by the priest after the confession of a penitent.[21] A Winchester manuscript, dated 1424 and described rather inadequately as 'Proprium sanctorum', was originally part of a two-volume set according to the detailed explanation and instructions inserted by William Vincent, who had entered St Swithun's around 1415/16. The set, so he specified, consisted of 'quoddam portiforium cum suo diurnale', in other words, probably a portable diurnal containing the day hours of the office. Vincent continues by stating that he was responsible for having one, or perhaps both, volumes made and that 'manibus meis propriis conscripsi'; he requested that after his death they were to be given to the sacrist or to another monk named by the sacrist, and so on *de uno ad alium*. The surviving volume is small, neatly written, and highly decorated and contains the propers of saints; the contents of the missing volume are uncertain.[22] *Portiforia* are also found at Norwich, the earliest mention being on the account of Ralph de Elingham, master of the cellar in 1278/9; he paid a total of 21s. 1d. for the purchase and preparation of the skins and the subsequent writing of the text on the finished parchment.[23] Among the contents of the upper chapel at the cell of St Leonard's in 1424 was a large *portiforium* donated by the monk Robert de Lakenham, who had died in 1404/5; and at the Yarmouth cell a fifteenth-century inventory includes two *portiforia*, a large one that had belonged to John de Hoo, prior of Yarmouth in the 1380s and between 1401 and 1406, and another described as *pro equitant'*, meaning, presumably, small enough to be easily carried when travelling.[24]

The liturgical seasons and the observances for fast and feast

The beginning of the liturgical year was and is the season of Advent, a season of waiting in expectation of the incarnation of the Saviour. It was therefore a period

---

[20] The volume is now BL MS Harley 4664; it may have been at the Durham cell of Coldingham at one stage and possibly at Oxford. Whitehead is C.1269 in *LVD*, iii and Crosby C.1321.

[21] The breviary is now CUL MS Ii.4.20; see Greatrex, 'Benedictine Observance at Ely', 77–98 at 88 and 91. Ker's dating in *MLGB* is a misprint.

[22] See *BRECP*, 743 for biographical details of Vincent, and note that some of the information that follows here corrects and amplifies what is given there; the manuscript is now Oxford, Bodley MS Rawlinson C.489 and the explanation occurs on fo 25v.

[23] For Elingham see *BRECP*, 505; the entry on the master of the cellar's account is transcribed in Sharpe, *EBL*, 293.

[24] The few details known about Lakenham are in *BRECP*, 532 and the *portiforium* is listed in Sharpe, *EBL*, at B62.6 along with the two others at B62.7 and 8. John de Hoo, also in *BRECP*, 525, probably left his *portiforium* for the use of the monks at Yarmouth, Sharpe, *EBL*, at B64.27; the other one for travelling monks is at B64.28.

of penance and preparation beginning in late November or early December on the fourth Sunday before Christmas; the first of the four annual sets of Ember days were assigned to the Wednesday, Friday, and Saturday of the third week of Advent.[25] St Benedict had urged his followers to love fasting; in fact, he went as far as to say that the life of a monk ought to be a continuous Lent.[26] However, by the late thirteenth century the regulations with regard to fasting as laid down in the Rule had been relaxed. Where Benedict had given permission for meat to be eaten by monks only when they were ill and, by extension, to the elderly, stratagems had gradually evolved by which it had become acceptable under certain conditions, that is in locations other than the monastic refectory.[27] Some of these alternative eating places can be identified. In his injunctions of 1276 Bishop Nicholas de Ely had told the Winchester monks that meat could be served *cum expedit et decet* in the infirmary or a suitable location other than the refectory.[28] At Worcester Archbishop Winchelsey's visitation injunction of 1301 allowed meat dishes to be consumed in the *camera* of the prior, the room called the *misericordia* and the infirmary; but this was to apply only when at least two-thirds of the community were dining in the refectory.[29] At around the same date Christ Church monks were also permitted to eat meat not only in the prior's *camera* and the infirmary but also in two other locations, the *mensa magistri* or table hall situated close to the infirmary, and the *deportum* which was near the kitchen and probably the equivalent of the *misericordia* elsewhere.[30] A *solarium caritatis* served a similar function for the monks at Durham; it was an upper room over the cellar and between the refectory and the dormitory. The few references on the obedientiary account rolls indicate that the bursar, sacrist, and almoner were jointly responsible for some of the expenses related to its upkeep.[31] The location of a subsidiary dining chamber, or *misericordia* at Ely remains a matter of conjecture, although the architect and surveyor T. D. Atkinson surmised that it was adjoining the prior's great hall and to the east of the monastic kitchen; he also suggests that it was commonly known as the Bougre.[32] There was a small dining hall at Norwich located at the western end of

---

[25] The other three sets were the same three days during the first week of Lent, after the feast of Pentecost and after the fourteenth Sunday following the feast of the Trinity; ordinations customarily took place on Ember days.

[26] *RB*, C.4, 13 where the Latin states... *ieiunium amare*, and C.49, 1.

[27] Ibid., C.36, 9. At Durham and probably elsewhere the almonry school boys were given meat in Advent, Fowler, *Account Rolls*, i, 227 (almoner's account 1418/19).

[28] *Reg. Pontissara*, 642; in this reference and the one immediately below the injunctions of a previous bishop had been copied into a later register.

[29] *Reg. Montacute*, 275.

[30] The *deportum* was under the infirmarer's jurisdiction; see *Reg. Winchelsey*, 819–20.

[31] In the *Rites of Durham* it is called the Lofte, 268. The bursar, for example, bought a seat cover for a bench in the *solarium* in 1335/6 and paid for unspecified repairs in 1425/6, Fowler, *Account Rolls*, ii, 529, iii, 620; the sacrist paid for wine in the prior's *camera*, the *solarium caritatis* and the refectory in 1358/9 and employed a mason to work on a window in the *solarium* at a cost of 48s. in 1396/7 (DCM sacrist's accounts for the years named); the almoner's account for 1431/2 records 6s. 8d. for repairs and again in 1436/7, Fowler, *Account Rolls*, i, 231, 233.

[32] T. D. Atkinson, 'The City of Ely', *VCH Cambridgeshire*, iv (1931), 79. It was repaired by the sacrist in 1325/6, Chapman, *Sacrist Rolls*, ii, 59, and was used by those undergoing *minutiones* according to the precentor's account for 1349/50, CUL Add. MS 2957, 43.

the infirmary complex and within easy range of the monastic kitchens; A. B. Whittingham's plan of the cathedral priory names a 'table hall' in this location which may have doubled as an *aula minutionum*.[33] The Winchester hordarian made annual payments to the sick in the infirmary which, in 1337 and before, were itemized as *ad misericordiam infirmorum*; on the next surviving roll, dated 1382, this payment was continued, but in the form of separate sums for individual monks based on the length of their stay in the infirmary. It is uncertain therefore whether the hordarian was using the word *misericordia* as an abstract noun or referring to a particular place.[34] No reference to a chamber where meat was allowed has been found at St Swithun's.[35] Although the location of a *misericordia* at Worcester is uncertain, its presence is clearly attested by several obedientiaries: the kitchener paid a small sum owing to Walter de la misericorde in 1361/2; the cellarer arranged for the repair of the windows in 1376/7; and the refectorer paid the servant in the *misericordia* an annual stipend of 3s. 4d. in the 1390s.[36]

Advent menus in the cathedral priory refectories were not short of choice but, apart from potage, cheese, and eggs, the fare was limited to different kinds of fish. How the fish was cooked and served is largely unknown, but variety of flavour may have been enhanced by the addition of spices and herbs.[37] The cellarers at Durham, Ely, and Norwich and the kitcheners at Winchester and Worcester provide some details of weekly and quarterly expenditures on food, at times specifying what items were purchased and what was provided from the monastery stores.[38] At Worcester the kitchener's method of identifying each week of the year was by means of the opening words of the introit of the Sunday mass. Thus, the first Sunday in Advent was recorded as *Ad te levavi* and, in 1386, the total sum spent in this particular week was 78s. 2½d. for a community which then numbered about forty monks.[39] The Durham cellarer's account was based on the lunar cycle of thirteen months (i.e. four weeks to the month). In 1333/4 during the weeks of Advent the community was served a variety of fish including whitefish, turbot, plaice, salmon, and codling.[40] A rare, if not unique, survival is a diet roll of St Swithun's which records the items of food purchased for every day of the year 1492/3. On the first Sunday in Advent (2nd December) the meals consisted of 150 eggs, 3s. worth of beef, 1s. 6d. worth of mutton, calves' feet for those ministering or serving at table, potage for supper

---

[33] See Whittingham's revised plan of the cathedral priory (1975), and Gilchrist, *Norwich Cathedral Close*, 180. For the practice of the periodic blood-letting see below 281–8.

[34] Kitchin, *Obedientiary Rolls*, 274, 279.

[35] Conjectural plans of the monastic precincts may show the possible location of a *misericordia*, but evidence is lacking.

[36] WCM C.116, 69, 419, and 417.

[37] However, the spices purchased were often associated with treats for anniversaries and celebrations; see below 247–50.

[38] At Canterbury there are only five uninformative cellarer's accounts surviving before 1420.

[39] WCM C.121, edited by Hamilton, *Compotus Rolls*, 24–6, but incorrectly dated 1387/8. The introits for the next three Sundays were listed as *Populus Syon*, *Gaudete*, and *Memento[mei]* which, along with other introits, are listed in the section 'Saints' days and festivals' in Cheney, *Handbook of Dates*.

[40] DCM cellarer's account 1333/4, which has been transcribed in Fowler, *Account Rolls*, i, 17–32, at 18–19. It is surprising to find pork and veal included unless these were intended for the infirmary.

(*cena*), wine for the prior and the chaplain, two dishes described as *interferculi*, one of which was shared by the subprior and hordarian, and a dish described as *moile*; the total cost for the day was 9s. 9d.[41] On succeeding days eggs frequently recur as does mustard and, of course, fish including whiting, eels, flounders, herring sometimes served with mushrooms, and oysters and fresh cod for the subprior.[42] The reason for the omission of bread and dairy produce from these menus can presumably be attributed to the fact that the former was baked within the precinct from wheat and other cereal crops usually grown on the priory manors, and the latter was similarly supplied especially from the nearby home farm of Barton.[43] Fruit is also absent from the menu, but the fourteenth-century customary for St Swithun's refectory notes that the monk gardener was required to produce apples in Advent and Lent on Monday, Wednesday, and Friday; the distribution on these days reflected the order of seniority: the prior was to be given fifteen and the subprior and obedientiaries ten.[44]

The O antiphons

In the week before Christmas the Advent season attained its liturgical culmination in the singing of the great O antiphons. They were so described because they all began with 'O' followed by one of the titles attributed to the Messiah in the Old Testament passages foretelling his coming. They were sung each evening at Vespers before and after the Magnificat between 16 and 23 December. At Worcester precise instructions for the performance were inserted at the appropriate place in the Worcester Antiphoner, and at Norwich there is a similar entry in a kalendar attached to a fourteenth-century psalter.[45] At Norwich and Worcester, and, in all probability elsewhere, the series began with *O sapientia*, the singing of which was fittingly assigned to the prior.[46] Among the obedientiaries named to sing several of the other antiphons the selection was also made, so it seems, by a perceived connection between the opening words and the office in question. For example, at both Norwich and Worcester the cellarer, who must have always had a clutch of keys attached to his belt, sang *O clavis David*; both the gardener at Norwich and the kitchener at Worcester, for their part, had good but different reasons to sing *O radix Jesse*. The *O oriens splendor* assigned to both sacrists may have been considered relevant to their onerous responsibilities in the care and embellishment of the cathedral church and its decoration and furnishings. Among the seven 'O'

---

[41] The roll is printed in Kitchin, *Obedientiary Rolls*, 307–30, the Advent days on 311–13; there were between thirty and thirty-five monks in the 1490s.

[42] Ibid., as to mushrooms, the Latin word *fungus* can also mean 'stockfish'.

[43] See the tables in my thesis, 'The Administration of Winchester Cathedral Priory in the time of Cardinal Beaufort', Ph.D., Ottawa, 1972, xix–xxxi.

[44] Kitchin, *Consuetudinary*, 18–19, 29.

[45] The instructions in the antiphoner were added in a fourteenth-century hand in the margin, WCL MS F.160, fos 10v–11; the Norwich psalter is now BL MS Harley 3950 and the kalendar details on fo 8v.

[46] *RB*, C.64, 2, outlines the qualities to be sought in choosing an abbot among which should be his *sapientiae doctrina*.

obedientiaries the infirmarer was given a place only at Norwich and the pittancer only at Worcester, while the subcellarer was included at Worcester and the master of St Paul's hospital at Norwich.[47]

The liturgical celebration was accompanied by gifts and treats toward which all the obedientiaries regularly contributed. The payments for the 'Os' are well documented at Worcester on the account rolls of the cellarer, kitchener, precentor, and pittancer, but the correct interpretation of this complex network of receipts and payments can be difficult to extract from the copious evidence. It seems clear that the pittancer was the chief collector of the 'O' money as he regularly records contributions, often of about 10s. from each of six or seven obedientiaries. Under the heading *O virgo virginum* which was the 'O' assigned to him, he paid for spices and fish for his brethren in celebration, and at the same time he distributed small amounts of money to every monk. In 1340/1, for example, he spent 7s. 6d. on fish and 6s. 8d. on spices and gave 3s. to the prior, 2s. to the subprior, 18d. to the precentor and 12d. to the other monks.[48] The kitchener's annual contribution to the pittancer was 10s., but he also spent *c*. 13s. for fish as the delicacy to be shared for his *O radix* treat.[49] Similarly, the precentor's *O Adonai* was marked by 10s. to the pittancer and spices, fish, and sometimes wine for his feast; in addition he followed the pittancers' practice of distributing pocket money in slightly larger amounts and according to a similarly graduated scale.[50] The chamberlain's *O Emmanuel* followed the pattern of money distributions among the Worcester community, but there is no evidence of any expenditure on spices.[51] As for the cellarer, he not only paid the pittancer for his 'O' but also for those of the prior, the sacrist, and the subcellarer on most of the years for which accounts survive and, like the other obedientiaries, he purchased wine, fish, and spices and made cash payments to his brethren.[52] Between *c*. 1399/1400 and 1411/12 the 'O' moneys were diverted to the cellarer's expense account for the building work in the Worcester cloister.[53]

Records of the 'O' celebrations at Norwich are lacking in similar detail although the contributions paid by the seven obedientiaries involved occur fairly regularly on the accounts. On several of the earliest communar's accounts the receipts for 'O' payments amounted to £10 to £12, but once the building operations were in full swing, on some of the succeeding accounts there is no sign of any 'O' celebrations.[54]

---

[47] No information has so far come to light at Bath, Canterbury, Coventry, or Rochester. At Durham the only known reference occurs in the *Rites of Durham* where the unknown author suggests that the communar 'dyd...keepe his o Sapie[ntia]', but this as the editor suggests is unreliable, *Rites*, 89 and note 283.
[48] WCM C.299.
[49] Ibid., C.109, 120–7.
[50] Ibid., C.351–70 etc.
[51] Ibid., C.11–25 *passim*.
[52] Ibid., C.55–77, C.476; in 1392/3 he spent 4s. on spices for the convent in Advent, C.76.
[53] E.g., ibid., C.80, 370, 374, 476.
[54] NRO DCN 1/12/2–4 (1288/9, 1290/2) and printed in Fernie and Whittingham, *Communar Rolls*, 51, 57, 61. Similarly, in 1316/17, 1323/4, and 1324/5 receipts are recorded, but there is no mention of the purchase of food or wine for these particular celebrations, ibid., 1/12/13–15 and *Communar Rolls*, 89, 96, 100.

This is presumably because the money was absorbed into the building funds, a practice which seems to have continued intermittently through much of the fourteenth century due to the ongoing building programme.[55] In 1344/7 the pittancer records the receipt of £9 6s. 8d. from the subprior, who from time to time appears as collector of the 'O' money, and who passed on the money to the cloister fund; the following year, after receiving the same amount the pittancer distributed some of it in cash among the brethren, namely 1s. to each of sixty-seven monks.[56] The master of the cellar, who had no 'O' of his own, had the responsibility for that of the prior for which he accounts under *camera prioris* on his rolls. He bought rice and salmon in the 1340s, fish in 1367/8 and spices and wine in 1379/80.[57] It was the cellarer who received 'O' payments from the subprior in 1350/1 and who proceeded to distribute 40s. among his brethren *de O... ad Pasch[am*. This surprising change of date has its origin in one of Bishop Bateman's injunctions intended to settle the annual cash payments allowed to the monks *pro suis secretis necessitatibus relevandis*; he prescribed that one of these payments, which was to be taken from the money contributions to the 'O' treats, was to be made within the Easter octave and to amount to 12d. for each monk.[58] In the 1390s after more than a decade without O contributions the Norwich chamberlain stated that he had paid 53s. 4d. *in Oo ad Pasch*.[59]

Ely references to the Advent 'O' feasts are found in the accounts of the chamberlain, precentor, and sacrist and consist of only a few entries between *c.* 1300 and 1360.[60] In 1334/5 under the heading *O et olla* the chamberlain made two payments, one of 13s. 4d. to the sacrist and the other of the same amount for the convent's spices. The following year he paid 16s. 1d. for spices and ale for his brethren, but in the years between 1336/7 and 1347/8 his *O et olla* contributions were diverted *ad opus novi chori*.[61] A similar pattern of payments appears on the surviving precentor's accounts, in Bentham's selective transcripts, according to which he gave 100s. toward the fabric of the new choir in 1343/4 in lieu of the *O et olla*.[62] More frequent entries appear on the sacrist's accounts where, for example, in 1322/3 he gave his contribution of 13s. 4d. to the subprior stipulating that it was to be used *iuxta disposicionem conventus*.[63] In 1339/40 his

---

[55] See above 199, 215.
[56] NRO DCN 1/12/24–7; see below, note 58, for the likely explanation for the cash distribution in 1348/9, and note that there is no reference as to when the payment was made.
[57] Ibid., 1/1/38, 42, 50, 57.
[58] Ibid., 1/2/19 and Cheney, 'Norwich Cathedral Priory', 110; the injunctions are undated and making use of other evidence, Cheney suggests *c.* 1346/7, ibid., 94. This date fits well with the pittancer's payment in 1348/9; see note 56 above and the related passage in the text.
[59] NRO DCN 1/5/26–9; the chamberlain's failure to pay may have been due to his 'overdraft'. Presumably the Easter 'O' distribution did not replace the Advent treats although it would have reduced the amount available.
[60] There is a later entry on the chamberlain's account dated 1388/9, but it states that nothing was spent, CUL EDC 1/F/3/22. The dearth of evidence is at least partially due to the poor state of the rolls, many of which are so worn and fragile as to be illegible.
[61] CUL EDC 1/F/3/1, 2, 3, 4, 6, 7, CUL Add MS 2957, 22, 23, 24; in 1348/9 the payment was made *ad opus dormitorii*, CUL Add MS 2957, 25, *Olla* may refer to a pot or measure of ale.
[62] CUL Add. MS 2957, 39, 42, 43.
[63] CUL EDC 1/F/10/3; this year saw the beginning of the 'new work'.

13s. 4d. went toward the construction of the new choir stalls, and in 1345/6 to the new choir.[64] The latest reference to *O et olla* is on the account for 1359/60.[65] The pittances or *gracie* as they were called at Ely, which were dispensed by the pittancer, in later years may have included the 'O' payments but the latter may also have continued to be swallowed up in the continuing building expenses.[66] The presence of 'O' celebrations at Winchester is well attested, but there are no details as to how they were carried out. Thus, we know merely that the chamberlain regularly paid for his 'O'; the receiver paid for the 'O' of the prior, curtarian, and bartoner in 1334/5; the hordarian paid frequently for his 'O', and in 1329 and later years he notes that he contributed 13s. 4d. to the *Espernium* and gave an additional 5s. for spices and wine.[67]

Particulars of the performance of the elaborate festal liturgies appointed for mass and office during the seasons of Christmas and Epiphany, and the other major festivals of the year, showed minor variations from one Benedictine house to another, being partly dependent on local usage.[68] The individual community's liturgical observances were based on the Rule and on its own traditional practice passed on from one generation to another and periodically revised by the consensus of the superior and senior monks. These alterations and additions were inscribed in chapter ordinances and usually recorded in the monastic customary, the essential directory compiled by each community. An addition to the lost Canterbury customary, for example, would have been made following the murder of their Archbishop Thomas Becket, in 1170 within the Christmas octave, after the Christ Church monks had inserted the date of his martyrdom (29 December) in their kalendar and proceeded to select and compose appropriate propers for the new feast.[69]

---

[64] CUL EDC, 1/F/10/8, 10.

[65] Ibid., 1/F/10/15.

[66] For these expenses see, for example, the sacrist's accounts for the years 1386–90 in CUL Add MS 2956, 162–3.

[67] The chamberlain's first known payment in his earliest surviving account was 16s. 6d. for wine and spices in 1399/1400, WCM W53/14/2; later accounts, of which there is only one before 1420, are in Kitchin, *Obedientiary Rolls*, e.g. 365 (1416/17). For the receiver's payments see also Kitchin, ibid., 232 and for the hordarian, ibid., 255 (1327), 258 (1329), 262 (1331), 265 (1333), 268 (1334) etc.; by 1409/10 the entry reads 'In solutis depositariis pro O hordarii xiijs. iijd', ibid., 291. For the *Espernium* and *depositarii* see above 164–5 and below 274–5.

[68] For example, the Durham kalendar in BL MS Harley 4664 includes seventy-three principal feasts of twelve or more lessons and sixty-eight minor feasts of three lessons, fos 126–131v. The kalendar in the Norwich customary has eighty-eight feasts of twelve lessons (which includes principal feasts, feasts *in albis* and *in capis*) and fifty-six of three lessons, Tolhurst, *Norwich Customary*, 1–12.

[69] Although no Christ Church customary has survived two diligent monks compiled a customary for Becket's shrine in 1428. One of them, John Viel, was sacrist at the time and the other, Edmund Kyngston, *custos martyrii*; the result survives in BL Add. MS 59616 and has been edited by Turner in *Canterbury Cathedral Chronicle*, no. 70, 16–22. For Viel and Kyngston see *BRECP*, 310 and 214–15 respectively. Priory Reg. A contains several early fourteenth-century chapter ordinances concerning liturgical observances for certain feasts, fos 389–90, as do BL MS Cotton Galba E.iv, fos 71–75v and Priory Reg. K, fos 213v–220. There is also an interesting request from the prior to the archbishop in 1331 seeking advice about the celebration of the feast of the translation of St Benedict, Priory Reg. L, fo 8–8v. Among cathedral priory customaries the only survival is a mid-thirteenth-century manuscript from Norwich; see above 65. However, it is to be noted that the Ely precentor in the 1370s paid for the illumination and the rebinding of a customary CUL Add. MS 2957, 45, EDC 1/F/9/5; and in the

Exchange of gifts in the community

Preparations for the convivial feasting and entertainment that accompanied the Christmas and Epiphany celebrations are indicated by certain seasonal expenditures itemized on many obedientiary accounts. Although there seems to have been little concern for consistency or precise detail with regard to financial record keeping in general, the items purchased and gifts dispensed reveal some particulars of the expenses incurred by the monks in a mutual exchange of tangible greetings, in gratuities to their lay officials and servants, in donations to friends and patrons, and in offerings to the poor. Examples of all of these categories are plentiful and fairly clearly indicated on the accounts, with the exception of the obedientiaries' gifts to one another and to their brethren, which defy attempts to unravel and explain the spider's web of transactions, actual or possibly token, that lay behind them. These small customary payments/gifts in cash and kind by the prior, subprior, and every obedientiary to some or all of their brethren must have had their origin in a remote past, possibly before the requirement to present annual accounts had been imposed and certainly before the earliest surviving late thirteenth-century accounts.[70] In time these exchanges acquired an apparently undisputed status to become long-established customs inherited by successive obedientiaries as obligations attached to their office.[71]

The Christ Church almoner stated that he had given £9 15s. 4d. to his *fratres* and *famuli* in 1360/1, and £7 8s. in 1391/2 to his brethren *in claustro*, when he also paid 17s. to himself, this last explained by the somewhat ambiguous phrase *quia non capit oblationes aliunde*; this practice occurs on other accounts at Canterbury and also at Durham.[72] The Canterbury bartoner used the heading 'foreign expenses' to record Christmas and Easter *oblationes fratrum* in 1404/5; they amounted to 68s. 4d. to which he added 16s. in *oblationibus propriis*.[73] *Caritates et oblationes* of £4 were given by the chamberlain to his fellow monks in the 1390s at Easter with an additional 34s. reserved for himself.[74] The sole surviving feretrars' account of 1397/8 lists payments from shrine receipts as 'pittances' to their

---

1380s the Worcester precentor bought vellum and paper *pro libro consuetudinar' claustri* and paid a scribe to write the kalendar for it, WCM C.366.

[70] Obedientiaries had to be reminded from time to time of the obligation to render an annual account: Bishop Walpole issued an injunction to this effect to the Ely monks in 1300, Evans, *Ely Chapter Ordinances*, 21; the monks of Durham included a similar statement in a chapter ordinance of c. 1316, DCM Locellus XXVII, 16; and Bishop Bateman addressed one of his injunctions of c. 1346/7 to the Norwich monks who were serving as priors of cells, Cheney, 'Norwich Cathedral Priory', 107, 108.

[71] An unresolved question is how these inter-office distributions originated and developed. An intimation of the kind of record that may have existed to regulate the payments at Canterbury would, perhaps, explain the insertion on a flyleaf in CCA DCc Reg. J 'Qualiter dande sunt oblationes de Thesauraria ad Natale[m] Domini et Pascham'. In the mid-fourteenth-century list that follows, the prior was to receive 10s., the subprior 5s., the third prior 3s., several like the fourth prior and lector 2s., and the rest 1s. Unfortunately, there is no possibility of verifying that these were paid by the treasurers on the few surviving accounts.

[72] CCA DCc almoner's accounts 49/50, 1.
[73] CCA DCc bartoner's account 70.
[74] Ibid., chamberlain's account 56.

brethren on several occasions during the year including Advent, and as 'oblations' of £4 13s. at Christmas.[75] The Durham feretrars' regular distribution of the shrine receipts confirms that this must have been the practice at Canterbury. In 1376/7, for example, payments at Durham were made to every monk including the two feretrars on five feasts days during the year, and the amount received varied from 2s. to 3s. per monk each time with larger amounts to the prior, subprior, the feretrars, and one or two others, and correspondingly less to the novices.[76] However, several other Durham obedientiaries, including the hostiller and the sacrist, like the Christ Church almoner, paid themselves *oblationes quia nichil percipit de feretro*, as the sacrist recorded on his account in 1377/8.[77] The earliest extant account of the Ely feretrar, that of 1421/2, follows a similar pattern, forty-one monks received 3s. 4d. each and the prior, subprior, and two other seniors twice that amount; these payments came under the heading of the *gracie* permitted by Bishop Walpole.[78] The Ely treasurers gave small sums to the monks in deacon's and subdeacon's orders at Christmas as did most of the other obedientiaries; the hostiller, almoner, and cellarer were also among those who gave *exennia* to the prior.[79] The Norwich obedientiaries accounted for similar cash distributions, and these were usually reckoned simply as *per annum* totals to their *sociis* and the prior. In 1345/6, however, the infirmarer recorded *oblationes* at Christmas of 7s. 5d. but with no reference to any intended recipients; and he added a payment of 20s. to himself, with the explanation *pro oblatione [sua]et labore*.[80] The precentor acted similarly by awarding himself 20s. and his succentor 6s. 8d.; the sacrist gave *pensiones* totalling 18s. 9d. to *fratribus de claustro* in 1320/1, and in other years he sometimes named the recipients who could include the prior and his chaplains, the subprior, precentor, subsacrist, and the master of the high altar.[81] The Winchester anniversarian made a practice of paying the *depositarii* 13s. 4d. to be distributed as pittances to the brethren on Christmas eve; the hordarian gave a small sum to the cellarer, hostiller, and infirmarer on the feast of the Holy Innocents within the Christmas octave; at Christmas, Easter, and the feast of St Michael in Monte Tumba (16th October) in 1399/1400 the infirmarer gave the sacrist 7s. 2d. in *curialitates*; and the prior chose to give *oblationes* at Christmas and Easter to his chaplains, the curtarian,

---

[75] CCA DCc, feretrars' accounts, 1. Feretrars' accounts of the cathedral priories, where they existed, are today few and far between; the earliest to survive at Durham is dated 1376/7; those of the *tumbarius* at Worcester begin in 1375/6 while none survive from Ely before 1421.

[76] The five feasts are named in footnote 295, page 208 above. For a detailed list of the payments for one of these feasts in 1408/9 see Fowler, *Account Rolls*, ii, 457; only the thirty-eight monks currently resident at Durham benefited from these distributions.

[77] For the hostiller see DCM accounts for 1366/7, 1379/80 etc., and for the sacrist, ibid., accounts for 1377/8, 1379/80A etc.

[78] CUL EDC 1/F/11/1; *gracie* was the term used at Ely for pocket money.

[79] See for example CUL EDC 1/F/13/13 (1389/90) and 1/F/13/14 (1392/3) treasurers; 1/F/3/12 (1357/8) chamberlain; 1/F/5/1 (1328/9) hostiller; 1/F/1/8 (1375/6) almoner, 1/F/2/16 (1360/1) cellarer.

[80] NRO DCN 1/10/4.

[81] E.g., ibid., 1/9/5 (1350/1) precentor; 1/4/20 (1320/1), 1/4/37 (1385/6) sacrist.

and receiver in the 1330s.[82] Most, probably all, of the Worcester obedientiaries recorded an annual expenditure in gifts to the prior at Christmas and Easter, and the precentor sometimes added to these the feasts of Pentecost and St Wulstan.[83] The almoner on occasion accounted for a few shillings given to the sick brothers in the infirmary, and the *custos* of the Lady chapel lumped his Christmas distributions together in 1392/3 stating merely to *monachis, clericis et aliis*, 4s.[84] These payments at Worcester appear under *expense forinsece* although they are described as *dona, exennia*, and *oblationes* apparently indiscriminately. In many of the entries there is no detail of the category of people who received the gratuity nor of the date when it was given; in 1397/8, for example, the infirmarer stated merely *in diversis donis datis diversis*, 6s. 9d.[85]

The distribution of small sums of money among members of the monastic community to mark festivals such as Christmas and Easter was one of the forms in which gifts were exchanged. However, some of these expenditures entered in the accounts may actually have been for the purchase of gifts, the particulars of which were not deemed to be information required by the auditors. Where details are given we are able to observe that it was customary for obedientiaries to regale their brethren with items of food and drink for the festal table, most often in the form of wine and spices, but meat and fish and other consumables also occur. The prior, as befitted his status, was the chief recipient of these delicacies, but every monk received a share in accordance with his rank.[86] At Canterbury, the three feasts of St Thomas, archbishop, one of which was celebrated during the Christmas octave, were prominent.[87] On the feretrars' only surviving account of 1397/8, for example, over £8 was recorded as spent on spices for the prior and convent on the feast of Becket's translation.[88] More unusual was the anniversarians' purchase of lampreys for Easter eve in 1374/5.[89] The Durham feretrars are also found to be providing wine for the prior on a number of unnamed occasions during the year, and often when the latter was taking a holiday on one of his manors. The chamberlain also regularly sent wine to the prior, and he undertook to bring cheer to those of his sick brethren by providing wine for the infirmary in 1361/2 and probably other years.[90]

---

[82] WCM C.531 (1369/70), C.534 (1384/5) etc., Winchester anniversarian accounts among the Worcester muniments; Kitchin, *Obedientiary Rolls*, 258, 262, 268 (1329/34), hordarian; WCL W53/11/2, 3, infirmarer; Kitchin, ibid., 237 (1334/5), prior.

[83] As in 1349/50 and 1365/6, WCM C.353, 359a; in 1362/3, 1383/4, and other years the feast of St Nicholas was included, C.359, 363.

[84] WCM C.176, 179 (almoner 1380s); C.251 (*custos capelle*).

[85] Ibid., C.246.

[86] Rank was based on the date of profession. It was also determined in some cases by office as, for example, the subprior was held to be next to the prior in seniority.

[87] The three dates are the martyrdom 29 December, the translation 7 July, and the return from exile 2 December.

[88] CCA DCc feretrars' account 1; there must have been over seventy monks at the time, possibly closer to eighty.

[89] Ibid., anniversarians' account 6.

[90] For the feretrars see DCM feretrars' accounts for the 1370s, 1380s, and 1390s; for the chamberlain, ibid., chamberlain's accounts 1345/6, 1361/2 and Fowler, *Account Rolls*, i, 166 (1334/5).

The sacrist frequently bought wine and pears, sometimes with dates and almonds for the community on the feast of St Aidan.[91] There were similar contributions by Norwich obedientiaries to enhance the community celebrations; the almoner provided wine for the prior and community on the feast of St Nicholas (6 December) and also at the times of recreation; the chamberlain supplied wine at Michaelmas and in some years at Christmas and Pentecost as well; the precentor furnished wine on the feast of St Eustace (2 November), and spices such as ginger for the feasts of the Assumption and Christmas.[92] The Winchester prior's feasts were complemented by gifts of wine from the hordarian, almoner, anniversarian, chamberlain, infirmarer, and the *custos operum* who noted on his account of 1408/9 that there were five of these feasts during the year. Details supplied by the *custos operum* on this same account and on the accounts of other obedientiaries named above record that they also provided wine for named obedientiaries for their feasts as well as those of the prior.[93] Gifts to the prior of Worcester by some of the obedientiaries may have alternated between sums of money and items of food and drink as an initial reading of their accounts would suggest. Thus the almoner provided fish on the feast of St Nicholas in 1377/8, the chamberlain twelve capons at Christmas and Easter in 1389/90, and the precentor wine in 1360/1.[94] However, in other years these and other obedientiaries limited the statements on their accounts to the amount spent on these gifts, usually listed as *dona et exennia*. When the precentor spent 6s. 3d. in gifts to the prior for the feasts of St Nicholas, Christmas, Easter, and Pentecost in 1362/3 this was most likely in the form of wine as his obligatory annual contribution to the prior's table; however, we cannot be certain.[95] Gifts in kind between obedientiaries of the Worcester community, apart from those on the occasion of appointment to office, cannot be identified on the accounts.

The boy bishop was also the recipient of small sums during the octave of Christmas. He was one of the boys in the almonry school chosen each year usually around the feast of the Holy Innocents. The Winchester hordarian made regular payments on that day to the *episcopo juvenum* and the almoner, chamberlain, and anniversarian gave wine or ale. The Durham bursar's accounts refer to the *episcopo puerorum de elemosinaria* to whom he and six other obedientiaries gave gifts in cash annually without specifying a date. At Norwich, however, the master of the cellar and other obedientiaries paid a few pence to the *clericis* of St Nicholas

---

[91] DCM chamberlain's accounts 1351/2, 1359/60, 1380/1A, 1383/4A and other years; the feast of St Aidan was celebrated on 31 August.

[92] NRO DCN almoner, 1/6/16 (1353/4), 1/6/19 (1378/9); chamberlain 1/5/4 (1309/10), 1/5/13 (1352/3), 1/5/28 (1396/7); precentor 1/9/4 (1325/6), 1/9/9 (1367), 1/9/6 (1352/3).

[93] Kitchin, *Obedientiary Rolls*, 255, 262, 280 (hordarian); 398, 406, 413 etc. (almoner); WCM C.531, 532, Kitchin, ibid., 204, 206 (anniversarian); WCL W53/14/2, Kitchin, ibid., 370 (chamberlain); W53/11/2 (infirmarer); Kitchin, ibid., 213 (*custos operum*). The feasts of the prior and obedientiaries are not identified.

[94] WCM C.174 (almoner); C.17 (chamberlain); C.357 (precentor).

[95] Ibid., C.359.

(6 December) who may have been the equivalent there since the feast of St Nicholas like that of Holy Innocents is associated with children.[96]

Distribution of gifts to others outside

Gifts to priory and manorial servants, officials, and tenants are referred to on many of the obedientiary account rolls; and a few examples will illustrate the variety of items given, as well as donations of money, to a considerable number of people, most of whom lived outside the monastery but were, to a greater or lesser extent, dependent on it for their livelihood. The Durham hostiller, for example, made annual gifts in cash and kind at Christmas to the *ministris abbatie* under various headings including *dona, exennia,* and *oblationes.* The earliest extant terrar's account, dated 1401/2 singled out the monastery cooks to whom he gave 20d. *ex curialitate* at Easter; the chamberlain distributed several items of clothing and bedding as well as small sums of money to workers who included masons and carpenters; and the almoner distributed gloves and hose to foresters and others in his employ in 1375/6 and gloves to armigers and other servants in 1399/1400.[97] The prior of Christ Church gave his *famuli* 4s. at Easter in 1332 and the cellarer 33s. 8d. to a group of unnamed *famuli* at Christmas and Easter in 1396/7.[98] The Ely sacrist, the Winchester *custos operum,* and the Worcester pittancer rewarded their *famuli* similarly at these festivals, while the Winchester hordarian named his clerk and other members of his *familia* in 1335/6.[99] At Norwich, on the master of the cellar's lengthy list of donations many of the priory personnel were regular recipients of his largesse; they included the infirmary cook, two medical attendants, and the prior's barber in 1299/1300; the chamberlain specified manorial servants in 1399/1400; the communar named the convent barbers and washermen at Christmas and Easter in 1316/17, and the cellarer expressed his thanks to the priory's steward with gifts of wine in the 1380s.[100]

---

[96] The existence of ceremonies attached to the boy bishop's feast day is shown by the presence of antiphons and responsories in some breviaries and antiphonals. Examples of the Winchester hordarian's payments are found in Kitchin, *Obedientiary Rolls,* 255 (1326/7), 280 (1381/2) etc.; for the almoner see ibid., 398 (1311/12), 411 (1352/3) etc.; for the chamberlain ibid., 364 (1416/7) and for the anniversarian ibid., 204 (1394/5). The Durham bursar's accounts in Fowler, *Account Rolls,* contain references *passim* after 1360/1, ii, 564ff, and the other obedientiaries concerned, also in Fowler, ibid., *passim,* are the hostiller, chamberlain, almoner, infirmarer, communar, and sacrist. For Norwich examples of the relevant accounts are NRO DCN 1/1/14 (1298/9), master of the cellar; 1/7/1 (1320/1) hostiller; 1/10/10 (1398/9) infirmarer; 1/6/28 (1399/1400) almoner.

[97] DCM hostiller's accounts, 1344/5, 1368/9, 1381/2 etc.; Fowler, *Account Rolls,* ii, 300 (terrar); Fowler, ibid., i, 167 (chamberlain 1334/5) and later years; DCM almoner's accounts for these years and for 1399/1400 see also Fowler, ibid., i, 216.

[98] CCA DCc DE 3, fo 2, DCc cellarer's account 2.

[99] Chapman, *Sacrist Rolls,* ii, 28 (1322/3), ibid., 144 (1349/50); WCL W53/15/1 (1408/9) *custos operum* Winchester; WCM C.298, 299 (1339/41) pittancer Worcester; Kitchin, *Obedientiary Rolls,* 278, hordarian Winchester.

[100] NRO DCN 1/1/14; 1/5/31; Fernie and Whittingham, *Communar Rolls,* 89 where *lavatoriis* could refer to washerwomen; DCN 1/2/25 and 26.

The episcopal overlords of the cathedral priories, with their nominal role as titular abbots, reckoned to receive appropriate, practical expressions of their unique relationship with the resident monastic chapter. Evidence that this obligation was fulfilled is not lacking and may be found here and there in surviving records. Items of food sent as gifts to the archbishop from the Christ Church monks at Christmas and Easter are listed on the preliminary folios of an anonymous fourteenth-century chronicle; and another, probably slightly earlier, list occurs in priory Register A which states that the annual expenditure this necessitated was just over £8.[101] In addition, the chamberlain accounted for the purchase of cloth for the archbishop in 1308/10 which he commuted to a cash payment of 70s. in 1320/1.[102]

To have a member of the monastic community, even a former prior, on the episcopal throne of a cathedral priory church was no guarantee against discord and contention as the monks of Rochester found to their cost on more than one occasion.[103] During the metropolitan visitation of Archbishop Simon de Meopham in 1329 the monks presented a lengthy list of complaints against their bishop, Hamo de Hethe; one of these concerned the customary *exennium* due to the bishop on the feast of St Andrew, to whom the cathedral was dedicated.[104] This gift entitlement, possibly dating back to Bishop Gundulf in the early twelfth century, had originally consisted of large quantities of meat, poultry, fish, and other items of food for the bishop's feast in his hall after the appropriate liturgical ceremonies in the cathedral. It had been understood that if he were absent the monks were authorized to use the gift for almsgiving and hospitality.[105] By the time of Hethe's episcopate it was valued at £10 to alleviate expenses incurred by the bishop in providing hospitality at his table in celebration of the feast. The monks accused the bishop of taking the gift and leaving the prior and chapter to provide the obligatory refreshments themselves and foot the bill as well. However, the archbishop acquitted Hethe on this and all other counts, to the continuing resentment of the monks.[106]

Elsewhere, at other cathedral priories, bishops were the recipients of a variety of gifts from their monastic chapters. The cellarer of Ely, for example, gave 15s. 4d. to the bishop at Christmas in 1334/5, while the sacrist provided him with meat and fowl costing almost £2 in 1301/2 and lampreys and bittern in 1341/2.[107] The bishop of Norwich was given a *donatio* of 8s. in 1305/6 from the sacrist, and in 1335/6 the same amount but under the section headed *camera*. Gifts such as these

---

[101] The so-called 'Anonymous Chronicle', covering the period from Prior Eastry's death in 1331 to the first years of the priorate of John Wodnesburgh, is CCA DCc Lit. MS C.14 and the list on fos 18–20; the later portion of this chronicle was transcribed and translated by Eveleigh Woodruff in *Archaeologia Cantiana*, xxix (1911), 56–82. On fo 387v of CCA DCc Reg. A the list is headed *Liberac' exhenn'*, and is followed by the comment that, since the archbishop owed the monks £8 per annum from the manor of Reculver, the monks are only 3d. out of pocket!
[102] CCA DCc chamberlain's accounts nos 1–3, 16; in 1372/3 the sum was only 59s., ibid., 51.
[103] See above 9–10.
[104] *Reg. Hethe*, 427; the feast of St Andrew occurs on 30 November.
[105] See Brett, 'The Church at Rochester', 15.
[106] Oakley, 'Rochester Priory', 33; also *Reg. Hethe*, 427, 431.
[107] CUL EDC 1/F/2/2; Chapman, *Sacrist Rolls*, ii, 17; ibid., ii, 114.

dried up in the 1390s during the lawsuit against Bishop Despenser and were replaced by contributions to the monks' legal expenses in pursuing their cause.[108] The chamberlains of both Ely and Norwich frequently supplied articles of clothing, often *pellicia*, slippers, and boots or a sum of money equivalent to their cost. At Ely one or more of these three items occurs fairly frequently along with those provided for the monks. The entry on the account of the Norwich chamberlain, however, alternates between naming the articles of clothing and merely stating *in exennia* and the sum spent.[109] The *dona et exennia prioris* on the Durham bursar's accounts from time to time include references to gifts sent to the bishop; two oxen, a cow, twelve calves, and a saddle-cloth for the episcopal palfrey in 1333/4 and six calves at Christmas in 1349/50. The reason that such presents appear to have been infrequent may, perhaps, be explained by the fact that the bishop of Durham seems to have been more excluded from the domestic life of the priory than most other bishops of monastic chapters.[110] A similar reason cannot be put forward to explain the frequent omission of gifts to their bishops on the part of the priors and obedientiaries of Winchester and Worcester, but a lack of surviving evidence does not mean that there were none. In fact, the receiver of St Swithun's Winchester gave substantial gifts to the bishop at Christmas and Easter of 1334/5 which included two carcasses of beef, seven of calves, and rabbits and partridges.[111] The Worcester cellarer bought salmon in the octave of Epiphany 1294 *pro sena episcopi*, and the chamberlain's account of 1320/1 included the item *in botis et pelliciis* for the bishop; in 1361/2 the bishop was similarly provided with a *pellicia* by this obedientiary, and in 1389/90 with *ocree*.[112] However, many sporadic entries such as these fail to distinguish between gifts as such and obligatory payments, possibly in recognition of some service due as was the case at Rochester above. It is also likely that the responsibility of the monastic chapter to contribute to the bishop's basic needs originated in the distant post-Conquest era when episcopal and monastic households had shared some form of common life.[113]

Monastic largesse throughout the year as well as at festivals extended beyond the many persons who were closely associated with the monastic community attached to the cathedral, to include an even more numerous group which took in all levels of society: the royal family and their retainers, court and government officials, papal emissaries, patrons, benefactors and local gentry, travelling musicians and entertainers, messengers constantly arriving and departing, and many named individuals whose connection with the monks remains largely unknown. The accounting

---

[108] NRO DCN 1/4/16, 1/4/31. In 1393/4 the sacrist contributed £4 15s. 9d. to the legal costs, ibid., 1/4/40.

[109] CUL EDC 1/F/3/2 (1335/6), 1/F/3/7 (1346/7), 1/F/3/16 (1367/8); NRO DCN 1/5/7 (1327/8), 1/5/9 (1334/5), 1/5/15 (1381/2).

[110] Fowler, *Account Rolls*, ii, 523, iii, 550. This is the view expressed by Meryl Foster in 'Durham Priory', 198, based on her study of the priory in the first half of the fourteenth century.

[111] Kitchin, *Obedientiary Rolls*, 289.

[112] Wilson and Gordon, *Early Compotus Rolls*, 6, on which the dating has been incorrectly transcribed; WCM C.14, 17. *Ocree* are thigh boots or leggings.

[113] Some bishops made generous gifts to their monastic chapters during their lifetime and in the form of bequests; see above 204–6.

obedientiaries leave no doubt that, despite the repeated warnings of the Rule, fourteenth-century Benedictines found themselves unavoidably inheritors of a situation in which they were enmeshed in worldly affairs and customs.[114] The monks could and did argue on many occasions that none of them owned anything individually; but, as a corporate body holding property and employing a work force, they were subject to many of the same customs, conventions, and laws as their secular neighbours, and they paid their taxes and tenths to king and pope.[115] Constant claims on their hospitality from all levels of society were costly and often entailed gifts in addition to the food and lodging provided for guests. The Winchester receiver's lengthy list of *dona et exennia* in 1337/8 amounted to £25, half of which was distributed to officials and staff of the king, queen, and archbishop; and minstrels who came to entertain the community on the feast of St Swithun on the same account received 17s.[116] The bursar at Durham in 1375/6 bestowed a succession of gifts to reward groups of minstrels who performed before the prior and community on the feasts of Easter, St Matthew, St Cross, and the two feasts of St Cuthbert.[117] Half a century earlier the monks had paid a heavy price in *dona et exennia* to the purveyors, officials, and servants of the royal family, whose presence in the vicinity was occasioned by Edward III's Scottish campaign; in order to prevent their depredations the terse explanation of the bursar and terrar stated merely *pro bladis et fenis et cariagio salvandis*.[118] However, it was the Christ Church community who probably suffered most from royal visitations. Prior Oxenden's notebook records that in 1333, during the visit of the king and queen, gifts to them, to their retinue and horde of servants, and to the accompanying magnates totalled over £109.[119] The Ely treasurers made an obligatory contribution of £10 on the occasion of the marriage of Edward III's sister, Eleanor, in 1332/3, and in 1389/90 delivered twelve cranes to London for the enjoyment of Richard II and his uncle, Thomas of Woodstock, duke of Gloucester.[120] The Ely sacrist favoured more local connections such as John de Lisle, who was probably the chief steward of the bishop, Thomas de Lisle; in 1349/50 he received a gift of wine from this obedientiary.[121] At Norwich the master of the cellar frequently bestowed gifts on city officials such as the coroners, the constable of Norwich castle, the county sheriff and his deputy, and the city bailiffs whom he presented with knives in 1359/60.

[114] *RB*, C.4, 20: *saeculi actibus se facere alienum*.
[115] *RB*, C.33 where the monks are reminded that everything is to be held in common and no one is permitted to own anything. Prior Henry Eastry explained this to the king in a letter quoted above 18.
[116] Kitchin, *Obedientiary Rolls*, 250–1.
[117] Fowler, *Account Rolls*, iii, 582; they were listed under the *exennia* of the prior and amounted to 63s. Minstrels of the king, the Black Prince, and the earl of March also gave performances and were suitably rewarded on this account which spans the period from January 1375 to Easter 1376.
[118] Ibid., ii, 528; on the bursar's account, 1335/6B these 'bribes' amounted to at least £10.
[119] CCA DCc DE3, fo 22–22v, and see Woodruff and Danks, *Memorials of Christ Church*, 146–7, who note that the gifts were in addition to the accommodation and entertainment provided.
[120] CUL EDC 1/F/13/9; 1/F/13/13, and the Duchess of York, the king's aunt, was sent 400 *quynsez* on the same account.
[121] Chapman, *Sacrist Rolls*, ii, 141, 169; de Lisle was also the bishop's brother, J. Aberth, *Criminal Churchmen in the Age of Edward III, the case of Bishop Thomas de Lisle* (Pennsylvania State University Press, University Park, Pa, 1996), 51.

Minstrels and players also make regular appearances on the accounts of the master of the cellar, at Christmas, Easter, on the feast of the Trinity, and on other unspecified occasions; the sacrist also contributed his share to minstrels at Pentecost in 1301/2 and on the feast of the Trinity in 1307/8.[122] A similar group of recipients benefited from the gifts of Worcester obedientiaries; the cellarer remembered local officials and dignitaries such as John de Beauchamp in 1356/7, but also more prominent figures like Henry of Grosmont, duke of Lancaster, and the papal penitentiary the following year. The sheriff was probably given an annual gratuity; this was 30s. in 1371/2. It was also the cellarer who rewarded the minstrels, among whom were the king's minstrels and the queen's harper in 1344/5 and the minstrels of William de Beauchamp in 1395/6.[123]

The proliferation of the obligations that may be broadly identified as gifts is a salient feature of all the accounts of cathedral priory obedientiaries, and they have therefore merited examination in some detail. The extent of time and amount of attention that lay behind the usually summary and often ambiguous entries on the final accounts cannot be gauged, but the inclusion of phrases such as *prout[patet] per papirum, ut patet per acquietanciam* and *precepto prioris* indicate that there may well have been a few headaches in the process of producing the final draft for the annual audit, which was compiled from the collection of memoranda and slips of parchment and paper on which the relevant information had been recorded.[124]

The Lenten fast

The number of weeks between Epiphany and the beginning of Lent varied from year to year because of the fluctuating date of Easter. The latter was determined by means of a complex exercise in computistical calculation for which Bede (673–735) had composed a helpful instruction manual *De temporum ratione*.[125] The Christian paschal feast following on from the dating of the Jewish Passover was, from an early date, celebrated on the first Sunday after the full moon falling on or after 21 March, the date defined for this purpose as that of the vernal equinox. Thus, Easter day may occur as early as 22 March and as late as 25 April or any date in between. In his computistical treatise Bede included tables providing the date of Easter for the years 533 to 1064, and later generations of monks were occupied with similar computations for their own life span.[126] Signs of these computistical concerns are to be

---

[122] NRO DCN 1/1/4, 15, 21, 22, 24, 32, 42, 46, 53, 55 (master of the cellar); ibid., 1/4/14, 17 (sacrist).
[123] WCM C.63, 64, 67, 59, 77.
[124] These particular phrases occur on Worcester obedientiary accounts; see Hamilton, *Compotus Rolls*, 16, 21.
[125] See Blackburn and Holford-Strevens, *Oxford Companion*, 780, 796–7, 809–14 where the dating complexities are skilfully unravelled.
[126] An edition of Bede's *De Temporum Ratione* edited by C. W. Jones is available in *CCSL*, 123B (1975), 268–544. The monks of Rochester had a volume in which this work of Bede was bound along with Helpericus of Auxerre's *Compotus*, Sharpe, *EBL*, at B77.66 (early twelfth century). Christ Church also lists at least one copy in two volumes in the Eastry catalogue, James, *ALCD*, nos 91, and 92, one of which is now BL MS Royal 12 D.iv, a collection of computistical writings including Helpericus; James,

found in a number of cathedral priory manuscripts. An early thirteenth-century Christ Church manuscript, which contains the relevant treatises by Bede, is provided with not only a kalendar but also Easter tables and tables of the lunar cycles, while an Ely manuscript of miscellaneous material opens with a kalendar on which the date of Easter has been inserted on 26 March followed by a series of tables.[127] A blank folio in the previously mentioned Ely breviary has been filled by instructions for calculating the date of Easter by following the formula based on the Alexandrian nineteen-year cycle.[128] The Ely precentor's involvement in this essential exercise is confirmed by two entries on his accounts; in 1300/01 he paid a scribe to write out and repair the *tabula pascalis*; and in 1302/3 he decided to have a new illuminated *tabula* prepared at a cost of 4s.[129] Also at Ely a chapter ordinance of 1314 reminded the precentor of his yearly duty in the chapter house, on the first Monday in Lent, to receive and mark off on his roll all the borrowed books brought in by members of the community and, if need be, permit them to be renewed.[130] At least two thirteenth/fourteenth-century Norwich manuscripts supplied useful information for the monks adept in computus; both contain kalendars and tables and one of them makes use of the nineteen-year cycle mentioned above.[131] Reference to the Lenten display of books at Norwich is recorded on the precentor's account for 1352/3 because he paid two boys 9d. *custod[iendis] libros*.[132] A reference work for priests among Worcester manuscripts refers to movable feasts and calculates the dates of Easter for the years 1405–56.[133]

Two separate but concurrent Ash Wednesday ceremonies at Worcester cathedral priory in 1291 were described in the *Annales Wigorniensis*. One took place in the cathedral church during which the bishop, Godfrey Giffard, was represented by his penitentiary who distributed the ashes to the people assembled in the nave. Meanwhile, in the chapter house the prior, Philip Aubyn, preached to the monastic community and, after blessing the ashes, gave them to his brethren.[134] However, in

---

op. cit., no. 957 may be another copy. Coventry possessed two copies of *Tabulas compoti*, one of them with a kalendar and the other in a psalter produced for the monk Robert de Honintona, the scribe responsible for both books being the monk John de Bruges c. 1240, Sharpe, *EBL*, at B23.27 and B23.28. The 1395 list of books in the library at Durham records two copies in *Cat. Vet. Durham*, 64E and F, which may be the two volumes that occur in the twelfth-century list ibid., 3.

[127] Both manuscripts are now in the British Library: MS Royal 12 D.iv (Christ Church) as noted in the preceding note, and MS Add. 33381 (Ely); the kalendar and tables in both occur on the opening folios.

[128] For the breviary see above 178 n.104, 240; the nineteen-year cycle formula has been inserted on fo 207v. For explanatory details with regard to the Alexandrian cycle see Blackburn and Holford-Stevens, *Oxford Companion*, 801–4 (note 125 above).

[129] CUL Add MS 2957, 40–1.

[130] Evans, *Ely Chapter Ordinances*, 40; this requirement originates in *RB*, C.48, 15–16, which do not specify the day but merely state at the beginning of Lent. Sixteenth-century chapter discussions at Durham included similar instructions to the *magister librorum*. DCM Locellus XXVII, 10.

[131] The two Norwich manuscripts are now Cambridge, Corpus Christi College MSS 347 and 470; the kalendar and tables are on fos 1–12v of the latter.

[132] NRO DCN 1/9/6.

[133] Now Oxford, Bodley MS Hatton 11 (thirteenth- to fifteenth-century contents); the *de festis mobilibus* is on fo 34 and the Easter reckonings on fo 35.

[134] *Annales Wigorn.*, 504. The remark that follows this entry, *nec de officio episcopo se intromisit*, probably reflects the strained relations between bishop and convent at the time, about which see

other years at Worcester the bishops, who seem to have considered it their prerogative to perform the Ash Wednesday liturgy in the cathedral on some occasions, commissioned the prior to discharge this office on their behalf. Two of the fourteenth-century bishops, William de Gainsborough (1302–7) and Henry de Wakefield (1375–95), issued mandates to the cathedral prior to execute the customary office for all the assembled faithful penitents.[135] The entry in the priory register, the *Liber Albus*, which immediately follows Wakefield's 1392 mandate, records for posterity that the prior performed the Ash Wednesday rites 'virtute consuetudinis antique in libro ordinis scripte et in eadem ecclesia usitate a tempore cuius contrarii memoria hominis non existit'. A year later a similar entry in the *Liber Albus* makes it clear that the bishop had been persuaded to waive his claimed prerogative; thus, the 1393 mandate was sent in the form of a request to the prior to officiate, and the latter responded by doing so in his own right and not by virtue of the episcopal mandate.[136]

Lenten fare was at times a costly item in the budget of some of the obedientiaries who were concerned with and contributed to the monastic menus. The Worcester kitchener's weekly expenses averaged about £4 in 1334, but rose to over £6 between the first Sunday of Lent and Passion Sunday of 1341. In the 1380s expenditures for the weeks of Lent were around £5, while in the weeks following Easter the weekly charges were in the neighbourhood of £3. Apart from the cellarer's purchase of beans and white fish for the convent in Lent 1314, no details of what was eaten at Worcester have been found.[137] Cellarers at both Ely and Norwich made quarterly summaries of food purchases, although weekly totals are also given on a few accounts; these indicate that Lenten meals were usually more costly than at other times of the year. In 1377/8, for example, weekly expenditures on food at Ely varied between about £6 and £7, but during one week of Lent in 1388 purchases of fish amounted to almost £14; the list included fresh herring and lampreys, salted salmon, porpoise, eels, and also rice and almonds.[138] Almonds were a much appreciated addition to the Lenten repast at Norwich as well as at Ely. The Norwich refectorer, who was responsible for their purchase and provision, spent 11s. in 1333/4 and 15s. in 1361/2 *ad usum conventus*.[139] The first week of Lent cost the Durham cellarer over £6 in 1308 with the result that the monks dined

---

BRECP, 772 under Aubyn. In 1283 the bishop had preached the Ash Wednesday sermon in the cathedral church, *Reg. Giffard*, 173. 'Giving of ashes' refers to the ceremony in which the priest imprints a cross with the thumb on the forehead of the penitents.

[135] *Reg. Gainsborough*, 5, 15, 147; *Reg. Wakefield*, no. 658.

[136] WCM Liber Albus, fos 345, 355, 357, 365v, during Wakefield's episcopate, of which only the third entry of the four in the Liber Albus has been recorded in the bishop's register as the volume appears today. One of Gainsborough's mandates, that of 1304, appears in the Liber Albus on fo 16v. Note that the quotation, which appears on fos 357 and 365v, makes explicit reference to the monastic customary and ordo.

[137] WCM C.110, 111 (1333/4, 1340/1); C.120, 121 (1382/3, 1384/5); C.482 (1313/14). Numbers had decreased slightly or, rather, had not regained the pre-plague figures and this probably helps to explain the decrease in weekly expenditures.

[138] In the 1370s and 1380s there were between forty-seven and fifty-two monks. CUL EDC 1/F/2/20, 1/F/2/28; in 1385 the cellarer bought figs as well as nuts all through Lent, ibid., 1/F/2/26.

[139] NRO DCN 1/8/31, 41.

on salmon, plaice, sprat, cod, turbot, whitefish, and mussels; in 1334 the expense was about £2 lower and included lobster, apples, and a pennyworth of saffron. With one or two exceptions the cellarer does not seem to have been burdened with higher costs in Lent, but variations in expenditure can be partially explained here and elsewhere by the use of food supplies that were home grown within the precinct or on the priory manors, or purchased previously and retained in the community stores.[140] Among the recollections of the author of the *Rites of Durham* was that the communar provided spices, figs, and walnuts for the community to alleviate the hardships endured in Lent. Unfortunately, the earliest surviving account of this obedientiary is for the year 1416/17, and its expenditures under the heading *Emptio specierum* casts doubt on the accuracy of the reminiscencer's long-term memory. In fact, the communar spent about 15s. that year and 24s. in 1430/31.[141] It is possible that he had substantial supplies on hand of some of the items that were included in this category, but another explanation may be more likely, namely that these pittances were given in cash rather than in kind. On four festal occasions during the year the Durham communar made payments to his brethren, one of these being the Purification of the Virgin Mary on 2 February, a date which occurs most frequently in Lent or not long before.[142] In the absence of a pittancer and/or a communar at Christ Church Canterbury pittances were distributed among the brethren by other obedientiaries: by the anniversarian, for example, on a number of feast days in celebration of the lives of past archbishops and priors, and by the almoner who specified the Lenten season as the focus of some of his contributions. These he generally provided in the *mensa magistri*, a dining hall within the infirmary complex where he, along with other obedientiaries, took turns in the distribution of pittances and wine at other times through the year. In 1338 on the feast of St Gregory, which fell on 12 March and was therefore in Lent, the almoner recorded spending 13s. 5d. for titbits for the monastic community. The sum of his contribution in Lent 1373 rose to 38s. 5d. and included a pittance of wine.[143] The *mensa magistri* was also the locus for the distribution of pittances on Sundays in Lent for which the treasurers footed the bill in the 1370s and 1380s.[144] Insight into the Lenten fare served at Winchester is only available on two occasions

---

[140] Fowler, *Account Rolls*, i, 4, 21. In the week leading up to Easter in 1334 the cellarer recorded that he had spent over £8, of which £2 was for a supply of sugar from Cyprus, no doubt in preparation for celebratory feasting, ibid., 21. It has been noted by Miranda Threlfall-Holmes that during a later year, 1449/50 the cellarer's diet accounts showed fluctuations in expenses from week to week, and were slightly higher in Lent when the average was just under £6, *Monks and Markets*, 72.

[141] The items included almonds and filberts in 1416/17, Fowler, *Account Rolls*, ii, 286, 288; there are no accounts in the intervening period between these two accounts. The seemingly large totals in both cases are misleading because the deficit from the previous year was added in.

[142] In 1416/17 the payment amounted to £9 3s. 4d., Fowler, ibid., ii, 287. The other three feasts on which payments were made were All Saints (1 November), the *Inventio sancte Crucis* (3 May), and St Peter *ad vincula* (1 August).

[143] CCA DCc almoner's accounts nos 32, 28; note that the accounts are not numbered in chronological order.

[144] Lambeth MS 243, fos 171v, 203; pittances were also provided by the almoner, treasurers and other obedientiaries in the *deportum*, a common or recreation room probably corresponding to the *misericordia* at other cathedral priories. For the *mensa magistri*, see above 241.

widely separated in time. In 1281 the receiver bought a quarter of a pound of barley sugar and half a pound of ginger to ease Prior Adam de Farnham's Lenten fast. On Ash Wednesday the receiver's purchases, presumably for all the monks, included fourteen pounds of figs and four pounds of raisins to be used in making rissoles.[145] The sole surviving diet account of 1492/3 reveals an average weekly expenditure close to £3 between November and May. Prominent on the menu in Lent in 1493 were mushrooms, prunes, mustard, raisins, figs, rice, and oatmeal in addition to quantities of fish both fresh and salted. Some of the dishes were reserved for the prior, subprior, third prior, and the hordarian, and others for the monk *ministrantes* who were carrying out the weekly rota of service in the refectory. The single instance of the purchase of eggs (for the subprior) suggests that there were enough available from hens kept in the precinct or on the home farm at Barton. For Good Friday, however, one thousand were bought, with herrings and figs, to sustain the monks on this day of solemn fast.[146] We need to be reminded that some basic items of food are often absent from the expense accounts of obedientiaries because bread, milk, butter and some cheese, meat, poultry, and fruit and vegetables were often, like eggs, home grown or products of the priory manors. The complex exchange of pittances within the monastic community during the forty-day fast was, in fact, another facet of the communal giving and receiving described variously as *dona, ex[h]ennia, pittancia* on the obedientiary accounts.[147]

Holy week, Easter, and Pentecost

The final week of Lent marked the climax of the preparations for the Easter festival. The ceremonies pertaining to Maundy Thursday and Good Friday, as well as those of Easter day, were described in the cathedral priory custumals with precise details of how the liturgical solemnities were to be observed. The late thirteenth-century Norwich customary lays down the procedure to be followed at the *missa chrismalis* in the cathedral on Maundy Thursday, at which the bishop as diocesan was meant to preside and to consecrate the oil for use in the coming year in all the churches within his see.[148] The *mandatum*, which followed, took place in the cloister where an unspecified number of poor men had their feet washed, and each received a drink and a penny (?*nummus*). Later that day the *mandatum magnum* took place in the chapter house; the bishop washed the feet of the prior and the senior monks, followed by the prior who washed the bishop's feet and, together with the subprior, washed the feet of the remaining brethren. A later addition copied into the last leaves of the customary describes the Maundy Thursday (*cena domini*) mass [in the

---

[145] Watkin, 'Receiver's Roll', 104.

[146] Kitchin, *Obedientiary Rolls*, 307–29; there were about thirty-five monks in the community during the 1490s.

[147] Let it be remembered that the monks numbered themselves among the *pauperes domini*.

[148] Tolhurst, *Norwich Customary*, 82–5; see also the fourteenth-century Durham missal, BL MS Harley 5289 fos 488v–91, extracts of which are transcribed in *Rites of Durham*, 182–5. The word *mandatum* is the first word of the antiphon, *Mandatum novum do vobis* (Jn 13, 34), which is said or sung at the beginning of the washing ritual.

cathedral] at which a sermon was preached to the people. There was also a daily *mandatum* throughout the year which, at Norwich, referred to the feeding of three poor men.[149] The observance of these rites is confirmed by entries on the Norwich obedientiary accounts: for example, the cellarer regularly contributed 6s. 8d. to the poor *in die cena*; the refectorer provided three long towels for drying the feet.[150] The sacrist, who was responsible for procuring the chrism, had to locate the diocesan or contact another bishop to arrange for its consecration in the cathedral, or negotiate to obtain his supply of the holy oil wherever he was able to discover a not too distant celebration of the Maundy Thursday rites.[151]

At Christ Church Canterbury the subalmoner played a central role in the Maundy Thursday celebration. After the morning chapter he called in a number of poor people and guided them through the cloister to the altar of St John, in the south-east transept of the cathedral, to attend mass. Afterwards they were taken to the [guest] hall where each received a loaf of bread, salted fish, three herrings, and as much as he desired to drink. Then followed the ritual foot washing in the cloister which was performed by the prior and monastic community. Before departing the poor waited to receive a *mandatum*.[152] Difficulties experienced in obtaining the next year's supply of chrism were also reported by the Canterbury sacrist. In 1324 the prior was obliged to confess to the archbishop that the rascal who had been sent to fetch the chrism from the archbishop at his manor of Otford had drunk too much on his return journey and consequently had lost the bottles.[153] An ordinance of 1322 required the cellarer to supply the bread and fish for the Maundy Thursday distribution to the poor and also three monks' loaves for the daily *mandatum*.[154] The anniversarian also spent some of his funds to treat the monks to salted sturgeon and wine on Maundy Thursday in 1399 and lampreys and wine on Holy Saturday in 1375.[155]

---

[149] Tolhurst, *Norwich Customary*, 82–7, 241. For the *mandatum per circulem anni*, ibid., 200; and note that it was omitted on Maundy Thursday, Holy Saturday, Easter, and several other days, ibid., 85, 93, 96, 121, 125.

[150] NRO DCN 1/2/1 (1284/5), 1/2/101 (1336/40), 1/2/19 (1351/2), 1/2/24 (1371/2) etc. (cellarer); ibid., 1/8/48 (1392/3), which includes an inventory listing three long towels *pro cena domini*. The prior of the cell of St Leonard's also recorded on his yearly account a gift of 13d. to the poor *in cena domini*, NRO DCN 2/3/2, 3, 4 etc. to 1399/1400, 2/3/18.

[151] That the Norwich sacrist sometimes had a problem is demonstrated by the presence of three entries in a priory register only a few days before Easter 1325. The prior, Robert de Langele, acting as vicar general for the absent bishop, sent a request to the bishop of Ely to consecrate an extra supply of chrism for Norwich cathedral; he also asked where the bishop would be celebrating the mass so that he could send a messenger to collect it, NRO DCN 40/9, fos 55v, 57v.

[152] CCA DCc Reg. B, fo 419v/438v; see also Reg. P, fo 83/183 and Reg. J, fo 420. Woodward and Danks in *Memorials of Christ Church*, 248, state that the number of *pauperes* corresponded to the number of monks, but I have not been able to confirm this. It is not specified in what form the *mandatum* was given, probably as an item of food or a small coin.

[153] Sheppard, *Lit. Cant.*, i, no. 119, from CCA DCc Reg. L, fo 138. Another problem arose in Lent 1333 when, in the absence of the archbishop, the prior, at the instigation of the sacrist, approached the bishop of Rochester and asked him to consecrate chrism for Christ Church, ibid., ii, no. 514 (Reg. L, fo 28).

[154] CCA DCc Reg. K, fos 212v, 213v.

[155] CCA DCc anniversarian's accounts 7, 6, and 5 (wine in 1359/60); there are only a half-dozen account rolls before 1420.

It is the almsgiving section of the Durham bursar's accounts that provides evidence for annual donations to the poor on Maundy Thursday, but further details are lacking.[156] The liturgical rite for this day is found in a surviving fourteenth-century missal which was assigned for use at the altar of St John the Baptist and St Margaret, one of the nine altars that, side by side, were placed against the easternmost wall of the cathedral.[157] The reminiscences of the elderly former monk which were written down c. 1600 relate that thirteen poor and aged men were chosen to come into the cloister to have their feet washed as they sat together on a long bench in the east walk. The prior performed this ceremony himself after which he gave each of them 30d. and refreshed them with bread, fish, wafers, and drink; his personal almsgiving, paid by the bursar, frequently makes specific reference to the poor *die cene*.[158] For the monastic community's Maundy Thursday repast in 1314 the cellarer produced apples and figs.[159] There are a few references to the observance of Holy Week on Ely obedientiary accounts, but the sacrist's purchase of four basins *pro mandatis* in 1354/5 may refer to the daily foot washing rather than the annual ceremony on Maundy Thursday.[160] The almoner set aside 20s. in 1337 and the 1370s *pro mandatis pauperum die cene* and provided wastel-bread for his brethren on Good Friday in the 1370s; the sacrist contributed salmon *in cena domini* in 1302; while the pittancer's *caritates* to the community in 1309 included 3s. 2d. on Holy Saturday and, almost certainly, in other years.[161]

The frequent references to the *mandatum* on the Winchester obedientiary accounts concern the chamber or hall of that name which was in the care of the almoner. It was therefore probably attached to the almoner's quarters; and it would have been the site for the daily foot washing of several poor men, and for the distribution of the dole of bread which was omitted, as at Norwich, on Maundy Thursday, a day of solemnity within the cloister observed by the entire community.[162] The almoner employed a servant described as *de mandato* to whom he regularly gave oblations at Christmas and Easter and, from time to time, he lists

---

[156] DCM bursar's account, 1297/8, 1360/1A, 1379/80, Fowler, *Account Rolls*, iii, 579; other references which state *ad mandatum* without specifying *die cena* probably relate to the daily *mandatum*, e.g. Fowler, ibid., ii, 497, 508, 544. The almoner provided towels for the Holy Week *mandatum* in 1416/17, Fowler, ibid., i, 225.

[157] The missal is now BL MS Harley 5289; extracts from the sections devoted to Lent and Holy Week are in *Rites of Durham*, 175–91.

[158] *Rites of Durham*, 77–8; DCM bursar's accounts 1370/1, 1377/8, 1394/5, 1404/5.

[159] Fowler, *Account Rolls*, i, 37; I would assume that this was not unusual, but was usually lumped with other items and therefore had disappeared by the time the final account was drawn up.

[160] Chapman, *Sacrist Rolls*, ii, 167. The almoner also was probably referring to the daily custom in 1369/70 when he paid for five *mandata*, CUL Add. MS 2957, 11; the chamberlain paid for the heating of the *mandatum* chamber in 1346/7, CUL EDC 1/F/3/8.

[161] CUL EDC 1/F/1/8, 1/F/1/10 (1370s) and CUL Add MS 2957, 9 (?1336/7), almoner; Chapman, *Sacrist Rolls*, ii, 17, sacrist; CUL EDC 1/F/8/1, pittancer.

[162] Kitchin, *Consuetudinary*, 22. The most recent archaeological investigations suggest that the almonry and attached *mandatum* were located on the west side of the little cloister of the infirmary, unpublished information courtesy of John Crook.

equipment purchased *pro mandato* and other expenses there.[163] The 1281 receiver's account records a series of purchases of wine through most of the year for which the frequent explanation given is the entertainment of guests; Maundy Thursday, the vigil of Easter, Easter day, and Easter week are the occasions frequently included. On Maundy Thursday in 1335 he gave a pittance to the convent of 40s. and another to the prior of 4s. 3d., and he also bought 12d. worth of small cakes (*nebulones*) for all the brethren for their community celebration in the refectory.[164] For Holy Week observance at Winchester, the fourteenth-century refectory custumal furnishes us with some additional interesting insights into the network of regulations. For example, it was incumbent on the prior to provide fresh straw for the refectory floor at certain set times of the year two of these being the vigils of Easter and of Pentecost.[165] The sacrist was expected to provide fresh candles on Maundy Thursday, and the *custos* of the altar of the Blessed Virgin Mary was responsible for the candles that stood before the cross in the middle of the refectory to provide light for the reader during collation.[166] The almoner's role was to give a clapper [*signum*] to the refectorer on Maundy Thursday, while the refectorer collected the knives of the brethren after lunch on Maundy Thursday so that they could be thoroughly washed and cleaned before being returned on the evening of Holy Saturday.[167]

A Maundy Thursday custom at Worcester comes to light on the account rolls of the almoner; it was probably not unique or even unusual, but is revealed more clearly and precisely than elsewhere among the cathedral priories.[168] Here, from at least 1342 onwards, the almoner was accustomed to give 3s. 3d. to the prior and 6d. to each monk *pro mandato die cene* which might seem to have been one of the several distributions throughout the year made by obedientiaries to their brethren. However, an entry in the fourteenth-century priory register cum customary makes clear the purpose of this particular distribution. To fulfil his share of the Maundy Thursday rite each monk was assigned by the almoner to wash the feet of two of the poor men he had brought into the cloister for the *mandatum*; this having been accomplished,

---

[163] Kitchin, *Obedientiary Rolls*, 399 (1311/12), utensils and mats and the servant; 401 (1316/17), construction of a *novum pallicium* and the servant; 404 (1317/18), the washer [wo]man *de mandato*, candles, and the servant; 417 (1389/90), construction and repairs costing 38s 8d.

[164] Watkin, 'Receiver's Roll', 99, Kitchin, *Obedientiary Rolls*, 252; it is most unfortunate that only a few receiver's accounts survive, and most of them are mere fragments. The curtarian recorded that he had bought honey for making the *nebulis in die cene* in 1412, WCL W53/14/9. *Nebula* and *nebulonis* are variants of the same word.

[165] Kitchin, *Consuetudinary*, 16.

[166] Ibid., 17, 19; collation, as described in Lanfranc's *Monastic Constitutions*, was a reading from the lives or conferences of the Fathers that took place in the refectory before compline, and on Maundy Thursday the reading was from the gospels and accompanied by a drink of wine, ibid., 56.

[167] Kitchin, *Consuetudinary*, 18, 21.

[168] The pittances at Ely that were distributed to the community on specified feasts, including the Easter vigil, and distributions referred to above at the other cathedral priories are similar practices; but they often fail to be spelled out clearly because of the truncated form in which they appear in many of the surviving accounts.

each monk gave 3d. to each of the poor whom he had washed.[169] The pittancer bought wine for the convent *in die cene* in the 1340s and in the 1370s and probably in the years between; and the kitchener set side 53s. 4d. for the community *cena* in the *domus misericordie* in 1477/8 and possibly earlier.[170] The daily *mandatum* was also the concern of the almoner at Worcester, who employed a servant to assist him and bought towels from time to time; and he received 6d. a week from the kitchener which in 1382/3 was explained as 'for the *mandatum* of St Wulstan'.[171]

Rogationtide was observed about four weeks after Easter, and Pentecost some ten days later; both receive frequent, although brief, mention on obedientiary accounts because they entailed a number of expenditures in addition to the purchasing of extra supplies of food and wine for the monastic community's celebrations and to the engaging of minstrels and other entertainers for the assembled company of monks and guests.[172] In May 1325 Prior Eastry of Christ Church Canterbury took it upon himself to draw Archbishop Reynolds' attention to the fact that the long-standing and laudable custom of solemn processions on the three Rogation days was suffering from neglect in the city, deanery, diocese, and province of Canterbury; Eastry urged him to issue orders to remedy the situation.[173] The anniversarian spent a sizeable portion of his small income on food for the monastic table on the Rogation days of 1375, and in 1399 he included more details on his expense account by listing the purchases on each of the three days. Among these were lampreys salted, flawns, and sturgeon salted, all served with wine.[174] At Durham the first Rogation Day was an occasion for pittances and wine distributed by the hostiller in the refectory for which he usually spent over a pound every year.[175] The Ely sacrist made a similar contribution, but in most cases he specified that it was for the third Rogation Day. Sturgeon, lampreys, and pike were recorded on his accounts, and the precentor often contributed wine.[176] Bishop Hugh de Balsham *c.* 1260 and one of his successors in the see, Thomas Arundel *c.* 1377, issued strong reminders to the clergy and laity of Ely deanery and diocese to take part in processions to the cathedral to make their offerings in the week of Pentecost.[177] The precentor's responsibility was to enlist the boys in the almonry school to collect and strew flowers in the choir of the cathedral at

---

[169] WCM C.170, 171, 172, 173 etc. The fourteenth-century *Registrum Prioratus*, 107a, implies that the prior washed the feet of thirteen men among whom he divided his alms of 3s 3d., and presumably the 6d. given to each monk was for the same purpose.

[170] WCM C.299, 300, 293, 305, 310; ibid., C.159.

[171] Ibid., C.171, 172, 176, 177; probably the *mandatum* of St Wulstan is a reference to the daily feeding of three poor men, *Registrum Prioratus* xciii.

[172] See above 255.

[173] Sheppard, *Lit. Cant.*, i, no. 150 (Reg. L, fo 140v). There was a similar problem at Winchester in 1286 with regard to the processions at Pentecost which the sacrist of St Swithun's reported to the bishop, Goodman, *Winchester Chartulary*, no. 37.

[174] CCA DCc anniversarian's accounts, 6 and 7; in 1375 he spent over £3 out of his total receipts of *c.* £25. Flawns (*flaconibus*) seem to have been some sort of savoury concoction, a flan perhaps.

[175] Fowler, *Account Rolls*, i, 115 (1333/5), DCM hostiller's accounts 1356/7, 1379/80, 1381/2, 1382/3A, 1390/1A, 1396/7.

[176] Chapman, *Sacrist Rolls*, ii, 26 (1322/3), 39 (1323/4), 53 (1325/6), 77 (1336/7), 88 (1339/40). For the precentor, CUL MS 2957, 38, 41, 42 (1301/2, 1302/3, 1321/2); these and other transcripts by Bentham contain only selections from the original accounts.

[177] CUL EDR G/3/28 (Liber M), 199; EDR G/1/2 (Reg. Arundel), fo 23v.

Pentecost, for which they were rewarded with 2d. to share among them.[178] There are some brief and imprecise references on the Norwich communar's accounts in the early fourteenth century with regard to a payment of 3d. for *oblationes* at Rogation. The recipients are not specified; and there is a sharp contrast between this paltry sum and the almoner's gifts to the lepers at the city gates and the prisoners in Norwich castle, whom he names among his distributions to the poor in the 1390s to receive a total of 10s. between them at Rogation.[179] The refectorer also entered a 3d. expenditure on alms at Rogation on two of his early fourteenth-century accounts.[180] The prior of St Leonard's cell with his three or four brethren enjoyed rations of butter and a drink of mead or wine on the days of Rogation according to a number of accounts between the 1370s and 1415; and in the latter year both mead and wine were served on the Vigil of Ascension day, which was the evening of the third Rogation day.[181] The relics of St Swithun and other Winchester saints accompanied by colourful banners were borne aloft on biers during Rogation day processions as recorded on the few existing receiver's accounts; and the presence of the custom of pentecostal offerings to the cathedral by the parishes of the archdeaconry of Winchester is attested by the sacrist's complaint to the bishop in 1286.[182] On these three days the customary of the refectory prescribed that butter was to be supplied, a practice that was continuing over one hundred and fifty years later according to the late fifteenth-century diet accounts. The monastic menu in 1493 included dried ling, eggs, milk, flawns, and mustard followed by beef, mutton, and venison on Ascension day.[183] Rogationtide at Worcester was also marked by processions in which the shrine chest and banners were carried by secular priests in 1394 to whom the cathedral priory precentor gave 19d. Thirty years later it was the sacrist who was responsible for paying the unidentified bearers.[184] The annual visit of the faithful to the mother church of the diocese in the week of Pentecost, here too had lost some of its appeal when in 1329 the sacrist, Robert de Clifton, complained to the bishop about the decline in pentecostal offerings and the latter ordered the rural deans to attend to the matter.[185]

---

[178] CUL Add. MS 2957, 42 (1321/2 and 1330/1), 43, 44 (1343/4, 1360/1) and CUL EDC 1/F/9/5 (1374/5).
[179] Fernie and Whittingham, *Communar Rolls*, 103; NRO DCN 1/6/26 and 27 almoner's accounts. The communar records oblations of 4d. on the three Rogation days of 1330 and adds *in missione flaonnes in villa* 8s., ibid.; for whom were the flawns purchased?
[180] NRO DCN 1/8/12, 25.
[181] NRO DCN 2/3/6, 9, 10, 17, 29, 30.
[182] Watkin, 'Receiver's Roll', 96 (1281), Kitchin, *Obedientiary Rolls*, 232, 247 (1330s); the bearers were paid 20s in each case. By the sixteenth century the responsibility had fallen to the sacrist, Kitchin and Madge, *Documents of Winchester*, 23.
[183] Kitchin, *Consuetudinary*, 16; Kitchin, *Obedientiary Rolls*, 349.
[184] WCM C.368, Hamilton, *Compotus Rolls*, 66 (C.425); these are the only two specific references to Rogation days on the obedientiary accounts at Worcester.
[185] *Reg. Orleton*, no. 573. At Worcester only the pentecostals from parishioners of the archdeaconry of Worcester pertained to the sacrist. Processions were not infrequently called for by the king and by bishops in times of war, plague, bad weather, or crises in church or state; in the 1390s, for example, the Worcester *tumbarius* lists expenses pertaining to processions *pro aere serenitatis* in which the shrine of St Oswald was carried, WCM C.457, 460, 462, 463, 464 etc.

The English Benedictine Cathedral Priories: Rule and Practice 265

Pittances in the form of food, drink, and small sums of money distributed among the monastic community at Easter and Pentecost have already been noted.[186] There are several references to suggest that celebrations at Pentecost continued for most of the following week. At Norwich the sacrist made use of several descriptive phrases; in the 1290s *in pascendo convent'* or *in procuracione convent'* for five days; in 1315 and 1331 *in cibacione convent'* for five days; in 1334 and later years *in recreacion[e] convent'* for five days. His expenses for these treats were substantial, varying from *c.* £3 10s. to over £5; and from the 1330/1 account he provided further details to the effect that he had paid 33s. 4d. for wine and 71s. 3d. for other items not counting what he was able to obtain from store.[187] Offerings received at the time of the Pentecost processions also appear on the Norwich sacrist's accounts; they varied considerably, from £8 in 1369 to just under £3 thirty years later.[188] The feretrar's accounts at Durham include similar entries with regard to receipts from offerings of the faithful who processed *cum vexillis ecclesiarum* of diocesan parishes to the cathedral in the week of Pentecost.[189]

Musical performance in the liturgy

That music played a major role in liturgical performance is well attested by the frequent expenses incurred by obedientiaries. Organs, organists, and singers occupied a prominent place in the monastic horarium of the cathedral priories. By their pre-eminent position as the episcopal seat and focal centre of the diocese and by the relatively larger size of their communities in comparison with the many small religious houses that dotted the landscape, they were able to attract potential musical talent, among both monastic recruits and secular musicians.[190] The skill and competence of precentors and, to a slightly lesser degree, of the succentors, can hardly be doubted for they were required to train and direct the monks in chant and to take a leading role themselves in singing. Unfortunately, the major part of what was sung has not been preserved although fragments have been recovered, many of them at Worcester where they had been cut up for use as binding leaves in library books in the wake of changing musical fashion.[191] By *c.* 1300 the newly constructed Lady chapels of some of the cathedral priories had become the setting for a

---

[186] See above 247–9; there were also other feasts scattered through the year—such as those of the Trinity, the Virgin Mary, and saints who were held in high regard by a particular cathedral priory such as St Oswald at Worcester and St Etheldreda at Ely.

[187] NRO DCN 1/4/10, 12, 19, 26, 29, 34, 36, 37, 38 etc.

[188] NRO DCN 1/4/36, 43; the Pentecost fair that took place in the lay cemetery, situated on the north side of the west front of the cathedral, also brought in a few pence in stallage, e.g. ibid., 1/4/26, 29, 31.

[189] In 1376 receipts amounted to 4s. 8d., Fowler, *Account Rolls*, ii, 421.

[190] Although Bath, Coventry, and Rochester, where there are few statistics as to the numbers of monks, probably averaged between twenty and thirty monks, their cathedral status raised them above monastic houses of similar size; the other six cathedral monasteries were close to double this number or more.

[191] See Thomson, *Medieval Manuscripts in Worcester Cathedral*, xxiv–xxv, xlvi.

daily Lady mass at which choral plainsong was sung, at first by monks alone but later, by or before 1400, with the addition of boys from the almonry school.[192] Details of the musical qualifications of those who were appointed to the office of precentor are largely unknown; but one may assume that Geoffrey Bonde was keenly alert to the superior musical prowess of Christ Church when he left St Alban's abbey in 1408/9 to seek admission to Canterbury where, after a due lapse of time, he was made precentor.[193] The cathedral archives still possess a few fragments of medieval polyphony some of which may have been composed at Christ Church. With its reputation as one of the major Benedictine monasteries whose cathedral church housed an archiepiscopal throne, it must have been one of the leaders in musical innovation and performance.[194] Organs, of which most if not all the cathedral priories had several, required constant repair and, from time to time, replacement. These expenses were paid by the sacrist at Canterbury, often with contributions from the prior and other monks as in the 1330s.[195] A few monk organists are known by name at Christ Church: William Bonyngton (d. 1412), who the prior rewarded with small sums of money and who was also commended for his singing, John Maghfeld (d. 1408), and John Cranbroke (d. 1447). None of these three are known to have been precentors; John Stanys (d. 1421), however, was noted for his singing as well as his skill on the organ, and John Borne (d. 1420) for his excellent voice; both of them were precentors.[196] There are scattered references to organs and liturgical singing on the accounts of several Durham obedientiaries, probably an indication that expenses related to musical performances were shared among some of the offices.[197] The hostiller, for example, in the 1340s rewarded his fellow monks Nicholas de Allerton for making (*fabricand'*) a missal and John de Goldsborough for making an antiphoner; the feretrars were responsible for organ repairs in 1378/9 and later years; the cellarer gave small sums to a clerk for blowing the organ in the Galilee chapel in the 1430s. The bursar's *exennia* of 10s. in 1377/8 to a fellow monk, Reginald de Wearmouth, in 1377/8 was a practical expression of the community's gratitude to him for building an organ. Wearmouth's musical accomplishments were not limited to the mechanics of organ construction because the following year he received 6s. 8d. from the almoner for playing the organ or singing and, soon after, was appointed precentor.[198] A cantor was employed in 1416/17 to teach young monks to play the organ

---

[192] Archbishop Winchelsey's injunctions to Christ Church reiterated the requirement that eight monks should be present at the Lady mass, *Reg. Winchelsey*, 820; for the almonry school see above 188–9.

[193] *BRECP*, 94.

[194] See Bowers, 'The Liturgy of the Cathedral and its Music', 415–19.

[195] In 1331 brother John de Copton gave 20s. toward a new organ CCA DCc DE3, fo 32; expenses for 1332/3 which were paid by the prior are listed in ibid., fos 18, 19; and in 1333/4 the prior contributed 71s., ibid., fo 35v. For Copton see *BRECP*, 129.

[196] *BRECP*, 94 (William Bonyngton I); 229 (Maghfeld); 132 (John Cranbroke I); 290 (Stanys); 95 (John Borne I).

[197] The loss of all the precentor's accounts is most unfortunate.

[198] DCM hostiller's accounts 1345/6, 1346/7; Fowler, *Account Rolls*, ii, 422; DCM feretrars' accounts 1385/6 etc; Fowler, *Account Rolls*, ii, 465 (making an organ); ibid., i, 73, 79 (cellarer). Biographical details of Allerton and Goldsborough are in *LVD*, iii, C.819 and C.835 respectively.

and was given 2s. 6d. by the communar; four years later it was the almoner who paid a cantor to instruct them either in chant or in organ playing or possibly both. They may have been making use of a book of *organum* which the hostiller had purchased for 3s. 4d. in 1387/8.[199] During that same year the hostiller had made several other contributions towards the enhancement of musical performance in the liturgy by procuring a processional which cost him 6s. 8d., and by giving money to cantors at Christmas and to one Nicholas the cantor for no specified date or season.[200] A monk cantor was given 3s. 4d. by the bursar in 1363/4 and an unidentified cantor singing *organum in choro* in the 1420s appears on the feretrar's accounts, as does the making of an organ.[201] This apparent distribution of the constant burden of expenses among obedientiaries to ensure the maintenance of a high standard of musical performance in the liturgy would presumably have evolved from periodic decisions made in chapter.[202]

Early to mid-fourteenth-century signs of the musical activity at Ely have been found on the precentor's accounts and in the binding of a copy of the *Liber Eliensis* chronicle. Extracts from one of the earliest accounts of the precentor, dated 1302/3, inform us that he paid a scribe the large sum of 7s. 10d. to correct and/or supply the missing sections of a book of antiphons.[203] The fragments of motets that were in use a few decades later have been identified as intended for three or four voices to be sung at the Lady mass.[204] The precentor's accounts reveal that he was expected to provide men to operate the organ bellows and to pay for the repairs. The latter must have involved a new instrument or an old one completely made over in 1396/7 since the total cost was over £7. Ten years later, having to foot another expensive repair bill, the monks gave up their *gracie* in order to pay for the work. In the same year, 1406/7, the precentor was also paying an unnamed person to teach his clerk to play the organ.[205] At Ely the accounts of the *custos* of the Lady chapel record this obedientiary's involvement with the musical performance under his supervision. There were clerks singing in the Lady chapel in 1364/5 and professed monks and 'others' in 1375/6, all of whom were remunerated by the *custos*; the 1383/4 account also recorded that monks and boys were rewarded for their singing at the Lady mass. A new organ was required for the chapel in 1381/2 at a cost of about £5, as

---

Wearmouth is C.951 in *LVD*, iii and appears, mistakenly, as Roger in Fowler, ibid., iii, 586 and again in i, 212 where the phrase is the ambiguous *ad organa*.

[199] Fowler, ibid., ii, 287, DCM almoner's accounts 1420/1A, Fowler, ibid., i, 134.
[200] Fowler, ibid., i, 134.
[201] DCM bursar's account for that year; Fowler, ibid., ii, 462, 463, 465.
[202] The fact that six obedientiaries were involved over a relatively short period probably reflects some of the chapter ordinances.
[203] CUL Add. MS 2957, 41; in fact, the precentor was constantly obliged to pay for the repair of antiphoners, graduals, and missals worn from frequent use, e.g. ibid., 44–6, and CUL EDC 1/F/9/5 (1374/5) where two tropers and an antiphoner were rebound and covered.
[204] R. Bowers, 'Liber Eliensis Music Fragments' in I. Fenlon (ed.), *Cambridge Music Manuscripts, 900–1700* (Cambridge University Press, Cambridge, 1982), no. 13, 44–7. For details of another fragment see Andrew Wathey, *Manuscripts of Polyphonic Music*, Supplement to RISM BIV 1–2, *The British Isles, 1100–1400* (G. Henle Verlag, Munich 1993), 15–17.
[205] CUL Add MS 2957, 46, 47; for *gracie* see above 248.

well as large amounts of tin previously purchased.[206] The Norwich precentor's expenses included the periodic mending and replacement of service books: repairs to a choir gradual in 1356, choir books in 1386/7, another gradual in 1398/9, and in 1418/19 the replacement of a processional that had been stolen.[207] Cantors occur frequently on the accounts of the precentor and of other obedientiaries, usually receiving small gifts of wine or money for their singing on various feasts as has already been noted. However, it is often not clear if they were members of the Norwich monastic community or outsiders. When, as in 1325/6, a cantor was given money for socks and other expenses it seems likely that he was not a monk; when, as in 1398/9, the precentor refers to the expenses and recreation of *socium cantorum* he may well be referring to those of his brethren who were involved in singing.[208] The late thirteenth-century Norwich customary contains a mere three references to boys (*pueri*) taking part in ceremonies on certain feast days, and on one occasion the only reference is to a boy beginning to sing the first antiphon while the young monks (*juvenes*) are to begin the remaining antiphons.[209] The dating of sections of the customary, though imprecise, ties in with the probable foundation of the almonry school in the 1270s or 1280s from which the boy singers would have been drawn. Later references to these boys are, unfortunately, non-existent apart from the almoner's payments for washing their surplices.[210] Organs were apparently the overall responsibility of the precentor with some contributions from fellow obedientiaries. The master of the cellar gave 20s. towards repairs in 1313/14 and the infirmarer and hostiller gave 6d. and 4d. respectively for repairs to the Lady chapel organ in 1345/6.[211] In 1332/3 the sacrist provided a robe for Adam, an organ builder (*organista*) who must have been engaged to do major work over a lengthy period if we can judge by the 10s. which the precentor paid the cellarer to cover the cost of his meals.[212] Major repairs cost the precentor 20s. in 1380/1, and there are frequent payments of 12d. or less to a servant *ad organa* in the 1380s and 1390s and later.[213] Robert de Burnham, who was elected prior in 1407, is one of two musical monks of Norwich known by name. It is not recorded that he served a turn as precentor, but few details about him have survived either before or after his election. It is rather the survival of a volume of musical treatises, one of which names him as the author, that provides evidence of his interests and skills.

[206] CUL EDC 1/F/7/3, 1/F/7/5B, 1/F/7/8, CUL Add. MS 2957, 58, 57. For the one monk organist known by name see Robert Colville in *BRECP*, 398–9.

[207] NRO DCN 1/9/8, 23, 25, 31. The precentor's choir book, which he used in directing the chant, had to be chained to his lectern or desk in 1382/3 as a precautionary measure, ibid., 1/9/20.

[208] Ibid., 1/9/4, 25.

[209] Tolhurst, *Norwich Customary*, 76, 135, 187; the master of the boys is included in the reference on 76 and the antiphons (for All Souls' day) on 187. See also Greatrex, 'Norwich Almonry School', 178–9. It should be remembered that Norwich lacked an obedientiary in charge of the Lady chapel; see above 169.

[210] NRO DCN 1/6/55 (1425/6), 1/6/62 (1436/7).

[211] NRO DCN 1/1/24; this is the account for 1314/15, but the repairs were made the previous year; ibid., 1/10/4, 1/7/8.

[212] NRO DCN 1/4/27, 1/2/101c; the 10s. occurs as a receipt on the cellarer's account but, unfortunately, there is a gap in the precentor's accounts between 1325 and 1350.

[213] Ibid., 1/9/19, 23, 24, 25, 31; what, precisely, did the servant do, perhaps operate the bellows?

The title of Burnham's composition is *Proportiones musicae mensurabilis*. Less than two folios in length, it is preceded by a longer treatise, *Tractatus de quatuor principalibus musicis*, which was copied into this composite manuscript by John Bergersh 'ad dei laudem et communem utilitatem sancte matris ecclesie anno domini 1421'. Bergersh had been precentor from 1411 to 1413, and in 1421 was appointed prior of St Leonard's on the outskirts of Norwich.[214]

The tenth-century organ in Winchester cathedral would have been capable of producing a loud noise reverberating through the length of the nave, but this was a far cry from anything that resembled the sound of music as we know it.[215] Around the middle of the twelfth century Bishop Henry de Blois' expressed concern about funding for organ repairs led him to make over the church of Elingdon, Wiltshire, to provide income for this purpose. Almost two centuries later a single reference on the almoner's account refers to a *clerico organiste scribenti rotulos* which presumably describes an organ player writing musical scores on rolls of parchment.[216] A lapse of almost another century ensued before the musical endeavours and practice of the Winchester monks come to light *c.* 1402. In that year they appointed John Tyes, a professional musician, to sing at the Lady mass, to play the organ in the Lady chapel, and also to instruct up to four boys of the almonry school in chant.[217] The extant polyphonic musical settings composed by Tyes during his lengthy tenure of office at St Swithun's are irrefutable evidence that there were competent singers among the monks of the cathedral priory.[218]

Fragments of music from Worcester cathedral priory continue to be discovered and already form an impressive collection dating from the 1220s onwards. Many of them were cut up in the early sixteenth century and used in rebinding worn manuscripts in the cathedral priory library, and some of these furnish precious examples of late thirteenth-century polyphony.[219] The earliest surviving accounts of the *custos capelle* record that in the 1390s he was buying robes for and paying stipends to three clerks and also clothing two or three boys; one of the clerks was

---

[214] For Burnham see *BRECP*, 489, and for Bergersh, ibid., 482; the identification of the names in this manuscript as Norwich monks was not made until after *BRECP* was published. This former Norwich manuscript is now Cambridge, Trinity College MS 1441, and Burnham's treatise is found on fos 53v to 55.

[215] J. W. McKinnon, 'The Tenth-Century Organ at Winchester', *Organ Yearbook*, 5 (1974), 4–19.

[216] Goodman, *Winchester Chartulary*, no. 10; Kitchin, *Obedientiary Rolls*, 402, 404 (1317/18). It is to be regretted that no precentor's accounts survive and that the earliest and only account of the *custos* of the Lady altar/chapel is dated 1529/30.

[217] Tyes may have been induced to leave his former post at Westminster abbey by the possibly greater potential in a cathedral setting and perhaps by the annual salary of £5 6s. 8d. See Greatrex, *Common Seal Register*, no. 53 and also the masterful and painstaking reconstruction of the Lady chapel choir and music at Winchester by Roger Bowers in 'The Musicians of the Lady Chapel of Winchester Cathedral Priory, 1402–1539', *Journal of Ecclesiastical History*, 45 (1994), 210–37.

[218] Some of Tyes' compositions written almost certainly for Winchester and preserved in BL Add. MS 57950, fos 15, 99v–100, have been transcribed in Bowers' article (preceding note), 236–7.

[219] One collection of fragments now forms Worcester Cathedral Add. MS 68 and another Oxford, Bodley MS Lat. liturgy. d. 20, and there are fragments remaining as binding leaves in BL Add MS 25031. Thomson, *Medieval Manuscripts in Worcester Cathedral* reports on the Worcester manuscripts from which music has been removed, viz., F.34, F.37, F.43, F.64, F.120, F.125, F.133, F.152, F.175, Q.19, Q.21, Q.24, Q.31, Q.50, Q.61, Q.66, Q.72, Q.94.

awarded a small sum *ad informandum pueros*, no doubt as a singing master. In his first year in office as precentor, in 1395/6, John de Worcestre bought parchment for the making of a book of *organum* in the form of a roll; four years later he spent 6d. *in j libro notando*.[220] Not until the 1460s does the *custos capelle* obligingly provide us with the names of any of the monks who sang in the Lady chapel choir; in 1467/8 there were three; Richard Myston, William Dene, and Thomas Streynsham. Evidence of musical talent in Myston and Dene is surely confirmed by their subsequent appointments, Myston to the precentor's office and Dene to that of *custos capelle*.[221] An organist, Thomas, is named in a late thirteenth-century deed, but other later references are few and unrevealing. The almoner reported on his 1387/8 account that he gave 7s. to a man who built an organ; and it was possibly the clerk of the Lady chapel who was instructing the boys in the 1390s and also teaching one or more of them the rudiments of organ playing.[222] Although there remain many lacunae in our knowledge of the medieval English musical performance of the liturgy, enough evidence has been recovered to impress historians and musicologists by the high standard of professional excellence achieved.

Priestly functions 1) the daily and weekly masses

Most, but not all, of the priestly functions of the monks were performed within the monastic precinct, which for the cathedral priories encompassed many chapels and altars in addition to the high altar with its daily sung mass and the Lady altar or chapel where a daily mass was also celebrated. Rotas were the essential means of ensuring that celebrants and their assistants were assigned to fulfil these duties; and *custodes* or *tabularii* were given the responsibility of drawing up the lists or tables (*tabulae*) of names.[223] This would have been a formidable task when one bears in mind the vicissitudes of daily life in a large monastic community in which individuals found themselves frequently immersed in a complex network of obligations in addition to the mass and office.[224] A Christ Church ordinance of 1305 shows the monastic chapter making changes with regard to the performance of the daily mass of the blessed Virgin Mary and prescribing that to the six brethren already on the weekly rota two more were to be added to assist them; their names were to be inserted on the *tabula* by the monk cantor on duty for the week.[225]

---

[220] WCM C.251, 252, 253, 255.
[221] Ibid., C.281; see also *BRECP*, 855 (Myston), 796–7 (Dene), 880 (Streynsham).
[222] WCM B.925, C.179; no other organists' names are known before 1420 and, as at Winchester, they were professional musicians.
[223] A number of obedientiaries recorded the payment of small sums to *tabularii*: the chamberlain at Norwich paid a clerk 3s. in 1396/7 for keeping the *tabulam pro missis*, NRO DCN 1/5/29; at Winchester the chamberlain, curtarian, *custos operum*, hordarian, almoner, and anniversarian all recorded a *curialitas* to their *tabularii* on most of the surviving accounts, e.g. Kitchin, *Obedientiary Rolls*, 365, HRO W53/14/9, Kitchin, ibid., 213, 256, 413, 204; and at Worcester there is one reference in WCM Reg. A.5, fo 151v. It is not known precisely what the Winchester *tabularii* were paid to do, probably to make lists required by the obedientiaries, but these are unlikely to have been all or only mass tables.
[224] See above 165–215 *passim*.
[225] CCA DCc Reg. K, fo 213v.

A monk priest was required to celebrate mass at least three or four times every week, but in a community numbering fifty or more monks the average monk might have been the celebrant at the daily high mass for only one or two weeks in the year.[226] During the rest of the year his name would have been entered on one or more of the *tabulae* prepared for the other chapels and altars in the cathedral church. How all the multiple assignments worked out in practice is uncertain apart from a momentary glimpse made possible through the survival of some rough notes from the 1440s probably made by a Norwich monk acting as *tabularius*.[227] Two lists for the high masses in 1447 and 1448 show that the *ebdomadarius*, or celebrant for the week, was one of a small number of monks who averaged two or three such assignments during the year.[228] In a monastic community numbering about fifty-five monks, in the 1440s, among whom at least five at any one time would have been either novices and not in priest's orders or elderly or ill in the infirmary, this means that only about one-quarter of the monks were on the rota for the high mass. It is significant that on this list one week of every month was unassigned, the word *nemo* being inserted in place of a name; this may have been to allow some flexibility in the event of last minute alterations. Most of the monks can be classed as seniors except for John de Chaumpeneys who had been a student at Oxford between 1439 and 1443. Many of the others would have been holders of obedientiary office, but the paucity of information in the extant records limits our knowledge to only two of them, namely Nicholas Burgate, who was refectorer between 1444 and 1448, and John Elmham, who was hostiller from 1445 to 1448.[229] A memorandum among the notes and lists on fo 77v of the same manuscript and dated Saturday 29 May 1445, states that Nicholas de Randworth had begun the new cursus for the *missa ebdomadaria* the previous week which was the octave of the feast of the Holy Trinity.[230] More rotas follow pertaining to five daily chantry masses which the monks had undertaken to celebrate on behalf of Bishop William Bateman (d. 1355), Bishop John Wakeryng (d. 1425), the monastic bishop and former Prior Alexander de Totyngton (d. 1413), and two lay benefactors, Sir Thomas

---

[226] The statutes issued by the Black Monk general chapter of 1277 stated that no more than four days were to elapse between celebrations, Pantin, *Black Monk Chapters*, i, 70. Archbishop Reynolds had to remind the Christ Church monks of this requirement in 1314, LPL Reg. Reynolds, fos 33, 44; in the same year the bishop of Durham, Richard de Kellawe, issued a similar reminder to the Durham monks, DCM Reg. Kellawe, II, fo 50v; it was the Ely monastic chapter, however, which passed an ordinance in 1315 to the effect that priests were to celebrate at least once every three days, Evans, *Ely Chapter Ordinances*, 37.

[227] Note the other duties in the Norwich customary that were written on *tabulae*, e.g. 'Feria quarta... missam pro Herberto episcopo cantabunt... tres[sacerdotes] positi, in tabula'; 'omnes qui ponuntur in tabula ad legendum et cantandum', Tolhurst, *Norwich Customary*, 78, 98.

[228] The lists are in Cambridge, Emmanuel College MS 142, fos 68 and 77v. Covered with untidy notes, lists, and tables they originally formed a wrapper containing a collection of letters, all of which were bound together, with other miscellaneous papers, into this manuscript; and thus the draft lists were inadvertently preserved. I am profoundly grateful to Dr Tessa Webber for helping to decipher these folios.

[229] For these three monks see *BRECP*, 494–5 (Chaumpeneys), 489 (Burgate), 505 (John Elmham I); Burgate was on the high mass rota four times in 1447 and three times in 1448, and Elmham three times and twice respectively.

[230] In 1444 Randworth was already elderly and frail, *BRECP*, 549.

Erpingham and Sir Peter de Tye, members of the East Anglian gentry.[231] These also appear as weekly rotas for fifteen to twenty-seven weeks and, although undated, they must have been compiled in the 1440s and no later than 1447 since two of the monks died that year. Five or six monks appear on both the high mass and chantry mass rotas and, surprisingly, those assigned to say the chantry masses are, with few exceptions, a small number of monks who were responsible for most of them. It would seem, therefore, that a group of about twenty-five members of the monastic community resident in Norwich—that is about half of the total—were being assigned to cover these chantry masses. There was remuneration provided for the performance of some of these obligations. Bateman, for example had arranged for each monk to receive 2s. for his week of duty, payment being made by the master of the cellar.[232]

A few details can be recovered with regard to the arrangements in place at Christ Church Canterbury for the celebration of high mass and some of the other masses. The almoner's 1337 account, for example, records an expenditure of 13s. 7d. for officiating at the high mass, and his account for 1361/2 was charged 37s. 7d. because he was on duty twice during the year.[233] Was this money used as a pittance for titbits and wine for himself and others, or was it treated as pocket money? On his 1326/7 account he includes wine in the week of [his] *magne misse* and in 1337/8 he spent 2s. on wine for his *socio ad magnam missam*.[234] The prior frequently favoured the monks who had celebrated the high mass with gifts of spices, some of whom, like Richard Hatfeld and William Woghope, were treasurers at the time.[235] Other Canterbury obedientiaries probably shared in making and receiving these distributions as single entries on three other obedientiary accounts suggest: those of the chamberlain in 1391/2 when he charged 16s. to his expenses, of the sacrist the same year when he paid himself and shared wine with his brethren, and of the bartoner in 1404/5 who charged 25s. on his account.[236] The Canterbury almoner's accounts make frequent references to secular chaplains who served the Black Prince's chantry and the almonry chapel. He not only paid their stipends—with contributions from the treasurers—but he also gave them food and lodging as

---

[231] For these and other chantries in the cathedral see Tanner, *The Church in Late Medieval Norwich*, 212–15.
[232] For example, NRO DCN 1/1/53, 55, 62. The details of Bateman's gifts to the monks and their consequent obligations are in NRO DCN 40/9, fo 46v; Totyngton's will, in LPL Reg. Arundel, II, fos 165v–166, does not mention any recompense and neither does Wakeryng's in NRO DCN 4/5. However, the earliest surviving chantry account of 1457/8 suggests that the monk accountant paid out a total of 52s. to those who had celebrated the masses for Wakeryng and Erpingham, i.e., as though they had been combined, DCN 4/7. It should be noted that at the foot of fo 77v in Cambridge, Emmanuel College MS 142 there was an attempt to keep a working account of the five chantries on which moneys received and still to be received show the totals anticipated as varying between 80s. (Bateman and Totyngton) and 40s. (Wakeryng, Erpingham, and Tye); however, to interpret these shorthand figures is impossible.
[233] CCA DCc almoner's accounts 42 (Epiphany to Michaelmas), 51.
[234] Ibid., almoner's accounts 38, 46.
[235] LPL MS 243, fo 171, 171v; the year is 1376/7. Others are named in ibid., fos 115, 120v, 203, 207 etc. For Hatfeld and Woghope see *BRECP*, 192, 324–5.
[236] CCA DCc chamberlain's account 56; sacrist's account 10; bartoner's account 70.

members of his *familia*.[237] Due to the loss of many account rolls, or because of insufficient details provided by most of the surviving rolls, further information is wanting.

The frequent celebration of masses incumbent on monk priests could not be performed legally without the presence of a fellow monk or clerk to assist them.[238] By the middle of the fourteenth century, probably because of an insufficient number of monks and clerks available to serve all the daily masses scheduled for the chapels and altars of Durham cathedral, the monastic chapter had begun to make use of boys in attendance at the almonry school.[239] It is not possible to follow the Durham monks in the planning and performance of the daily round of masses, but something similar to the customs and practice found in other cathedral priories is likely to have been in place. Several chantry masses are named on a few obedientiary accounts; the bursar, for example, in 1390/1 is found to be paying a pension of £4 to the monk chaplain of the chantry (? chantries) of the lord bishop and of Richard de Castrobernardi.[240] In 1395/6, Richard de Sedgebrook, an elderly monk and former master of Farne, was assigned to say mass at the Neville chantry in the south aisle of the nave.[241] The earliest extant communar's account, dated 1416/17, includes among its receipts of rents income for the support of this chantry and those of Prior John Fosser (d. 1374) and Bishop Walter Skirlaw (d. 1406); under his expenses he mentions, in his list of pensions and stipends, payments to the succentor *pro tabulacione* of Fosser's chantry and to the celebrant at Skirlaw's chantry.[242] The fortunate survival of one list of monks assigned to the Hatfield and Neville chantries confirms the presence of an arrangement similar to what was found at Norwich. In this case some thirty-three monk priests are named as responsible for the masses in these two chantries during the 1420s. Most of them were on the rota for both chantries, and among their number were senior but still active monks and junior monks who had recently been ordained to the priesthood.[243]

Ely records are virtually silent about the monastic community's arrangements for the celebration of masses in the cathedral church save for two small details. A note in a fifteenth-century hand inserted on one of the first few folios of a twelfth-century copy of the *Liber Eliensis* provides the following information: anniversary masses for Alexander de Bury, an Ely monk who died in 1392/3, were to be said by

---

[237] See for example CCA DCc almoner's accounts 3, 27, 24, 42, 54.
[238] Pantin, *Black Monk Chapters*, i, 99, in a statute issued in 1278 by the Benedictine chapter of Canterbury province and i, 258, dated 1287 by the chapter of York province; the latter, however, did not permit the assistance of a secular clerk. In 1343 the statute was re-enacted by the now single provincial chapter which accepted the alternative of clerks, ibid., ii, 33.
[239] For this purpose the boys selected were considered to be the 'honest clerks' permitted by the 1343 statute. In the 1390s their appointment became the almoner's responsibility, see Bowers, 'Almonry Schools', 192–3.
[240] Fowler, *Account Rolls*, iii, 597. The bishop may have been Thomas de Hatfield (d. 1381).
[241] DCM bursar's account 1395/6; for Sedgebrook see C.936 in *LVD*, iii. Several members of this prominent Durham family were buried in the chantry.
[242] Fowler, *Account Rolls*, ii, 295.
[243] DCM Misc. Charter 6080.

the two junior monks in priest's orders. There seems to have been nothing remarkable about this monk's forty years in the priory, and so this ruling may well have applied to other monks' anniversary masses.[244] There is a second reference to an anniversary mass in unusual circumstances requiring a licence from the bishop. In 1385 Bishop Thomas Arundel allowed the Ely monk John de Thornton to receive 6m. per annum, for a period of five years, for celebrating an anniversary mass for an unnamed person; the reason given was that his person was 'ere alieno graviter oneratam', with the additional general all-inclusive statement 'et ex certis aliis causis et legitimis'.[245] Evidence of memorial masses for deceased monks of Rochester has survived from the years between c. 1294 and c. 1307. This records the names of fifty-five monks, about whom in most cases little or nothing else is known, who were assigned to say mass for one or more of their brethren, the latter being also identified by name. Four masses were offered by four monks for each of the departed whose deaths had occurred a month earlier, hence the explanatory phrase *ad tricennale celebrandum*.[246]

On Winchester obedientiary accounts expenditures arising from the duty of presiding at the [high] mass feature more prominently than in the other cathedral priories. After serving his turn the celebrant was entitled to claim expenses, and at the same time was expected to distribute gifts of bread and wine, ale, and/or small sums of money to his brethren. The obedientiaries seem to have been on the mass rota once or twice a year; and the other monk priests among the *claustrales*, who would also have had their turn, receive frequent mention in this context. In 1311/12, for example, the almoner awarded himself 17s. 7d., gave bread and wine to the subprior, hordarian, and subalmoner and ale to 'diversis sociis existentibus in tabula missae'.[247] The hordarian gave bread to the subprior, third prior, and to his *socius* who was presumably an unidentified monk assistant; and to the *fratribus in tabula missa* he gave 26s. This was in 1333, and similar entries occurred in later years with only slight variations in the sums of money spent.[248] His own expenses, however, first appear in 1381/2 when he awarded himself 23s. 8d. In 1400/1, when he was on the mass rota twice, his 'expenses' increased to 36s. 9d.[249] For his part the chamberlain gave bread and wine to the subprior and third prior and paid himself 36s. for celebrating the high mass twice in 1416/17; he also gave 13s. 4d. to the *depositarii pro simili*, thus implying that these obedientiaries received money for pittances to which the celebrants contributed.[250] The anniversarian's account for 1394/5 suggests that the payment to the *depositarii* may have been for pittances

---

[244] Cambridge, Trinity College MS 1145, fo iiib; for Bury see *BRECP*, 395.
[245] CUL EDR G/1/2, fo 53v; for Thornton see *BRECP*, 450.
[246] The names are found in BL MS Cotton Vespasian A.xxii, fos 126v, 127; the manuscript is part chronicle, part customary, part record of manorial properties, with various additions such as the mass rotas.
[247] Kitchin, *Obedientiary Rolls*, 398, 401, 406; on other almoner's accounts the phrase was *fratribus existentibus*, 421, 427.
[248] Ibid., 265, 280, 287.
[249] Ibid., 280, 287; there are no hordarian's account rolls between 1337 and 1381/2.
[250] Ibid., 365; for the *depositarii* see also above 246. In 1399/1400 the subchamberlain was also included, WCL W/53/14/2.

for the monks after serving their turn on the mass rota, but the explanations for the expenditure are too condensed to be clear. Like other Winchester obedientiaries the anniversarian gave gifts to the subprior, third prior, and other monk priests who served their turn as celebrants; the fact that some of these other priests were given 10d. per week by him suggests that they may possibly have been assigned to masses other than the high mass.[251] Among these other masses there is some evidence of the monks undertaking to say masses in several chapels in the cathedral. In gratitude for certain benefactions received from the bishops, Nicholas de Ely and John de Pontissara, the prior and convent pledged themselves to assign two monks to celebrate a daily mass for each of them, their names to be inscribed in the appropriate mass table.[252] For Bishop William Wykeham they guaranteed to supply three monks to say three masses daily in his chantry chapel on the south side of the nave.[253] Records of two agreements survive, both made in the 1330s, with lay benefactors who desired monastic intercession on their behalf. Robert de Bokyngham and William de Dunstapele requested two masses each day and John Devenish a daily mass.[254] How and to what extent these obligations were carried out is unknown.

Evidence of the monks' arrangements for the celebration of masses at Worcester cathedral priory is scarce. When Archbishop Winchelsey issued an injunction that monk celebrants at private masses were always to be assisted by a fellow monk the community numbered forty-five to fifty.[255] However, there may have been difficulty in adhering to this requirement in later years with the likelihood of an increasing number of commitments to say frequent, if not daily, masses in response to benefactions and requests. Some of them were set up *in perpetuo* and others for a fixed term, like the three masses each week in 1294 while Edward I was overseas engaged in war with France.[256] Some details of the musical performance at the daily Lady mass can be gleaned from the surviving thirteenth-century antiphoner which clearly reveals the monks' devotion to the Blessed Virgin Mary to whom the medieval cathedral church was dedicated.[257] In 1300 a chapter ordinance made the infirmarer responsible for a contribution of 18d. to each monk on the feast of the nativity of the Virgin so that everyone would be free to have the spices that he preferred after taking part in the liturgical solemnities of the day.[258] The antiphoner also refers to weekly masses for Saints Oswald and Wulstan; but the only possible reference to mass *tabulae* occurs on the precentor's account for 1401/2.

---

[251] Ibid., 203; the *custos operum*, curtarian, and infirmarer made similar payments. The *custos operum*, hordarian, and infirmarer also paid their brethren who were *in tabula misse* through annual contributions to the *depositarii*, ibid., 213, 283, WCL W53/11/2.

[252] *Reg. Pontissara*, 83–4.

[253] *Common Seal Register*, no. 63; in return each monk was to receive a penny.

[254] Goodman, *Winchester Chartulary*, nos 134, 265.

[255] *Reg. Winchelsey*, 874. Almonry school boys were probably brought in later as at Durham; see above 273.

[256] A chapter ordinance recorded in *Annales Wigorn.*, 514.

[257] For a brief summary of Marian liturgical observance at Worcester and of the several altars as well as the chapel dedicated to the Virgin see Engel, *Worcester Cathedral*, 193–7.

[258] *Annales Wigorn.*, 547. In 1391/2 the pittance was still being paid, but the prior, subprior, and precentor received 3s., 2s. 3d., and 2s. 3d. respectively and the rest of the monks 18d., WCM C.243.

The purchase of parchment for the writing and correcting of liturgical and other manuscripts and for obituary notices frequently occurs, but on this one occasion he records that he bought three planks of willow *pro tabulis dominicalibus*.[259] At Worcester, as at Canterbury and elsewhere, secular priests were sometimes employed to say masses in the chapels, including those for deceased members of the community. William the chaplain, for example, received 53s. 4d., in addition to meals for celebrating masses for Prior John Grene and Thomas Hay, monk student at Oxford, for nine months after their deaths in 1395/6. In the same year a monk was assigned to say mass for Thomas Carter and was paid at the rate of 18d. a week; both of these arrangements were the responsibility of the almoner.[260] Finally, to this modicum of evidence should be added an undated list entitled 'De missis celebratis quotidie in ecclesia cathedralis'. There follows a list of names to be remembered by a mass of the Holy Spirit at St Edmund's altar; two of these are the monks John de Fordham, prior (d. 1438), and John de Dudley (d. post 1423); the other names are probably members of the cathedral confraternity and benefactors. Other altars such as that of St Cross are named where masses for Bishop Godfrey Giffard and others were to be said.[261]

In addition to the celebration of masses within the precincts of the monastery some monks said mass in parish churches and even in private houses. At Winchester, for example, Bishop William Wykeham licensed several of the cathedral priory hostillers in succession to administer the sacraments in the church at Littleton. The reason given in each case was the lack of funds to pay a chaplain.[262] In 1344 Bishop Richard de Bury issued a licence to the Durham subprior, William de Haltwhistle, and the monks permitting them to celebrate mass not only in the priory but also in the city and diocese wherever and whenever the need arose.[263] A problem was revealed at the Norwich cell of Lynn in 1362 when the bishop, Thomas Percy, received news of complaints from parishioners of the priory church of St Margaret, which functioned also as the parish church. It appears that monks had been celebrating mass in oratories and private houses without having obtained the requisite episcopal licence.[264]

---

[259] Hamilton, *Compotus Rolls*, 46. The full entry reads, 'in iij tabulis salicinis pro tabulis dominicalibus xijls et iijls in claustro xijd'; do *xijls et iijls* refer to the measurements of the mass tables?

[260] WCM C.182; Carter's mass was first mentioned in 1387/8, ibid., C.179. For Grene see *BRECP*, 812–13 (John Grene I) and for Hay, ibid., 819.

[261] WCM Reg. A.12, fo 133; for Dudley and Fordham see *BRECP*, 797–9 (John de Dudley I), 807. Most of this register contains either sixteenth-century material or sixteenth-century copies of earlier material.

[262] Both manor and church pertained to the office of hostiller, Goodman, *Winchester Chartulary*, nos 3, 25. The hostillers named were John Hyde, Thomas Stoke, and John Mideltone, *BRECP*, 704–5, 738, 719; no hostiller's accounts survive.

[263] *Reg. Bury*, 47–8; Haltwhistle is C.851 in *LVD*, iii. No evidence has been found of this authorization put into practice. In 1412 Bishop Burghill authorized the Coventry monks to say mass in oratories on their manors (which they would surely have been accustomed to doing) and also in other oratories wherever they happened to be staying within the diocese, LRO, Reg. Burghill, fo 203v.

[264] This may or may not have been an isolated instance; it is known only because of the survival of this sole piece of evidence in NRO DCN 43/76. The priors of some of the Norwich and Durham cells

Priestly functions 2) monk confessors

There are numerous examples of monks of the cathedral priories taking their turn as penitentiaries or confessors, both within the monastery for their brethren and in the city and diocese for the laity who visited the cathedral. It was usually an episcopal appointment, and at Canterbury the penitentiary, like several of the obedientiaries, was chosen by the archbishop from a list of three names sent to him by the prior and convent. Thus, James de Oxney was selected by Archbishop Islip in 1358 and commissioned to absolve penitents even in cases usually reserved to the archbishop, while Archbishop Langham named Thomas de Goodnyston as confessor to the monks in 1367.[265] It seems that Bishop Bateman's visitation of Norwich cathedral priory *c.* 1347 had uncovered the fact that, although confessors were expected to fulfil their responsibilities gratis, some were being given money by no doubt grateful penitents. He therefore ordered them to render account of their receipts and to share them with their brethren to the sum of twelve silver pennies annually.[266] Half a century later the bishop of Durham, Thomas Langley, was sufficiently concerned about this problem that he included a question in his articles of enquiry for the visitation of the cathedral priory 'an penitenciarii ... audiant confessiones libere sine exaccione pecunie'.[267] Ralph de Basyng, monk of Winchester and D. Cn.L, was appointed as confessor to the Benedictine nuns of Wherwell in 1393, to the nuns of Romsey in 1396 and two years later as penitentiary in the diocese. Two parish churches in Ely belonged to the sacrist who in 1397 was commissioned to hear the confessions of the parishioners of both.[268] The appointments of some fifteen monk penitentiaries at Worcester and a similar number at Winchester have been noted in the fourteenth-century episcopal registers, but not more because bishops increasingly tended to appoint secular priests as confessors to the laity.[269] It is surprising, however, that the registers of Rochester and Bath have yielded only one monk penitentiary each, while thirteen Coventry monks have been identified between 1349 and 1407.[270]

---

held the position of rector of the parish church where it was also the priory church; see above 232–3. The Durham cells of Coldingham, Lytham, and Stamford also included the cure of souls.

[265] LPL Reg. Islip, fo 144 and *BRECP*, 251 (James de Oxney I); *Reg. Langham*, 282–3 and *BRECP*, 179 (Thomas de Goodnyston I).

[266] Cheney, 'Norwich Cathedral Priory', 108–10. Twice in the 1340s the cellarer recorded the receipt of a few pennies on his account *pro absolucione habendo*, once from a woman of Hepton and once from *quodam extraneo*, NRO DCN 1/2/102b and c.

[267] *Reg. Langley*, i, 74, dated 1408; the injunctions do not survive. Langley commissioned a number of monks as penitentiaries, e.g., Robert Ripon and William de Kibblesworth, *LVD*, iii, C.985, C.1018.

[268] For Basyng see *BRECP*, 670, and for the Ely sacrist's appointment, CUL EDR G/1/3 (Reg. Fordham), fo clxxxix.

[269] In some cases monk confessors for their brethren would have been internal appointments which have left no records. A number of monks obtained a papal licence to choose their own confessor who would presumably have been a monk although, possibly, a secular priest from outside the monastic community, *BRECP passim*.

[270] Thomas Brouns (Rochester, 1400), *BRECP*, 594, where the alternative term used is *primarius*; Roger de Grutelyngthon (Bath, 1310, 1332) ibid., 26; for Coventry *passim*, 346–74, perhaps the result of more scrupulous record keeping?

Priestly functions 3) monks as benefice holders and papal chaplains

There are a few instances of cathedral monks holding benefices, but the precise circumstances and practical effect of this anomaly are unclear. Edmund de Totyngton, D.Th., monk of Ely, was probably sacrist in 1402 when he obtained papal dispensation to hold a benefice with or without cure of souls; he continued in the office of sacrist until at least 1407, and there is no evidence of his taking a benefice. The case of John de Cleve, hostiller at Worcester, is similar when, in 1411, he obtained papal authorization to hold a benefice. After six or seven years as hostiller he occupied the office of sacrist during most, if not all of the years between 1415 and 1430, and so the dispensation appears to have made no visible difference.[271] A later example offers more detail. By 1447, Robert Puryton D.Th., monk of Winchester, had made a distinguished contribution to his community, to the provincial Benedictine chapter, and to the crown as an ambassador to Spain. In that year he obtained a papal indult to hold *in commendam* any benefice with cure of souls and, at the same time, to retain his place in the monastic choir. Cardinal Beaufort's influence and that of his successor in the see of Winchester, William Waynflete, were used to justify the granting of this privilege; but, although Puryton continued to carry out his monastic responsibilities, it remains unknown if the indult was ever implemented.[272]

To seek appointment as an honorary papal chaplain was, in effect, a similar privilege acquired by some monks of the cathedral priories. Precisely what this entailed is also unclear but the motivation must have been prompted by personal dissatisfaction with his status by the monk in question within his community coupled with a desire to possess the means, on certain occasions at least, to bypass the regulatory routine of the monastery. For the cathedral priors and other monastic superiors it could lead to confrontation with the power that authorized the appointment and to which ultimately both they and their monks owed obedience; and within the cloister it undermined authority and provided cause for division.[273] One of the two John de Southams at Coventry, about whom little else is known, procured his dispensation in 1399 as did John de Tilney at Norwich in 1400, but the latter died within the year.[274] The only known papal chaplain among the Winchester monks within the time range of this study was William Gilers, whose dispensation stated that it was *registrata gratis*, evidence that these

---

[271] For Totyngton see *BRECP*, 451 and for Cleve ibid., 787–8.

[272] Puryton had been Beaufort's confessor, *BRECP*, 727–8. As early as 1332 a Coventry monk, Simon de Midlecombe, had prevailed on the pope to order the prior and chapter to reserve for him a benefice or dignity within their gift, but some years later he was condemned as a vagabond monk, ibid., 364. When Richard de Midelton at Norwich in 1412 was successful in acquiring the benefice of Marsham by means of a papal dispensation, the bishop soon procured a papal cancellation of the dispensation, ibid., 541. Papal licences for cathedral monks to hold benefices became more common in the late fifteenth and early sixteenth centuries.

[273] See the lucid survey of these papal dispensations—more aptly termed abuses in their disruptive effect on monastic community life—in Donald Logan's *Runaway Religious*, 51–63. See also Knowles, *RO*, ii, 170–4.

[274] *BRECP*, 370, 565.

privileges were normally purchased.[275] Of the two appointments of papal chaplains at Worcester, both were also claimed or obtained in the 1390s; one, John Severne, was forced by the bishop to renounce his claim, after which he disappeared and the other, William de Lodelowe, died soon after.[276] There were four monks at Durham who acquired the title between c. 1393 and 1414 one of whom, John Fishwick, was declared apostate within a year; another, John de Ripon, had his claim both to a benefice and a papal chaplaincy annulled, and he finished his days within the Durham cell of Wearmouth. The other two, John de Charlton and Hugh de Sherburn, obtained their dispensations while in Italy in 1393, and on their return continued as members of the Durham community, although the latter had to seek episcopal absolution for stabbing the subprior a few years later.[277] Prior Shepey's register at Rochester has preserved William de Reynham's renunciation, in 1387, of the dispensation, which had effectively made him answerable only to the pope, and his renewal of obedience to the prior and the bishop.[278] It is noteworthy that at Worcester and Rochester the prior and the bishop had combined forces to eradicate this potential source of dissension within the cloister. The apparent absence of papal chaplains among the monks of Bath and Ely may be due to the loss of relevant records, but this explanation is hardly satisfactory for Christ Church Canterbury for which primary sources abound; Christ Church had its share of apostate monks, but no papal chaplains have been identified.

Priestly functions 4) cathedral monks as preachers

Attention has been drawn above to the impressive collections of sermons and sermon manuals possessed by some of the cathedral priories, and also to a few monks like Robert Ripon of Durham and John Lawerne of Worcester, some of whose sermons have survived.[279] It is not possible to evaluate the degree of importance assigned by the cathedral monks to the pastoral ministry of preaching to the public. No doubt preaching within the community for the mutual edification of its members was a frequent if not daily occurrence in chapter; the Worcester MS Q.18, for example, which Neil Ker identified as a *Liber collationum*, is a late thirteenth- to early fourteenth-century collection of such homilies containing frequent references to the Rule and to 'our most holy father Benedict'.[280] Moreover, obedientiary accounts and episcopal and priory registers regularly record the occasions on which monks preached in the cathedral on greater festivals and solemnities when the laity would have been well represented, and again on other public

---

[275] Ibid., 695; this may have been authorized because of his impressive family connections.
[276] Ibid., 872, 839 (William de Lodelowe I).
[277] They are in *LVD*, iii, C.1030 (Fishwick), C.988 (Ripon), C.978 (Charlton), C.955 (Sherburn).
[278] *BRECP*, 629–30.
[279] Ripon is C.985 in *LVD*, iii; some of Lawerne's university sermons are found in his commonplace book now Oxford, Bodley MS 692, e.g., fos 122–3, and see *BRECP*, 830–1 (John Lawerne I).
[280] E.g., on fos 13 and 46; Professor Thomson has identified the hand of Henry Fouke, subprior and cellarer in the 1320s, on fos 38v–49v, *BRECP*, 807–8 and Thomson, *Medieval Manuscripts in Worcester Cathedral*, 130.

occasions such as the election, installation, and funeral of a prior, or the election and visitation of a bishop. Thus, at Worcester, the hostiller, John de Hatfeld, preached on the day of the election of Prior John Grene in 1388; and Thomas Ledbury still a student at Oxford, preached at the election of Philip Morgan as bishop in 1419. Similarly, at Christ Church Canterbury, Thomas Chillenden preached at the election of William Courtenay as archbishop in 1381, the year of his inception as D. Cn.L, and Richard Godmersham preached at the requiem mass for Prior John Wodnesburgh who died in 1428.[281] In 1309, during his tenure of the see of Worcester, Walter Reynolds encouraged the faithful to hear the preaching of the monks of the cathedral priory and authorized the prior, John de Wyke, to select and appoint some of his brethren to preach in locations that he deemed appropriate.[282] With the arrival of the plague in Winchester in 1349 Bishop William de Edington ordered Prior Alexander de Heriard and the abbot of Hyde to instruct and encourage the people by preaching on the doctrine of the resurrection.[283]

There is enough evidence of cathedral priory monks preaching in parish churches to confirm that it was not an unusual event. Most frequently occurring, no doubt, where the monastic church was also the parish church as at Yarmouth and Stamford, it nevertheless included other churches, both those pertaining to the cathedral priories and those authorized by episcopal licence. In the 1320s and 1330s, for example, the Durham monks John Fosser, John de Corbridge, and Robert de Cambois while resident in the cell of Stamford were licensed by the bishop of Lincoln to preach in churches within the diocese.[284] Details survive of three Durham monks who carried out preaching duties while acting as commissaries of the prior in the visitation of some of the priory churches. John de Barnard Castle preached at Norham in September 1369 and at Aycliffe, Heighington, and Merrington some time in 1376/7, and on the latter occasion the bursar paid him 4s. for his expenses.[285] In the 1380s Robert Ripon, while studying intermittently at Oxford, was commissioned by the prior to visit the two churches of Bywell Peter and Bedlington in March 1382, and Heighington, Billingham, and St Hild's chapel, South Shields during 1389/90. His expenses were again paid by the bursar. John de Newburn also visited and preached in the latter three churches during the same year. About two years later, between 8 and 14 July, Ripon made a visitatorial round of six churches preaching on different texts on each occasion;

---

[281] *BRECP*, 818 (Hatfeld), 833–4 (Ledbury), 119–21 (Thomas Chillenden I), 170–1 (Richard Godmersham I), 323–4 (John Wodnesburgh II). Godmersham's text was *transit de morte ad vitam*.

[282] *Reg. Reynolds*, 13; the bishop commended the preaching zeal of the prior and encouraged the laity to listen to the monks by granting an indulgence of forty days to those who had confessed their sins.

[283] *Reg. Edington*, ii, no. 201; this order directly followed an unfortunate incident in the lay cemetery of the cathedral where Ralph de Stanton, the monk who was officiating at a burial, was assaulted, *BRECP*, 737.

[284] *LVD*, iii, C.817 (Fosser), C.820 (Corbridge), C.833 (Cambois); Fosser and Cambois may have been priors of the cell at the time.

[285] Barnard Castle is C.926 in *LVD*, iii, and his payment is noted in Fowler, *Account Rolls*, iii, 585.

he then returned to Oxford where he incepted in theology the following year.[286] The Worcester monk Richard de Bromwych, D.Th. paid two supervisory visits to the priory manor of King's Norton in 1334/5, and on the first Sunday of Lent, 1335, he preached in the parish church; the diligent bailiff provided these details on the manorial expense account.[287] It is worthy of note that, from his accounts, the Worcester precentor appears to have been much occupied with the provision and refection of preachers, usually identified only as *fratres predicantes*, unless they were monk students recalled from Oxford whose travelling expenses were also charged to him.[288] The examples cited may assuredly be taken as indicative of frequent preaching on the part of the monks carrying out visitations and other duties in the service of both bishop and prior; the *sede vacante* register of Worcester cathedral priory records many commissions of this kind, but provides only a partial record of the monks officiating *in situ*.[289]

A pause in routine: *minutio* and *recreatio*

There were a number of occasions during the year when the monks of the cathedral priories benefited from a relaxation of routine. This respite or change of air was often preceded by the periodic blood-letting or *minutio* that was commonly observed by medieval religious. Although there is no mention of this practice in the Rule, Archbishop Lanfranc's Monastic Constitutions devotes a section to it in which he outlined the procedure to be followed and prescribed the day following for rest and recuperation.[290] Not surprisingly the recovery period allowed was later extended. In 1287 at Ely the prior, John de Hemmingstone, was persuaded by the precentor and almoner to grant an additional day to enable the monks to spend time away from the monastery, unless the day coincided with a double feast.[291] A few years later, in 1314, a chapter ordinance decreed that the prior and the major obedientiaries were to take it in turn to be responsible for supplying food and drink for three days for their brethren who had undergone *minutiones*.[292] The cellarer makes clear on his account rolls how this decision worked out in practice for him. He records expenditures averaging 3s. to 4s. a week for the weeks concerned, paying one of his brethren, viz., the sacrist, precentor, chamberlain, subprior, or prior for their *minutio* in company with from three to six fellow monks. This six-week cycle—it included himself—was then repeated barring interruptions caused

---

[286] Ripon is C.985 in *LVD*, iii, which provides all the sermon texts; and it notes that none of them are found in BL MS Harley 4894, which is a collection of his sermons. Newburn is C.989 in *LVD*, iii.
[287] WCM C.695 and *BRECP*, 782–3. For Ely monk students preaching in Cambridge see above 137.
[288] WCM C.351, 352, 355, 356 etc; the precentor's accounts only survive at Ely, Norwich, and Worcester. For the Worcester monk students see above 129.
[289] *Reg. Sed. Vac. passim*.
[290] Lanfranc, *Monastic Constitutions*, 138–41.
[291] CUL EDC 1/B, charter no. 152.
[292] Evans, *Ely Chapter Ordinances*, 42–3; in Lent and Advent their responsibility was extended to four days. Those named were the prior, or in his absence the monk steward of his hospice, the subprior, almoner, sacrist, cellarer, precentor, and chamberlain.

by the celebration of major feasts.[293] The fragment of the sacrist's account for 1341 shows how this obedientiary dealt with these arrangements for two sessions of blood-letting. In the first the expenses of the sacrist, Alan de Walsingham, on the eve of his election as prior, along with six other named monks, amounted to just over 4s. 6d. for three days without counting food that was provided from stock; the second session occurred seven weeks later for the same monks excluding Walsingham, and the cellarer reimbursed the sacrist's office to the sum of 6s. 6d.[294] While the close connection between blood-letting and recreation is apparent in the obedientiary accounts at Ely, it remains unclear precisely what was included in the latter term. The cellarer, for example, in 1350/1, explains one item charged as expenses *in recreatione fratrum*; and the sacrist's expenses in his *camera* in 1371/2 included the same phrase, suggesting that he entertained some of his brethren in his quarters from time to time on certain feasts.[295] It seems that both bishops, Thomas Arundel and John Fordham, were displeased with the *minutio* observance at Ely. It was no doubt the latter who visited the cathedral priory soon after his arrival at Ely in 1388 because the chamberlain's account of 1388/9 blames the increase in his expenses under *minutiones* on an episcopal ordinance prescribing that they were to be held more frequently.[296] Fragmentary extracts from what may have been a priory register record that Arundel required the *minuti* to have in attendance a *clericus lector* who would provide suitable reading for the convalescents; any conversation was to be in French or Latin with no frivolous chatting in English. Fordham, according to the same source, added the further restriction that the *minuti* were to remain in the *aula minutorum* and not to be allowed to go out.[297] Whether or not these restrictions had any permanent effect is uncertain but perhaps doubtful.

The Durham obedientiaries also link the expenditures on *minutiones* with those on recreation or *ludi*, but a survey of the account rolls and other primary source material gives the impression that more attention was paid to the provisions made for occasions devoted to *solacium*, or *ludi*, in other words to the monks *ludentes* more than the *minuti*. Nevertheless, the observance of periodic blood-letting is not in doubt, although details of its functioning are relatively few. It is noteworthy that the Durham hostiller on a number of occasions singled out the novices by giving them pittances *in minutione*; in 1334/5 the amount was 12d., and in other years he

---

[293] The cellarer's kitchen account of 1325/6, recently returned from Norwich, CUL EDC 1/F/2/1A and his account of 1344/5, ibid., 1/F/2/10 make this clear.

[294] Chapman, *Sacrist Rolls*, ii, 106; for these two sessions food purchased for the *minuti* specified poultry, ibid., 103, 105. These details are not repeated on later accounts, but the number of *minutiones* for which the sacrist was responsible during the accounting year is sometimes given and averaged eight or nine; the sums involved were often between £2 and £3. The chamberlain and precentor also acknowledged contributions from the cellarer to defray their expenses, e.g., CUL Add MS 2957, 26, 43 (1349/50 in both cases).

[295] CUL EDC 1/F/2/11, 1/F/10/18.

[296] CUL EDC 1/F/3/22; the treasurer makes a similar explanation in 1389/90 ibid. 1/F/13/13 and the precentor also makes reference to the change in 1396/7, CUL Add MS 2957, 45.

[297] LPL MS 448, fo 92, 92v; the location of the *aula minutorum* was within the infirmary complex as explained most recently by Anne Holton-Krayenbuhl in 'Ely Infirmary Complex', 152.

extended his generosity to novices and *alii minuti*.[298] The almoner included both in 1376/7 and in later years, but at other times, in the 1390s, he records merely expenses *circa seynes*; in 1414/15 he contributed 8s. 4d. *pro les seynes*.[299] A third obedientiary, the chamberlain, occasionally named the *minuti* among those to whom he gave *exennia*, as in 1337/8 and 1411/12; and in 1397/8 the infirmarer bought twelve earthenware dishes and a scalpel *pro fleubotimia*.[300] One may probably assume that most of the expenses involved in the *minutio* programme were, for the sake of conciseness, subsumed under general headings with other items and so lost to view.

Surviving ordinances emanating from both the monastic chapter and the bishop show concern for improvement in the recreational provisions for the Durham monks, but no signs have been noted of problems indicative of the need for reform of the *minutio* procedures. In 1314 Bishop Richard de Kellawe, the last monk of Durham to be elected to the see, reminded his brethren in an injunction that they were not to be deprived of their due and customary recreation; and, in a possible rewording of this injunction, another source, undated, recommends that a garden should be set aside within the precinct where both the healthy and the ailing could benefit from the fresh air. As a further elaboration, also undated, there is a reference recommending the provision of a certain place, along with financial support, where three or four monks could take it in turn to rest and relax.[301] Both old and young enjoying recreation were expected to converse in French or Latin, and no games of chess or dice were to be allowed.[302] In his episcopal injunctions of 1355 Thomas Hatfield repeated, with further qualifications, the order of his predecessor; the prior, or subprior, or a senior monk was to accompany monks *ad spaciandum* for which money was to be provided for their needs.[303] This envisages short sojourns away from the monastery and, indeed, there are numerous references to the prior and monks spending time *in ludis* at the prior's manor of Beaurepaire or Bearpark. Because of its proximity to Durham, situated about two and a half miles to the northwest of the city, it was a much favoured resort for the prior and monks. There is abundant evidence on the account rolls of many of the obedientiaries, constantly recording their contributions to the expenses of the prior and his fellow monks who were relaxing at Bearpark. Unfortunately, however, the accountants often neglected to state which of the *exennia* listed were exclusively for the holiday period; and the fact that the prior enjoyed prolonged spells at this manor and at Pittington several times a year should not imply that every visit was pure holiday.[304] The prior's

---

[298] DCM hostiller's accounts, 1334/5, 1390/1A, 1391/2 etc.; in 1396/7 he included wine in his pittances for both, and the cost was 4s. 6d.

[299] Ibid., almoner's accounts 1376/7A, 1377/8, 1378/9 etc., Fowler, *Account Rolls*, i, 215, 216, 225.

[300] DCM chamberlain's accounts 1337/8, 1411/12 which included wine; Fowler, *Account Rolls*, i, 266 (infirmarer); the room where the blood-letting operation was performed was presumably attached to the infirmary.

[301] DCM Priory Reg. II, fo 50v; Loc. XXVII, 16c.

[302] DCM Locellus XXVII, 16d.

[303] Harbottle, 'Hatfield's Visitation', 98–9; the subprior was to receive 6d. *pro coquina*, and his accompanying *socii* 2d. per day.

[304] Pittington was another of the prior's manors and also within easy reach of Durham, but to the north-east.

extensive itineraries of his manors, recorded and paid for by the bursar, were no doubt part business and part pleasure. In 1388/9, for example, the prior's expenses on the bursar's account included his *ludend' et spaciend'*, and items of food purchased amounted to almost £23; this would have included entertaining his brethren and often other visitors.[305] The chamberlain's earliest surviving account, dated 1334/5, lumped together his contributions to the prior's *ludi* at Bearpark and the novices' *minutiones*. In 1402/3 his entry under *dona et exennia* specified four *ludi* of the prior with his brethren, and wine was included; but he did not say where he sent the wine, merely that the cost was 58s. 2d.[306] The hostiller named the prior's *ludi* at both Bearpark and Pittington in 1344/5, 1381/2, and 1388/9; the almoner in 1351/2 sent his contribution to Bearpark and other unnamed locations, and in 1394/5 to Bearpark and Pittington.[307] The monks were not cut off from their families and friends after entering the monastery, and some periods of relaxation were spent in their company. Relatives were welcomed and entertained by the monastic community as the accounts of the hostiller and other obedientiaries at Durham record, and the monks themselves were permitted to visit their families and were provided with travelling expenses for this purpose.[308]

There can be no doubt that the monks of Christ Church Canterbury continued to follow the practice of periodic blood-letting and probably adhered to the main strictures imposed by Archbishop Lanfranc.[309] Nevertheless, it is surprising that few entries have been found on the obedientiary accounts, and only slight evidence in other records to confirm its regular observance.[310] One must therefore presume that expenses such as those described above at Ely and Durham, are hidden from view because they have been combined with other items under a heading which grouped together a number of regular payments on the obedientiary account rolls. The two most likely categories are those entitled *in* or *pro deporto* and *ad mensam magistri*, both of which refer to chambers or halls in which the dietary regulations were relaxed and to which the monks probably resorted after their blood-letting sessions.[311] Obedientiaries made frequent contributions under both headings: the chamberlain, for example, in 1391/2 gave 19s. *pro deporto* for the year and 10s. for wine *ad mensam magistri*; the almoner's account for this same year also survives and records the payment of 28s. 6d. *in deporto* and 20s. for wine *ad mensam magistri*.[312] In his concern for the monks who had been bled and for those among the

---

[305] DCM bursar's account 1388/9; see Dobson, *Durham Priory*, 92–99 for details of manorial visits by the priors.
[306] Fowler, *Account Rolls*, i, 166, DCM chamberlain's account, 1402/3A. The four *ludi* pertaining to the prior are mentioned from time to time; they were attached to the feasts of Saint John Baptist, All Saints, the Purification, and Easter; see Fowler, ibid., i, 243.
[307] DCM hostiller's accounts, 1344/5, 1381/2, 1388/9; almoner's accounts ibid., 1351/2, 1394/5. Similar entries occur in other years on many of the accounts.
[308] DCM hostiller's accounts *passim* and see *LVD*, iii, C.703–C.1091 *passim*.
[309] See above 281.
[310] There are references to a *minutor conventus* who was paid by the treasurer, e.g., in 1274 and 1328/9, LPL MS 242, fo 25v, ibid., MS 243, fo 11.
[311] R. A. L. Smith placed the *deportum* to the west of the refectory vestibule, *Canterbury Cathedral Priory*, 43 note 1; the *mensa magistri*, or table hall, was located within the infirmary complex.
[312] CCA DCc chamberlain's account, 56; almoner's account, 1.

community who were suffering from overwork Archbishop Reynolds in 1326 gave them the manor of Caldicote on the eastern outskirts of Canterbury, where the monks could benefit from a change of air and surroundings.[313] Archbishops Winchelsey and Sudbury both expressed concern for the monks' need of recreation and for its regulation, the former issuing instructions for the proper use of the *mensa magistri* and the *deportum* and the latter ordering that the *claustrales* as well as the obedientiaries were to have their customary recreation, *secundum laborem eorum*.[314] We are grateful to one of the Christ Church monks for a closer insight into a few holiday *exeats* permitted in 1439 which were recorded in a notebook. This rare survival belonged to William Glastynbury, a conscientious and industrious monk who entered Christ Church in 1415.[315] On one folio he lists the names of the brethren whose holidays had been approved in chapter and also the dates of their departure and return. For example, Walter Halstede and five other monks were allowed to be away from 7 to 20 January, 1439, and John Newton and six others from 20 to 31 January.[316]

Norwich monk obedientiaries were remarkably consistent in their treatment of blood-letting and recreation on their accounts, frequently referring to them both together as belonging to the same class of expenditure. The chamberlain, who spent 16s. 11d. on his own sessions *in minutione* in 1343/4, under his 'foreign expenses' for 1381/2 recorded his contribution 'circa minutos et in aliis recreationibus sociorum'; the *aliis* makes this close connection clear.[317] The almoner made frequent use of a similar phrase, as did the precentor, who several times added 'at St Leonard's' suggesting that he had spent some of his recreation days visiting his brethren there.[318] For his part the hostiller began to combine the two payments in 1349/50; the communar regularly sent wine to the *minutis*, and in 1363/4 he added *et aliorum recreationum*.[319] The gardener also supplied wine to his brethren *in minutis* annually from 1329/30 onwards, and in 1387/8 and later years he added the *aliis recreationibus*.[320] A slightly different perspective is visible in the sacrist's contributions to those of his brethren who were recuperating after being bled and to those enjoying periods of recreation. He sent wine to the *minuti* from time to time;[321] but, more regularly, from 1276/7 onwards he had the responsibility for providing his fellow monks with festal fare for five days at Pentecost, which in

---

[313] Ibid., Eastry Correspondence M.13, i, 53, and Smith, *Canterbury Cathedral Priory*, 46.
[314] *Reg. Winchelsey*, 820, dated 1298; LPL Reg. Sudbury, fo 32, dated 1377.
[315] *BRECP*, 169; see also Greatrex, 'Culture at Canterbury', which discusses the career of Glastynbury in the light of his notebook.
[316] Oxford, Corpus Christi College MS 256, fo 177v/182v; see also *BRECP*, 188 for Halstede and ibid., 241 for Newton.
[317] NRO DCN 1/5/12, 15; no separate sums are given in the later account.
[318] Ibid., 1/6/18 (1378/9), 1/6/24 (1390/1); 1/9/13 (1374/5), 1/9/16 (1377/8); 1/9/15 (1376/7), 1/9/23 (1386/7), 1/9/31.2 (1412/13).
[319] Ibid., 1/7/14, 15, 33 etc.; 1/12/16 and *passim*, 1/12/03, and see Fernie and Whittingham, *Communar Rolls*, 95, 99, 103.
[320] Noble, *Norwich Gardener's Rolls*, 31, 35, 36, 37, 39, 40 etc.
[321] The sacrist's donations to the *minuti* are found in 1363/4 and 1393/4, for example, NRO DCN 1/4/35, 40; but the extensive building operations for which he was responsible during much of the fourteenth century left him with reduced funds to spare.

1330/1 cost him over 71s., with another 33s. 4d. for wine. In some years he changed the descriptive term *in cibatione* or *pascend'* connoting food, to *in recreatione* which suggests a broader context but probably left the meaning unchanged.[322] However, there is a limit to our ability to interpret correctly such statements on the accounts and, in the case of recreation, food is not invariably the first or only thought that comes to mind. A *camera minutorum* is mentioned by several Norwich obedientiaries including the almoner who in 1396/7 sold several items including a bench and some cushions to the *camera minutorum*, presumably meaning to the infirmarer. The *camera* was almost certainly in the care of the infirmarer who regularly paid the stipend of a *servitor minutorum*.[323] It would seem that Norwich bishops did not consider it necessary to call for improvements in the arrangements in place for blood-letting in the cathedral priory, except indirectly. Bishop John Salmon, a former monk of Ely, expressed concern about the Norwich monks' recreation when, in 1319, he focused his attention on discipline in the infirmary. In his injunctions of that year he addressed the monks who had been authorized to retire to the infirmary *pretextu infirmitatis vel recreationis*; by 'recreation' he had in mind those who were beginning a prescribed period for recuperation with a short stay in the infirmary before going elsewhere for *aliam recepturi recreationem*. Both of these groups were enjoined to adhere to the rule of conventual silence, and those who were *recreatione inidigent[es]* were to be allowed to eat flesh meat according to their individual need.[324]

Only scraps of evidence remain to provide a glimpse of the St Swithun's monks undergoing their *minutiones* and enjoying recreation. With a few rare exceptions the obedientiaries omit any reference to either of them, the almoner, for example, confining himself to two early fourteenth-century entries on his account when he sent wine to the subprior *in ejus minutione*. The single extant infirmarer's roll of 1399/1400 renders briefly visible what might have helped to fill the gaps in our knowledge of the recreation of the monastic community. Among the customary expenses on this roll is a contribution of 40s. *in recreatione* of the obedientiaries at Christmas, the feast of St John Baptist, and Michaelmas; at the same time he contributed a further 43s. 4d. to the *depositorii* for the same feasts.[325] One can only assume that contributions to the *depositorii* funds were not specified as such by the obedientiary donors who invariably entered them as pittances for the *tabula misse* distributions; might contributions for *minutiones* and recreation be hidden under this heading?[326] That the infirmary was the place of convalescence for the monks after they had been bled is clear from a reference in the refectorer's customary which mentions the special dining table assigned to them within the

---

[322] NRO DCN 1/4/26 and also ibid., 1/4/31, 33, 36 etc.; *in recreatione* occurs in 1333/4, the 1340s and the 1360s, ibid., 1/4/29, 34, 35, 36. The sacrist's outlay at Pentecost may have allowed him a partial reprieve with regard to *minutiones*.
[323] NRO DCN 1/6/26; 1/10/4, 6, 9. In 1320/1 the hostiller paid for a glass window and a screen in the *camera*, ibid., 1/7/1.
[324] NRO DCN 92/2.
[325] Kitchin, *Obedientiary Rolls*, 401, 404; he spent 7½d. in each case.
[326] WCL W53/11/2.

infirmary precinct.[327] The late fifteenth-century diet account of the Winchester kitchener possibly hints at a rota of *minuti* in the abbreviation *Mi°* which appears at the top of many of the weekly headings; they are numbered one to four and generally occupy two or three days each. In the six months between November 1492 and May 1493 there were about twenty-six of these sessions which were suspended, as at Ely, during major feasts and solemnities. However, the menus, which itemized the weekly food purchases, were probably being prepared for the refectory and not concerned with the infirmary fare; the latter would probably have been supplied from the infirmary kitchen.[328] And so the mystery remains. Bishop Henry Woodlock, formerly prior of St Swithun's, issued injunctions to his fellow monks in 1315 in which a form of the word *recreatio* appears twice. The bishop ordered that the customary dues for pittances and for the *recreationes infirmorum* be collected and paid without fail, and he expressly forbade his successor in the office of prior, Richard de Enford, from displaying favouritism *in recreationibus faciendis*.[329] These two directives highlight the different contexts in which the word appears in the monastic vocabulary and alert us to the difficulty of interpreting the precise meaning in a particular context. In the first phrase used by Woodlock the reference is most likely to be to those recovering from blood-letting in the infirmary, but the second is surely to be associated with social occasions and therefore implies festive or holiday celebrations.

Apart from a single reference the word *recreatio* has not been found in Worcester cathedral priory records. The exception occurs in one of a set of injunctions of Bishop Thomas de Cobham (1327–37) in which he referred to the monks' *recreaciones et solacium*, taken both within the precinct and outside; he ordered that these should be made possible for every monk at appropriate times. Cobham commended the arrangements for blood-letting and the rest period afterwards which the monks were allowed to spend at the adjacent priory manor of Bevere or another convenient manor.[330] Two obedientiaries furnish details concerning the Worcester monks' *minutiones*. Both the pittancer and the cellarer introduced a separate section on their accounts in which the *minutio* payments are explained, the former from about 1324/5 onward and the latter from about 1344/5.[331] In 1324/5 the entry recorded the purchase of wine, which cost the pittancer 64s. Within a few years his entries become more informative, with the result that in 1344/5 we learn that the two monk students at Oxford and the two monks residing with Bishop Wulstan were also included, all of them receiving a pittance of 2d. for each bloodletting undergone. With the number of monks recorded as well as the total expense

---

[327] Kitchin, *Consuetudinary*, 20, 31.
[328] Perhaps there was no separate kitchen in the infirmary; the diet accounts are in Kitchin, *Obedientiary Rolls*, 307–50, and see above 242–3.
[329] *Reg. Woodlock*, 750; the collectors referred to were probably the *depositorii*.
[330] *Reg. Montacute*, item no. 1119; income from the weirs at Bevere, which was only a few miles north of Worcester, went to the kitchener.
[331] WCM C.296 (pittancer), C.59 (cellarer).

we may conclude that there were about eight *minutio* sessions for each of them.[332] Later entries become less detailed, but the pittances and the number of *minutiones* remain the same. The cellarer's account for 1344/5 presents details identical to those cited above for the pittancer, except that each monk received 4d. per session; and, for the second half of the year from Easter to Michaelmas, a small increment was added.[333] In the 1390s, as far as one can tell from the information recorded, the frequency of blood-letting and the pittances distributed continued as before. In addition, the kitchener began to specify an expenditure on spices *pro minutione* in the 1390s, but some of his earlier undifferentiated entries may have been purchases for the same purpose.[334] It might be tempting to think that the *minutio* pittances at Worcester were more efficiently managed than at the other cathedral priories, but this would be to forget the complex network of inter-office payments behind the scenes that would have provided the funding for them.[335]

In this chapter I have attempted to follow the cathedral monks in the daily rhythm of their conventual life within the monastic precinct through the liturgical seasons of the year. It must be remembered, however, that the otherworldly regime, centred on the spiritual preparation for eternal life as the Rule frequently enjoins, was at the same time pervaded by the intrusions of a secular world.[336] It not only surrounded them on the outside but mingled with them inside in the form of guests and pilgrims, messengers and envoys, corrodians and employees, both official and domestic. Moreover, the monks themselves were frequently called upon to mingle with their fellow human beings often in the course of duty. The need to procure the provisions, equipment, and other merchandise essential for their own well-being and the maintenance of their establishment, to administer and supervise their estates, to serve as proctors and envoys to protect their rights, and to fulfil royal and papal impositions and summonses—all of these I have set aside in the knowledge that they have been and continue to be the focus of scholarly research.[337] The constant interpenetration of the two worlds inevitably led to an undermining of discipline which is markedly evident in many visitation injunctions. But a harmonious balance between spiritual and material, between the *servitium divinum* and the human enterprise can be rarely achieved and never sustained in the individual or in the community.

---

[332] WCM, C.301; the bishop had previously been prior. It should be noted that the prior was always counted as two and therefore received 4d. for each of his *minutiones*.
[333] Ibid., C.59; the increment was less than 1d. per monk per *minutio*.
[334] Ibid., C.124, 125.
[335] See above 247.
[336] *RB*, C.4, 46; C.5, 10; C.7, 11; C.72, 2, 12.
[337] See the relevant bibliography in note 1 of Chapter IV above.

VI

The Closing Years: Illness, Age, Infirmity, and Death

> Mortem cotidie ante oculos suspectam habere... usque ad mortem in monasterio perseverantes.[1]

Illness and death were never far away from medieval man, and the monk was no exception.[2] Chapter thirty-six of the Rule, entitled *De infirmis fratribus* emphasizes that caring for the sick is of prime importance because in serving them the brethren were serving Christ. As for those who were ill, they were told to be reasonable in their requests to avoid overburdening those who were assigned to supply their needs. The abbot (or prior) was made responsible for the oversight of the sick and was required to ensure that the cellarer provided them with meat until they regained their strength. The following chapter, number thirty-seven, continuing in the same vein, is concerned with the elderly and the very young whose physical frailty required some relaxation of the Rule with regard to the prescribed hours for meals. While St Benedict urged his monks to have death daily before their eyes, he made no reference to the treatment of the dying and the burial of the dead. Lanfranc dealt with both in detail in his monastic constitutions, and these continued to be followed, no doubt, with slight local variations, by the English Benedictines.[3] The archbishop, himself a monk, also outlined the duties of the infirmarer and provided for a temporary release from the conventual duties for brethren who were indisposed but did not require admission to the infirmary.[4]

It is greatly to be regretted that many of the practical details of monastic life, such as those concerning the treatment of the sick and infirm members of the cathedral communities, are hidden from view. This is largely due to the random survival of the relevant primary sources, among which are the accounts of the obedientiary known as the infirmarer or master of the infirmary. Unfortunately, the majority of

---

[1] *RB*, C.4, 47; Prol. 50. The first phrase is one of the instruments of good works enjoining the young monks, as well as the seniors, to live each day as if it were their last; the second phrase emphasizes perseverance in the monastic vocation.
[2] The Benedictine monks' comparatively cloistered existence and the uncommonly high standard of their monasteries' sanitary arrangements have been taken into account. Barbara Harvey has reminded us of the health hazards latent in community life and also of the spread of infections brought in by the constant stream of visiting officials, pilgrims, relatives, and friends, Harvey, *Living and Dying*, 143, 81 and *passim*.
[3] Lanfranc, *Monastic Constitutions*, 132, 176–92. For later changes introduced by the Black Monk chapter, consult Pantin, *Black Monk Chapters*, iii, subject index under Dead.
[4] Lanfranc, *Monastic Constitutions*, 112, 176.

the extant accounts are brief and uninformative. At Canterbury the earliest infirmarer's roll is dated 1518; at Winchester there is only a single roll for the year 1399/1400, and at Ely one roll only of 1458/9. The Durham infirmarer's accounts begin in 1355/6 and those of Worcester comprise a short run between 1378/9 and 1412. The most extensive coverage and the most informative detail are to be found at Norwich where there are fourteen accounts between 1312/13 and 1421/2; in contrast, the twenty-five Durham accounts before 1420 are devoid of any references to the patients in the infirmarer's care.[5] Episcopal visitors and their deputies frequently heard complaints about the inadequate treatment received in the monastic infirmary, although the allegation that the death of one Durham monk, Thomas de Newcastle in 1313/14, had been due to Prior Geoffrey de Burdon's refusal to provide a competent doctor may have been a unique incident that arose during the heat of dissension and controversy within the convent.[6]

Infirmary care and personnel

Post-visitation injunctions, which bring to light many of the individual monk's *detecta* as reported during questioning, are mainly directed toward the absence of competent medical practitioners and varying degrees of callousness with regard to the welfare of the brethren confined in the infirmary.[7] Archbishop Winchelsey's injunctions survive for four of the cathedral priories that he visited between c. 1296 and 1304 and, in each case, he ordered improvements in the care of the sick. Detailed directions were given to the monks of Christ Church restricting the access of visitors, both from outside and inside the monastic community, requiring the attendants to be unfailingly diligent and vigilant, and ordering the prior or his deputy to visit in person at least once a week to ensure that every sick monk lacked nothing needful to promote his recovery. In addition, the archbishop laid stress on the necessity for cleanliness which was to be observed by the custodians in the infirmary and those who were admitted to visit.[8] At Worcester, as at Canterbury, Winchelsey allowed the eating of flesh meat in the infirmary but ordered that the sick were to cooperate by eating the food that had been specially prepared to suit their individual needs.[9] The Norwich monks seem to have been allowed to request the ministrations of a brother monk if this proved to be feasible.[10] At Rochester the cellarer's responsibilities were highlighted; he was admonished to make frequent

---

[5] No infirmarer's accounts of Bath and Coventry have been preserved and only a single cursory account of 1424/5 from Rochester.

[6] Newcastle is C.702 in *LVD*, iii, and Burdon C.731. The prior refuted this and other charges, but was obliged to resign in 1321 after eight contentious years in office; for the details of his priorate see Scammell, 'The Case of Geoffrey Burdon', 226–50.

[7] *Detecta* are the detections, i.e., the actual answers given and recorded during visitation.

[8] *Reg. Winchelsey*, 819–20 (AD 1298).

[9] Ibid., 876–7 (AD 1301); and for further regulations on when and where the eating of meat was permitted see above 241–2. See also *Reg. Montacute*, 276, which corrects the reading of this item in *Reg. Winchelsey*.

[10] NRO DCN 42/5–8, formerly no. 3928 (AD 1304).

visits to the infirmary to ascertain from every resident that he was receiving the nourishment suited to his condition.[11]

Further glimpses of conditions in cathedral priory infirmary cloisters can be inferred from other episcopal injunctions during the fourteenth century and from a few chapter ordinances. Bishop Ralph de Walpole commanded the Ely monks in 1300 to show more concern for the sick and infirm in body and mind; he enjoined quietness, some form of recreation where possible and companionship to console the dying. He also required those monks who were aged and frail to resign from office.[12] At Worcester both sets of William de Gainsborough's injunctions in 1304 and *c.* 1306/7 called for better care of the sick brethren; but it was Thomas de Cobham, his successor from 1317 to 1327, who spelled out the details of what this general prescription entailed. He reminded the monks of the relevant chapter of their Rule, ordered the appointment of an attendant (*garcio*) for every ill brother, and required the infirmarer to charge the cost of any treatment to his account. If he found himself short of funds the cellarer (receiver/bursar) was to come to his assistance; the food prescribed for the sick was to be prepared in the [convent] kitchen.[13] Henry Woodlock, monk of St Swithun's and bishop of Winchester, 1305–1316, visited his brethren in the cathedral priory on several occasions recorded in his register; but, in the two sets of surviving injunctions, he appears to have been content to confine his remarks on the infirmary to the necessity for frequent visits to the sick in accordance with the Rule, in order to ascertain their needs and to fulfil the *fraterne humanitatis debitum*.[14] The monastic chapter at Norwich in 1379 imposed several practical regulations regarding the infirmary which, no doubt, reveal the periodic need to reassess and reaffirm the community's shared responsibilities; the few surviving chapter ordinances such as these provide us with an insight into the probable complaints and difficulties expressed during the deliberations that may have preceded their issue. In this instance the communar was told to see to the repair of the doorway to the infirmary; the infirmarer was required to provide a competent doctor as had been past custom, and also to arrange for a lamp to light the entrance; and the hostiller was to be responsible for supplying a large candle for the infirmary whenever called upon to do so.[15]

Bishop Simon Sudbury was translated from London to Canterbury in 1375 and made his first official visitation of Christ Church early in January 1377. The reports he received, as well as his own observations, exposed the deplorable state of the infirmary; and there can be little doubt that his injunctions prompted the newly elected prior, Stephen de Mongeham, together with the subprior and nine other senior monks, to draw up a set of strict regulations for the care of the sick and

---

[11] *Reg. Winchelsey*, 841 (AD 1299).

[12] Evans, *Ely Chapter Ordinances*, 17, 20.

[13] *Reg. Montacute*, 266, 267, 272; there is no reference here to the existence of a separate kitchen in the infirmary.

[14] *Reg. Woodlock*, 508 (1308), 749 (1315); the wording is identical in both and there is no mention of those whose responsibility was in question.

[15] Cheney, 'Norwich Cathedral Priory', 118–19, transcribed from the flyleaves of a Norwich customary, Cambridge, Corpus Christi College MS 465, fos 161–2.

elderly brethren. These included extra funding for the anniversarian so that he could improve the quality of their food and pittances, and the preparation of a suitable dish each day by the cellarer along with bread and ale. Three laundrymen and a man in charge of baths were always to be on hand and additional attendants were to be brought in when need arose; furthermore, at the discretion of the subprior and almoner, the temporary services of an almonry schoolboy could offer additional help. The *claustrales* who were infirm but able to take their meals at the *mensa magistri* adjoining the infirmary were to receive 2d. each every day from the anniversarian, while the *stationarii*, for their pittances, were to have 12d. per week. However, it was decided that none of the monks who held obedientiary offices were to be eligible for these benefits, probably because their medical expenses were usually charged to their accounts.[16] Whether or not these self-imposed regulations were strictly adhered to remains unknown, although there are a few indications in the anniversarian's accounts that he was making the required distributions.[17]

In 1314 the visitation of Richard de Kellawe, monk and bishop of Durham, to his cathedral priory resulted in a brief admonition to those responsible for the infirmary to ensure that the food and drink served was sufficient to satisfy the needs of the sick brethren. He also ordered them to waste no time in appointing a qualified doctor.[18] Other surviving records concerning the infirmary at Durham draw attention to the recurring human tendency, in a situation fraught with dissatisfaction and dissent, to fasten blame on the person in authority, in this case the prior. Accusations against Prior William de Cowton (1321–1341), for example, during a visitation of Bishop Louis de Beaumont included the neglect of the sick and infirm who were resident in the cells.[19] The prior defended himself with regard to this and other charges in a written statement to the bishop; and his successor, John Fosser, reacted similarly when faced with Bishop Hatfield's allegations in 1355.[20] A later series of what appear to be *detecta* addressed to Fosser in 1371 by the same bishop reveals a divided community in which the prior's administrative abilities and leadership were again questioned in detail as well as his neglect of the sick.[21] Durham appears to have had more than its share of colourful priors in the fourteenth century, Richard de Hoton (1290–1309) and Geoffrey de Burdon (1313–1321) having also provoked contention and division within the monastery.[22] Fraught situations, such as those experienced by the

---

[16] Sheppard, *Lit. Cant.*, iii, 4–5; the refectorer and kitchener appear to have been minor offices at Canterbury and are not included. For the *mensa magistri* see above 258, and for the *stationarii*, who were permanent residents in the infirmary, see below 296–7. The doctor was required to produce an account of the medical expenses he incurred twice yearly.
[17] E.g., CCA DCc 7 (1396–1402).
[18] DCM Priory Reg. II, fo 50v.
[19] DCM Misc. Charter 2645, *c.* 1328; see also DCM Locellus XXVII, 12.
[20] DCM 2.9.Pont.6 (Cowton, ?1332), 2.8.Pont.5 (Fosser, 1355); see Harbottle, 'Hatfield's Visitation', 95–6.
[21] DCM 2.8.Pont.12; and see Piper, 'Size and Shape of Durham', 167–8.
[22] Prior Hoton's confrontation with Bishop Anthony Bek is related in detail in Fraser, *Antony Bek*, 123–75; for Prior Burdon see Scammell, 'The Case of Geoffrey Burdon', 226–50.

Durham monks under these four priors, suggest that they were all controversial figures, autocratic and self-willed or weak and incompetent, in either case stirring discontent and resentment if not overt opposition on the part of some monks. Allusions to the prior's failure to visit the sick monks in the infirmary and to ensure the attendance of a doctor to treat them were frequently recorded items among the monks' grievances at several cathedral priories, and the string of accusations impugning Cowton and Fosser may probably be considered exceptional only in so far as they happen to have been preserved. Moreover, Cowton was described by one of his brethren at the time of his election as 'vir utique Deo et hominibus amabilis'; and Fosser, who was chosen as prior at the age of fifty-seven and remained in office until his death at ninety, is surely to be commended for providing the necessary strong leadership to guide the convent to recovery after the ravages of the Black Death.[23]

There is no lack of evidence for the presence of doctors attending the sick in cathedral priory infirmaries despite the frequent complaints to the contrary. Ely, Winchester, and Worcester provided some of their medical practitioners with corrodies that included board and lodging. In the case of M. Adam de St Albans, a surgeon, appointed for life at Ely in 1272, the arrangement was that he was to pay rent to the infirmarer for a messuage close by and to receive daily supplies of food and drink. By the indenture drawn up between the prior and convent of Winchester and M. Thomas de Schaftesbury in 1320, the latter paid the substantial sum of 50m. in cash in return for room and board for life. M. John de Logwardyn, an Oxford graduate, was the recipient of a corrody at Worcester in 1338, the terms of which specified not only room and board but also one or two boys to serve him and stabling for two horses.[24] Payments as pensions to doctors occur frequently at Canterbury usually on the treasurer's accounts; for example, M. John Palmer, *medicus noster*, is named in the 1380s and received 53s. 4d. in 1382/3. Similarly, at Durham the bursar paid 20s. twice yearly to a M. John in the late 1370s and early 1380s in addition to a suitable robe in 1379/80. The Norwich master of the cellar gave small sums to doctors from time to time interspersed with occasional larger amounts, the latter probably to one who was summoned at a time of particular need. The infirmarer, on the other hand, seems to have been paying an annual pension of 20s. to M. Geoffrey de Suffeld in the 1340s; and in 1393/4 a *stipendium medicorum* of over £4 was entered on his account without further detail, but it probably included the purchase of medicines. No doubt there would have been

---

[23] The monk who wrote in praise of Cowton was Robert de Graystanes/Greystones, *LVD*, iii, C.801; see *HDST*, 120. Fosser's strength of character is evaluated by Piper in 'Size and Shape of Durham', 167–9, where the focus of attention is on the successful recruitment policy to make good the numbers lost when the plague struck the monastic community.

[24] The careers of the three doctors are in Talbot and Hammond, *Medieval Practitioners*, 8 (St Albans), 355–6 (Schaftesbury), 163 (Logwardyn), but two of them require qualification. Schaftesbury made a single payment of 50 marks as I have stated (Goodman, *Winchester Chartulary* no. 225) and not one silver mark per annum; and the details of Logwardyn's corrody are not given but they are to be found in WCM Liber Albus, fo 149.

times when the services of a resident doctor were lacking, but how often and for how long a time these gaps occurred cannot even be estimated.[25]

If monastic infirmarers managed at various times to carry out their responsibilities without a medical doctor in attendance, does it follow that those appointed to the office had themselves received some practical training in the diagnosis and treatment of common illnesses, perhaps serving for a period as assistants in the infirmary? Unfortunately there is little evidence to suggest that this may have been the case. In fact, few infirmarers of the cathedral priories during the century and a half under study are known by name, and little is known about most of them. There are only three, for example, at Canterbury, all of whom had been professed for thirty or more years; one was blind, and all died in office.[26] Nine or ten infirmarers' names have been found at Norwich between c. 1309 and the 1420s and a similar number at Worcester between 1302 and 1420. There is some indication that at least a few of the Norwich infirmarers had a degree of practical competence in the art of healing, for they seem to have been able to prepare some of their own medicines. Their accounts list purchases of essential ingredients in addition to ready-made remedies; and spices and herbs included pepper, nutmeg, saffron, and ginger, as well as sugar, oil, honey, and wine.[27] One mid-fifteenth-century monk, William Bokenham, although not known to have occupied the office of infirmarer, compiled two short treatises on the diagnosis of illnesses through the examination of the patients' urine.[28] At Worcester John de Dudley was appointed infirmarer immediately upon his return from Oxford after his inception in theology, and he seems to have remained in office for seven or more years before becoming subprior. John de Gloucestre, on the other hand, had held four obedientiary offices over a period of some thirty years before being named infirmarer. He would then have been in his early sixties and, possibly, not hale and hearty because he had to be replaced before the year was out and died the following year.[29] At Durham, where some sixteen infirmarers have been identified before 1420, both elderly monks and younger ones were appointed. Several like Michael de Chilton, John de Goldsborough, and Thomas Launcells had been professed for close to half a century, but two, Robert de Brackenbury and John de Langton, were monks of only about twenty years' standing.[30] Brackenbury is the only Durham

---

[25] A. M. Thomas was *medicus noster* in the 1280s at Christ Church, LPL MS 242, fos 105v, 98 and Palmer a century later, CCA DCc treasurer's account 26. The Durham bursar's accounts for 1378/9, DCM for that year and the three following years, name M. John; the master of the cellar at Norwich made small donations to medical men in 1309/10 and 1333/4 (NRO DCN 1/1/19, 1/1/32) and again in 1360/1 (ibid., 1/1/47) when the prior required a second opinion and specialist treatment. Suffeld's pension is on the infirmarer's accounts, ibid., 1/10/5, 1/10/6, and the *stipendium* on 1/10/9.

[26] The three monks are included in *BRECP*: John de Colchestre, who was blind, 127; Richard de Ikham, 207–8; John Elham I, 149.

[27] See the infirmarer's accounts *passim* NRO DCN 1/10/1–14; note also the remarks by Saunders in *Obedientiary Rolls*, 132–3 and Gilchrist, *Norwich Cathedral Close*, 180 (quoting Carole Rawcliffe).

[28] See *BRECP*, 485; the manuscript is now in the Wellcome Institute for the History of Medicine, MS 408.

[29] For John de Dudley I, see *BRECP*, 797–9, and for John de Gloucestre III ibid., 810–11.

[30] These are all in *LVD*, iii, and numbered as follows: Chilton C.677; Goldsborough C.835, Launcells C.945, Brackenbury C.894, Langton C.872.

monk known to have had in his possession a volume of medical treatises, namely some of those translated from Arabic and Latin sources by the eleventh century Constantinus Africanus, which were numbered among the basic medical handbooks in common use.[31] Only one fourteenth-century Rochester infirmarer has come to light, none at Ely, three at Winchester, all professed about forty years, but a fourth, appointed in 1402, had entered St Swithun's only fifteen or sixteen years before.[32] It would appear that the selection of infirmarers within the community was almost invariably pragmatic and probably determined by the aptitude and availability of the monks under consideration. To forestall any tendency toward generalization the case of the long-serving Coventry infirmarer John de Grenborough illustrates the significantly altered perspective opened up by a single chance survival, in this particular case of his medical handbook.[33] It is therefore possible, if not probable, that among both the identified and unidentified infirmarers in the cathedral priories there were others as dedicated and proficient as Grenborough.

Details of the layout of the infirmary complex of several of the cathedral priories have been reconstructed, and recent on-site investigations have added significantly to their accuracy. These confirm the impression of a separate mini-cloister within the monastic precinct with its own garden and *herbarium*. Ample room for the entire community seems to have been taken into account in the provision of a seven-bay infirmary hall at Canterbury in the twelfth century, while the slightly smaller monastic population at Norwich was content with six bays constructed at about the same date; the nine bays at Ely would have allowed more than enough room for the seventy or so monks in the twelfth century when the hall was built. The infirmary chapel, an eastern extension of the hall of several bays brought spiritual comfort and healing to the inmates of the infirmary through the daily liturgical celebration.[34] Infirmary halls at Durham, Canterbury, Norwich, and Ely began to be partially subdivided in the later fourteenth century to provide some private chambers for the inmates, and these were followed by the construction of additional chambers abutting or close by the hall.[35]

---

[31] DCL MS C.IV.12 and a second volume of the same author/translator, MS C.I.19 also bears Brackenbury's name. The book catalogue drawn up under Prior Eastry lists several copies of Constantinus's writings one of which had been owned by the previous prior, Thomas de Ryngmer, James, *ALCD*, item 1441; for his biography see *BRECP*, 269–70.

[32] These monks are included in *BRECP*: John de Wodestok, 648 (Rochester); Adam de Donytone, 686, William de Watford, 745, John Katerington, 706, William Bette, 673 (Winchester).

[33] See above 152.

[34] The most recent report on Christ Church infirmary is by Margaret Sparks in *Canterbury Precincts*, 33–4, 39–41. For Norwich see Gilchrist, *Norwich Cathedral Close*, 165–82 and for Ely, Holton-Krayenbuhl, 'Ely Infirmary Complex', 118–55.

[35] Nineteen *camerae* in the infirmary are mentioned at Durham in the early fifteenth century around the time that an extensive rebuilding programme was in progress, Dobson, *Durham Priory*, 78, 294. At Canterbury a similar desire for privacy is evident, Dobson, 'Monks of Canterbury', 131–2, while recent archaeological reports of the infirmary complex at Norwich and at Ely include plans of the reconstructed site, Gilchrist, *Norwich Cathedral Close*, 167–74 and Holton-Krayenbuhl, 'Ely Infirmary Complex', 158–64 with the later addition of chambers in both cases. The addition of a small dining hall or misericord adjoining the infirmary for those recovering from illness or blood-letting has been discussed above 241–2. As to separate infirmary kitchens, there was an infirmary cook at Durham whose stipend was 2s. for the year 1354/5, Fowler, *Account Rolls*, i, 261; a plan of the Ely infirmary in Holton-Krayenbuhl, 'Ely Infirmary Complex', 161, shows the location of the kitchen.

For the greater comfort and ease of monks confined in the infirmary at Durham tapestries were brought and hung in the hall in the 1380s, fireplaces and benches repaired, and cushions made. A small selection of books from the library was kept in a cupboard or chest at the entrance to the infirmary purportedly for use in the refectory; these included the Bible, saints' lives and sermons, suitable reading material for Durham monks who were alert and bookishly inclined.[36]

Other infirmary residents

In 1295 Martin de Clyve, monk of Christ Church, was serving as lector in teaching dialectic and theology in the cloister. Suffering from the encroaching disabilities that accompany old age he gratefully received a dispensation from Archbishop Winchelsey relieving him from his duties in choir, kitchen, and the reading rota in the refectory. There is no mention of his possible retirement to the infirmary, but it is to be noted that among the collection of books listed under his name in Prior Eastry's catalogue are several medical treatises; these allow us to speculate that in his last few years he may have been one of the unidentified infirmarers.[37] In the fifteenth century several Canterbury monks retired to the infirmary and were known as *stationarii*; one of them, William Chart, died in 1418 after occupying St John's chamber during his final years.[38] Pittances had been allocated to the *stationarii* resident in the infirmary in the ordinances drawn up in 1377 to put an end to the laxity in discipline and in the care of the sick and elderly monks. In this reform programme there is a clear reference to the assigning of chambers [*camerae*] to individual Christ Church monks.[39] Another example of the allocation of private quarters within the infirmary is found at Winchester in 1392. The recipient was John Langreod, and most of the details have fortunately been preserved in a lengthy but incomplete loose deed. In it the prior, Robert de Rodebourne, prompted it appears by a papal mandate on Langreod's behalf, rewarded him with this privilege because of his record of long and faithful service to the community of St Swithun's and because of age and infirmity following his fiftieth birthday. He had been the monastery treasurer during much of the 1380s and early 1390s prior to this concession. However, it in no way signalled a withdrawal from active duty for he filled the office of anniversarian from 1394 to 1396 and went on to be almoner from 1397 to 1404 and hordarian from 1404 to 1406 and possibly longer.[40] His

---

[36] DCM infirmarer's accounts 1384/5, 1385/6, 1387/8, 1389/90; *Cat. Vet. Durham*, 80–1.
[37] Brother Martin may have obtained a degree as he was addressed as *Magister*, BRECP, 125; his books are listed in James, *ACLD*, 131–3 where the titles of the medical texts are at item no. 1613.
[38] William Chart I, *BRECP*, 112–13; another *stationarius* was John Cantorbury I, who died in 1432; ibid., 108. A third Christ Church monk, John Holyngborne, a *stationarius* in the 1480s and early 1490s bought a volume of the medical tracts of Constantinus Africanus, *BRECP*, 202, where there are two monks by this name. I am now inclined to assign this book to the earlier monk (ibid., 201–2), rather than the later to whom James assigned it in his catalogue of the manuscripts of Oxford, Corpus Christi College (MS 189); James did not know of the existence of the first John Holyngborne.
[39] See above 291–2 for the new regulations and Sheppard, *Lit. Cant.*, iii, 4, for this reference.
[40] Langreod's career is in *BRECP*, 708–9; and what remains of the deed, along with a papal letter and the mandate, have been transcribed in Kitchin, *Obedientiary Rolls*, 163–9.

personal appeal to the pope—which was successful—seems somewhat surprising and raises several interesting and, as yet, unanswerable questions. Were such appeals common? Why, in this case, was it necessary? It may suggest a weak prior unable to keep peace and order and perhaps prone to favouritism within the community.

The case of Simon Crompe, monk of Worcester, some half century before Langreod has some features in common with those of the Winchester monk and of the Canterbury monk Martin de Clyve. Crompe had held the offices of pittancer, precentor and sacrist in succession over a period of some twenty years and was still serving as sacrist in 1333 when the prior, Wulstan de Bransford, dispensed him from participation at the night office of matins except on double feasts. The prior and chapter praised Crompe for risking his life for his brethren, notably when he journeyed to the Roman curia where he had laboured *viriliter et efficaciter* on their behalf. Crompe was assigned a clerk to minister to his needs for the rest of his life, with the latter's food and livery provided. There would have been no need for a room in the infirmary for Crompe because, as sacrist, he was probably occupying, or about to occupy, the newly built sacrist's house on the north side of the cathedral and attached to the outside wall of the choir between the western and eastern transepts.[41]

Priors and obedientiaries in their final years

The majority of the cathedral priors remained in office until death.[42] A few of them, like Nicholas de Hoo of Norwich, were assisted by a coadjutor to ease the burden of responsibility for their last year or two in office. Hoo resigned in 1381, in his twenty-fifth year as prior, and died only a few months later.[43] The priors who resigned from office expected to be supported by adequate means to enable them to maintain their dignity. It was no doubt a diplomatic arrangement on the part of the Durham chapter to send retired priors to one of the cells where they would be less tempted to interfere in Durham affairs. William de Tanfield, for example, was appointed master of the cell of Jarrow in 1313 with a pension of £10 per annum provided by the cell and an additional 6m. from the Durham exchequer; he was allowed to have two monk companions of his choice and was equipped with regulations to safeguard his authority.[44] Robert Bennington de Walworth, a later Durham prior, must have been in his late sixties when, in 1391, he was reported as infirm both in body and mind and consequently resigned. His remaining years

---

[41] There is no other record of Crompe's successful visit to the papal curia; it may have been connected with the appropriation of the church of Dodderhill to the cathedral priory in 1332; *Reg. Orleton*, no. 180. See Engel, *Worcester Cathedral*, 29. For Crompe, see *BRECP*, 792–3.

[42] Prior Fosser at Durham is a good example of longevity in the priorate, thirty-three active years in his case.

[43] *BRECP*, 525–6. Three decades earlier, in 1352, Prior Simon Bozoun resigned and took up residence as prior of St Leonard's; but he must have died within two years because John de Hedirset became prior of St Leonard's in 1353, ibid., 486, 518–19.

[44] DCM Priory Reg. II, fo 21v; he died within the year, *LVD*, i, 509–10; iii, C.1389.

were spent first at the cell of Finchale and, later, at Jarrow, where he also had two monks in attendance, one to be responsible for the liturgical services and the other for the administration of the cell.[45] When Thomas Crist resigned from the office of prior of Bath in 1340 it was the bishop, Ralph de Shrewsbury, who issued an ordinance to cover all his future needs. He was, first of all, to be provided with a suitable dwelling, probably inside the precinct as the food allowance for himself, his monk chaplain, and two servants seems to presuppose the priory kitchen as its source. His pension was to come from revenues derived from the manor and church of Northstoke pertaining to the priory over which he was given certain responsibilities with regard to maintenance.[46] William de Walpole's resignation at Ely took place during the visitation, *sede plene*, of Archbishop Thomas Arundel in 1401; details of the proceedings in the archiepiscopal register explained that the prior had recognized his 'insufficientiam et inhabilitatem ad tantam regendam ecclesiam'. The arrangements for his retirement included the income from the priory manor of Wodeley (estimated at £20 per annum), £10 a year for his clothing, and a chamber in the monastery, together with a chaplain and two servants; corrodies of food and drink were also to be supplied for the four of them.[47] In addition to Prior Fosser at Durham, Priors Henry Eastry and Thomas Chillenden of Christ Church Canterbury are examples of those who remained active in office until the end. Eastry was ninety-one when he died in 1331, and he was still advising and often admonishing the hapless archbishop, Simon de Meopham, the year before his death. Chillenden was probably in his early sixties when he attended the Council of Pisa in 1409 as a member of the English delegation; two years later on the eve of his death he was described as so emaciated that his body was reduced to skin and bone.[48] The monks of St Swithun's witnessed the unique and tragic fate of their prior, Thomas Nevyle, who had been unanimously elected bishop by them in 1404, only to have their choice overridden by the papal provision of Henry Beaufort. It was Beaufort who issued the commission for his arrest eleven years later; and the resignation deed which Nevyle signed in a room in the infirmary expressed the usual formula that no coercion had been exercised, that he had signed of his own free will 'propter grandevam etatemen ac corporis mei imbecillitatem et impotenciam'. He was not yet sixty years old. Taken to the Tower of London he disappeared from view. His death was only recorded by the almoner who on his account for 1415/16 made the customary distribution of bread and pittances for three named monks who died during the year; Nevyle was one of them.[49]

---

[45] *LVD*, iii, C.903; he had had a debilitating stroke in 1387, Piper, 'Monks of Durham and ... Old Age', 55.
[46] *BRECP*, 21.
[47] Evans, *Ely Chapter Ordinances*, 49; for Walpole see *BRECP*, 452–3 under William de Walpole I, where reference is made to two letters indicating that the provisions made for his retirement were considered inadequate by Archbishop Arundel.
[48] *BRECP*, 144–5 (Eastry), 119–21 (Thomas Chillenden I).
[49] *BRECP*, 721–2, where the suggestion, made by G. L. Harriss, is noted to the probability that Nevyle had been linked with the Southampton plot.

Many of the novices succumbed to infections and other ailments and were sent for short periods to the infirmary, but the older monks, potentially of retirement age, were often to be found there for longer spells if not permanently. Within the 'time frame' of this study, however, we are hampered by the loss of essential evidence, in this particular case the comparatively few recorded dates of the admission or profession of the great majority of monks and of their dates of death. Durham and Canterbury are the two exceptions among the cathedral priories, but at Canterbury the fairly complete admission/profession dates are not matched by the death dates, which for many monks remain unknown. Nevertheless, it seems fairly certain that many senior and elderly monks remained in harness, holding office until they were close to death. Alan Piper found that at Durham age did not appear as a bar to appointment to obedientiary office, and a similar practice can be discerned in the other cathedral priories. Does this imply that elderly incumbents of major offices were always blessed with a strong constitution as well as the mental agility required to ensure that their responsibilities were competently executed? It is certainly possible, if not probable, that at times they delegated some of their authority to younger and more physically active subordinates, but such persons, monastic or lay, remain largely unidentified. It is hardly surprising that the governance of cells was often, but by no means invariably, considered to be a suitable appointment for the active elderly monk as well as for retired priors. At the same time it is unlikely that a senior monk would have been posted against his will; nevertheless there must always have been some monks for whom the quieter and simpler life of a cell was attractive after the years of a lengthy and elaborate liturgy and the daily throngs of visitors, pilgrims, officials, and workmen who frequented the cathedral priory precinct. Some monk scholars like Uthred de Boldon would probably have found the surroundings congenial for their studious pursuits; in fact he spent most of the last twenty years of his life, from the late 1370s to 1396/7, as prior of Finchale apart from two relatively short intervals when he was recalled to Durham to be subprior.[50] John de Ripon, another Durham monk graduate, although not known as a writer, was master of Wearmouth from 1409 until his death four years later; thirty-eight years of monastic life before this appointment confirms his age and seniority.[51] At the Norwich cells of St Leonard's and Lynn several monks can be identified as having lengthy years of service behind them before being put in charge of these cells. Richard de Blakeneye was chamberlain at Norwich before being appointed prior of St Leonard's in 1386; he remained there for the next nineteen years until his death in 1405, except for a period of about five months when he was sent abroad on convent business. The absence of any biographical records before his assumption of the chamberlain's office

---

[50] *LVD*, iii, C.888; for Boldon's career and writings see also *ODNB*. It should be mentioned that during his years at Durham and Finchale he did not cease to be involved in monastic and ecclesiastical affairs.

[51] *LVD*, iii, C.988. There were, of course, exceptions to these late in life appointments: Richard de Sedgebrook, for example, became master of Farne in 1358 (*LVD*, iii, C.936), a mere five years after his admission/profession in *c*. 1353; however, it must be remembered that this was a time when the community at Durham was recovering from its heavy losses during the plague years, 1348 to 1352.

precludes any certainty as to his exact position in terms of seniority, but in 1386 he would have been between twenty and twenty-five years in the cathedral monastery.[52] Similar reckoning would date John de Hedirset's presence in the Norwich cathedral community to at least thirty-five years before he was sent to St Leonard's in 1353; there he remained until his death four years later.[53] Ralph de Martham's assignment to Lynn *c.* 1372, only ten years after his priestly ordination, would not be unusual if he had entered the monastery at a later than average age, and it seems to have been an appointment agreeable to his superiors and to himself for he remained there for twenty years until his death.[54] It is to be noted that the late appointments to the headship of cells alternated with those of monks in mid-career, and there could be a frequent turnover in this latter group. The incomplete state of existing records precludes the possibility of estimating which appointments were the more favoured.

The role of subprior was also subject to frequent changes of personnel.[55] As the prior's deputy when the latter was absent and the monk who oversaw the discipline and daily routine within the cloister, he was one of the senior brethren and sometimes an elderly one. His was another position often filled for short periods, but his responsibilities did not oblige him to render an annual financial statement and he appears only fleetingly in the obedientiary accounts. The unfortunate result is that with few dates obtainable the subpriors' periods of office can rarely be precisely determined. An example of the appointment of a monk of retirement age at Durham is William de Aislaby, who had over forty years of monastic life behind him when he was appointed subprior in 1398; he died two years later probably while still in office.[56] Others like Uthred de Boldon, as mentioned above, were appointed twice; his first term of office followed his recall from Finchale where he had been prior from 1367 to 1369. Then in his twenty-ninth year in the community and having completed several years as prior of Durham College Oxford, he would have been a mature and competent second in command to the ageing Prior Fosser. After about four years and a diplomatic mission to the papal curia he was allowed to return to Finchale, but again required in Durham in 1381 as subprior under Prior Walworth. His remaining years were mainly spent in charge of the cell at Finchale where he could benefit from the peaceful surroundings and remain in touch with affairs at Durham.[57]

It seems generally true that if subpriors were not chosen from the group of senior monks who were approaching the end of their active years in positions of responsibility they were monks whose maturity and competence had been previously tested

---

[52] *BRECP*, 484.
[53] Ibid., 518–19.
[54] Ibid., 539; the 1370/1 cell account lacks the name of the prior-accountant and is the earliest of the Lynn accounts. A monk named Nicholas may have filled the office briefly in 1373/4, ibid., 544 (Nicholas II).
[55] The archbishop of Canterbury and the bishops at Ely, Norwich, and Rochester had the right of final choice for the office of subprior; see above 15.
[56] *LVD*, iii, C.950.
[57] Ibid., iii, C.888. Unless the precise age is known my estimates are based on an average age of seventeen or eighteen at the time of profession.

in office. John de Goodnyston at Christ Church, for example, had been in the community at Canterbury for close to thirty years and had served in two obedientiary offices before his first appointment as subprior *c.* 1375/6 where he may have remained until 1381/2. He was then given the office of granator and, shortly after, moved to that of cellarer; but he was once again made subprior, this time until his death thirteen years later when he must have been in his late sixties. Another sexagenarian, Marcellus de Lese, is found serving as subprior in 1306, his forty-sixth year of monastic profession and the year of his death.[58] At Ely Henry de Wyke's career followed a similar path before he was given the office of subprior sometime between 1381 and 1390, that is in his thirty-fifth to forty-fifth year of monastic life; he died in 1392/3 at the approximate age of sixty- five.[59] John de Dudley at Worcester is first found as subprior *c.* 1409 when he had been professed for some thirty years and had obtained a doctorate in theology. Ten years later he was still, or again, in the office and attended a Black Monk chapter meeting at Northampton—no sign of ageing or infirmity here![60] The general state of health of these and other elderly subpriors remains unknown and, although their role was not one which could be described as physically exacting, the responsibilities could prove burdensome in the absence of the prior or when internal affairs were not running smoothly and an unforeseen crisis arose.

Senior monks at Durham, some of whom could be classed as eligible for retirement, were not infrequently charged with offices in which weighty responsibilities were placed on their shoulders. Among them are found the infirmarer, subprior, almoner, and sacrist in order of frequency. Alan Piper has been able to extract this information from the records because the dating details of monk obedientiaries of the Durham community have been preserved more fully than those of most monks in the other cathedral priories.[61] Any attempt to trace patterns of office holding in the cathedral monasteries of the southern province founders due to the preponderance of unknown dates in the lives of all but a very few monks; and estimates are often little more than rough guesses which, with the discovery of fresh biographical details, may prove to have been misleading. Nevertheless, it has been possible to draw a few comparisons with Durham among senior monks at Canterbury. Infirmarers and subpriors have been discussed above; and three active and elderly almoners can be singled out: two of them, Thomas de Borne in the late 1330s and Peter de Sales in the late 1350s, were in their early to mid-sixties, and the third, John de Otford, was said to have been in his late eighties when he died in office in 1413.[62] There are also enough biographical details of four sacrists to enable

---

[58] *BRECP*, 178 (John de Goodnyston I). There is an odd twist to Goodnyston's position as subprior. It seems that he successfully petitioned the pope to permit him to retain the office for life; but, although he had performed his duties in an exemplary manner, the prior and chapter made him renounce the privilege in 1381 because they asserted that it would have contravened their rights and customs. Nonetheless, he was reinstated as subprior only a few years later at the prior's recommendation, ibid., 178. For de Lese, ibid., 222–3, 230.
[59] *BRECP*, 464–5.
[60] Ibid., 797–9.
[61] Piper, 'Monks of Durham and...Old Age', 57.
[62] *BRECP*, 96 (Thomas de Borne I), 274 (Sales), 249 (John de Otford I).

us to calculate their approximate age. One of them, Henry Cranbroke, was about sixty-six when he was allowed to resign from office in 1421; it was his last post, and he retired to join the *stationarii* for the remaining years of his life. Richard de Sharstede must have been in his early seventies during his tenure of office and died in 1316, possibly still acting as sacrist. Robert de Dover would have been even more elderly as, on his third or fourth appointment to the office in the mid-1330s, he was in his fifty-fifth year of profession. In his twelfth consecutive year as sacrist in 1385 John de Guston was only three years behind the record of his predecessor, Robert de Dover; both would have been at least in their late sixties and possibly in their early seventies.[63]

The final hours of old and young

Details of the last rites performed for dying and dead monks within the century and a half covered by this study demonstrate a tender, brotherly concern on the part of their fellows. It is unfortunate, however, that surviving notices of some Christ Church obsequies are not prefaced by any details of the care and companionship with which they would have been surrounded during their final hours in accordance with the instructions given by Archbishop Lanfranc some two centuries earlier. He prescribed that two monks in rotation were to remain in the infirmary with their brother continuously, reading to and praying with and for him. When death appeared to be imminent the community was to be summoned to join in the appropriate prayers and rites at his bedside; and at the monk's passing the bells were to be tolled to announce the death.[64] The frequent inclusion of the detail of the precise time when death occurred confirms that the monk in question was, indeed, comforted by the presence of one or more members of the community. John Wykham, for example, third prior, died 'circa horam octavam ante mediam noctem' and Thomas Guston *tempore maioris misse*.[65] An ordinance, noted on the account of the chamberlain for the year 1422/3, states that the servant (*balneator*) in charge of the monks' bathing facilities, who was also an attendant in the infirmary, was to be one of those who kept watch at the dying monk's bedside and who assisted the infirmarer in anointing the sick when necessary. The monastic chapter must have felt the need to make clear that these were his responsibilities, but in no way could have intended that his required presence dispensed the monks from their bedside watch. John Grove, for example, as he lay dying after a fall in 1425 was assigned a young monk as his companion.[66]

---

[63] *BRECP*, 131–2 (Henry Cranbroke I), 285 (Sharstede), 139 (Dover), 184 (Guston).
[64] Lanfranc, *Monastic Constitutions*, 180–2.
[65] Wykham's death resulted *ex asthmatica passione* on the twenty-fifth of October 1421 and Guston on the seventh of May 1427, *Chronicle Stone*, 11, 13.
[66] CCA DCc chamberlain's account 63. William de London II, monk of Rochester, was attended by *diversis vigilantibus* as he lay on his death bed according to the chamberlain's account for 1396/7; they were paid 8d. for their services and were, therefore, probably not monks, *BRECP*, 618. The reason for their presence is unexplained. For John Grove see *Chronicle Stone*, 12 and *BRECP*, 183.

Obituaries of Christ Church monks present a variety of details. In the case of Thomas Wykyng the account is especially informative. We are told that the day before he died in 1407 he had received communion from the altar of the infirmary chapel, and he was anointed as he was about to draw his last breath. During his dying moments he had recited prayers to the Virgin Mary to whom he was especially devoted; it would not be surprising, the obituary writer added, if the blessed Virgin herself had at that moment summoned his spirit to herself. The account goes on to extol Wykyng's achievements and character. He was known as a monk who, by his presence and example, fostered peace in the monastic community while serving in the offices of penitentiary, sacrist, cellarer, warden of Canterbury College Oxford, feretrar, and *custos corone*. He was buried at the feet of his brother monk, William Richemond, opposite the tomb of St Thomas (Becket). The exceptional length of Wykyng's obituary reflects the reverence and love with which he was regarded by all his brethren.[67]

The sacramental rites of communion and extreme unction are also referred to in the obituaries of John Cantorbury and Henry Cranbroke, both of whom were *stationarii* residing in the infirmary before their deaths. John Islep collapsed and fell from his bed on to the dormitory floor in January 1401 and was taken to the infirmary; there he received the last rites and was able to make brief acts of faith and contrition before breathing his last.[68] Thomas Dover was another monk who made a lasting impression on his brethren at Canterbury. His demise occurred after he had recited first vespers of All Saints with his chaplains; the year was 1413, and the presence of chaplains in attendance may be explained by the fact that he was probably at the time subprior. He then began to say the *commendatio* prayers and continued until he came to the words of the litany which ask for the intercession of St Mary Magdalen to whom he had a special devotion; and at that moment, most appropriately, he expired.[69]

Durham records are devoid of details relating to the final moments of members of its monastic community. In the *Rites of Durham*, which was written some sixty years after the dissolution, the author recollected that the prior's chaplain was summoned to the infirmary to be at the bedside of the dying monk and to remain there until death occurred.[70] If this recollection is accurate it was probably this chaplain who performed the last rites. Several monks, among them Reginald de Wearmouth, the troublesome John Bonner, and William de Blakeston, are known to have finished their days in the Durham infirmary where there were reported to be nineteen individual *camerae* provided with fireplaces for the elderly and infirm.[71]

---

[67] *BRECP*, 328–9 and CCL Lit. MS D.12, fo 18v. For Richemond see William Richemond I, *BRECP*, 264–5 and Lit. MS D.12, fo 18v.

[68] John Cantorbury I died in 1432, *BRECP*, 108; Henry Cranbroke I in 1430, ibid., 132; Islep, ibid., 210 and CCL Lit. MS D.12, fo 18.

[69] *BRECP*, 139–40 and CCL Lit. MS D.12, fo 20.

[70] *Rites of Durham*, 51.

[71] For Wearmouth see *LVD*, iii, C.951 (d. 1400/01); for Bonner C.973 (d. 1418/19); for Blakeston C.993 (d. 1424/5). Reference to the private chambers is in DCM Locellus XXVII, 1b, which, though undated, is probably early to mid-fifteenth century.

A number of Durham monks died and were buried at one of the cells. Among those who died at Finchale were William Graper in 1375/6, John de Billesfield in 1393/4, and Thomas Hatfield in 1418/19; but the only monk whose burial has been recorded there is that of Uthred de Boldon, whose body was interred in the priory church at the entrance to the choir.[72] John de Whitrigg lived for about two decades at the cell on Farne Island where he died and was buried in 1372.[73] Simon de Darlington was at Jarrow when he passed away in 1368/9, and William Trollop died at Wearmouth in 1407/8 as did John de Ripon some six years later.[74] Two priors of the Scottish cell of Coldingham, Alexander de Lamesley and William de Bamburgh, died there; the books and bedding of the former were considered to be of sufficient value to be worth retrieving shortly after his death in 1338/9.[75]

The deaths of some Canterbury and Durham monks occurred at their respective colleges in Oxford. Between 1406/7 and 1417 no less than five Durham monks ended their days in Oxford; one of them, William Appleby, held the position of warden, and two of the others served as bursars.[76] Outbreaks of plague afflicted the residents of the university town during these years, and one of them in the summer of 1413 led Richard Holden, warden of Canterbury College, to seek refuge at the Christ Church manor of Monks Risborough in Buckinghamshire. He did not escape, however, but died there and was buried in haste in the parish church of St Dunstan close to the high altar.[77] Another monk, John Wy, who was a student at Canterbury College in 1418, died in December of that year; his bodily remains were taken back by cart to Canterbury with the aid of Thomas Guston, his fellow student.[78] The lengthy and expensive journey involved in transporting a corpse from Oxford to Canterbury for burial in the monastic precinct was probably a rare occurrence, and no other example has been found. In the case of John Wy it may have been due to the persistence and determination of his brother monk; the two had probably been friends since their admission to the cathedral priory on the same date more than eight years earlier.

There is, however, one record of a monk's body being conveyed a much shorter distance from one of the Norwich cells to the mother house, and it is to be noted that the monk in question was the prior of the cell of Lynn. The details have been preserved on the Lynn account roll for the year 1393 which records the cost of transporting not only the corpse of Ralph de Martham along with his books but also for the two-way journey of the other monks then residing at Lynn, who attended the funeral solemnities in the cathedral. The total expenditure amounted to over £6.[79] Monks who died while journeying abroad were generally buried *in*

---

[72] For Graper *LVD*, iii, C.952; Billesfield C.938; Hatfield C.1043; Boldon C.888.
[73] Ibid., C.933.
[74] Ibid., C.861 (Darlington), C.977 (Trollop), C.988 (Ripon).
[75] Ibid., C.790 (Lamesley), C.871 (Bamburgh); the latter died in office in 1362.
[76] *LVD*, iii, C.1001 (Appleby); C.1007 (John Harle), C.1049 (Walter Artret) bursars; the other two were John Kirkland (C.1041) and Robert Hornby (C.1047).
[77] *BRECP*, 201.
[78] Ibid., 327 (John Wy II), 184 (Guston); details of the funeral are given in *Chronicle Stone*, 9.
[79] *BRECP*, 539 under Martham.

situ; but if their books and other possessions were considered worth retrieving the necessary means of transport was arranged. The six barrels of Adam Easton's books, for example, finally reached London for delivery to Norwich ten years after his death in Rome in 1397.[80] A century earlier the Worcester monk Thomas de Segesbarowe had also died in Rome and was buried at the Dominican convent at Anagni; his books were reclaimed by a fellow monk, Henry de Newynton, who was sent by the prior and chapter in 1299 to secure their safe return to Worcester.[81] The contentious prior of Durham, Richard de Hoton, was the focal point of dissension and division among his brethren over a prolonged period both before and during his priorate. Controversy with the bishop, Antony Bek, was followed by appeals to king and pope, deprivation and suspension from office, and final restoration by the pope a month before his death in 1308 while still at the papal curia in Poitiers where, presumably, he was buried.[82]

Unexpected death abroad was a less likely eventuality than premature death at home when the cathedral priories were visited by one of the recurring epidemics such as the plague. Surviving records that provide details of date, place, and numbers of fatalities are relatively few and spasmodic; nevertheless they give some indication of the always unpredictable and sometimes devastating consequences, and they allow a few comparisons among the cathedral priories affected. Four deaths from the plague were reported at Canterbury within a few weeks in 1349 during May and June, but about twenty-five succumbed in the epidemic that struck the community in 1361 between June and October.[83] The next surviving set of figures is dated 1421 when, of eight who were taken, five deaths occurred *ex pestilentia* and three *ex asmatica passione*; two of them were young men who were not yet in priest's orders.[84] The death toll in the Durham community during the 1349/50 epidemic totalled no less than fifty-two out of a total of about eighty-five.[85] At Ely the chamberlain's account for the previous year, 1348/9, lists a payment for the sewing of fifteen pairs of *manycles* and *pedules* for dying monks, that is for about one third of the brethren.[86] Norwich monks also suffered a severe blow in the late 1340s which is incidentally disclosed through an annual charge levied on St Leonard's cell by the cathedral priory; in 1347/8 sixty-four monks benefited from the receipt of 2s. each, but in 1349/50 the same amount was

---

[80] Ibid., 502–3. Easton had been created cardinal priest of St Cecilia in Trastevere and his tomb may be seen today in the church.
[81] BRECP, 871, 858.
[82] LVD, iii, C.699.
[83] CCL Lit. MS D.12, fos 16v, 17; all the names are listed in both cases. However, the chamberlain provided clothing for sixty-four brethren in 1359/60 and for *c.* fifty-five in 1366/7, CCA DCc chamberlain's accounts 44, 45; this apparent discrepancy may be explained by the fact that the ravages of 1361 had already been largely offset by the admission of *c.* 30 between 1361 and 1365. Nevertheless, none of these figures can be regarded as unassailable; for example, the chamberlain did not necessarily outfit all the monks every year, and the five or six monks at Oxford may not always have been included in his reckoning.
[84] CCL Lit. MS D.12, fo 21v.
[85] BL MS Harley 4664, fo 130v, marginal addition.
[86] CUL Add. MS 2957, 25; these no doubt refer to some sort of coverings for hands and feet. In 1346/7 there were about forty-six monks according to the chamberlain, CUL EDC 1/F/3/8.

distributed among only thirty-four monks.[87] The degree to which the periodic epidemics affected Worcester are, for the most part, not detectable. When Prior John de Evesham sent a petition to the pope in 1364 to grant a dispensation for six monks to receive priest's orders at the age of twenty-two he explained the reason for his request as based on the fatalities caused by the plague. According to the prior the community had been depleted by two devastating attacks during which thirty-two had died.[88] It is not often possible to identify the years in which these deadly visitations occurred at Worcester as there are few records on surviving obedientiary accounts of more than the average of two to four deaths a year in a community numbering slightly under fifty. Between 1346/7 and 1349/50, however, numbers fell from forty-seven to thirty-two, and three included in the latter number were juniors and therefore recent arrivals.[89] Two other years, 1339/40 and 1419/20, were also noted as exceptional: in the first instance eight monks died and in the second eleven.[90] Little is known of Winchester, Bath, Coventry, and Rochester cathedral priory monks and their dates and circumstances of death. For the other five cathedral priories, as noted above, the years that were marked by onslaughts of pestilence varied, probably in line with regional outbreaks; those of 1348/50, the early 1360s, and 1419/21 seem to have been the most widespread, affecting most of them in their widely scattered locations.

Office of the dead, requiem mass, and interment

Funeral and burial rites and customs, where these are known, show a general similarity among the cathedral priories, but there are also slight differences of which we have a few details. The obits of some of the Canterbury monks, which have been preserved from *c.* 1268 onwards, are unique among the cathedral priories in furnishing a record of the post mortem procedures that were followed and the liturgical rites that were performed, concluding with the burial office at the grave. The corpse was first placed, with face exposed, on the appointed stone slab in the infirmary chapel. When this stone was replaced in 1403 its exact location was described: it was in front of the image of the holy cross in the 'interior chapel' of the infirmary.[91] The *commendam*, or commendatory prayers were then recited by monks assigned for this purpose and would probably have included vespers or vigils and lauds of the dead.[92] The subprior or master of the infirmary often presided at these funerary offices. The body was then removed to the choir of the cathedral church in preparation for the requiem mass. Some of the Christ Church

---

[87] NRO DCN 2/3/7, 1.
[88] *CPL*, iv (1362–1404), 91.
[89] WCM C.302, 292 (pittancer's account).
[90] Ibid., C.298 (pittancer's account), C.32 (chamberlain's account).
[91] See *Chronicle Stone*, 7–13 and CCL Lit. MS D.12, fo 18; there were several altars dedicated to saints, before some of which monks chose to be buried, as noted below 308. For similar procedures at Westminster see Harvey, *Living and Dying*, 112–13.
[92] I.e., the office of the dead. Vespers of the dead was often referred to as *Placebo* which was the first word of the opening antiphon, and vigils of the dead was commonly known as *Dirige* for a similar reason. The hour of death would presumably have determined the choice of office.

obituary notices are informative in their detailed recording of unusual circumstances in connection with the funeral rites and observances. This situation arose on the occasion of the death of John de Eynesford in 1355 only six months after his admission and clothing as a monk. Since he had died before profession a discussion ensued as to the proper form to be followed when no precedent could be recalled within the living memory of any of the senior monks. An ordinance was therefore issued to resolve the problem. The unfortunate monk was to have the same rites and observances performed for him as for a professed monk including the recitation of fifty psalms and the celebration of thirty masses; however, the five masses customarily offered by five [monk] priests and the *liberatio* known as *fenys* were to be omitted.[93] Another problematic situation occurred when Salamon Litelbourne died on Christmas Eve in 1408. In this case all the customary offices were performed in the infirmary chapel and not in the choir as was usual in normal circumstances, the other rites being postponed until 28 December (the feast of the Holy Innocents). In response to murmured objections on the part of some of the senior monks Prior Thomas Chillenden was able to restore order by producing a rubric which confirmed these arrangements.[94] Less than three years after Litelbourne's death the Canterbury obituarist was obliged to provide for posterity a detailed account of the impressive funeral services performed for Prior Chillenden by a grateful community, united in mourning his loss but also in celebrating his achievements during his twenty-year rule. He died on Saturday 15 August, the feast of the Assumption of the Virgin Mary. The following morning his body was brought to the infirmary chapel where the subprior, William Chart, and a group of monks designated for the occasion sang the *commendatio*, after which other monks intoned [*cum nota*] the exequies of the dead and the *Placebo* and *Dirige*. Next followed an intoned requiem mass before the office of prime. At the end of the high mass in the choir of the cathedral church the subprior and monks processed to the site selected for the burial in the nave while reciting the appointed psalms, responses, and prayers. Sunday afternoon vespers was followed by solemn exequies in choir for the late prior as decreed by a chapter ordinance. The Monday mass, celebrated by the subprior, was attended by the abbot and seventeen monks from the neighbouring Benedictine abbey of St Augustine's; and, finally, on 31 August the archbishop, Arundel, was joined by many prelates, clergy, and laymen from all ranks of society for a solemn requiem, followed the next day by a reception in the monastic refectory in the presence of the archbishop.[95]

When a monk died of a virulent disease like the plague the corpse was buried at once, and some of the customary ceremonies were curtailed while others were rearranged. Richard Holden, warden of Canterbury College Oxford when struck down by the plague and buried locally in 1413 was not forgotten by his brethren at

---

[93] CCL Lit. MS D.12, fos 16v–17; the span of living memory was stated as being forty-six years. See also *BRECP*, 156.

[94] CCL Lit. MS D.12, fo 19 and *BRECP*, 223 (Litelbourne), which states 26 rather than 28 December in error.

[95] CCL Lit. MS D.12, fo 19–19v and *BRECP*, 119–21.

Christ Church; they performed the exequies and other divine offices for him as prescribed by the rubric laid down for this contingency, and the prior celebrated a requiem mass for him.[96] Thus the particular circumstances surrounding a monk's death could necessitate a change in the funeral arrangements normally followed and, even when the customary procedures were adhered to, the arrangement of all the details had to be efficiently masterminded to ensure that each occasion ran smoothly.

The author or compiler of the *Rites of Durham* included a brief account of the procedures followed by the monks of St Cuthbert for the deceased members of their community. According to his recollections the corpse was placed in St Andrew's chapel, which is thought to have adjoined the infirmary. While it lay there awaiting the funeral two monks, who had been close friends of the deceased, were named by the prior to watch and pray beside the bier throughout the night. The infirmarer had at hand the relevant texts which had become worn through frequent use, and in 1423/4 he ordered new copies of the *Placebo* and part of the *Dirige*.[97] The monks were joined by boys from the almonry school who took their place in the stalls on either side and read through the psalter until eight o'clock in the morning. The body was then conveyed to the chapter house where the monks were assembled to recite matins of the dead, which was remembered as the 'Dergie and Devotio'. Burial followed in the monks' cemetery, the open ground located to the east of the chapter house on the south side of the choir of the cathedral church. The lack of any reference to the requiem mass must reflect the writer's failing memory and makes it clear that his account is far from complete. As to the procedures followed for deceased priors of Durham, he reported that these were similar to what was done for the monks with the exception that John Fosser and his successors were buried in the cathedral church rather than outside in the cemetery.[98] Monks of Canterbury, unlike those of Durham, were buried in a variety of places in their cathedral church and cloister, presumably in accord with their previously expressed wishes. James de Dover, who died in 1397, was buried in the cathedral crypt in front of the altar dedicated to St Nicholas, and the crypt was also the last resting place of William Gyllyngham in 1411 under a stone that he had prepared in advance.[99] Others chose the infirmary chapel, William Chart, for example, specifying at the altar of St Benedict and St Leonard, and John Molond before St Agnes' altar.[100] Two priors, Robert Hathbrande (d. 1370) and Richard de Oxenden (d. 1338), were buried in St Michael's chapel in the south-west transept, while a third prior, John Fynch (d. 1391), preferred to lie in the martyrdom chapel.[101]

---

[96] CCL Lit. MS D.12, fo 19v.
[97] *Rites of Durham*, 51–2, and Fowler, *Account Rolls*, i, 271; on this same account the infirmarer also bought chains for a volume containing the exequies of the dead and the *commendatio*.
[98] *Rites of Durham*, 52–3, and *LVD*, iii, C.817 for Fosser. The bursar paid for the making of the sepulchres for two monks: Thomas de Newthorpe in 1418/19, DCM bursar's account 1418/19, and Thomas de Stapeley the following year, Fowler, *Account Rolls*, iii, 618; these monks' careers are in *LVD*, iii, C.991 and C.1002.
[99] BRECP, 138 (Dover), 185–6 (William Gyllyngham I).
[100] Ibid., 112–13 for William Chart I, who died in 1418; ibid., 237, for John Molond I, who died in 1428.
[101] Ibid., 193 (Hathbrand), 250 (Oxenden), 163–4 (Fynch).

There is little or no evidence of burial customs and sites at the other cathedral priories apart from a few details, mostly concerning the funeral and interment of several of their priors. Dying in 1341 at Ely, John de Crauden was buried near the high altar of the cathedral at the feet of the bishop, William de Hotham, whose death had occurred only four years earlier. In their time and under their direction the extensive building programme was under way, and the new Lady chapel became the final resting place of John de Wisbech, the monk in charge of this section of the work; he died in 1349 and was buried at the chapel entrance.[102] The burial of Prior John de Bukton in 1396 cost over £28 according to the Ely treasurer who listed many of the items in some detail; these included black cloth for the livery of the priory servants, wax for making the funeral torches, and the expenses of the abbot of Walden to come to celebrate the funeral exequies and mass.[103] The Norwich sacrist's account for 1342/3 recorded an expenditure of 10s. 2d. on stone intended for the tombs of monks; does this suggest that most of the monks' graves were to be found in their cemetery on the south side of the east end of the cathedral in a position similar to the one at Durham?[104] Half a century later, in 1395/6, on the death of Joseph de Martham subprior, the sacrist paid *pro factura sepulcri*.[105] At Worcester there are several instances of the burial of priors in the cathedral church and cloister. Richard de Dumbleton, for example, whose death occurred in 1272, was buried in the cloister; Philip Aubyn was interred in front of the nave altar of the Holy Cross in 1296 and the abbot of Evesham presided at the burial.[106] The cellarer's account for 1369/70 displayed a separate heading under which were listed the expenses incurred at the death of Prior John de Evesham. They included fish, spices, and other items of food, wine, and ale for the mourners, and the distribution of alms to friars, nuns, and the poor; the total amounted to £23.[107] In 1382, six years before his death, Prior Walter de Legh adorned the altar of St Cecilia with alabaster images at the same time making clear that he had chosen that location for his burial.[108] The only monk whose final resting place is known is Thomas Hosyntre, whose unexpected death while a student at Oxford in 1444/5 proved costly for the cellarer. He paid for the body to be returned to Worcester as well as the remaining bills owed by the deceased. In addition, it was the cellarer who was responsible for employing a man to make the tomb for Hosyntre *in claustro*.[109] The sparsity of evidence in connection with the burial rites and practices of the cathedral priories is much to be regretted, but what survives is sufficient to make it clear that a general conformity to the established pattern of services did not discourage the appearance of some local differences in the way that these were carried out.

---

[102] *BRECP*, 401 (Crauden and Hotham); 462 (Wisbech).
[103] CUL EDC 1/F/13/16.
[104] NRO DCN 1/4/34; it seems surprising that this entry has been found only once, but the sacrist may have usually had supplies of stone at hand ready for use.
[105] *BRECP*, 539.
[106] Ibid., 801 (Dumbleton), 772–3 (Aubyn).
[107] Ibid., 802–4 and WCM C.66.
[108] *BRECP*, 835–6.
[109] Ibid., 825.

The dispatch of death notices and the distribution of alms

Following the death of a monk two undertakings on his behalf received immediate attention. One of these was the writing and dispatching of an announcement of the community's loss to other religious houses in the vicinity, with a request for prayers for the departed. The responsibility for seeing to the preparation of these briefs (*brevia*) was allocated to one or more of the obedientiaries and a brief bearer (*brevitor*) was employed to deliver the messages. The accounts of the almoner at Canterbury include a *brevitor* who received regular payments as one of his *famuli*; in 1361, because he was unusually busy in carrying the briefs for some twenty-five monks who had been struck down by the plague, he was given an extra 5s.[110] The *brevitor* was generally appointed for a year at a time and carried with him an official document giving his credentials and requesting that he be provided with food and other necessities.[111] At Durham it was also the almoner who paid the *brevitor*, in the form of an annual stipend of 4s.; in 1369/70 and 1377/8 the almoner states on his account that he paid 2s. to the precentor to write out the obits or have them written.[112] The *brevitor* at Ely, who was employed by the almoner in 1344/5 to bear the news of four monks' deaths, wore out his shoes and was given 2s. 8d. to replace them. Thirty years later another almoner made use of his *brevitor* not only for delivering the briefs but also for collecting rents for him from his Ely properties and elsewhere.[113] Different arrangements were in place at Norwich where the chamberlain was the obedientiary who was responsible for the *brevitor*. The latter's stipend varied according to the number of obits he carried during the year; it was usually 6s. 8d. for each one, but in the 1390s he was receiving only 10s. for two and on one occasion for three.[114] However, it was the precentor who employed a scribe to write the obits in 1315/16, 1386/7, and probably in the years between.[115] The meagre evidence from St Swithun's Winchester records a renewal of an appointment of a *brevitor* by the prior and chapter in 1331, and a payment of 10s. to a *brevitor* by the receiver, some six years later, for making the rounds with the obit notice of the retired prior, Richard de Enford.[116] Almost a century later, when a *brevitor* received his 10s. for conveying the obit of John Merke, it was from the chamberlain, who may have been the obedientiary usually responsible as at

---

[110] CCA DCc almoner's accounts 8, 10, 51 (1361/2).

[111] CUL MS Ee.5.31, fo 78v (appointment), CCA DCc Reg. H, fo 94 (printed in Sheppard, *HMC VIIIth Report*, 343). See also DCc CCA chamberlain's account 63 (1422/3) on the dorse of which there are regulations for the care of dying monks.

[112] DCM almoner's accounts for 1342/3, 1369/70, 1372/3A, 1377/8; the task of writing the obit briefs may sometimes have devolved on the succentor to whom the almoner paid 2s. in 1390/1 for parchment for the briefs, ibid., almoner's account for that year, both A and B copies.

[113] CUL Add. MS 2957, 12; CUL EDC 1/F/1/7.

[114] NRO DCN 1/5/5, 6, 7, 12, 16, 18, 28 etc. The *brevitor*'s attachment to the chamberlain's office may have been due to the fact that the chamberlain was in charge of selling the belongings of deceased monks, thereby receiving small sums which could be used to pay the *brevitor*.

[115] NRO DCN 1/9/3, 23, 14 (1375).

[116] Goodman, *Winchester Chartulary*, no. 152; Kitchin, *Obedientiary Rolls*, 247. Both brief bearers were named Walter and so they were probably one and the same person.

Norwich.[117] The arrangements at Worcester appear to have in part combined what has been found at other cathedral priories in that both the almoner and the chamberlain were actively involved with the *brevitor*. From 1341/2, the earliest surviving account, this servant received an annual stipend of 4s. from the almoner.[118] The precentor's regular purchase of parchment from time to time stated that some of it was intended for the writing of obits and occasionally implied that the actual writing was the responsibility of his office.[119] In addition, the chamberlain made frequent payments to the *brevitor* in the 1380s and 1390s and later; these occur on his account under the heading *Liberatio denariorum* or *Expense forinsece*, thus seeming to imply that it was a contribution possibly assigned to him on the strength of the fact that he benefited from the sale of the belongings of deceased monks.[120]

The second undertaking the monks were committed to perform on behalf of their defunct brethren was the distribution of alms among the poor who, on hearing the tolling of the monastery bell to announce the demise, would have made their way to the priory gate in hopeful anticipation. For the monks of the cathedral priories this particular occasion of almsgiving was the concern of several of the obedientiaries whose share of responsibility is often unclear; once again investigations are thwarted by the gaps in the evidence. The almoner, whose major involvement might reasonably have been assumed, seems to have played a relatively minor role occupied as he was with, if not overburdened by, his daily obligations in the dispensing of alms.[121] The almoner's accounts at Canterbury, although plentiful in number, fail to make any specific reference to this particular distribution. One reference has been noted, however, which states that on the day of the burial of Prior Eastry in 1331 the subprior, Thomas Stoyl, distributed the sum of 54s. to the poor; his involvement is probably explained by the fact that it concerned a deceased prior and not an ordinary monk.[122] At Durham, from at least 1306/7 the bursar gave 10s. in alms for each brother who had died during the year and the distribution was almost certainly made at the time of the interment; at the burial of Prior Cowton in 1341 this was clearly stated and the sum of £4 3s. was recorded.[123] Whether or not it was given in cash or in kind is unknown, except for one occasion

---

[117] Kitchin, *Obedientiary Rolls*, 370 (chamberlain's account for 1422/3); for Enford and Merke see *BRECP*, 689 and 718 respectively. In 1432/3 the chamberlain also made a payment to a *brevitor* (Kitchin, *Obedientiary Rolls*, 376), but the few extant rolls of this office shed no further light on this point; moreover, there is no indication that the almoner was involved, and there are no surviving precentor's rolls.

[118] WCM C.170, 171, 174 etc.; C.171 is printed in Hamilton, *Compotus Rolls*, 49–54.

[119] E.g. in 1362/3, WCM C.359, *pro brevibus... scribandis*, also C.359a, 361, 365, 369 etc.

[120] WCM C.13, 14, 20, 21, 23, 26 etc.; the sale of the goods of brethren after their deaths is discussed above 176 n.89 and below 316–7.

[121] See above 187.

[122] LPL MS 243, fo 24v; the almoner's involvement, and that of other obedientiaries, may be concealed on their accounts under the general heading of 'alms'. One reason that the subprior was made responsible in Eastry's case may hinge on a phrase which appears to be in the form of an explanation, viz., *in defectu panni*; this may refer to the fact that there was no clothing of the deceased for distribution.

[123] DCM bursar's accounts *passim*; it is gratifying that the name of the deceased monk is almost invariably stated. Cowton's death is on the account for 1340/1; see also *LVD*, iii, C.768.

in 1373/4 when it was stated that the money was used to buy bread.[124] A year after the loss of fifty-two Durham monks to the plague in 1349/50, the bursar doled out £13 6s. 8d., slightly over half the usual 10s. per monk; but these were lean years and the bursar was hard pressed for funds.[125]

At Ely it was the almoner who was given charge of the distribution on the day of inhumation. To assist him in this charitable enterprise he received contributions from the prior and fellow obedientiaries, usually at the rate of 5s. each. Thus in 1369/70 he was paid by the prior, sacrist, chamberlain, and precentor at the time of the death of William de Riston. The year before, when five monks had died, each obedientiary would have been expected to hand over 25s., and the chamberlain and sacrist are recorded as having done so.[126] The amount of money that the Ely almoner allocated for the poor at the death of each monk is, unfortunately, not revealed on the almoner's account. There is a problem of interpretation with regard to the almsgiving of Norwich monks on behalf of their deceased brothers. Not only did the chamberlain pay the *brevitor*, but from about the early 1380s he also included in his receipts small sums, classed as 'alms' from those who died during the year.[127] In 1398/9, for example, he accounted for the sum of 6s. 8d. in 'alms' from William de Gunton and Simon Harpele; this money may have been used for distribution at the time of their death, but it may not have been, in the strict sense, a death-bed donation.[128] No evidence has as yet come to light to provide any details of the alms distributed on the day of burial of a Norwich monk with the single exception of the prior, Henry de Lakenham, who died in 1310. In this instance it was William de Hadsto, master of the cellar, who paid £21 3s. *in usus pauperum* on that day.[129] The Rochester custumal dating from the time of John de Westerham, who was briefly prior from 1320 to 1321, contains a paragraph concerning almsgiving by the almoner on the day of burial. It specifies that 1s. was to be contributed by each of three obedientiaries, namely the sacrist, chamberlain, and cellarer, and another 2s. was to come from manorial revenues; this sum was to be collected and spent on the purchase of bread.[130] These obligations appeared to be still in force almost a century later according to entries on two of the three surviving chamberlain's accounts. In 1396/7 he paid 1s. to the almoner *in obitu* of William de London and in 1415/16 he gave 2s. because of the deaths of Nicholas de Frendesbury and William Sydyngbourne.[131]

---

[124] Fowler, *Account Rolls*, iii, 579; another example of the alms being distributed on the day of burial was specified in the entry *in exequiis* of William de Aislaby in 1399/1400, DCM bursar's account 1399/1400. For Aislaby C.950 in *LVD*, iii.
[125] DCM bursar's account, 1351/2 A, for this year only under the heading *expense necessarie* instead of the usual *elemosina consueta*; in fact the bursar was heavily in the red with a much reduced income.
[126] CUL Add. MS 2957, 11; CUL EDC 1/F/3/17 (chamberlain), CUL Add. MS 2956, 158 (sacrist); for Riston see *BRECP*, 434.
[127] NRO DCN 1/5/16 (1382/3), 1/5/20 (1386/7).
[128] Ibid., 1/5/26; see *BRECP*, 316 for Gunton and 317–18 for Harpele.
[129] NRO DCN 1/1/22 (1310/11).
[130] Thorpe, *Custumale Roffense*, 36.
[131] CKS DRc/F.14, F.15; for London see *BRECP*, 618 (William de London I), for Frendesbury ibid., 604 and Sydyngbourne, ibid., 642.

From 1311/12 onwards the Winchester almoner's accounts show a regular expenditure on bread for the poor on behalf of every deceased brother on the day of his burial. For Henry de Bromle and Alan de Bungey that year the sum spent was 13s. 4d. for each.[132] By 1389/90 the amount had been reduced to 10s. each and, since four monks passed away that year, his almsgiving on their burial days added £2 to his expenses.[133] The only other obedientiary of St Swithun's whose accounts reveal any involvement in these distributions is the receiver and then on only one occasion: in 1334/5 he spent 20s. on bread for each of four deceased monks.[134] The burial of Prior John de Evesham at Worcester on the first of April 1370 was a costly affair for the cellarer who had to provide a meal for the dignitaries present. The almsgiving portion of his expenses consisted of distributions to the poor amounting to £7 8s. of which the Franciscans received 13s. 4d., the Dominicans 10s., and nuns 3s. 3d. Charity was regularly dispensed to the friars and other religious through the year accompanied by the request for prayers, but only occasionally, as here, is giving on the day of burial specified.[135] On other occasions the almoner appears to have been responsible; in 1341/2, for example, his 'foreign expenses' included 12d. spent on bread for the poor at the time of Roger de Henley's death.[136] However, there is no further mention of this particular expense for half a century until 1391/2 when Robert Stanes was the beneficiary of the prayers of the poor, who received 2s. worth of bread on the day of his burial. In 1399/1400 only 12d. was spent by the almoner on behalf of John de Stanleye, but he also distributed a further 6s. 8d. among the Franciscans and Dominicans.[137] When four monks died in 1409/10 the poor benefited from 6s. 8d. worth of bread on each occasion.[138] On a number of accounts the Worcester almoner's almsgiving omitted these details, and the resulting impression gained is that he was not concerned about being questioned by the auditors; in the second half of the fourteenth century his finances were generally in a healthy state.[139]

The deceased monks benefited not only from prayers offered by the grateful poor and the friars, but also from those of their living brethren who partook of pittances on the burial day. Both procedures are clearly stated on the Winchester almoner's accounts from 1389/90 onwards. In that year four monks died, and the almoner's two payments for each consisted of 10s. of bread for the poor and 6s. 8d. for the monks, the latter amount being paid to the *depositorii* who spent it on spices or other treats for the brethren.[140] Distributions of pittances made by the almoner to

---

[132] *BRECP*, 677, 678; there are, unfortunately, two lengthy gaps in the almoner's accounts between 1319 and 1352 and again between 1353 and 1386.
[133] Kitchin, *Obedientiary Rolls*, 417.
[134] Ibid., 232. This account is the sole complete receiver's roll that has survived; the remaining five are fragmentary.
[135] WCM C.66; the cellarer at Worcester was equivalent to the bursar at Durham, the treasurers at Ely and Canterbury, and the master of the cellar at Norwich.
[136] WCM C.170, the earliest surviving almoner's account; for Henley see also *BRECP*, 819.
[137] WCM C.181, 184 and *BRECP*, 875, 876.
[138] WCM C.189; John de Malverne, prior, also died this year and the cellarer covered all the expenses.
[139] WCM C.173–83; in 1404/5 he shared his surplus with the hard pressed cellarer, ibid., C.187.
[140] Kitchin, *Obedientiary Rolls*, 417.

the convent on behalf of his brethren at the time of their burial are recorded, with the names of the departed, from about 1310/11, and from 1313/14 he states that his contribution is paid to the *depositorius* whose duty it was to distribute the pittances.[141] The first mention of alms for the poor at the time of a burial is in 1316/17; and the *custos depositi* occurs here and in later years as the monk who collected contributions toward the purchase of *crespi* (cakes) for the convent on All Souls' day.[142] These arbitrary differences from one year to another in the entries itemized on the account are probably indicative of no more than inconsistency and haste in compiling and writing up the account; as such they serve as a warning against the tendency to 'discover' policy changes or new impositions in the lack of uniform wording. Some of the other cathedral priories probably had arrangements similar to St Swithun's for the provision of pittances among the community after the burial of one of their number. Unfortunately, there are few details at our disposal. One of the few is the Durham hostiller's account for 1344/5 which includes a 10s. expenditure on pittances for the monks on the day that Ralph de Twizell was buried. The fact that Twizell had been serving as hostiller until a few months before his death probably explains the presence of the entry on this account; no other similar entries have been found.[143] It is likely, however, that the custom of pittances being shared by the monks after burying one of their brethren was a regular feature at Durham, but undetectable in the accounts because it was subsumed under the general category of pittances through the year on the accounts of one or more of the obedientiaries.[144] On the day that the Norwich monks buried their bishop, William de Ayermine, in March 1336, they shared pittances costing 30s. as recorded on the master of the cellar's account; this is the sole known reference that provides evidence of the custom at Norwich.[145] For Ely and Rochester cathedral priories no evidence has come to light, and for Worcester the little information that can be gleaned from the primary sources cannot be interpreted with any degree of certainty. The Worcester pittancer distributed pittances on a number of occasions during the year, such as those in the fourth week of Advent when the 'O' antiphons were sung.[146] Other distributions were identified as *pro obitibus*, which generally implied the annual commemorations of the deceased monks and their ecclesiastical and lay benefactors. The word *obitus* in this sense is synonymous with anniversary; but is also found at Worcester in the context of the day of death, *die obitus*, when alms were dispensed to the poor for the monk whose burial was taking place, as described above.[147]

---

[141] Kitchin, *Obedientiary Rolls*, 391, 392, 393, 394, 395 etc.
[142] Ibid., 401; the deceased monks would have been among those remembered on this day.
[143] DCM hostiller's account 1344/5; for Twizell see *LVD*, iii, C.813.
[144] For example, the almoner in 1351/2 gave pittances to his *sociis in claustro*, Fowler, *Account Rolls*, i, 207, and the hostiller in 1357/8, DCM hostiller's account, 1357/8.
[145] NRO DCN 1/1/33; unusually, this entry is found under 'foreign receipts' because the 30s. was taken out of a larger sum received from the cellarer in the form of arrears.
[146] See above 244.
[147] See above 313.

The status or inventory drawn up by the Durham almoner in 1344 lists a storage chest for the *pannis veteribus... de fratribus mortuis* and a second chest for their *staminibus et femoralibus*. These articles of clothing were to be dispensed among the poor if the statutes of earlier Benedictine provincial chapters were still being adhered to. The statutes of the 1277 chapter of the southern province had required the monk's old clothing to be returned when new clothing was issued so that it could be given to the poor. A similar regulation survives in the northern chapter of 1221, with the responsibility placed upon the chamberlain; it was succeeded in 1310 by a regulation condemning the increase in the adoption of distinctive clothing by individuals in place of monastic uniformity. Regulation clothing only was to be worn in future and everything else was to be confiscated and distributed among the poor by the almoner.[148] Episcopal injunctions furnish evidence that obedience to these precepts continued to be stressed at Ely and Norwich in the early fourteenth century. In 1300 Ralph de Walpole, bishop of Ely, held the almoner and/or the chamberlain responsible for collecting the monks' old and worn garments and distributing them to the poor, and in 1319 John Salmon at Norwich issued a similar admonition reminding the monks of the Rule by which they were bound. Salmon also denounced any attempt to sell old clothing, probably because this offence had come to his notice during the visitation.[149] Some years later, at Worcester and possibly at Norwich, the abuse of selling the clothing of monks who had recently died was openly acknowledged. In 1380/1 the Worcester chamberlain's 'foreign receipts' included the sum of slightly over £5 from the sale of the *panni* of John de Gloucestre and John de Kyderminstre.[150] It was Thomas de Wyke's *botes* that were sold the next year for a mere 12d.; and the sale of the *vestimenta* of Robert Shrovesbury in 1411/12 and of John de Stone in 1421/2 increased the chamberlain's receipts by £5.[151] The Norwich chamberlain's receipts from time to time listed small sums as alms from his brethren, both living and dead. In the one case they appear to have been genuine gifts to an obedientiary whose expenses far exceeded his receipts on the surviving accounts from the 1350s onwards. The other alms were from the recently dead, possibly in the form of death-bed donations of pocket money but, more likely, they represented the amounts received through the sale of the departed monk's clothing and belongings. The likelihood becomes a certainty when the chamberlain makes a clear distinction between alms and gifts as he does, for example, in 1395/6; in that year he received 20s. in alms from three deceased monks and 3s. 6d. in gifts from friends.[152] Alms received from unnamed monk *socii* appear in 1381/2, and the dead monks are named in 1386/7 and subsequent years. When seven monks died in 1419/20 the entry on the

---

[148] Pantin, *Black Monk Chapters*, i, 80, 236, 269.
[149] Evans, *Ely Chapter Ordinances*, 9, 17; NRO DCN 92/2.
[150] WCM C.13; *BRECP*, 810–11 for John de Gloucestre III, and 828 for John de Kyderminstre I and II.
[151] WCM C.14, 30, 33; the three monks are in *BRECP*, 898 (Wyke), 878 (Stone), 873 (Shrovesbury). *Panni* and *vestimenti* both refer to items of clothing; other items sold included bedding and harness, *BRECP*, 839, under William de Lodelowe I and 863 under Richard Pole.
[152] NRO DCN 1/5/27.

chamberlain's account records the receipt of a total of 101s. 5d. from the defunct brethren.[153] The source of these alms is never stated, but it seems a reasonable suggestion that the Norwich chamberlain was following a practice similar to that found at Worcester.

Monastic corrodies and commemorations

The Worcester accounts also reveal the use of the term 'corrody' in connection with deceased monks. All the cathedral priories were intermittently plagued by corrodies imposed on them by royal demand for retired court retainers, often in the form of accommodation as well as daily rations of food and drink. For their part the monks often felt obliged to offer corrodies to some of their own officials and to lay outsiders in return for much needed cash advances.[154] Monastic corrodies, however, are unique to Worcester among cathedral priories and, with the known exception of Westminster, appear to be rarely if ever found elsewhere.[155] A deceased monk's corrody at Worcester consisted of a daily food allowance or, more probably, the equivalent reckoned in cash, which was distributed to the poor for a period of up to a year. The evidence for this practice is found on the earliest surviving almoner's account roll of 1341/2, and on about half of the later rolls which number just over twenty for the period under study. In fact, these corrodies were often sold for cash as was the case with regard to Roger de Henley's in 1341/2. The result was an entry in the receipt section of the almoner's account to the effect that the corrody had been valued at the rate of 12d. per week for the first thirty days and at 9d. per week for the rest of the year, thus increasing the almoner's funds by a total of 46s. 6d.[156] Apart from the alms of 12d. given to the poor by the almoner on Henley's burial day it would seem that his soul had been deprived of its due. The almoner may have allocated some, possibly all, of the sum he received in the sale to his almsgiving through the year; having obtained more cash in selling he would have eliminated some of the burdens attached to organizing the frequent purchases and distributions of bread. Another corrody, that of Robert de Clifton in 1355/6, covering a period of twenty-three weeks from November to April, brought in 17s. 3d. at the rate of 9d. per week. Marmaduke de Pirie died the same year as Clifton, but his corrody money was diverted into the expense account for the almoner's *domus* or household.[157] A few years later, in 1380/1, the monks' corrodies for John de Gloucestre and John de Kyderminstre were distributed among the poor, and the almoner noted that he had therefore received nothing; but in 1395/6 the sale of Prior John Grene's corrody augmented his receipts by 52s. (1s. per week for a whole year as befitted the deceased prior's status).[158] If these sales of deceased monks' corrodies were,

---

[153] NRO DCN 1/5/15, 19, 47.
[154] This is an aspect of the monastic economy which is not treated in this study.
[155] Barbara Harvey's detailed examination of the Westminster corrodies appears in her *Living and Dying*, 13–14, 179–209.
[156] WCM C.170; for Henley see *BRECP*, 819.
[157] WCM C.172; for Clifton see *BRECP*, 789–90 (Robert de Clifton II), and for Pirie, ibid., 863.
[158] *BRECP*, 810–11 for John de Gloucestre III, ibid., 828 for John de Kyderminstre I, and ibid., 812–13 for John Grene I.

in effect, defrauding the poor and, in doing so, depriving the dead monk of the spiritual benefits attached to the almsgiving it is difficult to understand how this abuse originated and was allowed to continue.[159] Although the priory register known as the *Liber Albus* contains copies of many corrodies sold to various categories of people, the conditions specified in every case make it impossible for there to be any connection with the corrodies intended to benefit the souls of the deceased monks.[160] Apart from those which were sold it seems that the money for the distributions came from the cellarer from at least 1380/1, although there is no sign of these payments to the almoner on the cellarer's accounts, or of their receipt by the almoner, before the second half of the fifteenth century. In 1473/4 the almoner recorded that he had received 33s. 4d. from the cellarer for the corrody of Richard Lodelowe, but five years later, when six monks died and he noted that he should have received a total of £12, he received nothing because the cellarer had been excused from making the payment.[161] Were the deceased monks being given short shrift, or was the money forthcoming from sources hidden from view?

Other forms of commemoration ensured the continuing concern for the spiritual welfare of deceased brethren. Their names were entered in the monastery necrology, which was ordered like a calendar so that the obits for the appropriate date could be read to the monks assembled for the daily chapter. This practice is recorded in the customary of St Augustine's abbey Canterbury written in the first half of the fourteenth century.[162] No complete necrology has survived among the cathedral priories; but some partial lists of monks' obit days are found inserted in kalendars, such as those in a fourteenth-century Norwich psalter and a twelfth-century *Liber Eliensis*.[163] A composite volume formerly at Canterbury, which contains material written by hands dating from the fourteenth to the sixteenth century, records the names of benefactors and men and women admitted to the Christ Church confraternity as well as obits of monks.[164] The register of deceased monks which must have been kept by every monastic establishment is akin to, but distinct from, the profession lists in which were entered the names of monks and dates of profession. The Durham *Liber Vitae* for example, with entries ranging from the ninth to the sixteenth century, includes the names and profession dates of monks and the names of patrons, benefactors, and members of the confraternity of St Cuthbert in an incomplete and

---

[159] One might envisage it arising in a year of severe financial crisis or when the number of deaths was unusually high.
[160] These corrodies were sold for large sums and their duration was spelled out in terms of years if not for life.
[161] WCM C.203, 204; for Richard Lodelowe see *BRECP*, 839.
[162] Thompson, *Customary of St. Augustine*, i, 238.
[163] The Norwich psalter is BL Harley MS 3950 fos 3–8v; the names span the twelfth to the sixteenth centuries and the majority are priors. The Ely kalendar and obits in Cambridge, Trinity College MS 1105 are on fos 1–13.
[164] BL MS Arundel 68, fos 1–68; members of the confraternity were frequently benefactors. A twelfth-century list from Canterbury reveals that the Christ Church monks were linked with those of other cathedral priories—namely Durham, Ely, Rochester, Winchester, and Worcester—in offering mutual prayers and masses for the men and women commemorated by each of them, BL MS Cotton Claudius C.vi, fos 171–2.

somewhat haphazard combination.[165] Medieval scholars are indebted to Thomas Causton, a Christ Church monk of the second half of the fifteenth century, whose work represents neither a profession list nor a necrology but must have been based on both sources. He listed the names of Canterbury monks with their profession dates from the exile under King John (1207–14), and the record was continued after his death in 1504. A second section of the manuscript is made up of the dates of death covering the years between 1286 and 1507. Unfortunately, neither of these lists is complete; for example, there is a gap of some thirty years in the obits between 1361 and 1395, and scattered omissions among the professions.[166]

Lanfranc had ordered that a daily mass was to be offered for every deceased brother for a period of thirty days after his death, and this requirement appears in the customary of St Augustine's some two and a half centuries later.[167] The evidence for the continuity of this practice between *c.* 1295 and *c.* 1304 makes a brief appearance at Rochester cathedral priory where four named monks were assigned *ad tricennale celebrandum* for each deceased brother. William de Hoo, for example, during this decade was on the *tricennale* list on four occasions on behalf of four of his fellow monks. The dates of the admission and ordination of Hamo de Hethe, the future prior and bishop, remain unknown, but he was in priest's orders by *c.* 1302 when he was one of the four monks on the rota to celebrate masses for the soul of William de Ledes.[168] Masses celebrated for deceased monks on the anniversary of their death also come to light at Ely cathedral priory. An insertion in the kalendar section of the *Liber Eliensis* referred to above notes that the two junior monks in priest's orders were assigned to say masses for the anniversary of Alexander de Bury, who had been the monastery cellarer not long before he died in 1392/3.[169] Other cathedral priories must have included anniversary masses for their deceased brethren, but no evidence to this effect has yet been found.

Only Canterbury and Winchester and, possibly, Ely numbered anniversarians among their obedientiaries.[170] Of the many annual commemorations which appear on their accounts and those of other obedientiaries, however, only a few concerned

---

[165] The entire contents of the *Liber Vitae*, BL MS Cotton Domitian vii, have recently been subject to an exhaustive study by a team of experts under the general editorship of David and Lynda Rollason, *The Durham Liber Vitae*, 3 vols, British Library, 2007. There are also some early obits of Durham monks from the period before *c.* 1107, ibid., i, 24–6 (*LVD*).

[166] The Causton manuscript remains *in situ* at Canterbury where it is CCL Lit. MS D.12. The list of monks compiled by W. G. Searle in *Lists of Christ Church*, 172–96, is largely based on Causton; for Causton himself see *BRECP*, 110.

[167] Lanfranc, *Monastic Constitutions*, 188, Thompson, *Customary of St Augustine*, i, 368; the latter also required every monk priest to say ten masses on the deceased brother's behalf, ibid., 343.

[168] The lists of monks assigned to these masses are in BL MS Cotton Vespasian A. xxii fos 126v–127; this is a miscellaneous priory register mainly early thirteenth century in date. For Hoo see *BRECP*, 613 (William de Hoo II); for Hethe, ibid., 611; for Ledes, ibid., 616.

[169] Cambridge, Trinity College MS 1145, fo iiib; for Bury see *BRECP*, 395. This was probably the first anniversary, the year after Bury's death, if the Ely custom was in line with that of St Augustine's where no reference is made to anniversary celebrations in later years, Thompson, *Customary of St Augustine*, i, 369.

[170] The Ely treasurer's account for 1392/3 provides the sole evidence for the presence of an anniversarian in recording a payment made to him for the obit of two monks who had died that year, CUL EDC 1/F/13/14.

monks; and these were confined to a few priors and monk bishops, because only they had the means at their disposal to fund such projects. The two names most frequently occurring at Canterbury were the monk Archbishops Dunstan and Lanfranc, whose anniversaries continued to be observed throughout the fourteenth century. The ordination feast of Dunstan fell on 21 October; and it was the monk *granetarius* or granger, who was responsible for the grain supplies in the priory granary and who, for this celebration, supplied the wheat for the flour from which tarts were baked for the delectation of both the monks and their *familia*.[171] Other obedientiaries shared in this celebration in the form of pittances for the monastic community the cost of which was 8s. 2d. in 1386/7.[172] On Lanfranc's feast day, 28 May, 700 loaves of bread were distributed among the monks and their *familia* according to the mainly fourteenth-century priory Register B, and the almoner paid a servant to ring the bells in the great tower to alert the poor to the 3,400 loaves awaiting them at the priory gate.[173] The prior, cellarer, and hostiller at Durham played their part in the celebration of the two feasts of St Cuthbert (20 May and 4 September). It was the prior who frequently paid for minstrels to entertain the monks and their guests on these festive occasions; there were twelve minstrels who performed in 1374/5 at a cost of 20s. 8d.[174] The cellarer's generous outlay for the two feasts included, for example, turbot and salmon and olive oil in 1337/8, and in 1388/9 a large number of red herring, while the hostiller was obliged to order a fresh supply of drinking cups on several occasions in the 1340s.[175] The altar dedicated to St Nicholas and St Giles, which stood at the north end of the north transept, was the chosen resting place of Prior Fosser. He had assigned land and rents to the communar's office for the maintenance of this, his chantry, where he decreed that a daily mass was to be said for him. He had also provided for a pittance for the monks on his anniversary, which appears on the communar's account for 1416/17.[176] A pittance of wine for this same occasion was contributed by the sacrist to regale the brethren in 1393/4 and later years.[177] Prior Crauden and his successor, Prior Walsingham, were remembered at Ely with gratitude for their achievements in undertaking and directing the lengthy building programme. Their anniversaries were celebrated together on 15 May for which

[171] For example in 1322/3, CCA DCc granetarius'/granger's account 14; there are thirty-seven accounts, all very brief, before 1420. Dunstan, of course, is numbered among the saints and enjoyed two other feast days: 19 May, and 7 September which commemorated his translation.

[172] LPL MS 243, fo 9 (c. 1328), fo 203 (1386/7); these are rough drafts of accounts with no names of accountants.

[173] CCA DCc Reg. B, fo 419v/438v and recorded in Sheppard, *HMC VIIIth Report*, 326; CCA DCc almoner's accounts 26 (1324/5), 52 (1362/3).

[174] Fowler, *Account Rolls*, iii, 581 (bursar's account); other references are also in ibid., ii, 552, iii, 582, 599.

[175] Ibid., i, 33, 34, 49 (cellarer); ibid., i, 118, 119 (hostiller). The 'open house' celebrations on the feast of St Cuthbert in March are described in *Rites of Durham*, 4–5.

[176] *HDST*, 130–4 and Fowler, *Account Rolls*, iii, lxi; ii, 285, 286. In 1430/1 the pittance money was deflected to pay for expenses incurred in the care of the vestments pertaining to the Fosser chantry, Fowler, *Account Rolls*, ii, 288.

[177] Fowler, *Account Rolls*, ii, 292, 402.

funding was provided in each case by means of an appropriation and purchase of lands, the income from which was to be divided between alms for the poor and pittances for the convent. A day of recreation for the monks was to be set aside according to the deed for the memorial celebration.[178]

One of the chantry masses at Norwich for which a rota of monks was prepared was for Alexander de Totyngton, prior and bishop. It was to be celebrated at 6 am each morning in the Lady chapel, the site of his burial in 1406.[179] There is also evidence for the continuing commemoration of three former priors: Gerard (c. 1175–1202), William de Kirkeby (1272–89), and Henry de Lakenham (1289–1310). In 1316/17, for example, in a section headed *Anniversaria* among his receipts, the communar recorded the receipt of 1m. from the cellarer for Gerard and 26s. 8d. from the master of the cellar on the prior's behalf for William de Kirkeby. He then listed his purchases for the convent celebrations, which included porpoise, wine, spices, almonds, and figs.[180] All three anniversaries are listed on later accounts of the communar/pittancer; in 1348/9 among the pittancer's receipts were 26s. 8d. for Lakenham, the same amount for Kirkeby and 13s. 4d. for Gerard.[181] The chantry of Hamo de Hethe, prior and bishop of Rochester, was located at the altar where the Lady mass was celebrated. He gave directions for a daily celebration by a secular priest to be appointed by the prior and chapter. On his anniversary 10s. was to be set aside to feed the poor from the funds he had made available and another 10s. to provide pittances for the monastic community.[182] The Winchester anniversarian made an annual payment to the monk *depositorius* of 66s. 8d. for five of the founders and benefactors of St Swithun's to be commemorated by the community. Three twelfth-century bishops are named on a number of fourteenth-century anniversarian accounts, and the names of four eleventh- and twelfth-century priors who were commemorated appear in the surviving portions of a twelfth/thirteenth-century customary. Priors Simeon and Godfrey are followed by Geoffrey and Robert; for these last two no identification is possible because there were three priors in the twelfth century named Geoffrey and another three named Robert. There is also in the customary the unique case of a monk, Anschetill', included with the priors because, so it is stated, he had conferred many benefits on his brethren by his good works. Details of the sums to be spent and the dishes to be served to the monks on all of these anniversaries are given, but how or if they relate

---

[178] BL Add. MS 33181, fo 12 and Chapman, *Sacrist Rolls*, i, 161–3; for Crauden and Walsingham see *BRECP*, 401, 453–4.

[179] Totyngton's will is in LPL Reg. Arundel, II, fos 165v–6 and is summarized in Tanner, *The Church in Late Medieval Norwich*, 214.

[180] Fernie and Whittingham, *Communar Rolls*, 92; he spent a total of just over £9 15s., using money remaining from the previous account.

[181] NRO DCN 1/12/27; financial difficulties in the second half of the fourteenth century, especially in the wake of the plague and the fall of the cathedral spire in 1352, probably disrupted the enjoyment of pittances in order to pay for building materials and construction workers. The three priors are in *BRECP*, 514–15 (Gerard II), 531 (Kirkeby), 531–2 (Lakenham).

[182] CKS DRc T320, confirmation of the chantry dated 1341, eleven years before he died; it describes the altar as close to the tomb of St William of Perth, murdered in Rochester in 1201 while on pilgrimage to the Holy Land. See also Haines, 'Hamo de Hethe', 207.

to the anniversarian's account is unknown.[183] Wulstan was the prior and bishop of Worcester who continued to be commemorated and celebrated on two occasions during the year, his obit on 19 January and his translation on 7 June. The pittancer was a regular contributor to the translation feast day repast from 1296/7, the date of the earliest surviving account of this office. In 1318/19 he named the translation as one of the festal occasions during the year for which he supplied wine; in many of the later accounts, however, he failed to specify the feasts included.[184] For this annual pittance he received a contribution from the feretrar, or *tumbarius*, of Wulstan's shrine; in 1343/4, for example, it was 20s., in 1372/3 14s. 8d.; and in 1387/8 16s., the amount probably varying according to the size of the offerings made at the shrine.[185] The cellarer made up for the shortfall of supplies from the convent kitchen in 1351/2 by purchasing meat and cheese for Wulstan's obit, and from *c.* 1371/2 on, he records the payment of £4 for the obit, frequently in the list of expenditures caused by the *defectum coquine*.[186] The almoner was responsible for distributing among the poor what he described as Wulstan's bread in 1341/2. He was probably referring to the saint's maundy dole of food, which in 1355/6 he sold together with what he identified as Wulstan's corrody, thereby adding 25s. to his receipts. From *c.* 1377/8 until *c.* 1391/2 this corrody was assigned to a relative of the prior and so he received nothing. In the latter year he acknowledged the receipt of £4 for Wulstan's corrody and *coquina* and then proceeded to pay the £4 to the prior; this double transaction continued in the 1390s; it probably originated in the cellarer's £4 expenditure which was turned over to the almoner. In 1395/6, however, he provides more detail to the effect that he received £4 for the corrody and a further 13s. for the maundy; the maundy money would probably have come from the kitchener because he was named in the 1399/1400 account as having been excused payment.[187] There is evidence of continuing distributions in kind, usually bread and pulses, in Wulstan's memory, some of these listed on the dorse of the almoner's account.[188]

There is no doubt that the cathedral monks were conscientious about the commemoration of their deceased brethren, but some of the means by which this was effected are lost in the tangled network of inter-office transactions behind the scenes; the monks were, of course, preparing their accounts for those who were familiar with the day-to-day internal affairs of their monastery. At times, however, these accounts suggest that more of the letter of the law than of the spirit was at work in the implementation of the commemorative practices.

---

[183] The earliest known anniversarian is Philip Trenchefoil in 1250, *BRECP*, 740; the earliest account is WCM C.531 (1369/70), followed by eight others before 1400; these Winchester account rolls are preserved at Worcester cathedral. The customary is in BL Add MS 29436 and the bishops and priors are named on fos 75v and 78; on the feasts of St Swithun (2 and 15 July) the monks drank claret, ibid., fo 75.

[184] WCM C.294 (1318/19).

[185] Ibid., C.300, 309, 313; although the *tumbarius* (or *tumbarii*) had the responsibility for two shrines, the other being that of St Oswald, the latter's feast is not mentioned in these accounts.

[186] Wilson and Gordon, *Early Compotus Rolls*, 49, WCM C.67, 69, 71, 76 etc.

[187] WCM C.170 (the earliest extant almoner's account), C.172, 174, 179, 181 (1391/2), 182 (1395/6), 185; the almoner paid the £4 corrody to the prior in 1406/7, C.188.

[188] WCM C.172, 174, 177, 183.

VII

Conclusion

The preceding pages have been confined to the study of Benedictine life in the English cathedral priories between *c.* 1270 and *c.* 1420. It is now time to draw together some of the threads connecting the main topics that have been treated and, by way of conclusion, to extend the horizon in order to situate this 'slice' of history in its wider historical context.

St Benedict does not seem to have thought it necessary to order a daily public reading of his Rule in community; he was content to say that it should be read *saepius*, which is the comparative form of *saepe*, meaning 'often'.[1] It is uncertain how early a daily reading was introduced, but in the 1270s statutes issued by both the northern and southern provinces of the Black Monk chapter prescribed a daily reading from the Rule in chapter; and in the southern province this was to be followed by a summary given in English or French with an accompanying commentary by way of explanation.[2] Only a year or two later the southern chapter circulated a document entitled 'Tradicio generalis super mores et observanciis monachorum' which considered it necessary to affirm that absent monks, those confined in the infirmary and those on visits to the manors, were bound by the same obligation.[3] Later statutes promulgated *c.* 1363 included a stern reminder that, while it was compulsory for novices to attend the daily chapter in order to hear the reading from the Rule, they were to leave immediately afterwards; only the professed members of the community were eligible to participate in the discussion of the private and confidential matters dealt with by the chapter.[4]

It has been noted above that before profession the novice was expected to have committed the Rule to memory, but he would hardly have begun to attach more than a superficial meaning to the words he could recite by heart. Their stark simplicity and their focus on practical details could prove disarming and deceptive with regard to their deeper intent. As a result of the frequent and regular hearing of daily extracts from the Rule an increasing familiarity was expected to gradually awaken a more profound inner response and, simultaneously, to encourage an outward conformity to its precepts now understood as the way to fullness of life.

---

[1] *RB*, C.66, 8; a suitable translation would be 'very often'.
[2] It is interesting to note that one of the versions of the 1278 statutes of the southern (general) chapter was included under the heading *De reformacione regule*, Pantin, *Black Monk Chapters*, i, 94–5; the northern chapter in 1273 stated that the readings were to take place in every chapter in accordance with the statutes promulgated by the papal legate, Ottobonus, ibid., i, 250.
[3] Ibid., i, 111–12 and Thompson, *Customary of St. Augustine*, 390.
[4] Pantin, *Black Monk Chapters*, iii, 69–70.

The monks of the cathedral priories in the 1420s would have listened to the Rule just as their predecessors had done in the 1270s, but their reaction and interpretation in practical terms would have been conditioned by the impact of the constantly fluctuating world outside from which the monastic cloisters were never immune. The monks had been born and had grown up in it and their families continued to belong to it; the monastic community was dependent on it for its supplies of food and other basic necessities of life as well as for labour both within the precinct and on the priory manors; and this dependency extended to include a wide circle of patrons, benefactors, and friends among the great and the lowly who supported the monks by their gifts and offerings.

In the late thirteenth and early fourteenth centuries the Black Monk chapters, in which some cathedral priors played a leading role, were pressing for the reform of their liturgical office in the face of episcopal condemnation while at the same time episcopal visitation injunctions were denouncing the growth of abuses and decline in discipline in contravention to the Rule. In this same period the Benedictines joined the friars in the university halls of learning and, in so doing, exposed themselves to a range of new ideas and influences. By the time that the statutes of 1343 were published any signs of determined reforming zeal on the part of the monks seems to have petered out, and the document itself was little more than a set of statutes for the recently united English province compiled from the separate but similar sets of the two former provinces of Canterbury and York.[5] As for the bishops' injunctions, among the relatively few that are extant, there is little to suggest that they were having noticeable success in their attempt to raise the standard of discipline through closer adherence to the Rule.[6]

During the ecumenical council convened at Constance (1414–18) signs of a growing movement for reform among Benedictine monasteries in Europe were exposed to view. Among the English party at the council were John de Fordham, prior of Worcester, and Thomas Spofford, abbot of St Mary's York; while there, the latter had been chosen to play a leading role in the reform of German monasteries.[7] The need for reform of the English Black Monks was brought to the attention of Henry V on his return from France early in 1421. According to a contemporary chronicle written at the abbey of St Albans, the king was influenced by the accusations of 'false brethren' among whom, so the Croyland abbey chronicle affirms, the dominant figure was the prior of the Carthusian monastery of Mount Grace; this was Robert Layton, who, unsurprisingly, was a disaffected former Benedictine.[8] The king's response was to request the presidents of the

---

[5] Ibid., ii, 27–62. Another surviving set of statutes from 1363 is much shorter and deals with domestic affairs like the enforcement of uniform clothing for the monks and regulations for the welfare of the monk students.

[6] When Bishop Wykeham clamped down on the Winchester monks' pocket money in 1387 they retaliated by refusing to co-operate with him in his building project in the cathedral; they won, Greatrex, 'Injunction Book', 246.

[7] Knowles, *RO*, ii, 182–4, provides a clear and concise account of this episode.

[8] The St Alban's chronicle is that of Thomas Walsingham, *Historia Anglicana*, ii, 337–8. The later continuation of the chronicle of Croyland, or Crowland, abbey has been transcribed by William Fulman in *Rerum Anglicarum Scriptorum Veterum*, i, (Oxford, 1684), where details of the

Black Monk chapter (one of whom was John de Fordham, prior of Worcester) to summon their brethren to meet him at Westminster in order to discuss and remedy the underlying problems. The gathering that took place in May of that year consisted of some sixty prelates and more than 300 monk delegates, many of them university graduates.[9] Three men, one of them being the prior of Mount Grace, and six monks who included John de Fordham, John Wessington, prior of Durham, and the reform-minded Thomas Spofford, were chosen to represent the monks.[10] A further twenty-four monks were brought in to join the six and, together, they were given the task of negotiating with the king's representatives while considering the proposed articles of reform prepared by the latter. Henry came in person to greet the distinguished assembly, gathered in the chapter house of Westminster abbey, and in a movingly sincere address reminded the monks how much they owed to his royal progenitors and other benefactors who had founded and supported their monasteries and made over substantial gifts. In return they had confidently relied on the monks' regular prayers on their behalf, as had he most recently on the battlefield in France. He urged them to direct their attention to the urgent need for a return to a simpler, more disciplined way of life in stricter adherence to the Rule; only in so doing would their prayers continue to be efficacious.

Discussion of the king's proposed articles followed, resulting in a series of critical responses. These took the form of a *modificatio* of the articles which was drawn up by a committee of thirteen monks numbered among whom were two from Norwich cathedral priory: John de Dereham, who had recently completed his doctorate in theology, and William Worstede, who was in the final stages of his doctoral studies, also in theology.[11] This body gave its *placet* to a few of the king's reform measures such as the need for regulations to ensure uniformity in monastic dress; but a number of qualifications were attached to many of these acceptable items. It was agreed, for example, that monks should not leave the monastic precinct without permission; however, an exeat would be granted whenever, for a good reason, it was deemed necessary.[12] The committee members rejected the call for a return to a stricter, more literal interpretation of the Rule, however, with regard to personal possessions including books, private cells for monk graduates, private quarters for the abbot, and pocket money for the monks on the grounds that these matters were not contrary to the Rule; they were, in fact, permissible at the discretion of the abbot or prior. To support their case they quoted from chapter

---

Westminster meeting are recounted, 513–14; they are probably accurate as the abbot of Croyland was one of the monastic delegation appointed to discuss the king's articles. Layton is named in Pantin, *Black Monk Chapters*, ii, 107.

[9] Pantin, *Black Monk Chapters*, ii, 98–101.

[10] For Fordham, see *BRECP*, 805–7, for Wessington, *LVD*, iii, C.1028, and for Spofford, *BRUO*, iii, 1744.

[11] Pantin, *Black Monk Chapters*, ii, 100, 121; for Dereham see *BRECP*, 499–50 and for Worstede, who was soon to be elected prior, see ibid., 573–4.

[12] Pantin, *Black Monk Chapters*, ii, 120; the phrase is 'nisi ardua causa et racionabili exigente', and a 'special licence' was to be obtained.

thirty-three of the Rule in which the abbot's discretion is the ultimate, deciding factor.[13] A number of the committee's insertions were intended to reduce the impact of some of the unexceptionable reforms put forward by the king and his advisers such as, for example, the monks' substitution of the requirement that a certain course of action should require the consent of the whole community to the consent only of the *sanioris partis*.[14] A conspicuous feature of the surviving versions of the final set of articles approved by the monks is the frequency with which they reinforced their position by references to a range of authorities including papal and archiepiscopal constitutions, the early fathers of the church, namely Augustine, Jerome, John Chrysostom, Thomas Aquinas, William Durandus the canonist, and Bernard of Clairvaux. In general the items could be described as bearing resemblance to episcopal visitation injunctions; and they amount to little more than a reaffirmation of the status quo in spelling out in verbose detail regulations concerning clothing, the annual rendering of accounts, recreation, diet, and money allowances, all to continue to be subject to the final decision of the abbot or prior.[15]

Few noticeable signs indicative of reform are visible in the proceedings of later Black Monk chapters. Even so, the preamble to the statutes of 1444 affirmed that the committee responsible for its production was concerned to bring about a *sanctissimam reformacionem animarum*.[16] Their mandate had been the compilation of a new code to replace the previous one of a century earlier by incorporating additions from statutes promulgated in the intervening period.[17] In summary, once again its contents are a repetition of the familiar matters that continued to cause concern and to require legislation; but it is possible to discern in them the sincere intention of setting in motion a sober offensive against ingrained abuses and infringements of the Rule. All monks were to be present for the divine office which was to be celebrated *studiose* and *devote*, and the psalms were to be chanted *rotunde et viva voce*; all were to attend the daily chapter; university graduates and office holders among the monks were not to be given preference in rank of order; bedridden monks in the infirmary were to be provided with all their needs. These and many other regulations were spelled out in lengthy detail, but also with the continuing loophole of frequent allusions to the obligation to procure a licence from the superior when there were legitimate reasons for absence from office, chapter or monastic precinct.[18]

---

[13] *RB*, C.33, 5 with the addition that everything should be *in disposicione abbatis*, a phrase which may be a reference to chapter 65, 11. The article in question is no. 9 in Pantin, *Black Monk Chapters*, ii, 123 where the reference is to *RB*, C.30 instead of 33.

[14] Pantin, *Black Monk Chapters*, ii, 122.

[15] Ibid., ii, 125–34; two versions of the final articles are in manuscripts at Durham, DCL MSS B.IV.26, fo 236, B.III.30, fo 53.

[16] Pantin, *Black Monk Chapters*, ii, 187; in addition to the manuscript copies listed by Pantin, there is another in BL MS Egerton 3316, fos 1–9, the provenance of which is Bath cathedral priory.

[17] Pantin points out that sections in the 1444 set of statutes that appear to be new 'must represent the diffinitions of those chapters between 1343 and 1444 which are now lost', *Black Monk Chapters*, ii, 186.

[18] Ibid., ii, 195, 198, and *passim* 190–220; other sections dealt with almsgiving, university students, appropriate punishments for disobedient monks etc.

An earlier chapter has drawn attention to a renewed interest in the study of the origins and historical development of Benedictine monasticism together with a fresh look at the Rule and the provision of an up-to-date commentary.[19] The two Durham monk scholars, John de Beverley and Uthred de Boldon played a prominent role in this project around the middle of the fourteenth century and, from evidence based on surviving manuscripts, they were soon joined by monastic writers from Bury St Edmunds, Glastonbury and St Albans.[20] The project of re-examining the Benedictine past had initially been set in motion to respond to the challenge posed by the mendicants to their privileged position among the religious orders and in the field of higher learning.[21] In the early fifteenth century the compilations and writings of a third Durham monk, John Wessington, made a significant addition to the Benedictine corpus of Uthred and John de Beverley. Wessington had been appointed librarian/chancellor three years after his return from Oxford, and in 1416 was elected prior. Barrie Dobson has commented at length on the quality and variety of Wessington's literary productions which were concerned with two closely related subjects, namely the history of English Benedictine monasticism and the historical rights and customs of the cathedral church of Durham. His *De fundacione monasteriorum nigrorum in regno Angliae* took the form of a collection of historical notes on the origins of most of the major houses of Black Monks, and another work consisted of a series of biographies of distinguished monks of the past with the purpose of edifying his contemporaries in the Durham community through an appreciation of the impressive array of their divinely inspired predecessors.[22]

Although it is well nigh impossible to gauge the prevailing moral and spiritual climate within the Benedictine houses of the early fifteenth century, a surviving Latin sermon of *c.* 1400 may offer a glimpse. It was most probably delivered to the monks assembled for their triennial provincial chapter c. 1400 although, unfortunately, few details of the proceedings of the chapters between the 1390s and 1420 have been found. The sermon is one among many that were copied into a Worcester manuscript and the volume remains in the cathedral library to the present day.[23] The monastic preacher noted, in the form of a prayer, that they were gathered to beg for pardon for their transgressions and *pro ordinis monastici reformacione*, and went on to quote the desert father John Cassian (*c.* 360–?435) to the effect that the *prima doctrina* of the monk is to master his own will and to obey

---

[19] See above 78–9.
[20] Pantin, 'Origins of Monasticism', 189–90.
[21] The spread of heretical teaching by Wyclif and his adherents had also provided impetus to the need for a reasoned statement in defence of monastic and clerical orthodoxy; see Pantin, 'Uthred of Boldon', *passim*.
[22] Dobson, *Durham Priory*, 378–86; Wessington is C.1028 in *LVD*, iii.
[23] The manuscript is WCM F.10 and the sermon is on fo 81; it has been transcribed in 'A Sermon for a General Chapter' by W. A. Pantin, *Downside Review*, 51 (new series 32) (1933), 291–308. If the sermon was delivered by a Worcester monk it was probably John de Dudley, who was the proctor appointed to represent the prior and chapter at both the 1399 and 1402 meetings, *BRECP*, 798.

the commands of his seniors.[24] He recalled the early days of monasticism in the Egyptian desert and the conversion of their Anglo-Saxon forbears. Referring to Jerome's dictum that 'monachus non habet officum doctoris, set plorantis' he told his hearers that this stricture applied to anchorites and not to coenobites.[25] On the contrary, it behoved Benedictines to study scripture and preach to the people; and the monk students, he reminded them, should be assured of adequate support in their university studies. He extolled the unity among brethren as portrayed in Psalm 132 and reaffirmed by Augustine as the sign of true monks, who live as *una anima et unum cor* although *multa corpora*.[26] Rather than a timely call for the strengthening of the bonds of unity among the brethren in their communal life the preacher seems to be complimenting the delegates on the *status quo*, an attitude he endorses in his closing remarks about an incident in the life of Pachomius, the father of western monasticism. It was related that in a vision Pachomius had received a divine guarantee of the everlasting continuance of his monastic way of life and, for this reason, the preacher concluded, the monks should rejoice with St Paul that they had been chosen as *primicias in salutem*. In his closing words he prayed that the Black Monks might continue to live a devout life together in harmony and so receive, like Pachomius, the promised eternal rest.[27] A further comment on the contents of the sermon is pertinent in order to draw attention to the wide-ranging array of texts, in addition to the Bible, to which he had recourse. He included references to and quotations from Plato, Aristotle, Cicero, Ovid among pagan authors and Augustine, Bede, Bernard of Clairvaux, John of Salisbury, Robert Grosseteste, and others already mentioned among Christian writers. This would make it fairly certain that the unnamed monk preacher belonged to a community where there was a well-stocked library and that he himself was familiar with at least an impressive cross section of its contents.

This study has exposed to view many of the daily, weekly and seasonal activities that took place in the monastic cathedral church, cloister, and precinct. In the preceding pages we have observed that, even on their own home ground, the monks were constantly contending with the noise and confusion around them, akin to the market place, in sharp contrast to the silence and peace envisaged by St Benedict in his Rule. It was not that the daily mass and office failed to be performed; it was rather that the world was too much in their midst to allow their life of prayer, the life to which they had committed themselves on the day of profession, to have their undivided attention. Many of the persons who, no doubt unintentionally, distracted them from their primary responsibility, their sole *raison d'être*, were in the monks' employ, or had come to execute essential business affairs; others had

---

[24] Cassien *Institutions*, book iv, chapter 8, p. 130 for 'ut doceat primitus suas vincere voluntates' and chapters 10, 23 etc., pp. 132–4, 152 etc. for references to the necessity of obedience which occur *passim*, but the phrase *maiorum imperiis obedire* found in the sermon does not appear as such in the *Institutions*. In Pantin's transcription (note 23 above) the Latin phrases are on p. 305.

[25] Pantin, 'A Sermon for a General Chapter', 301 (note 23 above).

[26] Ibid., 306–7.

[27] Ibid., 307–8; Pachomius (290–346) was the author of the earliest rule for monks, which was influential on later monastic founders including St Benedict.

lodgings in the precinct and were supplied with daily rations; still others were pilgrims, visitors, relatives, or friends who expected hospitality in meals and accommodation. It is not surprising to find among these outsiders an increasing number who were becoming less impressed by and more critical of the monks' relatively comfortable life, no longer so different from their own secular interests and occupations. In an earlier age what had distinguished the monk and the monastic community was the visible pursuit of holiness which gave rise to a respect bordering on reverence on the part of those in the world outside and the desire to have their names remembered in the monks' masses and prayers. For their part the monks, especially those of the cathedral priories and other monasteries in an urban setting, became increasingly hard pressed by the practical problems involved in providing for the day-to-day necessities of the monastic community. Only by the regular oversight of their properties, either directly or through officials appointed to deal with rents, pensions, and produce due, were they able to ensure that the brethren were adequately fed and clothed. In addition, as we have seen, the level of disturbance within the monastic precinct during the fourteenth century was frequently augmented, sometimes for prolonged periods, due to building operations and the presence of workmen who were often resident and had to be provided with meals on site.

The absence of reform-inspired and inspiring leaders, however, does not preclude the continuing presence of devout and even holy monks; although their lives for the most part remain hidden, they formed an essential and enduring core on which the well-being of every community was dependent. Thanks to the survival of a few fragmentary notes we have been given a glimpse of the persevering faithfulness of a William Glastynbury of Canterbury and, from the Christ Church obituary notices we have learned of the pious and charitable lives of several of his brethren like Thomas Wykyng.[28] Some Durham monks are also remembered for their lives of prayer as attested by a collection of spiritual writings that survive in a Durham manuscript. John de Whitrigg and Richard de Sedgebrook were both resident on the island of Farne during the 1350s and 1360s, and one of them is the probable author of the meditations and devotions in the manuscript. Sedgebrook was master of the cell for some years and responsible for compiling the accounts of this tiny community of Durham monks, while Whitrigg is not known to have had any responsibilities during his stay there. Since the writer of the meditations was described as a solitary, and therefore living apart from his brethren, it is likely that the work should be attributed to Whitrigg.[29]

Among cathedral priors, at least a few would have striven resolutely to model themselves on St Benedict's abbot whose character and role he described in careful detail in two lengthy chapters of his Rule.[30] Since he held the place of Christ in the

---

[28] See above 285, 303.
[29] This is the conclusion of Richard Sharpe; see his entries for both monks in his *Latin Writers*. See also *LVD*, iii, C.933 for Whitrigg and C.936 for Sedgebrook. The relevant folios of the manuscript, now DCL B.IV.34, are 6–75v, and two articles may be consulted for descriptive details of their contents: Farmer, 'Meditations', and Pantin, 'The Monk-Solitary of Farne'.
[30] *RB*, C.2 and C.64; a third chapter (C.27) deals with the abbot's treatment of monks who infringe the Rule.

monastery he was required to be an example to the brethren in his actions as in his words, caring for the weak with compassion and, with wisdom and discernment, teaching and exhorting them to persevere more and more diligently in their monastic vocation. The cathedral priors who fulfilled this role cannot be singled out with any certainty, but there is enough surviving evidence to allow us to suggest the names of three possible candidates. The character of John de Crauden of Ely, for example, who died in 1341, was summed up in an Ely manuscript which described him as a *pastor pacificus*, a monk of profound spirituality who was found frequently absorbed in prayer and meditation in his chapel late into the night.[31] Another possible candidate for St Benedict's approval is John de Evesham, prior of Worcester between 1340 and 1370. His actions reveal him as a judicious and astute superior who led his community safely and unscathed through a series of crises with even-handed persistence, qualities which can do no more than suggest that their source was to be found hidden in a life of prayer.[32] A local monastic chronicle of Christ Church Canterbury refers to Prior John Fynch (1377–91) as a monk who was at once devout, innocent, and pure of heart, and whose achievements were the outcome of prayer.[33]

The presence of an unknown number of devout and faithful monks in some, probably all, monasteries does little to obscure the fact that there was a noticeable malaise within English Benedictine establishments in the fifteenth and early sixteenth centuries. Attention has been drawn to the gradual erosion of the common life in respect of absence from communal meals in the refectory and from communal participation in the full daily round of the monastic office, the daily chapter, and other regular observances. What has been brought to light and emphasized in this study is that the attention of most monks appears to have been caught up in a pressing round of long-established duties, obligations, and related practices. As a result there was little time left for the cultivation of that bond of fellowship that is indispensable, for it lies at the heart of the common life. An apparent disregard of the gravity of the problem was accompanied by a general lack of concern to review and strengthen the existing programme of instruction in the noviciate with the intent of inspiring the young monks to attain to a full and mature participation as professed members of their monastic community. Neither of the chapters relating to novices in the statutes of 1343 or 1444 reveals any awareness of the need for a more spiritually challenging approach and a greater degree of inner discipline for those entering St Benedict's 'school of the Lord's service'.[34] As we have seen, the energies of a few intellectually gifted Benedictines in the fourteenth and fifteenth centuries were directed

---

[31] LPL MS 448, fo 59–59v; see also *Anglia Sacra*, i, 649.
[32] See my 'Prior John de Evesham'.
[33] 'Anon. Chron.', 58–61 and *BRECP*, 163–4. It should be noted that the sermon addressed to the general chapter of the Blank Monks in 1343 (note 23 above) emphasized the role of monastic superiors (*prelati*) in being an example to their monks, but without any reference to the lifelong essential ingredients of *conversatio morum* and *compunctio* which applied to them as much as to the other members of their community.
[34] Pantin, *Black Monk Chapters*, ii, 49–50, 206–8; the quotation is from *RB*, Prol. 45.

toward composing accounts of the origins and historical development of monasticism and of extolling the glories of their saintly forbears, much of it being a kind of historical apologetic aimed at securing and enhancing the status of the Black Monks among religious orders.[35] Perhaps a few novices were inspired with fresh zeal when reading these productions.

The available evidence strongly suggests that during the greater part of the two centuries preceding the dissolution monks in the cathedral priories and other monastic houses in England were afflicted by a form of accidie. Often described as the monastic sin par excellence, it was a recurrent theme in the writings of the church fathers, including Cassian, who devoted a whole book to it in his *Institutions*.[36] Surprisingly, however, the word *accidia* does not appear in the Rule, although in the single reference to *otiositas* Benedict clearly had it in mind. He warns that *otiositas*, or idleness, is the enemy of the soul and his prescribed antidote was a timetable with specific hours divided between manual work and *lectio divina*.[37] In this he shows his awareness that it is not simply a matter of idleness that is at stake but rather that the state of idleness can lead from boredom to aversion and alienation, thus becoming an obstacle in the monk's striving to draw closer to God. Bernard of Clairvaux also described the state of being fed up with the monastic routine, which leads to negligence in prayer and regular observance.[38] In his *Summa theologiae* and his treatise *De malo* Thomas Aquinas dwelt at length on the moral and theological aspects of the sin of *accidia* and its various manifestations in the day-to-day experience of living the Christian life. His conclusions have recently been summed up succinctly and aptly by a French Benedictine theologian as having their source in 'la tentation du repli sur soi et de la fermeture à l'Autre'.[39]

The daily occupations of the monks as examined in detail in the present study point to the conclusion that many of the brethren were personally acquainted with one of the many subtle guises in which *accidia* presents itself. At the same time, however, and in the same monastery there would have been other monks who had remained untouched by the disease or had struggled against it, kept it at bay and overcome. As I have remarked above, it is unfortunate that members of this latter group remain for the most part unknown, often because they were *claustrales* and held no office, or were model monks whose exemplary lives caused no disturbance and left nothing to record.

In the past thirty years scholars have begun to revise, rewrite, and even to challenge the picture of late medieval English monasticism presented by David Knowles in his masterly three-volume study of the religious orders. This is as it should be because recent studies have been based on the prolonged examination of

---

[35] See above 78–9 and below 352–3.
[36] Cassien, *Institutions*, book x, 'De spiritu acediae', 382–425.
[37] *RB*, C.48, 17.
[38] See J.-C. Nault, *La saveur de Dieu, l'acédie dans la dynamisme de l'agir* (Les éditions du Cerf, Paris, 2006), 91–6, 142–3. Abbot Nault makes frequent reference to the earlier impressive work by Siegfried Wenzel, *The Sin of Sloth:* Acedia *in Medieval Thought and Literature* (University of North Carolina Press, Chapel Hill, 1968).
[39] Ibid., 358.

primary source material which was not available for Knowles' perusal half a century ago. His Epilogue, however, provides some pertinent insights in his critical assessment of what reduced the Black Monks and other religious to a state of non-resistance to Henry VIII's determined takeover of their monasteries and ejection of their members. He does not employ the word *accidia* to describe the internal condition of contemporary monasticism; but his reference to the breakdown of the community life of prayer and silence through increasing involvement in external secular affairs implies his awareness of its presence.[40]

Among recent judgements by some historians is the verdict that by, if not before, 1540 monasticism had become secularized, with the result that the monasteries no longer stood apart from the world around them, nor commanded the respect of former years. They had, therefore, run their course and the time was ripe for their replacement by the parish churches and the faithful congregations of supporting parishioners.[41] More recently others have begun to draw attention to signs of new life in several of the larger monasteries where an increase in young men seeking admission has been noted. In a discerning appraisal of the last generations of Durham monks Alan Piper regards 'the whole of the period 1500–39 as one of significant growth leading to impressive stability'; and he concludes that 'it was a period in which the health of the community, judged by its size, was considerably stronger than during the preceding forty years, 1460–99'.[42] In contrast, Barrie Dobson's pessimistic account of the closing years at Canterbury found the Christ Church monks to be increasingly pursuing 'their separate, individual ways' with resulting tension and division in the cloister.[43] However, another more positive judgement results from a consideration of the record of the latest available numbers of admissions and professions at Canterbury on the eve of the suppression; in 1527 there were twelve and in 1534 eight.[44] A similar favourable reckoning may be obtained at Worcester where, of the total of about thirty-eight monks in 1522/3, eight were not yet in priest's orders; and nine years later, in 1531/2, out of forty monks five were juniors, not yet ordained to the priesthood.[45] Even more striking is the discovery of ten junior monks not in major orders at Ely in 1534 when the senior monks numbered only twenty-three.[46]

These signs may so far be few; but they are sufficiently impressive to reject the verdict of terminal decline, even though the 1530s were particularly testing years

---

[40] Knowles, *RO*, published between 1948 and 1959; the Epilogue is in iii, 456–63.
[41] See B. Thompson, 'Monasteries, Society and Reform in Late Medieval England', in J. G. Clark (ed.), *The Religious Orders in Pre-Reformation England* (Boydell, Woodbridge, 2002), 165–95, *passim* and especially 194–5. In his *Late Monasticism and the Reformation* (Hambledon, London, 1994), A. G. Dickens described English monasticism as 'too old, too enfeebled, too forgotten to die violently amid dramatic passions', 23.
[42] Piper, 'Size and Shape of Durham', 163.
[43] Dobson, 'Monks of Canterbury', 153, and *BRECP*, 57.
[44] Searle, *Lists of Christ Church*, 195–6.
[45] WCM Reg. A.17, 204 (chamberlain's account), WCM C.414c (prior's account).
[46] They were listed by name at Bishop Goodrich's visitation, CUL EDR G/1/7, fo 90v. Similar late increases in numbers have also been detected at Glastonbury and Ramsey abbeys; see the references in my 'Recent Perspectives', 39.

for the Black Monks and all English religious. Cardinal Wolsey's summons to Benedictine prelates to meet him at Westminster in 1519/20, like the similar summons a century earlier, drew strong objections when an austere reform programme was put before the assembly. The monks argued that by agreeing to such a severe code they would cease to attract vocations and would become akin to the enclosed orders of Carthusians and Bridgettines or to the Observant Friars Minor.[47]

This study has witnessed changes in the interpretation and practice of the Benedictine Rule in the period *c.*1270 to *c.* 1420, changes encompassing both movements of reform and resistance to it. Periods of renewal and decline in this century and a half were both present and, to some degree, coexistent.[48] How else does one explain the continuing attraction of monastic life in the early sixteenth century, when it is clear that decline was more apparent than renewal both before and after 1420? It is perhaps tempting to condemn the Benedictines outright, but it was they, rather than Wolsey, who understood the problem when they told him that the implementation of his inflexible reforms would mean that there would be no more Black Monks. The underlying strength of St Benedict's Rule which is, paradoxically, at the same time its weakness is found in the lifelong commitment required of the monk. This is no more and no less than the *conversatio morum*, the daily practice of an inner conversion of heart and mind.[49] Whenever we observe the comfortable complacency manifest in the life style of, for example, some fifteenth-century Benedictines we might recall that there were also hidden seeds of renewal and reform waiting for their successors who, while striving to remain faithful to the Rule, would study to adapt its practice to meet the challenges of a new environment.

[47] Pantin, *Black Monk Chapters*, iii, 117–24.
[48] See the section on 'decline and renewal' in Fry, *RB*, 131–6.
[49] *RB*, C.58, 17.

APPENDICES
BOOKS FOR STUDY AND LEISURE

APPENDIX I
Grammar

Grammar and history are the two subjects selected here in order to demonstrate the potential fruitfulness of comparative studies of monastic library holdings in these as well as in other fields. It is to be hoped that even a brief survey of some of the authors and titles acquired by the cathedral monks in grammar and history will suffice to convince the reader that further endeavour in these and other subjects would be worthwhile.[1]

The two subjects selected here were both, in their different ways, indispensable for all monks. Grammar in its medieval context was defined by Hugh of St Victor (d. 1141) as 'la base de toute formation intellectuelle' because it was essential to the understanding and interpretation of texts.[2] In his *Corrogationes Promethei* Alexander Nequam, almost a century later, expressed the same conviction in slightly different terms: grammar is an *ars recte intelligendi* not merely an *ars recte scribendi* and *recte proferendi*.[3] The medieval grammar master, therefore, included in his teaching all the necessary skills that would result in the competent use of both the spoken and written word. This all-encompassing view of what the study of grammar entailed means that it not only comprised syntax, orthography, pronunciation, etymology, and *dictamen* but it also drew upon, and ventured into, other disciplines such as philosophical, classical, and scriptural studies. The introduction of a philosophical, in addition to a purely practical, approach to grammatical studies came to be distinguished as speculative grammar suitable for more advanced students; and the deployment of texts taken from classical literature and the Bible furnished models to illustrate correct usage for both levels of instruction.[4] The fundamental rules of Latin grammar had been laid down by the fourth-century Donatus Grammaticus and his fifth-century successor Priscianus Caesariensis; and many, if not most, of the later grammarians took up the task of writing commentaries on these two forerunners in the field whose works, nevertheless, continued to circulate, as exemplified in the medieval holdings of the cathedral priories. The later medieval teachers were especially concerned to facilitate the study of the Latin language for those who, unlike the pupils of the classical grammarians, were not native speakers, and at the same time to take account of the influence of the writings of the speculative or philosophical grammarians whose interest centred on the theory of language.

A mid-twelfth-century Durham inventory of books records that a monk by the name of Guarinus had an untitled work of Donatus and the *De constructionibus* of Priscian.[5] Later

---

[1] See above, 159.
[2] Jean Leclercq, 'Le De grammatica de Hugues de Saint-Victor', *Archives d'Histoire doctrinale et littéraire du Moyen Age*, 14 (1943/45), 263–322 at 263. See also Hugh's specific reference to Donatus, Priscian, and Servius as the prescribed grammatical texts, Jerome Taylor (ed.), *Didascalicon*, 90.
[3] R. W. Hunt, *The Schools and the Cloister: the life and writings of Alexander Nequam*, ed. and revised by Margaret Gibson (Clarendon Press, Oxford, 1984), 41.
[4] It was soon perceived, however, that there was an unavoidable contradiction between models extracted from classical pagan literature and those drawn from Christian sources.
[5] *Cat. Vet. Durham*, 9; a second unidentified work by Donatus and written in English is listed in the same catalogue, ibid., 6. The *De constructionibus* of Priscian, or Priscian minor, consists of Books 17 and 18 of his *Institutiones grammaticae*. For Guarinus or Warin see *LVD*, iii, C.232.

book lists from Christ Church indicate that the Canterbury monks had multiple copies of both, those by Priscian being by far the more numerous.[6] Despite the existence of several fourteenth-century book catalogues and a large number of surviving books at Durham, only a few contain copies of the antique grammarians, and Donatus is surprisingly rare; the anglicized work attributed to Donatus in the earliest catalogue contains grammatical texts by the English monks Aelfric and Aelfric Bata, whose principal sources were, of course, Donatus and Priscian.[7] The name of Priscian occurs in the same Durham book list which records five copies of the *Institutiones grammaticae*, two of the *De constructione* and, in addition, six glossed copies of the former and two glossed copies of the latter.[8] There is also a surviving manuscript, Cambridge, Jesus College MS 28, which has been identified as one of the 'Duo Prisciani' bequeathed to the monks by Bishop Hugh Puiset in 1195.[9] Canterbury College also had a copy of the *Institutiones* available for consultation in 1443; it was listed in the *Libri logicales* section of the inventory and described as the gift of Thomas Becket.[10] Although for the most part we have no knowledge of where, when, and by whom these texts were used, at Durham the novices' book cupboard had, in 1395, the *De constructione* of Priscian; and there can be little doubt that it was well worn.[11]

As to the presence of Donatus and Priscian in other cathedral monasteries, our knowledge of Rochester as of Durham benefits from the fortunate survival of an early (c. 1202) catalogue. Listed there are what was probably the *Ars minor* of Donatus, four copies of Priscian's *Institutiones* and three of his *De constructione*.[12] Extracts from the writings of Donatus and Priscian are found at Worcester in a fourteenth-century compilation of grammatical treatises and include the latter's *Institutiones grammaticae*; this volume seems to have passed through the hands of several early fifteenth-century monks, among whom were Richard Lychefeld and Thomas Blackwell.[13] A second collection of *grammatica* at Worcester also includes the *Institutiones grammaticae* of Priscian, and a third copy of this work is now a volume among the Royal manuscripts.[14] It may have been one of these copies, or possibly

---

[6] James, *ALCD*, Eastry catalogue: the *Ars maior* of Donatus, book 3 (or *De barbarismo*), item nos 98, 676, 677, 847, 1364, 1575, 1622; Priscian, *Institutiones grammaticae* nos 389–95, 846, 1480 (*Priscianus Magnus* or *Maior*), and *De constructione* nos 396–7, 518, 1530, 1561 (1681, Priscianus minor), 1791. (The first eighteen items of the c. 1170 catalogue are also various writings of Priscian, several with monks names attached, ibid., 7). Four items in the Eastry catalogue include works of both Donatus and Priscian, item nos 847, 1481, 1533, 1622.

[7] This volume, now MS 154 in St John's College Oxford, was identified by its second folio incipit that had been noted in two Durham inventories of books in *Cat. Vet. Durham*, 33E[2] and 111E.

[8] *Cat. Vet. Durham*, 3–4; later items, e.g., 32H[1], 33G[2], P[1], 49M, 111G, 111A[2] may have been identical with some of the early copies. Note that the *De constructione* and the *De constructionibus* refer to the same work.

[9] *Cat. Vet. Durham*, 49N, 119; this volume is the *Institutiones*.

[10] Pantin, *Canterbury College Oxford*, i, 6, item no. 101.

[11] *Cat. Vet. Durham*, 81C; there was also a 'Liber unus cum diversis regulis grammaticalibus', ibid., 81A[2].

[12] Sharpe, *EBL*, at B79.178 (Donatus); B79.173, B79.175 (Priscian) and a Quintus Prisciani, B79.174, that had previously belonged to a Magister Robert, perhaps Robert de Waletone, prior of the cell of Felixstowe; see *BRECP*, 646.

[13] WCM MS F.61; these two monks are in *BRECP*, 840 (Lychefeld), 776–7 (Blackwell); the insertion of their names on the verso of the end folio may have been merely pen-trials.

[14] WCM MS Q.5 (eleventh century); BL MS Royal 15 B.xiv. Two short extracts, *Expositio Donati*, and *Ridimus Donati*, occur in WCM MS Q.50 a thirteenth-century grammatical compendium.

another one, that was among the thirty books accompanying three young Worcester monks to Oxford in the 1430s or 1440s.[15]

The *Ars minor* of Donatus also occurs in a surviving manuscript from Coventry cathedral priory where it was bound with other grammatical treatises and texts to form a useful compilation and work of reference. The Coventry compilation is written by a single hand of the first half of the fifteenth century, and it has been suggested that we have here a teaching text for use in the almonry school attached to the cathedral priory.[16] The manuscript also contains the grammatical treatise *Memoriale iuniorum* written by Thomas Hanney, a grammar master about whom little is known apart from the fact that he completed the text in Lewes in 1313.[17] In the same Coventry volume are found a metrical tract on grammar, extracts from Bede's *De arte metrica*, a dictaminal exposition and the *Speculum grammaticale* of the fourteenth-century Oxford grammar master, John of Cornwall; this last, dated 1346, was intended for advanced students in introducing them to a philosophical, rather than a purely pedagogical, approach to grammar.[18]

Similar collections of grammatical treatises are found in other cathedral monasteries. A Christ Church grammatical miscellany, for example, now in the British Library, contains a collection of anonymous treatises and notes of various dates between 1396 and 1504; in the late fifteenth century it had belonged to Reginald Goldston, who passed it on to a young monk, William Ingram, for whom he had acted as *senior* during the latter's noviciate.[19] In addition to a Latin/English glossary the volume provides information on the declension of nouns, conjugation of verbs, a *De modo latine loquendi*, and the second half of a versified grammar known as *Graecismus* written in the thirteenth century by the little known Everard of Béthune.[20]

Among the surviving books that formerly belonged to Worcester cathedral library there is an impressive number of *grammaticalia*, most of them still *in situ*. One volume, which contained the *Ars minor* of Donatus, as mentioned above, also contained an anonymous

---

[15] Sharpe, *EBL*, at B116.25; the monks were John Broghton, John Lawerne, and Isaac Ledbury, all in *BRECP*, 780–1, 830–1, 832–3 respectively. Priscian was required reading for university students and, although monks were presumably exempt from this prescription, they were no doubt advised to bring copies for reference.

[16] The manuscript is now Oxford, Bodley Auct. F.3.9 and the suggestion as to its probable use was made by J. N. Miner, *The Grammar Schools of Medieval England, A. F. Leach in Historical Perspective* (McGill-Queen's University Press, Montreal, 1990), 138. Almonry school boys and novices were sometimes taught together; see above 103.

[17] See the references under his name in Sharpe, *Latin Writers*, 659–60; and note the remark of R. W. Hunt, 'Oxford Grammar Masters in the Middle Ages', *Oxford Studies Presented to D. A. Callus*, Oxford Historical Society, new series 16 (Oxford, 1964), 175n.: he states that Hanney's treatise also occurs anonymously in another Coventry manuscript, Oxford, Bodley Auct. F.5.23, with the title 'Obiectiones Donati'. Hunt's paper on Oxford grammar masters has been reprinted in a collection of his papers edited by G. L. Bursill-Hall, *The History of Grammar in the Middle Ages*, Amsterdam Studies in the Theory and History of Linguistic Science, series III, vol. 5 (Benjamins, Amsterdam, 1980), 167–91. This same treatise is also in the Worcester grammatical compendium WCM MS Q.50; see above note 14.

[18] For a brief history of medieval grammar see G. L. Bursill-Hall, *Speculative Grammars of the Middle Ages, the Doctrine of Partes Grationis of the Modistae* (Mouton, The Hague/Paris, 1971), 15–36, especially 24–9.

[19] The manuscript is BL Harley 1587. Both Reginald Goldston I and William Ingram I are in *BRECP*, 172–3 and 209 respectively. It is quite probable that Ingram attended the almonry school before entering the noviciate and that he himself later taught the novices grammar; but evidence is lacking.

[20] See below 340–1.

commentary on the *Ars minor* and several treatises of the late thirteenth-century Oxford grammar master Richard Hambury, which, as Richard Hunt has suggested, were probably 'put together at the instance of someone in authority in the monastic community at Worcester', perhaps one of the monk students who had been at Oxford in the early years of the fifteenth century and whose names occur in the manuscript.[21] In the same manuscript there were also a short tract by John Leyland, an Oxford grammar master who died in 1433, Bede's *De schematibus et tropis* on figurative language in the Scriptures, the *Tropi* of William de Montibus, and *De tropis loquendi* of Peter Cantor; these last two aimed to clarify the meanings and remove the ambiguities and contradictions found in scripture texts.[22] Finally, a lengthy section of this volume is taken up by William Brito's *Expositiones vocabulorum Bibliae*, one of the popular dictionaries recommended for gaining mastery of Latin nomenclature in the reading of Scripture.[23]

The writings on syntax of two less well-known grammarians are bound into a thirteenth-century Rochester priory manuscript along with glosses on two books of the Old Testament and a collection of sermons. These are the *Summa in arte grammaticae* of Robert Blund, a canon of Lincoln in the 1180s, and the *Summa* or commentary on Priscian Minor, usually known by its incipit *Absoluta*, by Peter Hispanus about whom little is known.[24] The Worcester monks also acquired the latter treatise together with the *Summa super Priscianum* of Peter Helias, a French grammarian of the mid-twelfth century; this manuscript is written in a single, early, fourteenth-century hand and probably came to Worcester about a century later.[25] The only other cathedral priory known to have had the text of Peter Hispanus was Christ Church where its presence is recorded in the Eastry catalogue.[26]

Commentaries on Priscian and other grammatical texts were often bound into volumes of which the contents can only be classed as miscellanea. One of the treatises frequently found in these compilations is a work by the prolific and versatile English writer and teacher Alexander Nequam, who died in 1217 as abbot of the Augustinian house at Cirencester. His *Corrogationes Promethei*, a popular introduction to grammar, was accompanied by a commentary on difficult words in the Bible.[27] Canterbury, Coventry, Durham, Ely,

---

[21] See note 13 above for the names of the monks in this manuscript, WCM F.61 (fourteenth century). See Hunt, 'Oxford Grammar Masters', 164 (note 17 above); these treatises include Hambury's *Summa grammaticae*, and several of the unascribed pieces are probably also by him, ibid., 165.

[22] There is a lengthy section devoted to the *Tropi* of William de Montibus in Joseph Goering's *William de Montibus (c. 1140–1213), The Schools and the Literature of Pastoral Care*, Studies and Texts 108, Pontifical Institute of Mediaeval Studies (Toronto, 1992), 349–88.

[23] A detailed list of the contents is in Thomson, *Medieval Manuscripts in Worcester Cathedral*, 37–9. It must be borne in mind that Latin was a second language for the monks, only acquired after diligent study and practice. For Brito see above 145, 148.

[24] BL MS Royal 2 D.xxx. See R. W. Hunt, 'The Summa of Petrus Hispanus on Priscianus Minor', *Historiographia Linguistica*, 2 (1975), 1–23. For Blund see *BRUO*, i, 206–7.

[25] WCM MS F.137; Helias has been described by G. L. Bursill-Hall as the 'most famous master of grammar in the twelfth century' who was one of the earliest to 'make a systematic attempt to relate the ideas of the new philosophy (Aristotle) to the study of grammar', Bursill-Hall, *Speculative Grammars* (note 18 above), 28, 16. A second copy of Helias' *Summa* at Worcester is found in WCM MS F.99, but the date of arrival of this manuscript at Worcester is unknown.

[26] James, *ALCD*, item no. 1528; Dover priory also lists a copy in its catalogue dated 1389, bound in a volume with six other grammatical treatises, Stoneman, *Dover Priory*, at BM1.387g.

[27] In *The Schools and the Cloister: the Life and Writings of Alexander Nequam*, ed. and revised by Margaret Gibson (Clarendon Press, Oxford, 1984), the author, R. W. Hunt, remarks that the *Corrogationes* appears to be mainly lecture notes on Donatus and Priscian, 37–8.

Norwich, and Worcester all had one, or more than one, copy according to surviving books and inventories.[28] Nequam's *Corrogationes* was one of the few grammatical treatises by an Englishman to have circulated on the continent, in contrast to the writings of numerous European grammar masters which found a favourable reception in England generally, as well as in the cathedral priories.[29]

From the many and various surviving texts and manuals—all originating on the continent—that proved most popular in the later middle ages in England, Professor Bursill-Hall has made a selection based on a survey of over 1,300 manuscripts.[30] Five of these, which occur in cathedral priory manuscripts and library catalogues, will be selected for discussion here.[31]

The works of three Italian grammarians belong to Bursill-Hall's selected group: Papias of Pavia (fl. 1050), Hugutio of Pisa (d. 1210), and John Balbus of Genoa or John Januensis (d. post 1286). The *Elementarium doctrinae rudimentum* of Papias was a useful dictionary of geographical and historical names together with their declensions and derivations, the *Liber derivationum* of Hugutius an etymological dictionary, and the *Catholicon* of Balbus a combined grammar and lexicon. Canterbury, Durham, and Norwich are known to have possessed copies of all three; Worcester had Papias and Hugutio while Rochester's early surviving catalogues and manuscripts only record Papias.[32] As for Balbus, the *Catholicon* is first mentioned at Christ Church in a list of books repaired in 1508, but two copies are recorded over a century earlier in a Durham inventory of books and one of these remains *in*

---

[28] James, *ALCD*, Eastry catalogue, item nos 650, 727, 1249, 1633, *Promotheus* [sic] *et glose super eundem* (Canterbury); Oxford, Bodley MS Auct. F.5.23 (Coventry); *Cat. Vet. Durham*, 33D³, 49F, the 1391 and 1395 inventories, respectively recording two different texts, one of which may have survived in part as CUL MS Kk.5.10 (thirteenth century) (Durham); Oxford, Bodley MS Laud misc. 112 (Ely); Cambridge, Corpus Christi College MS 460, thirteenth/fourteenth century (Norwich); WCM MS F.1 mid-thirteenth century and Cambridge, Corpus Christi College MS 217, fourteenth century (Worcester). It should be noted that the surviving Durham copy, which also contains the vulgate Bible, states on fo 8v 'iste liber assignatur armariolo noviciorum per magistrum Thomam Swalwell STP' (*LVD*, iii, C.1221) in the early sixteenth century.

[29] The *Panormia* or *Liber Derivationes* of Nequam's older contemporary, Osbern Pinnock, monk of Gloucester, is another exception. Among the cathedral priories only Canterbury and possibly Worcester are known to have had copies of the *Panormia* while over twenty survive on the continent; James, *ALCD*, Eastry catalogue item no. 531 and WCM MS Q.37 which may not have reached Worcester before the sixteenth century.

[30] See G. L. Bursill-Hall, 'Teaching Grammars of the Middle Ages, the Manuscript Tradition', *Historiographia Linguistica*, 4 (1977), 1–29.

[31] This is, of course, an arbitrary selection.

[32] Several Canterbury copies of Papias are recorded in the Eastry catalogue, James, *ALCD*, item nos 344, 526, 614, 1358 (imperfect); for Durham see *Cat. Vet. Durham*, 49I (1395 inventory); the Norwich copies are identified in note 35 below; Bishop Hamo de Hethe bequeathed his copy to the cathedral church of Rochester in 1346, Sharpe, *EBL*, at B82.12; the Worcester copy, of late thirteenth-century date and probably acquired at Oxford, is still *in situ* as WCM MS F.20.

Hugutio is also in the Eastry catalogue, James, *ALCD*, item no. 530, bound with Bruto (*recte* Brito) and formerly in the possession of Thomas de Stureye junior (d. 1298). This same volume had migrated to Canterbury College by or before 1443; see note 33 below. Stureye also owned two other grammatical works of reference, Isidore's *Etymologia* and Osbern Pinnock's *Panormia*, *BRECP*, 296 (Thomas Stureye II); item no. 1478 in the Eastry catalogue, Huguntio [sic], may also be a copy of the *Liber derivationum*. A Durham *Hugutio* survives *in situ*, DCL MS C.I.20 (later thirteenth and fourteenth century), bound with Isidore's Etymologia; three copies are listed in the 1395 inventory, *Cat. Vet. Durham*, 49K, L, M², one of which may be the surviving manuscript. Worcester cathedral library has also retained its Hugutio, now WCM MS F.22, a later thirteenth-century acquisition, again probably via Oxford.

situ.[33] The libraries of both the Oxford colleges had a copy of the *Catholicon*; it was found at Canterbury College, along with two copies of Hugutio's *Derivationes* in 1443; the Durham College *Catholicon* was listed in a late fourteenth-century inventory under the heading *Libri de diccionibus difficilibus*.[34]

A copy of the *Elementarium* of Papias is included in a fifteenth-century list of books at Yarmouth priory, a cell of Norwich; Hugutio's *Derivationes* was at St Leonard's priory, also a cell of Norwich on the outskirts of Norwich, in 1424, while the *prima pars* of the *Catholicon* of Balbus was among the books purchased by Prior Simon Bozoun during his short rule (1344–52) over the cathedral community and its dependent cells.[35] May we presume that the *secunda pars* was in the cathedral library and that this volume was possibly intended to replace one that had been lost? May we further presume that this evidence of book circulation between the mother house in Norwich and its dependencies suggests the presence of sufficient copies of the above three texts in the cathedral library to allow a monk to take one with him when sent to serve in a cell?

Bursill-Hall has described Papias, Hugutio, and Balbus as glossators whose writings for the most part took the form of commentaries on Donatus and Priscian, but these were little more than dictionaries. Alexander de Villa Dei (*c.* 1170–*c.* 1250), Everard de Béthune (early thirteenth century), and the prolific John of Garland (d. *c.* 1272) on the other hand, were teachers in their own right.[36] Alexander's *Doctrinale magnum* and Everard's *Graecismus*, commonly found together, were among the most frequently occurring grammatical texts, which appear to have been more widely received by several of the English cathedral monasteries than that of the native born John of Garland, who was highly critical of both foreigners.[37] The *Doctrinale* and *Graecismus* were designed as teaching texts in competition with the antique grammarians and intended for use by those who had mastered the fundamental rules of grammar. The Durham and Worcester monks had copies of both, bound together in single volumes along with other items; Canterbury seems to have possessed the *Graecismus* of which there were four copies listed in the Eastry catalogue.[38]

---

[33] James, *ALCD*, item no. 156 p. 158 and Pantin, *Canterbury College Oxford*, i, item no. 4, p. 3 (Christ Church); *Cat. Vet. Durham*, 49 A and B of which B is now DCL MS B.I.31.

[34] Pantin, *Canterbury College Oxford*, i, item no. 4 p. 3 (*Catholicon*); ibid., item nos 5 p. 3 and 102 p. 6 (*Derivationes*, the former, bound with Brito had belonged to Thomas Stureye; see note 32 above). Pantin, 'Durham College Catalogues', 244, item no. 86.

[35] Sharpe, *EBL*, at B64.9 (Yarmouth), B62.39 (St Leonard's), B58.21 (Bozoun).

[36] R. W. Hunt, *The History of Grammar in the Middle Ages*, Collected Papers ed. with introduction by G. L. Bursill-Hall. *Amsterdam Studies in the Theory and History of Linguistic Science*, iii, *Studies in the History of Linguistics*, 5, Amsterdam—John Benjamins B. V. (1980), introduction, xvii.

[37] Bursill-Hall, 'Teaching Grammars' (note 30 above), 6–14. For John of Garland, who taught mainly in France see A. G. Rigg, *A History of Anglo-Latin Literature 1066–1422* (Cambridge University Press, Cambridge, 1992), 163–6 and Bursill-Hall, 'Johannes de Garlandia—Forgotten Grammarian and the Manuscript Tradition', *Historiographia Linguistica*, 3 (1976) 155–77. Two Worcester manuscripts, WCM Q.50 and BL Harley 4967, included several of Garland's grammatical treatises and a Durham manuscript, DCL C.IV.26, also contains his work; the 1524 inventory of books at Canterbury College lists 'Johannes de Gerlandia de artificio ?grate/orate elocucionis', James, *ALCD*, item no. 284, p. 172.

[38] DCL MS C.IV.26, late thirteenth century (Durham), and a second incomplete copy of the *Graecismus* has survived in Bodley MS Laud Lat. 12 (Oxford, Durham College); WCM MS F.147 was probably written at Worcester in the late thirteenth century and there is a second copy of the *Graecismus* in WCM MS Q.50 (thirteenth century) with other grammatical material (Worcester); James, *ALCD*, Eastry catalogue, item nos 631, 687, 688, 1482, and an incomplete text survives in BL MS Harley 1587 that is dated 1396 (Canterbury). It should be noted that the *Doctrinale* and *Graecismus* are often found together and, in their turn gave rise to a number of commentaries often anonymous.

The English Benedictine Cathedral Priories: Rule and Practice 341

In the 1424 inventory compiled by the outgoing prior of St Leonard's next to Norwich the contents of the library included the *Graecismus*, while the community at the cathedral in the heart of the city had acquired the *Doctrinale* according to an early sixteenth-century select list; presumably it was not a recent addition to the library unless as a second or replacement copy.[39] One *Graecismus* can be associated with two Christ Church monks, Eudo de Bocton and Richard de Merstham. It would appear that the volume was relegated to the library before or at the time of Bocton's death in 1309, and that it was subsequently borrowed by Merstham, who had been professed in 1328. Since it was recorded as lost by 1338 it may have been assigned to him in the noviciate.[40] The *Graecismus* appears to have continued in use at Canterbury into the late fifteenth century when a volume of *grammatica* containing the second part of Everard's text was passed on from Reginald Goldston to William Ingram; the former was the latter's *senior* in the noviciate.[41] Several generations of Worcester monks may also be associated with copies of the *Graecismus*, Thomas de Hindelep' for one, who was sacrist in the 1280s and, less certainly, Robert de Hambury, John de Fordham, and John de Dudley who, taken together, spanned the years 1365 to 1438.[42]

The wide range of topics included in the medieval study of grammar has been exemplified by the contents of some of the volumes described above in which the basic rules of Latin construction are found in conjunction with particular aspects of grammar expounded by Bede, Peter Cantor, William Brito, and others. In addition to the known grammarians there were numerous anonymous or unidentified texts, many of them found in *grammatica* collections.[43] The breadth of the subject material covered by both known and unknown authors emphasizes the medieval view of grammar as not only a discipline for the young but as the gateway to the understanding of texts, both religious and secular, which in turn opened the way toward a true understanding of man and his relation to the world.[44] The goal of learning today is directed toward the same understanding, but the premises have shifted in a world dominated by secular desires and ambition.

Because the field of grammatical studies included the skills necessary for all forms of literary composition in both prose and verse the art of writing letters in accordance with the approved style was considered an essential part of monastic and clerical education. To this end manuals of instruction were prepared, usually accompanied by model letters illustrating the different classes of correspondence both official and personal.[45] These letter collections

---

[39] The St Leonard's *Graecismus* is listed in Sharpe, *EBL*, at B62.43; the *Doctrinale*, ibid., at B59.19.

[40] *BRECP*, 92 (Bocton) where I have incorrectly assigned the book to his contemporary John de Bocton; ibid., 243 (Merstham).

[41] The volume is now BL MS Harley 1587 (see also note 38 above); Reginald Goldston I and William Ingram I are in *BRECP*, 172–3 and 209 respectively.

[42] Hindelep's name is on fo 1 of WCM MS F.147 and the other three names appear as pen-trials on an end fly leaf of WCM MS Q.50. These monks are all in *BRECP*, 822 (Hindelep'), 816 (Hambury), 805–7 (Fordham), 797–9 (John de Dudley I) or 799 (John Dudley II); but note that only for Dudley I have I made reference to MS Q.50. R. M. Thomson identified Hambury and Fordham in *Medieval Manuscripts in Worcester Cathedral*, 150, for which I thank him; and it is he who suggests that the reference there is probably to the second John Dudley, ibid.

[43] For example, item no. 956 in the Eastry catalogue lists seven treatises in one volume including a 'dictionarius, libellus de regulis artis grammatice, libellus de prepositionibus, ars legendi in ecclesia', James, *ALCD*, 93. Again, a Master Hamo before 1202 left the Rochester monks 'Bina volumina de glossis diversis. Unum de Rhetorice aliud de dialectica et Grammatica cum pluribus summis', Sharpe, *EBL*, at B79.211.

[44] Bursill-Hall, 'Johannes de Garlandia', 155 (note 37 above).

[45] The historical value of all types of medieval correspondence has long been recognized as Martin Camargo pointed out in '*Ars dictaminis, Ars dictandi*', Typologie des Sources du moyen âge occidental', fasc. 60 (Brepols, Turnhout, 1991), 56–9.

were invaluable in furnishing examples to be imitated and adapted according to the particular circumstances for which a letter was to be written. The cathedral priory book collections display a variety of dictaminal texts and treatises, among which the skills required for epistolary composition figured prominently; but some of the masters of *dictamen*, or *dictatores*, dealt with other prose forms as well. Some of the texts remain unidentified, known only by the titles supplied by medieval cataloguers, the *Liber de modo dictandi*, for example, which appears three times in the Eastry catalogue at Canterbury along with two copies of a *Libellus epistolaris* in the same catalogue.[46] Another anonymous text also occurring in a Christ Church manuscript is one of the few extant copies of the *Regina sedens rhetorica* which forms part of a miscellany mainly devoted to *dictamen* and law. The volume was acquired by the monk Henry Cranbroke in 1452 possibly when he was still a student at Oxford.[47] There he may also have procured another dictaminal miscellany comprising *artes dictandi*. This latter contained short instructive treatises, one by Thomas Merke and another possibly by Simon Alcock, English writers who were active in the late fourteenth and early fifteenth centuries.[48]

Letter collections such as those of Peter de Blois and Peter de Vinea were found in several of the monastic cathedral libraries. The former, although of French birth and education, spent some years in England where he became archdeacon of Bath in the 1180s and produced his first letter collection for distribution.[49] Probably at the same time he composed a *Libellus de arte dictandi rhetorice* to accompany it, but the only surviving copy of this manual belonged to the monks of Reading; nevertheless, one may presume that it must have circulated with the letters.[50] The Italian jurist and diplomat Peter de Vinea has recently been described as 'the greatest stylist and rhetorician in the Latin language of the thirteenth century'.[51] Both men had developed their epistolary skills in the chanceries in which they were employed in England and on the Continent, and the fact that both were influential at the English court of their day ensured that their model letters were in popular demand.[52] The Canterbury monks were able to consult one of these dictaminal collections in Prior Eastry's day recorded as 'Epistole P. Blesensis abbreviate' in his catalogue and a fuller version, 'Epistole Petri Blesensis', listed in the section entitled *Libri poetrie* in the 1501

---

[46] James, *ALCD*, item nos 630, 684, 1427 and 676, 1574.

[47] This treatise has been edited and transcribed from the Canterbury manuscript, now BL MS Royal 10B.ix, by Martin Camargo in *Medieval Rhetorics of Prose Composition*, five English *Artes Dictandi* and their tradition, vol. 115, Medieval and Renaissance Texts and Studies (Medieval & Renaissance Texts & Studies, Binghamton, New York, 1995), 169–221. For Henry Cranbroke II see *BRECP*, 132.

[48] The manuscript is now Oxford, Bodley Selden supra 65. Merke, a monk of Westminster and later bishop of Carlisle, wrote the *Formula moderni et usitati dictaminis* which is described by R. G. Davies in the *ODNB* as a 'guide to letter-writing for apprentice estate managers' and therefore not out of place in monastic libraries. To Alcock, who may have taught at Oxford and was incorrectly named as Reginald in this manuscript, is ascribed a *De arte dictaminis*. See Pantin, *Canterbury College Oxford*, i, 112–13 and Camargo, *Medieval Rhetorics* (note 47 above), 110 where the contents of the manuscript are described.

[49] See the excellent summary of his career by Richard Southern in *ODNB*.

[50] The manuscript is now CUL Dd.9.38. In the article cited in the previous note Southern affirms the authenticity of Peter of Blois' authorship of the *Libellus*, a view which Camargo had challenged in 'The Libellus de arte dictandi attributed to Peter of Blois', *Speculum*, 59 (1984), 16–41. See also Sharpe, *Latin Writers*, 418–19 under Blois.

[51] Marie-Claire Gerard Zai, 'Pier della Vigna: a Latin manuscript discovered in the Lilly Library at Indiana University', *Scriptorium*, 32 (1978), 259–63 at 260.

[52] While Peter of Blois died *c*. 1212, Peter de Vinea was active during the first half of the thirteenth century.

inventory of the warden at Canterbury College Oxford.[53] The Eastry catalogue also included the much less common 'De modo loquendi et scribendi epistolam' of the early thirteenth-century Bolognese master Guido Faba.[54]

The Durham monks seem to have acquired a wider selection of dictaminal texts and treatises that did not, as far as we know, include Peter of Blois; but the *De forma dictandi* of Peter de Vinea and a collection of his letters have been preserved to this day among the Durham manuscripts in a volume containing other dictaminal material.[55] A late fourteenth-century paper register of letters, probably compiled by Robert de Lanchester while chancellor of the Durham chapter in the 1380s, was preserved for use as a formulary in all types of correspondence.[56] It was kept in the treasury at the north end of the west walk of the cloister beside other dictaminal treatises recorded there in 1421 by the then chancellor John Fishburn; these included two *Summae dictaminis*, one by Thomas de Capua (d. c. 1249), the other by Richard de Pophis (fourteenth century).[57] The *Practica dictaminis* of Laurence de Aquileia was also available at Durham with its useful compendium of epistolary salutations.[58]

The correspondence of Peter de Blois was bound with treatises of Priscian and Peter Helias in a Royal manuscript that belonged to Worcester.[59] Peter de Vinea's letters, together with some letters from a collection of *Epistole* by Thomas de Capua, which formed part of his *Flores dictaminum*, were also among volumes formerly belonging to Worcester and now in the Royal library.[60] The monks also had a second copy of the latter

---

[53] James, *ALCD*, item no. 1227 (p. 107) and Pantin, *Canterbury College Oxford*, i, 26, item no. 296. Dover Priory catalogue of 1389 lists both of these, Stoneman, *Dover Priory*, at BM1. 98p, 110h, 133a, 135a, all incomplete (Blois); BM1. 327d is the *Libellus*, see note 50 above. Lena Wahlgren's *The Letter Collections of Peter of Blois*, Studia Graeca et Latina Gothoburgensia 58 (Acta Universitatis Gothoburgensis, Göteborg, 1993) does not include reference to the provenance of the manuscripts she cites.

[54] Presumably the *Summa modo dictaminis*, James, *ALCD*, item no. 1508. There is another copy listed as *Dictamina M. Guydonis* in the same catalogue, item no. 528. For brief notes on Faba see N. Denholm-Young, 'The Cursus in England' in *Collected Papers on Mediaeval Subjects* (Blackwell, Oxford, 1946), 48–50, and Charles B. Faulhaber, 'The *Summa dictaminis* of Guido Faba' in James J. Murphy ed., *Medieval Eloquence, Studies in the Theory and Practice of Medieval Rhetoric* (University of California Press, Berkeley, 1978), 85–111.

[55] DCL MS C.IV.24 (thirteenth/fourteenth centuries); it is listed in a 1395 inventory of the cloister library, *Cat. Vet. Durham*, 48AG.

[56] Now DCL MS C.IV.25; see W. A. Pantin, 'English Monastic Letter-Books' in *Historical Essays in Honour of James Tait* (Manchester, 1933), 201–22, especially 210–11. For Lanchester see *LVD*, iii, C.948.

[57] *Cat. Vet. Durham*, 123–4, 124 I and P. The *Summa* of Richard de Pophis, compiled from papal registers, is one of the items in a volume inscribed with the name of Prior John Wessington (1416–46) (*LVD*, iii, C.1028) and now in the British Library MS Lansdowne 397. Durham MS C.IV.25 also contains dictaminal treatises, one by William Whalley, a monk of Whalley (n.d.), and several by anonymous authors; see also note 70 below. For Fishburn see *LVD*, iii, C.1031.

[58] Now Oxford, Bodley MS Laud misc. 402.

[59] BL MS Royal 15 B.iv. There may have been another copy of Blois in the Worcester cathedral library, viz., MS Q.25, which was listed as missing in 1821 according to J. K. Floyer and S. G. Hamilton in the *Catalogue of Manuscripts in the Chapter Library of Worcester Cathedral* (James Parker & Co, Oxford, 1906), 173, where they print a note from the chapter minutes of that year. On the other hand it may be the same volume, because the *Catalogue of Royal Manuscripts* states that 15 B.iv 'was not identified in the old catalogues of the Royal collection', ii, 155; moreover, the itemized description in both catalogues is a partial match and one cannot be sure if Floyer and Hamilton were quoting more than an incomplete summary of the contents.

[60] BL MS Royal 10 B.x (fourteenth century) contains both Peter de Vinea's letters and those of Thomas de Capua.

entitled *Summa dictaminis* which, however, may not have entered the cathedral library before *c.* 1530.[61] In 1303/4 the Norwich cloister acquired a collection of the letters of Peter de Blois itemized in the cellarer's account for that year *pro septem peciis epistolarum Petri Blesensis* which the prior, Henry de Lakenham, probably commissioned because the cost was included under the expenses of the *camera prioris*.[62]

Neither of the Peters occurs among the identified books formerly belonging to Rochester cathedral priory, but it must be borne in mind that there are no surviving library catalogues later than 1202. However, the monks there were able to consult a text by Geoffrey de Vinsauf which the monk compiler of the inventory of books in the *commune librarium* in that year listed only as *Versus magistri Ge' Vinisalvi*.[63] The author, an Englishman who probably lectured in Paris as well as in Northampton, produced a lengthy poem, *Poetria nova*, which proved to be the 'single most successful textbook on rhetorical composition written during the middle ages.' According to Martin Camargo it was 'accepted as the definitive synthesis of rhetoric and poetics, of theory and practice'.[64] One copy survives from Canterbury in an early fifteenth-century manuscript of *Artes dictandi* probably acquired by Henry Cranbroke as a monk student at Oxford in the middle of the century.[65] A Durham *Poetria nova* is one of the items found in a manuscript in the *communi armariolo . . . infra spendimentum* in 1391 and still *in situ* today.[66]

Despite the international popularity of the *Poetria nova*, amply attested by the large number of surviving manuscripts, the cathedral monasteries may have been more impressed by Vinsauf's 'Documentum de modo et arte dictandi et versificandi' and by a later augmented and anonymous version of it in which many passages in the latter were copied from the former.[67] The shorter version, which is considered to be authentically Vinsauf, was in the library at Canterbury College bound in the same volume as the *Poetria nova*.[68] There are also two surviving copies of the short *Documentum* formerly in the monastic library at Durham; both are fifteenth century and both are inscribed with names of monks. One which had belonged to Richard Bell, prior 1464 to 1478, was placed in the *novo armariolo in claustro* in the 1480s or 1490s.[69] The other copy remains at Durham in a register of letters, a manuscript which first occurs in an inventory of the monk chancellor John Fishburn in 1421.[70] A thirteenth-century copy of the short *Documentum* belonged to the Worcester

---

[61] WCM MS Q.62; see Thomson, *Medieval Manuscripts in Worcester Cathedral*, 158.

[62] Sharpe, *EBL*, at B57.19; the amount paid was 5s. 10d. For Lakenham, reputed to have been a *magister* and a collector of books, see *BRECP*, 531–2. A grammatical text (now Cambridge, Gonville and Caius College MS 136) assigned to the cell of Norwich at (King's) Lynn and ascribed to a prior, John Palmer, by Neil Ker (in *MLGB*, 127, 280) is a mistaken identification.

[63] Sharpe, *EBL*, at B79.124b where it has been suggested that this was probably Vinsauf's *Poetria nova*; however, since the latter was dedicated to Pope Innocent III (1198–1216) it is improbable that this work could have reached Rochester in time to have been included in the catalogue.

[64] Both statements were made by Martin Camargo, who probably overstates his case: the first is in *ODNB* under Geoffrey de Vinsauf (Galfridus Anglicus); the second is in '*Tria sunt*; the Long and the Short of Geoffrey of Vinsauf's *Documentum de modo et arte dictandi et versificandi*', *Speculum*, 74 (1999), 935–55 at 949.

[65] See above note 48 where the manuscript in which it occurs, Oxford, Bodley MS Selden supra 65, is described. This is probably the same volume which is listed only by its incipit *Papa stupor mundi* in a 1524 inventory of the Canterbury College library, James, *ALCD*, item no. 177 (p. 169).

[66] DCL MS C.IV.23.

[67] See Martin Camargo's article '*Tria sunt*' in note 64 which compares at length the 'short' and the 'long' *Documentum*.

[68] That is Oxford, Bodley MS Selden supra 65; see above note 48.

[69] It is now Cambridge, Sidney Sussex College MS 56. Prior Bell passed it on to another Durham monk, William Law; see Watson, *MLGB Supplement*, 86 under Bell, Ricardus. Bell is C.1109 and Law C.1169 in *LVD*, iii.

[70] Now DCL MS C.IV.23; see *Cat. Vet. Durham*, 124L.

monks; and the small, semi-independent community at Dover, with their own sizeable library numbering some 450 volumes in 1389, possessed Vinsauf's *Poetria nova*.[71]

Several of the cathedral monasteries are known to have made use of the works of other grammarians and lexicographers who were English by birth. One of these authors was Adam de Balsham, more frequently known as Petit Pont after the school in Paris where he taught in the first half of the twelfth century. His major work was the *Ars disserendi*, the aim of which was to instil the correct use of language in order to safeguard against faulty thinking. This volume was found at Rochester priory before 1202; and his more popular lexicographical *De utensilibus ad domum regendam*, a dictionary of everyday terms, was one item in a thirteenth-century grammatical compendium at Worcester.[72] In 1391 the Durham inventory of the Spendement listed Adam's lexicon under the title *Epistola Adae Parvipontani—partes magistri*; like the Worcester collection of grammatical texts the Durham volume also contained both Adam's and Alexander Nequam's *De nominibus utensilum*.[73] The presence among cathedral priory book collections of John of Garland's grammatical and lexicographical works, which may be compared with the similar writings of the above two earlier authors, has already been mentioned.[74] The *Panormia* of the mid-twelfth-century Gloucester Abbey monk Osbern Pinnock, also referred to above, should be considered in this group of English writers in the field of grammar of whom the earliest was Bede.[75] In his remote northern cell of Jarrow in the early eighth century this Benedictine monk did not confine himself to writing history and biblical commentaries; he composed several grammatical texts including *De arte metrica* dealing with the art of poetry, 'De schematibus et tropis sacrae scripturae' explaining difficult words in the Bible, and *De orthographia*, a glossary.[76] The earliest copy of the *De schematibus* at Worcester dates from the late tenth century and the latest was purchased by Prior More in 1531, a printed version of 1527. To what extent can this be taken as an indicator of continuing use?[77] Moreover, there were additional copies, one in a fourteenth-century volume of *grammatica* mentioned above, another of approximately similar date—both of these still remaining at Worcester—and a third in which only a brief extract has been preserved.[78] Rochester cathedral priory also furnishes evidence of the probable persistent use of the *De arte metrica* and the *De schematibus*: they were provided by a monk named as *magister* G. de Stratton not later than 1122/3 and probably consulted by a mid-fifteenth-century monk, Thomas Wybarn,

---

[71] The Worcester *Documentum* is now Cambridge, Corpus Christi College MS 217; Worcester MS Q.79, also Vinsauf, did not belong to the cathedral until long after the Dissolution. The Dover *Poetria*, bound with extracts from Priscian, is now Cambridge, Trinity College MS 624.

[72] Sharpe, *EBL*, at B79.163 (Rochester); WCM MS Q.50 (Worcester) which has been described above, 336 n.14. For a recent assessment of Adam's *De utensilibus* see Tony Hunt, *Teaching and Learning Latin in Thirteenth-Century England*, 3 vols (Woodbridge, 1991), i, 165–71; it is sometimes known as *Phaletolum* after its incipit.

[73] *Cat. Vet. Durham*, 33D³; the title in full was *Epistola Adami Balsamiensis ad Anselmum*. There were five copies of Adam's *Phaletolum* listed in the 1391 Dover Priory catalogue, Stoneman, *Dover Priory*, at BM1.408e, 412c, 440h, 440i, 442f.

[74] See note 37 above.

[75] See note 29 above.

[76] An informative summary of Bede's life and writings is provided by J. Campbell in *ODNB*; for his biblical exegesis see above 105 and for his historical achievements see below 353–4.

[77] The tenth-century copy is preserved at Worcester as MS Q.5; it also contains the *De arte metrica* and was probably in the monastic library by the twelfth century. Professor Thomson suggests that it may have come from the Christ Church scriptorium, *Medieval Manuscripts in Worcester Cathedral*, 120. The latest is listed in the record of More's acquisitions in Sharpe, *EBL*, at B117.63.

[78] WCM MSS F.61, and F.123; Cambridge, Corpus Christi College MS 217.

who took the trouble of adding his name on fo xv verso.[79] Extant manuscripts of the grammatical works of Bede formerly belonging to Canterbury and Durham cathedral libraries have yet to be found and references to copies in catalogues and inventories are sparse. In Prior Eastry's catalogue, for example, there is a single unambiguously identifiable reference to the *De arte metrica* and the *De schematibus* in one volume. Late fourteenth-century Durham library inventories place a copy of the *De arte* in the Spendement, and a copy of both in the cloister book cupboards.[80]

Finally, the sole known survivor of the Winchester monks' collection of grammatical works is a text which has so far not been identified as having belonged to any of the other cathedral priory libraries. This is the *Promptuarium parvulorum clericorum* attributed to Geoffrey the Grammarian. It is probably the earliest English–Latin dictionary and, as such, would surely have been well thumbed by Benedictine novices.[81] Its presence at Winchester prompts one to imagine what might have been its neighbours on the cathedral library bookshelves; and its apparent absence elsewhere may, in part, be the result of the dearth of book catalogues and inventories of the second half of the fifteenth century.[82]

The question arises as to how many of the above grammatical texts were placed in the hands of novices; to this Rodney Thomson offers his considered reply based on the surviving manuscripts in Worcester cathedral library. For him these would include Nequam's *Corrogationes*, Papias's *Elementarium*, Hugutio's *Liber derivationum*, Everard de Béthune's *Graecismus*, Pinnock's *Panormia*, and, of course, Donatus and Priscian and their later commentators like Peter Helias' *Summa super Priscianum*.[83] In all cases the reading of such texts would have been preceded and accompanied by oral instruction, a challenging task since the grammar being inculcated was that of a foreign tongue.[84]

Attention has recently been drawn to the possibility that the Benedictines may have made a far from insignificant contribution to the teaching of grammar, rhetoric, and *dictamen* in medieval England. The suggestion was put forward by Martin Camargo while taking note of the collections of key texts found among the books belonging to student monks at Oxford. Among the monks he names Henry Cranbroke of Canterbury College and Richard Bell and William Law of Durham College.[85] To these should be added John Lawerne and his fellow

---

[79] The manuscript in question is now Cambridge, Trinity College MS 1128; Stratton and Wybarn are both included in *BRECP*, 640 and 649–50 respectively. Bede's *De orthographia* is not included in the 1122/23 catalogue where the other two treatises are recorded at B77.67 in Sharpe, *EBL*; however, it occurs in the 1202 catalogue, ibid., at B.79.176.

[80] Eastry catalogue, James, *ALCD*, item no. 93. The Spendement inventory, dated 1391, is in *Cat. Vet. Durham* where the entry is at 20C², and the extensive 1395 list of books in the cloister book cupboards located 'in diversis locis infra claustrum' includes both, ibid., 64–5F.

[81] The *ODNB* article under Geoffrey the Grammarian is not reliable; see R. Sharpe, 'Thomas Tanner (1674–1735), the 1697 Catalogue and *Bibliotheca Britannica*', in *The Library*, 7th series, 6 (2005), 381–421, at 409–17.

[82] The *Promptorium* or *Promptuarium* remains in the cathedral library at Winchester where it is MS 15; it was edited by A. Way, Camden Society, old series, 3 vols (1843–65). See Sharpe, *Latin Writers*, 124.

[83] View expressed in conversation with the author.

[84] See above 65–6, 70, Episcopal injunctions reveal that speaking Latin was an uphill struggle. For example, Archbishop Sudbury in January 1377 ordered that the [Christ Church] monks *magis utantur loqui latinam*, Reg. Sudbury, fo 32.

[85] M. Camargo, 'Toward a Comprehensive Art of Written Discourse: Geoffrey of Vinsauf and the Ars dictaminis', *Rhetorica*, vi (1988), 167–94 at 178. For Cranbroke see Henry Cranbroke II, *BRECP*, 132 and for Bell and Law, *BRUO*, i, 161–2 and ii, 1111–12 respectively. Cranbroke was at Oxford in the 1440s, Bell in the 1430s, and Law in the 1460s. The careers of Bell and Law are also in *LVD*, iii, C.1109 and C.1169.

monks Isaac Ledbury and John [Broghton] of Worcester, and Thomas Wybarn of Rochester.[86] As Camargo points out it was often the Oxford trained monks who taught the novices; in so doing they may have been at least to some degree playing their part in attempting to implement Benedictine policy aimed at circumventing the faculty of theology requirement that graduation in arts was a necessary preliminary to the study of theology.[87] In addition, Camargo goes so far as to postulate that the 'Benedictine interest in rhetorical training seems to have led not only to the composition of new texts but also to the recovery of texts that had lain unused in monastic libraries since the thirteenth century.'[88] In support of this hypothesis he cites the anonymous *Tria sunt*, the earliest copies of which are of thirteenth-century origin. The survival of a number of fifteenth-century versions, such as those at Worcester and the Oxford colleges of Canterbury and Durham, points to its renewed popularity and leads Camargo to suggest that it may have been 'rediscovered' by monks who, in surveying their library holdings for suitable teaching material in grammar and rhetoric, came across the *Tria sunt* which had been left unnoticed for a century or more.[89]

Neither the contribution of Benedictine monks to the teaching of Latin grammar nor the degree of aptitude and standard of achievement found among the majority of their student novices can ever be accurately assessed. The lack of sufficient documentation to enable us to answer these and other related questions can be at least partly explained by the fact that much of the teaching was conducted orally and has left no written evidence. That the professed monk was adequately competent and comfortable in both the spoken and written language of the Church can, however, hardly be doubted.[90] The fact that the cathedral monasteries, as we have seen, were on the whole well stocked with a variety of grammatical teaching aids and manuals strongly suggests that novice masters in particular and members of the community in general kept abreast of developments in the field.

---

[86] Lawerne and his companions were at Gloucester College in the 1430s and 1440s taking with them some thirty volumes for which a list of titles has survived; it included Priscian's *Institutiones grammaticae*, see Sharpe, *EBL* at B116 and *BRECP*, 830–1 (John Lawerne I), 832–3 (Isaac Ledbury), 780–1 (John Broghton); Sharpe points out that the name Broghton is in part illegible, with the result that there is a slight doubt as to the correct reading. Wybarn was at Oxford in the 1460s with unknown and unnamed books in his possession. What is certain, however, is that he inserted his name and verselogo in a number of Rochester volumes, one of which is an early twelfth-century *Grammatica* described above (345–6); see *BRECP*, 649–50 for Wybarn.

[87] Camargo, 'Tria sunt', 953–4 (note 64 above).

[88] Ibid.

[89] Ibid., 937, 954. The fact that the *Tria sunt* incorporates a substantial amount of material from Geoffrey de Vinsauf's *Documentum* has led to its frequent inclusion among his works.

[90] One has only to read the letters composed by William Glastynbury to his Christ Church brethren at Canterbury College to observe the facility with which he expressed himself without the benefit of university training; see the entry under his name in *BRECP*, 169.

APPENDIX II
History

Benedictine monks did not confine their interests to the reading of historical works; they were also actively involved to the extent that they took up the pen to make their own contributions. This should not be the cause of surprise when we recall their own historical origins which, by AD 1200, were already in the distant past, and when we realize that they saw themselves as heirs of a living tradition the continuity of which they were concerned to preserve and transmit to their successors.[1] Christianity itself also looked back to its historical foundations and its expansion in the first few centuries after the death of Christ. The stories of missionary enterprise accompanied by perseverance and zeal in the conversion of western Europe, including the British Isles, remained to inspire future generations. The medieval approach to history was thus strongly influenced by the conviction of its universal significance as the definitive account of the redemption of fallen man. The diversity of forms and methods used in its recording, however, does not conceal the unanimity of purpose, which was to ensure the preservation, in the collective memory, of past events and deeds as lessons for future inspiration and guidance. However, the significance of historical study in the eyes of medieval monks and clerics and, indeed of everyone else, was not limited to the history of the church and the religious orders but encompassed all aspects of secular history, for these too served to demonstrate the unfolding of the divine plan in the rise and fall of earthly powers and kingdoms. Moreover, it is important to recognize that it was essential for the monks to maintain a record of their possessions, that is of their lands, rents, churches, and so on, and of their rights and privileges, many of them hard won at great expense. When controversy arose the evidence was thus readily available to defend their claims. Inventories of muniments, cartularies, and registers were, per se, a vital historical record to be preserved at all costs and handed on from one generation of monks to the next.[2]

For our present purposes selections will be made from the many types of ecclesiastical and secular history found in the cathedral priory book collections: examples of world or universal history, regional and local history, and the history of individual monasteries and the cathedral priories will be included. Some writings are no more than annals, recording major events year by year; others with more detail may be termed chronicles, while a few others are more ambitious in attempting to present a critical analysis of the events recorded with a degree of competence which has won the praise of historians today.[3] In summary, it is widely acknowledged that the twelfth century saw an impressive flowering of historical writing, which subsequently lost momentum, giving place to a more modest output in the

---

[1] There is no recent up-to-date study of the English Benedictine order in the middle ages but see the groundbreaking work of Knowles, *MO* and *RO*. For a résumé and critique of the writings of English medieval historians, including monks, see the monumental survey by Gransden, *Historical Writing*.

[2] This is not to exclude an interest in history for its own sake; man's innate curiosity to learn about the past is certainly a factor to be taken into account.

[3] William of Malmesbury provides an example here; see the collection of essays by R. M. Thomson in his *William of Malmesbury*, rev. edn. (Boydell, Woodbridge, 2005), especially Chapter 2, "William as Historian and Man of Letters", 14–39.

fourteenth and fifteenth centuries, most of which is disappointingly commonplace and of limited interest.[4]

In a tentative reconstruction of the cathedral priory holdings in the realm of history we must reluctantly accept the recurrent stumbling block of the untraced losses that have left gaps that can be filled only by conjecture. The advantage of a comparative study such as this, however, is that it is possible to obtain a more comprehensive picture by surveying the surviving corpus of books and inventories of books from the nine monastic houses which are the subject of the present study. This facilitates a potential replacement of at least some of the now absent volumes in one cathedral priory on the strength of volumes found in other cathedral priories. Communication between the major Benedictine establishments in England was both regular and frequent with regard to many common interests and problems as has been made clear in this study. Monk precentors and librarians, intent upon obtaining specific texts through purchase or loan, would have made inquiries among their counterparts in other monastic communities and negotiated with them over the acquisition of books both by means of loans, possibly for copying purposes, and by commissioning copies for purchase.

The historical collections of Canterbury and Durham would have proved more than adequate to meet the needs and satisfy the interests of even a seriously inquisitive scholarly monk. At Norwich one of the fourteenth-century priors has left evidence of his keen interest in obtaining historical texts, and the three library catalogues from Rochester, dated between the 1120s and 1202, already show an extensive collection that included historical writers, from antiquity as well as from later periods, side by side with patristic and classical authors.[5] Whether this interest was maintained in later years is unknown because of our scanty knowledge of the policies that were operative in monastic libraries including those of the cathedral monasteries. The general aims and specific objectives of those in charge can rarely if ever be glimpsed. In fact, with regard to acquisitions and development of collections, there could never have been a consistent or long-term policy because almost everything was dependent on the individual librarian. Since he was very frequently the monk who had been assigned to the obedientiary office of precentor, which required his daily concern with the direction of the monastic chant and the care of all liturgical books, he would scarcely have had time to do much more than to try to make sure that the library was kept in satisfactory order.

Several monastic cathedral librarians are known to have had a sufficiently keen interest in history to prompt them to produce historical works in one form or another. Senatus, precentor of Worcester *c.* 1175, for example, who described himself as *bibliothecarius*, wrote a life of St Wulstan in the form of an abridged version of the *Vita* which had been composed by William of Malmesbury sometime between 1113 and 1142 at the request of the Worcester monks.[6] At Christ Church Canterbury the historian Eadmer, a younger contemporary of Archbishop Anselm and a *familiaris* in the archiepiscopal household, is known to have held the office of precentor in the community, probably in the 1120s, and

---

[4] Why was this so?

[5] I refer to Prior Simon Bozoun whose list of purchases is given in Sharpe, *EBL*, at B58. His predecessor in the priorate, Henry de Lakenham, *BRECP*, 531–2, was also a bibliophile but his interests were not noticeably historical; see Dodwell, 'History and Norwich Monks', 41; Miss Dodwell estimates that Lakenham may have possessed eighteen books, ibid.

[6] See *BRECP*, 871–2, and *ODNB* under Senatus Bravonius. The only surviving copy from a cathedral priory is at Durham, DCL MS B.IV.39B which also contains a life of St Oswald, like Wulstan bishop of Worcester and later archbishop of York; this too may have been the work of Senatus, see Mason, *St Wulfstan*, 299.

with it almost certainly that of librarian. He wrote several saints' lives but is better known for his *Historia novorum*, a biography of Anselm's public life, and a *Vita Anselmi*, a record of the archbishop's personal and private life.[7] In the first decade of the twelfth century Symeon was precentor of Durham when, between 1104 and 1107, he wrote a history of the church of Durham at the command of his monastic superiors; it covers the history of the bishopric from 635 to 1096, that is from its foundation on Lindisfarne to Symeon's own day, and its earliest title was *Libellus de exordio atque procursu istius hoc est Dunhelmensis ecclesie*.[8]

There are a number of other cathedral-based monks who are not named as either precentors or librarians but who compiled and recorded historical events in the twelfth, thirteenth, and early fourteenth centuries; some of these are known by name: Gervase at Canterbury and Geoffrey de Coldingham and Robert de Graystanes (Greystones) at Durham are among the most well known. Gervase was a monk of Christ Church during the second half of the twelfth century and the first decade of the thirteenth century, an eventful period which included the murder of Archbishop Thomas Becket in 1170, the disastrous fire of 1174, and the bitter disputes with Archbishops Baldwin and Hubert Walter; his *Chronica* runs from 1100 to his own day. In addition he produced less detailed works of history, a *Gesta regum* and an *Acta pontificum Cantuariensis ecclesie*, both of these largely dependent on other sources.[9] Geoffrey de Coldingham wrote a continuation of Symeon's chronicle covering the years 1152 to 1215, the probable date of his death. Graystanes, a university graduate, is credited with writing a further continuation which dealt with the period from 1215 until his death in 1334. His contribution became part of a composite official record known as *Gesta episcoporum Dunelmensium* which is mainly concerned with domestic affairs.[10] Bartholomew de Cotton of Norwich is another; he

---

[7] See *BRECP*, 142–3. They are printed in M. Rule (ed.), *Eadmeri Historia novorum in Anglia*, Rolls Series 81 (Longman, London, 1884), and R. W. Southern (ed.), *Life of St Anselm Archbishop of Canterbury by Eadmer*, Oxford Medieval Texts (2nd edn, Clarendon Press, Oxford, 1972). See also R. W. Southern, *Saint Anselm and his Biographer: a study of monastic life and thought, 1059–c. 1130* (Oxford, 1963). Manuscript copies of the *Historia novorum* at Christ Church occur in the Eastry catalogue: James, *ALCD*, item nos 188, 189 (described as *maior*); one of these is now Cambridge, Corpus Christi College MS 452.

[8] For his writings see J. H. Hinde (ed.), *Symeonis Dunelmensis opera et collectanea*, Surtees Society 51 (Andrews, Durham, 1868), and T. Arnold (ed.), *Symeonis monachi opera omnia*, 2 vols, Rolls Series (Longman, London, 1882–5). See also Rollason, *Symeon of Durham*. (A new edition of the *Libellus* by Rollason for Oxford Medieval Texts was published in 2000.) Durham MS A.IV.36 is an early thirteenth-century copy of the writings of Symeon. Cambridge, Trinity College MS 1227 is largely extracts from his historical works and dates from the twelfth century, perhaps not long after Symeon's death *c.* 1130; both of these manuscripts belonged to Durham. Meryl Foster has aptly described the *Libellus* as 'a skilful piece of propaganda . . . intended to demonstrate the continuity between that [the Lindisfarne] community and the monks and bishops of the new Benedictine cathedral priory [at Durham]', the underlying theme bearing an implicit warning to Cuthbert's successors not to underestimate his sanctity and the prestige and privileges of his monastic community, Foster, 'Durham Priory', 14. For Symeon's biography see *LVD*, iii, C.40 where there is a detailed list of his writings and the manuscript sources.

[9] Gervase's historical works were edited by W. Stubbs, *Gervasii Cantuariensis Opera Historica*, Rolls Series 73, 2 vols (Longman, London, 1879–80). His career and achievements have been well summarized by Gransden, *Historical Writing*, i, 253–60, and more recently by G. H. Martin in *ODNB*. The Eastry catalogue in James, *ALCD* lists one copy, item no. 284; it is now BL MS Cotton Vespasian B.xix. For Gervase see also *BRECP*, 168.

[10] These Durham chronicles were edited by J. Raine, *Historiae Dunelmensis scriptores tres*, Surtees Society 9 (Durham, 1839); see also Foster, 'Durham Priory', 12–36 and *ODNB* under their respective names. For Graystanes' theological interests see above 114, 145, and for his career, *LVD*, iii, C.801; Coldingham is in ibid., C.194.

The English Benedictine Cathedral Priories: Rule and Practice 351

held the most senior obedientiary office there, that of master of the cellar, in the early 1280s. Most of his *Historia anglicana* consists of extracts from earlier writers; but some details of local history, such as the revolt of Norwich townsmen in 1272, their invasion of the cathedral precinct and the resulting conflagration were no doubt his own work.[11] The name of Richard, prior of Ely in the 1180s, has been attached to all or part of the *Liber Eliensis* while his contemporary, Thomas, may also have contributed to the text.[12] In answer to a request from his former prior at Winchester Richard de Devizes composed a *Chronicon de tempore regis Ricardi primi* in the 1190s. A recent evaluation of his work concludes that it 'represents monastic learning in the last phase of its pre-eminence before the emergence of the universities'.[13] In the first half of the twelfth century, a generation or two before Senatus of Worcester, a monk of that house by the name of John had compiled a *Chronica chronicarum*, a world history from creation to 1140, making extensive use of the text of an Irish monk, Marianus Scotus, who had died at Fulda in 1082. The evolution of John's text shows that he kept in touch with his monastic contemporaries at Durham and Canterbury who were also engaged in historical writing. There are fairly convincing reasons to suggest that Nicholas de Norton, a Worcester sacrist in the final decade of the thirteenth century, was also responsible for a section of John's Chronicle covering his own day.[14] At Rochester *c*. 1300 an *Annales ecclesiae Roffense*, which was then being compiled, was later attributed to Edmund de Hadenham; much of it is a version and continuation of the *Flores Historiarum* of Roger de Wendover, a monk of St Albans, with interpolations relating to Rochester.[15]

---

[11] A brief biographic account is in *BRECP*, 496–7, but it fails to mention his *Compilationes de libro Britonis* which is based on Brito's *Expositiones vocabulorum Bibliae* (now Cambridge, Corpus Christi College MS 460). Some of Cotton's historical writings have been edited by H. R. Luard, *Bartholomæi de Cotton, Monachi Norwicensis, Historia Anglicana; A.D. 449–1298*, Rolls Series, 16 (Longman, London, 1859). Antonia Gransden describes Cotton as an archivist because of his inclusion of the texts of many documents, *Historical Writing*, i, 444–5. Three copies formerly belonging to Norwich monks survive: DCL Ms.1 in the NRO which has Ralph de Fretenham's name inscribed (he was master of the cellar in 1273/4); BL MSS Royal 14 C.i, together with Cotton Nero C.v, a thirteenth/fourteenth-century text belonged to Geoffrey de Smalbergh; a section of Oxford, Magdalen College MS Lat.53 (thirteenth century) is inscribed with the name Thomas de Plumsted (d. *c*. 1323); see *BRECP*, 513, 556, and 548–9 respectively.

[12] For the most recent summary of Prior Richard, see the *ODNB* (under Richard of Ely) written by E. O. Blake, who transcribed and edited the *Liber Eliensis*. Written in the late twelfth century, this survives as Cambridge, Trinity College MS 1105, and a slightly later extant version remains in the hands of the dean and chapter of Ely. In his introduction Dr Blake discusses these and other related manuscripts, ibid., xxiii–xxvii.

[13] G. H. Martin, in *ODNB*; the text of the *Chronicon* has been edited by J. T. Appleby, Nelson's Medieval Texts (Nelson, Edinburgh, 1963). Cambridge, Corpus Christi College MS 339 (twelfth/thirteenth century) may have belonged to St Swithun's and also BL MS Cotton Domitian xiii, fos 1–87 (thirteenth century).

[14] This is the conclusion of P. McGurk in his article on John in *ODNB*; he is currently editing the text of which two volumes have appeared: *The Chronicle of John of Worcester*, vol. 2 (450–1066) with R. R. Darlington, Oxford Medieval Texts (Clarendon Press, Oxford, 1995), vol. 3 (1067–1140), Oxford Medieval Texts (Clarendon Press, Oxford, 1998). The former Worcester manuscript, now Trinity College Dublin, 503 (twelfth century) is the principal text. Another early twelfth-century copy now Oxford, Corpus Christi College MS 157, described as Florence of Worcester, was in the hands of the Worcester monk Thomas Streynsham in 1480, *BRECP*, 880. For Norton, see *BRECP*, 858–9.

[15] In the *ODNB*, M. C. Buck dismisses Hadenham as the 'supposed annalist', but then goes on to doubt his very existence for want of evidence. The evidence is, in fact, in the entry under Hadenham's name in *BRECP*, 608; and extracts of the annals are printed in *Anglia Sacra*, i, 341–55 from BL MS Cotton Nero D.ii. A recent suggested attribution of authorship of the annals names John de Reynham [Rainham], prior of Rochester (1262–83, 1292–4); see the references in Sharpe, *Latin Writers*, 299 and

Anonymous chronicles and diverse other historical records were among the volumes that formerly found a place among the volumes in cathedral priory book cupboards and presses or were preserved in the muniment collections. In most, but not all, cases the presence of these and other books and documents was due to the initiative of the successive individual holders of the office of precentor, librarian, chancellor (at Durham), or a vigorous and forward-looking prior with a strong interest in history; such were priors Henry de Lakenham (1289–1310) and Simon Bozoun (1344–52) at Norwich.[16] The fact that chronicles and their later continuations were often, as we have seen, little more than compilations based on a variety of sources, some of which are yet to be identified, makes it certain that these same sources in one form or another must have circulated among the cathedral priories, major Benedictine houses, and those of other religious orders. Some would have been borrowed for copying *in extenso* and others for copying selected extracts to combine with matters of local interest. These productions were gradually superseded by even less enterprising historical undertakings, as at Ely where several unknown monastic authors in the wake of Thomas and Richard continued into the late fifteenth century; but they more frequently limited themselves to organizing the cartularies and other documents in the Ely archives and to recording the episcopal careers of the successive incumbents of the see.[17]

However, a few exceptions to this downward trend may be found among late fourteenth- and fifteenth-century cathedral monks, three of whom were gratefully remembered by their respective communities. One of these, John de Malverne, who was prior of Worcester from 1395 to 1409, had served as precentor in the 1370s; during that time there are entries on his accounts recording the updating of a chronicle, described as *magnas chronicas pendentes* in the cathedral where it would have been available for public reading.[18] It was likely during these years that Malverne wrote a supplement to Ranulph Higden's *Polychronicon*, beginning where Higden had ended in 1348 and continuing until 1377.[19] John Wessington of Durham, another prior, was serving in the office of chancellor/librarian in the year that Malverne died. During his tenure he completed a major overhaul of the convent archives and of the book collections, the latter being rehoused in the new library by 1418 two years after his election to the priorate. According to R. Barrie Dobson this building was his 'greatest achievement as custodian of the Durham manuscripts'.[20] A recent judgement by the same writer concludes that although Wessington cannot be classed as a historian in the strict sense, he was 'one of the most historically minded of all late medieval English Benedictine monks'.[21] Two of Wessington's historical productions are worthy of note

---

BRECP, 629 (John de Reynham I). Roger de Wendover's historical works are described and evaluated in Gransden, *Historical Writing*, i, 359–60.

[16] Individual monks who purchased, copied, or were given historical texts may have retained them for life but they were consigned to the library on the possessor's death.

[17] *Anglia Sacra*, i, 631–74 has transcribed some of this material, taken from former Ely manuscripts like BL Cotton Domitian xv (thirteenth to fifteenth century), Cotton Titus A. i (twelfth to fifteenth century), Cotton Nero A. xv and A. xvi (fifteenth century), Oxford, Bodley MS Laud misc. 698 (fifteenth century).

[18] Greatrex, 'English Cathedral Priories and . . . Learning', 405 where the references to the specific accounts are given. Details of Malverne's monastic career are in *BRECP*, 843–4 under John de Malverne I. There is evidence of a hanging *tabula* at Durham used for historical notices, Piper, 'Historical Interests of Durham Monks', 307.

[19] A description of the *Polychronicon* will be found below 354–5; for Malverne's continuation see Gransden, *Historical Writing*, ii, 56.

[20] R. B. Dobson, *Durham Priory*, 365; further details of the new library and of Wessington's role in its construction and development are in ibid., 362–9.

[21] I am quoting from Dobson's article on Wessington in *ODNB*.

here: a new history of the church of Durham, and a history of the Benedictines in England. The former, *De primordio et progressu sedis episcopalis et monachicae conversationis ecclesiarum Lindisfarnensis et Dunelmensis*, incorporates extracts from Bede, Symeon, and others as well as copies of documents that would have proved useful in the event of legal challenges. The *De fundatione monasteriorum nigri ordinis S. Benedicti infra regnum Angliae* is a kind of historical guide furnishing details of the foundation of some forty English houses of the Black Monks.[22]

John Stone was a monk of Christ Church Canterbury for over half a century between c. 1417 and c. 1480 and therefore his historical endeavours lie outside the dates assigned to this study. However, his work furnishes us with an illustration of the narrowing range of interest and focus in the century before the Dissolution. Stone's chronicle is almost entirely concerned with community affairs interspersed with obituaries of his brethren but, as such, is useful for some of its graphic delineations.[23] None of these cathedral monks produced historical works to match the calibre of the national histories of William of Malmesbury in the twelfth century, Matthew Paris in the thirteenth, and his successor Thomas Walsingham in the late fourteenth/early fifteenth, or the scope of universal chronicles like that of Ranulph Higden in the fourteenth century. Nevertheless, these were also Benedictines of major abbeys, the first from Malmesbury, the next two from St Albans, and the fourth from Chester.[24] The St Swithun's monk Thomas Rudborne is also slightly beyond the scope of this study in that he was writing in the mid-fifteenth century; however, his historical treatises, especially the *Historia major de fundatione ecclesiae Wintoniensis et successionis episcoporum ejusdem ad annum 1138* and an *Epitome historiae majoris*, which ranges from Brutus to Henry VI, should be noted as they were much admired by his contemporaries.[25]

A survey of the manuscripts and treatises devoted to history that were available for reading and study in the cathedral priory libraries should begin with the writings of Bede, who lived, taught, wrote, and died at the monastery of Jarrow which five centuries later became a cell of Durham.[26] It is to be expected, therefore, that copies of his *Historia ecclesiastica gentis Anglorum* would have a prominent place in the cathedral priory.[27] In fact, only one copy of the *Ecclesiastica historia* occurs in a twelfth-century catalogue of books kept in the *armariolo* but a later catalogue of 1395 lists two copies, both of which are bound in

---

[22] See Dobson, *Durham Priory*, 379–81. Four copies of the *De fundatione* survive, the earliest and fullest being in Durham MS B.III.30. The History has been preserved in Oxford, Bodley MS Laud misc. 748, London, Lincoln's Inn, MS Hale 114, and BL MS Cotton Claudius D.iv, all former Durham priory manuscripts.

[23] Stone's biographical details are in *BRECP*, 293; most of the chronicle has been printed (from Cambridge, Corpus Christi College MS 417) in Searle, *Lists of Christ Church*, 5–118.

[24] For William of Malmesbury see above 348 n.3.

[25] Wharton's *Anglia Sacra*, i, 179–286 prints the *Historia major*; and the Epitome is found in Oxford, All Souls College MS 114. For Rudborne's career see *BRECP*, 731 and the *ODNB* where an *Annales breves ecclesiae Wintoniensis* is also included; he also wrote a short history of Durham to 1083. In addition, there was a Winchester monk, a John Exeter, who was either Rudborne's contemporary or lived a century later; one of them wrote a brief account of the cathedral priory and its bishops that ends in 1439, *BRECP*, 690–1.

[26] Bede's relics had been surreptitiously removed to Durham at an earlier date; see Piper, *Durham Monks at Jarrow*, 3–5.

[27] It has been edited by B. Colgrave and R. A. B. Mynors in the Oxford Medieval Texts series (Clarendon Press, Oxford, 1969). A satisfactory English rendering of the text is that of Leo Sherley-Price, *Bede, A History of the English Church and People* (Penguin Classics, Harmondsworth, 1955).

volumes of historical treatises that are still extant.[28] Several copies of the History are recorded in Prior Eastry's catalogue at Christ Church, one described as *vetus*, another as *nova*.[29] An extant Norwich copy occurs in Prior Simon Bozoun's list of purchases; it is bound with the last section of Roger de Wendover's *Flores historiarum* and may have been commissioned by Bozoun as the writing is in a fourteenth-century hand, the cost being stated as 10s.[30] The 1122/3 catalogue of Rochester books includes a two-volume set of Bede's *Historia Anglorum* which in 1202 was seemingly replaced by Hubert the precentor whose name is inscribed on the second folio of this latter volume, now preserved in the British Library.[31] An earlier, tenth/eleventh-century text belonged to St Swithun's but perhaps not before the fourteenth century when parts of it were marked for use as a lectionary, today it remains *in situ*.[32] The only known History by Bede at Worcester is a surviving post-Dissolution copy, but there are extracts in Old English in a surviving text which may have been at Worcester before the twelfth century. However, it would be most unlikely that no version in the original Latin of Bede was available for the cathedral monks.[33]

It may be a coincidence of the survival of particular manuscripts but evidence suggests that in its day Ranulf Higden's *Polychronicon*, or universal history, was a popular choice for many cathedral priory monk readers. The author's intention was to relate the history of mankind from creation to his own day, that is the mid-fourteenth century. In so doing he appealed to an English monastic audience because he gave them 'a clear and original picture of world history based upon medieval tradition, but with a new interest in antiquity, and with the early history of Britain related as part of the whole.[34] Norwich cathedral priory possessed at least four copies that still survive, one of them purchased by Prior Bozoun for 20s. in a volume of historical texts that included extracts from classical authors Gerald of Wales and Marco Polo. Since

---

[28] In medieval book lists Bede's history has various titles including this one, *Historia Anglorum*, and *De gestis Anglorum*; the name of the author is often omitted and so there is a possibility, as in the twelfth-century catalogue in *Cat. Vet. Durham*, 2, that the *Historia ecclesiastica* of Eusebius, the bishop of Caesaria (d. c. 339), probably in the translation of Rufinus, was intended. The later copies are also in *Cat. Vet. Durham*, 56 G and N under *Libri historiarum* and repeated in the same list, 65 G² and N under *Libri venerabilis Bedae* and *Baedae, Gildae* respectively. The first of these (56 G and 65 G²) is preserved at Durham as MS B.II.35 and contains a fifteenth-century *tabula* to Bede's history; the second (56 N and 65 N) is now BL MS Burney 310 which was copied by the scribe William de Stiphol for the monk Uthred de Boldon, probably in the 1380s. There was also an *Ecclesiastica historia* sent to Durham College Oxford before 1416, *Cat. Vet. Durham*, 40 A². Another incomplete version appears in a list of books in the Spendement in 1416 under *Vitae Sanctorum*, bound with Bede's life of Cuthbert, ibid., 107 C. Boldon is C.888 in *LVD*, iii.

[29] James, *ALCD*, Eastry catalogue item no. 187, *Historia Anglorum vetus* (which specifies that it was written in five books, thus validating the identification); item no. 356, *Hystoria Anglorum nova*; item nos 522 and 911, *Hystoria ecclesiastica* (probably, Rufinus' translation of Eusebius); also item no. 150 of the books repaired in 1508 (p. 157), 'Venerabilis Bede presbiteri super historiam ecclesiasticam'.

[30] Now Cambridge, Corpus Christi College MS 264; the list of purchases is in Sharpe, *EBL*, at B58.

[31] Sharpe, *EBL*, at B79.50 in one volume, now BL MS Harley 3680; the earlier listing is in Sharpe, *EBL*, at B77.65. For Hubert see *BRECP*, 613.

[32] WCL MS 1; for a detailed description see Ker, *MMBL*, iv, 578–9.

[33] The History given to the cathedral in the seventeenth century is in a hand of the fifteenth century and is now WCM MS F.148. The Old English text is now BL MS Cotton Otho C.i, vol. 2; for further details see N. R. Ker, *Catalogue of Manuscripts containing Anglo-Saxon* (Clarendon Press, Oxford, 1957), no. 182.

[34] John Taylor in *ODNB*, and see also his *The Universal Chronicle of Ranulf Higden* (Clarendon Press, Oxford, 1966). Like all medieval authors Higden incorporated into his text much material from earlier sources, but the unifying narrative is refreshingly his own.

Bozoun died in 1352 the book must have been acquired soon after its completion.[35] Two later fourteenth-century copies were also available for the monks, and a fourth is embellished by a portrait of Peter de Dereham, who was master of the cellar between 1379 and 1390.[36] It seems almost certain that Worcester cathedral priory had a *Polychronicon* since John Malverne would have wanted to consult it when working on his continuation.[37] The Bath monks' *Polychronicon* was produced by a scribe named John Lutton and acquired by a monk named William Salford *quem Deus coronet in celestibus*.[38] The two Canterbury copies are written in fourteenth-century hands, although one of them may not have been at Christ Church before John Broke obtained it; he was professed in 1459 and was still active in 1511.[39]

Another universal history, that of the thirteenth-century French Dominican Vincent de Beauvais, had served as a model for Higden and was one of the sources on which he relied.[40] A late thirteenth-century copy of a section of Beauvais' *Speculum historiale* bears the name of John de Cawston, who served as master of the cellar at Norwich in the mid-1280s and as chamberlain in the 1290s. A massive volume in pristine condition, that must have been acquired soon after the author's death c. 1264, it lacked an adequate finding aid in the search for information until Prior Simon Bozoun procured a *Tabula super Speculum historiale* for 8s. between 1344 and 1352.[41]

The second part of the *Speculum historiale*, dated AD 1448, survives at Durham, and a *Repertorium super Speculum historiale* was assigned to a new book cupboard in the cloister by Prior John Auckland (prior 1484–92).[42] While the *Repertorium*, a form of index, written in a fifteenth-century hand, may have served as a convenient guide to the hefty original there is no evidence to allow us to assume the latter's presence. Nevertheless, it seems unlikely that part of the *Speculum* would have been sought if the other part was not present on the library shelf. Like their Norwich brethren the Canterbury monks had an index to the *Speculum*, a mid-fourteenth-century manuscript still in its original home. However, the earliest datable evidence that both the *Speculum* and the *Tabula* were in the monastic library

---

[35] This manuscript, listed in Bozoun's inventory, Sharpe, *EBL*, at B59.29, is now BL MS Royal 14 C.xiii.

[36] These are now BL MS Harley 3634 and BL Add. MS 15759; Peter de Dereham's portrait, with a scroll reading 'celorum munus petro det trinus et unus' is now in Paris, B. N. MS Lat. 4922. See *BRECP*, 500, where another incomplete version, Oxford, Bodley MS 316, is described as possibly the work of the Norwich cathedral *scriptorium* although not produced for its monastic library.

[37] See above 352.

[38] The monk's name and inscription are on the last folio, 124v, of BL MS Arundel 86; the problem is that there are two William Salfords and Lutton's dates are unknown; the hand is fourteenth/fifteenth century; for the Salfords see *BRECP*, 40.

[39] Oxford, Bodley MS Rawlinson B.191 has been assigned to Christ Church because of its distinctive marks in the margins. Broke's copy is now CUL MS Ii.3.1; it is beautifully written, has rubricated chapter numbers and headings, and is provided with an alphabetical index. For Broke see *BRECP*, 101.

[40] There must have been a copy available at Chester abbey, but no record of its presence survives. For Higden's sources see Gransden, *Historical Writing*, ii, 47–50.

[41] Sharpe, *EBL*, at B58.19. Book four of the *Speculum historiale* is now Oxford, Magdalen College MS lat. 180; it has been dated by Ralph Hanna in his recently completed catalogue (p. 852) in which he also refers to a second monk, Geoffrey de Wroxham, whose name can be distinguished under a bookplate. These two monks are in *BRECP*, 494 (Cawston) and 574–5 (Wroxham).

[42] The second part of the *Speculum* is DCL MS B.I.32 and the *Repertorium* is Cambridge, Jesus College MS 45; see Piper, 'The Libraries of the Monks of Durham', 228 and *passim*. John of Tynemouth's *Historia aurea*, a lesser known and inferior world history, from creation to the mid-fourteenth century was in the Durham library by and probably before 1395, *Cat. Vet. Durham*, in 3 parts, 56 D, E, F; it is now in LPL MSS 10–12.

is the year 1508 when they were sent for repair by William Ingram, *custos* of the shrine of St Thomas.[43]

Several national histories, that is those concerned mainly with English affairs, were penned by monastic authors, William of Malmesbury and Matthew Paris and his successors at St Albans being the most well known. In his unremittingly diligent search for information William travelled far from his abbey; before 1130 he had visited Canterbury and Worcester, and he also made visits to Bath, Coventry, Durham, Rochester, and Winchester.[44] From his contacts with monks of these monasteries one might expect to find copies of his completed volumes in their libraries. One copy of both his *Gesta regum* and *Gesta pontificum* commissioned by Elias, while very probably serving as precentor, is recorded in the Rochester library catalogue of 1202; a second copy of similar date inscribed with the name of Alexander precentor has survived, as has also a third, an early fourteenth-century copy of the *Gesta regum* which belonged to John de Whytefeld.[45] St Swithun's monks may have had a twelfth-century volume of the *Gesta regum* if a sixteenth-century list now in the Vatican library can be relied on and if BL MS Arundel 35 is the book in question.[46] The only trace of a possible text of the *Gesta pontificum* at Canterbury is a book with this title in the Eastry catalogue; however, there are several works by other writers with the same or a similar title.[47] Prior Simon Bozoun may have picked up a *Gesta pontificum* for 12s. although the description names only the author and omits the title.[48]

As to Matthew Paris and the school of historians at St Albans, their writings or, more frequently, extracts of varying length, were copied *ad libitum* and incorporated into the texts of other writers who did not hesitate to adapt their borrowings to suit their individual objectives. Selections from and sections of these St Albans productions are still to be discovered in some of the many volumes which consist of a collection of historical (and other) texts bound together. Attributions of authorship, even when provided, can be confusing if not misleading, and caution is necessary. In fact, the *Chronica majora* and other histories by Matthew Paris do not seem to have circulated among the cathedral monasteries. The *Flores historiarum* of Roger de Wendover was, however, without doubt a popular choice among Norwich monks, and its historical span extended from creation to the

---

[43] The *Tabula* is now Canterbury Cathedral MS 100 (B.12), and in 1508 it was kept in close proximity to the *Speculum*. Ingram's list of repaired volumes is in James, *ALCD*, where they are item no. 141 (p. 157, *Tabula*), and item no. 151 (p. 158, *Speculum*). For William Ingram I see *BRECP*, 209. Peter Comestor's *Historia scholastica* is of a similar genre as Higden's *Polychronicon* and Beauvais' *Speculum* except that it was confined to the period covered by the Bible.

[44] R. M. Thomson, *William of Malmesbury* (Boydell, Woodbridge, 2003), 72–3.

[45] Sharpe, *EBL*, at B79.120 and B81.19; Elias was later prior from *c.* 1214 to 1217, see *BRECP*, 602 (Elias III, which is corrected and amplified here). A new edition of the *Gesta Regum Anglorum* with commentary has been published in the Oxford Medieval Texts series by R. A. B. Mynors, R. M. Thomson, and M. Winterbottom, 2 vols (Clarendon Press, Oxford, 1998–9); the *Gesta Pontificum Anglorum* has also been completed by R. M. Thomson and M. Winterbottom in the same series, 2 vols (Clarendon Press, Oxford, 2007). The copy procured by Alexander, now BL MS Harley 261, does not feature in the list of books he copied or acquired, Sharpe, *EBL*, at B80; Alexander II, *BRECP*, 589, omits this manuscript. John de Whytefeld's copy is now Oxford, Bodley MS Hatton 54; for his monastic career see *BRECP*, 647.

[46] The Vatican Library reference is supplied by Sharpe in *EBL*, at B113.12 and B4; the name 'St Swithun' can be found written in capital letters on fo 33.

[47] James, *ALCD*, item no. 298, where the title does specify *Gesta pontificum Anglie*.

[48] Sharpe, *EBL*, at B58.28; when Bale visited Robert Talbot, prebendary of Norwich in the mid-sixteenth century, he noted a copy of the *Gesta pontificum*, ibid.

year before the author's death in 1236.[49] Three *Flores* manuscripts from Norwich survive: one was Prior Bozoun's selection, a fourteenth-century volume for which he paid 20s.; two others of similar date were noticed by Bale, one of which he attributed to the fictitious Westminster 'Matthew', and the other he recorded as consisting only of book six.[50] The Winchester book collection included an early fourteenth-century *Flores*, and the Rochester volume that contained the *Chronicon Roffense* included other historical texts one of which was the *Flores*.[51]

Histories of the ancient and early medieval world are most frequently represented in the cathedral priory collections by Dares Phrygius, Josephus Flavius, and Eusebius bishop of Caesarea. The Rochester monks' early twelfth-century catalogue describes a volume in which were bound together Dares' *De excidio Troiae* and a collection of other texts including the *Historia Britonum*.[52] A Norwich copy is also bound in a book of mixed contents, some of which were previously in the Benedictine alien cell of Horsham St Faith.[53] The items described in a Canterbury volume in the Eastry catalogue are remarkably similar to those at Norwich, an indication that they may be closely related. Prior Eastry himself had a *Historia Troianorum* listed among his books on civil law, and John Holyngborne bought a copy in 1503 from *quodam fratre* for 20d.[54] The first/second-century Jewish historian Josephus wrote the *Antiquitates iudaicae* and *De bello iudaico* to relate both the former greatness and the subsequent downfall of his own people. Both volumes occur at Rochester in the early twelfth century and two-volume sets of similar date were also acquired by Canterbury and Durham.[55] The prefaces only, along with the prefaces of other ancient and medieval writers on history, were available at Norwich where they were bound with a copy of the

---

[49] R. Vaughan, *Matthew Paris* (Cambridge University Press, Cambridge, 1958), 154, where he says that although the *Chronica majora* was 'the fullest and most detailed of all mediaeval English chronicles [it] was virtually unknown outside St Albans in the later Middle Ages'. It was edited by H. R. Luard in the Rolls Series, 7 vols, 57 (Longman, London, 1872–84); the *Flores* is in the same series, 3 vols, 84 (Longman, London, 1886–9) ed. by H. G. Hewlett.

[50] The Bozoun *Flores* is bound with miscellaneous extracts and is now Oxford, Bodley MS Fairfax 20; Bale probably saw BL MS Cotton Claudius E.viii and Cambridge, Corpus Christi College MS 264 which is book six of the *Flores*. These three books are listed and described in Sharpe, *EBL*, at B58.27, B61.6 ('Matthew'), B61.10 (book six). At least part of the contents of LPL MS 188, which includes a version of the *Flores*, has the pressmark of Norwich priory library and may have been an additional copy.

[51] Both manuscripts survive: Oxford, Bodley MS Laud misc. 572 (Winchester), BL MS Cotton Nero D.ii (Rochester).

[52] The contents of this volume are now divided into two separate manuscripts, BL Royal 15 A.xxii and Cotton Vespasian D.xxi; a detailed description is given in Sharpe, *EBL*, at B77.91 and B79.100.

[53] Now Cambridge, Trinity College MS 884; see Watson, *MLGB Supplement*, 50.

[54] James, *ALCD*, item no. 244 and now BL MS Cotton Vespasian B.xxv (twelfth century). For Holyngborne see *BRECP*, 202 under John Holyngborne II; his purchase is recorded on a flyleaf. Eastry's personal copy is in James, *ALCD*, item no. 61 (p. 145). There are several other entries in the Eastry catalogue that have similar titles but fail to name an author, e.g., item nos 709, 820, 1421 (*Historie Troianorum et Britonum*); no. 431 is, however, *Daret de bello Troiano versifice*. BL MS Add. 45103 (a later thirteenth-century abridgement) has been identified as the copy repaired by William Ingram in 1508, James, ibid., item no. 161 (p. 158).

[55] The Rochester volumes are described in Sharpe, *EBL*, at B77.90. The Canterbury Josephus is in the Eastry catalogue, James, *ALCD*, item nos 339 and 340 and it survives as CUL MS Dd. 1. 4 (part 1) and Cambridge, St John's College MS 8 (part ii); both of them must have been well used since they were singled out for repair in 1508, James, ibid., item nos 149, 148 (p. 157). The Durham copy, listed in the 1395 inventory in *Cat. Vet. Durham*, 56 A, remains at Durham as MS B.II.1; there is also a Josephus Antiquitatus in the twelfth-century catalogue, *Cat. Vet. Durham*, 1.

Polychronicon.[56] At least five of the cathedral priory libraries had the *Historia ecclesiastica* of Eusebius in the Latin translation by Rufinus; it was, and remains a principal source for Christian history from the time of the Apostles to the early fourth century. Two Canterbury manuscripts are listed in the Eastry catalogue both of which have survived, and one of which belonged to the subprior Salomon.[57] Richard, a monk of Rochester, gave his brethren an early twelfth-century Eusebius, and Prior Bozoun at Norwich bought a copy in the mid-fourteenth century.[58] The Durham copy, dated AD 1381, was acquired by Uthred de Boldon by means of a commission to the scribe William de Stiphol to make a copy for him.[59] The earliest surviving copy among cathedral priory manuscripts is at Worcester. It is an early tenth-century work of continental manufacture which may have come to Worcester by way of Canterbury.[60]

For monks who displayed an interest in far away peoples and places Norwich cathedral library offered Martin Polonus' *Chronica pontificum et imperatorum*, a copy of which was spotted by Leland during his visit in the 1530s, and Jacques de Vitry's *Historia orientalis* procured by Prior Bozoun.[61] Durham and Canterbury both possessed Polonus, the Durham copy having belonged to Robert de Brackenbury who served in the office of infirmarer in the 1360s, and the Canterbury copy appearing in the Eastry catalogue as *Cronica de gestis pontificum et imperatorum* without authorial attribution.[62] Ralph de Pretelwelle, a Christ Church monk who must have been much occupied serving as warden of manors and treasurer in the 1280s and 1290s, also appears to have had a keen interest in distant lands and peoples; his name was attached to a *Hystoria de lege et natura Saracenorum, et de vita et origine et lege Mathomethe [sic] prophete*.[63]

The prolific and provocative writer Gerald of Wales not only pursued a career in the church in the late twelfth and early thirteenth century, but also produced several books on the history and geography of Wales and Ireland. That some of these found favour with cathedral monks is attested by their presence in library lists and/or their physical survival to the present day. The Eastry catalogue of Canterbury, for example, records his *Descriptio Hibernie* together with his *Expugnatio Hibernica* (the latter entitled *Vaticinalis*), and an

---

[56] Bound with or copied in to the *Polychronicon*, now BL MS Royal 14 C.xiii; see above 153 n.350.

[57] Cambridge, Corpus Christi College MSS 51 and 187, both twelfth century, are item nos 282 and 186 respectively in James, *ALCD*. Salomon II is in *BRECP*, 276 and his name is in the Corpus MS 51. Both of these needed repair in 1508, James, *ALCD*, item nos 152 (Corpus MS 51) and 155 (Corpus MS 187), both on p. 158. See note 28 above.

[58] The Rochester volume is in Sharpe, *EBL*, at B77.55 and now Cambridge, Corpus Christi College MS 184, and there are seven Richards in *BRECP*, 630; Bozoun's text is in Sharpe, ibid., at B58.6a.

[59] Now BL MS Burney 310, which also contains Bede's Ecclesiastical History, it must surely have been a replacement for a lost or worn copy, although the only possible evidence of an earlier copy of Eusebius is the twelfth-century listing of an *Ecclesiastica historia* which could refer to Bede or to both, *Cat. Vet. Durham*, 2. See also note 28 above.

[60] Now WCM MS Q.28; see Thomson, *Medieval Manuscripts in Worcester Cathedral*, 135 where he proposes this likely explanation of its migration.

[61] Leland's list is in Sharpe, *EBL*, at B60.2; Vitry is contained in BL MS Royal 14 C.xiii.

[62] The Durham Polonus is now Oxford, Bodley MS Laud misc. 603; for Brackenbury's books, see Watson, *MLGB Supplement*, 87 and for his career *LVD*, iii, C.894. The Eastry catalogue in James, *ALCD*, item no. 686, is almost certainly Polonus.

[63] For Pretelwelle see *BRECP*, 258–9; his book is listed in the Eastry catalogue, James, *ALCD*, item no. 711 and may refer to a work with a similar title by Robert de Ketton for whom see Sharpe, *Latin Writers*, 559–60.

Itinerarium [*Kambriae*] with the *Descriptio Cambrie*; the latter duo being on a list of up to eighteen books belonging to Roger de la Lee, who was prior of Christ Church from 1239 to 1244.[64] A surviving volume comprising Gerald's *Descriptio Hiberniae*, his *Expugnatio Hiberniae*, and *Itinerarium Kambriae* of thirteenth-century date was in the hands of another Canterbury monk, William Bonyngton, by whom it was repaired in 1483.[65] A *De mirabilibus Hiberniae* which occurs twice in the inventory of Durham books dated 1395, is probably Gerald's *Topographia Hiberniae*.[66] It has been noted that Prior Bozoun's purchase of the *Polychronicon* manuscript brought with it in the same volume a collection of other writings; among them was the preface to Gerald's *Expugnatio Hibernica*.[67] Leland found a copy of this work when he visited Norwich cathedral priory a few years before the Dissolution, while Bale, in the mid-fifteenth century recorded spotting there a copy of the preface to the *Expugnatio* and also the *Topographia*.[68]

The *Historia regum Britanniae*, written by Geoffrey of Monmouth in the 1130s, is regarded today as a work of pseudo-historical interest. It purports to relate the story of the monarchy in Britain from its mythical origin in the so-called Trojan exile Brutus and, in so doing, it incorporates extracts from earlier works like the *Historia Brittonum* and the *De excidio Britannie* of the sixth-century Gildas.[69] These often appear under one, or possibly more than one, title in a wide-ranging confusion of permutations and combinations. Geoffrey's works appear to have been the 'historical novels' of their day, and the reliability of the factual details was insignificant in comparison with the dramatic portrayal and romantic glorification of the heroes of early Britain. Canterbury copies are difficult to identify in the Eastry catalogue; however, some of them may have been included in items listed under the fictitious title Brutus to which Geoffrey of Monmouth referred as one of his sources.[70] In fact, there are two references in the catalogue which strongly suggest that they were an earlier work of Geoffrey entitled *Prophetia Merlini* which he later incorporated into the *Historia*, although it also continued to have an independent existence.[71] Extracts from Geoffrey's *Historia* are also found in a surviving late thirteenth-century Canterbury

---

[64] James, *ALCD*, item no. 299 (*Descriptio* and *Expugnatio*); item no. 586 (*Itinerarium* and *Descriptio*). For Roger de la Lee see *BRECP*, 221. The *Descriptio Hibernie* is more accurately entitled *Topographia Hibernie*; all three works were edited by J. F. Dimock, Rolls Series 21, vols 5 and 6 (Longman, London, 1867–8).

[65] Now Oxford, Bodley MS Rawlinson B.188; for William Bonyngton II see *BRECP*, 95. Cambridge, Corpus Christi College MS 400 contains a version of the *Descriptio Cambriae* which may have had a Canterbury origin.

[66] *Cat. Vet. Durham*, 79 K, 83 K; they are one and the same book.

[67] Sharpe, *EBL*, at B58.29c.

[68] Sharpe, *EBL*, at B60.4 (Leland); B61.3, B61.5 (Bale); B61.3 is, according to Sharpe, the preface also found in BL MS Royal 14 C.xiii.

[69] The most recent research on Geoffrey of Monmouth is summarized in the *ODNB*; see also Gransden, *Historical Writing*, i, 200–8. The best edition of the *Historia regum Britanniae* to date is by E. Faral, *La Légende arthurienne* (Paris, 1929). The writings of Gildas were edited by T. Mommsen in *Monumenta Germaniae Historia, Auctores antiquissimi*, 13 (1895–8).

[70] *Brutus latine* occurs in the catalogue in James, *ALCD*, item nos 214, 674, and 708, and *Brutus gallice* in item no. 675, while item no. 1546 was both *latine* and *gallice*. One of these (214) was listed in a text containing a collection of treatises, and the same may have been true of other volumes; this, along with the variations in title, may explain the apparent absence of Geoffrey of Monmouth's *Historia regum Britanniae* with the exception of item no. 244 where it is found with Dares Phrygius.

[71] These are item nos 110 (*Prophetia Merlini*) and 214 (*Expositio super Merlinum imperfecta*).

manuscript which includes an *Historia Troianorum et Grecorum*.[72] The history section of a 1395 Durham inventory of library books describes two volumes containing works attributed to Gildas, one a *Gesta Britonum* by *Gilda vel Nennio* and another a *Historia Britonum*; both of these works have received mention above because they also contain Bede's Ecclesiastical History, and one of them includes the Ecclesiastical History by Eusebius.[73] There is also a fourteenth-century Durham book, now in the Cotton manuscript collection in the British Library, which has among its miscellaneous contents Geoffrey of Monmouth's *Historia Britonum*.[74] One of the mere handful of books known to have been in the monastic library at Coventry is Geoffrey of Monmouth's *Prophetia Merlini* which was copied out by John de Bruges around the middle of the thirteenth century; he was a monk scribe responsible for the production of more than thirty books, most of them liturgical, at the command of his prior, Roger de Walton.[75] The Norwich priors' predilection for history has already been established; however, further evidence is provided in the account of the master of the cellar for the year 1294/5. In the section *camera prioris*, Henry de Lakenham is charged with the expenditure of 16d. for the purchase of three *pecia* of parchment for *Bruto*. It has been assumed that this probably refers to Geoffrey of Monmouth's *Historia regum Britanniae*.[76] In addition, there is a surviving fourteenth-century copy that belonged to Roger de Blikling some time during his long life as a professed monk of Norwich (*c.* 1313 to 1376) and later passed on to Richard Salthous, who was master of the cellar in 1460.[77] Although the early date of the 1122/3 Rochester catalogue would seem to preclude the likelihood of the presence of any work by Geoffrey of Monmouth, there is a *Historia Britonum* included in one of the surviving volumes that are listed in it. In addition, one item in the 1202 catalogue consists of a collection of treatises one of which was an *Annales de gestis Britonum, Saxonum, Danorum*; this manuscript also survives but the *Annales* is now missing.[78] A monk named Leonard, about whom nothing else is known, gave this latter volume and another, containing prayers and meditations by Anselm, to his monastic community at Rochester.[79]

---

[72] BL Add MS 45103 which was repaired in 1508 and placed in the upper library where it was chained; see the list compiled by William Ingram, James, *ALCD*, item no. 161 (p. 158). May we take this chaining as a strong indication that the volume had had a popular appeal within the community?

[73] *Cat. Vet. Durham*, 56 G and N. The manuscript containing the *Gesta Britonum* or, probably more correctly, the *Historia Britonum* survives at Durham as MS B.II.35 in which the title appears as *Eulogium brevissimum Britannie insule*; its appearance today is the result of the binding together of four separate sections around 1500.

[74] BL MS Cotton Titus A.xviii in which the name of Prior John Auckland (1484–94) is inscribed; Auckland is C.1156 in *LVD*, iii.

[75] It is item B23.14C in the list printed in Sharpe, *EBL*, 110–13. Both Bruges and Walton are in *BRECP*, 348 and 372 respectively.

[76] See Sharpe, *EBL*, at B57.8 where the account details are printed and the interpretation proposed. For the binding of two volumes, one of which was the Bruto, a further 18d. was charged to the account, ibid. Cambridge, Trinity College MS 883 (thirteenth/early fourteenth century) may be this volume, most of which is taken up with a rule for nuns; it is inscribed with the name of the Norwich monk Geoffrey de Wroxham, *BRECP*, 574–5.

[77] Now CUL MS Ii.4.12 where it is bound with the *Summa* of Richard de Wetheringsett. For Blikling and Salthous see *BRECP*, 484 and 554 respectively.

[78] The *Historia Britonum* is listed in Sharpe, *EBL*, at B77.91e and is to be found today in BL MS Royal 15 A.xxii which also contained Dares Phrygius as noted above; this *Historia* is often attributed to the fictitious 'Nennius'. The annals are not mentioned in Sharpe, *EBL*, at B79.144 which only cites one item of the contents, namely the *Vita S. Malchi* by Reginald of Canterbury; this manuscript is now Oxford, Bodley MS Laud misc. 40.

[79] No dates can be assigned to Leonard although the *terminus ad quem* cannot be more than a few years later than 1202; see *BRECP*, 616.

In an age when there was almost universal belief in the virtue of holiness, models of sanctity were readily available for admiration and imitation. In a monastic setting, in particular, the lives of holy men and women were read and studied with the avowed aim of emulating their pattern of life and behaviour. Benedict himself had encouraged his disciples to read the Lives of their Fathers in the faith, a practice which he included among the *instrumenta virtutum* in his Rule.[80] Hagiography was therefore a popular choice in private reading material; moreover, it was prescribed for the readings during mealtimes in the refectory and for the appropriate *lectiones* on saints' days which were appointed for the liturgical office, and often selected for use as sermon material. Saints' lives abounded in monastic libraries, sometimes as individual monographs, often sandwiched into volumes containing miscellaneous treatises, or as a collective work possibly arranged for liturgical use.

Among the cathedral priories the records of individual monks' choices of reading material have disappeared with the sole exception of Canterbury. The Christ Church evidence demonstrates the popularity of the local saint and martyr Thomas Becket, whose *Vita* must have existed in numerous copies, three of which were reported lost in 1338. One of the careless monks who had failed to return his copy was William de Cantorbury, who was professed less than five years earlier and so would have been given it, or have chosen it, to read while still a novice.[81] A second monk, Richard de Wylardeseye, was acting as chamberlain when he was charged with the loss of his *Vita*; it was the copy identified as having once belonged to Simon a former subprior.[82] A third *Vita*, formerly belonging to Humphrey de Malling, was lost while on loan to Thomas de Goodnyston, who was feretrar in 1336.[83]

With the possible exception of Thomas Becket's *Vita* at Canterbury, books consisting of the life of a single saint occur less frequently than in gatherings of two, three or more. At Coventry, however, a small, illustrated book devoted to Bede's life of St Cuthbert and written in the twelfth century found a home in the library *ex dono* of Prior Richard Crosby (1399–1437).[84] The lengthy *Vita S. Godrici* by Reginald, monk of Durham, in the twelfth century, is another such text; it occurs at Durham in the 1391 inventory in the section *Vitae Sanctorum*, and still survives.[85] Matthew Paris's life of St Edmund of Canterbury, on the other hand, is tucked into a Worcester cathedral volume which is a miscellaneous collection of sixteen texts by Augustine, Isidore, William de Montibus, and others; this is a fourteenth-century manuscript which is associated with John Lawerne when he was at Oxford in the 1430s and 1440s.[86]

---

[80] *RB*, C.73, 4–6.

[81] See William de Cantorbury I in *BRECP*, 108–9, and James, *ALCD*, item no. 13 (p. 147), where the book is described as belonging to the *de communi* section of the library.

[82] Wylardeseye and Simon are in *BRECP*, 329 and 288–9 respectively; there are six monks named Simon, the first and last of whom are known to have been subpriors. The entry in the inventory of lost books in James, *ALCD*, is item no. 16 (p. 147).

[83] Humphrey de Mallyng does not occur as such in *BRECP*, but is probably M. Humphrey, the monk who died in Rome in 1188, ibid., 206; evidence for this identification is found in James, *ALCD*, item nos 1044–?1049 (p. 99) in conjunction with the inventory of lost books, James, *ALCD*, item no. 24 (p. 148) which is in the list of books formerly in the hands of dead monks. See Thomas de Goodnyston I, *BRECP*, 179 which has failed to note his negligence in 1338.

[84] Now Cambridge, Trinity College MS 1088; for Crosby see *BRECP*, 352–3.

[85] For Reginald see *ODNB* and *LVD*, iii, C.164; the *Vita* was edited by J. Stevenson, *Vita S. Godrici*, Surtees Society (Durham, 1847). The listing in *Cat. Vet. Durham*, is 29 L and the volume is now Oxford, Bodley MS Laud misc. 413.

[86] The manuscript remains at Worcester as Q.27; for John Lawerne see *BRECP*, John Lawerne I, 830–1. There is a modern edition of this work by C. H. Lawrence, *St. Edmund of Abingdon* (Clarendon Press, Oxford, 1960).

A late fourteenth-century list of books for reading in the Durham refectory includes some that contain biographies of several English saints and of saintly popes and archbishops; but there is also an impressive *Legenda sanctorum sive passionarium* in six volumes that covers all twelve months of the year.[87] Such collections, of which there were many, vary in their choice of contents although the major saints were always represented. The Ely monks, for example, compiled a *Vitae sanctorum* during the twelfth century which highlighted their local luminaries as well as honouring St Benedict and his sister St Scholastica. In it the life of St Werburga is followed by seven *lectiones* for her feast day while the local Sts Sexburga and Ermenilda are each given eight.[88] There is a late eleventh-century *Vitae sanctorum* which was in use at St Swithun's Winchester and an early fourteenth-century *Legenda sanctorum* from Christ Church Canterbury both of which have survived.[89] Among the books bequeathed by Prior Henry Eastry there is also a *Legenda sanctorum* as well as a *Legenda dominicalis et sanctorum xii Lectionum per totum annum*; these may well have been used by him and his chaplain for the daily office.[90] Another Canterbury *Legenda* is actually an early copy of what is more usually known as the *Legenda aurea* compiled by the Dominican friar James de Voragine (Genoa) in the 1260s; this was owned by John de Frome, lector to the monks in the 1350s.[91] It was a highly successful hagiographical collection, copies of which have survived at three other cathedral priories and a fourth is known to have possessed it. The Durham monks procured a late thirteenth-century *Legenda sanctorum* by Voragine which was ideally arranged for use by preachers in preparing their sermons; and a Worcester copy, entitled *Legenda aurea* and of a late fourteenth-century date, was similar.[92] Two Winchester manuscripts entitled *Legenda aurea* and dating from the thirteenth/fourteenth century have migrated to Cambridge libraries; both appear to have been gifts, one *ex dono* Robert Cramborne, who was not a monk, and the other inscribed with the *memoriale* of John de Drayton, who was alive and well in the monastery in 1307.[93] A fifteenth-century inventory of the Yarmouth cell of Norwich included a copy of Voragine's *Legenda aurea* bearing a cathedral priory pressmark, a fact which surely encourages us to assume that the cathedral priory was not being deprived of its one and only copy of this work.[94]

---

[87] *Cat. Vet. Durham*, 80 E, F, G², H², I, K; the same set of volumes was also listed in ibid., 54 E, F, G, H, I, K. There were other collections such as the surviving *Legenda sanctorum*, now DCL MS B. IV.14 an early twelfth-century volume that also appears in *Cat. Vet. Durham*, 54 L and 80 L.

[88] Now BL MS Cotton Caligula A.viii, fos 59–191. The last Ely prior, Robert Steward (Wells), inserted his arms on fo 169 in the year 1531; for his career see *BRECP*, 457–8.

[89] The Winchester volume is now Oxford, Bodley MS 535; the Canterbury *Legenda* is probably Oxford, Bodley MS 336 and may be the item listed in the Eastry catalogue, James, *ALCD*, item no. 1793. There was also a copy at Canterbury College Oxford in 1524, James, ibid., item no. 70 (p. 167), and another copy had been repaired a few years earlier in 1508, ibid., item no. 265 (p. 162).

[90] Eastry's gifts are in ibid., item nos 10 and 9 (p. 143).

[91] The Canterbury volume in question is now CUL MS Ff.5.31, a late thirteenth-century production; for Frome see *BRECP*, 163. The text of the *Legenda Aurea* was edited by T. Graesse (Breslau, 1890³, reprinted Osnabrück, 1965). There is also a recent edition in English: W. G. Ryan, *The Golden Legend*, 2 vols (Princeton University Press, Princeton, 1993).

[92] The Durham *Legenda aurea sanctorum* is now Oxford, Bodley MS Laud misc. 489; there is another two-volume set of the early thirteenth/fourteenth century still in Durham as MSS B.IV.39A and B; the Worcester volume also remains *in situ* as WCM MS F.45. It is uncertain when the Worcester copy was acquired, possibly not before the early sixteenth century when Roger Neckham's name was inscribed; for Neckham see *BRECP*, 855–6, which does not mention this inscription.

[93] Robert Cramborne, who gave Cambridge, Trinity College MS 338, may have had a monk relative as there was a Peter Cranbourne at St Swithun's in the early fifteenth century; see *BRECP*, 684. Drayton's gift is now CUL MS Gg.2.18; for his career see ibid., 686–7.

[94] Sharpe, *EBL*, at B64.8.

It is very likely that the Rochester community possessed the *Legenda aurea* but there remains no evidence of its presence. In the 1202 catalogue, however, there was a similar collection entitled *Vita sanctorum patrum* in two volumes; like the *Legenda* collections the contents of books with this or a similar title varied, but some inclusions tended to be common to all.[95] An early sixteenth-century *Vitae*, or *Vitas*, *patrum* that belonged to Norwich cathedral priory is written in a clear, upright hand and has added stress marks in red presumably as an aid in public reading.[96] The Worcester monks used a much earlier copy of eleventh- and twelfth-century date with marginal notes that may be in the hand of the monk Coleman.[97] There is some uncertainty as to the Winchester monks' ownership of the extant two-volume version of a late twelfth-century *Vitas patrum*, but there is little doubt as to its connection with Winchester.[98] The monks of Christ Church and their brethren of St Cuthbert at Durham had several copies of the *Vitae patrum* from which to choose. An R. de Gyllyngham, otherwise unknown, had owned a copy which was listed in the Eastry catalogue along with two other copies, one being among the *libri de armariolo claustri*, and a fourth copy being recorded as sent for repair in 1508.[99] When Bishop William of St Calais died in 1096 he left some of his books to his monastic chapter at Durham; one of them was the *Vitas patrum* which was numbered among the books set aside for the selection of readings at the office of matins.[100]

Finally, two individual monks emerge for a moment from the obscurity of their respective cathedral chapters to offer a glimpse of personal relationships and activity that have historical writing as their focus. Insignificant events in the daily routine of medieval monastic life went, no doubt, often unnoticed even by contemporaries within the community, and usually unknown to us; the following, however, are two revealing exceptions. The authorship of a brief treatise of a mere fifteen folios entitled *Peregrinacio totius terre sancte* is attributed to Ralph de Iklingham, monk of Ely, whose years in the monastery, apart from the record of his ordination as acolyte by bishop de Lisle in 1352, have been lost to view.[101] Did his interest in the Holy Land arise from a visit made in person or was he restricted to collecting information from others? He appears to have been especially interested in recording the indulgences and absolutions offered to pilgrims on their journey; an unusual preoccupation it may seem to us. The second monk, John Blakeneye of Norwich, was professed in 1427 and ordained priest a few years later; no details of his later monastic career have survived with the sole exception of an inscription in a small fifteenth-century manuscript with the title *De institutione fratrum carmelitarum ordinis*. It was written by Thomas Scrope, a Carmelite friar of the Norwich convent close by the cathedral; and the inscription reads 'Frater Thomas Bradley... anachorita carissimo fratri suo Johanni Blakeneye nigro

---

[95] Sharpe, ibid., at B79.58 where this section of the catalogue is headed *commune librarium*.
[96] Now Cambridge, Corpus Christi College MS 36.
[97] Still *in situ* as WCM MS F.48; for Coleman see *BRECP*, 790–1.
[98] These are Winchester Cathedral MS 14 and Winchester College MS 18 which is now reunited with its companion in the cathedral. See Ker, *MMBL*, iv, 591–2, item no. 14.
[99] James, *ALCD*, Eastry catalogue item nos 270 (p. 47) (Gyllyngham), 269 (p. 47), 355 (p. 52) (*armariolo*); the volume repaired is ibid., item no. 267 (p. 162).
[100] *Cat. Vet. Durham*, 118.
[101] The manuscript, formerly at Ely and now Oxford, Bodley MS Rawlinson C.958, measures only 4" by 6" and contains several other treatises of which this is the first. In bishop de Lisle's register the surname is given as Ikelynton; but episcopal clerks were often careless and inaccurate in copying names; see *BRECP*, 418 which does not mention this recent discovery. Unfortunately, there are many gaps in the records of Ely cathedral priory, and Iklingham is but one of a large number of monks about whom little is known.

monacho salutem...'[102] Scrope/Bradley lived as an anchorite within his convent for some time during the 1430s, but later was consecrated as bishop of Dromore and then acted for some years as suffragan in Norwich. How did these two men meet and what sparked their friendship? Did Scrope's zeal for preaching and his mystical bent meet a kindred spirit in Blakeney?

This selection of historical works present in the book cupboards and presses of the cathedral priories is only the tip of the iceberg in the context of the total collection of holdings in each case. However, the true size of the iceberg, including the extent of its depth below the surface of the water, when metaphorically applied to the measure of the entire accumulation of books in these libraries, can only be conjectured due to the ravages of time. Furthermore, even if the choice of books in any given subject was impressive, how often were they in circulation? It is surely advisable to give the monks the benefit of doubt by concluding that there were always some monk readers and at times more than a few.[103]

---

[102] The manuscript, now CUL Ff. 6.11, was probably in the cathedral library of Norwich although it lacks any identifying shelf mark. For Blakeneye see *BRECP*, 484 and for the life and career of Thomas Scrope de Bradbury, *ODNB* in an article by Richard Copsey, O. Carm., who first drew my attention to this manuscript.

[103] It is a misreading of the evidence to state that medieval monks were indifferent to historical truth and accuracy and that their interest in the past was for the sole purpose of finding in it lessons to apply to the present; this is to deny that they were curious, intelligent, reasoning, and questioning human beings not totally different from present-day writers and readers of history. I am here taking issue with some of the remarks made by Janet Coleman in *Ancient and Medieval Memories, Studies in the Reconstruction of the Past* (Cambridge University Press, Cambridge, 1992), especially 135–9, 275–85, 299.

Bibliography

A. MANUSCRIPT SOURCES

Note: the location of the documents below is given and, where necessary, the individual class mark assigned for the purpose of identification. The archiepiscopal registers in Lambeth Palace Library, along with most of the Durham muniments are mercifully free of any such additional classification. For registers that have been printed see below under Registers.

Bath

1) Episcopal Registers, Somerset Record Office (SRO)

Reg. [John] Drokensford/Droxford (1309–29)	D/D/B.Reg.1
Reg. [Ralph] Shrewsbury (1329–63)	D/D/B.Reg.2
Reg. [Henry] Bowett (1401–7)	D/D/B.Reg.3
Reg. [Nicholas] Bubwith (1408–24)	D/D/B.Reg.4
Reg. [John] Stafford (1425–43)	D/D/B.Reg.5
Reg. [Thomas] Bekynton/Beckington (1443–65)	D/D/B.Reg.6
Reg. [Robert] Stillington (1466–91)	D/D/B.Reg.7

2) Bath Priory Reg., London, Lincoln's Inn, MS 185 (MS Hale); *c.* 1200 to mid-14th c.

Note: this has been paginated, although some of the numbering has been crossed through. I have followed the page references in the ms which are also in Hunt.

Canterbury

1) Archiepiscopal Registers, Lambeth Palace Library (LPL)

Reg. abp [John] Pecham (1279–92)

Reg. abp [Robert] Winchelsey (1294–1313)

Reg. abp [Walter] Reynolds (1313–27)

Reg. abp [Simon] Islip (1349–66)

Reg. abp [Simon] Langham (1366–8)

Reg. abp [William] Wittlesey (1368–74)

Reg. abp [Simon] Sudbury (1375–81)

Reg. abp [William] Courtenay (1381–96), 2 vols, of which vol. ii is bound in Reg. abp Morton, fos 181–228.

Reg. abp [Thomas] Arundel (1396–7, 1399–1414), 2 vols.

Reg. abp [Henry] Chichele (1414–43), 2 vols.

Reg. abp [John] Stafford (1443–52)

2) Canterbury Cathedral Archives (CCA DCc)

Priory Registers A, B, C, D, E, G, H, I, J, K, L, O, P, Q, S

3) Obedientiary accounts

Coventry

1) Episcopal Registers, Lichfield Record Office (LRO)

Reg. [Walter] Langton (1296–1321)			B/A/1/1, fos 1–142
Reg. [Roger] Northburgh (1322–58) 3 vols:		i	B/A/1/1, fos 143–216 (ordinations)
		ii	B/A/1/2
		iii	B/A/1/3
Reg. [Robert] Stretton (1360–85) 3 vols:		i	B/A/1/4
		ii	B/A/1/5i
		iii	B/A/1/5ii
Reg. [Walter] Skirlaw (1386)			B/A/1/6
Reg. [Richard] Scrope (1386–98)			B/A/1/6
Reg. [John] Burghill (1398–1414)			B/A/1/7
Reg. [John] Catterick (1415–19)			B/A/1/8
Reg. [William] Heyworth (1420–47)			B/A/1/9
Reg. [William] Booth (1447–52)			B/A/1/10
Reg. [Reginald] Boulers (1453–9)			B/A/1/11
Reg. [John] Hales (1459–90)			B/A/1/12

2) Priory Registers

Magnum Reg. Album   Lichfield Cathedral Library MS 28

Reg. Haloughton   TNA, E164/21

Durham

Note: Comprehensive bibliographies have been provided in *BRECP* covering all the cathedral priories with the exception of Durham. It has been deemed unnecessary to repeat them *in extenso* here because full references to the primary sources cited have been given in the accompanying footnotes. For Durham some extra bibliographical information with regard to manuscript materials is included below.

Identification of most of the muniments at Durham has not been complicated by the use of a lengthy array of numbers and letters interspersed with slashes; these are impossible to remember and virtually meaningless to all but the archivist *in situ*. The name of the manuscript has long been and remains sufficient and, in the case of obedientiary accounts, the year of the account should be added.

1) Episcopal Registers

Reg. [Richard] Kellawe (1311–16), TNA, Durham 3/1

Durham Cathedral Muniments (DCM)

Reg. [Richard] Bury (1333–45)

Reg. [Thomas] Hatfield (1345–81)
Reg. [Thomas] Langley (1406–37)

2) Priory Registers (DCM)

Reg. II	Letter-Book of the prior and chapter, 1312–1401
Reg. III	Letter-Book, 1401–44
Reg. Parvum I	Prior's small register, *c.* 1322–1406, now BL MS Cotton Faustina A.vi
Reg. Parvum II	Prior's letter-book, 1407–45

3) Other primary sources

Liber Vitae		BL MS Cotton Domitian A. VII
Locelli	DCM	A miscellaneous collection of loose documents arranged by subject matter
Miscellaneous charters	DCM	A large class of documents, loosely catalogued, similar to the above
Obedientiary accounts	DCM	
Pontificalia (Pont.)	DCM	A collection of materials concerning relations between bishop and prior and chapter including visitations and elections

4) Unpublished Thesis

Foster, 'Durham Priory'   M. Foster, 'Durham Cathedral Priory 1229–1333: aspects of the ecclesiastical history and interests of the monastic community', Cambridge, Ph.D. 1979.

Ely

1) Episcopal Registers, Cambridge University Library (CUL)

Reg. [Simon de] Montacute (1337–45)	EDR G/1/1, fos 1–101
Reg. [Thomas] de Lisle (1345–61)	EDR G/1/1, fos 1–125, second foliation
Reg. [Thomas] Arundel (1374–88)	EDR G/1/2
Reg. [John] Fordham (1388–1425)	EDR G/1/3
Reg. [Thomas] Bourgchier (1443–54)	EDR G/1/4

2) Priory Registers, Cambridge University Library (CUL) and (BL)

Liber B	CUL EDR G/2/3
Liber M (cartulary)	CUL EDR G/3/28
Reg. Walsingham	CUL EDC 1/E/1
MS Add. 9822	BL
MS Add. 41612	BL

3) Obedientiary accounts

CUL EDC 1/F–
CUL Add. MS 2957

Norwich

1) Episcopal Registers, Norfolk Record Office (NRO)

Reg. [John] Salmon (1299–1325)	DN Reg/1/1
Reg. [William] Ayermine (1325–36)	DN Reg/1/2
Reg. [Anthony] Bek (1337–43)	DN Reg/1/3
Reg. [William] Bateman (1344–55)	DN Reg/2/4
Reg. [Thomas] Percy (1356–69)	DN Reg/2/5
Reg. [Henry] Despenser (1370–1406)	DN Reg/3/6
Reg. [Alexander] Totyington (1407–13)	DN Reg/4/7, fos 1–71
Reg. [Richard] Courtenay (1413–15)	bound with the above, fos 72–104
Reg. [John] Wakeryng (1416–25)	DN Reg/4/8
Reg. [William] Alnwick (1426–36)	DN Reg/5/9
Reg. [Thomas] Brouns (1436–45)	DN Reg/5/10
Reg. [Walter] Lyhert (1446–72)	DN Reg/6/11

2) Priory Registers (NRO)

Reg. I	DCN 40/1
Almoner's Reg. / Reg. II, i	DCN 40/2/1
Reg. II, ii	DCN 40/2/2
Reg. IV	DCN 40/4
Reg. V	DCN 40/5
Reg. VI	DCN 40/6
Reg. IX	DCN 40/9
Reg. X	DCN 40/10
Reg. XI	DCN 40/11

3) Obedientiary accounts   DCN 1/1, 1/2, 1/3 etc

4) Unpublished thesis C. Noble, 'Aspects of Life at Norwich Cathedral Priory in the Later Medieval Period', University of East Anglia, Ph.D., 2001.

Rochester

1) Episcopal Registers, Maidstone, Centre for Kentish Studies (CKS)

Reg. [Hamo de] Hethe (1319–52)	DRb Ar1/1
Reg. [John] Shepey (1353–60)	DRb Ar1/2
Reg. [William] Wittlesey (1362–4)	DRb Ar1/3
Reg. [Thomas] Trillek (1364–72)	DRb Ar1/4
Reg. William Bottlesham (1389–1400)	DRb Ar1/5
Reg. John Bottlesham (1400–4)	DRb Ar1/6
Reg. [Richard] Young (1404–18)	DRb Ar1/7
Reg. [John] Langdon (1422–34)	DRb Ar1/8

Reg. [Thomas] Brouns (1435–6)   DRb Ar1/9
Reg. [William] Wells (1437–44)   DRb Ar1/10

2) Priory Registers

Reg. Prior Shepey   BL MS Cotton Faustina C.v.
Reg./Liber temporalium   CKS DRb/Ar2

3) Obedientiary accounts   CKS DRc/F–

Winchester
1) Episcopal Registers, Hampshire Record Office (HRO)

Reg. [John de] Pontissara/Pontoise (1282–1304)   21M65/A1/1
Reg. [Henry] Woodlock (1305–16)   21M65/A1/2
Reg. [John] Sandale (1316–19)   21M65/A1/3
Reg. [Rigaud de] Asserio/Assier (1320–3)   21M65/A1/4
Reg. [John de] Stratford (1323–33)   21M65/A1/5
Reg. [Adam de] Orleton (1333–45)   21M65/A1/6, 7
Reg. [William de] Edington (1346–66)   21M65/A1/8, 9
Reg. [William de] Wykeham (1367–1404)   21M65/A1/10, 11
Reg. [Henry] Beaufort (1405–47)   21M65/A1/; only one vol. extant for 1405–18.

2) Priory Registers, Winchester Cathedral Library (WCL)

Reg. I   Common Seal Register, 1345–1497

3) Obedientiary accounts   W53/–

Worcester
1) Episcopal Registers, Worcestershire County Record Office (WRO)

Reg. [Godfrey] Giffard (1268–1302)   b.716.093-BA.2648/1 (i)
Reg. [William de] Gainsborough (1303–7)   b.716.093-BA.2648/1 (ii)
Reg. [Walter] Reynolds (1308–13)   b.716.093-BA.2648/1 (iii)
Reg. [Walter de] Maidstone (1313–17)   b.716.093-BA.2648/1 (iv)
Reg. [Thomas de] Cobham (1317–27)   b.716.093-BA.2648/2 (i)
Reg. [Adam de] Orleton (1327–33)   b.716.093-BA.2648/2 (ii)
Reg. [Simon de] Montacute (1334–7)   b.716.093-BA.2648/2 (iii)
Reg. [Thomas de] Hemenhale (1337–8)   b.716.093-BA.2648/2 (iv)
Reg. [Wulstan de] Bransford (1339–49)   b.716.093-BA.2648/3 (i)
Reg. [John] Thoresby (1350–2)   b.716.093-BA.2648/3 (ii)
Reg. [Reginald] Bryan (1353–61)   b.716.093-BA.2648/3 (iii) (vol. i) and iv (vol. ii)

Reg. [John] Barnet (1362–3)	b.716.093-BA.2648/4 (i)
Reg. [William] Wittlesey (1364–8)	b.716.093-BA.2648/4 (ii)
Reg. [William] Lynn (1369–73)	b.716.093-BA.2648/4 (iii)
Reg. [Henry] Wakefield (1375–95)	b.716.093-BA.2648/4 (iv)
Reg. [Tideman de] Winchcombe (1395–1401)	b.716.093-BA.2648/4 (v)
Reg. [Richard] Clifford (1401–7)	b.716.093-BA.2648/5 (i)
Reg. [Thomas] Peverel (1407–19)	b.716.093-BA.2648/5 (ii)
Reg. [Philip] Morgan (1419–26)	b.716.093-BA.2648/5 (iii)
Reg. [Thomas] Polton (1426–33)	b.716.093-BA.2648/5 (iv)
Reg. [Thomas] Bourgchier (1435–43)	b.716.093-BA.2648/6 (i)

Note: These have been paginated in pencil.

2) Priory Registers, Worcester Cathedral Manuscripts and Muniments (WCM)

Reg. A.1 (Sede Vacante)

Reg. A.5 (Liber Albus), 2 vols, continuous pagination.

3) Obedientiary accounts   C.1–

B. WORKS IN PRINT WITH ABBREVIATIONS

Note: Full reference details of some works mentioned only once are included in the relevant footnotes.

Acta Stephani Langton	K. Major (ed.), *Acta Stephani Langton (1207–1228)*, Canterbury and York Society, 1950.
Anglia Sacra	H. Wharton, *Anglia Sacra*, 2 vols, London, 1691.
Annales Burton	H. R. Luard (ed.), *Annales Monastici*, 5 vols, Rolls Series, 1864–9, i.
Annales Wigorn.	Ibid., iv.
Annales Winton.	Ibid., ii.
'Anon. Chron.'	C. E. Woodruff, 'A Monastic Chronicle of Christ Church (1331–1414) Lately Discovered', *Archaeologia Cantiana*, 29 (1911), 47–84; transcription and translation of Canterbury Cathedral, Literary MS C.14.
Atherton, *Norwich Cathedral*	I. Atherton *et al.* (eds), *Norwich Cathedral: Church, City and Diocese, 1096–1996*, London, 1996.
Atkins, 'Church of Worcester'	Ivor Atkins, 'The Church of Worcester from the Eighth to the Twelfth Century', *Antiquaries Journal*, 17 (1937), 371–91 (pt i) and 20 (1940), 1–38 and 203–28 (pt ii).

Atkins, *Office of Organist*	Ivor Atkins, *The Early Occupants of the Office of Organist and Master of the Choristers of the Cathedral Church of Christ and the Blessed Virgin Mary, Worcester*, London, 1918.
Barlow, *Durham Annals and Documents*	F. Barlow (ed.), *Durham Annals and Documents in the Thirteenth Century*, Surtees Society, 155 (1945).
Bath Priory Reg.	W. Hunt (ed.), *Two Chartularies of the Priory of St Peter at Bath: i, The Chartulary in MS cxi in the Library of Corpus Christi College, Cambridge; ii, Calendar of the MS Register in the Library of the Hon. Society of Lincoln's Inn*, Somerset Record Society 7, 1893. In the latter the entries have been numbered.
Beeching and James, 'Norwich Library'	H. C. Beeching and M. R. James, 'The Library of the Cathedral Church of Norwich with an Appendix of Priory Manuscripts now in English Libraries', *Norfolk Archaeology*, xix (1917), 67–116.
Bensly, 'St Leonard's Priory'	W. T. Bensly, 'St Leonard's Priory, Norwich', *Norfolk Archaeology*, xii (1895), 190–227; includes a transcription of inventories of 1424 and 1452/3.
BL	British Library.
Blackburn and Holford-Strevens, *Oxford Companion*	B. Blackburn and L. Holford-Strevens, *The Oxford Companion to the Year*, Oxford, 1999.
Blakiston, 'Some Durham College Rolls'	H. E. D. Blakiston, 'Some Durham College Rolls', *Oxford Historical Society, Collectanea* 3rd series, 32 (1896), 1–76.
Blomefield, *Norfolk*	F. Blomefield and C. Parkin, *An Essay Towards a Topographical History of the County of Norfolk*, 11 vols, London, 1805–10.
Bloom, *Liber Ecclesiae*	J. Bloom, *Liber Ecclesiae Wigorniensis: A Letter Book of the Priors of Worcester*, Worcestershire Historical Society, 1912.
Bloom, *Original Charters*	J. Bloom (ed.), *Original Charters Relating to the City of Worcester in Possession of the Dean and Chapter*, Worcestershire Historical Society, 1909.
Blyth, *Visitations*	P. Heath (ed.) *Bishop Geoffrey Blythe's Visitations c.1515–1525*, Staffordshire Record Society, 4th series, 7, 1973.
Bowers, 'Almonry Schools'	R. Bowers, 'The Almonry Schools of the English Monasteries c. 1265–1540', in Benjamin Thompson (ed.), *Monasteries and Society in Medieval Britain*, Harlaxton Medieval Studies, vi, Stamford, 1999, 177–222.

Bowers, 'The Lady Chapel and its Musicians'	R. Bowers, 'The Lady Chapel and its Musicians', in Crook, *Winchester Cathedral*, q.v., 247–56.
Bowers, 'The Liturgy of the Cathedral and its Music'	R. Bowers, 'The Liturgy of the Cathedral and its Music, *c.* 1075–1642', in Collinson, *History of Canterbury Cathedral*, 408–50.
BRECP	J. Greatrex, *Biographical Register of the English Cathedral Priories of the Province of Canterbury, c. 1066–1540*, Oxford, 1997.
Brett, 'The Church at Rochester'	M. Brett, 'The church at Rochester, 604–1185', in N. Yates, *Rochester Cathedral*, 1–28.
Brett, 'Forgery at Rochester'	M. Brett, 'Forgery at Rochester', *Falschungen im Mittelalter Monumenta Germaniae Historica Schriften*, 33, iv (1988), 397–412.
Brett, 'John of Worcester'	M. Brett, 'John of Worcester and his Contemporaries', in R. H. C. Davis and J. Wallace-Hadrill (eds), *The Writing of History in the Middle Ages: Essays Presented to R. W. Southern*, Oxford, 1981, 101–26.
Brown, 'Financial System of Rochester'	A. Brown, 'The Financial System of Rochester Cathedral Priory: A Reconsideration', *Bulletin of the Institute of Historical Research*, 50 (1977), 115–20.
BRUC	A. B. Emden, *A Biographical Register of the University of Cambridge to A.D. 1500*, Cambridge, 1963.
BRUO	A. B. Emden, *A Biographical Register of the University of Oxford to A.D. 1500*, 3 vols, Oxford, 1957–59.
BRUO (1501–40)	A. B. Emden, *A Biographical Register of the University of Oxford, A.D. 1501–1540*, Oxford, 1974.
Cal. Inq. A. Q. D.	*Calendar of Inquisitions ad quod Damnum*, Record Commissioners, 1803–.
Cal. Inq. Misc.	*Calendar of Inquisitions Miscellaneous*, Public Record Office Texts and Calendars, 1916–.
Cassien, *Institutions*	Jean Cassien, *Institutions Cénobitiques*, ed. J. C. Guy, Sources chrétiennes, 109, Paris, 1965.
Cat. Vet. Durham	B. Botfield (ed.) [and J. Raine], *Catalogi Veteres Librorum Cathedralis Dunelm*, Surtees Society, 7 (1840).
CCA DCc	Canterbury Cathedral Archives, Dean and Chapter.
CCCM	*Corpus Christianorum Continuatio Medievalis*, i— (Brepols, Turnholti, 1971–).
CCL	Canterbury Cathedral Library.
CCR	*Calendar of Close Rolls preserved in the Public Record Office*, Public Record Office Texts and Calendars, 1892–.

CCSL	*Corpus Christianorum, Series Latina* i—(Turnhout 1954–).
Chapman, *Sacrist Rolls*	F. R. Chapman (ed.), *The Sacrist Rolls of Ely*, 2 vols, Cambridge, 1907, printed for private circulation only; vol. ii contains transcriptions of the first fifteen accounts.
Cheney, *Handbook of Dates*	C. R. Cheney (ed.), *A Handbook of Dates for Students of History*, revised by Michael Jones, Cambridge, 2000.
Cheney, 'Norwich Cathedral Priory'	C. R. Cheney, 'Norwich Cathedral Priory in the Fourteenth Century', *Bulletin of the John Rylands Library*, 20 (1936), 93–120.
'Chron. William Glastynbury'	C. W. Woodruff (ed.), 'Chronicle of William Glastynbury, Monk of the Priory of Christ Church, Canterbury', *Archaeologia Cantiana*, 37 (1925), 121–51; an incomplete transcript, partly in translation, of Oxford, Corpus Christi College MS 256.
Chronicle Stone	W. Searle (ed. and comp.), *The Chronicle of John Stone, Monk of Christ Church, 1415–1471*, Cambridge Antiquarian Society, Octavo Publications, no. 34 (1902); transcript of Cambridge, Corpus Christi College MS 417.
Churchill, *Cant. Admin.*	I. J. Churchill, *Canterbury Administration: The Administrative Machinery of the Archbishop of Canterbury Illustrated from Original Records*, 2 vols, London, 1933.
CKS	Centre for Kentish Studies.
Close Rolls	TNA Chancery Records, 1902–38.
Collinson, *History of Canterbury Cathedral*	P. Collinson *et al.*, *A History of Canterbury Cathedral*, Oxford, 1995.
CPL	*Calendar of Entries in the Papal Registers Relating to Great Britain and Ireland*, TNA Calendars, 1894–.
CPP	*Calendar of Entries in the Papal Registers Relating to Great Britain and Ireland, Petitions to the pope*, TNA Calendars, 1897, i (1342–1419).
CPR	*Calendar of Patent Rolls Preserved in the Public Record Office*, TNA Calendars, 1891–.
Crook, 'East Arm and Crypt of Winchester'	J. Crook, 'The Romanesque East Arm and Crypt of Winchester Cathedral', *Journal of British Archaeological Association*, cxlii (1989), 1–36.
Crook, 'Monastic Buildings of St Swithun's'	J. Crook, 'The Monastic Buildings of St Swithun's Priory, 1079–1540', unpublished typescript.

Crook, *Winchester Cathedral*	J. Crook (ed.), *Winchester Cathedral, Nine Hundred Years, 1093–1993*, Chichester, 1993.
CUL	Cambridge University Library.
Darlington, *Worcester Cartulary*	R. Darlington (ed.), *The Cartulary of Worcester Cathedral Priory*, Publications of the Pipe Roll Society, new series, 38, 1968.
Dart, *Antiq. Cant.*	J. Dart, *History and Antiquities of the Cathedral Church of Canterbury*, London, 1726; the appendices include extracts from BL MS Cotton Galba E.iv.
DCL	Durham Cathedral Library.
DCM	Durham Cathedral Muniments.
Delisle, *Rouleau des Morts*	L. Delisle, *Rouleau des Morts du IXe au XVe siècle*, Paris, 1866.
Demidowicz, *Coventry's First Cathedral*	G. Demidowicz (ed.), *Coventry's First Cathedral Priory of St Mary*, Papers from the 1993 Anniversary Symposium, Stamford, 1994.
Dobson, *Durham Priory*	R. B. Dobson, *Durham Priory, 1400–1450*, Cambridge, 1973.
Dobson, 'Monks of Canterbury'	Barrie Dobson, 'The Monks of Canterbury in the Later Middle Ages, 1220–1540', in Collinson, *History of Canterbury Cathedral*, 69–153.
Dodwell, 'The Foundation of Norwich Cathedral'	B. Dodwell, 'The Foundation of Norwich Cathedral', *Transactions of the Royal Historical Society*, 5th series, 7 (1957), 1–18.
Dodwell, 'History and Norwich Monks'	B. Dodwell, 'History and the Monks of Norwich Cathedral Priory', *Reading Medieval Studies*, 5 (1979), 38–56.
Dugdale, *Monasticon*	W. Dugdale, *Monasticon Anglicanum*, rev. edn. by J. Caley, H. Ellis, and B. Bandinel, 6 vols in 8, London, 1817–1830.
Edwards, *Secular Cathedrals*	K. Edwards, *The English Secular Cathedrals in the Middle Ages*, Manchester, 1967.
Engel, *Worcester Cathedral*	U. Engel, *Worcester Cathedral, an Architectural History*, Chichester, 2007.
Epist. Peckham	C. T. Martin (ed.), *Registrum epistolarum fratris Johannis Peckham, archiepiscopi Cantuariensis*, Rolls Series, 3 vols, 1882–5; the volumes are paginated continuously throughout and the letters numbered likewise. Vol. i, pp. 1–392, vol. ii, pp. 393–743, vol. iii, pp. 773–.

Evans, 'Ely Almonry Boys'	S. J. A. Evans, 'Ely Almonry Boys and Choristers in the Later Middle Ages', in J. C. Davies (ed.), *Studies Presented to Sir Hilary Jenkinson*, London, 1957, 155–69.
Evans, *Ely Chapter Ordinances*	S. J. A. Evans, *Ely Chapter Ordinances and Visitation Records, 1241–1515*, Camden Miscellany, 3rd series, xvii, 1940, 1–74.
Evans, 'The Purchase of Mepal'	S. J. A. Evans, 'The Purchase and Mortification of Mepal by the Prior and Convent of Ely', *English Historical Review*, li (1936), 113–20.
Farmer, 'Meditations'	H. Farmer, 'The Meditations of the Monk of Farne', *Studia Anselmiana*, 4th series, 41 (1957), 141–245.
Fasti, ii	D. E. Greenway, comp., *John Le Neve, Fasti Ecclesiae Anglicanae, 1066–1300*, ii, *Monastic Cathedrals*, London, 1971.
Fasti, iv	B. Jones, comp., *John Le Neve, Fasti Ecclesiae Anglicanae, 1300–1541*, iv, *Monastic Cathedrals*, London, 1963.
Fasti, vi	B. Jones, comp., *John Le Neve, Fasti Ecclesiae Anglicanae, 1300–1541*, vi, *Northern Province*, London, 1963.
Fegan, *Journal of William More*	E. Fegan (ed.), *Journal of Prior William More*, Worcestershire Historical Society, 1914.
Feodarium	W. Greenwell (ed.), *Feodarium Prioratus Dunelmensis*, Surtees Society 58 (1872).
Fernie, *Architectural History . . . Norwich*	E. Fernie, *An Architectural History of Norwich Cathedral*, Oxford, 1993.
Fernie and Whittingham, *Communar Rolls*	E. C. Fernie and A. B. Whittingham (eds), *The Early Communar and Pittancer Rolls of Norwich Cathedral Priory with an Account of the Building of the Cloister*, Norfolk Record Society 41, 1972.
Flight, *Bishops and Monks of Rochester*	C. Flight, *The Bishops and Monks of Rochester 1076–1214*, Kent Archaeological Society, Monograph Series no VI, 1997.
Foster, 'Durham Priory'	See under Durham Manuscripts, Thesis.
Fowler, *Account Rolls*	J. T. Fowler (ed.), *Extracts from the Account Rolls of the Abbey of Durham*, 3 vols, Surtees Society, 99, 100, 103 (1898–1901).
Fraser, *Antony Bek*	C. M. Fraser, *A History of Antony Bek*, Oxford, 1957.
Gervase, *Opera Historica*	W. Stubbs (ed.), *Gervasii Cantuariensis Opera Historica*, Rolls Series, 2 vols, 1879–80.

Gibson, *Lanfranc*	M. Gibson and H. Clover (eds), *The Letters of Lanfranc, Archbishop of Canterbury*, Oxford Medieval Texts, Oxford, 1979.
Gilchrist, *Norwich Cathedral Close*	R. Gilchrist, *Norwich Cathedral Close: The Evolution of the English Cathedral Landscape*, Woodbridge, 2005.
Goodman, *Winchester Chartulary*	A. W. Goodman (ed.), *Chartulary of Winchester Cathedral*, Winchester, 1927.
Gransden, *Historical Writing*	A. Gransden, *Historical Writing in England*, i, *c. 550 to c. 1307*. London, 1974; ii, *c. 1307 to the early 16th century*, London, 1982.
Greatrex, 'Benedictine Monk Scholars'	J. Greatrex, 'Benedictine Monk Scholars as Teachers and Preachers in the Later Middle Ages: Evidence from Worcester Cathedral Priory', *Monastic Studies*, ii (1991), 213–25.
Greatrex, 'Benedictine Observance at Ely'	J. Greatrex, 'Benedictine Observance at Ely: The Intellectual, Liturgical and Spiritual Evidence Considered', in P. Meadows and N. Ramsay (eds), *A History of Ely Cathedral*, Woodbridge, 2003, 77–93.
Greatrex, 'Cathedral Monasteries'	J. Greatrex, 'The Cathedral Monasteries in the Later Middle Ages', in D. Rees (ed.), *Monks of England: The Benedictines in England from Augustine to the Present Day*, London, 1997, 118–34.
Greatrex, *Common Seal Register*	J. Greatrex (ed.), *The Register of the Common Seal of the Priory of St Swithun, Winchester, 1345–1497*, Hampshire Record Series, ii, Hampshire County Council, 1978.
Greatrex, 'Culture at Canterbury'	J. Greatrex, 'Culture at Canterbury in the Fifteenth Century: Some Indications of the Cultural Environment of a Monk of Christ Church', in J. Clark (ed.), *The Culture of Medieval English Monasticism*, Woodbridge, 2007, 169–76.
Greatrex, 'English Cathedral Priories and . . . Learning'	J. Greatrex, 'The English Cathedral Priories and the Pursuit of Learning in the Later Middle Ages', *Journal of Ecclesiastical History*, 45 (1994), 396–411.
	J. Greatrex, 'From Cathedral Cloister to Gloucester College', in H. Wansbrough, 48–60.
Greatrex, 'Horoscopes and Healing'	J. Greatrex, 'Horoscopes and Healing at Norwich Cathedral Priory in the Later Middle Ages', in C. M. Barron and J. Stratford (eds), *The Church and Learning in Later Medieval Society: Essays in Honour of R. B.*

	Dobson, Harlaxton Medieval Studies XI, Shaun Tyas, Donington, 2002, 170–7.
Greatrex, 'Injunction Book'	J. Greatrex, 'A Fourteenth-Century Injunction Book from Winchester', *Bulletin of the Institute of Historical Research*, 50 (1977), 242–6.
Greatrex, 'Innocent III's Writings'	J. Greatrex, 'Innocent III's Writings in English Benedictine Libraries', in Anne Duggan, Joan Greatrex, and Brenda Bolton (eds), *Omnia Disce—Medieval Studies in Memory of Leonard Boyle, O. P.*, Aldershot, 2005, 183–95.
Greatrex, 'The Layout of Worcester'	J. Greatrex, 'The Layout of the Monastic Church, Cloister and Precinct of Worcester: Evidence in the Written Records', in C. Guy (ed.), *Archaeology at Worcester Cathedral*, Report of the Eighth Annual Symposium, 1998, 12–18.
Greatrex, 'The Local Origins of the Monks of Worcester'	J. Greatrex, 'The Local Origins of the Monks of Worcester Cathedral Priory', *Transactions of the Worcestershire Archaeological Society*, 3rd series, xvi (1998), 143–53.
Greatrex, 'Marian Studies'	J. Greatrex, 'Marian Studies and Devotion in the Benedictine Cathedral Priories in Later Medieval England', *Studies in Church History*, 39 (2004), 157–67.
	J. Greatrex, *Monastic or Episcopal Obedience: The Problem of the Sacrists of Worcester*, Worcestershire Historical Society, Occasional Publications no 3, 1980.
Greatrex, 'Monk Students from Norwich'	J. Greatrex, 'Monk Students from Norwich Cathedral Priory at Oxford and Cambridge *c*. 1300 to 1530', *English Historical Review*, 106 (1991), 555–83.
Greatrex, 'Norwich Almonry School'	J. Greatrex, 'The Almonry School of Norwich Cathedral Priory', *The Church and Childhood*, Studies in Church History, 31 (1994), 169–81.
Greatrex, 'Prior John de Evesham'	J. Greatrex, 'Prior John de Evesham of Worcester, One of St Benedict's Worthy Stewards?', in V. King and A. V. M. Horton (eds), *Essays Presented to Father Robert Nicholl on the 85th Anniversary of his Birth, 27 March 1995*, University of Hull, 1995, 64–76.
Greatrex, 'Prosopographical Perspectives'	J. Greatrex, 'Prosopographical Perspectives, or What Can Be Done with Five Thousand Monastic Biographies?' *Medieval Prosopography*, 20 (1999), 129–45.

	J. Greatrex, 'Prosopography of English Benedictine Cathedral Chapters: Some Monastic *Curricula Vitae*', *Medieval Prosopography*, 16 (1995), 1–26.
Greatrex, 'Rabbits and Eels'	J. Greatrex, 'Rabbits and Eels at High Table: Monks of Ely at the University of Cambridge, *c.* 1337–1539', *Monasteries and Society in Medieval Britain*, Harlaxton Medieval Studies, 6 (1999), 312–28.
Greatrex, 'Recent Perspectives'	J. Greatrex, 'Recent Perspectives in Monastic History', in *The Religious Orders in Pre-Reformation England*, ed. J. G. Clark, Woodbridge, 2002, 35–47.
	J. Greatrex, 'The Reconciliation of Spiritual and Temporal Responsibilities: Some Aspects of the Monks of St Swithun's as Landowners and Estate Managers (*c.* 1380–1450)', *Hampshire Studies*, 51 (1996), 77–87.
	J. Greatrex, 'Some Statistics of Religious Motivation', *Studies in Church History*, 15 (1978), 179–86.
Greatrex, 'Who were the Monks of Rochester?'	J. Greatrex, 'Who were the Monks of Rochester?', T. Ayers and T. Tatton-Brown (eds), *Medieval Art, Architecture and Archaeology at Rochester*, The British Archaeological Association Conference Transactions, xxviii, Leeds, 2006, 205–17.
Haines, *Dover Priory*	C. Haines, *Dover Priory: A History of the Priory of St Mary the Virgin and St Martin of the New Work*, Cambridge, 1930.
Haines, 'Hamo de Hethe'	R. M. Haines, 'The Episcopate of a Benedictine Monk: Hamo de Hethe, Bishop of Rochester (1317–1352)', *Revue Bénédictine*, 102 (1992), 192–207.
	R. M. Haines, 'Some Visitation Injunctions for Worcester Cathedral Priory Appended to the Register of Bishop Simon de Montacute', *Revue Bénédictine*, 106 (1996), 332–55.
	R. M. Haines, 'Wolstan de Bransford, Prior and Bishop of Worcester, *c.* 1280–1349', *University of Birmingham Historical Journal*, 8 (1962), 97–113. Note: This article has been revised and brought up to date, 'Wolstan de Bransford OSB: A Fourteenth-Century Prior and Bishop of Worcester', *Transactions of the Worcestershire Archaeological Society*, 3rd series, xxi (2008), 179–93.
Hamilton, *Compotus Rolls*	S. G. Hamilton (ed.), *Compotus Rolls of the Priory of Worcester of the 14th and 15th Centuries*, Worcestershire Historical Society, 1910.

Hancock, *Dunster*	F. Hancock, *Dunster Church and Priory*, Taunton, 1905.
Harbottle, 'Hatfield's Visitation'	B. Harbottle, 'Bishop Hatfield's Visitation of Durham Priory in 1354', *Archaeologia Aeliana*, 4th series, 36 (1958), 81–99.
Harriss, *Beaufort*	G. L. Harriss, *Cardinal Beaufort: A Study of Lancastrian Ascendancy and Decline*, Oxford, 1988.
Harvey, *Living and Dying*	B. Harvey, *Living and Dying in England 1100–1540: The Monastic Experience*, Oxford, 1993.
Harvey, *Monastic Dress*	B. Harvey, *Monastic Dress in the Middle Ages, Precept and Practice*, The William Urry Memorial Trust, 1988.
Harvey, *English Medieval Architects*	J. Harvey, *English Medieval Architects: A Biographical Dictionary Down to 1550*, revised edn, 1987.
	J. Hatcher *et al.*, 'Monastic Mortality: Durham Priory, 1395–1529', *Economic History Review*, 59 (2006), 667–87.
HDST	J. Raine (ed.), *Historiae Dunelmensis scriptores tres*, Surtees Society, 9 (1839), 33–122.
Heale, *Dependent Priories*	M. Heale, *The Dependent Priories of Medieval English Monasteries*, Woodbridge, 2004.
HMC	*Royal Commission on Historical Manuscripts*. Appendices to Reports and Calendars, London, 1870–.
Holton-Krayenbuhl, 'Ely Infirmary Complex'	A. Holton-Krayenbuhl, 'The Infirmary Complex at Ely', *The Archaeological Journal*, 154 (1997), 118–72.
HRH	*The Heads of Religious Houses: England and Wales*, D. Knowles, C. N. L. Brooke, V. London (eds), i (*940–1216*), 2001; D. Smith, V. London, ii (*1216–1377*), 2001; D. Smith, iii (*1377–1540*), 2008.
HRO	Hampshire Record Office.
James, *ALCD*	M. R. James, *The Ancient Libraries of Canterbury and Dover*, Cambridge, 1903.
Jessopp, *Visitations of Norwich*	A. Jessopp (ed.), *Visitations of the Diocese of Norwich, A.D. 1492–1532*, Camden Society, new series 43 (1888).
Ker, 'Manuscripts from Norwich'	N. R. Ker, 'Medieval Manuscripts from Norwich Cathedral Priory', *Transactions of the Cambridge Bibliographical Society* (1949–53), 1–28; reprinted in A. G. Watson (ed.), N. R. Ker, *Books, Collectors and*

	Libraries, Studies in the Medieval Heritage, London, 1985, 243–72; references are to the reprinted article.
Ker, *MLGB*	N. R. Ker, *Medieval Libraries of Great Britain*, 2nd edn, Royal Historical Society, 1964.
Ker, *MMBL*	N. R. Ker, *Medieval Manuscripts in British Libraries*, 4 vols, Oxford, 1969–92; vol. iv completed by A. J. Piper.
Ker and Watson, *MLGB Supplement*	N. R. Ker and A. G. Watson, see under Watson.
Kitchin, *Consuetudinary*	G. W. Kitchin, *A Consuetudinary of the Fourteenth Century for the Refectory of the House of S. Swithun in Winchester*, London and Winchester, 1886.
Kitchin, *Obedientiary Rolls*	G. W. Kitchin (ed.), *Compotus Rolls of the Obedientiaries of St. Swithun's Priory, Winchester*, Hampshire Record Society, 1892.
Kitchin and Madge, *Documents of Winchester*	G. W. Kitchin and F. T. Madge, *Documents Relating to the Foundation of the Chapter of Winchester, A.D. 1541–47*, Hampshire Record Society, 1889.
Knowles, *MO*	D. Knowles, *The Monastic Orders in England*, Cambridge, 1966.
Knowles, *RO*	D. Knowles, *The Religious Orders in England*, 3 vols, Cambridge, 1948–59.
Knowles and Hadcock, *Medieval Religious Houses*	D. Knowles and R. N. Hadcock, *Medieval Religious Houses, England and Wales*, London, 1971.
Lanfranc, *Monastic Constitutions*	D. Knowles and C. N. L. Brooke (eds), *The Monastic Constitutions of Lanfranc*, OMT, Oxford, 2002; note that this is the revised edition.
Leach, *Documents . . . Education*	A. F. Leach, *Documents Illustrating Early Education in Worcester, 685 to 1700*, Worcester Historical Society, 1913.
Leclercq, *Love of Learning*	J. Leclercq, *The Love of Learning and the Desire for God: A Study of Monastic Culture*, transl. Catharine Misrahi, Fordham University Press, 1961 (published as a Mentor Omega Book, 1962).
Liber Albus	J. M. Wilson (ed.), *The Liber Albus of the Priory of Worcester, Parts 1 and 2, 1301–1339*, short abstract of documents, Worcestershire Historical Society, 1919.
Liber Eliensis	E. O. Blake (ed.), *Liber Eliensis*, Camden Society, 3rd series, xcii (1962); transcript of early versions of a 12th c. cartulary *cum* chronicle.
Liber Pensionum	C. Price (ed.), *Liber Pensionum Prioratus Wigorn*, Worcester Historical Society, 1925.

Lindley, 'Architectural Programme at Ely'	P. Lindley, 'The Fourteenth-Century Architectural Programme at Ely Cathedral', in W. M. Ormrod (ed.), *England in the Fourteenth Century: Proceedings of the 1985 Harlaxton Symposium*, Woodbridge, 1986, 119–29.
Logan, *Runaway Religious*	F. D. Logan, *Runaway Religious in Medieval England, c. 1240–1540*, Cambridge, 1996.
	R. A. Lomas, 'The Priory of Durham and its Demesnes in the Fourteenth and Fifteenth Centuries', *Economic History Review*, 2nd series, 31 (1978), 339–53.
LPL	Lambeth Palace Library (London).
LRO	Lichfield Record Office.
	H. R. Luard, *Bartholomæi de Cotton, Monachi Norwicensis, Historia Anglicana; A.D. 449–1298*, Rolls Series, 16 (London, 1859).
LVD	A. J. Piper with Lynda Rollason, 'Durham Monks: Biographical Register of Durham Cathedral Priory (1083–1539)' in The Durham *Liber Vitae*, London British Library, MS Cotton Domitian A.VII, edition and digital facsimile (eds), David and Lynda Rollason, 3 vols, British Library, 2007, iii, 129–436.
	J.P. McAleer, *Rochester Cathedral, 604–1540, an architectural history*, University of Toronto Press, 1999.
Magnum Reg. Album	H. E. Savage (ed.), *The Great Register of Lichfield Cathedral Known as Magnum Registrum Album*, William Salt Archaeological Society, 3rd series, 1924 (1926).
Manco, 'Bath Priory'	J. Manco, 'The Buildings of Bath Priory', *Somerset Archaeology and Natural History*, 137 (1993), 75–109.
Mason, *St Wulfstan*	E. Mason, *St. Wulfstan of Worcester, c. 1008–1095*, Oxford, 1990.
	M. Mate, 'Agrarian Economy after the Black Death: The Manors of Canterbury Cathedral Priory 1348–91', *Economic History Review*, 2nd series, 37, iii (1984), 341–54.
	M. Mate, 'The Farming Out of Manors: A New Look at the Evidence from Canterbury Cathedral Priory', *Journal of Medieval History*, 9 (1983), 331–43.
	M. Mate, 'The Indebtedness of Canterbury Cathedral Priory', *Economic History Review*, 2nd series, 26 (1973), 183–97.

Maxwell Lyte, *Dunster*	H. C. Maxwell Lyte, *A History of Dunster and the Families of Mohun and Luttrell*, 2 vols, London, 1909.
Miller, *The Abbey and Bishopric of Ely*	E. Miller, *The Abbey and Bishopric of Ely: The Social History of an Ecclesiastical Estate from the Tenth Century to the Early Fourteenth Century*, Cambridge, 1969.
Morgan and Thomson, *The Book in Britain*	N. J. Morgan and R. M. Thomson (eds), *The Cambridge History of the Book in Britain*, ii, 1100–1400, Cambridge, 2008.
Morris, *Cathedrals and Abbeys*	R. Morris, *Cathedrals and Abbeys of England and Wales: The Building Church, 600–1540*, London, 1979.
Nilson, *Cathedral Shrines*	B. Nilson, *Cathedral Shrines of Medieval England*, Woodbridge, 1998.
Noake, *Worcester Cathedral*	J. Noake, *The Monastery and Cathedral of Worcester*, London, 1866.
Noble, *Norwich Gardener's Rolls*	C. Noble (ed.), *Farming and Gardening in Late Medieval Norfolk*, Norfolk Record Society 61, 1996, 1–93.
NRO	Norfolk Record Office.
Oakley, 'Rochester Priory'	A. Oakley, 'Rochester Priory, 1185–1540', in N. Yates (ed.), *Faith and Fabric: A History of Rochester Cathedral 604–1994*, Woodbridge, 1996, 29–56.
ODNB	*Oxford Dictionary of National Biography*.
Orme, *English Schools*	N. Orme, *English Schools of the Middle Ages*, London, 1973.
Owen, *King's Lynn*	D. M. Owen (ed.), *The Making of King's Lynn: A Documentary Survey*, British Academy, London, 1985.
Oxford, Bodley	Oxford, Bodleian Library.
Pantin, *Black Monk Chapters*	W. A. Pantin (ed.), *Documents Illustrating the Activities of the General and Provincial Chapters of the English Black Monks, 1215–1540*, Camden Society, 3rd series, 45[i], 47[ii], 54[iii], 1931–7.
Pantin, *Canterbury College Oxford*	W. A. Pantin, *Canterbury College Oxford*, Oxford Historical Society, new series, 4 vols, i and ii (1947), iii (1950), iv (1985).
Pantin, 'Durham College Catalogue'	W. A. Pantin, 'Catalogue of the Books of Durham College, Oxford, c. 1390–1400' in H. Salter, W. A. Pantin, and H. Richardson (eds), *Formularies which Bear on the History of Oxford, c. 1204–1420*, Oxford Historical Society, new series, iv, vol. 1 (1942), 240–5.

Pantin, 'The Monk-Solitary of Farne'	W. A. Pantin, 'The Monk-Solitary of Farne: A Fourteenth-Century English Mystic', *English Historical Review*, 59 (1944), 162–86.
Pantin, 'Origins of Monasticism'	W. A. Pantin, 'Some Medieval Treatises on the Origins of Monasticism', in V. Ruffer and A. J. Taylor (eds), *Medieval Studies Presented to Rose Graham*, Oxford, 1950, 189–215.
Pantin, 'Uthred of Boldon'	W. A. Pantin, 'Two Treatises by Uthred of Boldon on the Monastic Life', in R. W. Hunt, W. A. Pantin, and R. W. Southern (eds), *Studies in Medieval History Presented to F. M. Powicke*, Oxford, 1948, 363–85.
Paris, *Chronica Majora*	H. R. Luard (ed.), *Matthaei Parisiensis, monachi sancti Albani, Chronica Majora*, Rolls Series, 7 vols, 1872–1883.
	R. W. Pfaff, *The Liturgy in Medieval England, a History*, Cambridge, 2009.
Piper, *Durham Monks at Jarrow*	A. J. Piper, *The Durham Monks at Jarrow*, Jarrow Lecture, 1986.
Piper, 'Historical Interests of Durham Monks'	A. J. Piper, 'The Historical Interests of the Monks of Durham', in D. W. Rollason (ed.), *Symeon of Durham, Historian of Durham and the North*, Stamford, 1998, 301–32.
Piper, 'The Libraries of the Monks of Durham'	A. J. Piper, 'The Libraries of the Monks of Durham', in M. B. Parkes and A. G. Watson (eds), *Medieval Scribes, Manuscripts and Libraries: Essays Presented to N. R. Ker*, London, 1978, 213–49.
Piper, 'Monks of Durham and... Old Age'	A. J. Piper, 'The Monks of Durham and Patterns of Activity in Old Age', in C. Barron and J. Stratford (eds), *The Church and Learning in Later Medieval Society: Essays in Honour of R. B. Dobson*, Harlaxton Medieval Studies, xi, Donington, 2002, 51–63.
	A. J. Piper, 'The Monks of Durham and the Study of Scripture', in J. E. Clark (ed.), *The Culture of Medieval English Monasticism*, Woodbridge, 2007, 86–103.
Piper, 'Size and Shape of Durham'	A. J. Piper, 'The Size and Shape of Durham's Monastic Community, 1274–1539', in C. Liddy and R. Britnell (eds), *North-East England in the Later Middle Ages*, Woodbridge, 2005, 153–71.
Piper, 'Stamford Priory'	A. J. Piper, 'St Leonard's Priory, Stamford', in the *Stamford Historian* (Stamford Historical Society and the Stamford Survey Group), no. 5 (Sept. 1980), 5–25 (pt 1), no. 6 (Feb. 1982), 1–23.

PL	J. P. Migne, *Patrologia Latina*, 217 vols, Paris, 1844–55.
Raine, *Coldingham*	J. Raine (ed.), *The Priory of Coldingham: The Correspondence, Inventories, Account Rolls and Law Proceedings of the Priory of Coldingham*, Surtees Society, 12 (1841).
Raine, *Finchale*	J. Raine (ed.), *The Priory of Finchale: The Charters of Endowment, Inventories and Account Rolls of the Priory of Finchale in the County of Durham*, Surtees Society, 6 (1837).
Raine, *Jarrow/Wearmouth*	J. Raine (ed.), *The Inventories and Account Rolls of the Benedictine Houses or Cells of Jarrow and Monk-Wearmouth in the County of Durham*, Surtees Society, 29 (1854).
RB	1) T. Fry, *RB 1980, The Rule of St. Benedict: In Latin and English with Notes*, Collegeville, 1981;
	2) T. Kardong, *Benedict's Rule: A Translation and Commentary*, Collegeville, 1996;
	3) H. Rochais and E. Manning (eds), *Règle de Saint Benoît*, les Éditions la Documentation Cistercienne, Paris, 1980.
	(Note: These may be distinguished as Fry, *RB*, Kardong, *RB*, and Manning, *RB* respectively, when referring to the translation or commentary; references to the Latin text of the Rule will be identified simply as *RB* as they may be found in all editions of the Rule which have numbers for both chapter and verse.)

Registers, episcopal and priory, by diocese and in chronological order

Bath

Reg. Giffard	T. S. Holmes (ed.), *The Registers of Walter Giffard, Bishop of Bath and Wells, 1265/6, and of Henry Bowett, Bishop of Bath and Wells, 1401–7*, Somerset Record Society 13, 1899.
Reg. Drokensford	E. Hobhouse (ed.), *Calendar of the Register of John de Drokensford, Bishop of Bath and Wells (AD 1309–1329)*, Somerset Record Society 1, 1887.
Reg. Shrewsbury	T. S. Holmes (ed.), *The Register of Ralph of Shrewsbury, Bishop of Bath and Wells, 1329–1363*, Somerset Record Society, 2 vols, 9, 10, 1896.
Reg. Bowett	See under *Reg. Giffard* above.

Reg. Bubwith	T. S. Holmes (ed.), *The Register of Nicholas Bubwith, Bishop of Bath and Wells, 1407–1424*, Somerset Record Society, 2 vols, 29, 30, 1914.
Reg. Stafford	T. S. Holmes (ed.), *The Register of John Stafford, Bishop of Bath and Wells, 1425–1443*, Somerset Record Society, 2 vols, 31, 32, 1915–16.
Reg. Bekynton	H. C. Maxwell Lyte and M. C. B. Dawes (eds), *The Register of Thomas Bekynton, Bishop of Bath and Wells, 1443–1465*, Somerset Record Society, 2 vols, 49, 50, 1934–35.
Reg. Clerk	H. C. Maxwell Lyte (ed.), Somerset Record Society, 55 (1940), 1–26 (printed with registers of Thomas Wolsey, William Knyght, and Gilbert Bourne).

Canterbury

Reg. Pecham	F. N. Davis *et al.* (eds), *The Register of John Pecham, Archbishop of Canterbury, 1279–1292*, Canterbury and York Society, 2 vols, 64, 65, i (1969); Decima Douie (ed.), *ib.*, ii (1968).
Reg. Winchelsey	Rose Graham (ed.), *Registrum Roberti Winchelsey Cantuariensis Archiepiscopi, A.D. 1294–1313*, Canterbury and York Society, 2 vols, 51, 52 (1952, 1956); vol. i (pp. 1–511), vol. ii (pp. 513–1473).
Reg. Langham	A. C. Wood (ed.), *Registrum Simonis Langham, Cantuariensis Archiepiscopi [1366–8]*, Canterbury and York Society 53, 1956.
Reg. Chichele	E. F. Jacob (ed.), *The Register of Henry Chichele, Archbishop of Canterbury, 1414–1443*, Canterbury and York Society, 4 vols, 45, 42, 46, 47 (1943–7).

Coventry

Reg. Stretton (1907)	R. A. Wilson (ed.), *The Registers or Act Books of the Bishops of Coventry and Lichfield, Book 4, being the register of the guardians of the spiritualities during the vacancy of the see, and the first register of Bishop Robert de Stretton, 1358–1385: An Abstract of the Contents.* William Salt Archaeological Society, new series 10, part 2, 1907.
Reg. Stretton (1905)	R. A. Wilson (ed.), *The Registers or Act Books of the Bishops of Coventry and Lichfield, Book 5, being the second register of Bishop Robert de Stretton, A.D. 1360–1385: An Abstract of the Contents.* William Salt Archaeological Society, new series, 8, 1905.

Reg. Catterick	R. N. Swanson (ed.), *The Register of John Catterick, Bishop of Coventry and Lichfield, 1415–1419*. Canterbury and York Society 77 (1990).
Durham	
Reg. Kellawe	*Registrum Palatinum Dunelmense: The Register of Richard de Kellawe*, ed. T. Duffus Hardy, 4 vols, Rolls Series (1873–8).
Reg. Bury	G. W. Kitchin (ed.), *Richard d'Aungerville, of Bury: Fragments of his Register and Other Documents*, Surtees Society, 119 (1910).
Reg. Langley	*The Register of Thomas Langley, Bishop of Durham, 1406–1437*, ed. R. L. Storey, 6 vols, Surtees Society, 164, 166, 169, 170, 177, 182 (1956–70).
Norwich	
Reg. Bateman	P. E. Pobst (ed.), *The Register of William Bateman, Bishop of Norwich, 1344–1355*, 2 vols, Canterbury and York Society (1996, 2000).
Rochester	
Reg. Hethe	C. Johnson (ed.), *Registrum Hamonis Hethe, Diocesis Roffensis, AD 1319–1352*, 2 vols, Canterbury and York Society, 48, 49 (1948); continuous pagination; vol. ii begins on p. 593.
Reg. Roffense	J. Thorpe (ed.), *Registrum Roffense*, London, 1769.
Winchester	
Reg. Pontissara	C. Deedes (ed.), *Registrum Johannis de Pontissara, episcopi Wintoniensis, A.D. MCCLXXXII–MCCCIV*, Canterbury and York Society, 2 vols 19, 30 (1915–24). Pagination continuous throughout.
Reg. Woodlock	A. W. Goodman (ed.), *Registrum Henrici Woodlock, diocesis Wintoniensis, A.D. 1305–1316*, Canterbury and York Society, 2 vols 43, 44 (1940–41). Pagination continuous throughout.
Reg. Sandale / Reg. Asserio	F. Baigent (ed.), *The Registers of John de Sandale and Rigaud de Asserio, Bishops of Winchester (A.D. 1316–1323) with an Appendix of Contemporaneous and Other Illustrative Documents*, Hampshire Record Society, 1897.
Reg. Edington	S. Hockey (ed.) *The Register of William Edington, Bishop of Winchester, 1346–1366*, Hampshire Record Series, 2 vols, 1986–7.

Reg. Wykeham	T. F. Kirby (ed.), *Wykeham's Register*, Hampshire Record Society, 2 vols, 1896–9.
Priory Register	
Reg. Common Seal	J. Greatrex (ed.), *The Register of the Common Seal of the Priory of St. Swithun, Winchester, 1345–1497*, Hampshire Record Series, 1978.
Worcester	
Reg. Giffard	J. W. Willis Bund (ed.), *Episcopal Registers, Diocese of Worcester: Register of Bishop Godfrey Giffard, September 23rd 1268 to August 15th 1301*, Worcestershire Historical Society, 2 vols, 1902; continuous pagination.
Reg. Gainsborough	J. W. Willis Bund (ed.), *The Register of William de Geynesburgh, Bishop of Worcester, 1302–1307*, Worcestershire Historical Society, 1907.
Reg. Reynolds	R. A. Wilson (ed.), *The Register of Walter Reynolds, Bishop of Worcester, 1308–1313*, Worcestershire Historical Society, 1927.
Reg. Cobham	E. H. Pearce (ed.), *The Register of Thomas de Cobham, Bishop of Worcester, 1317–1327*, Worcestershire Historical Society, 1930.
Reg. Orleton	R. Haines (ed.), *Calendar of the Register of Adam de Orleton, Bishop of Worcester, 1327–1333*, Worcestershire Historical Society, new series, and Historical Manuscripts Commission Joint Publication, 1980.
Reg. Montacute	R. Haines (ed.), *Calendar of the Register of Simon de Montacute, Bishop of Worcester, 1334–1337*, Worcestershire Historical Society, 1996.
Reg. Bransford	R. Haines (ed.), *A Calendar of the Register of Wolstan de Bransford, Bishop of Worcester, 1339–49*, Worcestershire Historical Society new series and Historical Manuscripts Commission Joint Publication, 1966.
Reg. Wakefield	W. Marett (ed.), *A Calendar of the Register of Henry Wakefield, Bishop of Worcester, 1375–95*, Worcestershire Historical Society, new series, 1972.
Reg. Clifford	W. E. L. Smith, *The Register of Richard Clifford, Bishop of Worcester, 1401–1407: A Calendar*. Pontifical Institute of Mediaeval Studies, Toronto (Subsidia Mediaevalia), 1976.
Priory Registers	
Liber Albus	J. M. Wilson (ed.), *The Liber Albus of the Priory of Worcester, Parts 1 and 2, Priors John de Wyke, 1301–*

	1317, and Wulstan de Bransford, 1317–1339, folios 1–162, Worcestershire Historical Society, 1919.
Reg. Almoner	J. Bloom (ed.), *Liber Elemosinarii: The Almoner's Book of the Priory of Worcester*, Worcestershire Historical Society, 1911.
Reg. Prioratus	W. Hale (ed.), *Registrum sive Liber Irrotulatus et Consuetudinarius Prioratus beate Marie Wigorniensis*, Camden Society, old series 91, 1865.
Reg. Sed. Vac.	J. Willis Bund (ed.), *The Register of the Diocese of Worcester During the Vacancy of the See, Usually called Registrum Sede Vacante, 1301–1435*, Worcestershire Historical Society, 1893–97.
	M. P. Richards, 'Texts and their Traditions in the Medieval Library of Rochester Cathedral Priory', *Transactions of the American Philosophical Society*, lxxviii/3 (1988).
Rites of Durham	J. T. Fowler (ed.), *Rites of Durham*, Surtees Society, 107, 1903.
Rollason, *Symeon of Durham*	D. Rollason (ed.), *Symeon of Durham: Historian of Durham and the North*, Stamford, 1998.
Rouse, *Authentic Witnesses*	M. A. and R. H. Rouse, *Authentic Witnesses: Approaches to Medieval Texts and Manuscripts*, Notre Dame, 1991.
Rouse, *Reg. Anglie de Libris*	R. H. and M. A. Rouse and R. A. B. Mynors, *Registrum Anglie de Libris Doctorum et Auctorum Veterum*, Corpus of British Medieval Library Catalogues, 2, British Library/British Academy, 1991.
Rouse, 'Verbal Concordance'	R. H. and M. A. Rouse, 'The Verbal Concordance to the Scriptures', *Archivum Fratrum Predicatorum*, 44 (1974), 5–30.
Rud, *Codices . . . Dunelmensis*	T. Rud, *Codices Manuscripti Ecclesiae Dunelmensis*, Durham, 1825.
Rymer, *Foedera*	T. Rymer, *Foedera, Conventiones, Litterae, et cujuscumque Generis Acta Publica inter Reges Angliae et alios quosvis Imperatores, Reges, Pontifices, Principes, vel Communitates, 1101–1654*, new ed., 1069–1381 ed. by A. Clark, F. Holbrooke, and J. Caley, 4 vols in 7 parts, Record Commission, 1816–69.
Salter, *Snappe's Formulary*	H. Salter (ed.), *Snappe's Formulary and Other Records*, Oxford Historical Society, 1924.
Saltman, *Theobald*	A. Saltman, *Theobald Archbishop of Canterbury*, University of London Historical Studies II, London, 1955, reprinted New York, 1969.

Saunders, *Obedientiary Rolls*	H. W. Saunders, *An Introduction to the Obedientiary and Manor Rolls of Norwich Cathedral Priory*, London, 1930.
Scammell, 'The Case of Geoffrey Burdon'	J. Scammell, 'Some Aspects of Medieval English Monastic Government: The Case of Geoffrey Burdon, Prior of Durham (1313–1321)', *Revue Bénédictine*, 68 (1958), 226–50.
Scammell, *Puiset*	G. V. Scammell, *Hugh de Puiset, Bishop of Durham*, Cambridge, 1956.
Searle, *Lists of Christ Church*	W. G. Searle, comp., *Lists of the Deans, Priors and Monks of Christ Church Monastery*, Cambridge Antiquarian Society, Octavo Publications, no. 34 (1902); compiled from Canterbury, Lit. MS D.12 and Cambridge, Corpus Christi College MS 298.
Sharpe, *EBL*	R. Sharpe, J. Carley, R. Thomson, and A. Watson, *English Benedictine Libraries: The Shorter Catalogues*, Corpus of British Medieval Library Catalogues, 4, British Library/British Academy, 1996.
Sharpe, *Latin Writers*	R. Sharpe, *A Handlist of the Latin Writers of Great Britain and Ireland Before 1540*, Publications of the Journal of Medieval Latin, 1, Brepols, 1997.
Sheppard, *HMC Vth (VIIIth, IXth) Report*	J. B. Sheppard, *Historical Manuscripts Commission, Appendix to the Vth Report* (1876), *VIIIth Report* (1881), *IXth Report* (1883).
Sheppard, *Lit. Cant.*	J. B. Sheppard (ed.), *Litterae Cantuarienses*, Rolls Series, 3 vols, 1887–9; extracts mainly from priory registers; the items are numbered continuously throughout.
Smalley, *Study of the Bible*	B. Smalley, *The Study of the Bible in the Middle Ages*, 3rd edn, Oxford, 1982.
Smith, *Masters of the Sacred Page*	Lesley Smith, *Masters of the Sacred Page: Manuscripts of Theology in the Latin West to 1274*, Notre Dame, 2001.
Smith, *Canterbury Cathedral Priory*	R. A. L. Smith, *Canterbury Cathedral Priory: A Study in Monastic Administration*, Cambridge, 1969.
Smith, 'Rochester Cathedral Priory'	R. A. L. Smith, 'The Financial System of Rochester Cathedral Priory', *English Historical Review*, 1940 and reprinted in his *Collected Papers*, London, 1947, 42–53.
Somner, *Antiquities of Canterbury*	W. Somner and N. Battely, *The Antiquities of Canterbury*, 2nd edn, London, 1703.
Southern, *Scholastic Humanism*	R. W. Southern, *Scholastic Humanism and the Unification of Europe*, 2 vols, Oxford, 1995, 2001.

Sparks, *Canterbury Precincts*	M. Sparks, *Canterbury Cathedral Precincts, a Historical Survey*, Canterbury, 2007.
SRO	Somerset Record Office.
Stewart, *Architectural History of Ely*	D. J. Stewart, *Architectural History of Ely Cathedral*, London, 1868.
Stoneman, *Dover Priory*	W. P. Stoneman (ed.), *Dover Priory*, Corpus of British Medieval Library Catalogues, v, British Library/British Academy, 1999.
	T. Symons (ed.), *Regularis Concordia: The Monastic Agreement*, NMT, Edinburgh, 1953.
Talbot and Hammond, *Medical Practitioners*	C. H. Talbot and E. A. Hammond, *The Medical Practitioners in Medieval England*, London, 1965.
Tanner, *The Church in Late Medieval Norwich*	N. Tanner, *The Church in Late Medieval Norwich, 1370–1532*, Toronto, 1984.
	T. Tanner, *Notitia Monastica*, London, 1744.
Tatton-Brown, *Archaeology of Cathedrals*	T. Tatton-Brown and J. Munby (eds), *The Archaeology of Cathedrals*, Oxford University Committee for Archaeology, Monograph no. 42 (1996).
	T. Tatton-Brown, 'Three Great Benedictine Houses in Kent: Their Buildings and Topography', *Archaeologia Cantiana*, 100 (1984), 171–88.
	Jerome Taylor, *The Didascalicon of Hugh of St Victor*, London, 1961.
Thompson, *Customary of St. Augustine*	E. M. Thompson (ed.), *Customary of the Benedictine Monasteries of St. Augustine, Canterbury and St. Peter, Westminster*, Henry Bradshaw Society, 2 vols, 1902–4; Note: St. Aug. is vol. i; St. Peter is vol. ii.
Thomson, *Medieval Manuscripts in Worcester Cathedral*	R. M. Thomson (ed.), *A Descriptive Catalogue of the Medieval Manuscripts in Worcester Cathedral Library*, Woodbridge, 2001.
	J. Thorpe (ed.), *Custumale Roffense*, London, 1788.
Threlfall-Holmes, *Monks and Markets*	M. Threlfall-Holmes, *Monks and Markets: Durham Cathedral Priory 1460–1520*, Oxford, 2005.
TNA	The National Archives (formerly Public Record Office).
Tolhurst, *Norwich Customary*	J. Tolhurst (ed.), *The Customary of the Cathedral Priory Church of Norwich*, Henry Bradshaw Society, 1948.
	J. Tolhurst (ed.), *The Monastic Breviary of Hyde Abbey: Winchester*, 6 vols, Henry Bradshaw Society, 1932–43.

Turner, 'Customary of St. Thomas Becket'	D. H. Turner, 'The Customary of the Shrine of St. Thomas Becket', *Canterbury Cathedral Chronicle*, no. 70 (1976), 16–22.
Turner and Coxe, *Charters and Rolls*	W. H. Turner and H. O. Coxe (eds), *Calendar of the Charters and Rolls in the Bodleian Library*, Oxford, 1878.
	R. Twysden, *Historiae Anglicanae Scriptores X*, 2 vols, London, 1652.
VCH	*The Victoria History of the Counties of England*, London, 1900–.
	J. and J. A. Venn, comps, *Alumni Cantabrigiensis: A Biographical List of all Known Students, Graduates and Holders of Office at the University of Cambridge, from the Earliest Times to 1900*, pt 1, 4 vols, Cambridge, 1922.
	J. Venn, comp., *Biographical History of Gonville and Caius College, 1349–1891*, i, *1349–1713*, Cambridge, 1897.
Walsingham, *Gesta Abbatum*	H. Riley (ed.), *Gesta Abbatum Monasterii sancti Albani: A Thoma Walsingham*, Rolls Series, 3 vols, 1867–1869.
Walsingham, *Historia Anglicana*	H. Riley (ed.), *Thomae Walsingham quondam Monachi S. Albani, Historia Anglicana*, Rolls Series, 2 vols, 1863–4.
Wansbrough, *Benedictines in Oxford*	H. Wansbrough and A. Marett-Crosby (eds), *Benedictines in Oxford*, London, 1997.
Watkin, 'Receiver's Roll'	A. Watkin (ed.), 'Fragment of a Thirteenth Century Receiver's Roll from Winchester Cathedral Priory', *English Historical Review*, 61 (1946), 89–105.
Watson, *Dated and Datable Manuscripts*	A.G. Watson, *Catalogue of Dated and Datable Manuscripts c. 435–1600 in Oxford Libraries*, 2 vols, Oxford, 1984.
Watson, *MLGB Supplement*	A. G. Watson (ed.), *Medieval Libraries of Great Britain*, a list of surviving books, supplement to Ker, *MLGB*, 2nd edn, London, 1987.
WCL	Winchester Cathedral Library.
WCM	Worcester Cathedral Manuscripts and Muniments.
	F. W. Weaver, *Somerset Incumbents*, Bristol, 1889 (privately printed).
	F. W. Weaver, *Somerset Medieval Wills*, Somerset Record Society, 2 vols (1st series, 16, 1383–1500; 2nd series, 19, 1501–1530), 1901, 1903.
	Wells Liber Albus, i and ii, *Wells Liber Ruber*, *Wells Charters*, W. H. Bird and W. P. Baildon (eds),

	Historical Manuscripts Commission, 10th Report Appendix 3, Calendar of the Manuscripts of the Dean and Chapter of Wells, 2 vols, 1907, 1914. *Liber Albus* i and ii and *Liber Ruber* are in the 1st volume, 1–304, 305–528 and 529–51 respectively; *Wells Charters* is in vol. ii, 546–724.
Wilkins, *Concilia*	D. Wilkins, *Concilia Magnae Britanniae et Hiberniae*, 4 vols, London, 1737.
Willis, *Architectural History*	R. Willis, *Architectural History of Some English Cathedrals; A Collection in Two Parts of Papers Delivered During the Years 1842–1863*, Chicheley, 1972–3.
Wilson, *Accounts for . . . Henry VIII*	J. M. Wilson (ed.), *Accounts of the Priory of Worcester for the Year 13–14 Henry VIII, A.D. 1521/2*, Worcester Historical Society, 1907, Appendix vii, 58–61 (a Winchester hordarian's account, *c*. 1330).
Wilson and Gordon, *Early Compotus Rolls*	J. M. Wilson and C. Gordon (eds), *Early Compotus Rolls of the Priory of Worcester*, Worcestershire Historical Society, 1908.
Wilson, 'John de Wyke'	J. M. Wilson, 'John de Wyke, Prior of Worcester, 1301–1317: Some Glimpses of the Early Years of his Priorate from the "Liber Albus"', *Associated Architectural Societies' Reports and Papers*, 34 (1917–18), pt 1, 131–52.
Wood, *English Monasteries*	S. Wood, *English Monasteries and their Patrons in the Thirteenth Century*, Oxford, 1955.
Woodruff, 'Sacrist's Rolls'	C. Woodruff, 'The Sacrist's Rolls of Christ Church, Canterbury', *Archaeologia Cantiana*, 48 (1936), 38–80.
Woodruff and Danks, *Memorials of Christ Church*	C. Woodruff and W. Danks, *Memorials of the Cathedral and Priory of Christ Church in Canterbury*, London, 1912.
Wormald, *English Benedictine Kalendars*	F. Wormald, *English Benedictine Kalendars after A.D. 1100*, 2 vols, Henry Bradshaw Society, 77, 81, 1939–46.
WRO	Worcestershire County Record Office.
Yates, *Rochester Cathedral*	N. Yates (ed.), *Faith and Fabric: A History of Rochester Cathedral 604–1994*, Woodbridge, 1996.

Index of Manuscripts

Aberdeen, University Library
  MS 2740 97 n.

Cambridge
  Clare College
    MS 30 105 n.
  Corpus Christi College
    MS 36 214 n., 363 n.
    MS 51 358 n.
    MS 137 76
    MS 157 351 n.
    MS 178 72 n.
    MS 184 358 n.
    MS 187 358 n.
    MS 217 339 n., 345 n.
    MS 252 153 n.
    MS 264 153 n., 354 n., 357 n.
    MS 298 37 n., 149 n.
    MS 339 351 n.
    MS 347 256 n.
    MS 400 359 n.
    MS 407 153 n.
    MS 416 96 n.
    MS 417 353 n.
    MS 441 63 n., 66 n.
    MS 452 350 n.
    MS 460 339 n., 351 n.
    MS 465 171 n., 291 n.
    MS 470 256 n.
    MS 473 239 n.
  Emmanuel College
    MS 142 79 n., 271 n., 272 n.
  Fitzwilliam Museum
    MS McClean 169 69 n.
  Gonville and Caius College
    MS 136 344 n.
  Jesus College
    MS 15 122 n.
    MS 22 239 n.
    MS 23 237 n.
    MS 28 336 n.
    MS 41 73, 80
    MS 45 355 n.
    MS 57 145 n.
    MS 61 73
  King's College
    MS 22 96
  Peterhouse
    MS 71 122 n.
  Sidney Sussex College
    MS 56 344 n.
  St John's College
    MS 8 357 n.
    MS 51 114 n.
    MS 130 96 n.
    S.5.24 early printed book 156 n.
  Trinity College
    MS 46 105 n.
    MS 79 105 n.
    MS 123 106 n.
    MS 132 108
    MS 133 108
    MS 338 362 n.
    MS 342 119 n.
    MS 346 96 n.
    MS 384 123 n.
    MS 624 345 n.
    MS 883 360 n.
    MS 884 357 n.
    MS 987 22 n.
    MS 1005 178 n.
    MS 1088 361 n.
    MS 1105 317 n., 351 n.
    MS 1128 346 n.
    MS 1145 99 n., 274 n., 318 n.
    MS 1227 150 n., 350 n.
    MS 1441 269 n.
  University Library
    Add. MS 2956 40 n., 99 n., 136 n., 203 n., 204 n., 205 n., 246 n., 312 n.
    Add. MS 2957 28 n., 29 n., 35 n., 40 n., 65 n., 103 n., 135 n., 136 n., 170 n., 174 n., 175 n., 176 n., 178 n., 179 n., 180 n., 181 n., 191 n., 241 n., 245 n., 246 n., 256 n., 261 n., 263 n., 264 n., 267 n., 268 n., 282 n., 305 n., 310 n., 312 n.
    MS Dd.1.4 357 n.
    MS Dd.9.38 342 n.
    MS Ee.5.31 36 n., 186 n., 310 n.
    MS Ff.3.19 121 n.
    MS Ff.4.43 81 n.
    MS Ff.5.28 96 n.
    MS Ff.5.31 362 n.
    MS Ff.6.11 364 n.
    MS Gg.2.18 155 n., 362 n.
    MS Ii.1.22 95 n.
    MS Ii.1.23 110 n.
    MS Ii.1.32 152 n.
    MS Ii.2.7 95 n.
    MS Ii.2.15 122 n.
    MS Ii.2.19 214 n.
    MS Ii.2.22 106 n.
    MS Ii.3.1 355 n.
    MS Ii.3.7 115 n.
    MS Ii.3.24 113 n.
    MS Ii.4.2 152 n.

Index of Manuscripts

Cambridge (cont.)
  MS Ii.4.12 95 n., 360 n.
  MS Ii.4.15 81 n., 152 n.
  MS Ii.4.20 178 n., 240 n.
  MS Ii.4.25 152 n.
  MS Ii.4.35 81 n.
  MS Ii.4.38 122 n.
  MS Kk.2.19 113 n.
  MS Kk.2.21 81 n., 153 n.
  MS Kk.3.26 72 n., 80 n.
  MS Kk.4.6 97 n.
  MS Kk.4.13 214 n.
  MS Kk.5.10 339 n.
  MS Ll.5.21 153 n.
  MS Mm.1.19 158 n.
  MS Mm.3.14 151 n.
Canterbury, Cathedral Library
  MS 24 (C.14) 201 n., 252 n.
  MS 26 (D.12) 37 n., 303 n., 305 n., 306 n., 307 n., 308 n., 318 n.
  MS 27 (C.11) 170 n.
  MS 53 (D.8) 95 n.
  MS 54 (D.9) 95 n.
  MS 62 (E.17) 237 n.
  MS 100 (B.12) 117 n., 356 n.
  Add MS 6 239 n.

Downside Abbey
  MS 26524 239 n.
Dublin, Trinity College
  MS 503 351 n.
Durham
  Cathedral Library
    MS A.I.2 114 n.
    MSS A.I.3–5 110 n.
    MS A.I.6 109 n.
    MS A.I.8 108 n.
    MS A.I.11 108 n.
    MSS A.I.12–16 108 n.
    MS A.I.13 112 n.
    MSS A.II.11–13 112 n.
    MS A.II.9 112 n.
    MS A.II.10 112 n.
    MS A.II.16 105 n.
    MS A.III.7 112 n., 150 n.
    MS A.III.9 112 n.
    MS A.III.10 112
    MS A.III.11 105 n.
    MS A.III.12 114 n.
    MS A.III.13 112 n.
    MS A.III.31 109 n.
    MS A.III.35 117 n.
    MS A.IV.2 112 n.
    MS A.IV.3 379 n.
    MS A.IV.36 350 n.
    MSS B.I.1–4 122 n.
    MS B.I.6 123
    MSS B.I.8–17 123 n.
    MS B.I.9 150 n.
    MS B.I.10 145 n.
    MS B.I.17 123
    MS B.I.31 340 n.
    MS B.I.32 355 n.
    MS B.I.33 119 n.
    MS B.I.34 119 n.
    MS B.II.1 357 n.
    MS B.II.27 105 n.
    MS B.II.30 113 n.
    MS B.II.32 106 n.
    MS B.II.33 82 n.
    MS B.II.35 354 n., 360 n.
    MS B.II.36 119 n.
    MS B.III.8 73
    MS B.III.10 106 n.
    MS B.III.20 119 n.
    MS B.III.22 114 n.
    MS B.III.27 117 n.
    MS B.III.28 117 n.
    MS B.III.29 117 n.
    MS B.III.30 78 n., 325 n., 353 n.
    MS B.III.31 117 n.
    MS B.IV.14 362 n.
    MS B.IV.15 150 n.
    MS B.IV.24 73
    MS B.IV.26 73, 325 n.,
    MS B.IV.34 78 n., 79 n., 222, 328 n.
    MS B.IV.39 A and B 349 n., 362 n.
    MS B.IV.41 73
    MS B.IV.42 80 n., 117 n.
    MS B.IV.43 117 n.
    MS C.I.19 150 n., 295 n.
    MS C.I.20 339 n.
    MS C.II.3 150 n.
    MS C.III.13 117 n.
    MS C.IV.12 150 n., 295 n.
    MS C.IV.21 117 n.
    MS C.IV.23 344 n.
    MS C.IV.24 68 n., 150 n., 343 n.
    MS C.IV.25 343 n.
    MS C.IV.26 151 n., 340 n.
  Ushaw, St Cuthbert's College
    MS 7 238 n.

Leyden, University Library
  MS Voss lat. F.93 155 n.
London
  British Library
    Add. MS 6162 78 n.
    Add. MS 15759 355 n.
    Add. MS 25031 269 n.
    Add. MS 29436 65 n., 321 n.
    Add. MS 33381 256 n.
    Add. MS 41612 28 n., 168 n., 191 n.
    Add. MS 45103 357 n., 360 n.
    Add. MS 57950 269 n.
    Add. MS 59616 208 n., 246 n.
    MS Arundel 35 356

MS Arundel 68 62 n., 72 n., 87 n., 93 n., 317 n.
MS Arundel 86 355 n.
MS Arundel 155 237 n.
MS Arundel 292 83 n.
MS Arundel 507 222
MS Burney 310 354 n., 358 n.
MS Cotton Caligula A.viii 362 n.
MS Cotton Claudius C.vi 317 n.
MS Cotton Claudius C.ix 69 n.
MS Cotton Claudius D.iv 353 n.
MS Cotton Claudius E.viii 357 n.
MS Cotton Domitian vii 318 n. (the *LVD* has Domitian A.vii)
MS Cotton Domitian xiii 351 n.
MS Cotton Domitian xv 352 n.
MS Cotton Faustina A.vi 141 n., 150 n., 219 n., 222 n., 224 n.
MS Cotton Faustina C.v 16 n., 41 n., 56 n., 228 n.
MS Cotton Faustina C.xii 60 n., 65 n., 85 n.
MS Cotton Galba E.iv 62 n., 246 n.
MS Cotton Nero A.xv 352 n.
MS Cotton Nero A.xvi 352 n.
MS Cotton Nero C.iv 238 n.
MS Cotton Nero C.v 351 n.
MS Cotton Nero D.ii 351 n., 357 n.
MS Cotton Otho C.i 354 n.
MS Cotton Tiberius A.iii 72 n.
MS Cotton Titus A.i 352 n.
MS Cotton Titus A.xviii 360 n.
MS Cotton Vespasian A.xxii 274 n., 318 n.
MS Cotton Vespasian B.xix 350 n.
MS Cotton Vespasian B.xxv 357 n.
MS Cotton Vespasian D.xxi 357 n.
MS Egerton 3316 163 n., 325 n.
MS Harley 23 119 n.
MS Harley 261 356 n.
MS Harley 315 155 n.
MS Harley 328 37 n.
MS Harley 491 150 n.
MS Harley 547 238 n.
MS Harley 1587 337 n., 340 n., 341 n.
MS Harley 3066 131 n.
MS Harley 3634 355 n.
MS Harley 3680 354 n.
MS Harley 3950 238 n., 243 n., 317 n.
MS Harley 4664 35 n., 240 n., 246 n., 305 n.
MS Harley 4725 96 n.
MS Harley 4894 281 n.
MS Harley 4967 340 n.
MS Harley 5234 95 n., 150
MS Harley 5289 239 n., 259 n., 261 n.
MS Lansdowne 397 343 n.
MS Royal 4A.xv 110 n.
MS Royal 5A.x 154 n.
MS Royal 6A.xi 97 n.
MS Royal 10A.xii 155 n.
MS Royal 10A.xvi 116
MS Royal 15A.xxii 357 n., 360 n.
MS Royal 3B.i 154 n.
MS Royal 4B.ii 154 n.
MS Royal 4B.vii 69 n.
MS Royal 4B.xiii 105 n., 106
MS Royal 6B.ii 105 n.
MS Royal 10B.ii 95 n., 154 n.
MS Royal 10B.ix 342 n.
MS Royal 10B.x 343 n.
MS Royal 15B.iv 343 n.
MS Royal 15B.xiv 336 n.
MS Royal 2C.i 119
MS Royal 2C.v 109 n., 113, 154 n.
MS Royal 3C.iv 106 n.
MS Royal 3C.vii 118 n.
MS Royal 5C.i 105 n.
MS Royal 6C.iv 154 n.
MS Royal 6C.vi 106 n.
MS Royal 9C.iv 124 n., 155 n.
MS Royal 11C.i 123 n.
MS Royal 14C.i 351 n.
MS Royal 14C.xiii 153 n., 355 n., 358 n., 359 n.
MS Royal 2D.vi 96 n.
MS Royal 2D.xxx 338 n.
MS Royal 4D.xii 118 n.
MS Royal 6D.vii 106 n., 154 n.
MS Royal 8D.v* 96 n.
MS Royal 8D.xiii 81 n.
MS Royal 12D.iv 255 n., 256 n.
MS Royal 4E.v 115 n.
MS Royal 5E.ii 105 n.
MS Royal 7E.vi 72 n.
MS Royal 9E.xi 155 n.
MS Royal 7F.iv 154 n.
MS Royal 12G.iv 152 n.
BL IA.3420 early printed book 155 n.
Lambeth Palace
  MSS 10–12 355 n.
  MS 20 62 n., 63 n., 72 n., 87 n., 100 n.
  MS 23 117 n.
  MS 78 149 n.
  MS 180 81 n.
  MS 188 357 n.
  MS 204 105 n.
  MS 242 284 n., 294 n.
  MS 243 258 n., 272 n., 284 n., 311 n., 319 n.
  MS 368 238 n.
  MS 448 58 n., 67, 68 n., 115 n., 282 n., 329 n.
  MS 558 237 n.
Lincoln's Inn
  MS Hale 114 353 n.
Wellcome Institute for the History of Medicine
  MS 408 294 n.

Index of Manuscripts

Norwich
  Bridewell Museum
    MS 99.20 232 n.
  Record Office
    DCL MS 1 351 n.

Oxford
  All Souls College
    MS 114 353 n.
  Balliol College
    MS 15 106 n.
  Bodleian Library
    MS Auct. D.4.8 116 n.
    MS Auct. F.3.9 337 n.
    MS Auct. F.5.23 337 n., 339 n.
    MS Bodley 58 156 n.
    MS Bodley 196 96 n., 97 n.
    MS Bodley 217 105 n.
    MS Bodley 251 109 n.
    MS Bodley 316 355 n.
    MS Bodley 336 362 n.
    MS Bodley 345 108 n.
    MS Bodley 379 96 n.
    MS Bodley 535 362 n.
    MS Bodley 692 146 n., 279 n.
    MS Bodley 775 239 n.
    MS Bodley 828 95 n.
    MS Bodley 862 114 n.
    MS Digby 4 97 n.
    MS Digby 31 156 n.
    MS Douce 366 178 n., 238 n.
    MS Fairfax 20 153 n., 357 n.
    MS Hatton 11 95 n., 157 n., 256 n.
    MS Hatton 40 81 n.
    MS Hatton 48 72 n.
    MS Hatton 54 356 n.
    MS Lat. liturg. d.20 269 n.
    MS Lat. liturg. f.19 238 n.
    MS Laud lat. 12 340 n.
    MS Laud lat. 95 238 n.
    MS Laud misc. 40 360 n.
    MS Laud misc. 112 72 n., 82 n., 339 n.
    MS Laud misc. 161 109 n.
    MS Laud misc. 402 343 n.
    MS Laud misc. 413 361 n.
    MS Laud misc. 489 362 n.
    MS Laud misc. 572 357 n.
    MS Laud misc. 603 150 n., 358 n.
    MS Laud misc. 641 150 n.
    MS Laud misc. 698 352 n.
    MS Laud misc. 748 353 n.
    MS Lyell 19 72 n.
    MS Rawlinson B.188 359 n.
    MS Rawlinson B.191 355 n.
    MS Rawlinson C.4 95 n.
    MS Rawlinson C.428 157 n.
    MS Rawlinson C.489 240 n.
    MS Rawlinson C.958 363 n.
    MS Seldon supra 65 342 n., 344 n.
    MS Tanner 4 79
  Corpus Christi College
    MS 157 351 n.
    MS 189 296 n.
    MS 256 59 n., 147 n., 285 n.
  Magdalen College
    MS lat. 53 351 n.
    MS lat. 100 238 n.
    MS lat. 180 355 n.
  St John's College
    MS 154 336 n.
  Wadham College
    MS A13.7 238 n.

Paris
  Bibliothèque nationale
    MS lat. 770 237 n.
    MS lat. 4922 355 n.
    MS nouv.acq.lat. 1670 237 n.

Winchester, Cathedral Library
  MS 1 354 n.
  MS 4 113 n.
  MS 8 118 n.
  MS 14 363 n.
  MS 15 346 n.
  Winchester College MS 18, in cathedral library 82 n., 363 n.

Worcester, Cathedral Library
  MS F.1 120, 339 n.
  MS F.2 157 n.
  MS F.8 122 n., 157 n.
  MS F.10 158 n.
  MS F.16 157 n.
  MS F.20 339 n.
  MS F.22 339 n.
  MSS F.25–8 110 n.
  MS F.34 269 n.
  MS F.37 120, 269 n.
  MS F.43 269 n.
  MS F.45 362 n.
  MS F.46 122 n.
  MS F.47 113 n.
  MS F.48 363 n.
  MS F.53 122 n.
  MS F.61 336 n., 338 n., 345 n.
  MS F.62 157 n.
  MS F.64 122 n., 269 n.
  MS F.67 109 n.
  MS F.71 95 n., 97 n., 113 n., 120 n.
  MS F.77 157 n.
  MS F.79 144
  MS F.80 117 n.
  MS F.88 122 n.
  MS F.93 158 n.
  MS F.98 122
  MS F.99 338 n.
  MSS F.101–4 124 n.

Index of Manuscripts

MSS F.107–9 124 n.
MS F.120 269 n.
MS F.123 345 n.
MS F.124 97 n., 144, 157 n.
MS F.125 157 n., 269 n.
MS F.128 117 n.
MS F.129 97 n.
MS F.130 116 n., 131 n.
MS F.131 118 n., 157 n.
MS F.133 120 n., 269 n.
MS F.134 122
MS F.137 338 n.
MS F.139 124 n., 157 n.
MS F.141 157 n.
MS F.147 340 n., 341 n.
MS F.148 354 n.
MS F.152 269 n.
MS F.157 118 n., 157 n.
MS F.160 178 n., 238 n., 239 n., 243 n.
MS F.163 113 n.
MS F.170 157 n.
MS F.175 116 n., 269 n.
MS F.176 122 n.
MS Q.5 336 n., 345 n.
MS Q.12 157 n.
MS Q.13 144 n.
MS Q.17 158 n.
MS Q.18 157 n., 279
MS Q.19 269 n.
MS Q.21 269 n.
MS Q.22 95 n.
MS Q.24 106 n., 157 n., 269 n.
MS Q.25 106 n., 343 n.
MS Q.26 239 n.
MS Q.27 95 n., 361 n.
MS Q.28 358 n.
MS Q.31 269 n.
MS Q.32 122 n.
MS Q.33 144 n.
MS Q.37 339 n.
MS Q.42 116 n., 156 n.
MS Q.44 120
MS Q.46 157 n.
MS Q.47 122 n.
MS Q.48 108 n.
MS Q.50 269 n., 336 n., 337 n., 340 n., 341 n., 345 n.
MS Q.51 120 n.
MS Q.53 157 n.
MS Q.61 269 n.
MS Q.62 344 n.
MS Q.64 118 n., 157 n.
MS Q.65 118 n.
MS Q.66 97 n., 269 n.
MS Q.72 269 n.
MS Q.79 345 n.
MS Q.85 157 n.
MS Q.94 269 n.
Add MS 68 269 n.

General Index

Note: The following abbreviations have been used: abp (archbishop), abt (abbot), bp (bishop), mk (monk), pr (prior); B. (Bath), C. (Canterbury), Co. (Coventry), D. (Durham), E. (Ely), N. (Norwich), R. (Rochester), W. (Winchester), Wo. (Worcester). Medieval names are indexed by Christian names and modern names by surnames.

Abergavenny, priory 102 n.
Abingdon, Berkshire 12, 46
Abingdon abbey 51, 85
Absalom 111 n.
accidie 236 n., 330
acolyte 38, 40, 41–2, 94, 98
Adam, organ builder 268
Adam, organist N. 179
Adam de Aldeby, mk N. 232
Adam de Balsham/Petit Pont 345
Adam de Bedingham, mk N. 232 n.
Adam de Belagh, mk N. 232 n.
Adam de Cirencestre, mk Wo. 42
Adam de Donytone, mk W. 295 n.
Adam Easton, mk N. 129, 134 n., 140, 305
Adam de Farnham, pr W. 259
Adam de Hyda, mk W. 194
Adam de Neubir', mk W. 166 n.
Adam Orleton, bp Wo. 51, 56, 210
Adam de Schipdam, mk N. 234
Adam de St Albans, surgeon 293
Adam de Wyg', mk W. 170
Adrian the Carthusian 153
Advent, season of 28, 164, 190, 194, 236, 240–1, 242–3, 245, 248, 281 n., 314
Aelfric 336
Aelfric Bata 336
Aelmer/Elmer II, pr C. 76 n.
Aidan, *see under* saints
Ailricus, mk C. 172
Alan II, mk E. 166 n.
Alan de Bungey, mk W. 313
Alan de Soham, mk E. 164 n.
Alan de Walsingham, pr E. 49, 203 n., 204, 282, 319
Alcock, John, *see* John Alcock
Aldeby priory, N. 31, 228, 231–3
Alexander II, mk R. 155 n., 356 n.
Alexander V, pope 92 n.
Alexander de Bury, mk E. 211 n., 273, 318
Alexander de Glanvill, pr R. 118
Alexander of Hales 155
Alexander de Heriard, pr W. 162, 280
Alexander de Lamesley, mk D. 304
Alexander London, mk C. 184 n.
Alexander Nequam/Neckham 76 n., 82, 335, 338, 345, 346
Alexander de Sprowston, mk N. 134 n.

Alexander Staple I, mk C. 99 n.
Alexander de Totyngton, pr N. 93, 271, 320
Alexander de Villa Dei 151, 340
All Saints, feast of, *see under* saints
All Souls' Day 268 n., 314
almoner 26, 28, 132, 135, 141, 176 n., 186–97, 241, 247–50, 251, 258, 261–4, 301–2, 310–17, 321
almonry school 39 n., 52, 103, 154 n., 186–90, 192–4, 250, 263, 266, 268, 269, 273, 308, 337
almsgiving 161, 187, 189, 190, 193, 197, 252, 261, 311–13, 316–17, 325 n.
Alured, hermit 111
Amalarius of Metz 96
Ambrose, *see under* saints
Anagni, Dominican friary of 305
Andrew, *see under* saints
Andrew, mk C. 172
Andrew de Hardys, mk C. 123, 127
Andrew de London, pr W. 9 n., 11
anniversarian 39, 133, 162, 164, 191, 204, 214–15, 248–9, 258, 260, 263, 274–5, 292, 318
Anschetill', mk W. 320
Anselm, mk W. 172
Anselm of Bec, abp C., *see under* saints
Anselm of Laon 111–14
Antony Bek, bp D. 292 n., 305
Aristotle 327, 338 n.
Arundel, *see* Thomas Arundel
Ascelin, bp R. 9, 10 n., 113 n.
Ascension Day 118, 264
Ash Wednesday 256–7, 259
Atkinson, T. D. 241
Aufredus, mk R. 227–8
Augustine of Hippo, *see under* saints
Augustinians 2, 5 n., 51, 74, 82
Avignon 199, 200 n.
Avon, river 21, 22
Aycliffe, Co. Durham 280
Azo, mk C. 111, 112 n.

Baldwin, abt Forde, bp Wo., abp C. 7, 8 n., 9 n., 18, 121, 350
Bale, *see* John Bale
Bamburgh, Northumberland 46
Barnard Castle, Co. Durham 46

Bartholomew de Cotton, mk N. 350, 351 n.
Bartholomew of Salerno 156
Bartholomew de Scrowtby, mk N. 40
Barton, Winchester 243, 259
bartoner 166, 246, 247, 272
Bateman, *see* William Bateman
Bath, church: St Mary of Stalls 29
Bath, cathedral priory, *passim*
  cloister and precinct 21–30
  Lady chapel 162 n., 169
  dependent priories, *see* Dunster; Waterford
Bathampton, Somerset 44
Battenhall, Worcester 22
Bearpark/Beaurepaire, Durham 283–4
Beaumont, Louis de, *see* Louis de Beaumont
Bec, abbey 6
Bede, mk Jarrow 96, 104–6, 111, 145, 153, 223, 255–6, 337, 338, 341, 345, 346, 353–4, 360, 361
Bedlington, Northumberland 280
Bedwardine, Worcester 45
Beechen Cliff, Bath 22
Benedict, Saint *passim*
  rule of, *passim*
Benedict XII, pope 66 n.
  constitutions of 70, 80, 100 n., 101, 131
Benedict Biscop, mk 223
Bentham, James 245
Bernard, abt Clairvaux 71, 74–8, 80–2, 150, 325, 327, 330
Bernard Aiglerius, abt Monte Cassino 76, 81 n., 153
Bertram, pr D. 11 n.
Bertram de Eastry, mk C. 186 n.
Bertram de Middleton, pr D. 11 n., 108
Berwick-upon-Tweed 31, 218
Bevere, Worcestershire 287
Beverle, almonry school boy N. 193
Beverley, east Yorkshire 46
Billingham, Co. Durham 280
Binham, priory 32 n.
Bishop Auckland, Co. Durham 30
Bishopstone, *see* Bushton
Black Death 4, 35, 36, 38, 71, 192, 194, 293
Black Monk Chapter, *passim*
Black Prince 254 n.
  chantry of 272
Blackwell, Worcestershire 132
Blois, *see* Henry de Blois
Blomefield, Francis 231
blood-letting, *see* minutiones
Bonaventure, *see under* saints
Boniface IX, pope 57
Bossall, north Yorkshire 138 n.
boy bishop 39 n., 250, 251 n.
Bredgar, Kent 188 n.
brevitor 310–12
Bridgettines 332
Brinton, Thomas, *see* Thomas Brinton

Bristol 44
Brutus 353, 359
Buckingham, John, *see* John Buckingham
building operations 183, 199–200, 202, 204–6, 244–5, 319, 328
Bungay, convent of 232
bursar/master of the cellar 108, 114, 134, 139, 153, 164, 165–8, 176 n., 181, 206 n., 211–212, 230, 241, 245, 253, 254, 261, 266, 284, 291; *see also* treasurer/receiver
Bursill-Hall, G. L. 337 n., 338 n., 339, 340
Bury, J. B. 1
Bury St Edmunds, abbey and abbots 5, 9, 65, 79 n., 93 n., 100 n., 326
Bushton, Wiltshire 52 n., 215
Bywell St Peter, Northumberland 280

Caen, Normandy, abbot of 6
Caesarius of Arles 77 n.
Caldicote, near Canterbury 285
Calthorpe, Oxfordshire 47 n.
Camargo, Martin 341 n., 342 n., 344, 346–7
Cambridge:
  Black Monk hostel 136
  churches:
    St Andrew the Great 137 n.
    St Mary, Trumpington 98
  university studies 2, 102, 125, 127, 128, 132, 135–6, 137, 140 n., 141–2, 146
Canterbury, churches:
  St Elphege 45
  St Margaret 45, 90 n., 94 n.
  St Mildred 45
  St Paul 45
  St Peter 45
Canterbury, cathedral priory, *passim*
  Black Prince, chantry of 272
  chapels and altars:
    Lady chapel 169–70
    Martyrdom chapel 170, 308
    St Agnes' altar 308
    St Andrew's chapel 308
    St Benedict and St Leonard, altar of 308
    St John's altar 260
    St Mary in crypt chapel 170
    St Michael's chapel 308
    St Nicholas' altar 308
    Trinity chapel 170
  cloister and precinct 20–30, 44 n., 126 n., 145, 149, 260, 295, 308
  dependent priories, *see* Canterbury College *under* Oxford; Dover priory
  Meister Omers 27, 167 n.
Canterbury College, *see under* Oxford
Carlisle, cathedral 5 n.
Carthusians 153, 332, 333
Cassian, *see* John Cassian
Cassiodorus 113
Catton, Norwich 43

cellarer 15, 135–6, 144, 163–8, 187, 211–14, 242–5, 252, 253, 255, 257, 260, 266, 281–2, 278, 290, 309, 319
chamberlain 15, 26, 28–9, 37–8, 61–2, 132, 133–6, 162, 171, 172–6, 245, 247, 249, 250, 281–5, 310–12, 315–16
chancellor 182–4, 352
chantries 194, 272, 273, 275, 319, 320
chaplain of prior 81, 151, 169, 182–5, 207 n.
Chapman, F. R. 16
Chapters, Black Monk, *passim*
Charleton, almonry school boy, N. 193
Chartres, Benedictine monks of 74
Chatham, Kent 45
Chester, abbey 117, 353, 355 n.
Christmas, season of 129, 236, 243, 246–50, 251–3, 286, 307
Cicero 327
Cirencester, Gloucestershire 43
    abbot of 338
Cistercians 2, 34 n., 64, 74
Cîteaux, abbey 64
claustrales 161 n., 183, 274, 292, 330
Clement VI, pope 132 n.
Clementine Constitutions 92
Clement Thornage, mk N. 40
Cluny, Cluniacs 2, 6, 34 n., 64
Cobham, *see* Thomas de Cobham
Colchester, Essex 45, 192
Coldingham, priory, D. 31, 139, 217–9, 240 n.
Coleman, mk Wo. 363
Combe, nr Bath 44
communar 98, 129 n., 134–5, 164, 191, 200, 214–15, 258, 273, 319–20
Compline, office of 68, 71, 237 n., 262 n.
Constance, council of 323
Constantinus Africanus 150, 295, 296 n.
Cork, house of St John, B. 31 n.
Corley, Warwickshire 44
corrodies 22 n.
    monastic 195–7, 298, 316–17
    secular 27, 195, 222, 293
Corston, Somerset 44
Courtenay, Richard, *see* Richard Courtenay
Courtenay, William, *see* William Courtenay
Coventry, church: St Nicholas 44
Coventry, cathedral priory, *passim*
    cloister and precinct 21–30
Cropthorne, Worcestershire 132
Crowle, Worcestershire 45
Croyland, abbey 323–4
curtarian (Winchester) 164–6, 270 n.; *see also* cellarer
customaries 64–5, 83, 87 n., 180 n., 236 n., 246, 259
    of the abbey of St Augustine 51 n., 60 n., 62, 65, 84, 85, 87 n., 317, 318
    of Ely 67, 246 n.
    of Canterbury 208, 246

of Norwich 214 n., 246 n. 259, 268, 271 n., 291 n.
of Winchester refectory 165, 213, 243, 262, 264, 286, 320
of Worcester 180 n., 247 n., 257 n.
custos capelle (Lady chapel) 136 n., 162 n., 169–70, 178, 249, 267, 269, 270
custos corone (Canterbury) 170
custos martyrii (Canterbury) 170, 208
custos operum 132, 139, 163, 198, 250–1; see also *magister operum*
custos tumbe (Canterbury) 170; see also *tumbarius*
Cuthbert, *see under* saints
Cyprus 258 n.
Cyril of Alexandria 153

Dares Phrygius 357, 359 n., 360 n.
Daventry, Northamptonshire 44
David de Presthmede, mk Wo. 86 n.
David of Augsburg 77, 80
Denys de St Margaret, mk C. 94 n.
depositarius, W. 164–5, 246 n., 248, 274–5, 286
Derby 44
Despenser, *see* Henry Despenser
diet and dining arrangements 83, 193, 242–3, 257–9, 264
Ditton/Fen Ditton, Cambridgeshire 98
Dobson, Barrie 35 n., 36, 96 n., 161 n., 216 n., 326, 331, 352
Dodderhill, Worcestershire 297 n.
Dodwell, Barbara 6 n., 152, 349 n.
Dominicans 76, 104, 108–9, 114–15, 123, 153, 313
Donatus Grammaticus 335–8, 340, 346
Douie, Decima 101
Dover 44, 45
Dover priory, C. 32, 77, 85, 119, 216, 225–6, 345 n.
Downham [Market], Norfolk 43
Droitwich, Worcestershire 45
Dunstable, Bedfordshire 44
Dunstan, abp C., *see under* saints
Dunster, priory, B. 14, 31, 36 n., 161, 226–7
Durham, church: St Oswald 167
Durham, cathedral priory, *passim*
    chapels and altars:
        Galilee chapel 113, 170, 202, 223, 266
        St Andrew's chapel 308
        St John the Baptist and St Margaret, altar of 238, 261
        St Nicholas and St Giles, altar of 319
    cloister and precinct 21–30, 68, 126 n., 295–6
    dependent priories, *see* Coldingham; Durham College *under* Oxford; Farne; Finchale; Holy Island; Jarrow; Lytham; Stamford; Wearmouth

hospitals:
  Kepier 31 n.
  Magdalen 31 n., 189, 206, 303
  Witton Gilbert 189
  Neville chantry 273
Durham College, *see under* Oxford
Dymock, Gloucestershire 43 n.

Eadmer, mk C. 76 n., 349
Eadwine, psalter of 22 n.
Easter 10, 236, 245, 247, 248, 249, 251, 253, 255, 259–63, 284 n., 288
  Easter tables 157, 181, 237, 256
Eastry, Kent 45, 75
Eastry, Henry, *see* Henry Eastry
Ebbe, *see under* saints
Edmund of Abingdon, abp C., *see under* saints
Edmund de Basyng 51
Edmund de Hadenham, mk R. 351
Edmund Kyngston, mk C. 208, 246 n.
Edmund de Thomeston, mk E. 209 n.
Edmund de Totyngton, mk E. 137, 278
Edmund Walsingham, pr E. 203 n.
Edward II 27, 195 n.
Edward III 18, 47 n., 51, 130 n., 254
Edward, master 52
Edward Coudray 166 n.
Eleanor, sister of Edward III 254
elections:
  archiepiscopal 8, 142, 280
  episcopal 8–10, 11, 17, 121 n., 142, 217
  prioral 10–12, 142, 217, 228
Elias III, mk R. 105
Elingdon, Wiltshire 269
Elizabeth (of Juliers), countess of Kent 47
Elmer II/Aelmer, pr C. 76 n.
Elphege, abp C., *see under* saints
Elvet[hall], Durham 46, 167
Ely, Nicholas, *see* Nicholas de Ely
Ely, cathedral priory, *passim*
  Lady chapel 98, 136, 177, 179 n., 204, 267, 309
  church: St Cross/St Peter 204 n.
  cloister and precinct 21–30, 67–8, 126 n., 295
  hospital of St John 203
Elyas de Hoxne, mk N. 215 n.
Elys, almonry school boy N. 193
Ember days, Embertide 10, 98, 241
Emery de Lumley, mk D. 150, 223
Enford, Wiltshire 44
Epiphany, season of 229, 246, 247, 253, 255
Ermenilda, *see under* saints
Ernulf, pr C. 170
Etheldreda, *see under* saints
Eudo de Bocton, mk C. 341
Eugenius IV, pope 92
Eusebius, bp Caesarea 354 n., 357–8, 360
'Eusebius Gallicanus' 76, 77

Eustace, *see under* saints
Everard de Béthune 148, 337, 340–1, 346
Evesham 45
Evesham, abbot of 108, 309
Exeter 44
exorcist 41
Eynsham, abbey 65

Farne, priory, D. 31, 221–3, 224, 273, 299 n., 304, 328
Farnham, Surrey 44
Fasts, *see* Advent; Lent
Feasts, *see* Ascension; Christmas; Easter; Pentecost; Trinity *and under* saints
Fécamp 191
Felix III, mk C. 111 n., 112 n.
Felixstowe, priory, R. 31, 227–8, 336 n.
feretrar/shrine-keeper 15, 86, 139, 162, 206–11, 247–9, 266; see also *tumbarius*
Fernie, Eric 215
Fen Ditton, Cambridgeshire 98
Finchale priory, D. 9, 31, 47, 113, 150, 217, 218, 219, 223, 298, 299, 300, 304
Fisher, John, *see* John Fisher
Fishlake, west Yorkshire 138 n.
'Florence of Worcester' 158, 351 n.
Forde abbey 9 n., 18
Fordham, John, *see* John de Fordham bp
Foster, Meryl 12 n., 47 n., 145 n., 150, 253 n., 350 n.
Fountains, abbey 9
Frampton, Lincolnshire 138 n.
Franciscans 77, 100–1, 105 n., 109, 118, 158, 313
Fulda 351

G. de Stratton, mk R. 345
gardener 28–9, 135, 163–4, 243, 285
Geoffrey, pr W. 320
Geoffrey Bonde, mk C. 177 n., 266
Geoffrey de Burdon, mk D. 217, 219, 290, 292
Geoffrey de Coldingham, mk D. 350
Geoffrey the grammarian 346
Geoffrey of Monmouth 359–60
Geoffrey de Norwich, mk N. 231
Geoffrey Poterel, mk C. 180 n., 185
Geoffrey de Romenal, mk C. 119 n.
Geoffrey Sall, mk N. 39 n.
Geoffrey de Smalbergh, mk N. 351 n.
Geoffrey de Suffeld, *medicus* 293
Geoffrey de Totyngton, mk N. 171
Geoffrey de Vinsauf 344, 346 n., 347 n.
Geoffrey de Wroxham, mk N. 355 n.
Gerald of Wales 354, 358–9
Gerard II, pr N. 192 n., 320
Gervase I, mk C. 350
Giffard, Godfrey, *see* Godfrey Giffard
Giffard, William, *see* William Giffard
Gilbert de Bisshoppiston, mk C. 186 n.

Gilbert de Dodynham, mk Wo. 116 n.
Gilbert de Elwick, mk D. 114 n., 322
Gilbert of Poitiers 111, 112, 113
Gilbert of Tournai 157
Gilbertus Anglicus 152
Gildas 359–60
Glastonbury 45
Glastonbury, abbey and abbots 5, 6, 9, 44, 52, 326, 331 n.
Gloucester, abbey 10, 45
Gloucester, duke of, *see* Thomas of Woodstock
Gloucester Hall, *see under* Oxford
Godfrey I, pr W. 320
Godfrey Giffard, bp Wo. 15, 86, 205 n., 256, 276
Godric, *see under* saints
Godricus, mk Wo. 172
Good Friday 129, 259, 261
granator 135, 136, 165
Grandisson, John, *see* John Grandisson
Gratian 117 n.
Greatham, Co. Durham 46
Great Malvern, priory 45, 158
Gregory I, II and/or III, mks C. 111 n.
Gregory the Great, pope, *see under* saints
Gregory IX, pope 11–12, 13, 150
Grimley, Worcestershire 132
Guarinus, mk D. 335 n.
Guido de Calumpnis 158
Guido Faba 343
Guildford, Surrey 44
Gullick, Michael 72 n., 180 n.
Gundulf, bp R. 10, 252
Guy d'Evreux 157
Guy de Smerdon, mk C. 187 n.
Guy de St Edmund, mk N. 43, 184 n.

H. de Merleburg, mk W. 155
Haddenham, Buckinghamshire 166 n.
Hainault 47
Hamo, master 341 n.
Hamo de Hethe, mk and bp R. 41, 119, 184, 252, 318, 320, 339 n.
Hartlebury castle 30
Hartlepool, Co. Durham 46
Harvey, Barbara 60 n., 88 n., 93 n., 173 n., 196 n., 189 n., 316 n.
Hatfield, Thomas, *see* Thomas Hatfield
Hay on Wye, Herefordshire 45
Heighington, Co. Durham 280
Helpericus of Auxerre 255 n.
Henry IV 22 n.
Henry V 2, 323, 324
Henry VI 353
Henry VIII 20, 93 n., 331
Henry de Annochia, mk Wo. 171
Henry Beaufort, bp W. 20, 39, 278, 298
Henry de Blois, bp W. 6, 9, 15, 168, 269
Henry Bradelegh, mk B. 41 n.

Henry de Bromle, mk W. 313
Henry Bruyn 27
Henry Chichele, abp C. 137 n., 142, 226
Henry Cranbroke I, mk C. 302, 303
Henry Cranbroke II, mk C. 342, 344, 346
Henry Despenser, bp N. 13, 57, 253
Henry Eastry, pr C. 18, 25, 73, 94, 120, 121 n., 127, 185, 200, 237 n., 295 n., 296, 298, 311, 342, 354, 357, 362
Henry Ferriby, mk D. 113, 237
Henry Fouke, mk Wo. 86, 117, 118 n., 122, 124 n., 156, 279 n.
Henry of Ghent 144
Henry of Grosmont, duke of Lancaster 255
Henry, Lord of Harley 47
Henry Helay, mk D. 119, 169, 221
Henry Henfeld, mk C. 140
Henry de Kirkstede, mk Bury St Edmunds 100 n.
Henry de Lakenham, pr N. 81, 152, 199, 200 n., 312, 320, 344, 349 n., 352, 360
Henry Langham/Ely, mk E. 49
Henry Langrake, mk N. 152
Henry de Leycester I, pr Co. 11 n.
Henry Madyngle, mk E. 137 n.
Henry de Mepeham, mk R. 154
Henry de Newynton, mk Wo. 120, 124, 305
Henry Raundes, mk R. 228
Henry de Selverton, mk C. 51, 84 n.
Henry de Soilli, abt Glastonbury 9 n.
Henry Stoke, mk R. 41 n., 94 n.
Henry Stordy, mk C. 215 n.
Henry de Stratton, mk Co. 211 n.
Henry de Wakefield, bp Wo. 206, 210, 257
Henry Wild 46
Henry de Wodehull, mk Abingdon and C. 51, 85
Henry Woodlock, mk and bp W. 11 n., 44, 287, 291
Henry de Wyke, mk E. 301
Henry de Wynchestre, mk W. 213 n.
Henry de Wyrmintone, mk Wo. 116 n.
Henwick, Worcestershire 22
Herbert de Bosham 111 n., 149 n.
Herbert Losinga, bp N. 6, 30, 191, 192, 214, 228, 232, 271 n.
Hereford, St Guthlac's priory 45
Hervey de Swafham, mk N. 126
Hethe, Hamo, *see* Hamo de Hethe
Hexham, Northumberland 46
Hilarius, mk D. 172
Hinton (Ampner), Hampshire 194
Hobley, Brian 21 n.
Holt, Norfolk 98
Holy Cross, *inventio* of, *see under* saints
Holy Innocents, *see under* saints
Holy Island/Lindisfarne, priory, D. 31, 46, 208, 221, 222–3, 350
Holy Land 207, 320 n., 363

Holy Week 259–63
Honorius III, pr C. 121
Honorius Augustodunensis 76, 96, 97 n., 150
hordarian (Winchester) 25 n., 39, 133, 164, 166, 242–3, 250, 259, 274
Horsham St Faith priory, Norfolk 357
hostiller 25 n., 100, 135, 167–9, 266, 276, 281, 285
Howden, east Yorkshire 52 n.
Hoxne priory, N. 16, 31, 43, 228, 231
Hubert I (?II), mk R. 354
Hubert Walter, abp C. 350
Huddington, Worcestershire 45
Hugh II, mk B. 14 n.
Hugh de Balsham, mk and bp E. 263
Hugh de Dovor, mk B. 227
Hugh de Folieto 71, 77, 80–1, 152, 153
Hugh de Geround, mk C. 213 n.
Hugh de Inceberg, mk Wo. 116 n.
Hugh de Monte Alto (Mohaut), mk D. 31 n.
Hugh du Puiset, bp D. 8, 11, 15, 336
Hugh de Sherburn, mk D. 279
Hugh de Sprowston 113
Hugh of St Cher, cardinal 108, 112, 114
Hugh de St Edmund, mk N. 43
Hugh de St Ives, mk C. 127 n.
Hugh of St Victor 62, 66, 69, 71, 74, 75, 76, 77, 96, 107, 108, 231, 335
Hugh Warkworth, mk D. 177 n., 182 n.
Hugh Whitehead, pr D. 239
Hugutio of Pisa, grammarian 339–40, 346
Humphrey I (de Malling), mk C. 111 n., 112 n., 119 n., 121, 361 n.
Hunt, Richard 338
Hunt, William 14
Hurstbourne, Hampshire 133
Hyde, Winchester 29, 44
Hyde, abbey 280

Impington, Cambridgeshire 137 n.
infirmarer 134, 152, 171–2, 248, 275, 283, 289–90, 293–5
Inkberrow, Worcestershire 45
Innocent III, pope 16, 76 n., 95, 97 n., 121, 150, 344 n.
Innocent IV, pope 157
Innocent V, pope 144
Ipswich, Suffolk 98
Isaac Ledbury, mk Wo. 143, 337 n., 347
Isidore of Seville 75 n., 150, 154 n., 339 n., 361
Isleham, Cambridgeshire 43
Islip, Simon, *see* Simon Islip
Itchen, river, Winchester 21, 30
Ithamar, bp R., *see under* saints
Ivo of Chartres 112

Jacques de Vitry 358
James Aubyn 42
James de Cessolis 155–6

James de Dover, mk C. 308
James Hegham, mk C. 61
James of Milan 153
James de Oxney I, mk C. 127 n., 277
James de Oxney II/Stone, mk C. 83 n.
James de Voragine (Januensis) 151, 155, 157, 234, 362
James Whyte I, mk C. 84 n.
Jarrow, priory, D. 31, 217, 223–4, 297–8, 304, 345, 353
Jerome, *see under* saints
Jocelin of Wells, bp B. 9 n.
John, king 8, 11, 121, 318
John XXIII, pope 92
John, earl of Kent 47
John I, pr R. 122, 123
John III, mk B. 163 n.
John V, mk B. 163 n.
John I, mk Wo. 350
John, *frater* 101
John, *medicus*, D. 293, 294 n.
John Abel, mk D. 202
John Alcock, bp Wo. 56 n.
John Aleyn I, mk C. 140
John de Allerton, mk D. 170 n., 208 n.
John Amundesham, mk St Albans 144
John de Ankerdom, mk Wo. 195 n.
John Appleby, mk D. 41 n.
John de Aston, mk Wo. 144
John Auckland, pr D. 360 n.
John de Aycliffe, mk D. 89, 119, 139 n., 151, 218
John Balbus of Genoa 339–40
John Bale 356, 357, 359
John the Baptist, nativity of, *see under* saints
John de Barnard Castle, mk D. 182 n., 221, 280
John de Basyng I, mk W. 166 n.
John Basyng III, mk W. 163 n.
John de Bathonia, physician 28
John de Beauchamp 255
John de Bedingfeld, mk N. 232
John de Begbroke, mk C. 170 n.
John de Bekkles, mk E. 136
John Beleth 96, 97 n.
John Bergersh, mk N. 269
John Bertram, mk C. 83
John de Betele, mk N. 135
John de Beverley, mk D. 75 n., 76 n., 77, 78, 326
John de Billesfield, mk D. 304
John de Bishopton, mk D. 223
John Blakeneye, mk N. 363
John de Bloxham, mk B. 227
John de Bocton, mk C. 148
John de Bolton, mk D. 119, 151
John Bonner, mk D. 303
John de Borden, mk R. 185 n.
John Borne, I, mk C. 177, 266
John de Bosco 28

John de Bradefeld, mk and bp R. 9, 52
John de Briera, mk Wo. 210
John Broghton, mk Wo. 143–4, 337 n., 347
John Broke, mk C. 355
John de Bromesgrove, mk Wo. 120, 156
John de Bromlegh, mk Co. 215 n.
John of Bromyard, op. 153, 154
John de Bruges, mk Co. 72, 111 n., 120, 238, 256 n., 360
John Buckingham, bp Lincoln 27
John de Bukton I, pr E. 309
John de Bukton II, mk E. 213 n.
John Burghill, bp Co. and Lichfield 161 n., 233 n., 276 n.
John de Burgo 156
John Bywell, mk D. 142, 143 n.
John Cantorbury I, mk C. 296 n., 303
John de Carleton, mk N. 211 n., 234
John Cassian 326, 330
John de Cauz, pr W. 9 n.
John de Cawston, mk N. 355
John de Charlton, mk D. 279
John de Chatham, pr C. 12
John de Chaumpeneys, mk N. 271
John Chrysostom 325
John de Cleve, mk Wo. 130, 157–8, 179 n., 278
John de Clipesby, mk N. 186
John de Colchestre, mk C. 294 n.
John Coleshull, mk C. 162 n., 171 n.
John Conversus/Mason, mk Wo. 49, 163 n.
John de Copton, mk C. 171 n., 178, 266
John de Corbridge, mk D. 280
John of Cornwall, grammar master 337
John Coumbe II, mk C. 226
John Cranbroke I, mk C. 179, 266
John de Crauden, pr E. 127, 309, 319, 320 n., 329
John de Croxton, mk E. 209
John Dallyng, scribe 181
John of Damascus 151
John de Dereham, mk N. 124 n., 234–5, 324
John de Derl[?yn]ton, *clericus* 27
John Devenish 275
John le Devenish, mk W. 42, 44
John Dounham, junior 103
John de Drayton, mk W. 155, 362
John de Drokensford, bp B. and Wells 14, 41, 86
John de Dudley I, mk Wo. 47, 130–1, 136, 175 n., 176 n., 276, 294, 301, 326 n., 341
John Dudley II, mk Wo. 341 n.
John de Dumbleton, mk Wo. 116, 126, 216 n.
John Durham senior, mk D. 208 n.
John de Ealding, mk R. 141, 180 n., 228
John de Eastry II, mk C. 180 n.
John Eccleshall, mk Co. 168 n.
John de Ekynton, schoolmaster, Wo. 197
John de Elham I, mk C. 294 n.

John Elmham, mk N. 271
John de Ely IV, mk E. 186, 203 n., 283
John Ely VII, mk E. 166
John de Eston, mk B. 14
John de Evesham, pr Wo. 57, 183, 198 n., 306, 309, 313, 329
John de Exeter, mk C. 84 n.
John Exeter I and/or II, mks W. 353 n.
John of Exeter, bp W. 9
John de Eynesford, mk C. 307
John de Faversham I, mk R. 185 n.
John Fishburn jr, mk D. 143
John Fishburn sr, mk D. 237, 343, 344
John Fisher, bp R. 41 n.
John Fishwick, mk D. 279
John Folsham, mk N. 108
John de Fordham, pr Wo. 117, 126 n., 142, 175 n., 276, 323–4, 341
John de Fordham, bp D. and E. 137 n., 142, 184, 217 n., 282
John de Fornsete, mk N. 39 n.
John Fosser, pr D. 163, 174, 218, 220, 224, 273, 280, 292, 293, 297 n., 298, 300, 308, 319
John of Freiburg 157
John de Frome, mk C. 362
John Fynch, pr C. 308, 329
John of Garland, grammarian 340, 341 n., 345
John Gloucestre I, mk C. 93 n.
John de Gloucestre II, mk Wo. 212 n.
John de Gloucestre III, mk Wo. 196 n., 294 n., 315, 316
John de Goldsborough, mk D. 178 n., 266, 294
John de Goodnyston, mk C. 301
John de Gore, mk C. 183 n.
John Grandisson, bp Exeter 149 n.
John de Grenborough, mk Co. 152, 171, 295
John Grene I, pr Wo. 110, 196, 276, 280, 316
John de Grenestrete, mk R. 185 n.
John de Grey, bp N. 192
John Grove, mk C. 302
John de Guston, mk C. 201 n., 302
John Harle, mk D. 304 n.
John de Harleye, mk Wo. 47, 63 n., 116 n., 205 n.
John de Haselwode, mk W. 63 n.
John de Hatfeld, mk Wo. 179 n., 183 n., 280
John de Haywoode, mk W. 184
John de Hedirset, mk N. 230, 297 n., 300
John de Hemingbrough, pr D. 17 n., 92–4, 220 n.
John de Hemmingstone, pr E. 281
John de Hengham I, mk N. 184 n.
John de Hertlepe I, pr R. 228
John de Hethe, mk Wo. 210
John Holyngborne I, mk C. 237, 296 n.
John Holyngborne II, mk C. 357
John de Holyngbourne, mk R. 90, 141
John de Hoo, mk N. 134, 135 n., 234, 340
John Horold/de Roffa I, mk R. 42
John de Hotham, bp E. 20, 204
John Hyde, mk W. 168 n., 276 n.

John de Iford, mk B. 227
John Islep, mk C. 203
John Januensis, *see* John Balbus
John de Jernmuth, mk N. 231
John Katerington, mk W. 295 n.
John Kirkland, mk D. 304 n.
John de Kyderminstre I, mk Wo. 196 n., 315, 316
John de Kyderminstre II, mk Wo. 315 n.
John Kynton, mk C. 85 n.
John Lacok, mk B. 162 n., 215
John Lamport, mk B. 227
John Langdon I, mk C. 130, 142
John Langreod, mk W. 296–7
John de Langton, mk D. 294
John Lawerne I, mk Wo. 102, 141, 143–4, 146, 279, 337 n., 346–7, 361
John de Layton, mk D. 182
John de Legh II, mk Wo. 90 n., 163 n., 212 n.
John Leland, antiquary 72 n., 105, 206 n., 358, 359
John de Lemenstre I, mk Wo. 132, 179 n.
John de Lenham, mk C. 94 n.
John de Leycestria, mk R. 168 n.
John Leyland, grammar master 338
John de Lisle 254
John de Logwardyn, *medicus* 293
John de London I, mk C. 215 n.
John de London II, mk R. 41 n.
John Lutton, scribe 355
John Luttrell, mk D. 46, 168
John de Lyndeseye, mk Wo. 205 n., 206
John Maghfeld, mk C. 179, 266
John de Malverne I, pr Wo. 142, 179 n., 180 n., 183 n., 205 n., 313 n., 352, 355
John Manby, mk D. 119 n.
John Marchall I, mk C. 85, 225
John de Marchia, mk R. 166 n.
John de Mari, mk N. 143, 234
John Mascal 47
John de Mepeham II, mk R. 185 n.
John Merke, mk W. 310
John de Merlawe I, pr W. 162 n.
John de Merstone, mk Co. 164 n.
John Mideltone, mk W. 168 n., 276 n.
John Mody, mk D. 150
John Molond I, mk C. 171 n., 308
John Morel, mk R. 228
John Morton II, mk W. 156
John Musard, mk Wo. 158
John de Newburn, mk D. 280, 281 n.
John de Newport, mk Wo. 196 n.
John Newton, mk C. 285
John Noble, mk R. 155
John de Northborne I, mk C. 184 n.
John de Norton, mk D. 224
John Norton II, mk B. 214 n.
John Oll, mk D. 237
John de Orewell, mk E. 162 n.

John de Ostillaria (John III), mk W. 49 n.
John de Otford I, mk C. 301
John de Pagham, bp Wo. 113
John Palmer, *medicus* 293, 294 n.
John Pecham, abp C. 101 n., 166
John Pleme, mk R. 177 n.
John de Plumstede, mk N. 230
John de Pontissara, bp W. 12, 15, 193 n., 275
John Pope, mk Co. 162 n.
John Potynger, *magister* 103
John de Powik, mk Wo. 198, 205 n.
John de Preston II, mk Wo. 102, 120, 122
John Pyrye, mk C. 91 n.
John de Ramesey II, mk E. 213 n.
John de Ramesey I, mason 199 n.
John Redyng II, mk W. 213 n.
John de Reynham, pr R. 351–2 n.
John de Reynham, mk N. 153
John de Ripon, mk D. 279, 299, 304
John de Roffa I, *see* John Horold
John Ryton, mk D. 113
John de St Briavel, mk Wo. 186, 205
John de St Germans, mk Wo. 102, 122, 126, 127 n.
John of Salisbury 327
John Salisbury III, mk C. 149
John Sall II, mk N. 146
John Salmon, pr E., bp N. 30, 49, 65 n., 143 n., 177, 186, 199 n., 231, 286, 315
John Sandwich I, mk C. 93 n.
John de Sautre, mk E. 136
John Severne, mk Wo. 279
John Shepay I, mk C. 171 n.
John Shepey, mk Co. 162 n.
John de Shepey II, (pr I) pr R. 228
John de Shepey III, (pr II) pr R. 41, 56, 90, 141 n., 185, 228
John de Sittingborne, mk C. 121
John de Southam I or II, mks Co. 278
John le Spycer, mk C. 49 n., 121 n., 165 n., 186 n.
John de Stanleye, mk Wo. 196 n., 238, 313
John Stanys, mk C. 179, 266
John Stone I, mk C. 179 n., 353
John de Stone I, mk B. 227
John de Stone, mk Wo. 315
John de Stratford, bp W., abp C. 53–4, 57, 84, 193
John de Stukle, mk N. 134–5
John de Teukesbury I, mk Wo. 83, 210
John de Thaneto II, mk C. 170 n., 177
John de Thoresby, bp Wo. 56, 186, 210
John de Thornton, mk E. 274
John de Thurgarton, mk N. 184 n., 232
John Thurston, mk W. 165 n.
John Thwarton[er], mk Wo. 210
John de Tickhill, mk D. 163
John de Tilney, mk N. 184 n., 278
John Tyes, organist 269
John of Tynemouth 355 n.

John de Upton, mk Wo. 163 n.
John de Valoyns, mk C. 94 n.
John Viel, mk C. 208, 246 n.
John de Villula, bp B. 14
John Volney, mk Co. 214
John Wakeryng, bp N. 199 n., 271, 272 n.
John Waltham I, mk C. 226
John Waltham, II, mk C. 237
John Wessington, pr D. 52 n., 73 n., 94, 145, 182 n., 190, 324, 326, 343 n., 352
John de Westbury, mk Wo. 179 n.
John de Westerham, pr R. 123, 155, 312
John Westgate III, mk C. 183
John Wethamstede, abt St Albans 144
John de Whitrigg, mk D. 304, 328
John Whytefeld, mk Dover 77
John de Whytefeld, mk R. 110, 356
John de Wisbech, mk E. 204 n., 309
John de Wodestok, mk R. 295 n.
John Wodeward, mk Wo. 129
John Wodnesburgh II, pr C. 147, 183 n., 252, 280
John de Worcestre, mk Wo. 270
John de Wy I, mk C. 117
John Wy II, mk C. 304
John Wyclif 78, 326 n.
John Wycliffe, mk D. 92 n.
John Wydecombe, mk B. 41 n.
John de Wygornia, mk Glastonbury 52, 53 n.
John de Wyke, pr Wo. 55, 63 n., 86, 102, 108, 116, 120, 132, 156, 205, 280
John Wykham I, mk C. 302
John de Yaxham, mk E. 135, 209
Joseph de Martham, mk N. 309
Josephus Flavius 357
Joybert, pr Co. 10, 11 n.
Juliana Gray 203 n.
Juliers, *see* Elizabeth, countess of Kent
juvenes 38–40, 89 n., 98, 104 n., 194, 268

Kellawe, Richard, *see* Richard de Kellawe
Kelloe, Co. Durham 46
Kenilworth, priory 51, 84 n.
Kepier hospital, *see under* Durham
Ker, Neil 279
Kingsland, Herefordshire 45
King's Norton, Worcestershire 281
kitchener 139, 164, 211–14, 244
Knowles, Dom David 4 n., 66, 323 n., 330–1, 348 n.
Koran, the 153

Lakenham, Norfolk 43
Lakenheath, Suffolk 43, 136
Lanchester, Durham 46
Lanfranc, abp C. 6, 73, 188 n., 284, 302, 319
 Constitutions of 13, 62–3, 66, 158 n., 186, 198 n., 262 n., 281, 289
Langham, Simon, *see* Simon Langham

Langley, Thomas, *see* Thomas Langley
Lateran Councils:
 third 101
 fourth 8, 101, 121
Laurence, pr. D. 112
Laurence de Aquileia 343
Laurence de Badminton, mk Wo. 116 n., 209 n.
Laurence de Leck, pr N. 232
Laurence Tent, mk C. 93 n.
Laurence de Tunstale, mk N. 234
Laurence Wade, mk C. 149
Leclercq, Jean 5 n., 69, 76 n., 104
lector 99–102, 140
Ledbury, Herefordshire 45, 46
Leeds, Kent 45
Le Goff, Jacques 4
Leicester 44, 45
Leland, *see* John Leland
Lent, season of 28, 180, 181, 192, 194, 197 n., 212 n., 214, 236, 241, 243, 255–9, 260 n., 281
Leominster, priory 45
Leonard, *see under* saints
Leonard, mk R. 360
Lewes, Sussex 337
librarian 182
Lichfield 13, 14, 17, 20 n., 30
Lincoln 43, 46, 220
Lindisfarne, Northumberland, *see* Holy Island
Lisle, Thomas de, *see* Thomas de Lisle
Little Malvern, priory 216
Littleton, nr. Winchester 168, 176
Lombardy, medical schools of 152
London 44, 45, 46, 55 n., 106, 199, 210, 220, 254, 291, 305
 Tower of 298
Losinga, Herbert, *see* Herbert Losinga
Louis de Beaumont, bp D. 292
Ludlow, Shropshire 45, 46
Ludolf of Saxony 155
Lumley, Co. Durham 46
Lynn (King's Lynn) priory, N. 31, 43, 228, 232–5, 276, 299, 300, 304, 344 n.
Lytham priory, D. 31, 46, 219–20, 223, 237

Macrobius 155
Magdalen hospice, *see* under Durham
magister operum 163
Maidstone, Kent 45
Maidstone, Walter, *see* Walter Maidstone
Malmesbury abbey 353
Malvern, *see* Great Malvern and Little Malvern
mandatum 259–63
Marcellus de Capella, mk C. 49 n.
Marcellus de Lese, mk C. 170 n., 301
March, earl of 254 n.
Marco Polo 354
Margaret *dicta* Porter 191 n.
Margery Kempe 234–5

Marianus Scotus 351
Marlborough, Wiltshire 44
Marmaduke de Pirie, mk Wo. 316
Marsham, Norfolk 278 n.
Martin II, mk B. 172 n.
Martin de Clyve, mk C. 101, 296, 297
Martin de Middleton, mk N. 143
Martin Polonus 115, 150, 358
Mary, Virgin, *see under* Virgin Mary
Mary Magdalen, *see under* saints
Masham, north Yorkshire 46
Mass rotas 270–5
Matins, office of 68, 71, 229, 237 n., 297, 308, 363
Matthew, *see under* saints
Matthew Parker, abp C. 66 n.
Matthew Paris 75 n., 353, 356, 361
Maundy Thursday 259–62
Maurice the Englishman (Hibernicus) 116–17
Maxstoke, Warwickshire 44
Medway, river, Kent 21
Meister Omers, *see under* Canterbury
Meopham, Kent 45
Meopham, Simon, *see* Simon de Meopham
Merrington/Kirk Merrington, Co. Durham 280
Michael in Monte Tumba, *see under* saints
Michael de Chilton, mk D. 294
Michaelmas 250, 286, 288
Micheldever, Hampshire 44
minstrels 254–5, 263
minutiones 236, 241 n., 242, 281, 282–8, 295 n.
Molicourt/Mullicourt 'priory', E. 32 n., 216
Monks Risborough, Buckinghamshire 304
Moses, pr Co. 10, 11 n.
Mount Grace, prior and priory 323–4
Much Wenlock, Shropshire 45
music and chant 22, 82–3, 147, 169 n., 177–9, 237 n., 238–40, 253, 265–70, 275, 349

N. mk E. 215 n.
'Nennius' 360 n.
Newcastle, Northumberland 46
New Minster 29; *see also* Hyde
Newton, nr Cambridge 137 n.
Newton St Loe, Somerset 44
Nicholas, *see under* saints
Nicholas II, mk N. 300 n.
Nicholas IV, mk Co. 177 n.
Nicholas, cantor D. 267
Nicholas, organist E. 179
Nicholas, scribe E. 180
Nicholas de Allerton, mk D. 178 n., 266
Nicholas de Bath I, mk B. 163 n.
Nicholas de Bradefeld, mk Wo. 210, 215
Nicholas Burgate, mk N. 43, 271
Nicholas de Bysshopestone, mk W. 52
Nicholas de Caldecote, mk Co. 165 n.
Nicholas de Cayton, chaplain 191 n.
Nicholas de Coulsdon, mk Wo. 116 n.

Nicholas Derby, mk. E. 166
Nicholas de Ely, bp Wo. and W. 193, 205, 241, 275
Nicholas de Enford, mk W. 98
Nicholas de Frendesbury, mk R. 312
Nicholas Galeye, mk C. 163 n.
Nicholas Geyton, mk N. 231
Nicholas Gorran 109, 112, 113, 154, 157
Nicholas Hambury, mk Wo. 131
Nicholas de Haywode I, mk W. 184 n.
Nicholas de Hindolveston mk N. 200 n.
Nicholas de Hoo, pr N. 297
Nicholas de Kirkeby II, mk N. 39–40
Nicholas de Lusby, mk D. 221
Nicholas de Lyra 109, 110, 111
Nicholas Morton, mk Wo. 90
Nicholas de Norton, mk Wo. 205, 351
Nicholas de Randworth, mk N. 271
Nicholas Russel, mk D. 46
Nicholas Salisbury I, mk W. 165 n.
Nicholas de Stanlake, mk Wo. 186
Nicholas de Tarente, pr W. 155
Nigel Wireker, mk C. 119 n., 121 n.
Norham, Northumberland 280
Normanspital, *see* St Paul's hospital
Northallerton, north Yorkshire 46, 52 n.
Northampton 44, 344
Northampton, Cluniac priory 141, 163, 220, 301
North Holmes, Canterbury 21
Northstoke/North Stoke, Somerset 298
Norwich, church: St Mary in the Marsh 29 n., 113
Norwich, cathedral priory, *passim*
  chapels:
    Lady chapel 23 n., 169, 268, 320
    St Catherine's chapel 201
    St Michael's chapel 124
    St William's chapel 200 n., 207, 320 n.
  cloister and precinct 21, 23–30, 171, 200–1, 215, 261, 295
  dependent priories, *see* Aldeby; Hoxne; Lynn; St Leonard's, Norwich; St Paul's hospital, Norwich; Yarmouth
Nottingham, Nottinghamshire 44
novice master 65–6, 68, 74, 79, 80, 82, 86–7
novices:
  admission 37–8, 40, 41, 50–7, 61–3, 67–8, 79, 226
  clothing 38, 58, 60–3, 174–5
  profession 38, 39–42, 83–8, 90–4, 105, 226, 322
  study 64–6, 68–71, 73–5, 77–83, 89, 99–106, 124–6, 346–7

'O' antiphons 243–6, 314
obedientiaries, *see*:
  almoner

obedientiaries, see (cont.)
  anniversarian
  bartoner
  bursar
  cellarer
  chamberlain
  chancellor
  chaplain of prior
  communar
  curtarian
  custos capelle (Lady chapel)
  depositarius
  feretrar/shrine-keeper
  gardener
  granator
  hordarian
  hostiller
  infirmarer
  kitchener
  librarian
  magister operum
  pittancer
  precentor
  refectorer
  sacrist
  senescallus terrarum/warden of manors
  speciarius
  terrar
  treasurer
  tumbarius
Observant Friars Minor 332
Odo, clerk 134
Omers, Meister 27, 167 n.
ordinations 10, 38, 40–2, 53, 88, 89–99, 103, 241 n., 319
organs, organists 178–9, 265–70
Orleton, Adam, *see* Adam Orleton
Osbern Pinnock, mk Gloucester 339 n., 345, 346
Oswald, bp Wo., *see under* saints
Oswald, king, *see under* saints
Ottobonus, papal legate, constitutions of 75
Ouse, Great, river, Cambridgeshire 21, 232
Otford, Kent 260
Overbury, Worcestershire 132
Ovid 327
Oxford, *passim*
  churches:
    St Frideswide, priory of 138 n.
    St Peter-in-the-East 32
  colleges:
    Canterbury (Christ Church) 32, 68, 90, 97, 106, 109 n., 121 n., 128, 130, 137, 138 n., 139, 140, 142, 144, 145 n., 303 n., 304, 307, 336, 339 n., 340, 343, 344, 346, 347, 262
    Durham (Trinity) 32, 78, 106, 112, 119, 126, 127 n., 128, 137–9, 141–5, 151, 184 n., 220 n., 300, 304, 346, 347

    Gloucester Hall/College 126, 127, 129 n., 131, 134, 137, 138 n., 140, 142, 144, 152 n., 347
    New 52, 103 n.
  university studies 47, 51 n., 70, 85, 90, 101–2, 107, 108, 120, 124, 125–7, 129–30, 130–3, 146, 149, 155, 221

Pachomius 327
Packington, Warwickshire 44
Pagham, Sussex 138
Pandulf Masca, bp N. 8
Pantin, W. A. 51 n., 60, 68, 70, 79, 80, 139, 325 n.
Papias of Pavia, grammarian 339–40, 346
Paris 111, 156, 344
  abbey and school of St Victor 74, 107, 118
  convent of St Jacques 108–9, 114, 115
  schools of Paris 107 n., 109 n., 121 n., 123, 147, 345
  school of Notre Dame 118–19
  university of Paris 101, 122, 123, 127, 148 n.
Paul, *see under* saints
Paulinus, bp R. and saint 207 n.
Pecham, John, *see* John Pecham
penitentiaries 119, 277, 303
Pentecost, feast of 10, 241 n., 249, 250, 255, 259–65, 285, 286 n.
Pershore, Worcestershire 44–5, 47
Peter *ad vincula, see under* saints
Peterborough, abbey 10, 95
Peter de Blois 342–4
Peter Cantor 82, 116, 338, 341
Peter Chrysologus 150
Peter Comestor 113, 118, 120, 145, 151, 156, 158, 356 n.
Peter of Cornwall 154
Peter Cranbourne, mk W. 362
Peter de Dereham, mk N. 355
Peter de Donewich, mk N. 231
Peter de Durham, mk D. 182 n., 221, 222 n.
Peter Helias 338, 343, 346
Peter de Hethe, mk R. 41 n., 185 n.
Peter Hispanus 338
Peter de Ikham, mk C. 170 n.
Peter Lombard 102, 111–13, 120, 122, 123, 124, 143, 145, 148, 150, 151, 155, 156, 157
Peter de Norwich II, mk E. 180, 184 n.
Peter de Oxney, mk C. 83
Peter de Sales, mk C. 301
Peter de Tye 272
Peter de Vinea 342–3
Philip Aubyn, pr Wo. 42, 45, 156, 256, 309
Philip de Dallyng, mk E. 163 n.
Philip de Lusteshall, mk W. 128 n.
Philip Morgan, bp Wo. 280
Philip Trenchefoil, mk W. 215 n., 321 n.

Philip de Wykham, mk C. 147
Philippa of Hainault, wife of Edward III 47 n.
Piper, Alan 35 n., 37 n., 43 n., 47 n., 53 n., 86, 91 n., 94, 100 n., 151 n., 158 n., 224, 293 n., 299, 301, 331
Pisa, council of 298
pittancer 214–15, 244, 246, 251, 287, 314; *see also* communar
Pittington, Co. Durham 283, 284
Plato 327
Plumstead, Norfolk 43
Poitiers, papal curia at 305
preaching 99, 103, 115 n., 124, 129, 137, 142, 146 n., 256, 257 n., 260, 279–81, 326, 327, 362
precentor 15, 29, 52, 98, 135, 156, 176–82, 244, 248, 250, 263, 267–8, 275–6
Presteigne, Shropshire 45
Priscian[us Caesariensis] 335, 336, 337, 338, 340, 343, 346

R II, mk B. 14 n.
R. de Gyllingham 363
R. de Yakesham, mk E. 162 n.
Rainham, Kent 45
Ralph I, mk B. 171
Ralph III, mk R. 172
Ralph de Apuldor, mk C. 89 n.
Ralph de Basyng, mk W. 133, 277
Ralph de Derham, mk E. 98
Ralph de Elingham, mk N. 240
Ralph de Fretenham, mk N. 351 n.
Ralph de Hulme, mk N. 184 n.
Ralph de (Iklingham), Ikelynton, mk E. 363
Ralph de Martham, mk N. 233, 300, 304
Ralph Mascal, mk W. 47
Ralph de Neville, bp Chichester 9 n.
Ralph de Pretelwelle, mk C. 358
Ralph de Shrewsbury, bp B. and Wells 298
Ralph de Stanton, mk W. 280 n.
Ralph de Stisted, mk E. 213 n.
Ralph de Stoke, mk R. 119
Ralph de Twizell, mk D. 314
Ralph de Walpole, bp E. 50, 172 n., 174 n., 190, 247 n., 291, 315
Ramsey, abbey 102, 331 n.
Ranfredus of Benevento 157
Rankin, Susan 239 n.
Ranulph de Calthrop (Scot), mk Wo. 47, 102, 131 n., 144
Ranulph Higden, mk Chester 117, 153, 352, 353, 354
Raymond Pennafort 157 n.
Reading 8 n.
Reading, abbey 10, 45, 342
recreation, monastic 28, 31, 83, 153, 218, 250, 265, 281–4, 287, 291, 320; see also *minutiones*
Reculver, Kent 252 n.

refectorer 28, 39, 211–14, 262, 264, 286–7
Reginald, mk D. 361
Reginald de Barnby, mk D. 163 n.
Reginald Bryan, bp Wo. 57, 198
Reginald of Canterbury 360 n.
Reginald Dyere, mk Wo. 161 n., 178 n., 180
Reginald Goldston I, mk C. 337, 341
Reginald de Thurtlestane, *clericus* 51
Reginald de Wearmouth, mk D. 178, 266, 303
Reinald, mk W. 207 n.
Reiner, mk R. 21 n.
Repp, almonry school boy, N. 193
Reynolds, Walter, *see* Walter Reynolds
Richard II 57, 205, 254
Richard, pr E. 351–2
Richard ?IV, mk R. 358
Richard Barndesley, mk Wo. 129
Richard Bell, pr D. 344, 346
Richard de Blakeneye, mk N. 230, 299
Richard de Brompton, mk D. 202 n.
Richard de Bromwych, mk Wo. 102, 109, 124, 144, 157, 179 n., 281
Richard de Bury, bp D. 9 n., 218 n., 276
Richard de Castrobernardi 273
Richard de Claverlye, mk W. 164 n.
Richard Clifton, mk Wo. 142 n.
Richard de Clyve, mk C. 127
Richard Colys, mk Wo. 186
Richard Courtenay, bp N. 39, 109 n.
Richard Crosby, pr Co. 361
Richard Crosby, mk D. 239
Richard de Devizes, mk W. 351
Richard Drowte, mk Co. 162 n.
Richard de Dumbleton, pr Wo. 309
Richard Dunster, mk B. 41 n.
Richard de Eastgate, mk R. 171 n.
Richard de Enford, pr W. 287, 310
Richard de Feckenham, pr Wo. 15
Richard de Folsham, mk N. 234
Richard Godmersham I, mk C. 130, 280
Richard Godmersham II, mk C. 99 n.
Richard de Grafton, mk Wo. 157
Richard Hambury, grammar master 338
Richard de Haselarton, mk 54 n.
Richard Haswell, mk D. 219, 220
Richard Hatfeld, mk C. 272
Richard de Hecham II, mk N. 180 n., 199–200
Richard de Hegham, mk C. 163 n.
Richard de Helyngton, mk N. 193 n.
Richard de Herrington, mk D. 172 n.
Richard Holden, mk C. 304, 307
Richard de Hoton, pr D. 219, 224 n., 292, 305
Richard de Ikham, mk C. 294 n.
Richard de Kellawe, mk and bp D. 9, 35 n., 161 n., 171, 220, 271 n., 283, 292
Richard Kidderminster, abt Winchcombe 146
Richard de Lakenham, mk N. 200 n.
Richard de Lodbrok, mk Co. 198
Richard Lodelowe, mk Wo. 317

410 *General Index*

Richard Luff, mk Co. 152
Richard Lychefeld, mk Wo. 336
Richard de Merstham, mk C. 148, 341
Richard de Midelton, mk N. 199 n., 278 n.
Richard Mulleward 47
Richard Myston, mk Wo. 270
Richard Norwich II, mk N. 146
Richard de Oxenden, pr C. 54, 84, 178, 254, 308
Richard Pole, mk Wo. 315 n.
Richard Poore, bp D. 15
Richard de Pophis 343
Richard Praemonstratensis 76
Richard Salthous, mk N. 360
Richard de Sedgebrook, mk D. 222, 273, 299 n., 328
Richard de Sharstede, mk C. 302
Richard de Skerninge, mk N. 230
Richard de Spalding, mk E. 213 n.
Richard de Stockton, mk D. 151
Richard Stoke, mk Co. 169
Richard Stone, mk C. 149
Richard of St Victor 80, 151
Richard Vaughan, mk C. 27, 54 n., 85 n.
Richard de Wallingford, abt St Albans 78 n.
Richard de Walsham, mk N. 153, 230
Richard Warrewyk, mk Co. 161 n.
Richard de Wenlok, mk Wo. 216 n.
Richard de Wetheringsett 75, 95, 360 n.
Richard de Whitworth, mk D. 217
Richard Winchcombe 27
Richard Wylardeseye, mk C. 361
Richard de Wynchepe, mk C. 66, 225 n
Richer de Baldeswell, mk N. 172
Ripon, west Yorkshire 46
Robert, pr W. 320
Robert II, mk B. 165 n.
Robert de Aldon, mk C. 94 n.
Robert de Basevorn 151
Robert de Basyng, mk W. 164 n.
Robert Bennington, *see* Robert de Walworth
Robert de Blacklaw, mk D. 110, 138, 140–2
Robert Blund, canon, Lincoln 338
Robert de Bokyngham 275
Robert de Brackenbury, mk D. 112 n., 150, 151 n., 294, 358
Robert de Burnham, pr N. 268
Robert de Cambois, mk D. 280
Robert Catton, mk N. 110 n.
Robert de Chattegrove, mk N. 13 n.
Robert Chiew, mk B. 41 n.
Robert de Claxton, mk D. 169, 218 n.
Robert de Clifton II, mk Wo. 205 n., 264, 316
Robert de Clopcote, mk B. 226 n., 227
Robert Colville, pr E. 179, 268 n.
Robert Constable, mk D. 151
Robert Cramborne 362
Robert de Crull, *lector* 101 n.
Robert de Diclesdone, mk Wo. 122, 156

Robert de Donewich, mk N. 81, 153
Robert de Dover, mk C. 201, 302
Robert de Duffelde, mk C. 84 n.
Robert de Dymok 42
Robert Ebchester, pr D. 52 n.
Robert de Elham, mk C. 170 n.
Robert [Longchamp] de Ely, pr E. 72 n.
Robert de Ely, mk N. 180 n.
Robert Embleton II, mk D. 69 n.
Robert Foxton 203 n.
Robert Fulham, *lector* 100 n.
Robert de Gelham, mk R. 113, 154
Robert de Godeshulle, mk W. 213 n.
Robert de Graystanes, mk D. 9 n., 114, 145, 218, 293 n., 350
Robert Grosseteste, bp Lincoln 327
Robert de Hallington, mk D. 221
Robert de Hambury, mk Wo. 196, 341
Robert Hardwyk, mk N. 39 n.
Robert IV (de Hastings), mk C., abt Chester 119 n.
Robert Hathbrande, pr C. 54, 308
Robert de Hecham, mk R. 165–6 n.
Robert Hendeman, mk B. 226
Robert de Hexham, mk D. 220 n.
Robert de Honintona, mk Co. 256 n.
Robert Hornby, mk. D. 139, 143, 304 n.
Robert de Insula, mk and bp D. 9
Robert de Ketton 358 n.
Robert de Lakenham, mk N. 240
Robert de Lanchester, mk D. 182 n., 343
Robert de Langele, pr N. 143, 231–2, 260 n.
Robert Lawerne, mk Wo. 47
Robert Layton, pr Mount Grace 323
Robert Lynton II, mk C. 225
Robert Marmion, mk D. 46
Robert de Masham, mk D. 139
Robert atte More 166 n.
Robert de Morton, mk Wo. 157
Robert de Orford, pr and bp E. 172 n., 174 n., 177
Robert de Ormesby, mk N. 178 n., 231, 238
Robert de Picton/Pigdon, mk D. 142, 220
Robert de Popham, mk W. 184 n.
Robert Poucyn, mk C. 117, 121 n., 123, 145, 207
Robert Puryton, mk W. 278
Robert Ripon, mk D. 142, 277 n., 279, 280
Robert de Rodebourne, pr W. 296
Robert de Rykelyng, mk E. 209
Robert Shorne, mk R. 93
Robert Shrovesbury, mk Wo. 315
Robert de Southflete II, pr R. 228
Robert de Southflete III, mk R. 185 n.
Robert Stanes, mk Wo. 313
Robert de Stichill, mk and bp D. 9, 12 n., 47
Robert de Sutton, pr B. 14 n., 226 n.
Robert de Sutton I, mk E. 204
Robert de Sutton II, mk E. 102, 103 n., 184 n.

Robert de Swanton, mk N. 180 n.
Robert Talbot, prebendary N. 356 n.
Robert de Thaneto (Hayward), mk C. 49
Robert Tideman de Winchcombe, *see* Tideman de Winchcombe
Robert de Waletone, mk R. 228, 336 n.
Robert de Walworth[Bennington], pr D. 37 n., 217, 297, 300
Robert Wells/Steward, pr E. 67, 72 n., 362 n.
Robert de Weston, mk Wo. 52, 205 n.
Robert de Wich, mk Wo. 116 n.
Robert Winchelsey, abp C. 16 n., 50, 54, 99 n., 100 n., 101, 165, 185, 188, 193–4, 196 n., 201 n., 205 n., 241, 266 n., 275, 285, 290, 296
Robert de Wodeheye, *lector* 100 n.
Robert de Wodehirst, mason 204 n.
Rochester, church: St Nicholas 29 n.
Rochester, cathedral priory, *passim*
  cloister and precinct 21, 23–4, 29–31
  Lady chapel 169 n.
rogation days 263–4
Roger, scribe, E. 180–1
Roger Bacon 118 n.
Roger de Blikling, mk N. 360
Roger de Bosbury, mk Wo. 183 n.
Roger of Caen 76 n.
Roger Coton, pr Co. 14
Roger de Dorobina, mk N. 215 n.
Roger de Eston, mk N. 143 n., 199 n.
Roger de Evesham, mk Wo. 169, 212 n.
Roger de Godmersham, mk C. 127 n.
Roger de Grutelyngthon, mk B. 277 n.
Roger de Henley, mk Wo. 313, 316
Roger de la Lee, pr C. 359
Roger de Mainsforth, mk D. 219 n., 237
Roger Neckham, mk Wo. 81, 362 n.
Roger de Northburgh, bp Co. and Lichfield 198
Roger de Norwich I, mk E. 102, 130, 136–7
Roger Postle, mk D. 46
Roger de Shrovesbury, mk Wo. 176 n.
Roger de Skerning, pr and bp N. 9
Roger de Stanhope, mk D. 202 n.
Roger de Staplehurst, mk R. 180 n.
Roger de Stevintone, mk Wo. 86 n., 210
Roger de Thurston, mk N. 182 n.
Roger de Walton, pr Co. 238, 360
Roger de Wendover, mk St Albans 153, 351, 352 n., 354, 356
Roger de Wrotham, mk C. 207
Romanus de Roma 157 n.
Rome, Italy 57, 119 n., 120–1, 124, 305, 361 n.
Romsey, abbey 277
Rothbury, Northumberland 46
Rouse, Richard and Mary 114
Rud, T. 73
Rufinus 354 n., 358
Rupert of Deutz 96

sacrist 15, 26, 132, 135, 163, 197–206, 250, 252, 254, 262–3, 265, 285–6, 301–2
Saint Andrews, bp of 318
saints
  Aidan 221, 250
  All Saints, feast of 208 n., 248 n., 258 n., 284 n., 303
  Ambrose 71, 96, 97 n., 104–6, 154
  Andrew 252
  Anselm of Bec, abp C. 70 n., 76 n., 145, 148, 149, 208, 349–50, 360
  Augustine, bp Hippo 62, 77, 80, 82, 97 n., 105, 106, 111, 113, 117, 131, 147, 155, 325, 327, 361
  Benedict, *passim*
  Bonaventure 121 n., 152, 156
  Cuthbert 6, 86, 99, 151, 202, 208, 221, 254, 319, 350 n., 354 n., 361
  Dunstan 149, 208, 319
  Ebbe 213 n.
  Edmund of Abingdon, abp C. 12, 361
  Elphege, abp C. 208
  Ermenilda 362
  Etheldreda 204 n., 209, 265 n.
  Eustace 250
  Godric 218, 361
  Gregory (the Great), pope 71, 80 n., 96, 97 n., 105–6, 117, 145, 146, 154
  Holy Cross, *inventio* of 208 n., 254
  Holy Innocents, feast of 39 n., 42, 250–1, 307
  Ithamar 207 n.
  Jerome 77, 105–6, 111, 113, 116, 146, 147, 153, 154, 325, 327
  John the Baptist, nativity of 173 n., 284 n., 286
  Leonard 230
  Mary, *see under* Virgin Mary
  Mary Magdalen 303
  Matthew 254
  Michael in Monte Tumba 248
  Nicholas 249 n., 250, 251, 308, 319
  Oswald, bp Wo. 209, 211, 264 n., 265 n., 275, 321 n., 349 n.
  Oswald, king 151
  Paul 327
  Peter *ad vincula* 208 n., 209 n., 258 n.
  Scholastica 362
  Sexburga 362
  Swithun 207, 254, 264, 321 n.
  Thomas the apostle 206
  Thomas Becket, abp C. 7 n., 51, 76 n., 85, 111 n., 170, 207, 249, 350
  Werburga 362
  William of Norwich 200, 207
  William of Perth 207, 320 n.
  Wulstan, bp Wo. 6, 15, 45, 197, 209, 211, 249, 263, 321, 349 n.

St Albans, abbey 32 n., 226 n., 266, 323, 326, 351, 353, 356
St Andrews, bishop of 218
St Andrew the Great, church of, *see under* Cambridge
St Augustine, abbey 45, 102, 307
St Catherine, chapel of, *see under* Norwich
St Cross/St Peter, church of, *see under* Ely
St Dunstan, church of, Monks Risborough 304
St Elphege, church of, *see under* Canterbury
St Frideswide, priory of, *see under* Oxford
St Giles, fair of, W. 39
St Guthlac, priory of, Hereford 45
St Jacques, convent of, *see under* Paris
St James, church of, Bath cathedral priory precinct 29 n.
St John Bedwardine, church of Worcester 45
St John the Evangelist, priory of, Waterford 31, 161, 226–7
St Leonard, priory of, N. 17 n., 31, 43 n., 105 n., 106 n., 115, 120, 122–4, 134, 153, 228–30, 240, 264, 269, 285, 297 n., 299–300, 305, 340, 341
St Loe, *see* Newton St Loe
St Margaret, church of, *see under* Canterbury
St Margaret, church of, Lynn 276
St Mary, abbey of, York 56, 74 n., 100, 224 n., 323
St Mary, Trumpington, church of, *see under* Cambridge
St Mary Magdalene, chapel of, Warkworth 31 n.
St Mary in the Marsh, church of, *see under* Norwich
St Mary of Stalls, church of, *see under* Bath
St Michael, chapel of, *see under* Norwich
St Michael, church of, *see under* Worcester
St Mildred, church of, *see under* Canterbury
St Nicholas, church of, *see under* Coventry
St Nicholas, church of, *see under* Rochester
St-Omer, monastery of 121 n.
St Oswald, church of, *see under* Durham
St Osyth, priory of, Essex 56
St Paul, church of, *see under* Canterbury
St Paul's hospital, Norwich 17 n., 31, 192, 228, 230 n., 244
St Peter, church of, *see under* Canterbury
St Peter-in-the-East, church of, *see under* Oxford
St Victor, abbey and school of, *see under* Paris
St William, chapel of, *see under* Norwich
St Wulstan, church of, *see under* Worcester
Salamon Litelbourne, mk C. 307
Salerno, medical school of 152
Salisbury, Wiltshire 44, 98
Salomon, goldsmith 49
Salomon II, mk C. 358
Savaric Fitzgeldewin, bp B. 9 n.
Scholastica, *see under* saints
Senatus, pr Wo. 349, 351

senescallus terrarum/warden of manors 165–6
Septuagesima 194
Severn river 21, 22, 30
Sexburga, *see under* saints
Sheppey, isle of 45
Sherbourne, river, Coventry 21, 23 n.
Sherburn, Durham 46
Shrewsbury, Shropshire 45
shrines 15, 167 n., 200, 202, 206–11, 246 n., 247–8, 321; see also *feretrar, tumbarius*
Sidbury, Worcester 45
Silvester, mk C. 237 n.
Silvester de Evesham, mk and bp Wo. 9
Simeon, pr W. 320
Simon ?VI, mk C. 361
Simon III, mk Co. 172
Simon *dictus* Porter 191 n.
Simon Alcock 342
Simon de Banham, mk E. 136, 209
Simon Bozoun, pr N. 81, 117, 124, 152, 153 n., 182, 229, 297 n., 340, 349 n., 352, 354–6, 358, 359
Simon Crompe, mk Wo. 45, 86 n., 179 n., 180 n., 205 n., 297
Simon de Darlington, mk D. 214, 304
Simon de Elmham I, pr N. 96 n.
Simon de Elmham II, mk N. 96
Simon Gillyngham, mk R. 93 n.
Simon Harpele, mk N. 40, 312
Simon Islip, abp C. 54, 171, 173, 188, 225, 277
Simon Langham, abt Westminster, bp E., abp C. 185, 277
Simon Meopham, abp C. 185, 227, 252, 298
Simon de Midlecombe, mk Co. 278 n.
Simon de Montacute, bp E. 204
Simon de St Paul, mk C. 148, 185 n.
Simon de Solers, mk Wo. 86 n.
Simon Sudbury, abp C. 55, 285, 291, 346 n.
Simon de Wyre, mk Wo. 116 n., 179 n., 180 n.
Sittingbourne, Kent 45
Smalley, Beryl 109
Smaragdus, abt St-Mihiel 77, 80, 81, 82, 158
Soham, Cambridgeshire 43
Southfleet, Kent 45, 119, 165 n.
Southampton Plot 298 n.
South Shields, Co. Durham 280
Spain 278
Spalding, Lincolnshire 43
Sparsholt, Hampshire 44
speciarius 165
Spinney, cell E. 32 n., 216
Sprowston, Norfolk 43, 133, 134, 135
Stamford priory, D. 31, 46, 108 n., 113 n., 119, 220–1, 280
Stanhope, Co. Durham 46
stationarii 296–7, 292, 302, 303
Stavanger, Norway 207 n.
Stephen, king 6
Stephen Byrchyngton mk C. 183 n.

Stephen de Feversham II, mk C. 101, 123, 127, 148 n.
Stephen de Howden, mk D. 53 n.
Stephen de Mongeham, pr C. 291
Stephen Tygh, mk C. 225
Stephen de Wytton, mk Wo. 205 n.
Stockton, Wiltshire 47
Stoke, near Coventry 44
Stour, river, Canterbury 21
Stratford John, *see* John de Stratford
Stretham, Cambridgeshire 43
Strood, Kent 45
Stunteney, Cambridgeshire 43
subprior, office of 14–15, 100 n., 134, 139 n., 162–3, 245, 249 n., 259, 283, 291–2, 300–1, 306–7, 311 n.
Sudbourne, Suffolk 120
Sudbury, Simon, *see* Simon Sudbury
Surrey, archdeacon of 11
Swaffham Prior, Cambridgeshire 137 n.
Swithun, *see under* saints
Symeon, mk D. 7, 350, 353

tabularius 270–1
Temple Laugherne, Worcestershire 47
Tenbury, Worcestershire 45
terrar 28, 165, 167
Tewkesbury, abbey 10
Thanet, Kent 45
Thetford, Norfolk 98
Thomas the apostle, *see under* saints
Thomas, *medicus*, C. 294 n.
Thomas, organist, Wo. 179, 270
Thomas I, pr D. 11
Thomas Aquinas 108, 109, 110, 123, 145, 148, 150, 155, 325, 330
Thomas Arundel, bp E., abp C. 16 n., 17, 57, 142, 172 n., 175 n., 186, 190, 205, 263, 274, 282, 298, 307
Thomas Baa [Elsyng] 172 n.
Thomas de Barndesley II, mk Wo. 89
Thomas Becket, abp C., *see under* saints
Thomas Blackwell I, mk Wo. 162 n., 336
Thomas de Borne I, mk C. 301
Thomas Bradwardine, abp C. 69 n.
Thomas de Brinton, mk N., bp R. 129, 185
Thomas de Broghton, mk Wo. 89, 98, 157, 179 n.
Thomas de Brok, mk N. 214
Thomas Broun (Bruyn), mk R. 124, 155
Thomas Brouns, bp N. 57 n., 277 n.
Thomas Browne, mk C. 90
Thomas Bungay, mk C. 184 n.
Thomas Caly, mk D. 150
Thomas de Capua 343
Thomas Carter 197, 276
Thomas Causton, mk C. 91, 318
Thomas Cawmbridge I, mk N. 234
Thomas de Chilbolton I, mk W. 133, 142 n.

Thomas Chillenden I, pr C. 68 n., 138 n., 201, 207, 211, 280, 298, 307
Thomas de Cobham, bp Wo. 56, 206, 210, 287, 291
Thomas Crist, pr B. 298
Thomas Cromwell 93
Thomas de Cyrcestre, mk. B. 227
Thomas D'Autre, mk D. 202
Thomas Dene, mk Wo. 196
Thomas de Depedale, mk N. 172 n.
Thomas Dover, mk C. 140, 303
Thomas de Dovorr, mk R. 177 n.
Thomas de Ealding, mk R. 93 n.
Thomas [Baa] de Elsyng, mk N. 172 n.
Thomas Erpingham 271–2
Thomas Esh, mk D. 224
Thomas Everard, mk C. 140
Thomas de Foxcote, mk B. 227
Thomas de Goodnyston I, mk C. 185, 277, 361
Thomas Goodrich, bp E. 331n.
Thomas Grene, mk Wo. 158
Thomas Guston, mk C. 302, 304
Thomas Gyllyngham, mk C. 84 n.
Thomas Hamsterley, mk D. 142
Thomas Hanney, grammar master 337
Thomas Hatfield, bp D. 19 n., 127, 163, 224, 273 n., 283, 292
Thomas Hatfield, mk D. 304
Thomas Hay, mk Wo. 196 n., 276
Thomas de Henton, mk W. 171
Thomas Herne, mk C. 173 n.
Thomas de Hevyngham, mk N. 234
Thomas de Hindelep, mk Wo. 341
Thomas de Holyngborne, mk C. 212
Thomas de Horsted, mk R. 106 n., 115, 154, 155
Thomas Hosyntre, mk Wo. 131, 309
Thomas Knyghton, mk Co. 162 n.
Thomas Lacok, pr B. 226
Thomas Langley, bp D. 20, 92 n., 143, 277
Thomas Launcells, mk D. 46, 294
Thomas Ledbury, pr Wo. 126 n., 130, 142 n., 280
Thomas Legat, mk D. 223
Thomas de Lincoln, mk E. 136
Thomas de Lisle, bp E. 254, 363
Thomas de London, mk W. 90 n.
Thomas Lund, mk D. 114 n., 117, 122
Thomas de Lymynton, mk W. 63 n.
Thomas Melsonby, pr D. 86
Thomas Merke, mk Westminster 342
Thomas Mildenham, pr Wo. 158
Thomas atte More I, mk Wo. 212
Thomas Morton, mk N. 146
Thomas Nesbitt, mk D. 92 n.
Thomas Nevyle, pr W. 133, 141, 142, 298
Thomas de Newcastle, mk D. 122, 290
Thomas de Newthorpe, mk D. 308 n.
Thomas Newton, mk W. 213

Thomas Percy, bp N. 233 n., 276
Thomas Pickering, mk D. 119 n.
Thomas de Plumsted, mk N. 351 n.
Thomas de Qwermington, smith 28
Thomas de Ramesey I, mk E. 168 n.
Thomas de Rillington, mk D. 215
Thomas Rome, mk D. 112, 141, 182 n.
Thomas Rudborne, mk W. 142 n., 353
Thomas Ryngmer, pr C. 295 n.
Thomas de Sandwyco, mk C. 94 n.
Thomas de Schaftesbury, *medicus* 293
Thomas Scheldesley, mk Wo. 158
Thomas Scrope/Bradley, Carmelite 363, 364 n.
Thomas de Segesbarowe, mk Wo. 120, 124, 156, 305
Thomas Shirebourne, pr W. 133, 142 n.
Thomas Spofford, abt, St Mary's, York 323–4
Thomas de Stapeley, mk D. 308 n.
Thomas de Stoke, mk W. 168 n., 276 n.
Thomas Stoyl, mk C. 311
Thomas Streynsham, mk Wo. 158, 270, 351 n.
Thomas de Stureye I, mk C. 97, 109, 340 n.
Thomas de Stureye II, mk C. 97 n., 144, 145 n., 339 n.
Thomas de St Valerico, mk C. 111 n., 112 n.
Thomas Swalwell, mk D. 96, 112 n., 339 n.
Thomas Talbot, mk Wo. 83
Thomas de Tilmerstone, mk C. 184 n.
Thomas Undyrdown I, mk C. 148
Thomas Waleys, op 115 n.
Thomas Walsingham, mk St Albans 323 n., 353
Thomas de Westoe, mk D. 123, 145
Thomas de Winton, pr B. 11 n.
Thomas Wolsey, cardinal 332
Thomas de Wolviston, mk D. 150, 157
Thomas of Woodstock, duke of Gloucester 47, 130, 254
Thomas de Wouldham, pr and bp R. 10, 185
Thomas Wulstan, mk Wo. 81, 158
Thomas Wybarn, mk R. 106 n., 345, 347
Thomas de Wych I, mk Wo. 116 n., 179 n.
Thomas de Wyke, mk Wo. 315
Thomas Wykyng, mk C. 303, 328
Thomson, Rodney 116, 346
Thorney, abbey and abt 126 n., 181 n.
Thorpe (Wood), Norwich 31, 43, 229
Tichborne, Hampshire 44
Tideman de Winchcombe, bp Wo. 56
Tintern (de Voto), Ireland, C. 32 n.
treasurer/receiver 135, 140, 162, 164, 206 n., 211, 248, 254, 259, 262
Trinity, feast of the 229, 241 n., 255, 265, 271
Trumpington, Cambridge 298
tumbarius 15, 209–11, 321
Tyne, river 31

university studies, *see under* Cambridge, Oxford, Paris
Urban II, mk B. 211 n.

Urban III, pope 16 n.
Uthred de Boldon, mk D. 75, 78–80, 139, 219, 221, 299, 300, 304, 326, 354 n., 358

Vale of the White Horse, Berkshire 44
Vegetius 155
Vespers, office of 68, 229, 237 n., 243, 303, 307
of the dead 306
Vicarii in choro 161 n.
Vincent de Beauvais 117 n., 355
Virgin Mary 75, 169, 170, 173 n., 238 n., 248 n., 258, 262, 265 n., 270, 275, 303, 307
assumption 129, 204 n., 250, 307
nativity 275
purification 173 n., 208 n., 229, 248 n., 258, 284 n.
visitations:
archiepiscopal 50, 103, 142, 185, 227, 241, 252
Black Monk Chapter 70 n., 100, 142
episcopal 4, 5, 39, 41 n., 42, 48 n., 142–3, 146, 163, 172 n., 192–3, 217, 218, 221, 223, 224, 228–9, 277, 291–2, 315, 331 n.
Vitruvius 155

Wakefield, Henry, *see* Henry de Wakefield
Wakeryng, John, *see* John Wakeryng
Walden, abt of 309
Walkelin, bp W. 7
Walpole, Ralph, *see* Ralph de Walpole
Walsingham, Norfolk 43
Walter, *brevitor*, W. 310 n.
Walter III, pr C. 121
Walter V, mk B. 214
Walter VII, mk B. 214
Walter de Anno, pr B. 11 n.
Walter Artret, mk D. 304 n.
Walter Causton, mk C. 186 n., 225
Walter Durdent, pr C., bp Co. 9, 111
Walter de Eastry, mk C. 171 n.
Walter Halstede, mk C. 285
Walter de Kirkeby, mk Wo. 169
Walter de Legh, pr Wo. 197 n., 309
Walter Maidstone, bp Wo. 55 n., 186, 205 n., 210
Walter de la Misericorde, servant Wo. 242
Walter de Norwyco, mk C. 46, 123 n., 148
Walter de Rawe, mk R. 168 n.
Walter Reynolds, bp Wo., abp C. 55, 86, 183, 185, 205, 210, 263, 271 n., 280, 285
Walter de Scarisbrick, mk D. 169
Walter Skirlaw, bp D. 17 n., 273
Walter de Stokton, mk N. 124 n., 229
Walter de Teesdale, mk D. 142
Walter de Walpole, mk E. 171 n.
Walter de Walsoken, mk E. 136
Walton St Felix, *see* Felixstowe
wardens of manors 148, 166, 177, 183 n., 358

Ware, Hertfordshire 98
Warin, mk C., pr Dover 111 n., 112 n., 119 n., 121 n.
Warin (Guarinus) mk D. 335 n.
Warkworth, Northumberland 31 n.
Waterford, Ireland, priory of St John the Evangelist, B. 31 n., 161, 226–7
Waynflete, William, *see* William Waynflete
Wear, river, Durham 21, 22 n., 31, 218, 223 n.
Wearmouth, priory, D. 31, 46, 223–4, 279, 299, 304
Wells, Somerset 14, 17, 20, 30, 44
Wenlock [Much], Shropshire 45
Wensum, river, Norwich 21, 31, 229
Werburga, *see under* saints
Westerham, rectory, Kent 173
Westminster 2, 8 n., 65, 324, 332
  abbey 53 n., 60 n., 93 n., 185, 269 n., 316, 324, 342 n.
Weston, Somerset 52
Wetheral, priory, Cumberland 224 n.
Wherwell, abbey, Hampshire 277
Whitchurch, Hampshire 98, 133
Whittingham, A. B. 215, 242
Wibert, pr C. 111, 112 n.
William the Conqueror 6
William II (Rufus) 7
William the chaplain, Wo. 196, 276
William, mk D. 86
William IV, mk R. 211 n.
William de Aislaby, mk D. 300, 312 n.
William Appleby, mk D. 117, 117 n., 141, 142–3, 182, 304
William de Ayermine, bp N. 233 n., 314
William de Bamburgh, mk D. 304
William Barry, mk D. 46 n.
William Bateman, bp N. 20, 39, 127, 173 n., 228, 245, 247 n., 271–2
William Beauchamp 255
William Bette, mk W. 295 n.
William de Bitton, bp B. and Wells 10
William de Blakeston, mk D. 303
William de Blois, bp Wo. 209–10
William Bokenham, mk N. 294
William Bonar, mk B. 41 n.
William Bonyngton I, mk C. 179, 266
William Bonyngton II, mk C. 359
William de Bottlesham, bp R. 115
William de Bradebourne, mk R. 214
William Brito, mk C. 111 n., 112 n.
William Brito, ofm. 145, 148, 338, 339 n., 340 n., 341, 351 n.
William de Brythwalton, pr Co. 14, 215
William Burdeleys, mk E. 161 n.
William de Camel, mk W. 163 n.
William de Cantorbury I, mk C. 147, 148 n., 361
William Chart I, mk C. 296, 307, 308
William Chartham II, mk C. 61 n., 149

William Chichele I, mk C. 61 n.
William de Cirencester I, mk Wo. 205 n.
William de Claxton, pr N. 234
William de Corston, *see* William Uppehull
William Courtenay, abp C. 56, 186 n., 280
William de Cowton, pr D. 100 n., 190 n., 217, 222, 224, 292, 293, 311
William de Dalton, mk D. 213 n.
William de Dene, mk Wo. 270
William de Dover III, mk C. 93 n., 137, 138 n., 225
William de Dunelm, mk E. 46 n.
William de Dunstapele 275
William Durandus, the elder, canonist 97, 325
William de Durham, mk D. 113, 182, 237
William Ebchester, pr D. 130 n., 150 n., 190
William de Edington, bp W. 280
William Elmore, mk C. 184 n.
William de Eltisle 168 n.
William de Ely I, *see* William Powcher
William de Eythorne, mk C. 184 n.
William de Farindone, mk R. 41 n.
William Fordham, mk Wo. 158
William de Gainsborough, bp Wo. 196 n., 257, 291
William Gemeticensis 150
William Giffard, bp W. 7
William Gilers/Julers, mk W. 47, 278
William Glastynbury, mk C. 59, 61, 147, 149, 226, 285, 328, 347 n.
William de Goldsborough, mk D. 217 n.
William Graper, mk D. 304
William de Greneburgh, pr Co. 92 n.
William de Grymeley, mk Wo. 122, 179 n.
William de Guisborough senior, pr D. 150
William de Gunton, mk N. 312
William Gyllyngham I, mk C. 140, 308
William Hadlegh I, mk C. 237
William de Hadlo, mk R. 41 n.
William de Hadsto, mk N. 312
William Haloughton, mk Co. 152 n., 162 n.
William de Haltwhistle, mk D. 276
William de Hampton I, mk B. 163 n.
William de Hertilbury, mk Wo. 129
William de Hethe I, mk C. 140
William de Hexham, mk D. 222
William de Hoo II, mk R. 318
William de Hotham, bp E. 309
William de Hydeshale, mk Wo. 89
William Ingram I, mk C. 81 n., 106, 117 n., 123, 149, 237, 337, 341, 356, 357 n., 360 n.
William Julers, *see* William Gilers
William de Kelloe, mk D. 89
William de Kibblesworth, mk D. 100 n., 143, 277 n.
William de Killerby, mk D. 151
William de Kirkeby, pr N. 192, 320
William Lane, mk W. 164 n.

William Laud, abp C. 72 n.
William Law, mk D. 344 n., 346
William de Ledebery, mk C. 108, 121 n., 123 n.
William de Ledes, mk R. 318
William de Lenn I, mk N. 17 n.
William de Lodelowe I, mk Wo. 279, 315 n.
William de London II, mk R. 302 n.
William de London, mk Wo. 209 n., 312
William de Lynn, bp Wo. 206
William de Malling, mk C. 94 n.
William of Malmesbury, mk Malmesbury 348 n., 349, 353, 356
William Manwode, mk W. 156
William de Martham, mk N. 201 n.
William de Mawfeld I, mk R. 41 n., 94 n.
William de Maydenstone I, mk R. 163 n.
William Molassh, pr C. 92, 93
William de Molendis 197
William de Montibus 115, 338, 361
William More, pr Wo. 97 n., 106, 115, 116 n., 345
William of Norwich, *see under* saints
William de Nubbeley, mk B. 49 n.
William of Pagula 95, 118, 156, 157, 158 n., 231
William Pensford, mk B. 41 n.
William Penteney, mk N. 234
William Peper, mk R. 185 n.
William Peraldus 76, 77, 80, 152, 153, 154
William of Perth, *see under* saints
William Pocklington, mk D. 112 n., 113
William Powcher, pr E. 203 n., 204, 205 n.
William Power, mk Wo. 183 n
William de Ralegh, bp N. 9 n.
William Regeway, mk C. 94 n.
William de Reyersh, mk R. 154, 185 n.
William Reynham, mk R. 279
William Richemond I, mk C. 303
William de Riston, mk E. 312
William Rufus/William II 7
William de Rykinghale, mk N. 230
William de Sancta Barbara, bp D. 8 n.
William de St Calais (Carilef), bp D. 6, 7, 73 n., 223, 363
William Salford I or II, mk B. 162 n., 168 n., 169 n., 355
William Seton, mk D. 117
William Sever, bp D. 9
William Shirborn, mk B. 41 n.
William de Silton, mk N. 199 n.
William Skyllyng, mk W. 184 n.
William de Stiphol, scribe 110, 354 n., 358
William de Strode I, mk R. 41 n.
William Sydyngbourne, mk R. 312
William de Tanfield, pr D. 224, 297
William de Taunton, pr W. 9 n.
William de Thornham, mk R. 118
William de Thorpe, mk E. 168 n., 179
William de Thrulegh, mk C. 94 n.
William Tonebregg II, mk R. 41 n.
William Trollop, mk D. 304

William de Turba, bp N. 9 n.
William Uppehull, mk B. 42
William Vavasour, mk D. 46
William Vincent, mk W. 240
William de Walpole I, pr E. 203 n., 298
William de Walpole, mk N. 39 n.
William de Watford, mk W. 295 n.
William Waynflete, bp W. 11 n., 39, 278
William Wells/Martin, mk E. 49
William Wells, bp R. 41 n., 56
William Weston, chaplain 195, 197 n.
William Whalley, mk Whalley 343 n.
William Wittlesey, abp C. 55
William Woghope I, mk C. 272
William Worstede, pr N. 43, 130, 234, 324
William Wykeham, bp W. 20, 37 n., 50, 52, 142, 195, 275, 276, 323 n.
Winchcombe, abbey 45, 146
Winchelsea, Sussex 45
Winchelsey, Robert, *see* Robert Winchelsey
Winchester, fair, St Giles 39
Winchester, cathedral priory, *passim*
  cloister and precinct 20–26, 28–31, 261 n., 296
  Lady chapel 23 n., 177 n., 269
Winchester College 52–3, 103 n.
Winnall, Hampshire 44
Witton, near Norwich 43
Witton Gilbert, hospital, *see under* Durham
Wodeley, ?Cambridgeshire 298
Wolsey, Thomas, *see* Thomas Wolsey
Woolstone, Berkshire 133
Worcester, churches:
  St Michael 29 n.
  St Wulstan 45
Worcester, cathedral priory, *passim*
  chapels and altars:
    Lady chapel 86, 206, 249, 270
    St Mary Magdalene's chapel 206
    St Thomas' chapel 206
    St Cecilia's altar 309
    St Cross' altar 276
    St Edmund's altar 276
  cloister and precinct 21–8, 29–31, 49, 126 n., 244, 309
Wulstan, pr and bp Wo., *see under* saints
Wulstan de Bransford, pr and bp Wo. 56, 86 n., 132, 186, 210, 287, 297
Wykeham, William, *see* William Wykeham
Wymondham, priory 32 n.

Yare, river, Norfolk 232
Yarmouth, priory, N. 31, 43, 108, 110, 115, 117, 193 n., 228, 231–5, 240, 280, 340, 362
York, city 46, 64, 126, 220 n., 273 n.
  abbey, *see* St Mary
York, duchess of 254 n.

Zacharias Chrysopolitanus 118

Show downside + losses with
month movement
overlay.

Show all collected priors though.